S0-CFQ-907

8.95

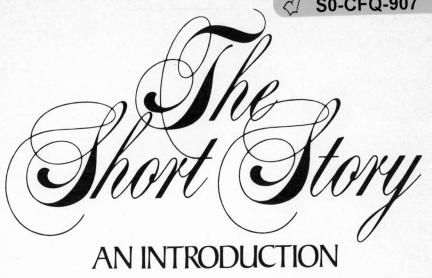

The Short Story

AN INTRODUCTION

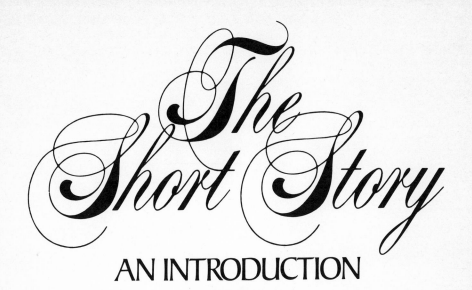

AN INTRODUCTION

Wilfred Stone
Professor of English
Stanford University

Nancy Huddleston Packer
Associate Professor of English
Stanford University

Robert Hoopes
Professor of English
University of Massachusetts

McGRAW-HILL BOOK COMPANY

New York St. Louis San Francisco Auckland Düsseldorf Johannesburg
Kuala Lumpur London Mexico Montreal New Delhi Panama
Paris São Paulo Singapore Sydney Tokyo Toronto

The Short Story:
An Introduction

Copyright © 1976 by McGraw-Hill, Inc. All rights reserved. Printed in the United States of America. No part of this publication may be reproduced, stored in a retrieval system, or transmitted, in any form or by any means, electronic, mechanical, photocopying, recording, or otherwise, without the prior written permission of the publisher.

34567890 KPKP 7987

See Additional Acknowledgments on page 593. Copyrights included on this page by reference.

This book was set in Times Roman by Rocappi, Inc. The editors were Ellen B. Fuchs and Phyllis T. Dulan; the cover was designed by Joseph Gillians; cover photo by Hiag Akmakjian; the production supervisor was Charles Hess.
Kingsport Press, Inc., was printer and binder.

Library of Congress Cataloging in Publication Data
Main entry under title:

The Short story.

    Bibliography: p.
    Includes index.
    1. Short stories. I. Stone, Wilfred Healey,
    date II. Packer, Nancy Huddleston. III. Hoopes, Robert.
PZ1.S5577 [PN6014]   808.83′1   75-15849
ISBN 0-07-061689-2

Contents

Preface

We had two objectives in mind in making this book. First, we aimed to gather a collection of stories richly representative of the short story genre; second, we aimed to make a book that would be, owing to its critical and introductory material, as useful to the beginning writer as to the critical reader and teacher.

Any gathering that covers so many years (roughly from 1800 to the present—with bows to a farther past) represents some painful compromises and omissions. We have steadfastly tried to adhere to the following two tests for inclusion: Is the story good in and of itself, that is, is it an outstanding achievement as a work of art? And is it representative, that is, does it in its writing, technique, or theme represent an important event in the historical development of the short story? We believe that, in the main, our goals have been achieved.

We have prefaced the book with a fairly long introduction which provides, among other things, most of the information about technique that the reader (or writer) needs to know. The work of each writer is preceded by a short introduction which provides biographical information together with enough critical discussion about the particular story to get the student-critic on his way. At the end of the book is a Thematic Table of Contents—which will assist the reader who wants an entry into the range of human experiences the stories deal with—a Brief Glossary of Terms, and a List of Useful Books. Finally, we have tried to make our Index genuinely valuable by listing there all critical terms or other matters from the Introductions that we thought would be useful. We have avoided the detailed questions and other apparatus that can make a book like this look more like an instrument of pedagogy than a book of wonderful readings. When the life of the reader intersects with the life of the story—that is when criticism ought to begin. In designing our critical aids, we have attempted to enhance rather than to stifle that moment.

Throughout we have used "he" when we mean "he or she" and the word "man" when we mean all human beings. The language is in need of generic nouns and pronouns that will reflect reality with more accuracy and less prejudice. But this book is not the place to start the reform, so we have followed the old ways.

We think it is worth mentioning that the editors of this volume include a short story writer as well as two persons with more usual academic credentials and experience. We hope that the crossing of the critical and creative strains has brought a useful focus to what we have selected and to what we have written. In the short introductions no attempt has been made to "homogenize" the writing styles of the three editors.

This volume has been several years on the fire, and in that time many people have helped us, in large and small ways, to put it together. We hope that a mere listing of their names will signal our genuine gratitude: Nancy Bazin, Betty Brereton, George Brown, Christine Gwynn, John Felstiner, Suzanne Ferguson, Guelfo Frulla, Roger Harm, Arturo Islas, Barbara Baer, Dana Levitt, Eric Lindquist, Emily Olmstead, Thomas G. Parker, Lawrence Ryan, and Scott Turow.

                                                             Wilfred Stone
                                                Nancy Huddleston Packer
                                                            Robert Hoopes

Introduction

1

Storytelling is as old as campfires. The impulse to embody human experience in narrative form is probably as old as human consciousness itself. Drawn together by the warmth of the fire, by terror of strange sounds in the dark, our early ancestors gave voice in story form to their fears and beliefs—and thus made for themselves a magic against the trials of life. The earliest stories, traveling from campfire to campfire and down the generations, marked man's slow emergence from his animal status. Their forms, like the forms of other rituals, helped create for early man his history and identity—and were part of the creative impulse that made him consciously human.

All "primitive" cultures have their myths and legends—narratives of how things began, how the humans came, how the tribe survived, how the heroes fought. Though these tales are sometimes funny, their purpose is intensely serious. For the tribe that related them, they were the gospel, the sacred word—matter not of mere make-believe but of belief itself. Since we no longer see the world as primitive storytellers did, a lot of this folklore can seem alien and strange. But increasingly, in this latter day of ours, we read such lore with nostalgia, moved by the power of things we have lost: the kinship with nature, sense of community, the certainty of belief.

Much of our earliest written literature—the Gilgamesh epic, the Old Testament stories, the Greek and Roman myths, Beowulf—borrows heavily from such prehistoric lore. They are in great part the forms of such stories that have been developed, sophisticated, and written down.

But "modern" fiction has come a long way from those early beginnings (though it often reshapes those ancient forms to new uses). One cannot read a modern novel or story after an ancient myth without realizing that it exists in a vastly different world of value. Myths, as Frank Kermode points out, are for explaining things "as they are and were," whereas fictions "are for finding things out." "Myths are the agents of stability, fictions the agents of change. Myths call for absolute, fictions for conditional assent." Today in the West we accept no one or no "correct" way to view truth or reality. Our culture for the past three hundred years has been one of fantastic change and instability. The forces of science, industry, capitalism, and democracy that swept away the feudal order (along with many of its injustices) also swept away many of the traditional grounds for human confidence. Centuries-old beliefs were challenged, institutions radically altered or destroyed, and the Christian myths that supported the old order lost much of their power to explain and comfort. The new age became as much an age of anxiety as of optimism, and in this century it has seemed to many more like an age of despair. It is the age of fiction.

The impulses that make the modern fiction writer are probably, at heart, no different from those of the "primitive" storyteller. He too would like to be a myth maker, and often is, but his problem is vastly complicated. Early stories were vehicles of assertion. Modern fiction is one of search. Early stories spoke for a whole community, modern fiction for lonely individuals called "authors." Myths record a completed vision of something true; fiction often represents, for writer and for reader, a crisis of belief and a groping for certainty. The modern writer does not receive his worldview, he discovers it. He does not, like the ancient myth maker, inherit his rituals, he invents them. But—and this is the vital point—though he may not give voice to universal truths, he is nevertheless making a statement about values. "Our whole age," said the poet Mallarmé, "is seeking to bring forth a sacred book."

Gogol's "The Overcoat" may not, like the myth of Adam and Eve in the Garden, identify the source of original sin, but it unforgettably reminds us of the perversity that prevents people from being their brothers' keepers. Karel Čapek's "The Last Judgment" is only a tattered remnant of Christian eschatology, yet it prefigures the human longing for justice. "The Lottery," horrible and grotesque as it is, is nevertheless a rite of sacrifice—and who can call it merely a fantasy when we note in our modern world similar human sacrifices in concentration camps and insane wars? The human sacrifice in Yukio Mishima's "Patriotism" is a traditional ritual, and, perhaps, less grotesque, yet it is rendered pitiable, even absurd, by its modern setting. Finally, Forster's "The Rock" is anything but scriptural in tone, yet it is basically a fable testing Christ's admonition: "Go and sell that thou hast, and give to the poor."

Stories are not sermons. They tend to present rather than to preach; their values are more often implicit than explicit. Yet no matter how objective a writer is, no matter how given to *showing* over telling, his values seep into his story—into his subject matter, his style, his way of defining character, his plots, his very tone of voice. The careful reader will learn to read these signs.

When Guy de Maupassant writes that the mother in "A Country Outing" uncovered "a leg whose erstwhile slenderness was vanishing under the invasion of flesh coming down from her thighs," but writes that the daughter was "one of those women who, met in the street, fill a man with a sudden, whipping desire and leave that vague disturbance and agitation of the senses with him until he goes to sleep," he tells us what he valued, giving voice to the unrefined sexual code of what the French call *l'homme moyen sensuel*. When Updike at the close of "Wife-wooing" turns his story into a fable with an actual moral at the end ("An expected gift is not worth giving"), he delivers a half-comic summation of what the story dramatizes: that love is a human and not a sublime event, and it exists, if it is to exist at all, in the middle of the mess we call human life.

As the historical progression of the stories in this volume approach the present day, the values they express become more difficult to decipher. A story like "Gogol's Wife" may seem no more than a gag, a *jeu d'esprit*. Böll's "Action Will Be Taken" may seem only the game-playing of a clever wordsmith. And Brautigan's "The Cleveland Wrecking Yard" in its comic surrealism may seem as pointless as it is discontinuous. Certainly in such works there is a radical turning away from "realism," from the "manners and morals" that Lionel Trilling called the proper subject for fiction, toward fantasy, absurdity, and far-out allegorical invention. Many of these writers—especially American writers of the last two decades—are responding to their sense of cultural break-up, and to a sense that the old fictional conventions are inadequate for expressing it. They are especially sensitive to what they feel to be the corruption of language via the mass media, government, and advertising; to that world of Doublespeak where peace is war, the lie merely something "inoperative," aggression against the enemy a "protective reaction strike," and official illegalities merely "inappropriate." To many such writers the modern "wasteland" is a waste of words, a flood of *dreck* in Barthelme's terms, and they have sought their artistic integrity partly through opposing that flood: by eliminating plot, fracturing syntax, and in every way imaginable and unimaginable defying the lexical and fictional patterns that were conventional in earlier decades. They are responding not only to the corruption of language, but to its shrinkage. As George Steiner says:

> Large areas of meaning and praxis now belong to such non-verbal languages as mathematics, symbolic logic, and formulas of chemical or electronic relation. Other areas belong to the sub-languages or anti-languages of non-objective art and *musique concrète*. The world of words has shrunk.

All the arts have reflected these trends, and the short story is no exception.

But it would be a mistake to suppose that these writers have abandoned values. To say that they have atomized the conventional short story is not to say that they have made nihilism or pointlessness or craziness their new creed. They are, it is true, deeply aware of what T. S. Eliot has called "the immense panorama of futility and anarchy which is contemporary history," and, ironically, their reaction has been largely apolitical and personal rather than polemical and engaged. Yet they are making their positive comment, though making it in surprising, and sometimes shocking, new ways.

Barthelme's "Report," for example, parodies the deadly officialese of the military, the business-as-usual vocabulary used in merchandising the instruments of terror, and, most terrible of all, the computerized "moral sense" that is supposed to keep this arsenal under human control. It is a trenchant satire. In "The Shore," Alain Robbe-Grillet gives us a story in which he has removed any human observer, a fitting device for depicting a depersonalized culture. And William Gass's "In the Heart of the Heart of the Country" uses language that lifts the spirit even as it announces a cultural disintegration.

But in all these tales there is the implicit wish that *things were not this way.* "I want to go to some other country . . . I want to go somewhere where everything is different," says a character in one of Barthelme's early stories, and that unspoken desire almost defines these modernist writers, and perhaps tells us why they have gone in for fantasy. Even in such a bizarre piece as "The Cleveland Wrecking Yard," where Brautigan good-naturedly shows the American dream as a junkyard, we are reminded that that dream still has a place in the author's imagination.

These experimental writers deserve our careful attention, whether or not they express experiences the reader can easily share. For the form of fiction as well as the content, the technique as well as the subject matter, are vital indicators of what is happening to us—and vital purveyors of value. In his important anthology *Anti-Story,* Philip Stevick has rightfully classified these antitraditional tendencies as a series of negations:

"Against Mimesis" or dismissal of the traditional goal of imitating "real life."
(Compare Melville's "Bartleby, the Scrivener" with Schwartz's "In Dreams Begin Responsibilities.")

"Against 'Reality'" or the indulgence in fantasy and dream. (See Čapek's "The Last Judgment" or Borges's "Everything and Nothing.")

"Against Event" a tendency in the direction of plotless stories. (See William Gass's "In the Heart of the Heart of the Country.")

"Against Subject" or fiction in search of something to say. (Consider Brautigan's "The Cleveland Wrecking Yard.")

"Against the Middle Range of Experience" or new forms of extremity. (Consider Jackson's "The Lottery" or Rosenfeld's "The Brigadier.")

"Against Analysis" the objective depiction of the phenomenal world. (Consider Robbe-Grillet's "The Shore.")

"Against Meaning" or forms of the absurd. (Consider Cortázar's "Axolōtl.")

"Against Scale" the minimal story, the epigram. Here, for the record, is an entire "minimal" story that Stevick includes; it is "Taboo" by Enrique Anderson Imbert:

His guardian angel whispered to Fabián, behind his shoulder:
"Careful, Fabián! It is decreed that you will die the minute you pronounce the word *doyen.*"
"Doyen?" asks Fabián, intrigued.
And he dies.

But negation—even perverse negation—is a sign that the moral sense is not dead. It is too early to say whether these experimental stories are classics or these trends permanent. It is enough to say that they represent something undeniably present in our culture: a sense of despair, break-up, horror, absurdity, violence and often as well a saving humor. But not all contemporary writers are working with these "against" techniques, for the good reason that they do not all share this kind of vision. Traditional techniques and traditional attitudes toward the human condition seem to go hand in hand. The contemporaries using more traditional techniques—Welty, Malamud, Rulfo, Olsen, Updike—seem less concerned with the forces breaking up our culture than with the forces holding it together.

Flannery O'Connor wrote: "People without hope not only don't write novels, but what is more to the point, they don't read them." The act of writing is in itself a kind of act of faith. The search for redemption, if we look deeply and tolerantly enough, can be found in all the stories in this book.

2

What is the short story? Is it only a truncated and incomplete version of the novel? Or is it a genre, that is, a category of art with a distinctive content, form, and style? This question has occupied a great many thoughtful practitioners of the form, Frank O'Connor, Sean O'Faolain, H. E. Bates eminent among them. Generally speaking these writer-critics do not think of a story as merely a work that happens to be short, but as a unique literary form, with techniques and effects that cannot be achieved through another medium. What are those effects, those techniques?

One of the most useful answers came from Edgar Allan Poe in 1842 when the short story was in its infancy. He believed that the prose tale stood just below the lyric poem in the hierarchy of literary art. For Poe, the "unity of effect or impression" was of prime importance, but, he felt, this unity could be obtained only in works that could be read "at one sitting." For Poe, the novel does not have this unity, is incapable of achieving the "immense force derivable from *totality*." Poe believed the short story is different from the novel, and superior to it. It was not shortness but intensity of impact that Poe the romantic valued most highly.

Although Poe's concern with effect, particularly the effects he chiefly sought— terror, passion, horror—has had little influence on important writers of the short story, his views on singleness and unity are widely shared. Elizabeth Bowen wrote in *Collected Impressions*:

> The story should have the valid central emotion and inner spontaneity of the lyric. . . .
> It must have tautness and clearness. . . . Poetic tautness and clarity are so essential to
> it that it may be said to stand at the edge of prose.

While this analogy with lyric poetry is a tricky one, it is also illuminating, and a great many writers have suggested it. Faulkner, no doubt only half in earnest, said in his *Paris Review* interview (1956):

> Maybe every novelist wants to write poetry first, finds he can't, and then tries the
> short story, which is the most demanding form after poetry. And, failing at that, only
> then does he take up novel writing.

Like a fine lyric poem, the short story requires the reader's utmost attention, a focusing of the mind on each detail in order to realize the final fullness of effect. The short story depends on concreteness, on sensual impressions that deliver their meaning without waste. Like the lyric, it is a lean form; it can tolerate little if any digression, and it stays within the world it creates. The action of a conventional short story is compressed within a short (usually continuous) time frame and space. The characters, few in number, are revealed, not developed. The background and setting are implied, not rendered. Like most drama, the short story's action begins *in medias res*. The story gets going as quickly as possible: "Once upon a time in a distant land there lived a princess . . ." and the story is off and running. ("Beginners," said Chekhov, "often have to . . . fold in two and tear up the first half. . . . The first half is superfluous.") The effects are, as Poe said, intense and total.

Consider Chekhov's brilliant "Ninochka." In fewer than 2,000 words we are given an ironic minidrama—a love triangle in which the cuckolded husband, miserable over his wife's infidelity with his best "friend," goes helplessly to that friend for advice. ("Tell me, what is Ninochka supposed to do now? Should she go on living with me, or do you think it would be better if she moved in with you?") The solution is given without emotion, the writer carefully repressing his pity so the reader can provide it himself:

> Having deliberated briefly, we left it at this: Ninochka would continue to live at Vikhlyenev's; I would go to see her whenever I liked, and he would take the corner room, which formerly had been the storeroom, for himself. This room was rather dark and damp, and the entrance to it was through the kitchen, but, on the other hand, he could perfectly well shut himself up in it and not be a nuisance to anyone.

If a writer attempted that kind of concentration of energy for, say, 300 pages, he would surely exhaust the reader, and would not in any case be able to maintain such emotional tension. The pace of a novel can be leisurely, its settings, characters, and events slowly developed until fully rendered.[1] The novelist—at least the conventional novelist—can tolerate subplots and digressions from the main thrust of his story; he can even desire them in order to achieve changes in pace and intensity. But that kind of pacing and development is not appropriate to the short story, and it is revealing that great novelists like Henry James, Joseph Conrad, and Thomas Mann found the short-story form troublesome. They were sticklers for fullness of presentation, for the richly rendered context, and for the slow unfolding. The James and Mann stories in this volume will indicate how difficult it was for these authors to squeeze into the short-story form, to sacrifice expansiveness to compression.

There are in the main three qualities that mark the short story as clearly different from other forms of prose fiction, that make it a "genre." The first quality is of course brevity. The second is its power of compensating for the consequences of shortness. And the third is the interaction of one and two.

How does the story manage to tell it all in such a brief space? Such a fine story as Gogol's "The Overcoat" seems quaintly old-fashioned today: the lengthy biography of the main character, the thorough development of each scene, the slow pacing of the action. Even Chekhov, that master of the form, was sometimes unwilling to sacrifice such embellishments for tautness. But the development of the short story has been continually toward greater and greater compression. Katherine Mansfield's "Marriage à la Mode," for example, is more than coincidentally close in theme and event to a story by Chekhov (not included here) called "La Cigale." "La Cigale" is about a foolish philandering woman who discovers after her doctor-husband is dead that he was the great man she had always sought. The story comes in eight "chapters"—with episodes from the time of the marriage through the infidelity to the husband's death,

---

[1] There is a fictional form called the "lyrical novel" which includes such books as Virginia Woolf's *The Waves*, Herman Hesse's *Demian*, and André Gide's *Les Faux-Monnayeurs*, and there are modern novelists like John Hawkes who would like to eliminate "plot, theme, character, and structure," thus carrying fictional compression almost to the point, if such wishes could be fulfilled, of nihilism. But these facts do not, we believe, contradict seriously the above generalizations.

and the wife's too-late recognition that she had let his greatness "slip by, slip by." But "Marriage à la Mode" is continuous action, and action covering only a weekend. The story opens with William, the husband, traveling to spend the weekend at his country house, where he is met by his wife and her friends. Later he overhears all of them, Isabel included, discussing him in a condescending way. The next day he returns to the city and writes his wife a letter in which he tells her he wishes only for her happiness. Isabel reads this letter to her friends, who laugh at it. Momentarily, she realizes what a terrible thing she has done; then, she puts the letter away and goes swimming with her friends, "laughing in the new way."

Mansfield has followed the master's advice to "fold in two and tear up the first half." Her story has a tight unity, the rising action being uninterrupted until the drama is complete, whereas Chekhov's story is loose and long, with many startings and stoppings. But something has been sacrificed. Compression can exact a price, and the Mansfield story pays it. The artist Bill in Mansfield's story is virtually a caricature; when Isabel suggests he paint the group he can only say, rudely, "Light's wrong. . . . Far too much yellow." And when the remark seems to charm Isabel, it tends to caricature her as well. As Elizabeth Bowen has said, the short story's disadvantage is an "emotional narrowness," and here we see it. In contrast the artist Riabovski in Chekhov's "La Cigale" is presented in such depth that we can believe him to be an important artist, and when he criticizes Olga's painting we witness a genuine struggle between his artistic integrity and his desire for Olga.

Writing in 1917, Herbert Ellsworth Cory said, "The very technique of the short-story is pathological, and titillates our nerves in our pathological moments. The short-story is the blood kinsman of the quick-lunch, the vaudeville, and the joy-ride." No doubt the short story is one manifestation of the modern speedup, though Cory's rather shuddering vision of a world full of "pathological moments" is one that even Kafka might reject. However, he does touch on the short-story writer's chief difficulty: how to be succinct without being shallow, how to create a single effect without creating a merely transitory one.

How does the short story achieve depth, or the feeling of depth? As we have noted, the short-story writer cannot, like certain novelists, stop his narrative while his characters' psyches are analyzed or their portraits painted. He cannot take time out to draw a scene. The story writer must intimate the setting, imply the complexity, insinuate the character, and the reader must infer the rest. When a story writer violates these practices—as when Melville in "Bartleby, the Scrivener" stops the story to summarize background—the result seems awkward and static, inimical to the spirit of the short story (however fitting to that of the novella). There are ways of avoiding such summarization, and they are all encompassed on one vital word: *suggestion.* The story reveals the "tip of the iceberg" in Hemingway's phrase; the rest of the iceberg is *suggested.* Consider that scene in Thurber's "The Secret Life of Walter Mitty" in which the henpecked husband is sitting in the car, cowed and dumb, while his wife tells him to wear his overshoes and not to forget the puppy biscuit. He is outraged, frustrated, impotent, and bent on revenge. How do we know? In one phrase, we are given his experience of that moment: "He raced the engine a little." Or consider that haunting dialogue between the old man and the boy in McCullers' "A Tree · A Rock · A Cloud" in which the old man, battered by life, tells the boy about love, and about the "science of love" he found could heal the hurt of being abandoned by the one woman he ever loved. His whole life is encompassed in those five pages, yet we learn only a few facts. When he tells the boy that, in trying to love a woman, he had begun at "the wrong end" of love, at the "climax," and that love should be begun with "A tree. A rock. A cloud," we are by these few words taken into the very center of his life and into the heartbreak that defined it. His "science" is the last desperate resource of an alienated man:

> Son. I can love anything. . . . I see a street full of people and a beautiful light comes in me. I watch a bird in the sky. Or I meet a traveller on the road. Everything, Son. And anybody. All stranger and all loved! Do you realize what a science like mine can mean?

Was he drunk? Was he a dope fiend? the boy wanted to know. Was he crazy? Leo, the stingy café owner, answered no to the first two questions, but was silent as to the third, though he felt himself to be an expert on craziness. But the reader must answer, for the tale lives by its suggestions and is incomplete on the printed page; it is completed in the imagination of the reader.

Sometimes a single detail will stand for a wealth of meaning—a whole social class or a character's background. Such an "emblem"—less than a symbol yet more than a thing—is a potent means of suggestion. The milkman's cart in Maupassant's "A Country Outing" identifies the family as lower-middle class, of modest means, just as the higher status of the young oarsman becomes clear from the description of "two splendid skiffs, fine and worked like costly pieces of furniture." The drink of Anis del Toro in Hemingway's "Hills Like White Elephants" tells us that these are sophisticated and worldly people. In the same story the repetition of the word "perfectly"—perfectly natural, perfectly simple—pegs the speaker as disingenuous, a manipulator, not to be trusted. In the first paragraph of "Vierochka," we learn that the protagonist's hat "lies in the dust underneath his bed" and we learn a good deal about the life he leads—that he is probably alone, certainly uncared for.

In a letter to his brother, an aspiring writer, Chekhov wrote:

> In my opinion, descriptions of nature should be extremely brief and offered by the way, as it were . . . you will evoke a moonlit night by writing that on the mill dam the glass fragments of a broken bottle flashed like a bright little star, and that the black shadow of a dog or a wolf rolled along like a ball, and so on.

And to Maxim Gorki he wrote:

> It is intelligible when I write, "The man sat down on the grass"; it is intelligible because it is clear and does not impede the reader's attention. Conversely, it will be unintelligible and tax the reader's brain if I write: "The tall, narrow-chested man of average build, who had a short, red beard, sat down on the green grass, already trampled by passers-by; sat down noiselessly, timidly and fearfully glancing around him." One's brain cannot grasp this at once, yet fiction must be grasped at once—on the spot.

Sometimes the setting is an emblem (the star-point on the neck of the broken bottle), sometimes it is not; but it is in the short story always abbreviated, caught in passing, out of the corner of the eye, as other things get done.

Compression and suggestion working together create what Sean O'Faolain calls "the point of illumination," and that in a nutshell is what the short story is all about.

"Every short story," O'Faolain writes, "has some bright destination and . . . every step into the story must imperceptibly lead toward its point of illumination." He continues:

> I believe the whole craft of the short story is summed up in those last half-dozen words—"that it must lead imperceptibly toward its point of illumination," with the maximum of emphasis on the word "imperceptibly." The main fun of writing short stories and part of the fun of reading them, consists in being led onward, of leading the reader onward to the moment of surprised pleasure when the story behind the story, the meaning behind the Yarn, the interior significance of the event, makes us utter a delighted "Ah!"—as when a train comes around a headland and there, in front of us, is the place to which we have been travelling on a Mystery Tour the destination of which until that moment we did not realize.

The point of illumination is the essential unifying element in the story. It is the light at the end of the tunnel, the target all the story elements are deployed to reach. At that moment the plot has come to its climax, the characters have been revealed, the relationship between character and environment has achieved at least a tentative equilibrium. The human significance of the story is manifest. Thereafter, there is a unity of feeling and of understanding. Such an "exaltation of the soul" cannot, as Poe said of the poem, "be long sustained," but what a moving experience it can be! As V. S. Pritchett says, "every short story is a drama, but every writer of short stories has his own idea of what is dramatic. A story moves towards a disclosure and that may be an event, a complete revelation of character, the close of a mood, the changing of an emotion, the clinching of an idea, the statement of a situation now completed." The beauty of the short story is that all its elements can be drawn to a single point that shines with such brightness that all the past moments of the tale are bathed in light—seen as a whole, as a radiance.

For this experience James Joyce used the word *epiphany,* a term borrowed from Christian thought and signifying the manifestation of God in the world. In *Stephen Hero* Joyce said:

> First we recognize that the object is *one* integral thing, then we recognize that it is an organized composite structure, a *thing* in fact: finally, when the relation of the parts is exquisite, when the parts are adjusted to the special point, we recognize that it is that *thing* which it is. Its soul, its whatness, leaps to us from the vestment of its appearance.

In Joyce's story "Araby" there are several small epiphanies, all building towards a final, surprising, one. The lovesick narrator, clinging to his romantic "love" for Mangan's sister, seeks out places of darkness and isolation in order the better to realize, in imagination, its rare splendor. "All my senses seemed to desire to veil themselves and, feeling that I was about to slip from them, I pressed the palms of my hands together until they trembled, murmuring, 'O love! O love!' many times." In places of darkness, his passion seemed more visible; the "high cold empty gloomy rooms liberated me" and from them he pondered the "dark house" where she lived, "seeing nothing but the brown-clad figure cast by my imagination." These epiphanies precede his visit to the bazaar (called *Araby*) where his purpose was to buy a gift for his lady. But he comes late, the great hall is already half in darkness, and he increasingly finds himself "remembering with difficulty why [he] had come." Failing to buy the gift, the story ends with this moment of revelation (like the others, tied to a concrete emblem and action): "Gazing up into the darkness I saw myself as a creature driven and derided by vanity; and my eyes burned with anguish and anger." This is the moment of "luminous intensity," an epiphany—and it is even cast in quasi-religious terms, since in the hall of the bazaar he "recognized a silence like that which pervades a church after a service." But it is an empty silence—the "worship" is over, the mystery has—for subtle psychological reasons which the story leaks to us—departed. For the reader who shares that epiphany, it is the moment when the elements of the story coalesce into a meaning.

Similarly in Isaac Babel's brilliant tale, "My First Goose." From the narrator's first fearful, admiring glance at the Commander (". . . and I wondered at the beauty of his giant's body. . . . His long legs were like girls sheathed to the neck in shining riding boots") to his rejection by the Cossacks (when the steam from the cook-pot was "like the far-off smoke of home in the village") to the killing of the goose, the cruel act that gained him acceptance ("the moon hung . . . like a cheap earring"), we are fascinated by the progression of events. But though the events are consecutive, causative, they seem to have no special meaning. Then in the last two lines, that master Babel provides the point of illumination: "I dreamed, and in my dreams saw women, but my heart, stained with bloodshed, grated and brimmed over."

Is such a story the blood kin of the quick lunch? Is it just a fragment of a novel or a digest of what would be superior if it were fleshed out? Has compression impaired the possibilities of depth and meaning? We think not. We think the short story at its best is an art form responsive to the highest reaches of the human imagination.

But *epiphany* is a word with echoes from an age of faith, and many contemporary writers react to our age as one of doubt and despair. As Philip Stevick says in *Anti-Story*, speaking of the work of certain avant-garde writers:

> Characters . . . do not learn. There are no insights. Relationships are not grasped in an instant. Structurally, the stories are flat, or circular, or cyclic, or mosaic constructions, or finally indeterminate or incomprehensible in their shape—they are not climactic. What we start with is pretty much what we have at the end. No epiphanies.

Illumination is not "in" these days. To point the way, to shine the light, implies that one knows—or has some idea—where one is going. The idea of where one is going used to be called a *plot*. The idea of what one means used to be called a *theme*. The idea of what a person is used to be called a *character*. Many modernist storytellers are in flight from these assertions, and their chapters of the "sacred book" open more often into absurdity than into transcendence, into the wilderness than into any promised land. Only time will tell whether they represent a new tradition or a dead end.

3

Henry James said, "Nothing . . . will ever take the place of the good old fashion of 'liking' a work of art or not liking it!" Literature begins where the life of the story intersects with the life of the reader. And it is this fresh, unmediated, immediate response that the reader should treasure above all else.

But criticism is important as well. The pale cast of afterthought can yield rich rewards. What caused the immediate response? Why was I so torn between love and hate for a character? Why did the plot disappear—or never emerge? Why did that technical trick bother me? By analyzing the parts of a story and seeing how they work together, we can enlarge the impact of the work upon us—and enlarge our understanding of literature and how it is made.

The creative life of a writer is a mystery. He makes many decisions unconsciously; his choices in matters of tone or point of view are not usually the result of critical analysis. The old adage, "How do I know what I think until I hear what I say?" applies frequently to writers. Writing is a process of *discovering* the story and its meaning. Faulkner said, "With me, a story usually begins with a single idea or memory or mental picture. The writing . . . is simply a matter of working up to that moment, to explain why it happened or what it caused to follow."

This process of *discovering* can be a disaster for the would-be writer who has no control of techniques; without craft, he can discover very little, for himself or for the reader. Yet with most writers, technique is not a matter of first priority. Sean O'Faolain writes:

> I do not deny that there are some technical tricks to be learned, and quickly forgotten, having become second nature. . . . The things I like in a story are punch and poetry . . . "technique" is the least part of the business.

But making something "second nature" is usually the result of a long, dedicated apprenticeship. "Art is the habit of the artist," writes Flannery O'Connor; "and habits have to be rooted deep in the whole personality." For her,

> The only way, I think, to learn to write short stories is to write them, and then to try to discover what you have done. The time to think of technique is when you've actually got the story in front of you.

In the following pages we discuss, in reference to the stories in this volume, such elements as point of view, tone, characterization, dialogue, setting, symbol, and theme. A story is a whole greater than the sum of its parts, but seeing how those parts work is often to see into the heart of the whole.

Point of View

Some writers believe that the second most important decision they make, after selecting that "idea or memory or mental picture" Faulkner identified as the source of a story, is point of view. Point of view is a term of art which refers to the relationships between the storyteller, the story, and the reader. What vantage point has the writer selected from which to relate his story? Does the story come directly as a happening to the reader, or is it filtered through another mind or personality? Through what window is the reader permitted to see the characters and actions?

Every story has a storyteller. He may announce his role or he may conceal himself. In Eudora Welty's "A Worn Path," the storyteller seems to be a kind of disembodied spirit hovering near the old woman—all-knowing, yet invisible. In Gogol's "The Overcoat," the narrator calls attention to himself in the first sentence and reappears frequently, always as a narrator outside the story, not as a character. The storyteller is the character in Poe's "The Black Cat." Sometimes there is hardly a trace of him anywhere, as in Rulfo's "Macario." It was Joyce's theory and practice that the writer, "like the God of Creation, remains within or behind or beyond or above his handiwork, invisible, refined out of existence, indifferent, paring his fingernails."

But invisible or not, unobtrusive or participating, he is always there, controlling the story. His tone and his subject matter govern the reader's responses; it is his plot that will carry the meaning. Above all, it is he who determines the window through which the reader views the story.

There are many possible windows on a story. If the window is remote from the characters, the view will be long and very likely wide. If the reader is close up, he will feel the intimacy, but he may find it difficult to see around the character's biases to the truth. With one view, the reader may be privy to mental states; with another, he may be limited to what can be seen or heard. These are just some of the possibilities. Each window, each point of view has opportunities and limitations. In the four points of view discussed below, we get some idea of their range.

Omniscient point of view

"None of them knew the color of the sky" is the opening sentence of Stephen Crane's "The Open Boat," and it tells the reader that the storyteller is omniscient. There will be no limitation on the storyteller's knowledge, his power to range widely wherever he chooses. The storyteller knows what the men know, and more. He knows they believe they are near a lifesaving station, and he knows they are wrong. He knows the color of the sky, and the ache in the muscles of the oarsmen. He can be two places at once, in many minds, enjoying many perspectives. And he shares his freedom and knowledge, so that the reader as well can take a broad overview.

Omniscience also permits philosophic depth. Crane's storyteller, for instance, comments not alone on these shipwrecked men but on all men lost at sea ("When it occurs to a man that nature does not regard him as important. ...." "A high cold wind on a winter's night is the word he feels she says to him"). The omniscient narrator is free to bring his own views into the story.

Omniscience has limitations. Crane's wide angle requires distance, making close identification with characters difficult. Our experience therefore tends not to be intimate or intense. Crane attempts to overcome this limitation by frequently restricting his focus to the mind of the correspondent. But—and this is the problem—he still maintains his detached, mildly ironic and philosophic tone:

> The correspondent wondered ingenuously how in the name of all that was sane could there be people who thought it amusing to row a boat. It was not an amusement; it was a diabolical punishment.

This from a man who is struggling for his life against a raging sea! It is all right for gods to be omniscient, but when writers play that game, they can sometimes seem to know too much—and thereby to impair the reader's sense of participation and discovery as he reads the story.

A more successful effort, though not for that a better story, is Mishima's "Patriotism." This chronicle of a ritual suicide moves from a broad view of a culture to a most intimate view of two lovers. "Their lives were lived beneath the solemn protection of the gods and were filled with an intense happiness which set every fiber in their bodies trembling." The tone remains the same throughout, reverential and mystical. Though the narrator is omniscient, he has little emotional distance from the two. As their relationship is profoundly sensual, yet ritualized, so is his attitude. He is at one with the values of what he narrates. He offers no ironic perspective: as they view themselves so their creator views them. Thus, Mishima knows what only an omniscient narrator can know, but he presents it from the point of view of a participant.

Direct observer

Almost the exact opposite of the omniscient is the direct observer. As the omniscient storyteller goes everywhere, knows everything, and comments when he chooses, the direct observer has no memory of the past, no understanding of the present; he is little more than a fly on the wall, recording the scene. This kind of story approaches pure drama: all action, dialogue, setting, stage directions. The audience does the rest.

But a short story, even one with this point of view, is not a play, as a look at Hemingway's "Hills Like White Elephants" shows. About seven-eighths of the story is enclosed within quotation marks, but in that little which is not dialogue is the difference between a story and a play. The story opens with a paragraph of description which concludes: "It was very hot and the express from Barcelona would come in forty minutes. It stopped at this junction for two minutes and went on to Madrid." This passage sets the physical and psychological stage for the story. The time interval and the place are established; the barren quality of the crossroads is a comment on the lives of two characters. Each detail counts, laden with meaning. The reader's eyes and imagination are insistently led to those elements the storyteller wishes him to notice. Although the two characters are discussing abortion, the subject is not named. Finally the man carries out their bags:

> Coming back, he walked through the barroom, where people waiting for the train were drinking. He drank an Anis at the bar and looked at the people. They were all waiting reasonably for the train.

Notice how smoothly and quickly the reader is taken through time and space, avoiding the irrelevant. A crowd of people is suggested in a line; minutes pass in a phrase. Although quick cutting to condense time is possible in a movie, and a play can suggest a setting without filling in details, neither can create a dense and rapid scene with such quick brushstrokes. The direct observer moves rapidly through time and space; his eye is always on the story's center. Of all points of view, the direct observer provides the greatest dramatic intensity and compactness, as this story or as Shirley Jackson's "The Lottery" shows. No storyteller stands between the reader and the scene. The storyteller focuses our senses on the relevant details. We are there.

The disadvantages of this method are obvious. Limited as he is to speech, gesture, action, and setting, the direct observer will find it difficult to render subtly shifting psychological states or to provide a wide range of understanding and feeling. Complexity and subtlety can only be suggested. The drama must speak for itself.

First-person narration

First-person narration can avoid the sprawling quality of omniscience and the narrowness of direct observer. But it has other limitations.

With this point of view, the reader is told what he knows by a "person" who speaks in his own voice. The reader knows only what that person knows and when he knows it and tells it. The reader cannot witness scenes the narrator has not witnessed, nor witness them from angles the narrator does not provide. He cannot be taken into other minds. But first person has a special authenticity and a special vibrancy. The reader feels in touch with a real person who cares about what he is telling. In Maupassant's "A Country Outing"—told by an omniscient narrator—the reader never for a moment believes the teller is involved in his story. But in first person, the words come to us with the force of the narrator's commitment.

The narrator may not be the main character in the story, as he is not in Anderson's "The Egg"; but typically he is an active participant, as in Updike's "Wife-wooing." To compare these two is to glimpse the great flexibility of first-person strategy.

Updike's story is narrated in first person and present tense, which greatly increases the reader's sense of immediacy. The reader identifies closely with the narrator who is telling and seeing it all—inevitably in a light favorable to himself. But the narrator's self-interested tone creates a subtle credibility gap between himself and the reader, and the resultant tension is never fully resolved. Updike takes full advantage of the irony thus created: by the end of the story the reader's sympathies have shifted several times between the narrator and his wife.

Anderson's narrator looks back at his father and mother and the events of their lives from a perspective of many years. Sufficient time has elapsed for all the ambiguities of his early experience to be laid to rest. He knows what he thinks of all the characters, has weighed them in an ultimate scale. There is little risk involved for him in telling his story, and he firmly guides the reader to the appropriate conclusions. In the process, the reader has been so distanced from the heart of the narrative that a good deal of the intimacy and excitement of first person has been sacrificed.

One might say that the closer the narrator is to the story, emotionally and physically, the less certain he is, the less reliable as an interpreter to the reader. The point of view of "an unreliable witness" can be very useful to a writer. This narrator may not actually tell lies, but he interprets incorrectly, or gets scared or rattled, or forgets or weasles; his perspective is too limited or self-serving or emotional for him to report accurately the significance of the events.

Some fine effects can be achieved this way. In Rosenfeld's "The Brigadier," we move from belief in the narrator to doubt of his reliability to utter disbelief in his sanity. Because the narrator's perceptions are askew, the close emotional relationship of the beginning is severed. But something is gained: an ironic glimpse of the reality the writer is exposing; the speaker may be crazy but not much crazier than many presumably sane people we know. His paranoic search for the enemy that isn't there brings to mind some of our own holy wars, and the wisdom of Pogo: "We has met the enemy, and they is us."

Third person intimate

Third person intimate provides a double vision. The reader not only observes the main character, he is also intimately involved with the character's feelings and thoughts. This point of view creates tension between what the storyteller and the reader understand and what the character knows, between external action and internal reaction, between the grossness of gesture and the refinement of thought, between what really is and what the character thinks. Third person intimate can be flexibly adapted to a writer's intentions. At one end of the spectrum is "The Beast in the Jungle" by Henry James; at the other end is "The Grave" by Katherine Anne Porter.

Henry James made many contributions to the craft of fiction, and two of them converge here. In his maturity, James came to believe that the writer should *show* rather than *tell* the reader, that everything should be "rendered," dramatized. He also believed that the most effective point of view for a story was to submerge the story-teller into a character he called the "central intelligence." As the character sees, the reader sees; as he knows, the reader knows. The scenes in "The Beast in the Jungle" come to us through the consciousness of John Marcher, but it is a consciousness rendered in the language of Henry James. Thus we understand more than Marcher does. We can "see" the drama of his shifting mental states, and his blindness. Despite our intimate contact with his mind, we can judge him and his experience from the distance of our own moral perspective, and James's.

"The Grave" illustrates a different use of third person intimate. Its anonymous storyteller directs the reader's attention to setting, characters, situation. Then she steps offstage and turns the reader loose to share the thoughts and feelings of the main character, Miranda. The storyteller remains in the wings, however, occasionally call-ing out directions for the next scene, dropping comments to help the reader under-stand Miranda. Thus, we see Miranda from the outside, in a context of action which is presented objectively, and we understand her from the inside. Under Porter's skillful direction we feel no disruption in the shift, no cracking of the "single effect."

Between these two uses are any number of possibilities. This volume contains numerous examples. Perhaps the most striking is that mixed approach in Delmore Schwartz's "In Dreams Begin Responsibilities." The first-person narrator *imagines* a film about his parents in their youth. The film is described in third person intimate and is believable in its own right; it is believable also as a projection of the narrator's subjectivity. This fictionalized "memory" provides the reader with a multidimensional psychological experience, an experience made possible by the rich artistic resources of point of view.

Tone

The tone of a story is the "voice" in which it is conveyed and the attitude that voice expresses. Even when there is no obvious storyteller or "I," a story has a voice, a style, a special signature that conveys the author's conscious or unconscious intentions.

Part of the meaning of words is carried by pitch, cadence, tempo, rhythm, and syntactical arrangement. Together with the subject matter, these create the personality of a story. Imagine a Chekhov story told by Hemingway, a Mann story in the tone of Robbe-Grillet. The results would probably be grotesque; they would certainly be different. Tone is the load of meaning that cannot be paraphrased but that nonetheless shapes the reader's responses. Even before he makes the plot apparent, the writer begins to create the universe of feeling in which the story takes place. "For forty-seven years they had been married," begins Tillie Olsen's "Tell Me a Riddle":

> How deep back the stubborn, gnarled roots of the quarrel reached, no one could say—but only now, when tending to the needs of others no longer shackled them together, the roots swelled up visible, split the earth between them, and the tearing shook even to the children, long since grown.

A paraphrase: "Once the children were gone the old couple really began to fight." The difference is, of course, a difference in tone. The paraphrase lacks the sense of complexity, the promise of intense feeling, the foreshadowing of sadness, the weight of the bare events. In short, it lacks the passion of Tillie Olsen conveyed by her lovely language.

Here is the beginning of Poe's "The Black Cat":

For the most wild, yet most homely narrative which I am about to pen, I neither expect nor solicit belief. Mad indeed would I be to expect it, in a case where my very senses reject their own evidence. Yet, mad am I not—and very surely do I not dream. But tomorrow I die, and today I would unburthen my soul.

The reader is thus prepared to have his fears aroused, his spine tingled, his credulity stretched. The inversions, slow cadence, archaic literary expressions are used not only to convey information but to solidify a mood of mystery and unreality.

The range of possible tones is as wide as the range of human attitudes. But one tone needs special notice: irony. Irony, whether verbal or situational, always involves a tension between such opposites as appearance and reality, the ideal and the real, or the literal and the implied. Bernard Malamud's "The Magic Barrel," for example, begins in an ironic tone. As soon as we are told that Leo Finkle, a rabbinical student, is pondering the advice that "he might find it easier to win himself a congregation if he were married" we are in an ironic situation. Ideally one marries for love, not expediency. Of course, the final irony of the story is that he marries for love in spite of his intentions—and marries a prostitute at that.

Irony is not only a tone, it may also be a mode of organization, since conflict between the expected and the actual, for example, can be registered in the plot as well as the voice of a story. Though irony can be funny, as in Walter Mitty's struggle between an ideal and a real world, it can also be serious, as in Isaac Rosenfeld's "The Brigadier." More often it is somewhere between, as in Böll's "Action Will Be Taken" were the plastic waitresses programmed for cheerfulness are described as "as crammed with unsung songs as chickens with unlaid eggs"; or as in Landolfi's "Gogol's Wife" where a man tries to shape reality to his ideal by taking a rubber doll as his wife. In all these instances the ironic tone controls the whole story and not just a part.

Plot

In *Aspects of the Novel,* E. M. Forster distinguishes the simple story from the more complex plot: "'The king died and then the queen died' is a story. 'The king died and then the queen died of grief' is a plot." The story, with its "then . . . and then," is only, writes Forster, "the chopped-off length of the tape-worm of time," and satisfies nothing better than mindless, time-killing curiosity. But over the plot "will hover the memory of the reader (that dull glow of the mind of which intelligence is the bright advancing edge)." The intelligent reader wants to know not only what happened, but why, and what it means. The acts are not merely consecutive, as in the simple "story," they are consequential. Implicit in the idea of plot is the belief that human beings shape their lives and are shaped by their experiences. "What is character," asks Henry James, "but the determination of incident? What is incident but the illustration of character?"

The James dictum and the Forster distinction between story and plot would rule out the "surprise ending" story. Life is in some measure unpredictable, flowerpots do fall fourteen floors and land on innocent heads, people do behave in ways even their analysts find strange. But if the ending of a story is an accident or a coincidence, or if the characters act "out of character" in capricious ways, the reader will be unprepared for the ending, and the body of the story will seem literally of no consequence.

Plot is not life; a plot is a writer's arrangement of events that will express his attitude toward the human condition. Most of the stories in this volume have conventional plots. Indeed, the reader might diagram the plots of such stories as Gogol's "The Overcoat," or Lawrence's "The Blind Man," or Flannery O'Connor's "Greenleaf," and discover that they follow quite nicely the classic contours of situation, complication, rising action, climax, falling action, and dénouement. Consider this diagram of "The Overcoat":

1. Akakii is content in his dull civil service job.   SITUATION
2. His overcoat is in rags, and he must have a new one. He has no money.   COMPLICATION
3. By dint of scrimping and saving, he finally gets his coat. It transforms him. He begins to come out of his shell.   RISING ACTION
4. The overcoat is stolen.   CRISIS
5. Akakii seeks justice but encounters only bureaucratic indifference and delay.   FALLING ACTION
6. He sickens and dies; but his ghost haunts all the city's petty bureaucrats and busies itself snatching off their overcoats.   DÉNOUEMENT (POETIC JUSTICE)

Not all stories are so strong in plot as the three mentioned; indeed, Chekhov, the master himself, was noted for the slightness of his plots. Somerset Maugham once said, "If you try to tell one of [Chekhov's] stories, you will find there is nothing to tell. The anecdote, stripped of its trimmings, is insignificant and often inane."

Stories may promise movement, change, development without relying upon external action. The opposing force the hero is up against may be the elements, the universe, other people, the social system, or it may be his own inner need, ambition, sensitivity. When the real battlefield of a story is inside a character, rather than between him and external forces, then the movement of plot from situation through complication to resolution is most likely to be interior also. In Carson McCullers' delicate story, "A Tree · A Rock · A Cloud," there is almost no action at all, yet some profound movements of mood and insight occur. In Bernard Malamud's "The Magic Barrel," things happen, but the drama lies in the psychic change.

It has become commonplace today to deny the necessity of plot. Many avant-garde writers no longer see events as connected or sequential, but rather as products of chance, randomness, coincidence. Thus does art reflect, perhaps unconsciously, such commonplaces of modern science as Werner Heisenberg's "Principle of Uncertainty"—which says that "no events, not even atomic events, can be described with certainty." Orderly plots with beginnings, middles, and ends do not express the way things seem to these writers. Plots imply a faith in history and in the future, but this is not the view expressed in Robbe-Grillet's "The Shore" or Brautigan's "The Cleveland Wrecking Yard" or Gass's "In the Heart of the Heart of the Country." Many modernists agree in greater or lesser degree with Ronald Sukenick:

God was the omniscient author, but he died; now no one knows the plot, and since our reality lacks the sanction of a creator, there's no guarantee as to the authenticity of the received version. Time is reduced to presence, the content of a series of discontinuous moments. Time is no longer purposive, and so there is no destiny, only chance.

Philip Stevick, in *Anti-Story,* says a character "doesn't have to do anything at all, just talk to us. . . ." He cites Gass's story as an example of "against event." Yet, from another point of view, that story can be seen as a subtle and oblique narrative of event. It is without a scrap of dialogue, and certainly there is no drama. Little is shown, much is told. When the story begins, the all-affecting love affair is over, the narrator is seeking a new equilibrium. Nevertheless the story is a kind of journey through his psychic states, a journey brought about and validated by his experiences ("I was raking leaves when Uncle Halley introduced himself to me. . . ." "Friday night. Girls in dark skirts and white blouses sit in ranks and scream in concert"). These experiences carry him to the fine conclusion: "There's no one to hear the music but myself, and though I'm listening, I'm no longer certain. Perhaps the record's playing something else."

Setting and Dialogue

"Nothing," says Elizabeth Bowen, "can happen nowhere." The place where the action happens can powerfully focus the reader's expectations. Without it, there would be vagueness, uncertainty.

In "The Three Strangers"—an expanded anecdote with important connections to the "ballad" tradition (which minimizes setting)—Hardy gives us pages of description before the action begins. The procedure is unusual for a short-story writer but not for Hardy, who is famous for vitalizing his settings. Here, as Suzanne Ferguson has shown, he pans in on his scene almost like a film cameraman: "Hardy narrows his view from a panorama of the windswept downs to the lonely shepherd's cottage at the crossing of two footpaths, then moves to the contrast-cheeriness of the interior. . . . The crossing footpaths place the cottage at a symbolic intersection of men's journeys and prepare for the appearance of the three strangers. . . . But Hardy is idiosyncratic in his practice. Most story writers try to render the setting swiftly, sparsely, or impressionistically, by slipping representative concrete details into other parts of the narrative. Thus does Kafka give us the wintry setting of "A Country Doctor":

> I had to start on an urgent journey; a seriously ill patient was waiting for me in a village ten miles off; a thick blizzard of snow filled all the wide spaces between him and me; I had a gig, a light gig with big wheels, exactly right for our country roads; . . . but there was no horse to be had, no horse.

The doctor has to *get somewhere*—the snow, the gig, and all other descriptive details are relevant to that fact, and to no other. The setting is, quite literally, given us on the run.

Dialogue appears in almost all stories. Few writers are willing to sacrifice the talk of the characters. Talk creates a sense of verisimilitude and immediacy. They speak, therefore they are; we overhear, therefore we believe. Nothing defines characters and relationships more quickly than speech. Consider this exchange in Kipling's "The Wish House":

> "You're as free-tongued as ever, Liz," Mrs. Ashcroft observed.
> "Only when I'm with you. Otherwhiles, I'm Granny—three times over. . . ."

and a little later at tea time:

> ". . . I dunno as I've ever owed me belly much," said Mrs. Ashcroft thoughtfully. "We only go through this world once."
> "But don't it lay heavy on ye, sometimes?" her guest suggested.

Almost solely by means of interchanges like these, Kipling establishes the situation, defines the characters, moves the story forward. Nothing goes on but talk, and yet the reader has profoundly experienced these two old ladies and their whole lives.

In the first scene of O'Connor's "Greenleaf," Mrs. May imagined what Greenleaf would say if she asked him to get the bull out of her garden:

> "Hit looks to me like one or both of them boys would not make their maw ride out in the middle of the night this away. If hit was my boys, they would have got thet bull up theirself."

And a little later: "If your boys had any pride, Mr. Greenleaf," she would like to say to him someday, "there are many things that they would not *allow* their mother to do." Through accent and cadence as well as vocabulary and intended meaning, these two characters are indelibly engraved on the reader's imagination: Mrs. May, threatened, defensive, inadequate, superior: and Mr. Greenleaf, insolent in a sneaky way, undermining, proud. What is of special interest here is that the exchange is not actual speech but what Mrs. May imagines. Even in her fantasy, Greenleaf's and her own character are expressed in what is said and how it is said.

Generally, dialogue is not used as a vehicle for exposition. Although frequently a character will by his words drop important information, conveying facts is not a primary function of dialogue. Its primary function is human interaction. Effective dialogue sounds the way people talk, but few writers attempt a phonographic representation of speech—partly because much day-to-day speech (Pass the butter. May I have the car?) is non-functional in a short story. Dialogue is interaction, and interaction pushes the story toward its conclusions. For instance, after the imagined dialogue, Mrs. May decides to let the bull root in the yard rather than call Greenleaf.

Of course monologue, reverie, self-confession—as in Joyce's "Araby" or Gass's story or Landolfi's "Gogol's Wife"—are variations on dialogue that can have similar effects. (In fact, Mrs. May's imagined dialogue is only a dramatic form of reverie.) But whether we hear inner or outer voices, nothing quite takes the place of letting the reader overhear significant interchanges.

Character

We engage in characterization almost every day of our lives. We tell our family or friends what happened at work or school, who said what, who did what, maybe why. Perhaps we mimic a voice or a gesture; we may even invent mannerisms to convey what we felt about a person. Yet common as characterization is, it is one of the mysteries of tale-telling. T. S. Eliot said:

> A "living character" is not necessarily "true to life." It is a person whom we can see and hear, whether he be true or false to human nature as we know it. What the creator of character needs is not so much knowledge of motives as keen sensibility; the dramatist need not understand people, but he must be exceptionally aware of them.

What goes into a living character? How does a writer create the breath of life on a page with mere words? Perhaps a few notions will cast a little light on the mystery. All that we have said about point of view touches on character, for the way we see the character determines the character we see. If the omniscient narrator of Maupassant's "A Country Outing" had been inside the ridiculed mother's mind, the reader might, instead of despising her as a foolish woman, have shared her hope for pleasure, her fear of ridicule, her sense of isolation from an indifferent husband. Third-person intimate or first person would have changed the character—and our attitude.

Tone also creates character. If the author's tone is contemptuous or humorous, the reader will likely see the character as contemptible or funny. Imagine the difference had Verga in "The She-Wolf" treated the lusting old woman humorously, or if Thurber's tone in "The Secret Life of Walter Mitty" had been solemn, finding pathos in Mitty's need for fantasy. We would have seen those characters differently.

Everything about a character defines him and contributes to the impact on us: looks, gestures, attire, social class, words spoken, views held, motives revealed, deeds done or not done. Discussing how these qualities are conveyed brings us again to *showing* versus *telling*. Some writers prefer to tell about their characters. The lawyer in "Bartleby, the Scrivener" simply informs the reader about his work, personal qualities, values. In "Little Herr Friedemann," Mann goes so far in telling as to summarize and evaluate the emotional state of the character:

> But in his twenty-first year his mother died, after a lingering illness.
>
> This was a sore blow for Johannes Friedemann, and the pain of it endured. He cherished his grief, he gave himself up to it as one gives oneself to a great joy, he fed it with a thousand childhood memories; it was the first important event in his life and he made the most of it.

In cases like these two, telling provides a richness of background difficult to achieve by showing.

But Henry James believed that if details were rendered sharply enough, the reader would be able to infer character. In *Collected Impressions,* Elizabeth Bowen says,

> Characters must *materialize*—that is, must have a palpable physical reality. They must be not only see-able (visualizable): they must be able to be felt. . . . Physical personality belongs to action. . . . Pictures must be in movement. Eyes, hands, stature, etc. must appear, and only appear, in play.

In "A Simple Heart," Flaubert introduces Félicité's only lover: "a smart young fellow, who had been leaning on the shaft of a cart, came up and asked her to dance." And the seducer takes shape before our eyes!

In first-person and third-person-intimate point of view, there is often a simultaneous characterization of two characters. In Babel's "My First Goose," the narrator, upon seeing the commanding officer,

> wondered at the beauty of his giant's body. He rose, the purple of his riding breeches and the crimson of his little tilted cap and the decorations stuck on his chest cleaving the hut as a standard cleaves the sky.

A character can be revealed in the way others see him and in his view of others.

There are, as E. M. Forster says, flat characters and round characters. Flat characters do not change or develop, and though usually humorous they are apt to be less interesting than round ones. Yet they must be given life adequate to their function in the story. Sometimes simple naming assists this function, as Dickens brilliantly shows with his Gradgrinds and Pecksniffs. (Although Akakii Akakiievich in Gogol's "The Overcoat" is not really flat, his name, which in Russian refers to feces or defecation, fixes him as one of the offal of human society.) Sometimes a character is pinpointed by a physical characteristic, like the after-lunch anger of the clerk Turkey in "Bartleby, the Scrivener." Sometimes a flat character can be identified by an emblem: the artist's silly phrases ("A Lady in Love with a Pineapple") in Mansfield's "Marriage à la Mode."

Flat characters are often types and easily tagged: the "nagging wife" and the "henpecked husband" in "The Secret Life of Walter Mitty," the "super-patriot" in "The Brigadier." Yet even as we laugh at characters whose souls have been solidified by early rigor mortis or who are beset by an *idée fixe,* we may catch a glimpse of the tragedy as well as the comedy of life.

Though a round character may be no more difficult to create than a flat one, he is almost by definition more complex. Each appearance of a round character adds to our understanding of him *and* is consistent, of a piece, with what we already know. Each gesture, each word spoken opens a door to the whole person, seems to imply a wholeness of personality. In "The Magic Barrel" we are introduced to Leo Finkle as a rabbinical student who seeks a wife in order to obtain a congregation. Thus far, he is flat and somewhat laughable. The next characterization occurs when Malamud tells us that the look of sadness in the marriage broker's eyes "put Leo a little at ease although the situation, for him, was inherently tense." Leo is thus rounded, and the rest of the story is further evidence of his complex, touching humanity.

Sometimes stories seem not to be concerned with character at all. In "In the Heart of the Heart of the Country" Gass has substituted a poetic sensibility for characterization. Sometimes when the main purpose of a story is its theme or moral, as in Aesop's *Fables,* or Bunyan's *The Pilgrim's Progress,* or modern counterparts like Čapek's "The Last Judgment," the characters are only ends towards means.

People, ideally, are ends in themselves, not means to ends. But artists are creators and, for the sake of their compositions, often treat their people with the freedom a musician takes with his notes: manipulating, foreshortening, flattening, rounding. For, the characters in a story are only part of a whole; it is within the whole context that we finally read the story.

Symbolism

A symbol is a sign standing for a meaning. It can be a *stipulated* meaning—as, for example, when a new nation "decides" on the symbolic colors for its new flag—but usually it is a *derived* meaning, one born from the history and experience of a culture, as the blindfolds on our statues of Justice stand for that impartiality of the law which is rooted in our Western tradition. Broadly speaking, all words are symbols (since they are signs standing for meanings); but in literature we limit the term to those words which have, in the context of the work, collected unto themselves—like iron filings unto a magnet—something of the story's essential point or meaning. Such a sign can light up a single character, an event, a scene, a whole story—can be, in fact, inseparable from its point of illumination. Indeed, the very titles of some stories in this volume name the symbols that unite them: "The Overcoat," "The Black Cat," "The Blind Man," "A Worn Path." Unlike traditional symbols—the Cross of Christianity, the Star of David, the dove of peace—the symbols in these stories are not inherited, but created by the writers, shaped by the pressures of their narratives. We no longer live, as Joseph Campbell has reminded us, in a "mythologically instructed community" that comes fully equipped with the traditional symbols embodying the traditional values and beliefs of that community. Instead, we are symbol-poor; as Carl Jung has said, "only an unparalleled impoverishment of symbolism could enable us to rediscover the gods as psychic features . . . as archetypes of the unconscious." But the need persists, in literature and in life, to focus our feelings and beliefs—or, more likely, our longing for belief and our groping for assurance. Writers, in their explorations of human experience, in their pursuit of the art (in Kermode's words) of "finding things out," are in some measure supplying those needs. Not all writers are clearly symbolists, and not all symbols in stories are big flags waving in our eyes; symbols can be quite unpretentious and, often, are no more than simple *things* or *acts* around which the meaning of the story clusters.

Thus that simple path in Welty's "A Worn Path" is a symbol. It is the *way* of Old Phoenix's suffering just as the stations of the Cross have, in Christian tradition, become ritualized as the *way* of Christ's suffering. Less portentously, "The wide w, the receptive o. Womb" of Updike's "Wife-wooing" are symbols reminding the lustful hero of warm thighs and vaginas ("They say rose windows in cathedrals are vaginal symbols") but also, comically, of "the white O of the plate upon which the children discarded with squeals of disgust the rings of translucent onion that came squeezed in the hamburgers." Wife-wooing and child-raising are in desperate conflict, and out of the pressure of that conflict even onion rings become symbolic. Joyce is mentioned in that story, which puts one in mind of "Araby"—a story in which romantic promise and sordid reality are in similar conflict, and in which that one word *Araby,* with its connotations of Eastern mystery and romance, becomes symbolic of a shriveled dream. And much the same could be said of the "magic barrel" in Malamud's story— for in that barrel rest all the hopes and fears of that story.

Emblems are symbols of limited scope, and are sometimes mere impressionistic details—like Chekhov's bit of bottle shining in the starlight (see p. 8). In Saul Bellow's "Looking for Mr. Green" the character of Staika, whose power "expressed the war of flesh and blood" against the sordid misery of slum existence, is seen in flaming colors, flaming reds and golds, and this quality of her spirit colors everything the narrator sees that day: "the spirit of Staika somehow presided over the whole district for him, and it took color from her; he saw her color, in the spotty curb fires and the fires under the El, the straight alley of flamy gloom." Compared with her, the repressed children were "silent and white." Thus do colors become emblems of character, flashes on the mind's eye that connect the outer world and the inner. Are the details of the following passage from Wright's "Almos' a Man" emblems or just details?

> [Dave] came in sight of Joe's store. A yellow lantern glowed on the front porch. He mounted steps and went through the screen door, hearing it bang behind him. There was a strong smell of coal oil and mackerel fish.

The central symbol of that story is the gun—the symbol of Joe's rage and frustrated manhood—but these details spell his poverty, the condition that subsidizes, so to speak, the meaning of that gun. Emblems or details? The question is academic; the important thing is that we recognize how the particulars of a story can have profound and wide-ranging reverberations.

In the hands of a clumsy writer, a symbol may seem pasted onto a story, as if the writer were saying, "This way to the meaning." To be effective, a symbol will emerge from the story's own life, and help the reader back into the story. The snow in Aiken's story is such a symbol, and we must read its meaning in order to understand the trouble of the boy (see pp. 317-329). Unfortunately, however, symbol hunting has become an overindulged indoor sport with some readers. Such readers should be reminded that Freud himself said that sometimes a cigar is only a cigar.

Theme

As we pointed out in Part I of the Introduction, a story expresses the values of a writer and his conception of the human condition. In that sense, the whole story embodies his theme.

But the thoughts and feelings that a writer embodies in a story are seldom very simple. Most stories cannot be reduced, like Aesop's *Fables*, to a simple moral. A modern short story is not fertile soil in which to plant a sermon. Chekhov wrote to his editor:

> You upbraid me about objectivity, styling it indifference to good and evil, absence of ideals and ideas, etc. You would have me say, in depicting horse thieves, that stealing horses is an evil. But then, that has been known a long while, even without me. Let jurors judge them, for my business is only to show them as they are. . . . Of course, it would be gratifying to couple art with sermonizing, but, personally, I find this exceedingly difficult and, because of conditions imposed by technique, all but impossible.

Nor can a story be translated into a philosophic treatise or a sociological tract. Weighty ideas need systematic presentation as free as possible from the mess that is human beings. Organized knowledge by its very nature deals in generalities, but fiction deals with the specific person in the specific situation. And sometimes characters can take on a life of their own—almost in defiance of their creator's intention.

Still and all, as Chekhov well knew, serious readers demand more than an accounting of events; they demand that these events in some way illumine their own lives—that events be shaped into a meaning. After the pleasure or pain, excitement or perplexity caused by the story has receded, the reader is left with a residue, a distillation that we call its *theme*. After we lay aside Böll's "Action Will Be Taken," we can abstract its point: the alienation of modern man. When we have recovered from the discomfort at the odd confrontation of the two men in "The Blind Man," we understand that Lawrence is saying that there is a knowing and a loving that only those who are alive in their senses can have.

The reader should be cautioned against overemphasizing theme. Writers seldom consciously set out to imbed ideas in their stories. If you had asked William Faulkner what "Barn Burning" was about, he might mention the subject but he probably would not abstract the meaning. If you asked the authors of "The Lottery" or "Report" what their theme was, they would probably refer you back to their stories. For, just as the light at the end of the tunnel is inconceivable without the tunnel and inseparable from it, so the theme is inseparable from the totality of the tale.

Part One

Beginnings: Forms of Early Stories

Myth and Legend

Myth: HOW THINGS GOT STARTED

How and where to draw the line between myth and legend is a vexed question with anthropologists and folklorists. It is usually said that a legend is the story of some wonderful or miraculous human event, or saint's life, which is believed to have a historical (though unverifiable) basis; whereas a myth more often deals with divinities and heroes, and with ultimate natural events like the origin of man, or of the customs, rites, and institutions of a people. Of course, in their native milieus myths are held to be historically true, just as some Christians hold the Genesis story to be a literal account of the Creation. But myths normally deal with matters antecedent even to vestigial human memory, whereas legends approach historical time. To complicate things, there is also that generic term "folktale," which is almost synonymous with "legend," but not quite. Here is how Géza Róheim, a great pioneer in cultural anthropology and psychoanalysis, makes the distinction:

> In a myth the actors are mostly divine and sometimes human. In a folktale the *dramatis personae* are mostly human and especially the hero is human, frequently with supernatural beings as his opponents. In a myth we have definite locality; in a folktale the actors are nameless, the scene is just anywhere. A myth is part of a creed; it is believed by the narrator. The folktale is purely fiction, and not intended to be anything else.

The Genesis myth begins, "In the beginning God created the heaven and the earth"; the creation myth of the native American Kiowa tribe begins, "You know, everything had to begin, and this is how it was. . . ." In the one the actors are both human and divine, in the other only human; the "definite locality" in the one is the Garden of Eden, in the other a "hollow log." But they are both parts of creeds and are both, in their living cultural contexts, believed to be true.

If that is how things began, the other Kiowa stories from N. Scott Momaday's beautiful collection are about how things went on as the tribe accumulated its history and values. The first two (about the talking dog and the girl who married the sun) are doubtless "folktales" in Róheim's sense; the third (an exploit against a Kiowa enemy) is unquestionably a legend, since it reflects an honorific memory of real events by real people.

In the two excerpts from the *Dialogues* of St. Gregory the Great detailing the holy life of St. Benedict, we get a similar mix of the miraculous and the historical. St. Benedict really lived, but whether we call these stories fictional or historical depends on whether we are true believers or not.

But whatever we call them, these stories out of a believing past have increasing charm for modern readers. Perhaps, as Philip Rahv says, "the craze for myth is the fear of history." "To some people," he writes, "it appears as though the past, all of it together with its gods and sacred books, were being ground to pieces in the powerhouse of change, senselessly used up in the fabrication of an unthinkable future." But mythic time and—to a lesser extent—legendary time, have the advantage of "confounding past, present, and future in an undifferentiated unity," thus giving us timeless events "endlessly present," rather than historical events that occur "once only." To say this is to say in a particular way that myths and legends are part of sacred lore, whereas the genre of the short story is secular. Perhaps Saul Bellow has put it best in saying: "Myth, rising from the unconscious, is superior to mere 'story,' but myth will not come near while ordinary trivial ideas of self remain. The powers of myth can be raised up only when the well-known pretensions of selfhood are surrendered. Therefore consciousness must abase itself, and every hidden thing must be exhumed."

Yet one of the paradoxes of this collection is that, as we approach the present, those stories which ostensibly record despair, absurdity, and cultural break-up are, at the same time, those stories most close in form to myth and legend. The events of "The Lottery" or "The Cleveland Wrecking Yard" hardly seem events that occur "once only"—like the events in Forster's "The Rock" or Joyce's "Araby." Rather they seem like timeless events "endlessly present"—and such effects may tell us that the search for final value via fiction is also endless.

The First Book of Moses, called Genesis

CHAPTER 1

1 In the beginning God created the heaven and the earth.

2 And the earth was without form, and void; and darkness *was*[1] upon the face of the deep. And the Spirit of God moved upon the face of the waters.

3 And God said, Let there be light: and there was light.

[1] Italics indicate words inserted by the original translators to make better English sense.

4 And God saw the light, that *it was* good: and God divided the light from the darkness.

5 And God called the light Day, and the darkness he called Night. And the evening and the morning were the first day.

6 ¶ And God said, Let there be a firmament in the midst of the waters, and let it divide the waters from the waters.

7 And God made the firmament, and divided the waters which *were* under the firmament from the waters which *were* above the firmament: and it was so.

8 And God called the firmament Heaven. And the evening and the morning were the second day.

9 ¶ And God said, Let the waters under the heaven be gathered together unto one place, and let the dry *land* appear: and it was so.

10 And God called the dry *land* Earth; and the gathering together of the waters called he Seas: and God saw that *it was* good.

11 And God said, Let the earth bring forth grass, the herb yielding seed, *and* the fruit tree yielding fruit after his kind, whose seed *is* in itself, upon the earth: and it was so.

12 And the earth brought forth grass, *and* herb yielding seed after his kind, and the tree yielding fruit, whose seed *was* in itself, after his kind: and God saw that *it was* good.

13 And the evening and the morning were the third day.

14 ¶ And God said, Let there be lights in the firmament of the heaven to divide the day from the night; and let them be for signs, and for seasons, and for days, and years:

15 And let them be for lights in the firmament of the heaven to give light upon the earth: and it was so.

16 And God made two great lights; the greater light to rule the day, and the lesser light to rule the night: *he made* the stars also.

17 And God set them in the firmament of the heaven to give light upon the earth,

18 And to rule over the day and over the night, and to divide the light from the darkness: and God saw that *it was* good.

19 And the evening and the morning were the fourth day.

20 And God said, Let the waters bring forth abundantly the moving creature that hath life, and fowl *that* may fly above the earth in the open firmament of heaven.

21 And God created great whales, and every living creature that moveth, which the waters brought forth abundantly, after their kind, and every winged fowl after his kind: and God saw that *it was* good.

22 And God blessed them, saying, Be fruitful, and multiply, and fill the waters in the seas, and let fowl multiply in the earth.

23 And the evening and the morning were the fifth day.

24 ¶ And God said, Let the earth bring forth the living creature after his kind, cattle, and creeping thing, and beast of the earth after his kind: and it was so.

25 And God made the beast of the earth after his kind, and cattle after their kind, and every thing that creepeth upon the earth after his kind: and God saw that *it was* good.

26 ¶ And God said, Let us make man in our image, after our likeness: and let them have dominion over the fish of the sea, and over the fowl of the air, and over the cattle, and over all the earth, and over every creeping thing that creepeth upon the earth.

27 So God created man in his *own* image, in the image of God created he him; male and female created he them.

28 And God blessed them, and God said unto them, Be fruitful, and multiply, and replenish the earth, and subdue it: and have dominion over the fish of the sea, and over the fowl of the air, and over every living thing that moveth upon the earth.

29 ¶ And God said, Behold, I have given you every herb bearing seed, which *is* upon the face of all the earth, and every tree, in the which *is* the fruit of a tree yielding seed; to you it shall be for meat.

30 And to every beast of the earth, and to every fowl of the air, and to every thing that creepeth upon the earth, wherein *there is* life, *I have given* every green herb for meat: and it was so.

31 And God saw every thing that he had made, and, behold, *it was* very good. And the evening and the morning were the sixth day.

CHAPTER 2

1 Thus the heavens and the earth were finished, and all the host of them.

2 And on the seventh day God ended his work which he had made; and he rested on the seventh day from all his work which he had made.

3 And God blessed the seventh day, and sanctified it: because that in it he had rested from all his work which God created and made.

4 ¶ These *are* the generations of the heavens and of the earth when they were created, in the day that the LORD God made the earth and the heavens,

5 And every plant of the field before it was in the earth, and every herb of the field before it grew: for the LORD God had not caused it to rain upon the earth, and *there was* not a man to till the ground.

6 But there went up a mist from the earth, and watered the whole face of the ground.

7 And the LORD God formed man *of* the dust of the ground, and breathed into his nostrils the breath of life; and man became a living soul.

8 ¶ And the LORD God planted a garden eastward in Ē'-dĕn; and there he put the man whom he had formed.

9 And out of the ground made the LORD God to grow every tree that is pleasant to the sight, and good for food; the tree of life also in the midst of the garden, and the tree of knowledge of good and evil.

10 And a river went out of Ē'-dĕn to water the garden; and from thence it was parted, and became into four heads.

11 The name of the first *is* Pī'-sŏn: that *is* it which compasseth the whole land of Hăv'-i-läh, where *there is* gold;

12 And the gold of that land *is* good: there *is* bdellium and the onyx stone.

13 And the name of the second river *is* Gī'-hŏn: the same *is* it that compasseth the whole land of Ē-thĭ-ō'-pĭ-ă.

14 And the name of the third river *is* Hĭd'-dĕ-kĕl: that *is* it which goeth toward the east of Ăs-sўr'-ĭ-ă. And the fourth river *is* Êu-phrā'-tēs̀.

15 And the LORD God took the man, and put him into the garden of Ē'-dĕn to dress it and to keep it.

16 And the LORD God commanded the man, saying, Of every tree of the garden thou mayest freely eat:

17 But of the tree of the knowledge of good and evil, thou shalt not eat of it: for in the day that thou eatest thereof thou shalt surely die.

18 ¶ And the LORD God said, *It is* not good that the man should be alone; I will make him an help meet for him.

19 And out of the ground the LORD God formed every beast of the field, and every fowl of the air; and brought *them* unto Ăd′-ăm to see what he would call them: and whatsoever Ăd′-ăm called every living creature, that *was* the name thereof.

20 And Ăd′-ăm gave names to all cattle, and to the fowl of the air, and to every beast of the field; but for Ăd′-ăm there was not found an help meet for him.

21 And the LORD God caused a deep sleep to fall upon Ăd′-ăm, and he slept: and he took one of his ribs, and closed up the flesh instead thereof;

22 And the rib, which the LORD God had taken from man, made he a woman, and brought her unto the man.

23 And Ăd′-ăm said, This *is* now bone of my bones, and flesh of my flesh: she shall be called Woman, because she was taken out of Man.

24 Therefore shall a man leave his father and his mother, and shall cleave unto his wife: and they shall be one flesh.

25 And they were both naked, the man and his wife, and were not ashamed.

CHAPTER 3

1 Now the serpent was more subtil than any beast of the field which the LORD God had made. And he said unto the woman, Yea, hath God said, Ye shall not eat of every tree of the garden?

2 And the woman said unto the serpent, We may eat of the fruit of the trees of the garden:

3 But of the fruit of the tree which *is* in the midst of the garden, God hath said, Ye shall not eat of it, neither shall ye touch it, lest ye die.

4 And the serpent said unto the woman, Ye shall not surely die:

5 For God doth know that in the day ye eat thereof, then your eyes shall be opened, and ye shall be as gods, knowing good and evil.

6 And when the woman saw that the tree *was* good for food, and that is *was* pleasant to the eyes, and a tree to be desired to make *one* wise, she took of the fruit thereof, and did eat, and gave also unto her husband with her; and he did eat.

7 And the eyes of them both were opened, and they knew that they *were* naked; and they sewed fig leaves together, and made themselves aprons.

8 And they heard the voice of the LORD God walking in the garden in the cool of the day: and Ăd′-ăm and his wife hid themselves from the presence of the LORD God amongst the trees of the garden.

9 And the LORD God called unto Ăd′-ăm, and said unto him, Where *art* thou?

10 And he said, I heard thy voice in the garden, and I was afraid, because I *was* naked; and I hid myself.

11 And he said, Who told thee that thou *wast* naked? Hast thou eaten of the tree, whereof I commanded thee that thou shouldest not eat?

12 And the man said, The woman whom thou gavest *to be* with me, she gave me of the tree, and I did eat.

13 And the LORD God said unto the woman, What *is* this *that* thou hast done? And the woman said, The serpent beguiled me, and I did eat.

14 And the LORD God said unto the serpent, Because thou hast done this, thou *art* cursed above all cattle, and above every beast of the field; upon thy belly shalt thou go, and dust shalt thou eat all the days of thy life:

15 And I will put enmity between thee and the woman, and between thy seed and her seed; it shall bruise thy head, and thou shalt bruise his heel.

16 Unto the woman he said, I will greatly multiply thy sorrow and thy conception, in sorrow thou shalt bring forth children; and thy desire *shall be* to thy husband, and he shall rule over thee.

17 And unto Ăd'-ăm he said, Because thou has hearkened unto the voice of thy wife, and hast eaten of the tree, of which I commanded thee, saying, Thou shalt not eat of it: cursed *is* the ground for thy sake; in sorrow shalt thou eat *of* it all the days of thy life;

18 Thorns also and thistles shall it bring forth to thee; and thou shalt eat the herb of the field;

19 In the sweat of thy face shalt thou eat bread, till thou return unto the ground; for out of it wast thou taken: for dust thou *art,* and unto dust shalt thou return.

20 And Ăd'-ăm called his wife's name Ēve; because she was the mother of all living.

21 Unto Ăd'-ăm also and to his wife did the LORD God make coats of skins, and clothed them.

22 ¶ And the LORD God said, Behold, the man is become as one of us, to know good and evil: and now, lest he put forth his hand, and take also of the tree of life, and eat and live for ever:

23 Therefore the LORD God sent him forth from the garden of Ē'-dēn, to till the ground from whence he was taken.

24 So he drove out the man; and he placed at the east of the garden of Ē'-dēn Chĕr'-ū-bims, and a flaming sword which turned every way, to keep the way of the tree of life.

Kiowa Creation Myth

I

You know, everything had to begin, and this is how it was: the Kiowas came one by one into the world through a hollow log. They were many more than now, but not all of them got out. There was a woman whose body was swollen up with child, and she got stuck in the log. After that, no one could get through, and that is why the Kiowas are a small tribe in number. They looked all around and saw the world. It made them glad to see so many things. They called themselves *Kwuda,* "coming out."

From *The Way to Rainy Mountain* by N. Scott Momaday, pp. 16, 20, 22, 46. Copyright 1969 by The University of New Mexico Press. Reprinted by permission.

Legend: HOW THINGS WENT ON

Kiowa Legends

II

Before there were horses the Kiowas had need of dogs. That was a long time ago, when dogs could talk. There was a man who lived alone; he had been thrown away, and he made his camp here and there on the high ground. Now it was dangerous to be alone, for there were enemies all around. The man spent his arrows hunting food. He had one arrow left, and he shot a bear; but the bear was only wounded and it ran away. The man wondered what to do. Then a dog came up to him and said that many enemies were coming; they were close by and all around. The man could think of no way to save himself. But the dog said: "You know, I have puppies. They are young and weak and they have nothing to eat. If you will take care of my puppies, I will show you how to get away." The dog led the man here and there, around, and around, and they came to safety.

III

They lived at first in the mountains. They did not yet know of Tai-me, but this is what they knew: There was a man and his wife. They had a beautiful child, a little girl whom they would not allow to go out of their sight. But one day a friend of the family came and asked if she might take the child outside to play. The mother guessed that would be all right, but she told the friend to leave the child in its cradle and to place the cradle in a tree. While the child was in the tree, a redbird came among the branches. It was not like any bird that you have seen; it was very beautiful, and it did not fly away. It kept still upon a limb, close to the child. After a while the child got out of its cradle and began to climb after the redbird. And at the same time the tree began to grow taller, and the child was borne up into the sky. She was then a woman, and she found herself in a strange place. Instead of a redbird, there was a young man standing before her. The man spoke to her and said: "I have been watching you for a long time, and I knew that I would find a way to bring you here. I have brought you here to be my wife." The woman looked all around; she saw that he was the only living man there. She saw that he was the sun.

IV

If an arrow is well made, it will have tooth marks upon it. That is how you know. The Kiowas made fine arrows and straightened them in their teeth. Then they drew them to the bow to see if they were straight. Once there was a man and his wife. They were alone at night in their tipi. By the light of the fire the man was making arrows. After a while he caught sight of something. There was a small opening in the tipi where two hides were sewn together. Someone was there on the outside, looking in. The man went on with his work, but he said to his wife: "Someone is standing outside. Do not be afraid. Let us talk easily, as of ordinary things." He took up an arrow and straightened it in his teeth; then, as it was right for him to do, he drew it to the bow and took aim, first in this direction and then in that. And all the while he was talking, as if to his wife. But this is how he spoke: "I know that you are there on the outside, for I can feel your eyes upon me. If you are a Kiowa, you will understand what I am saying, and you will speak your name." But there was no answer, and the man went on in the same way, pointing the arrow all around. At last his aim fell upon the place where his enemy stood, and he let go of the string. The arrow went straight to the enemy's heart.

St. Gregory: Dialogue Two

When Benedict abandoned his studies to go into solitude, he was accompanied only by his nurse, who loved him dearly. As they were passing through Affile, a number of devout men invited them to stay there and provided them with lodging near the Church of St. Peter. One day, after asking her neighbors to lend her a tray for cleaning wheat, the nurse happened to leave it on the edge of the table and when she came back found it had slipped off and broken in two. The poor woman burst into tears; she had only borrowed this tray and now it was ruined. Benedict, who had always been a devout and thoughtful boy, felt sorry for his nurse when he saw her weeping. Quietly picking up both the pieces, he knelt down by himself and prayed earnestly to God, even to the point of tears. No sooner had he finished his prayer then he noticed that the two pieces were joined together again, without even a mark to show where the tray had been broken. Hurrying back at once, he cheerfully reassured his nurse and handed her the tray in perfect condition.

News of the miracle spread to all the country around Affile and stirred up so much admiration among the people that they hung the tray at the entrance of their church. Ever since then it has been a reminder to all of the great holiness Benedict had acquired at the very outset of his monastic life. The tray remained there many years for everyone to see, and it is still hanging over the doorway of the church in these days of Lombard rule.[1] Benedict, however, preferred to suffer ill-treatment from the world rather than enjoy its praises. He wanted to spend himself laboring for God, not to be honored by the applause of men. So he stole away secretly from his nurse and fled to a lonely wilderness about thirty-five miles from Rome called Subiaco. A stream of cold, clear water running through the region broadens out at this point to form a lake, then flows off and continues on its course.[2] On his way there Benedict met a monk named Romanus, who asked him where he was going. After discovering the young man's purpose, Romanus kept it secret and even helped carry it out by clothing him with the monastic habit and supplying his needs as well as he could.

At Subiaco, Benedict made his home in a narrow cave and for three years remained concealed there, unknown to anyone except the monk Romanus, who lived in a monastery close by under the rule of Abbot Deodatus. With fatherly concern this monk regularly set aside as much bread as he could from his own portion; then from time to time, unnoticed by his abbot, he left the monastery long enough to take the bread to Benedict. There was no path leading from the monastery down to his cave

---

[1] The Lombards, a Germanic people, left their homes along the upper Danube and invaded Italy in 568, establishing a kingdom there which lasted until 774.

[2] Subiaco lies along the Anio River about five miles north of Affile. The lake St. Gregory speaks of gave the site its Latin name of *Sublacum*. It was formed by a dam which Emperor Claudius had built across the river, and lasted until 1305 when the dam was destroyed by floods.

From St. Gregory the Great, *Dialogues*. Translated by Odo John Zimmerman, O.S.B. New York: Fathers of the Church, Inc., 1959.

because of a cliff that rose directly over it. To reach him Romanus had to tie the bread to the end of a long rope and lower it over the cliff. A little bell attached to the rope let Benedict know when the bread was there, and he would come out to get it. The ancient Enemy of mankind grew envious of the kindness shown by the older monk in supplying Benedict with food, and one day, as the bread was being lowered, he threw a stone at the bell and broke it. In spite of this, Romanus kept on with his faithful service.

At length the time came when almighty God wished to grant him rest from his toil and reveal Benedict's virtuous life to others. Like a shining lamp his example was to be set on a lampstand to give light to everyone in God's house.[3] The Lord therefore appeared in a vision to a priest some distance away, who had just prepared his Easter dinner. "How can you prepare these delicacies for yourself," He asked, "while my servant is out there in the wilds suffering from hunger?"

Rising at once, the priest wrapped up the food and set out to find the man of God that very day. He searched for him along the rough mountainsides, in the valleys, and through the caverns, until he found him hidden in the cave. They said a prayer of thanksgiving together and then sat down to talk about the spiritual life. After a while the priest suggested that they take their meal. "Today is the great feast of Easter," he added.

"It must be a great feast to have brought me this kind visit," the man of God replied, not realizing after his long separation from men that it was Easter Sunday.

"Today is really Easter," the priest insisted, "the feast of our Lord's Resurrection. On such a solemn occasion you should not be fasting. Besides, I was sent here by almighty God so that both of us could share in His gifts."

After that they said grace and began their meal. When it was over they conversed some more and then the priest went back to his church.[4]

At about the same time some shepherds also discovered Benedict's hiding place. When they first looked through the thickets and caught sight of him clothed in rough skins, they mistook him for some wild animal. Soon, however, they recognized in him a servant of God, and many of them gave up their sinful ways for a life of holiness. As a result, his name became known to all the people in that locality and great numbers visited his cave, supplying him with the food he needed and receiving from his lips in return spiritual food for their souls.

One day, while the saint was alone, the Tempter came in the form of a little blackbird, which began to flutter in front of his face. It kept so close that he could easily have caught it in his hand. Instead, he made the sign of the cross and the bird flew away. The moment it left, he was seized with an unusually violent temptation. The evil spirit recalled to his mind a woman he had once seen, and before he realized it his emotions were carrying him away. Almost overcome in the struggle, he was on the point of abandoning the lonely wilderness, when suddenly with the help of God's grace he came to himself.

He then noticed a thick patch of nettles and briers next to him. Throwing his garment aside he flung himself into the sharp thorns and stinging nettles. There he rolled and tossed until his whole body was in pain and covered with blood. Yet, once he had conquered pleasure through suffering, his torn and bleeding skin served to drain the poison of temptation from his body. Before long, the pain that was burning his whole body had put out the fires of evil in his heart. It was by exchanging these two

---

[3] Cf. Matt. 5.15.
[4] Cf. Acts 9.10-19.

fires that he gained the victory over sin. So complete was his triumph that from then on, as he later told his disciples, he never experienced another temptation of this kind.

One day while the monks were constructing a section of the abbey, they noticed a rock lying close at hand and decided to use it in the building. When two or three did not succeed in lifting it, others joined in to help. Yet it remained fixed in its place as though it was rooted to the ground. Then they were sure that the Devil himself was sitting on this stone and preventing them from moving it in spite of all their efforts.

Faced with this difficulty, they asked Abbot Benedict to come and use his prayers to drive away the Devil who was holding down the rock. The saint began to pray as soon as he got there, and after he had finished and made the sign of the cross, the monks picked up the rock with such ease that it seemed to have lost all its previous weight.

The abbot then directed them to spade up the earth where the stone had been. When they had dug a little way into the ground they came upon a bronze idol, which they threw into the kitchen for the time being. Suddenly the kitchen appeared to be on fire and everyone felt that the entire building was going up in flames. The noise and commotion they made in their attempt to put out the blaze by pouring on buckets of water brought Benedict to the scene. Unable to see the fire which appeared so real to his monks, he quietly bowed his head in prayer and soon had opened their eyes to the foolish mistake they were making. Now, instead of the flames the evil spirit had devised, they once more saw the kitchen standing intact.

On another occasion they were working on one of the walls that had to be built a little higher. The man of God was in his room at the time, praying, when the Devil appeared to him and remarked sarcastically that he was on his way to visit the brethren at their work. Benedict quickly sent them word to be on their guard against the evil spirit who would soon be with them. Just as they received his warning, the Devil overturned the wall, crushing under its ruins the body of a very young monk who was the son of a tax collector.

Unconcerned about the damaged wall in their grief and dismay over the loss of their brother, the monks hurried to Abbot Benedict to let him know of the dreadful accident. He told them to bring the mangled body to his room. It had to be carried in on a blanket, for the wall had not only broken the boy's arms and legs but had crushed all the bones in his body. The saint had the remains placed on the reed matting where he used to pray and after that told them all to leave. Then he closed the door and knelt down to offer his most earnest prayers to God. That very hour, to the astonishment of all, he sent the boy back to his work as sound and healthy as he had been before. Thus, in spite of the Devil's attempt to mock the man of God by causing this tragic death, the young monk was able to rejoin his brethren and help them finish the wall.

Fable, Parable, Exemplum, Allegory

The earliest fables were beast fables, stories about animals who behave like humans and convey a moral lesson. The Greek slave Aesop (ca. 620–560 B.C.) is, of course, the great exemplar here. Through his dogs and crows, foxes and lions, he speaks cautionary wisdom that is still taken to heart. And lest we miss the point, the moral is explicitly stated at the end ("familiarity breeds contempt" or "little by little does the trick")—a device that satirical fabulists like George Ade and James Thurber have used with delightful effect. A fable need not have animals as actors, but it must always have a moral, implied or explicit: that is its chief identifying characteristic. The stories by Hawthorne, Forster, Čapek, Updike, and Barthelme in this volume can all, with more or less accuracy, be called fables.

Teaching moral lessons via fiction is an ancient custom, and one specialized way of doing this is with the *exemplum* ("example"), a story used to spice up a sermon. One of the great exempla in our literature is Chaucer's *The Pardoner's Tale*, in which a priestly con man fleeces his congregation with the help of a tale containing the moral: *radix malorum est cupiditas* ("greed is the root of all evil"). In a more serious vein, St. Gregory's sermon about Adam's sin is brought to life by the story of the woman who gives birth to a babe in a dungeon. How can the mother ever describe to her boy what the sun, moon, and stars are like? How can we, born in the darkness of Adam's sin, ever know the glory of the unfallen state? The point is clear: the reaches of the unknown or the unimaginable are brought home by a simple illustration.

A parable is like an exemplum except that it is more short and pithy and has a more or less clear-cut allegorical twist. The New Testament is full of parables, like that of the talents and of the five wise and foolish virgins; and the sermons of Jesus are continually spiced with these homely illustrations that made clear to an unlettered audience the meaning of his words ("Ye are the salt of the earth: but if the salt have lost his savour, wherewith shall it be salted?" [Matt. 5:13]). A parable is perhaps best defined as a short fable; excellent modern examples are Borges's "Everything and Nothing" and "Borges and I."

Allegory is more complex, and the interested student would do well to consult Angus Fletcher's *Allegory: The Theory of a Symbolic Mode* (1964). In an allegory the characters are not individuals but personified abstractions, and the happenings are purely symbolic. Like the above forms, allegories are designed to teach something—an idea, a moral lesson—but they sometimes have a wayward habit of lapsing into fictions pure and simple. As Fletcher says, allegory embraces "a quite extraordinary variety of literary kinds." One of the purest examples of the mode is John Bunyan's *The Pilgrim's Progress* (1675), which had a prodigious popularity with Puritan readers who scorned other kinds of fiction as snares of the Devil. Bunyan is a born storyteller, and a particularly memorable part of his tale is the experience of Christian and Faithful in the town of Vanity, with its famous Fair, where everything is for sale from titles to bawds to souls. In an allegory like this, everything stands for something else, everything is symbolic (see Symbol, pp. 21-23), so the reader is inevitably involved in a process of discovery and interpretation. It is a clever device, since it relieves the reader of the feeling that he is being preached at; instead he is participating in the story, in a sense *creating* it. Strangely enough, allegory, though it is an ancient form, seems to have a renewed appeal for certain modernist story writers like Kafka ("A Country Doctor"), Čapek ("The Last Judgment"), Jackson ("The Lottery"), Rosenfeld ("The Brigadier"), and Oates ("Stalking"). The stories of these writers are mixed modes, but they all show that allegorical bent toward the symbolic—where character and event mean more than themselves and suggest the timeless.

Fables: Aesop

THE FOX AND THE CROW

A Fox once saw a Crow fly off with a piece of cheese in its beak and settle on a branch of a tree. "That's for me, as I am a Fox," said Master Reynard, and he walked up to the foot of the tree. "Good-day, Mistress Crow," he cried. "How well you are looking to-day: how glossy your feathers; how bright your eye. I feel sure your voice must surpass that of other birds, just as your figure does; let me hear but one song from you that I may greet you as the Queen of Birds." The Crow lifted up her head and began to caw her best, but the moment she opened her mouth the piece of cheese fell to the ground, only to be snapped up by Master Fox. "That will do," said he. "That was all I wanted. In exchange for your cheese I will give you a piece of advice for the future—

> *Do not trust flatterers."*

> *The Flatterer doth rob by stealth,*
> *His victim, both of Wit and Wealth.*

THE DOG IN THE MANGER

A Dog looking out for its afternoon nap jumped into the Manger of an Ox and lay there cosily upon the straw. But soon the Ox, returning from its afternoon work, came up to the Manger and wanted to eat some of the straw. The Dog in a rage, being awakened from its slumber, stood up and barked at the Ox, and whenever it came near attempted to bite it. At last the Ox had to give up the hope of getting at the straw, and went away muttering:

> *"Ah, people often grudge others what they cannot enjoy themselves."*

Parables: Matthew 25

Then shall the kingdom of heaven be likened unto ten virgins, which took their lamps, and went forth to meet the bridegroom.

2 And five of them were wise, and five *were* foolish.

3 They that *were* foolish took their lamps, and took no oil with them:

4 But the wise took oil in their vessels with their lamps.

5 While the bridegroom tarried, they all slumbered and slept.

6 And at midnight there was a cry made, Behold, the bridegroom cometh; go ye out to meet him.

7 Then all those virgins arose, and trimmed their lamps.

8 And the foolish said unto the wise, Give us of your oil, for our lamps are gone out.

9 But the wise answered, saying, *Not so;* lest there be not enough for us and you: but go ye rather to them that sell, and buy for yourselves.

10 And while they went to buy, the bridegroom came; and they that were ready went in with him to the marriage: and the door was shut.

11 Afterward came also the other virgins, saying, Lord, Lord, open to us.

12 But he answered and said, Verily I say unto you, I know you not.

13 Watch therefore, for ye know neither the day nor the hour wherein the Son of man cometh.

14 ¶ For *the kingdom of heaven is* as a man traveling into a far country, *who* called his own servants, and delivered unto them his goods.

15 And unto one he gave five talents, to another two, and to another one; to every man according to his several ability; and straightway took his journey.

16 Then he that had received the five talents went and traded with the same, and made *them* other five talents.

17 And likewise he that *had received* two, he also gained other two.

18 But he that had received one went and digged in the earth, and hid his lord's money.

19 After a long time the lord of those servants cometh, and reckoneth with them.

20 And so he that had received five talents came and brought other five talents, saying, Lord, thou deliveredst unto me five talents: behold, I have gained beside them five talents more.

21 His lord said unto him, Well done, *thou* good and faithful servant: thou hast been faithful over a few things, I will make thee ruler over many things: enter thou into the joy of thy lord.

22 He also that had received two talents came and said, Lord, thou deliveredst unto me two talents: behold, I have gained two other talents beside them.

23 His lord said unto him, Well done, good and faithful servant; thou hast been faithful over a few things, I will make thee ruler over many things: enter thou into the joy of thy lord.

24 Then he which had received the one talent came and said, Lord, I knew thee that thou art an hard man, reaping where thou hast not sown, and gathering where thou hast not strawed:

25 And I was afraid, and went and hid thy talent in the earth: lo, *there* thou hast *that is* thine.

26 His lord answered and said unto him, *Thou* wicked and slothful servant, thou knewest that I reap where I sowed not, and gather where I have not strawed:

27 Thou oughtest therefore to have put my money to the exchangers, and *then* at my coming I should have received mine own with usury.

28 Take therefore the talent from him, and give *it* unto him which hath ten talents.

29 For unto every one that hath shall be given, and he shall have abundance: but from him that hath not shall be taken away even that which he hath.

Exemplum: From St. Gregory's *Dialogues*

After Adam, the father of the human race, was driven from the joys of paradise as a result of sin, he entered upon the distress of this dark exile we are now suffering. Driven outside of himself by his sinful act, he was no longer able to perceive the joys of heaven which had been the object of his contemplation before. In paradise he habitually enjoyed converse with God and in purity of heart and loftiness of vision mingled with holy, angelic spirits. After falling from that noble state he also lost the inner light which enlightened his mind. Born as we are of his flesh into the darkness of this exile, we hear, of course, that there is a heavenly country, that angels are its citizens, and that the spirits of the just live in company with them; but being carnal men without any experimental knowledge of the invisible, we wonder about the existence of anything we cannot see with our bodily eyes. Adam could not possibly have entertained such doubts, for, although he was excluded from the happiness of paradise, he remembered what he had lost, because he had once known it. Carnal men, on the other hand, cannot remember or appreciate these joys when they hear about them, because, unlike him, they have no past experience to fall back on.

Take the case of an expectant mother cast into a dungeon where she gives birth to a son. He stays there with her and grows up in the darkness. Suppose this boy's mother described to him the sun, the moon, and the stars, the mountains and fields, birds flying in the air and horses running in the fields. Born and raised in the dungeon, knowing only the perpetual darkness around him, he would doubt whether the things he heard his mother describe actually existed, since he had no experience of them. So it is with men born into the darkness of this earthly exile. They hear about lofty and invisible things, but hesitate to believe in them, because they know only the lowly, visible things of earth into which they were born. It was for this reason that the Creator of the visible and invisible worlds came as the Only-begotten of the Father to redeem the human race and to send the Holy Spirit into our hearts. From Him we were to receive new life in order to believe those truths of which we as yet had no knowledge through experience. All of us, therefore, who have received this Spirit as the pledge of our inheritance are no longer in doubt about the existence of invisible beings. On the other hand, anyone who is not yet solidly grounded in this faith ought to accept what his elders say, putting his trust in them, since they have experimental knowledge of the invisible world through the Holy Spirit. In our story, too, it would have been foolish for the little boy to think his mother was telling him lies about the light, merely because he himself knew nothing but the darkness of the dungeon.

Allegory: Bunyan's *The Pilgrim's Progress*

Evang. My Sons, you have heard in the words of the truth of the Gospel, that you must through many tribulations enter into the Kingdom of Heaven. And again, that in every City, bonds and afflictions abide in you; and therefore you cannot expect that you should go long on your Pilgrimage without them, in some sort or other. You have found something of the truth of these testimonies upon you already, and more will immediately follow: for now, as you see, you are almost out of this Wilderness, and therefore you will soon come into a Town that you will by and by see before you: and in that Town you will be hardly beset with enemies, who will strain hard but they will kill you: and be you sure that one or both of you must seal the testimony which you hold, with blood: but be you faithful unto death, and the King will give you a Crown of life. He that shall die there, although his death will be unnatural, and his pain perhaps great, he will yet have the better of his fellow; not only because he will be

From John Bunyan, *The Pilgrims Progress*. London: Oxford (Humphrey Milford 1926)

arrived at the Cœlestial City soonest, but because he will escape many miseries that the other will meet with in the rest of his Journey. But when you are come to the Town, and shall find fulfilled what I have here related, then remember your friend, and quit your selves like men; and commit the keeping of your souls to your God in well-doing, as unto a faithful Creator.

Then I saw in my Dream, that when they were got out of the Wilderness, they presently saw a Town before them, and the name of that Town is *Vanity;* and at the town there is a *Fair* kept, called *Vanity-Fair.* It is kept all the Year long: it beareth the name of *Vanity-Fair,* because the Town where 'tis kept, *is lighter than* Vanity; and also, because all that is there sold, or that cometh thither, is *Vanity.* As is the saying of the wise, *All that cometh is Vanity.*

This Fair is no new erected business, but a thing of ancient standing; I will shew you the original of it.

Almost five thousand years agone, there were Pilgrims walking to the Cœlestial City, as these two honest persons are; and *Beelzebub, Apollyon,* and *Legion,* with their Companions, perceiving by the path that the Pilgrims made, that their way to the City lay through *this Town of Vanity,* they contrived here to set up a Fair[1]; a Fair wherein should be sold of *all sorts of Vanity,* and that it should last all the year long. Therefore at *this Fair* are all such Merchandize sold, as Houses, Lands, Trades, Places, Honors, Preferments, Titles, Countries, Kingdoms, Lusts, Pleasures and Delights of all sorts, as Whores, Bawds, Wives, Husbands, Children, Masters, Servants, Lives, Blood, Bodies, Souls, Silver, Gold, Pearls, Precious Stones, and what not.

And moreover, at this Fair there is at all times to be seen Jugglings, Cheats, Games, Plays, Fools, Apes, Knaves, and Rogues, and that of every kind.

Here are to be seen too, and that for nothing, Thefts, Murders, Adulteries, False-swearers, and that of a blood-red colour.

And as in other fairs of less moment, there are the several Rows and Streets, under their proper names, where such and such Wares are vended: So here likewise, you have the proper Places, Rows, Streets, (*viz.* Countreys and Kingdoms,) where the Wares of this Fair are soonest to be found: Here is the *Britain* Row, the *French* Row, the *Italian* Row, the *Spanish* Row, the *German* Row, where several sorts of Vanities are to be sold. But as in other *fairs,* some one Commodity is as the chief of all the *fair,* so the Ware of *Rome* and her Merchandize is greatly promoted in *this fair:* Only our *English* Nation, with some others, have taken a dislike thereat.

Now, as I said, the way to the Cœlestial City lies just through *this Town,* where this lusty Fair is kept; and he that will go to the City, and yet not go through this Town, *must* needs *go out of the World.* The Prince of Princes himself, when here, went through *this Town* to his own Country, and that upon a *Fair-day too:* Yea, and as I think, it was *Beelzebub* the chief Lord of this *Fair,* that invited him to buy of his Vanities; yea, would have made him Lord of the *Fair,* would he but have done him Reverence as he went through the *Town.* Yea, because he was such a person of Honour, *Beelzebub* had him from *Street* to *Street,* and shewed him all the Kingdoms of the

[1]Behold Vanity Fair! the Pilgrims there
    Are chain'd and stand beside:
    Even so it was our Lord pass'd here,
    And on Mount *Calvary* dy'd.

World in a little time, that he might, if possible, allure that Blessed One, to *cheapen* and *buy* some of his *Vanities*. But he had no mind to the Merchandize, and therefore left the *Town*, without laying out so much as one Farthing upon these *Vanities*. This *Fair* therefore is an Ancient thing, of long standing, and a very great *Fair*.

A Variety Of Secular Tales

In the centuries before the rise of the short story, the Western world saw a great variety of secular tales, in prose and verse. Preeminent among them were the short prose tales of Giovanni Boccaccio (1313–1375) called *novelle* (sing. *novella)*. Unlike *romances* (idealized, poetic, and often improbable tales of chivalry and love) the novella dealt with the actual cause-and-effect world of imperfect men and women. The very word *novella* suggests their secular nature: they are something new (fr. Italian *novello*), not the retelling of the traditional and the sacred, and it is appropriate that from *novella* came the modern word *novel. The Decameron,* Boccaccio's most famous work, is a series of 100 tales told by seven ladies and three men who have fled the plague that visited Florence in 1348. They visit neighboring villas between Settingnano and Fiesole, agreeing to spend part of each of ten days (hence the title) telling stories, each giving one story per day. This "frame" for a series of tales became a familiar medieval device and was used by Chaucer in *The Canterbury Tales.* But with Chaucer the storytellers of the frame are as lively as the stories; with Boccaccio the storytellers remain "flat" while the tales take on all the life. In either case they are secular tales: they deal with earthly, not heavenly, love and are often deliberately bawdy, scandalous, and irreverent. Though the *novella* has a reputation for "epigrammatic terseness," it is, like the age of its origin, a leisurely form compared to what we know as the short story. If the following tale by Philostratus seems to betray some male chauvinism, be assured that in others the ladies get some of their own back.

The Miller's Tale is a *fabliau,* a humorous tale of French origin that had wide popularity in the twelfth and thirteenth centuries. Normally in verse (octosyllabic couplets), it was a favorite of the medieval *jongleurs,* or minstrels, who spread them throughout France. They were full of bawdy humor and irreverent practical jokes, and favorite butts of their satire were the clergy and women as the daughters of Eve. In the Prologue to *The Canterbury Tales,* Chaucer describes the Miller as stocky, fat-faced, and red-bearded, with a wart atop his flat nose—all characteristics that Chaucer's contemporaries (ca. 1340–1400) would have associated with a "choleric" man: quarrelsome, hot-tempered, loudmouthed, and lecherous. The fabliau is his perfect métier: its lusty vulgarity fits his character perfectly.

Although *fabliau* means "little fable," the form has little in common with fables: its characters are always human and its "moral"—when it exists—is not meant for the ears of puritans.

As we near the nineteenth century, many new story forms appear—satires, gothic tales, rogue stories, didactic tales, and others. The form represented here in "The Vision of Mirzah" is perhaps best described as an "Oriental tale," a genre very popular for cautionary and satiric purposes in the eighteenth century. A traveler brings back from a far-off (and presumably inferior) land a tale embodying wisdom that puts to shame—or at least instructs—the "civilized" reader. This sample by Joseph Addison (1672–1719) appeared in the *Spectator* papers and is more instructional than satiric—a mere sketch or vignette with a moralizing edge. Mirzah's "vision" of the Vale of Misery and the Tide of Eternity, and the Bridge with threescore and ten arches under which human beings are continually being swept to death, is an elaborate, highly ornate allegory of the misery of human fate. Static and sentimental, it captures what an Englishman of the eighteenth century took to be the Oriental mode, an effect enhanced when the Genius shows Mirzah the Paradise that lurks in the thick Mists where the Tide of Eternity runs. The moral is a simple one: good men will be rewarded after death. It is the kind of artificial allegory that appeared in an age already half secularized, in which orthodoxy was on the decline. To read it is to know why the far more vital short story, which was soon to replace this sort of thing, has such a tremendous appeal.

Novella: Boccaccio's *The Decameron*[1]

THE THIRD DAY

Upon which Day, all matters to be discoursed on, doe passe under the regiment of Madam Neiphila: concerning such persons as (by their wit and industry) have attained to their long wished desires, or recovered something, supposed to be lost.

THE INDUCTION TO THE ENSUING DISCOURSES

The morning put on a vermillion countenance and made the Sunne to rise blushing red, when the Queene (and all the faire company) were come abroad forth of their Chambers; the Seneshall or great Master of the Houshold, having (long before) sent all things necessary to the place of their next intended meeting. And the people which prepared there every needfull matter, suddainely when they saw the Queene was setting forward, charged all the rest of their followers, as if it had beene preparation for a Campe; to make hast away with the carriages, the rest of the Familie remaining behind, to attend upon the Ladies and Gentlemen.

With a milde, majesticke, and gentle pace, the Queene rode on, being followed by the other Ladies, and the three young Gentlemen, taking their way towards the West; conducted by the musicall notes of sweete singing Nightingales, and infinite other pretty Birds beside, riding in a tract not much frequented, but richly abounding with faire hearbes and flowres, which by reason of the Sunnes high mounting, beganne to open their bosome, and fill the fresh Ayre with their odorifferous perfumes. Before they had travelled two small miles distance, all of them pleasantly conversing together; they arrived at another goodly Palace, which being somewhat mounted above the plaine, was seated on the side of a little rising hill.

When they were entred thereinto, and had seene the great Hall, the Parlors, and beautifull Chambers, every one so stupendiously furnished, withall convenient commodities to them belonging, and nothing wanting, that could be desired; they highly commended it, reputing the Lord thereof for a most worthy man, that had adorned it in such Princely manner. Afterward, being descended lower, and noting the most spacious and pleasant Court, the Sellars stored with the choysest Wines, and delicate Springs of waters every where running, their prayses then exceeded more and more.

[1] From the English edition of 1625.

And being weary with beholding such variety of pleasures, they sate downe in a faire Gallery, which tooke the view of the whole Court, it being round engirt with trees and flowres, whereof the season then yeelded great plenty. And then came the discreete Master of the Houshold, with divers servants attending on him, presenting them with Comfits, and other Banquetting, as also very singular Wines, to serve in stead of a breakefast.

Having thus reposed themselves a while, a Garden gate was set open to them, coasting on one side of the Pallace, and round enclosed with high mounted walles. Whereinto when they were entred, they found it to be a most beautifull Garden, stored with all varieties that possibly could be devised; and therefore they observed it the more respectively. The walkes and allyes were long and spacious, yet directly straite as an arrow, environed with spreading vines, whereon the grapes hung in copious clusters; which being come to their full ripenesse, gave so rare a smel throughout the Garden, with other sweete savours intermixed among, that they supposed to feele the fresh spiceries of the East.

It would require large length of time, to describe all the rarities of this place, deserving much more to be commended, then my best faculties will affoord me. In the middest of the Garden, was a square plot, after the resemblance of a Meadow, flourishing with high grasse, hearbes, and plants, beside a thousand diversities of flowres, even as if by the Art of painting they had beene there deputed. Round was it circled with very verdant Orenge and Cedar Trees, their branches plentiously stored with fruit both old and new, as also the flowres growing freshly among them, yeelding not onely a rare aspect to the eye, but also a delicate savour to the smell.

In the middest of this Meadow, stood a Fountaine of white Marble, whereon was engraven most admirable workemanship, and within it (I know not whether it were by a naturall veine, or artificiall) flowing from a figure, standing on a Collumne in the midst of the Fountaine, such aboundance of water, and so mounting up towards the Skies, that it was a wonder to behold. For after the high ascent, it fell downe againe into the wombe of the Fountaine, with such a noyse and pleasing murmure, as the streame that glideth from a mill. When the receptacle of the Fountaine did over-flow the bounds, it streamed along the Meadow, by secret passages and chanels, very faire and artificially made, returning againe into every part of the Meadow, by the like wayes of cunning conveighance, which allowed it full course into the Garden, running swiftly thence down towards the plaine; but before it came thether, the very swift current of the streame, did drive two goodly Milles, which brought in great benefit to the Lord of the soile.

The sight of this Garden, the goodly grafts, plants, trees, hearbes, frutages, and flowres, the Springs, Fountaines, and pretty rivolets streaming from it, so highly pleased the Ladies and Gentlemen, that among other infinite commendations, they spared not to say: if any Paradise remayned on the earth to be seene, it could not possibly be in any other place, but onely was contained within the compasse of this Garden. With no meane pleasure and delight they walked round about it, making Chaplets of flowers, and other faire branches of the trees, continually hearing the Birds in melodious notes, ecchoing and warbling one to another, even as if they envied each others felicities.

But yet another beauty (which before had not presented it selfe to them) on a sodaine they perceyved; namely divers pretty creatures in many parts of the Gardens. In one place Conies[2] tripping about; in another place Hares; in a third part Goats

2 Rabbits

browsing on the hearbes, and little yong Hindes feeding every where: yet without strife or warring together, but rather living in such a Domesticke and pleasing kinde of company, even as if they were appointed to enstruct the most noble of all creatures, to imitate their sociable conversation.

When their senses had sufficiently banquetted on those severall beauties, the tables were sodainly prepared about the Fountaine; where first they sung six Canzonets[3]; and having paced two or three dances, they sate downe to dinner, according as the Queene ordained, being served in very sumptuous manner, with all kinde of costly and delicate viands, yet not any babling noise among them. The Tables being withdrawne, they played againe upon their instruments, singing and dancing gracefully together: till, in regard of the extreame heate, the Queene commanded to give over, and permitted such as were so pleased, to take their ease and rest. But some, as not satisfied with the places pleasures, gave themselves to walking: others fell to reading the lives of the Romanes; some to the Chesse, and the rest to other recreations.

But, after the dayes warmth was more mildely qualified, and every one had made benefit of their best content: they went (by order sent from the Queene) into the Meadow where the Fountaine stood, and being set about it, as they used to do in telling their Tales (the argument appointed by the Queene being propounded) the first that had the charge imposed, was Philostratus, who began in this manner.

Massetto di Lamporechio, by counterfetting himselfe to be dumbe, became a Gardiner in a Monasterie of Nunnes, where he had familiar conversation with them all.

THE FIRST NOVELL

Wherein is declared, that Virginity is very hardly to be kept in all places.

Most worthy Ladies, there wants no store of men and women, that are so simple, as to credit for a certainty, that so soon as a yong virgin hath the veile put on hir head, and the black Cowle given to cover her withall, she is no longer a woman, nor more sensible of feminine affections, then as if in turning Nun, shee became converted to a stone. And if (perchance) they heard some matters, contrary to their former perswasion; then they grow so furiously offended, as if one had committed a most foule and enormous sinne, directly against the course of Nature. And the torrent of this opinion hurries them on so violently, that they will admit no leisure to consider, how (in such a scope of liberty) they have power to doe what they list, yea beyond all meanes of sufficient satisfying, never remembring how potent the priviledge of idlenes is, especially when it is backt by solitude. In like manner, there are other people now, who verily beleeve, that the Spade and Pickaxe, grosse feeding and labour, do quench al sensual and fleshly concupiscence, yea in such as till and husband the ground, by making them dull, blockish, and (almost) meere senslesse of understanding. But I will approve (according as the Queene hath commanded me, and within the compasse of her direction) by a short and pleasant Tale; how greatly they are abused by errour, that build upon so weake a foundation.

Not farre from Alexandria, there was a great and goodly Monasterie, belonging to the Lord of those parts, who is termed the Admirall. And therein, under the care and trust of one woman, divers virgins were kept as recluses, or Nuns, vowed to chastity of life; out of whose number, the Soldan[4] of Babylon (under whom they lived in subjection) at every three yeers end, had usually three of these virgins sent him. At

[3] Short, lighthearted songs, or airs.
[4] See note p. 46.

the time wherof I am now to speake, there remained in the Monastery, no more but eight religious Sisters only, beside the Lady Abbesse, and an honest poor man, who was a Gardiner, and kept the Garden in commendable order.

His wages being small, and he not well contented therewith, would serve there no longer: but making his accounts even, with the Factotum or Bayliffe belonging to the house, returned thence to the village of Lamporechio, being a native of the place. Among many other that gave him welcom home, was a yong Hebrew pezant of the country, sturdy, strong and yet comely of person, being named Masset. But because he was born not farre off from Lamporechio, and had there bin brought up all his yonger dayes, his name of Masset (according to their vulgar speech) was turned to Massetto, and therefore he was usually called and knowne by the name of Massetto of Lampo-rechio.

Massetto, falling in talke with the honest poore man, whose name was Lurco, demanded of him what services hee had done in the Monasterie, having continued there so long a time? Quoth Lurco, I laboured in the Garden, which is very faire and great; then I went to the Forest to fetch home wood, and cleft it for their Chamber fuell, drawing up all theyr water beside, with many other toilsome services else: but the allowance of my wages was so little, as it would not pay for the shoes I wore. And that which was worst of all, they being all yong women, I thinke the divel dwels among them, for a man cannot doe any thing to please them. When I have bene busie at my worke in the garden, one would come and say, Put this heere, put that there; and others would take the dibble[5] out of my hand, telling me, that I did not performe any thing well, making me so weary of their continuall trifling, as I have lefte all busines, given over the Garden, and what for one mollestation, as also many other; I intended to tarry no longer there, but came away, as thou seest. And yet the Factotum desired me at my departing, that if I knew any one who would undertake the aforesaid labours, I should send him thither, as (indeed) I promised to do: but let mee fall sicke and dye, before I helpe to send them any.

When Massetto had heard the words of Lurco, hee was so desirous to dwell among the Nunnes, that nothing else now hammered in his head: for he meant more subtilly than poore Lurco did, and made no doubt to please them sufficiently. Then considering with himselfe, how best he might bring his intent to effect; which appeared not easily to bee done. He could question no further therein with Lurco, but onely demaunded other matter of him, saying: Introth thou didst well Lurco, to come away from so tedious a dwelling, had he not need to be more then a man that is to live with such women? It were better for him to dwell among so many divels, because they understand not the tenth part that womens wily wits can dive into.

After their conference was ended, Massetto began to beate his braines how he might compasse to dwell among them, and knowing that he could wel enough per-forme all the labours whereof Lurco had made mention, he cared not for any losse he should sustaine thereby, but onely stood in doubt of his entertainment, because he was too yong and sprightly. Having pondered on many imaginations, he said to himselfe. The place is farre enough distant hence, and none there can take knowledge of mee; if I have wit sufficient, cleanely to make them beleeve that I am dumbe, then (question-les) I shal be received. And resolving to prosecute this determination, he tooke a Spade on his shoulder, and without revealing to any body whether hee went, in the disguise of a poore labouring Countryman, he travelled to the Monastery.

[5] A gardening tool for making holes in the ground for bulbs or seedlings.

When he was there arrived, he found the great gate open, and entering in boldly, it was his good hap to espy the Factotum in the court, according as Lurco had given description of him. Making signes before him, as if he were both dumbe and deafe; he manifested, that he craved an Almes for Gods sake, making shewes beside, that if need required, he could cleave wood, or doe any reasonable kinde of service. The Factotum gladly gave him food and afterward shewed him divers knotty logs of wood, which the weake strength of Lurco had left uncloven; but this fellow being more active and lusty, quickly rent them all to pieces. Now it so fell out, that the Factotum must needs go to the Forrest, and tooke Massetto along with him thither: where causing him to fell divers Trees, by signes he bad him to lade the two Asses therewith, which commonly carried home all the wood, and so drive them to the Monasterie before him, which Massetto knew well enough how to do, and performed it very effectually.

Many other servile Offices were there to bee done, which caused the Factotum to make use of his paines divers other dayes beside; in which time, the Lady Abbesse chancing to see him, demanded of the Factotum what he was? Madam (quoth hee) a poore labouring man, who is both deafe and dumbe, hither he came to crave an almes the other day, the which in charity I could do no lesse but give him; for which, hee hath done many honest services about the house. It seemes beside, that hee hath pretty skill in Gardening, so that if I can perswade him to continue here, I make no question of his able services: for the old silly man is gon, and we have need of such a stout fellow, to do the busines belonging to the Monastery, and one fitter for the turne, comes sildome hither. Moreover, in regard of his double imperfections, the Sisters can sustaine no impeachment by him. Whereto the Abbesse answered, saying; By the faith of my body, you speake but the truth: understand then, if hee have any knowledge in Gardening, and whether hee will dwell heere, or no: which compasse so kindly as you can. Let him have a new paire of shoes, fill his belly daily full of meate, flatter, and make much of him, for wee shall finde him worke enough to do. All which, the Factotum promised to fulfill sufficiently.

Massetto, who was not far off from them all this while, but seemed seriously busied about sweeping and making cleane the Court, heard all these speeches; and being not a little joyful of them; said to himselfe. If once I come to worke in your Garden, let the proofe yeeld praise of my skill and knowledge. When the Factotum perceived, that he knew perfectly how to undergo his businesse, and had questioned him by signes, concerning his willingnesse to serve there still, and received the like answere also, of his dutifull readinesse thereto; he gave him order to worke in the Garden, because the season did now require it; and to leave all other affayres for the Monastery, attending now onely the Gardens preparation.

As Massetto was thus about his Garden emploiment, the Nunnes began to resort thither, and thinking the man to be dumbe and deafe indeede, were the more lavish of their language, mocking and flowting him very immodestly, as being perswaded, that he heard them not. And the Lady Abbesse, thinking he might as well be an Eunuch, as deprived both of hearing and speaking, stood the lesse in feare of the Sisters walkes, but referred them to their owne care and providence. On a day, Massetto having laboured somewhat extraordinarily, lay downe to rest himselfe awhile under the trees, and two delicate yong Nunnes, walking there to take the aire, drew neere to the place where he dissembled sleeping; and both of them observing his comelinesse of person, began to pitty the poverty of his condition; but much more the misery of his great defectes. Then one of them, who had a little livelier spirit then the other, thinking Massetto to be fast asleepe, began in this manner.

Sister (quoth she) if I were faithfully assured of thy secrecie, I would tell thee a thing which I have often thought on, and it may (perhaps) redound to thy profit. Sister, replyed the other Nun, speake your minde boldly, and beleeve it (on my Maiden-head) that I will never reveale it to any creature living. Encouraged by this solemne answere, the first Nun thus prosecuted her former purpose, saying. I know not Sister, whether it hath entred into thine understanding or no, how strictly we are here kept and attended, never any man daring to adventure among us, except our good and honest Factotum, who is very aged; and this dumbe fellow, maimed, and made imperfect by nature, and therefore not worthy the title of a man. Ah Sister, it hath oftentimes bin told me, by Gentlewomen comming hither to visite us, that all other sweetes in the world, are mockeries, to the incomparable pleasures of man and woman, of which we are barred by our unkind parents, binding us to perpetuall chastity, which they were never able to observe themselves.

A Sister of this house once told me, that before her turne came to be sent to the Soldane,[6] she fell in frailty with a man that was both lame and blinde, and discovering the same to her Ghostly Father in confession; he absolved her of that sinne; affirming, that she had not transgressed with a man, because he wanted his rationall and understanding parts. Behold Sister, heere lyes a creature, almost formed in the self-same mold, dumbe and deafe, which are two the most rationall and understanding parts that do belong to any man, and therefore no Man, wanting them. If folly and frailty would be committed with him (as many times since hee came hither it hath run in my minde) hee is by Nature, sworne to such secrecie, that he cannot (if he would) be a blabbe thereof. Beside, the Laws and constitution of our Religion doth teach us, that a sinne so assuredly concealed, is more than halfe absolved.

Ave Maria Sister (saide the other Nun) what kinde of words are these you utter? Doe not you know, that we have promised our virginity to God? Oh Sister (answered the other) how many things are promised to him every day, and not one of a thousand kept or performed? If wee have made him such a promise, and some of our weaker-witted sisters do performe it for us, no doubt but he will accept it in part of payment. Yea but Sister, replied the second Nun againe, there is another danger lying in the way: If we prove to be with childe, how shall we doe then? Sister (quoth our couragious wench) thou art affraide of harme before it happen: if it come so to passe, let us consider on it then: thou art but a Novice in matters of such moment, we are provided of a thousand meanes, whereby to prevent conception. Or, if they should faile, we are so surely fitted, that the world shall never know it. Let it suffice, our lives must not be by any so much as suspected, our Monastery questioned, or our Religion rashly scandalized. Thus shee schooled her younger Sister in wit, albeit as forward as shee in will, and longed as desirouslie, to know what kinde of creature man was.

After some other questions, how this intention of theirs might bee safely brought to full effect: the sprightly Nun that had wit at will, thus answered. You see Sister

---

[6] Literally "sultan." This usage represents an attempt by an early editor to remove the scene of Massetto's rise and fall from a Christian to a pagan environment. The present translator had evidently consulted the version of Lionardo Salviati which read as follows:

"Not far from *Alexandria,* there was (and yet is) a great & goodly Monastery, belonging to the Lord of those parts, who is termed the Admiral. And therein, vnder the care and trust of one woman, diuers virgins were kept as recluses or Nunnes, vowed to chastity of life; out of whose number, the Soldan of *Babylon* (vnder whom they liued in subiection) at euery three yeares end, had vsually three of these virgins sent him."

[Quoted in Herbert G. Wright, *The First English Translation of the "Decameron"* (1620). Upsala: A. B. Lundequistska Bokhandeln, 1953, p. 162.]

(quoth she) it is now the houre of midday, when all the rest of our sisterhood are quiet in their Chambers, because we are then allowed to sleep, for our earlier rising to morning Mattins. Here are none in the Garden now but our selves, and while I awake him, bee you the watch, and afterward follow mee in my fortune, for I will valiantly leade you the way. Massetto immitating a Dogges sleepe, heard all this conspiracie intended against him, and longed as earnestly till shee came to awake him. Which being done, he seeming very simple and sottish, and she chearing him with flattering behaviour: into the close Arbour they went, which the Sunnes bright eye could not pierce into, and there I leave it to the Nunnes owne approbation, whether Massetto was a man rationall, or no. Ill deeds require longer time to contrive, then act; and both the Nuns having bene with Massetto at this new forme of confession, were enjoyned (by him) such an easie and silent penance, as brought them the oftner to shrift, and made him to proove a very perfect Confessour.

Desires obtayned, but not fully satisfied, doe commonly urge more frequent accesse, then wisedome thinkes expedient, or can continue without discovery. Our two joviall Nunnes, not a little proud of their private stolne pleasures, so long resorted to the close Arbour, till another Sister, who had often observed their haunt thither, by meanes of a little hole in her Window; that shee began to suspect them with Massetto, and imparted the same to two other Sisters, all three concluding, to accuse them before the Lady Abbesse. But upon a further conference had with the Offenders, they changed opinion, tooke the same oath as the forewomen had done; and because they would be free from any taxation at all: they revealed their adventures to the other three ignorants, and so fell all eight into one formall confederacie, but by good and warie observation, least the Abbesse her selfe should descry them; finding poore Massetto such plenty of Garden-worke, as made him verie doubtfull in pleasing them all.

It came to passe in the end, that the Lady Abbesse who all this while imagined no such matter, walking all alone in the garden on a day, found Massetto sleeping under an Almond tree, having then very little businesse to doe, because he had wrought hard all the night before. She observed him to be an hansome man, young, lusty, well-limbde and proportioned, having a mercifull commisseration of his dumbenesse and deafenes, being perswaded also in like manner, that if hee were an Eunuch too, hee deserved a thousand times the more to be pittied. The season was exceeding hot, and he lay downe so carelesly to sleepe, that somthing was noted, wherein shee intended to be better resolved, almost falling sicke of the other Nunnes disease. Having awaked him, she commanded him by signes that he should follow her to her chamber, where he was kept close so long, that the Nunnes grew offended, because the Gardiner came not to his daily labour.

Well may you imagine that Massetto was no misse-proud man now, to be thus advanced from the Garden to the Chamber, and by no worse woman then the Lady Abbesse her selfe: what signes, shews, or what language he speaks there, I am not able to expresse; onely it appeared, that his behaviour pleased her so well, as it procured his daily repairing thether; and acquainted her with such familiar conversation, as she would have condemned in the Nunnes her daughters, but that they were wise enough to keep it from her. Now began Massetto to consider, that hee had undertaken a taske belonging to great Hercules, in giving content to so many, and by continuing dumbe in this maner, it would redound to his no meane detriment. Whereupon, as he was one night sitting by the Abbesse, the string that retained his tongue from speech, brake on a sodaine, and thus he spake.

Madam, I have often heard it said, that one Cocke may doe service to ten several Hennes, but ten men can very hardly even with all their best endeavour, give full satisfaction every way to one woman; and yet I am tied to content nine, which is farre beyond the compasse of my power to do. Already have I performed so much Garden and Chamber-work, that I confesse my selfe starke tired, and can travaile no further, and therefore let me entreate you to lycense my departure hence, or finde some meanes for my better ease. The Abbesse hearing him speake, who had so long bene there dumbe, being stricken into admiration, and accounting it almost a miracle, said. How commeth this to passe? I verily beleeved thee to be dumbe. Madam (quoth Massetto) so I was indeed, but not by Nature; onely I had a long lingering sicknes which bereft me of speech, and which I have not onely recovered againe this night, but shal ever remaine thankfull to you for it.

The Abbesse verily credited his answer, demanding what he meant in saying, that he did service to nine? Madam, quoth he, this were a dangerous question, and not easily answered before all the eight Sisters. Upon this reply, the Abbesse plainely perceived, that not onely she had fallen into folly, but all the Nunnes likewise cried guilty too: wherfore being a woman of sound discretion, she would not grant that Massetto should depart, but to keepe him still about the Nunnes businesse, because the Monastery should not be scandalized by him. And the Factotum being dead a little before, his strange recovery of speech revealed, and some things else more neerely concerning them: by generall consent, and with the good liking of Massetto, he was created the Factotum of the Monasterie.

All the neighboring people dwelling thereabout, who knew Massetto to be dumbe, by fetching home wood daily from the Forest, and divers employments in other places, were made to beleeve, that by the Nunnes devout prayers and discipline, as also the merite of the Saint, in whose honour the Monastery was built and erected, Massetto had his long restrained speech restored, and was now become their sole Factotum, having power now to employ others in drudgeries, and ease himselfe of all such labours. And albeit he made the Nunnes to be fruitfull, by encreasing some store of yonger sisters, yet all matters were so close and cleanly carried, as it was never talkt of, till after the death of the Ladie Abbesse, when Massetto beganne to grow in good yeeres, and desired to returne home to his native abiding, which (within a while after) was granted him.

Thus Massetto being rich and olde, returned home like a wealthy father, taking no care for the nursing of his children, but bequeathed them to the place where they were bred and borne, having (by his wit and ingenious apprehension) made such a benefit of his youthfull yeeres, that now he merrily tooke ease in his age.

Fabliau: Chaucer's *The Miller's Tale*

WORDS BETWEEN THE HOST AND THE MILLER

When we had heard the tale the Knight had told,
Not one among the pilgrims, young or old,
But said it was indeed a noble story
Worthy to be remembered for its glory,
And it especially pleased the gentlefolk.

Geoffrey Chaucer's "The Miller's Tale" from *The Canterbury Tales* translated by Nevill Coghill. Copyright 1971 Penguin Book Ltd. Reprinted by permission.

Our Host began to laugh and swore in joke:
'It's going well, we've opened up the bale;
Now, let me see. Who'll tell another tale?
Upon my soul the game was well begun!
Come on, Sir Monk, and show what can be done;
Repay the Knight a little for his tale!'
   The Miller, very drunk and rather pale,
Was straddled on his horse half-on half-off
And in no mood for manners or to doff
His hood or hat, or wait on any man,
But in a voice like Pilate's he began
To huff and swear. 'By blood and bones and belly,
I've got a noble story I can tell 'ee,
I'll pay the Knight his wages, not the Monk.'
   Our Host perceived at once that he was drunk
And said, 'Now hold on, Robin, dear old brother;
We'll get some better man to tell another;
You wait a bit. Let's have some common sense.'
'God's soul, I won't!' said he. 'At all events
I mean to talk, or else I'll go my way.'
Our Host replied, 'Well, blast you then, you may.
You're just a fool; your wits are overcome.'
   'Now listen,' said the Miller, 'all and some,
To what I have to say. But first I'm bound
To say I'm drunk, I know it by my sound.
And if the words get muddled in my tale
Just put it down to too much Southwark ale.
I mean to tell a legend and a life
Of an old carpenter and of his wife,
And how a student came and set his cap . . .'
   The Reeve looked up and shouted, 'Shut your trap!
Give over with your drunken harlotry.
It is a sin and foolishness,' said he,
'To slander any man or bring a scandal
On wives in general. Why can't you handle
Some other tale? There's other things beside,'
   To this the drunken Miller then replied,
'My dear old brother Oswald, such is life.
A man's no cuckold if he has no wife.
For all that, I'm not saying you are one;
There's many virtuous wives, all said and done,
Ever a thousand good for one that's bad,
As well you know yourself, unless you're mad.
What's biting you? Can't I tell stories too?
I've got a wife, Lord knows, as well as you,
Yet for the oxen in my plough, indeed,
I wouldn't take it on me, more than need,
To think myself a cuckold, just because.

I'm pretty sure I'm not, and never was.
One shouldn't be too inquisitive in life
Either about God's secrets or one's wife.
You'll find God's plenty all you could desire;
Of the remainder, better not enquire.'
    What can I add? The Miller had begun,
He would not hold his peace for anyone,
But told his churl's tale his own way, I fear.
And I regret I must repeat it here,
And so I beg of all who are refined
For God's love not to think me ill-inclined
Or evil in my purpose. I rehearse
Their tales as told, for better or for worse,
For else I should be false to what occurred.
So if this tale had better not be heard,
Just turn the page and choose another sort;
You'll find them here in plenty, long and short;
Many historical, that will profess
Morality, good breeding, saintliness.
Do not blame me if you should choose amiss.
The Miller was a churl, I've told you this,
So was the Reeve, and other some as well,
And harlotry was all they had to tell.
Consider then and hold me free of blame;
And why be serious about a game?

THE MILLER'S TALE

Some time ago there was a rich old codger
Who lived in Oxford and who took a lodger.
The fellow was a carpenter by trade,
His lodger a poor student who had made
Some studies in the arts, but all his fancy
Turned to astrology and geomancy,
And he could deal with certain propositions
And make a forecast under some conditions
About the likelihood of drought or showers
For those who asked at favourable hours,
Or put a question how their luck would fall
In this or that, I can't describe them all.
    This lad was known as Nicholas the Gallant,
And making love in secret was his talent,
For he was very close and sly, and took
Advantage of his meek and girlish look.
He rented a small chamber in the kip
All by himself without companionship.
He decked it charmingly with herbs and fruit
And he himself was sweeter than the root

Of liquorice, or any fragrant herb.
His astronomic text-books were superb,
He had an astrolabe to match his art
And calculating counters laid apart
On handy shelves that stood above his bed.
His press was curtained coarsely and in red;
Above there lay a gallant harp in sight
On which he played melodiously at night
With such a touch that all the chamber rang;
It was *The Virgin's Angelus* he sang,
And after that he sang *King William's Note,*
And people often blessed his merry throat.
And that was how this charming scholar spent
His time and money, which his friends had sent.

This carpenter had married a young wife
Not long before, and loved her more than life.
She was a girl of eighteen years of age.
Jealous he was and kept her in the cage,
For he was old and she was wild and young;
He thought himself quite likely to be stung.

He might have known, were Cato on his shelf,
A man should marry someone like himself;
A man should pick an equal for his mate.
Youth and old age are often in debate.
His wits were dull, he'd fallen in the snare
And had to bear his cross as others bear.

She was a pretty creature, fair and tender,
And had a weasel's body, softly slender.
She used to wear a girdle of striped silk,
Her apron was as white as morning milk
To deck her loins, all gusseted and pleated.
Her smock was white; embroidery repeated
Its pattern on the collar front and back,
Inside and out; it was of silk, and black.
And all the ribbons on her milky mutch
Were made to match her collar, even such.
She wore a broad silk fillet rather high,
And certainly she had a lecherous eye.
And she had plucked her eyebrows into bows,
Slenderly arched they were, and black as sloes.
And a more truly blissful sight to see
She was than blossom on a cherry-tree,
And softer than the wool upon a wether.
And by her girdle hung a purse of leather,
Tasselled in silk, with metal droplets, pearled.
If you went seeking up and down the world
The wisest man you met would have to wrench
His fancy to imagine such a wench.

She had a shining colour, gaily tinted,
And brighter than a florin newly minted,
And when she sang it was as loud and quick
As any swallow perched above a rick.
And she would skip or play some game or other
Like any kid or calf behind its mother.
Her mouth was sweet as mead or honey—say
A hoard of apples lying in the hay.
Skittish she was, and jolly as a colt,
Tall as a mast and upright as a bolt
Out of a bow. Her collaret revealed
A brooch as big as boss upon a shield.
High shoes she wore, and laced them to the top.
She was a daisy, O a lollypop
For any nobleman to take to bed
Or some good man of yeoman stock to wed.
   Now, gentlemen, this Gallant Nicholas
Began to romp about and make a pass
At this young woman, happening on her one day,
Her husband being out, down Osney way.
Students are sly, and giving way to whim,
He made a grab and caught her by the quim
And said, 'O God, I love you! Can't you see
If I don't have you it's the end of me?'
Then held her haunches hard and gave a cry
'O love-me-all-at-once or I shall die!'
She gave a spring, just like a skittish colt
Boxed in a frame for shoeing, and with a jolt
Managed in time to wrench her head away,
And said, 'Give over, Nicholas, I say!
No, I won't kiss you! Stop it! Let me go
Or I shall scream! I'll let the neighbours know!
Where are your manners? Take away your paws!'
   Then Nicholas began to plead his cause
And spoke so fair in proffering what he could
That in the end she promised him she would,
Swearing she'd love him, with a solemn promise
To be at his disposal, by St Thomas,
When she could spy an opportunity.
'My husband is so full of jealousy,
Unless you watch your step and hold your breath
I know for certain it will be my death,'
She said, 'So keep it well under your hat.'
'Oh, never mind about a thing like that,'
Said he; 'A scholar doesn't have to stir
His wits so much to trick a carpenter.'
   And so they both agreed to it, and swore
To watch their chance, as I have said before.

When things were settled thus as they thought fit,
And Nicholas had stroked her loins a bit
And kissed her sweetly, he took down his harp
And played away, a merry tune and sharp.
  It happened later she went off to church,
This worthy wife, one holiday, to search
Her conscience and to do the works of Christ.
She put her work aside and she enticed
The colour to her face to make her mark;
Her forehead shone. There was a parish clerk
Serving the church, whose name was Absalon.
His hair was all in golden curls and shone;
Just like a fan it strutted outwards, starting
To left and right from an accomplished parting.
Ruddy his face, his eyes as grey as goose,
His shoes cut out in tracery, as in use
In old St Paul's. The hose upon his feet
Showed scarlet through, and all his clothes were neat
And proper. In a jacket of light blue,
Flounced at the waist and tagged with laces too,
He went, and wore a surplice just as gay
And white as any blossom on the spray.
God bless my soul, he was a merry knave!
He knew how to let blood, cut hair and shave,
And draw up legal deeds; at other whiles
He used to dance in twenty different styles
(After the current school at Oxford though,
Casting his legs about him to and fro).
He played a two-stringed fiddle, did it proud,
And sang a high falsetto rather loud;
And he was just as good on the guitar
There was no public-house in town or bar
He didn't visit with his merry face
If there were saucy barmaids round the place.
He was a little squeamish in the matter
Of farting, and satirical in chatter.
This Absalon, so jolly in his ways,
Would bear the censer round on holy days
And cense the parish women. He would cast
Many a love-lorn look before he passed,
Especially at this carpenter's young wife;
Looking at her would make a happy life
He thought, so neat, so sweet, so lecherous.
And I dare say if she had been a mouse
And he a cat, she'd have been pounced upon.
  In taking the collection Absalon
Would find his heart was set in such a whirl
Of love, he would take nothing from a girl,

For courtesy, he said, it wasn't right.
    That evening, when the moon was shining bright
He ups with his guitar and off he tours
On the look-out for any paramours.
Larky and amorous, away he strode
Until he reached the carpenter's abode
A little after cock-crow, took his stand
Beside the casement window close at hand
(It was set low upon the cottage-face)
And started singing softly and with grace,
    'Now dearest lady, if thy pleasure be
    In thoughts of love, think tenderly of me!'
On his guitar he plucked a tuneful string.
    This carpenter awoke and heard him sing
And turning to his wife said, 'Alison!
Wife! Do you hear him? There goes Absalon
Chanting away under our chamber wall.'
And she replied, 'Yes, John, I hear it all.'
If she thought more of it she didn't tell.
    So things went on. What's better than 'All's well'?
From day to day this jolly Absalon,
Wooing away, became quite woe-begone;
He lay awake all night, and all the day
Combed his thick locks and tried to pass for gay,
Wooed her by go-between and wooed by proxy,
Swore to be page and servant to his doxy,
Thrilled and rouladed like a nightingale,
Sent her sweet wine and mead and spicy ale,
And wafers piping hot and jars of honey,
And, as she lived in town, he offered money.
For there are some a money-bag provokes
And some are won by kindness, some by strokes.
    Once, in the hope his talent might engage,
He played the part of Herod on the stage.
What was the good? Were he as bold as brass,
She was in love with gallant Nicholas;
However Absalon might blow his horn
His labour won him nothing but her scorn.
She looked upon him as her private ape
And held his earnest wooing all a jape.
There is a proverb—and it is no lie—
You'll often hear repeated: *'Nigh-and-Sly*
Wins against Fair-and-Square who isn't there.'
For much as Absalon might tear his hair
And rage at being seldom in her sight,
Nicholas, nigh and sly, stood in his light.
Now, show your paces, Nicholas you spark!
And leave lamenting to the parish clerk.
    And so it happened that one Saturday,

When the old carpenter was safe away
At Osney, Nicholas and Alison
Agreed at last in what was to be done.
Nicholas was to exercise his wits
On her suspicious husband's foolish fits,
And, if so be the trick worked out all right,
She then would sleep with Nicholas all night,
For such was his desire and hers as well;
And even quicker than it takes to tell,
Young Nicholas, who simply couldn't wait,
Went to his room on tip-toe with a plate
Of food and drink, enough to last a day
Or two, and Alison was told to say,
In case her husband asked for Nicholas,
That she had no idea where he was,
And that she hadn't set eyes on him all day
And thought he must be ill, she couldn't say;
And more than once the maid had given a call
And shouted but no answer came at all.
    So things went on the whole of Saturday
Without a sound from Nicholas, who lay
Upstairs, and ate or slept as pleased him best
Till Sunday when the sun went down to rest.
    This foolish carpenter was lost in wonder
At Nicholas; what could have got him under?
He said, 'I can't help thinking, by the Mass,
Things can't be going right with Nicholas.
What if he took and died? God guard his ways!
A ticklish place the world is, nowadays.
I saw a corpse this morning borne to kirk
That only Monday last I saw at work.
Run up,' he told the serving-lad, 'be quick,
Shout at his door, or knock it with a brick.
Take a good look and tell me how he fares.'
    The serving-boy went sturdily upstairs,
Stopped at the door and, standing there, the lad
Shouted away and, hammering like mad,
Cried, 'Ho! What's up? Hi! Master Nicholay!
How can you lie up there asleep all day?'
    But all for nought, he didn't hear a soul.
He found a broken panel with a hole
Right at the bottom, useful to the cat
For creeping in; he took a look through that,
And so at last by peering through the crack
He saw this scholar gaping on his back
As if he caught a glimpse of the new moon.
Down went the boy and told his master soon
About the state in which he found the man.
    On hearing this the carpenter began

To cross himself and said, 'St Frideswide bless us!
We little know what's coming to distress us.
The man has fallen, with this here astromy,
Into a fit, or lunacy maybe.
I always thought that was how it would go.
God has some secrets that we shouldn't know.
How blessed are the simple, aye, indeed,
That only know enough to say their creed!
Happened just so with such another student
Of astromy and he was so imprudent
As to stare upwards while he crossed a field,
Busy foreseeing what the stars revealed;
And what should happen but he fell down flat
Into a marl-pit. He didn't foresee that!
But by the Saints we've reached a sorry pass;
I can't help worrying for Nicholas.
He shall be scolded for his studying
If I know how to scold, by Christ the King!
Get me a staff to prise against the floor.
Robin, you put your shoulder to the door.
We'll shake the study out of him, I guess!'
      The pair of them began to heave and press
Against the door. Happened the lad was strong
And so it didn't take them very long
To heave it off its hinges; down it came.
Still as a stone lay Nicholas, with the same
Expression, gaping upwards into air.
The carpenter supposed it was despair
And shook him by the shoulders with a stout
And purposeful attack, and gave a shout:
'What, Nicholas! Hey! Look down! Is that a fashion
To act? Wake up and think upon Christ's passion.
I sign you with the cross from elves and sprites!'
And he began the spell for use at nights
In all four corners of the room and out
Across the threshold too and round about:
      Jesu Christ and Benedict Sainted
      Bless this house from creature tainted,
      Drive away night-hags, white Pater-noster,
      Where did you go St Peter's soster?
      And in the end the dandy Nicholas
Began to sigh, 'And must it come to pass?'
He said, 'Must all the world be cast away?'
The carpenter replied, 'What's that you say?
Put trust in God as we do, working men.'
Nicholas answered, 'Fetch some liquor then,
And afterwards, in strictest secrecy,
I'll speak of something touching you and me,

But not another soul must know, that's plain.'
   This carpenter went down and came again
Bringing some powerful ale—a largeish quart.
When each had had his share of this support
Young Nicholas got up and shut the door
And, sitting down beside him on the floor,
Said to the carpenter, 'Now, John, my dear,
My excellent host, swear on your honour here
Not to repeat a syllable I say,
For here are Christ's intentions, to betray
Which to a soul puts you among the lost,
And vengeance for it at a bitter cost
Shall fall upon you. You'll be driven mad!'
'Christ and His holy blood forbid it, lad!'
The silly fellow answered. 'I'm no blab,
Though I should say it. I'm not given to gab.
Say what you like, for I shall never tell
Man, woman or child by Him that harrowed Hell!'
   'Now, John,' said Nicholas, 'believe you me,
I have found out by my astrology,
And looking at the moon when it was bright,
That Monday next, a quarter way through night,
Rain is to fall in torrents, such a scud
It will be twice as bad as Noah's Flood.
This world,' he said, 'in just about an hour,
Shall all be drowned, it's such a hideous shower,
And all mankind, with total loss of life.'
   The carpenter exclaimed, 'Alas, my wife!
My little Alison! Is she to drown?'
And in his grief he very near fell down.
'Is there no remedy,' he said, 'for this?'
'Thanks be to God,' said Nicholas, 'there is,
If you will do exactly what I say
And don't start thinking up some other way.
In wise old Solomon you'll find the verse
"Who takes advice shall never fare the worse,"
And so if good advice is to prevail
I undertake with neither mast nor sail
To save her yet, and save myself and you.
Haven't you heard how Noah was saved too
When God Forewarned him and his sons and daughters
That all the world should sink beneath the waters?'
·'Yes,' said the carpenter, 'a long time back.'
'Haven't you heard,' said Nicholas, 'what a black
Business it was, when Noah tried to whip
His wife (who wouldn't come) on board the ship?
He'd have been better pleased, I'll undertake,
With all that weather just about to break,

If she had had a vessel of her own.
Now, what are we to do? We can't postpone
The thing; it's coming soon, as I was saying,
It calls for haste, not preaching or delaying.
  'I want you, now, at once, to hurry off
And fetch a shallow tub or kneading-trough
For each of us, but see that they are large
And such as we can float in, like a barge.
And have them loaded with sufficient victual
To last a day—we only need a little.
The waters will abate and flow away
Round nine o'clock upon the following day.
Robin the lad mayn't know of this, poor knave,
Nor Jill the maid, those two I cannot save.
Don't ask me why; and even if you do
I can't disclose God's secret thoughts to you.
You should be satisfied, unless you're mad,
To find as great a grace as Noah had.
And I shall save your wife, you needn't doubt it,
Now off you go, and hurry up about it.
  'And when the tubs have been collected, three,
That's one for her and for yourself and me,
Then hang them in the roof below the thatching
That no one may discover what we're hatching.
When you have finished doing what I said
And stowed the victuals in them overhead,
Also an axe to hack the ropes apart,
So, when the water rises, we can start,
And, lastly, when you've broken out the gable,
The garden one that's just above the stable,
So that we may cast free without delay
After the mighty shower has gone away,
You'll float as merrily, I undertake,
As any lily-white duck, behind her drake.
And I'll call out, "Hey, Alison! Hey, John!
Cheer yourselves up! The flood will soon be gone."
And you'll shout back, "Hail, Master Nicholay!
Good morning! I can see you well. It's day!"
We shall be lords for all the rest of life
Of all the world, like Noah and his wife.
  'One thing I warn you of; it's only right.
We must be very careful on the night,
Once we have safely managed to embark,
To hold our tongues, to utter no remark,
No cry or call, for we must fall to prayer.
This is the Lord's dear will, so have a care.
  'Your wife and you must hang some way apart,
For there must be no sin before we start,
No more in longing looks than in the deed.
Those are your orders. Off with you! God speed!

To-morrow night when everyone's asleep
We'll all go quietly upstairs and creep
Into our tubs, awaiting Heaven's grace.
And now be off. No time to put the case
At greater length, no time to sermonize;
The proverb says, "Say nothing, send the wise."
You're wise enough, I do not have to teach you.
Go, save our lives for us, as I beseech you.'
   This silly carpenter then went his way
Muttering to himself, 'Alas the day!'
And told his wife in strictest secrecy.
She was aware, far more indeed than he,
What this quaint stratagem might have in sight,
But she pretended to be dead with fright.
'Alas!' she said. 'Whatever it may cost,
Hurry and help, or we shall all be lost.
I am your honest, true and wedded wife,
Go, dearest husband, help to save my life!'
   How fancy throws us into perturbation!
People can die of mere imagination,
So deep is the impression one can take.
This silly carpenter began to quake,
Before his eyes there verily seemed to be
The floods of Noah, wallowing like the sea
And drowning Alison his honey-pet.
He wept and wailed, his features were all set
In grief, he sighed with many a doleful grunt.
He went and got a tub, began to hunt
For kneading-troughs, found two, and had them sent
Home to his house in secret; then he went
And, unbeknowns, he hung them from a rafter.
With his own hands he made three ladders after,
Uprights and rungs, to help them in their scheme
Of climbing where they hung upon the beam.
He victualled tub and trough, and made all snug
With bread and cheese, and ale in a large jug,
Enough for three of them to last the day,
And, just before completing this array,
Packed off the maid and his apprentice too
To London on a job they had to do.
And on the Monday when it drew to night
He shut his door and dowsed the candle-light
And made quite sure all was as it should be.
And shortly, up they clambered, all the three,
Silent and separate. They began to pray
And '*Pater Noster* mum', said Nicholay,
And 'mum' said John, and 'mum' said Alison.
The carpenter's devotions being done,
He sat quite still, then fell to prayer again

And waited anxiously to hear the rain.
  The carpenter, with all the work he'd seen,
Fell dead asleep—round curfew, must have been,
Maybe a little later on the whole.
He groaned in sleep for travail of his soul
And snored because his head was turned awry.
  Down by their ladders, stalking from on high
Came Nicholas and Alison, and sped
Softly downstairs, without a word, to bed,
And where this carpenter was wont to be
The revels started and the melody.
And thus lay Nicholas and Alison
At busy play in eager quest of fun,
Until the bell for lauds had started ringing
And in the chancel Friars began their singing.
  This parish clerk, this amorous Absalon,
Love-stricken still and very woe-begone,
Upon the Monday was in company
At Osney with his friends for jollity,
And chanced to ask a resident cloisterer
What had become of John the carpenter.
The fellow drew him out of church to say,
'Don't know; not been at work since Saturday.
I can't say where he is; I think he went
To fetch the Abbot timber. He is sent
Often enough for timber, has to go
Out to the Grange and stop a day or so;
If not, he's certainly at home to-day,
But where he is I can't exactly say.'
  Absalon was a jolly lad and light
Of heart; he thought, 'I'll stay awake to-night;
I'm certain that I haven't seen him stirring
About his door since dawn; it's safe inferring
That he's away. As I'm alive I'll go
And tap his window softly at the crow
Of cock—the sill is low-set on the wall.
I shall see Alison and tell her all
My love-longing, and I can hardly miss
Some favour from her, at the least a kiss.
I'll get some satisfaction anyway;
There's been an itching in my mouth all day
And that's a sign of kissing at the least.
And all last night I dreamt about a feast.
I think I'll go and sleep an hour or two,
Then wake and have some fun, that's what I'll do.'
  The first cock crew at last, and thereupon
Up rose this jolly lover Absalon
In gayest clothes, garnished with that and this;
But first he chewed a grain of liquorice
To charm his breath before he combed his hair.

Under his tongue the comfit nestling there
Would make him gracious. He began to roam
To where old John and Alison kept home
And by the casement window took his stand.
Breast-high it stood, no higher than his hand.
He gave a cough, no more than half a sound:
'Alison, honey-comb, are you around?
Sweet cinnamon, my little pretty bird,
Sweetheart, wake up and say a little word!
You seldom think of me in all my woe,
I sweat for love of you wherever I go!
No wonder if I do, I pine and bleat
As any lambkin hungering for the teat,
Believe me, darling, I'm so deep in love
I croon with longing like a turtle-dove,
I eat as little as a girl at school.'
'You go away,' she answered, 'you Tom-fool!
There's no come-up-and-kiss-me here for you.
I love another and why shouldn't I too?
Better than you, by Jesu, Absalon!
Take yourself off or I shall throw a stone.
I want to get some sleep. You go to Hell!'
'Alas!' said Absalon. 'I knew it well;
True love is always mocked and girded at;
So kiss me, if you can't do more than that,
For Jesu's love and for the love of me!'
'And if I do, will you be off?' said she.
'Promise you, darling,' answered Absalon.
'Get ready then; wait, I'll put something on,'
She said and then she added under breath
To Nicholas, 'Hush . . . we shall laugh to death!'
    This Absalon went down upon his knees;
'I am a lord!' he thought, 'And by degrees
There may be more to come; the plot may thicken.'
'Mercy, my love!' he said, 'Your mouth, my chicken!'
    She flung the window open then in haste
And said, 'Have done, come on, no time to waste,
The neighbours here are always on the spy.'
    Absalon started wiping his mouth dry.
Dark was the night as pitch, as black as coal,
And at the window out she put her hole,
And Absalon, so fortune framed the farce,
Put up his mouth and kissed her naked arse
Most savorously before he knew of this.
    And back he started. Something was amiss;
He knew quite well a woman has no beard,
Yet something rough and hairy had appeared.
'What have I done?' he said. 'Can that be you?'
'Teehee!' she cried and clapped the window to.
Off went poor Absalon sadly through the dark.

'A beard! a beard!' cried Nicholas the Spark.
'God's body, that was something like a joke!'
And Absalon, overhearing what he spoke,
Bit on his lips and nearly threw a fit
In rage and thought, 'I'll pay you back for it!'
　　Who's busy rubbing, scraping at his lips
With dust, with sand, with straw, with cloth, with chips,
But Absalon? He thought, 'I'll bring him down!
I wouldn't let this go for all the town.
I'd take my soul and sell it to the Devil
To be revenged upon him! I'll get level.
O God, why did I let myself be fooled?'
　　The fiery heat of love by now had cooled,
For from the time he kissed her hinder parts
He didn't give a tinker's curse for tarts;
His malady was cured by this endeavour
And he defied all paramours whatever.
　　So, weeping like a child that has been whipped,
He turned away; across the road he slipped
And called on Gervase. Gervase was a smith;
His forge was full of things for ploughing with
And he was busy sharpening a share.
　　Absalon knocked, and with an easy air
Called, 'Gervase! Open up the door, come on!'
'What's that? Who's there?' 'It's me, it's Absalon.'
'What, Absalon? By Jesu's blessed tree
You're early up! Hey, *benedicite,*
What's wrong? Some jolly girl as like as not
Has coaxed you out and set you on the trot.
Blessed St. Neot! You know the thing I mean.'
　　But Absalon, who didn't give a bean
For all his joking, offered no debate.
He had a good deal more upon his plate
Than Gervase knew and said, 'Would it be fair
To borrow that coulter in the chimney there,
The hot one, see it? I've a job to do;
It won't take long, I'll bring it back to you.'
Gervase replied, 'Why, if you asked for gold,
A bag of sovereigns or for wealth untold,
It should be yours, as I'm an honest smith.
But, Christ, why borrow that to do it with?'
'Let that,' said Absalon, 'be as it may;
You'll hear about it all some other day.'
　　He caught the coulter up—the haft was cool—
And left the smithy softly with the tool,
Crept to the little window in the wall
And coughed. He knocked and gave a little call
Under the window as he had before.
　　Alison said, 'There's someone at the door.
Who's knocking there? I'll warrant it's a thief.'

'Why, no,' said he, 'my little flower-leaf,
It's your own Absalon, my sweety-thing!
Look what I've brought you—it's a golden ring
My mother gave me, as I may be saved.
It's very fine, and prettily engraved;
I'll give it to you, darling, for a kiss.'
   Now Nicholas had risen for a piss,
And thought he could improve upon the jape
And make him kiss his arse ere he escape,
And opening the window with a jerk,
Struck out his arse, a handsome piece of work,
Buttocks and all, as far as to the haunch.
   Said Absalon, all set to make a launch,
'Speak, pretty bird, I know not where thou art!'
This Nicholas at once let fly a fart
As loud as if it were a thunder-clap.
He was near blinded by the blast, poor chap,
But his hot iron was ready; with a thump
He smote him in the middle of the rump.
   Off went the skin a hand's-breadth round about
Where the hot coulter struck and burnt it out.
Such was the pain, he thought he must be dying
And, mad with agony, he started crying,
'Help! Water! Water! Help! For Heaven's love!'
   The carpenter, startled from sleep above,
And hearing shouts for water and a thud,
Thought, 'Heaven help us! Here comes Nowel's Flood!'
And up he sat and with no more ado
He took his axe and smote the ropes in two
And down went everything. He didn't stop
To sell his bread and ale, but came down flop
Upon the floor and fainted right away.
   Up started Alison and Nicholay
And shouted, 'Help!' and 'Murder!' in the street.
The neighbours all came running up in heat
And stood there staring at the wretched man.
He lay there fainting, pale beneath his tan;
His arm in falling had been broken double.
But still he was obliged to face his trouble,
For when he spoke he was at once borne down
By Nicholas and his wife. They told the town
That he was mad, there'd got into his blood
Some sort of nonsense about 'Nowel's Flood',
That vain imaginings and fantasy
Had made him buy the kneading-tubs, that he
Had hung them in the rafters up above
And that he'd begged them both for heaven's love
To sit up in the roof for company.
   All started laughing at this lunacy
And streamed upstairs to gape and pry and poke,

And treated all his sufferings as a joke.
No matter what the carpenter asserted
It went for nothing, no one was converted;
With powerful oaths they swore the fellow down
And he was held for mad by all the town;
Even the learned said to one another,
'The fellow must be crazy, my dear brother.'
So to a general laughter he succumbed.
   That's how the carpenter's young wife was plumbed
For all the tricks his jealousy could try,
And Absalon has kissed her nether eye
And Nicholas is branded on the bum.
And God bring all of us to Kingdom Come.

Oriental Tale: Addison, *The Spectator,* No. 159 (Sept. 1, 1711)

. . . Omnem, quae nunc obducta tuenti
Mortales hebetat visus tibi, & humida circum
Caligat, nubem eripiam . . .—Virg.[1]

When I was at *Grand Cairo* I picked up several Oriental Manuscripts, which I have still by me. Among others I met with one, entituled *The Visions of Mirzah,* which I have read over with great Pleasure. I intend to give it to the Publick when I have no other Entertainment for them; and shall begin with the first Vision, which I have translated Word for Word as follows.

   On the fifth Day of the Moon, which according to the Custom of my Forefathers I always keep holy, after having washed my self and offered up my Morning Devotions, I ascended the high Hills of *Bagdat,* in order to pass the rest of the Day in Meditation and Prayer. As I was here airing my self on the Tops of the Mountains, I fell into a profound Contemplation on the Vanity of humane Life; and passing from one Thought to another, Surely, said I, Man is but a Shadow and Life a Dream. Whilst I was thus musing, I cast my Eyes towards the Summit of a Rock that was not far from me, where I discovered one in the Habit of a Shepherd, with a little Musical Instrument in his Hand. As I looked upon him he applied it to his Lips, and began to play upon it. The Sound of it was exceeding sweet, and wrought into a Variety of Tunes that was inexpressibly melodious, and altogether different from any thing I had ever heard. They put me in mind of those heavenly Airs that are played to the departed Souls of good Men upon their first Arrival in Paradise, to wear out the Impressions of the last Agonies, and qualify them for the Pleasures of that happy Place. My Heart melted away in secret Raptures.

   I had been often told that the Rock before me was the Haunt of a Genius; and that several had been entertained with Musick who had passed by it, but never heard that the Musician had before made himself visible. When he had raised my Thoughts, by those transporting Airs which he played, to taste the Pleasures of his Conversation, as I looked upon him like one astonished, he beckoned to me, and by the waving of his

[1] From Virgil, Aeneid, Book II, lines 604-606, "I shall tear away all the cloud, which now, drawn over your sight, dulls your mortal vision with dark pall enshrouds
you." [Venus addressing her son Aeneas.]

Hand directed me to approach the Place where he sat. I drew near with that Reverence which is due to a superior Nature; and as my Heart was entirely subdued by the captivating Strains I had heard, I fell down at his Feet and wept. The Genius smiled upon me with a Look of Compassion and Affability that familiarized him to my Imagination, and at once dispelled all the Fears and Apprehensions with which I approached him. He lifted me from the Ground, and taking me by the Hand, *Mirzah,* said he, I have heard thee in thy Soliloquies, follow me.

He then led me to the highest Pinnacle of the Rock, and placing me on the Top of it, Cast thy Eyes Eastward, said he, and tell me what thou seest. I see, said I, a huge Valley and a prodigious Tide of Water rolling through it. The Valley that thou seest, said he, is the Vale of Misery, and the Tide of Water that thou seest is Part of the great Tide of Eternity. What is the Reason, said I, that the Tide I see rises out of a thick Mist at one End, and again loses it self in a thick Mist at the other? What thou seest, said he, is that Portion of Eternity which is called Time, measured out by the Sun, and reaching from the Beginning of the World to its Consummation. Examine now, said he, this Sea that is bounded with Darkness at both Ends, and tell me what thou discoverest in it. I see a Bridge, said I, standing in the Midst of the Tide. The Bridge thou seest, said he, is humane Life; consider it attentively. Upon a more leisurely Survey of it, I found that it consisted of threescore and ten entire Arches, with several broken Arches, which added to those that were entire, made up the Number about an hundred. As I was counting the Arches, the Genius told me that this Bridge consisted at first of a thousand Arches; but that a great Flood swept away the rest, and left the Bridge in the ruinous Condition I now beheld it. But tell me further, said he, what thou discoverest on it. I see Multitudes of People passing over it, said I, and a black Cloud hanging on each End of it. As I looked more attentively, I saw several of the Passengers dropping thro' the Bridge, into the great Tide that flowed underneath it; and upon further Examination, perceived there were innumerable Trap-doors that lay concealed in the Bridge, which the Passengers no sooner trod upon, but they fell through them into the Tide and immediately disappeared. These hidden Pit-falls were set very thick at the Entrance of the Bridge, so that Throngs of People no sooner broke through the Cloud, but many of them fell into them. They grew thinner towards the Middle, but multiplied and lay closer together towards the End of the Arches that were entire.

There were indeed some Persons, but their Number was very small, that continued a kind of hobbling March on the broken Arches, but fell through one after another, being quite tired and spent with so long a Walk.

I passed some Time in the Contemplation of this wonderful Structure, and the great Variety of Objects which it presented. My Heart was filled with a deep Melancholy to see several dropping unexpectedly in the Midst of Mirth and Jollity, and catching at every thing that stood by them to save themselves. Some were looking up towards the Heavens in a thoughtful Posture, and in the Midst of a Speculation stumbled and fell out of Sight. Multitudes were very busy in the Pursuit of Bubbles that glittered in their Eyes and danced before them, but often when they thought themselves within the Reach of them their Footing failed and down they sunk. In this Confusion of Objects, I observed some with Scymetars[2] in their Hands, and others with Urinals,[2] who ran to and fro upon the Bridge, thrusting several Persons on Trap-doors which did not seem to lie in their Way, and which they might have escaped had they not been thus forced upon them.

The Genius seeing me indulge my self in this melancholy Prospect, told me I had

[2] That is, soldiers and physicians.

dwelt long enough upon it: Take thine Eyes off the Bridge, said he, and tell me if thou yet seest any thing thou dost not comprehend. Upon looking up, What mean, said I, those great Flights of Birds that are perpetually hovering about the Bridge, and settling upon it from Time to Time? I see Vultures, Harpyes, Ravens, Cormorants; and among many other feathered Creatures several little winged Boys, that perch in great Numbers upon the middle Arches. These said the Genius, are Envy, Avarice, Superstitition, Despair, Love, with the like Cares and Passions that infest humane Life.

I here fetched a deep Sigh. Alas, said I, Man was made in vain! How is he given away to Misery and Mortality! tortured in Life, and swallowed up in Death! The Genius being moved with Compassion towards me, bid me quit so uncomfortable a Prospect: Look no more, said he, on Man in the first Stage of his Existence, in his setting out for Eternity; but cast thine Eye on that thick Mist into which the Tide bears the several Generations of Mortals that fall into it. I directed my Sight as I was ordered, and (whether or no the good Genius strengthened it with any supernatural Force, or dissipated Part of the Mist that was before too thick for the Eye to penetrate) I saw the Valley opening at the further End, and spreading forth into an immense Ocean, that had a huge Rock of Adamant running through the Midst of it, and dividing it into two equal Parts. The Clouds still rested on one Half of it, insomuch that I could discover nothing in it; but the other appeared to me a vast Ocean planted with innumerable Islands, that were covered with Fruits and Flowers, and interwoven with a thousand little shining Seas that ran among them. I could see Persons dressed in glorious Habits, with Garlands upon their Heads, passing among the Trees, lying down by the Sides of Fountains, or resting on Beds of Flowers; and could hear a confused Harmony of singing Birds, falling Waters, humane Voices, and musical Instruments. Gladness grew in me upon the Discovery of so delightful a Scene. I wished for the Wings of an Eagle, that I might fly away to those happy Seats; but the Genius told me there was no Passage to them, except through the Gates of Death that I saw opening every Moment upon the Bridge. The Islands, said he, that lie so fresh and green before thee, and with which the whole Face of the Ocean appears spotted as far as thou canst see, are more in Number than the Sands on the Sea-shore; there are Myriads of Islands behind those which thou here discoverest, reaching further than thine Eye or even thine Imagination can extend it self. These are the Mansions of good Men after Death, who according to the Degree and Kinds of Virtue in which they excelled, are distributed among these several Islands, which abound with Pleasures of different Kinds and Degrees, suitable to the Relishes and Perfections of those who are settled in them; every Island is a Paradise accommodated to its respective Inhabitants. Are not these, O *Mirzah*, Habitations worth contending for? Does Life appear miserable, that gives thee Opportunities of earning such a Reward? Is Death to be feared, that will convey thee to so happy an Existence? Think not Man was made in vain, who has such an Eternity reserved for him. I gazed with inexpressible Pleasure on these happy Islands. At length, said I, shew me now, I beseech thee, the Secrets that lie hid under those dark Clouds which cover the Ocean on the other Side of the Rock of Adamant. The Genius making me no Answer, I turned about to address my self to him a second time, but I found that he had left me; I then turned again to the Vision which I had been so long contemplating, but instead of the rolling Tide, the arched Bridge, and the happy Islands, I saw nothing but the long hollow Valley of *Bagdat*, with Oxen, Sheep, and Camels grazing upon the Sides of it.

The End of the first Vision of *Mirzah*.

Part Two

The Short Story Proper: The First Age

Nikolai Gogol (1809–1852)

Nikolai Gogol is considered the father of realism in Russian Literature, yet he has been called a romantic and even, by Vladimir Nabokov, a "fantast." These apparently disparate qualities converged to create one of the most influential short stories ever written. "The Overcoat," along with the work of Edgar Allan Poe, Nathaniel Hawthorne, and a few other writers of the age, stands as the bridge between the tale, that simple recital of happenings, and the modern short story, with its moral view and social commentary and complex psychology.

Frank O'Connor said that an alternate title for his fine study of the short story *The Lonely Voice* might have been a line from "The Overcoat": "I am your brother." These words—uttered by the harassed and ridiculed little clerk—so moved one of his colleagues, who here represents the narrator, that "many a time in his life thereafter did he shudder, seeing how much inhumanity there is in man." O'Connor points out that in this story is "the first appearance in fiction of the Little Man. . . . Everything about Akakii Akakiievich, from his absurd name to his absurd job, is on the same level of mediocrity, and yet his absurdity is somehow transfigured by Gogol."

Though obviously not every story is set in a city, in a way the modern short story is an expression of the life led in the modern city, with its estrangement and anonymity and its special awareness. Gogol spends a good deal of time describing St. Petersburg, especially life among the bureaucrats. "The Overcoat" is as much a story of that society as it is of the Little Man we laugh at and are moved by. A decent coat is hardly his only deprivation. The "formidable foe" against which even "Titular Councilors are sometimes utterly defenseless" is as much the isolation and loneliness of the city as it is the northern frost. To make this point and paint this picture, Gogol brilliantly uses techniques of realism, romanticism, and fantasy.

"We all came out from under Gogol's 'Overcoat'" is a remark variously attributed to Dostoevsky and Turgenev. That either or both might have said it is a sign of the story's wide significance.

Gogol, whose name translates as "wild duck," was born in 1809 in the Ukraine, but before he was twenty went seeking literary fame and fortune in St. Petersburg, which was the artistic capital of czarist Russia. In 1836 his satirical play *The Inspector General* caused such a storm of criticism that he was forced into an exile that lasted twelve years. *Dead Souls,* his satirical novel, was published in 1837 and *Taras Bulba,* a novel which deals with the Cossack struggles in the sixteenth century, in 1842. Gogol died, quite mad, in 1852.

The Overcoat

In the Bureau of . . . but it might be better not to mention the Bureau by its precise name. There is nothing more touchy than all these Bureaus, Regiments, Chancelleries of every sort, and, in a word, every sort of person belonging to the administrative classes. Nowadays every civilian, even, considers all of society insulted in his own person. Quite recently, so they say, a petition came through from a certain Captain of Rural Police in some town or other (I can't recall its name), in which he explained clearly that the whole social structure was headed for ruin and that his sacred name was actually being taken entirely in vain, and, in proof, he documented his petition with the enormous tome of some romantic work or other wherein, every ten pages or so, a Captain of Rural Police appeared—in some passages even in an out-and-out drunken state. And so, to avoid any and all unpleasantnesses, we'd better call the Bureau in question *a certain Bureau.* And so, in *a certain Bureau* there served *a certain clerk*—a clerk whom one could hardly style very remarkable: quite low of stature, somewhat pockmarked, somewhat rusty-hued of hair, even somewhat purblind, at first glance; rather bald at the temples, with wrinkles along both cheeks, and his face of that complexion which is usually called hemorrhoidal. Well, what would you? It's the Petersburg climate that's to blame. As far as his rank is concerned (for among us the rank must be made known first of all), why, he was what they call a Perpetual Titular Councilor[1] a rank which, as everybody knows, various writers who have a praiseworthy wont of throwing their weight about among those who are in no position to hit back, have twitted and exercised their keen wits against often and long. This clerk's

[1] A relatively low-level civil servant.

Nikolai Gogol, "The Overcoat," from *A Treasury of Russian Literature,* edited and translated by Bernard Guilbert Guerney. Copyright, 1943, by Vanguard Press. Reprinted by permission of Vanguard Press.

family name was Bashmachkin. It's quite evident, by the very name, that it sprang from *bashmak* or shoe, but at what time, just when and how it sprang from a shoe— of that nothing is known. For not only this clerk's father but his grandfather and even his brother-in-law, and absolutely all the Bashmachkins, walked about in boots, merely resoling them three times a year.

His name and patronymic were Akakii Akakiievich. It may, perhaps, strike the reader as somewhat odd and out of the way, but the reader may rest assured that the author has not gone out of his way at all to find it, but that certain circumstances had come about of themselves in such fashion that there was absolutely no way of giving him any other name. And the precise way this came about was as follows. Akakii Akakiievich was born—unless my memory plays me false—on the night of the twenty-third of March. His late mother, a government clerk's wife, and a very good woman, was all set to christen her child, all fit and proper. She was still lying in bed, facing the door, while on her right stood the godfather, a most excellent man by the name of Ivan Ivanovich Eroshkin, who had charge of some Department or other in a certain Administrative Office, and the godmother, the wife of the precinct police officer, a woman of rare virtues, by the name of Arina Semenovna Byelobrushkina. The mother was offered the choice of any one of three names: Mokii, Sossii—or the child could even be given the name of that great martyr, Hozdavat. "No," the late lamented had reflected, "what sort of names are these?" In order to please her they opened the calendar at another place—and the result was again three names: Triphilii, Dula, and Varahasii. "What a visitation!" said the elderly woman. "What names all these be! To tell you the truth, I've never even heard the likes of them. If it were at least Baradat or Baruch, but why do Triphilii and Varahasii have to turn up?" They turned over another page—and came up with Pavsikahii and Vahtissii. "Well, I can see now," said the mother, "that such is evidently his fate. In that case it would be better if he were called after his father. His father was an Akakii—let the son be an Akakii also." And that's how Akakii Akakiievich came to be Akakii Akakiievich.

The child was baptized, during which rite he began to bawl and made terrible faces as if anticipating that it would be his lot to become a Perpetual Titular Councilor. And so that's the way it had all come about. We have brought the matter up so that the reader might see for himself that all this had come about through sheer inevitability and it had been utterly impossible to bestow any other name upon Akakii Akakiievich.

When, at precisely what time, he entered the Bureau, and who gave him the berth, were things which no one could recall. No matter how many Directors and his superiors of one sort or another came and went, he was always to be seen in the one and the same spot, in the same posture, in the very same post, always the same Clerk of Correspondence, so that subsequently people became convinced that he evidently had come into the world just the way he was, all done and set, in a uniform frock and bald at the temples. No respect whatsoever was shown him in the Bureau. The porters not only didn't jump up from their places whenever he happened to pass by, but didn't even as much as glance at him, as if nothing more than a common housefly had passed through the reception hall. His superiors treated him with a certain chill despotism. Some assistant or other of some Head of a Department would simply shove papers under his nose, without as much as saying "Transcribe these," or "Here's a rather pretty, interesting little case," or any of those small pleasantries that are current in well-conducted administrative institutions. And he would take the work, merely glancing at the paper, without looking up to see who had put it down before him and whether that person had the right to do so; he took it and right then and there went to work on it. The young clerks made fun of him and sharpened their wits at his expense, to whatever extent their quill-driving wittiness sufficed, retailing in his very presence the various stories made up about him; they said of his landlady, a crone of seventy, that she beat him, and asked him when their wedding would take place, they scattered torn paper over his head, maintaining it was snow.

But not a word did Akakii Akakiievich say in answer to all this, as if there were actually nobody before him. It did not even affect his work: in the midst of all these annoyances he did not make a single clerical error. Only when the jest was past all bearing, when they jostled his arm, hindering him from doing his work, would he say: "Leave me alone! Why do you pick on me?" And there was something odd about his words and in the voice with which he uttered them. In that voice could be heard something that moved one to pity—so much so that one young man, a recent entrant, who, following the example of the others, had permitted himself to make fun of Akakii Akakiievich, stopped suddenly, as if pierced to the quick, and from that time on everything seemed to change in his eyes and appeared in a different light. Some sort of preternatural force seemed to repel him from the companions he had made, having taken them for decent, sociable people. And for a long time afterward, in the very midst of his most cheerful moments, the little squat clerk would appear before him, with the small bald patches on each side of his forehead, and he would hear his heart-piercing words "Leave me alone! Why do you pick on me?" And in these heart-piercing words he caught the ringing sound of others: "I am your brother." And the poor young man would cover his eyes with his hand, and many a time in his life thereafter did he shudder, seeing how much inhumanity there is in man, how much hidden ferocious coarseness lurks in refined, cultured worldliness and, O God! even in that very man whom the world holds to be noble and honorable. . . .

It is doubtful if you could find anywhere a man whose life lay so much in his work. It would hardly do to say that he worked with zeal; no, it was a labor of love. Thus, in this transcription of his, he visioned some sort of diversified and pleasant world all its own. His face expressed delight; certain letters were favorites of his and whenever he came across them he would be beside himself with rapture: he'd chuckle, and wink, and help things along by working his lips, so that it seemed as if one could read on his face every letter his quill was outlining. If rewards had been meted out to him commensurately with his zeal, he might have, to his astonishment, actually found himself among the State Councilors; but, as none other than those wits, his own co-workers, expressed it, all he'd worked himself up to was a button in a buttonhole too wide, and piles in his backside.

However, it would not be quite correct to say that absolutely no attention was paid him. One Director, being a kindly man and wishing to reward him for his long service, gave orders that some work of a more important nature than the usual transcription be assigned to him; to be precise, he was told to make a certain referral to another Administrative Department out of a docket already prepared; the matter consisted, all in all, of changing the main title as well as some pronouns here and there from the first person singular to the third person singular. This made so much work for him that he was all of a sweat, kept mopping his forehead, and finally said: "No, better let me transcribe something." Thenceforth they left him to his transcription for all time. Outside of this transcription, it seemed, nothing existed for him.

He gave no thought whatsoever to his dress; the uniform frock coat on him wasn't the prescribed green at all, but rather of some rusty-flour hue. His collar was very tight and very low, so that his neck, even though it wasn't a long one, seemed extraordinarily long emerging therefrom, like those gypsum kittens with nodding heads which certain outlanders balance by the dozen atop their heads and peddle throughout Russia. And, always, something was bound to stick to his coat: a wisp of hay or some bit of thread; in addition to that, he had a peculiar knack whenever he walked through the streets of getting under some window at the precise moment when garbage of every sort was being thrown out of it, and for that reason always bore off on his hat watermelon and cantaloupe rinds and other such trifles. Not once in all his life had he ever turned his attention to the everyday things and doings out in the street—something, as everybody knows, that is always watched with eager interest by Akakii Akakiievich's confrère, the young government clerk, the penetration of whose lively gaze is so extensive that he will even take in somebody on the opposite sidewalk who has ripped loose his trouser strap—a thing that never fails to evoke a sly smile on the young clerk's face. But even if Akakii Akakiievich did look at anything, he saw thereon nothing but his own neatly, evenly penned lines of script, and only when some horse's nose, bobbing up from no one knew where, would be placed on his shoulder and let a whole gust of wind in his face through its nostrils, would he notice that he was not in the middle of a line of script but, rather, in the middle of the roadway.

On coming home he would immediately sit down at the table, gulp down his cabbage soup and bolt a piece of veal with onions, without noticing in the least the taste of either, eating everything together with the flies and whatever else God may have sent at that particular time of the year. On perceiving that his belly was beginning to swell out, he'd get up from the table, take out a small bottle of ink, and transcribe the papers he had brought home. If there were no homework, he would deliberately, for his own edification, make a copy of some paper for himself, especially if the document were remarkable not for its beauty of style but merely addressed to some new or important person.

Even at those hours when the gray sky of Petersburg became entirely extinguished and all the pettifogging tribe has eaten its fill and finished dinner, each as best he could, in accordance with the salary he receives and his own bent, when everybody has already rested up after the scraping of quills in various departments, the running around, the unavoidable cares about their own affairs and the affairs of others, and all that which restless man sets himself as a task voluntarily and to an even greater extent than necessary—at a time when the petty bureaucrats hasten to devote whatever time remained to enjoyment: he who is of the more lively sort hastening to the theater; another for a saunter through the streets, devoting the time to an inspection of certain pretty little hats; still another to some evening party, to spend that time in paying compliments to some comely young lady, the star of a small bureaucratic circle; a fourth (and this happened most frequently of all) would simply go for a call on a confrère in a flat up three or four flights of stairs, consisting of two small rooms with an entry and a kitchen and one or two attempts at the latest improvements—a kerosene lamp instead of candles, or some other elegant little thing that had cost many sacrifices, such as going without dinners or good times—in short, even at the time when all the pretty bureaucrats scatter through the small apartments of their friends for a session of dummy whist, sipping tea out of tumblers and nibbling at cheap zweiback, drawing deep at their pipes, the stems thereof as long as walking sticks, retailing, during the shuffling and dealing, some bit of gossip or other from high society that had reached them at long last (something which no Russian, under any circumstances, and of whatever estate he be, can ever deny himself), or even, when there was nothing whatsoever to talk about, retelling the eternal chestnut of the commandant to whom people came to say that the tail of the horse on the Falconetti monument had been docked—in short, even at the time when every soul yearns to be diverted, Akakii Akakiievich did not give himself up to any diversion. No man could claim having ever seen him at any evening gathering. Having had his sweet fill of quill-driving, he would lie down to sleep, smiling at the thought of the next day: just what would God send him on the morrow?

Such was the peaceful course of life of a man who, with a yearly salary of four hundred, knew how to be content with his lot, and that course might even have continued to a ripe old age had it not been for sundry calamities, such as are stewn along the path of life, not only of Titular, but even Privy, Actual, Court, and all other sorts of Councilors, even those who never give any counsel to anybody nor ever accept any counsel from others for themselves.

There is, in Petersburg, a formidable foe of all those whose salary runs to four hundred a year or thereabouts. This foe is none other than our Northern frost—even though, by the bye, they do say that it's the most healthful thing for you. At nine in the morning, precisely at that hour when the streets are thronged with those on their way to sundry bureaus, it begins dealing out such powerful and penetrating fillips to all noses, without any discrimination, that the poor bureaucrats absolutely do not know how to hide them. At this time, when even those who fill the higher posts feel their foreheads aching because of the frost and the tears come to their eyes, the poor Titular Councilors are sometimes utterly defenseless. The sole salvation, if one's overcoat is of the thinnest, lies in dashing, as quickly as possible, through five or six blocks and then stamping one's feet plenty in the porter's room, until the faculties and gifts for administrative duties, which have been frozen on the way, are thus thawed out at last.

For some time Akakii Akakiievich had begun to notice that the cold was somehow penetrating his back and shoulders with especial ferocity, despite the fact that he tried to run the required distance as quickly as possible. It occurred to him, at last, that there might be some defects about this overcoat. After looking it over rather thoroughly at home he discovered that in two or three places—in the back and at the shoulders, to be exact—it had become no better than the coarsest of sacking; the cloth was rubbed to such an extent that one could see through it, and the lining had crept apart. The reader must be informed that Akakii Akakiievich's overcoat, too, was a butt for the jokes of the petty bureaucrats; it had been deprived of the honorable name of an overcoat, even, and dubbed a *negligée*. And, really, it was of a rather queer cut; its collar grew smaller with every year, inasmuch as it was utilized to supplement the other parts of the garment. This supplementing was not at all a compliment to the skill of the tailor, and the effect really was baggy and unsightly.

Perceiving what the matter was, Akakii Akakiievich decided that the overcoat would have to go to Petrovich the tailor, who lived somewhere up four flights of backstairs and who, despite a squint-eye and pockmarks all over his face, did quite well at repairing bureaucratic as well as all other trousers and coats—of course, be it understood, when he was in a sober state and not hatching some nonsartorial scheme in his head. One shouldn't, really, mention this tailor at great length, but since there is already a precedent for each character in a tale being clearly defined, there's no help for it, and so let's trot out Petrovich as well. In the beginning he had been called simply Gregory and had been the serf of some squire or other; he had begun calling himself Petrovich only after obtaining his freedom papers and taking to drinking rather hard on any and every holiday—at first on the red-letter ones and then, without any discrimination, on all those designated by the church: wherever there was a little cross marking the day on the calendar. In this respect he was loyal to the customs of our grandsires, and, when bickering with his wife, would call her a worldly woman and a German frau. And, since we've already been inadvertent enough to mention his wife, it will be necessary to say a word or two about her as well; but, regrettably, little was known about her—unless, perhaps, the fact that Petrovich had a wife, or that she even wore a house-cap and not a kerchief; but as for beauty, it appears that she could hardly boast of any; at least the soldiers in the Guards were the only ones with hardihood enough to bend down for a peep under her cap, twitching their mustache as they did so and emitting a certain peculiar sound.

As he clambered up the staircase that led to Petrovich—the staircase, to render it its just due, was dripping all over from water and slops and thoroughly permeated with that alcoholic odor which makes the eyes smart and is, as everybody knows, unfailingly present on all the backstairs of all the houses in Petersburg—as he clambered up this staircase Akakii Akakiievich was already conjecturing how stiff Petrovich's asking-price would be and mentally determined not to give him more than two rubles. The door was open, because the mistress of the place, being busy preparing some fish, had filled the kitchen with so much smoke that one actually couldn't see the very cockroaches for it. Akakii Akakiievich made his way through the kitchen, unperceived even by the mistress herself, and at last entered the room wherein he beheld Petrovich, sitting on a wide table of unpainted deal with his feet tucked in under him like a Turkish Pasha. His feet, as is the wont of tailors seated at their work, were bare, and the first thing that struck one's eyes was the big toe of one, very familiar to Akakii Akakiievich, with some sort of deformed nail, as thick and strong as a turtle's shell. About Petrovich's neck were loops of silk and cotton thread, while some sort of ragged garment was lying on his knees. For the last three minutes he had been trying to put a thread through the eye of a needle, couldn't hit the mark, and because of that was very wroth against the darkness of the room and even the thread itself, grumbling under his breath: "She won't go through, the heathen! You've spoiled my heart's blood, you damned good-for-nothing!"

Akakii Akakiievich felt upset because he had come at just the moment when Petrovich was very angry; he liked to give in his work when the latter was already under the influence or, as his wife put it, "He's already full of rot-gut, the one-eyed devil." In such a state Petrovich usually gave in willingly and agreed to everything; he even bowed and was grateful every time. Afterward, true enough, his wife would come around and complain weepily that, now, her husband had been drunk and for that reason had taken on the work too cheaply; but all you had to do was to tack on another ten kopecks—and the thing was in the bag. But now, it seemed, Petrovich was in a sober state, and for that reason on his high horse, hard to win over, and bent on boosting his prices to the devil knows what heights. Akakii Akakiievich surmised this and, as the saying goes, was all set to make back tracks, but the deal had already been started. Petrovich puckered up his one good eye against him very fixedly and Akakii Akakiievich involuntarily said, "Greetings, Petrovich!" "Greetings to you, Sir," said Petrovich and looked askance at Akakii Akakiievich's hands, wishing to see what sort of booty the other bore.

"Well, now, I've come to see you, now, Petrovich!"

Akakii Akakiievich, the reader must be informed, explained himself for the most part in prepositions, adverbs, and such verbal oddments as have absolutely no significance. But if the matter was exceedingly difficult, he actually had a way of not finishing his phrase at all, so that, quite frequently, beginning his speech with such words as "This, really, is perfectly, you know—"—he would have nothing at all to follow up with, and he himself would be likely to forget the matter, thinking that he had already said everything in full.

"Well, just what is it?" asked Petrovich, and at the same time, with his one good eye, surveyed the entire garment, beginning with the collar and going on to the sleeves, the back, the coat-skirts, and the buttonholes, for it was all very familiar to him, inasmuch as it was all his own handiwork. That's a way all tailors have; it's the first thing a tailor will do on meeting you.

"Why, what I'm after, now, Petrovich . . . the overcoat, now, the cloth . . . there, you see, in all the other places it's strong as can be . . . its gotten a trifle dusty and only seems to be old, but it's really new, there's only one spot . . . a little sort of . . . in the back . . . and also one shoulder, a trifle rubbed through—and this shoulder, too, a trifle—do you see? Not a lot of work, really—"

Petrovich took up the *negligée,* spread it out over the table as a preliminary, examined it for a long time, shook his head, and then groped with his hand on the window sill for a round snuffbox with the portrait of some general or other on its lid— just which one nobody could tell, inasmuch as the place occupied by the face had been holed through with a finger and then pasted over with a small square of paper. After duly taking tobacco, Petrovich held the *negligée* taut in his hands and scrutinized it against the light, and again shook his head; after this he turned it with the lining up and again shook his head, again took off the lid with the general's face pasted over with paper and, having fully loaded both nostrils with snuff, covered the snuffbox, put it away, and at long last, gave his verdict:

"No, there's no fixin' this thing: your wardrobe's in a bad way!"

Akakii Akakiievich's heart skipped a beat at these words.

"But why not, Petrovich?" he asked, almost in the imploring voice of a child. "All that ails it, now . . . it's rubbed through at the shoulders. Surely you must have some small scraps of cloth or other—"

"Why, yes, one could find the scraps—the scraps will turn up," said Petrovich. "Only there's no sewing them on: the whole thing's all rotten: touch a needle to it— and it just crawls apart on you."

"Well, let it crawl—and you just slap a patch right on to it."

"Yes, but there's nothing to slap them little patches on to; there ain't nothing for the patch to take hold on—there's been far too much wear. It's cloth in name only, but if a gust of wind was to blow on it it would scatter."

"Well, now, you just fix it up. That, really, now . . . how can it be?"

"No," said Petrovich decisively, "there ain't a thing to be done. The whole thing's in a bad way. You'd better, when the cold winter spell comes, make footcloths out of it, because stockings ain't so warm. It's them Germans that invented them stockings, so's to rake in more money for themselves. [Petrovich loved to needle the Germans whenever the chance turned up.] But as for that there overcoat, it looks like you'll have to make yourself a new one."

At the word *new* a mist swam before Akakii Akakiievich's eyes and everything in the room became a hotchpotch. All he could see clearly was the general on the lid of Petrovich's snuffbox, his face pasted over with a piece of paper.

"A new one? But how?" he asked, still as if he were in a dream. "Why, I have no money for that."

"Yes, a new one," said Petrovich with a heathenish imperturbability.

"Well, if there's no getting out of it, how much, now—"

"You mean, how much it would cost?"

"Yes."

"Why, you'd have to cough up three fifties and a bit over," pronounced Petrovich and significantly pursed up his lips at this. He was very fond of strong effects, was fond of somehow nonplusing somebody, utterly and suddenly, and then eyeing his victim sidelong, to see what sort of wry face the nonplusee would pull after his words.

"A hundred and fifty for an overcoat!" poor Akakii Akakiievich cried out—cried out perhaps for the first time since he was born, for he was always distinguished for his low voice.

"Yes, Sir!" said Petrovich. "And what an overcoat, at that! If you put a marten collar on it and add a silk-lined hood it might stand you even two hundred.

"Petrovich, please!" Akakii Akakiievich was saying in an imploring voice, without grasping and without even trying to grasp the words uttered by Petrovich and all his effects. "Fix it somehow or other, now, so's it may do a little longer, at least—"

"Why, no, that'll be only having the work go to waste and spending your money for nothing," said Petrovich, and after these words Akakii Akakiievich walked out annihilated. But Petrovich, after his departure, remained as he was for a long time, with meaningfully pursed lips and without resuming his work, satisfied with neither having lowered himself nor having betrayed the sartorial art.

Out in the street, Akakii Akakiievich walked along like a somnambulist. "What a business, now, what a business," he kept saying to himself. "Really, I never even thought that it, now . . . would turn out like that. . . ." And then, after a pause, added: "So that's it! That's how it's turned out after all. Really, now, I couldn't even suppose that it . . . like that, now—" This was followed by another long pause, after which he uttered aloud: "So that's how it is! This, really, now, is something that's beyond all, now, expectation . . . well, I never! What a fix, now!"

Having said this, instead of heading for home, he started off in an entirely different direction without himself suspecting it. On the way a chimney sweep caught him square with his whole sooty side and covered his whole shoulder with soot; enough quicklime to cover his whole hat tumbled down on him from the top of a building under construction. He noticed nothing of all this and only later, when he ran up against a policeman near his sentry box (who, having placed his halberd near him, was shaking some tobacco out of a paper cornucopia on to his calloused palm), did Akakii Akakiievich come a little to himself, and that only because the policeman said: "What's the idea of shoving your face right into mine? Ain't the sidewalk big enough for you?" This made him look about him and turn homeward.

Only here did he begin to pull his wits together; he perceived his situation in its clear and real light; he started talking to himself no longer in snatches but reasoningly and frankly, as with a judicious friend with whom one might discuss a matter most heartfelt and intimate. "Well, no," said Akakii Akakiievich, "there's no use reasoning with Petrovich now; he's, now, that way. . . . His wife had a chance to give him a drubbing, it looks like. No, it'll be better if I come to him on a Sunday morning; after Saturday night's good time he'll be squinting his eye and very sleepy, so he'll have to have a hair of the dog that bit him, but his wife won't give him any money, now, and just then I'll up with ten kopecks or so and into his hand with it—so he'll be more reasonable to talk with, like, and the overcoat will then be sort of. . . ."

That was the way Akakii Akakiievich reasoned things out to himself, bolstering up his spirits. And, having bided his time till the next Sunday and spied from afar that

Petrovich's wife was going off somewhere out of the house, he went straight up to him. Petrovich, sure enough, was squinting his eye hard after the Saturday night before, kept his head bowed down to the floor, and was no end sleepy; but, found that, as soon as he learned what was up, it was as though the Devil himself nudged him.

"Can't be done," said he. "You'll have to order a new overcoat."

Akakii Akakiievich thrust a ten-kopeck coin on him right then and there.

"I'm grateful to you, Sir; I'll have a little something to get me strength back and will drink to your health," said Petrovich, "but as for your overcoat, please don't fret about it; it's of no earthly use any more. As for a new overcoat, I'll tailor a glorious one for you; I'll see to that."

Just the same, Akakii Akakiievich started babbling again about fixing the old one, but Petrovich simply would not listen to him and said: "Yes, I'll tailor a new one for you without fail; you may rely on that, I'll try my very best. We might even do it the way it's all the fashion now—the collar will button with silver catches under appliqué."

It was then that Akakii Akakiievich perceived that there was no doing without a new overcoat, and his spirits sank utterly. Really, now, with what means, with what money would he make this overcoat? Of course he could rely, in part, on the coming holiday bonus, but this money had been apportioned and budgeted ahead long ago. There was an imperative need of outfitting himself with new trousers, paying the shoemaker an old debt for a new pair of vamps to an old pair of bootlegs, and he had to order from a sempstress three shirts and two pair of those nethergarments which it is impolite to mention in print; in short, all the money was bound to be expended entirely, and even if the Director was so gracious as to decide on giving him five and forty, or even fifty rubles as a bonus, instead of forty, why, even then only the veriest trifle would be left over, which, in the capital sum required for the overcoat, would be as a drop in a bucket. Even though Akakii Akakiievich was, of course, aware of Petrovich's maggot of popping out with the devil knows how inordinate an asking price, so that even his wife herself could not restrain herself on occasion from crying out: "What, are you going out of your mind, fool that you are! There's times when he won't take on work for anything, but the Foul One has egged him on to ask a bigger price than all of him is worth"—even though he knew, of course, that Petrovich would probably undertake the work for eighty rubles, nevertheless and notwithstanding where was he to get those eighty rubles? Half of that sum might, perhaps, be found: half of it could have been found, maybe even a little more—but where was he going to get the other half?

But first the reader must be informed where the first half was to come from. Akakii Akakiievich had a custom of putting away a copper or so from every ruble he expended, into a little box under lock and key, with a small opening cut through the lid for dropping money therein. At the expiration of every half-year he made an accounting of the entire sum accumulated in coppers and changed it into small silver. He had kept this up a long time, and in this manner, during the course of several years, the accumulated sum turned out to be more than forty rubles. And so he had half the sum for the overcoat on hand; but where was he to get the other half? Where was he to get the other forty rubles? Akakii Akakiievich mulled the matter over and over and decided that it would be necessary to curtail his ordinary expenses, for the duration of a year at the very least; banish the indulgence in tea of evenings; also, of evenings, to do without lighting candles, but, if there should be need of doing something, to go to his landlady's room and work by her candle; when walking along the streets he would set his foot as lightly and carefully as possible on the cobbles and flagstones, walking almost on tiptoes, and thus avoid wearing out his soles prematurely; his linen would have to be given as infrequently as possible to the laundress and, in order that it might not become too soiled, every time he came home all of it must be taken off, the wearer having to remain only in his jean bathrobe, a most ancient garment and spared even by time itself.

It was, the truth must be told, most difficult for him in the beginning to get habituated to such limitations, but later it did turn into a matter of habit, somehow, and everything went well; he even became perfectly trained to going hungry of evenings; on the other hand, however, he had spiritual sustenance, always carrying about in his thoughts the eternal idea of the new overcoat. From this time forth it seemed as if his very existence had become somehow fuller, as though he had taken unto himself a wife, as though another person was always present with him, as though he were not alone but as if an amiable feminine helpmate had consented to traverse the path of life side by side with him—and this feminine helpmate was none other than this very same overcoat, with a thick quilting of cotton wool, with a strong lining that would never wear out.

He became more animated, somehow, even firmer of character, like a man who has already defined and set a goal for himself. Doubt, indecision—in a word, all vacillating and indeterminate traits—vanished of themselves from his face and actions. At times a sparkle appeared in his eyes; the boldest and most daring of thoughts actually flashed through his head: Shouldn't he, after all, put marten on the collar? Meditations on this subject almost caused him to make absent-minded blunders. And on one occasion, as he was transcribing a paper, he all but made an error, so that he emitted an almost audible "Ugh," and made the sign of the cross.

During the course of each month he would make at least one call on Petrovich, to discuss the overcoat: Where would it be best to buy the cloth, and of what color and at what price—and even though somewhat preoccupied he always came home satisfied, thinking that the time would come, at last, when all the necessary things would be bought and the overcoat made.

The matter went even more quickly than he had expected. Contrary to all his anticipations, the Director designated a bonus not of forty or forty-five rubles for Akakii Akakiievich, but all of sixty. Whether he had a premonition that Akakii Akakiievich needed a new overcoat, or whether this had come about of its own self, the fact nevertheless remained: Akakii Akakiievich thus found himself the possessor of an extra twenty rubles. This circumstance hastened the course of things. Some two or three months more of slight starvation—and lo! Akakii Akakiievich had accumulated around eighty rubles. His heart, in general quite calm, began to palpitate. On the very first day possible he set out with Petrovich to the shops. The cloth they bought was very good, and no great wonder, since they had been thinking over its purchase as much as half a year before and hardly a month had gone by without their making a round of the shops to compare prices; but then, Petrovich himself said that there couldn't be better cloth than that. For lining they chose calico, but of such good quality and so closely woven that, to quote Petrovich's words, it was still better than silk and, to look at, even more showy and glossy. Marten they did not buy, for, to be sure, it was expensive, but instead they picked out the best catskin the shop boasted—catskin that could, at a great enough distance, be taken for marten.

Petrovich spent only a fortnight in fussing about with the making of the overcoat, for there was a great deal of stitching to it, and if it hadn't been for that it would have been ready considerably earlier. For his work Petrovich took twelve rubles—he couldn't have taken any less; everything was positively sewn with silk thread, with a small double stitch, and after the stitching Petrovich went over every seam with his own teeth, pressing out various figures with them.

It was on . . . it would be hard to say on precisely what day, but it was, most probably, the most triumphant day in Akakii Akakiievich's life when Petrovich, at last, brought the overcoat. He brought it in the morning, just before Akakii Akakiievich had to set out for his Bureau. Never, at any other time, would the overcoat have come in so handy, because rather hard frosts were already setting in and, apparently, were threatening to become still more severe. Petrovich's entrance with the overcoat was one befitting a good tailor. Such a portentous expression appeared on his face as Akakii Akakiievich had never yet beheld. Petrovich felt to the fullest, it seemed, that he had performed no petty labor and that he had suddenly evinced in himself that abyss which lies between those tailors who merely put in linings and alter and fix garments and those who create new ones.

He extracted the overcoat from the bandanna in which he had brought it. (The bandanna was fresh from the laundress; it was only later on that he thrust it in his pocket for practical use.) Having drawn out the overcoat, he looked at it quite proudly and, holding it in both hands, threw it deftly over the shoulders of Akakii Akakiievich, pulled it and smoothed it down the back with his hand, then draped it on Akakii Akakiievich somewhat loosely. Akakiievich, as a man along in his years, wanted to try it on with his arms through the sleeves. Petrovich helped him on with it: it turned out to be fine, even with his arms through the sleeves. In a word, the overcoat proved to be perfect and had come in the very nick of time. Petrovich did not let slip the opportunity of saying that he had done the work so cheaply only because he lived in a place without a sign, on a side street, and, besides, had known Akakii Akakiievich for a long time; *but* on the Nevski Prospect they would have taken seventy-five rubles from him for the labor alone. Akakii Akakiievich did not feel like arguing the matter with Petrovich and, besides, he had a dread of all the fancy sums with which Petrovich liked to throw dust in people's eyes. He paid the tailor off, thanked him, and walked right out in the new overcoat on his way to the Bureau. Petrovich walked out at his heels and, staying behind on the street, for a long while kept looking after the overcoat from afar, and then deliberately went out of his way so that, after cutting across a crooked lane, he might run out again into the street and have another glance at his overcoat from a different angle—that is, full front.

In the meantime Akakii Akakiievich walked along feeling in the most festive of moods. He was conscious every second of every minute that he had a new overcoat on his shoulders, and several times even smiled slightly because of his inward pleasure. In reality he was a gainer on two points: for one, the overcoat was warm, for the other, it was a fine thing. He did not notice the walk at all and suddenly found himself at the Bureau; in the porter's room he took off his overcoat, looked it all over, and entrusted it to the particular care of the doorman. None knows in what manner everybody in the Bureau suddenly learned that Akakii Akakiievich had a new overcoat, and that the *negligée* was no longer in existence. They all immediately ran out into the vestibule to inspect Akakii Akakiievich's new overcoat. They fell to congratulating him, to saying agreeable things to him, so that at first he could merely smile, and in a short time became actually embarrassed. And when all of them, having besieged him, began telling him that the new overcoat ought to be baptized and that he ought, at the least, to get up an evening party for them, Akakii Akakiievich was utterly at a loss, not

knowing what to do with himself, what answers to make, nor how to get out of inviting
them. It was only a few minutes later that he began assuring them, quite simple-
heartedly, that it wasn't a new overcoat at all, that it was just an ordinary overcoat,
that in fact it was an old overcoat. Finally one of the bureaucrats—some sort of an
Assistant to a Head of a Department, actually—probably in order to show that he was
not at all a proud stick and willing to mingle even with those beneath him, said: "So
be it, then; I'm giving a party this evening and ask all of you to have tea with me;
today, appropriately enough, happens to be my birthday."

The clerks, naturally, at once thanked the Assistant to a Head of a Department
and accepted the invitation with enthusiasm. Akakii Akakiievich attempted to excuse
himself at first, but all began saying that it would show disrespect to decline, that it
would be simply a shame and a disgrace, and after that there was absolutely no way
for him to back out. However, when it was all over, he felt a pleasant glow as he
reminded himself that this would give him a chance to take a walk in his new overcoat
even in the evening. The whole day was for Akakii Akakiievich something in the
nature of the greatest and most triumphant of holidays.

Akakii Akakiievich returned home in the happiest mood, took off the overcoat,
and hung it carefully on the wall, once more getting his fill of admiring the cloth and
the lining, and then purposely dragged out, for comparison, his former *negligée,* which
by now had practically disintegrated. He glanced at it and he himself had to laugh, so
great was the difference! And for a long while thereafter, as he ate dinner, he kept on
smiling slightly whenever the present state of the *negligée* came to his mind. He dined
gaily, and after dinner did not write a single stroke; there were no papers of any kind,
for that matter; he just simply played the sybarite a little, lounging on his bed, until it
became dark. Then, without putting matters off any longer, he dressed, threw the
overcoat over his shoulders, and walked out into the street.

We are, to our regret, unable to say just where the official who had extended the
invitation lived; our memory is beginning to play us false—very much so—and everything in Petersburg, no matter what, including all its streets and houses, has become so
muddled in our mind that it's quite hard to get anything out therefrom in any sort of
decent shape. But wherever it may have been, at least this much is certain: that official
lived in the best part of town; consequently a very long way from Akakii Akakiievich's
quarters. First of all Akakii Akakiievich had to traverse certain deserted streets with
but scant illumination; however, in keeping with his progress toward the official's
domicile, the streets became more animated; the pedestrians flitted by more and more
often; he began meeting even ladies, handsomely dressed; the men he came upon had
beaver collars on their overcoats; more and more rarely did he encounter jehus with
latticed wooden sleighs, studded over with gilt nails—on the contrary, he kept coming
across first-class drivers in caps of raspberry-hued velvet, their sleighs lacquered and
with bearskin robes, while the carriages had decorated seats for the drivers and raced
down the roadway, their wheels screeching over the snow.

Akakii Akakiievich eyed all this as a novelty—it was several years by now since
he had set foot out of his house in the evening. He stopped with curiosity before the
illuminated window of a shop to look at a picture, depicting some handsome woman
or other, who was taking off her shoe, thus revealing her whole leg (very far from ill-
formed), while behind her back some gentleman or other, sporting side whiskers and a
handsome goatee, was poking his head out of the door of an adjoining room. Akakii
Akakiievich shook his head and smiled, after which he went on his way. Why had he
smiled? Was it because he had encountered something utterly unfamiliar, yet about

which, nevertheless, everyone preserves a certain instinct? Or did he think, like so many other petty clerks, "My, the French they are a funny race! No use talking! If there's anything they get a notion of, then, sure enough, there it is!" And yet, perhaps, he did not think even that; after all, there's no way of insinuating one's self into a man's soul, of finding out all that he might be thinking about.

At last he reached the house in which the Assistant to a Head of a Department lived. The Assistant to a Head of a Department lived on a grand footing; there was a lantern on the staircase; his apartment was only one flight up. On entering the foyer of the apartment Akakii Akakiievich beheld row after row of galoshes. In their midst, in the center of the room, stood a samovar, noisy and emitting clouds of steam. The walls were covered with hanging overcoats and capes, among which were even such as had beaver collars or lapels of velvet. On the other side of the wall he could hear much noise and talk, which suddenly became distinct and resounding when the door opened and a flunky came out with a tray full of empty tumblers, a cream pitcher, and a basket of biscuits. It was evident that the bureaucrats had gathered long since and had already had their first glasses of tea.

Akakii Akakiievich, hanging up his overcoat himself, entered the room and simultaneously all the candles, bureaucrats, tobacco-pipes and card tables flickered before him, and the continuous conversation and the scraping of moving chairs, coming from all sides, struck dully on his ears. He halted quite awkwardly in the center of the room, at a loss and trying to think what he ought to do. But he had already been noticed, was received with much shouting, and everyone immediately went to the foyer and again inspected his overcoat. Akakii Akakiievich, even though he was somewhat embarrassed, still could not but rejoice on seeing them all bestow such praises on his overcoat, since he was a man with an honest heart. Then, of course, they all dropped him and his overcoat and, as is usual, directed their attention to the whist tables.

All this—the din, the talk, and the throng of people—all this was somehow a matter of wonder to Akakii Akakiievich. He simply did not know what to do, how to dispose of his hands, his feet, and his whole body; finally he sat down near the card-players, watched their cards, looked now at the face of this man, now of that, and after some time began to feel bored, to yawn—all the more so since his usual bedtime had long since passed. He wanted to say good-by to his host but they wouldn't let him, saying that they absolutely must toast his new acquisition in a goblet of champagne. An hour later supper was served, consisting of mixed salad, cold veal, meat pie, patties from a pastry cook's, and champagne. They forced Akakii Akakiievich to empty two goblets, after which he felt that the room had become ever so much more cheerful. However, he absolutely could not forget that it was already twelve o'clock and that it was long since time for him to go home. So that his host might not somehow get the idea of detaining him, he crept out of the room, managed to find his overcoat—which, not without regret, he saw lying on the floor; then, shaking the overcoat and taking every bit of fluff off it, he threw it over his shoulders and made his way down the stairs and out of the house.

It was still dusk out in the street. Here and there small general stores, those round-the-clock clubs for domestics and all other servants, were still open; other shops, which were closed, nevertheless showed, by a long streak of light along the crack either at the outer edge or the bottom, that they were not yet without social life and that, probably, the serving wenches and lads were still winding up their discussions and conversations, thus throwing their masters into utter bewilderment as to their whereabouts. Akakii Akakiievich walked along in gay spirits; he even actually made a sudden dash, for some unknown reason, after some lady or other, who had passed by him like a flash of lightning, and every part of whose body was filled with buoyancy. However, he stopped right then and there and resumed his former exceedingly gentle pace, actually wondering himself at the sprightliness that had come upon him from none knows where.

Soon he again was passing stretch after stretch of those desolate streets which are never too gay even in the daytime, but are even less so in the evening. Now they had become still more deserted and lonely; he came upon glimmering street lamps more and more infrequently—the allotment of oil was now evidently decreasing; there was a succession of wooden houses and fences, with never another soul about; the snow alone glittered on the street, and the squat hovels, with their shutters closed in sleep, showed like depressing dark blotches. He approached a spot where the street was cut in two by an unending square, with the houses on the other side of it barely visible— a square that loomed ahead like an awesome desert.

Far in the distance, God knows where, a little light flickered in a policeman's sentry box that seemed to stand at the end of the world. Akakii Akakiievich's gay mood somehow diminished considerably at this point. He set foot in the square, not without a premonition of something evil. He looked back and on each side of him—it was as though he were in the midst of a sea. "No, it's better even not to look," he reflected and went on with his eyes shut. And when he did open them to see if the end of the square were near, he suddenly saw standing before him, almost at his very nose, two strangers with mustaches—just what sort of men they were was something he couldn't even make out. A mist arose before his eyes and his heart began to pound.

"Why, that there overcoat is mine!" said one of the men in a thunderous voice, grabbing him by the collar. Akakii Akakiievich was just about to yell "Police!" when the other put a fist right up to his mouth, a fist as big as any government clerk's head, adding: "There, you just let one peep out of you!"

All that Akakii Akakiievich felt was that they had taken the overcoat off him, given him a kick in the back with the knee, and that he had fallen flat on his back in the snow, after which he felt nothing more. In a few minutes he came to and got up on his feet, but there was no longer anybody around. He felt that it was cold out in that open space and that he no longer had the overcoat, and began to yell; but his voice, it seemed, had no intention whatsoever of reaching the other end of the square. Desperate, without ceasing to yell, he started off at a run across the square directly toward the sentry box near which the policeman was standing and, leaning on his halberd, was watching the running man, apparently with curiosity, as if he wished to know why the devil anybody should be running toward him from afar and yelling. Akakii Akakiievich, having run up to him, began to shout in a stifling voice that he, the policeman, had been asleep, that he was not watching and couldn't see that a man was being robbed. The policeman answered that he hadn't seen anything, that he had seen two men of some sort stop him in the middle of the square, but he had thought they were friends of Akakii Akakiievich's, and that instead of cursing him out for nothing he'd better go on the morrow to the Inspector, and the Inspector would find out who had taken his overcoat.

Akakii Akakiievich ran home in utter disorder; whatever little hair still lingered on his temples and the nape of his neck was all disheveled; his side and his breast and his trousers were all wet with snow. The old woman, his landlady, hearing the dreadful racket at the door, hurriedly jumped out of bed, and, with a shoe on only one foot, ran down to open the door, modestly holding the shift at her breast with one hand; but, on opening the door and seeing Akakii Akakiievich in such a state, she staggered back. When he had told her what the matter was, however, she wrung her hands and said that he ought to go directly to the Justice of the Peace; the District Officer of Police would take him in, would make promises to him and then lead him about by the nose; yes, it would be best of all to go straight to the Justice. Why, she was even acquainted with him, seeing as how Anna, the Finnish woman who had formerly been her cook, had now gotten a place as a nurse at the Justice's; that she, the landlady herself, sees the Justice often when he drives past her house, and also that he went to church every Sunday, praying, yet at the same time looking so cheerfully at all the folks, and that consequently, as one could see by all the signs, he was a kindhearted man. Having heard this solution of his troubles through to the end, the saddened Akakii Akakiievich shuffled off to his room, and how he passed the night there may be left to the discernment of him who can in any degree imagine the situation of another.

Early in the morning he set out for the Justice's, but was told there that he was sleeping; he came at ten o'clock, and was told again, "He's sleeping." He came at eleven; they told him, "Why, His Honor's not at home." He tried at lunchtime, but the clerks in the reception room would not let him through to the presence under any circumstances and absolutely had to know what business he had come on and what had occurred, so that, at last, Akakii Akakiievich for once in his life wanted to evince firmness of character and said sharply and categorically that he had to see the Justice personally, that they dared not keep him out, that he had come from his own Bureau on a Government matter, and that now, when he'd lodge a complaint against them, why, they would see, then. The clerks dared not say anything in answer to this and one of them went to call out the Justice of the Peace.

The Justice's reaction to Akakii Akakiievich's story of how he had been robbed of his overcoat was somehow exceedingly odd. Instead of turning his attention to the main point of the matter, he began interrogating Akakii Akakiievich: Just why had he been coming home at so late an hour? Had he, perhaps, looked in at, or hadn't he actually visited, some disorderly house? Akakii Akakiievich became utterly confused and walked out of the office without himself knowing whether the investigation about the overcoat would be instituted or not.

This whole day he stayed away from his Bureau (the only time in his life he had done so). On the following day he put in an appearance, all pale and in his old *negligée,* which had become more woebegone than ever. The recital of the robbery of the overcoat, despite the fact that there proved to be certain ones among his co-workers who did not let pass even this opportunity to make fun of Akakii Akakiievich, nevertheless touched many. They decided on the spot to make up a collection for him, but they collected the utmost trifle, inasmuch as the petty officials had spent a lot even without this, having subscribed for a portrait of the Director and for some book or other, at the invitation of the Chief of the Department, who was a friend of the writer's; and so the sum proved to be most trifling. One of them, moved by compassion, decided, at the least, to aid Akakii Akakiievich with good advice telling him that he oughtn't to go to the precinct officer of the police, because, even though it might come about that the precinct officer, wishing to merit the approval of his superiors, might locate the overcoat in some way, the overcoat would in the end remain with the police, if Akakii Akakiievich could not present legal proofs that it belonged to him; but that the best thing of all would be to turn to a *certain important person;* that this important person, after conferring and corresponding with the proper people in the proper quarters, could speed things up.

There was no help for it; Akakii Akakiievich summoned up his courage to go to the important person. Precisely what the important person's post was and what the work of that post consisted of, has remained unknown up to now. It is necessary to know that the certain important person had only recently become an Important Person, but, up to then, had been an unimportant person. However, his post was not considered an important one even now in comparison with more important ones. But there will always be found a circle of people who perceive the importance of that which is unimportant in the eyes of others. However, he tried to augment his importance by many other means, to wit: he inaugurated the custom of having the subordinate clerks meet him while he was still on the staircase when he arrived at his office; another, of no one coming directly into his presence, but having everything follow the most rigorous precedence: a Collegiate Registrar was to report to the Provincial Secretary, the Provincial Secretary to a Titular one, or whomever else it was necessary to report to, and only thus was any matter to come to him. For it is thus in our Holy Russia that everything is infected with imitativeness; everyone apes his superior and postures like him. They even say that a certain Titular Councilor, when they put him at the helm of some small individual chancellery, immediately had a separate room for himself partitioned off, dubbing it the Reception Center, and had placed at the door some doormen or other with red collars and gold braid, who turned the doorknob and opened the door for every visitor, even though there was hardly room in the Reception Center to hold even an ordinary desk.

The manners and ways of the important person were imposing and majestic, but not at all complex. The chief basis of his system was strictness. "Strictness, strictness, and—strictness," he was wont to say, and when uttering the last word he usually looked very significantly into the face of the person to whom he was speaking, even though, by the way, there was no reason for all this, inasmuch as the half-score of clerks constituting the whole administrative mechanism of his chancellery was under the proper state of fear and trembling even as it was: catching sight of him from afar the staff would at once drop whatever it was doing and wait, at attention, until the Chief had passed through the room. His ordinary speech with his subordinates reeked of strictness and consisted almost entirely of three phrases: "How dare you? Do you know whom you're talking to? Do you realize in whose presence you are?" However, at soul he was a kindly man, treated his friends well, and was obliging; but the rank of General had knocked him completely off his base. Having received a General's rank he had somehow become muddled, had lost his sense of direction, and did not know how to act. If he happened to be with his equals he was still as human as need be, a most decent man, in many respects—even a man not at all foolish; but whenever he happened to be in a group where there were people even one rank below him, why, there was no holding him; he was taciturn, and his situation aroused pity, all the more since he himself felt that he could have passed the time infinitely more pleasantly. In his eyes one could at times see a strong desire to join in some circle and its interesting conversation, but he was stopped by the thought: Wouldn't this be too much unbending on his part, wouldn't it be a familiar action, and wouldn't he lower his importance thereby? And as a consequence of such considerations he remained forever aloof in that invariably taciturn state, only uttering some monosyllabic sounds at rare intervals, and had thus acquired the reputation of a most boring individual.

It was before such an *important person* that our Akakii Akakiievich appeared, and he appeared at a most inauspicious moment, quite inopportune for himself—although, by the bye, most opportune for the important person. The important person was seated in his private office and had gotten into very, very jolly talk with a certain recently arrived old friend and childhood companion whom he had not seen for several years. It was at this point that they announced to the important person that some Bashmachkin or other had come to see him. He asked abruptly, "Who is he?" and was told, "Some petty clerk or other." "Ah. He can wait; this isn't the right time for him to come," said the important man.

At this point it must be said that the important man had fibbed a little: he had the time; he and his old friend had long since talked over everything and had been long eking out their conversation with protracted silences, merely patting each other lightly on the thigh from time to time and adding, "That's how it is, Ivan Abramovich!" and "That's just how it is, Stepan Varlaamovich!" But for all that he gave orders for the petty clerk to wait a while just the same, in order to show his friend, a man who had been long out of the Civil Service and rusticating in his village, how long petty clerks had to cool their heels in his anteroom.

Finally, having had his fill of talk, yet having had a still greater fill of silences, and after each had smoked a cigar to the end in a quite restful armchair with an adjustable back, he at last appeared to recall the matter and said to his secretary, who had halted in the doorway with some papers for a report, "Why, I think there's a clerk waiting out there. Tell him he may come in."

On beholding the meek appearance of Akakii Akakiievich and his rather old, skimpy frock coat, he suddenly turned to him and asked, "What is it you wish?"—in a voice abrupt and firm, which he had purposely rehearsed beforehand in his room at home in solitude and before a mirror, actually a week before he had received his present post and his rank of General.

Akakii Akakiievich already had plenty of time to experience the requisite awe, was somewhat abashed, and, as best he could, in so far as his poor freedom of tongue would allow him, explained, adding even more *now's* than he would have at another time, that his overcoat had been perfectly new, and that, now, he had been robbed of it in a perfectly inhuman fashion, and that he was turning to him, now, so that he might interest himself through his . . . now . . . might correspond with the Head of Police or somebody else, and find his overcoat, now. . . . Such conduct, for some unknown reason, appeared familiar to the General.

"What are you up to, my dear Sir?" he resumed abruptly. "Don't you know the proper procedure? Where have you come to? Don't you know how matters ought to be conducted? As far as this is concerned, you should have first of all submitted a petition to the Chancellery; it would have gone from there to the head of the proper Division, then would have been transferred to the Secretary, and the Secretary would in due time have brought it to my attention—"

"But, Your Excellency," said Akakii Akakiievich, trying to collect whatever little pinch of presence of mind he had, yet feeling at the same time that he was in a dreadful sweat. "I ventured to trouble you, Your Excellency, because secretaries, now . . . aren't any too much to be relied upon—"

"What? What? What?" said the important person. "Where did you get such a tone from? Where did you get such notions? What sort of rebellious feeling has spread among the young people against the administrators and their superiors?" The important person had, it seems, failed to notice that Akakii Akakiievich would never see fifty again, consequently, even if he could have been called a young man it could be applied only relatively, that is, to someone who was already seventy. "Do you know whom you're saying this to? Do you realize in whose presence you are? Do you realize? Do you realize, I'm asking you!" Here he stamped his foot, bringing his voice to such an overwhelming note that even another than an Akakii Akakiievich would have been frightened. Akakii Akakiievich was simply bereft of his senses, swayed, shook all over, and simply could not stand on his feet. If a couple of doormen had not run up right then and there to support him he would have slumped to the floor; they carried him out in a practically cataleptic state. But the important person, satisfied because the effect had surpassed even anything he had expected, and inebriated by the idea that a word from him could actually deprive a man of his senses, looked out of the corner of his eye to learn how his friend was taking this and noticed, not without satisfaction, that his friend was in a most indeterminate state and was even beginning to experience fear on his own account.

How he went down the stairs, how he came out into the street—that was something Akakii Akakiievich was no longer conscious of. He felt neither his hands nor his feet; never in all his life had he been dragged over such hot coals by a General—and a General outside his bureau, at that! With his mouth gaping, stumbling off the sidewalk, he breasted the blizzard that was whistling and howling through the streets; the wind, as is its wont in Petersburg, blew upon him from all the four quarters, from every cross lane. In a second it had blown a quinsy down his throat, and he crawled home without the strength to utter a word; he became all swollen and took to his bed. That's how effective a proper hauling over the coals can be at times!

On the next day he was running a high fever. Thanks to the magnanimous all-round help of the Petersburg climate, the disease progressed more rapidly than could have been expected, and when the doctor appeared he, after having felt the patient's pulse, could not strike on anything to do save prescribing hot compresses, and that solely so that the sick man might not be left without the beneficial help of medicine; but, on the whole, he announced on the spot that in another day and a half it would be curtains for Akakii Akakiievich, after which he turned to the landlady and said, "As for you, Mother, don't you be losing any time for nothing; order a pine coffin for him right now, because a coffin of oak will be beyond his means."

Whether Akakii Akakiievich heard the doctor utter these words, so fateful for him, and, even if he did hear them, whether they had a staggering effect on him, whether he felt regrets over his life of hard sledding—about that nothing is known, inasmuch as he was all the time running a temperature and was in delirium. Visions, each one stranger than the one before, appeared before him ceaselessly: now he saw Petrovich and was ordering him to make an overcoat with some sort of traps to catch thieves, whom he ceaselessly imagined to be under his bed, at every minute calling his landlady to pull out from under his blanket one of them who had actually crawled under there; then he would ask why his old *negligée* was hanging in front of him, for he had a new overcoat; then once more he had a hallucination that he was standing before the General, getting a proper raking over the coals, and saying, "Forgive me, Your Excellency!"; then, finally, he actually took to swearing foully, uttering such dreadful words that his old landlady could do nothing but cross herself, having never in her life heard anything of the sort from him, all the more so since these words followed immediately after "Your Excellency!"

After that he spoke utter nonsense, so that there was no understanding anything; all one could perceive was that his incoherent words and thoughts all revolved about that overcoat and nothing else.

Finally poor Akakii Akakiievich gave up the ghost. Neither his room nor his things were put under seal; in the first place because he had no heirs, and in the second because there was very little left for anybody to inherit, to wit: a bundle of goose quills, a quire of white governmental paper, three pairs of socks, two or three buttons that had come off his trousers, and the *negligée* which the reader is already familiar with. Who fell heir to all this treasure-trove, God knows; I confess that even the narrator of this tale was not much interested in the matter. They bore Akakii Akakiievich off and buried him. And Petersburg was left without Akakii Akakiievich, as if he had never been therein. There vanished and disappeared a being protected by none, endeared to no one, of no interest to anyone, a being that actually had failed to attract to itself the attention of even a naturalist who wouldn't let a chance slip of sticking an ordinary housefly on a pin and of examining it through a microscope; a being that had submissively endured the jests of the whole chancellery and that had gone to its grave without any extraordinary fuss, but before which, nevertheless, even before the very end of its life, there had flitted a radiant guest in the guise of an overcoat, which had animated for an instant a poor life, and upon which being calamity had come crashing down just as unbearably as it comes crashing down upon the heads of the mighty ones of this earth!

A few days after his death a doorman was sent to his house from the Bureau with an injunction for Akakii Akakiievich to appear immediately; the Chief, now, was asking for him; but the doorman had to return empty-handed, reporting back that "he weren't able to come no more," and to the question, "Why not?" expressed himself in the words, "Why, just so; he up and died; they buried him four days back." Thus did they learn at the Bureau about the death of Akakii Akakiievich, and the very next day a new pettifogger, considerably taller than Akakii Akakiievich, was already sitting in his place and putting down the letters no longer in such a straight hand, but considerably more on the slant and downhill.

But whoever could imagine that this wouldn't be all about Akakii Akakiievich, that he was fated to live for several noisy days after his death, as though in reward for a life that had gone by utterly unnoticed? Yet that is how things fell out, and our poor history is taking on a fantastic ending.

Rumors suddenly spread through Petersburg that near the Kalinkin Bridge, and much farther out still, a dead man had started haunting of nights, in the guise of a petty government clerk, seeking for some overcoat or other that had been purloined from him and, because of that stolen overcoat, snatching from all and sundry shoulders, without differentiating among the various ranks and titles, all sorts of overcoats: whether they had collars of catskin or beaver, whether they were quilted with cotton wool, whether they were lined with raccoon, with fox, with bear—in a word, every sort of fur and skin that man has ever thought of for covering his own hide. One of the clerks in the Bureau had seen the dead man with his own eyes and had immediately recognized in him Akakii Akakiievich. This had inspired him with such horror, however, that he started running for all his legs were worth and for that reason could not make him out very well but had merely seen the other shake his finger at him from afar. From all sides came an uninterrupted flow of complaints that backs and shoulders—it wouldn't matter so much if they were merely those of Titular Councilors, but even those of Privy Councilors were affected—were exposed to the danger of catching thorough colds, because of this oft-repeated snatching-off of overcoats.

An order was put through to the police to capture the dead man, at any cost, dead or alive, and to punish him in the severest manner as an example to others—and they all but succeeded in this. To be precise, a policeman at a sentry box on a certain block of the Kirushkin Lane had already gotten a perfect grip on the dead man by his coat collar, at the very scene of his malefaction, while attempting to snatch off the frieze overcoat of some retired musician, who in his time had tootled a flute. Seizing the dead man by the collar, the policeman had summoned two of his colleagues by shouting and had entrusted the ghost to them to hold him, the while he himself took just a moment to reach down in his bootleg for his snuffbox, to relieve temporarily a nose that had been frostbitten six times in his life; but the snuff, probably, was of such a nature as even a dead man could not stand. Hardly had the policeman, after stopping his right nostril with a finger, succeeded in drawing half a handful of rapee up his left, than the dead man sneezed so heartily that he completely bespattered the eyes of all the three myrmidons. While they were bringing their fists up to rub their eyes, the dead man vanished without leaving as much as a trace, so that they actually did not know whether he had really been in their hands or not.

From then on the policemen developed such a phobia of dead men that they were afraid to lay hands even on living ones and merely shouted from a distance, "Hey, there, get going!" and the dead government clerk began to do his haunting even beyond the Kalinkin Bridge, inspiring not a little fear in all timid folk.

However, we have dropped entirely a certain *important person,* who, in reality, had been all but the cause of the fantastic trend taken by what is, by the bye, a perfectly true story. First of all, a sense of justice compels us to say that the *certain important person,* soon after the departure of poor Akakii Akakiievich, done to a turn in the raking over the hot coals, had felt something in the nature of compunction. He was no stranger to compassion; many kind impulses found access to his heart, despite the fact that his rank often stood in the way of their revealing themselves. As soon as the visiting friend had left his private office, he actually fell into a brown study over Akakii Akakiievich. And from that time on, almost every day, there appeared before him the pale Akakii Akakiievich, who had not been able to stand up under an administrative hauling over the coals. The thought concerning him disquieted the certain important person to such a degree that, a week later, he even decided to send a clerk to him to find out what the man had wanted, and how he was, and whether it were really possible to help him in some way. And when he was informed that Akakii Akakiievich had died suddenly in a fever he was left actually stunned, hearkening to the reproaches of conscience, and was out of sorts the whole day.

Wishing to distract himself to some extent and to forget the unpleasant impression this news had made upon him, he set out for an evening party to one of his friends, where he found a suitable social gathering, and, what was best of all, all the men there were of almost the same rank, so that he absolutely could not feel constrained in any way. This had an astonishing effect on the state of his spirits. He relaxed, became amiable and pleasant to converse with—in a word, he passed the time very agreeably. At supper he drank off a goblet or two of champagne—a remedy which, as everybody knows, has not at all an ill effect upon one's gaiety. The champagne predisposed him to certain extracurricular considerations; to be precise, he decided not to go home yet but to drop in on a certain lady of his acquaintance, a

Caroline Ivanovna—a lady of German extraction, apparently, toward whom his feelings and relations were friendly. It must be pointed out the important person was no longer a young man, that he was a good spouse, a respected *paterfamilias.* He had two sons, one of whom was already serving in a chancellery, and a pretty daughter of sixteen, with a somewhat humped yet very charming little nose, who came to kiss his hand every day, adding, "*Bonjour,* papa," as she did so. His wife, a woman who still had not lost her freshness and was not even in the least hard to look at, would allow him to kiss her hand first, then, turning her own over, kissed the hand that was holding hers.

Yet *the important person,* who, by the bye, was perfectly contented with domestic tendernesses, found it respectable to have a lady friend in another part of the city. This lady friend was not in the least fresher or younger than his wife, but such are the enigmas that exist in this world, and to sit in judgment upon them is none of our affair. And so the important person came down the steps, climbed into his sleigh, and told his driver, "To Caroline Ivanovna's!"—while he himself, after muffling up rather luxuriously in his warm overcoat, remained in that pleasant state than which no better could even be thought of for a Russian—that is, when one isn't even thinking of his own volition, but the thoughts in the meanwhile troop into one's head by themselves, each more pleasant than the other, without giving one even the trouble of pursuing them and seeking them. Filled with agreeable feelings, he lightly recalled all the gay episodes of the evening he had spent, all his *mots* that had made the select circle go off into peals of laughter; many of them he even repeated in a low voice and found that they were still just as amusing as before, and for that reason it is not to be wondered at that even he chuckled at them heartily.

Occasionally, however, he became annoyed with the gusty wind which, suddenly escaping from God knows where and no one knows for what reason, simply cut the face, tossing tatters of snow thereat, making the collar of his overcoat belly out like a sail, or suddenly, with unnatural force, throwing it over his head and in this manner giving him ceaseless trouble in extricating himself from it.

Suddenly the important person felt that someone had seized him rather hard by his collar. Turning around, he noticed a man of no great height, in an old, much worn frock coat, and, not without horror, recognized in him Akakii Akakiievich. The petty clerk's face was wan as snow and looked utterly like the face of a dead man. But the horror of the important person passed all bounds when he saw that the mouth of the man became twisted and, horribly wafting upon him the odor of the grave, uttered the following speech: "Ah, so there you are, now, at last! At last I have collared you, now! Your overcoat is just the one I need! You didn't put yourself out any about mine, and on top of that hauled me over the coals—so now let me have yours!"

The poor important person almost passed away. No matter how firm of character he was in his chancellery and before his inferiors in general, and although after but one look merely at his manly appearance and his figure everyone said, "My, what character he has!"—in this instance, nevertheless, like quite a number of men who have the appearance of doughty knights, he experienced such terror that, not without reason, he even began to fear an attack of some physical disorder. He even hastened to throw his overcoat off his shoulders himself and cried out to the driver in a voice that was not his own. "Go home—fast as you can!"

The driver, on hearing the voice that the important person used only at critical moments and which he often accompanied by something of a far more physical nature, drew his head in between his shoulders just to be on the safe side, swung his whip, and flew off like an arrow. In just a little over six minutes the important person was already at the entrance to his own house. Pale, frightened out of his wits, and minus his overcoat, he had come home instead of to Caroline Ivanovna's, somehow made his way stumblingly to his room, and spent the night in quite considerable distress, so that the next day, during the morning tea, his daughter told him outright, "You're all pale today, papa." But papa kept silent and said not a word to anybody of what had befallen him, and where he had been, and where he had intended to go.

This adventure made a strong impression on him. He even badgered his subordinates at rarer intervals with his, "How dare you? Do you realize in whose presence you are?"—and even if he did utter these phrases he did not do so before he had first heard through to the end just what was what. But still more remarkable is the fact that from that time forth the apparition of the dead clerk ceased its visitations utterly; evidently the General's overcoat fitted him to a *t;* at least, no cases of overcoats being snatched off anybody were heard of any more, anywhere. However, many energetic and solicitous people simply would not calm down and kept on saying from time to time that the dead government clerk was still haunting the remoter parts of the city.

And, sure enough, one policeman at a sentry box in Colomna had with his own eyes seen the apparition coming out of a house; but, being by nature somewhat puny, so that on one occasion an ordinary well-grown shoat, darting out of a private yard, had knocked him off his feet, to the profound amusement of the cab drivers who were standing around, from whom he had exacted a copper each for humiliating him so greatly, to buy snuff with—well, being puny, he had not dared to halt him but simply followed him in the dark until such time as the apparition suddenly looked over its shoulder, and, halting, asked him, "What are you after?" and shook a fist at him whose like for size was not to be found among the living. The policeman said, "Nothing," and at once turned back. The apparition, however, was considerably taller by now and was sporting a pair of enormous mustachios; setting its steps apparently in the direction of the Obuhov Bridge, it disappeared utterly in the darkness of night.

Edgar Allan Poe (1809–1849)

The short story was particularly suited to life in the United States where it flourished so well that some critics believe it is essentially an American form of literature. Frontier life remote from the centers of culture and social contact promoted the growth of magazines, and magazines certainly encouraged the writing of short fiction. Edgar Allan Poe became the outstanding American theorist and practitioner of the fledgling genre. He argued that the short story was a legitimate and important literary form, capable of intense emotional and aesthetic effects. Because it relied upon the "single effect" it was, to him, second only to the lyric poem in its ability to "induce an exaltation of the soul." In his own work, he was the most self-conscious of artists.

> I prefer commencing with the consideration of an effect. . . . I say to myself . . . "Of the innumerable effects, or impressions, of which the heart, the intellect, or (more generally) the soul is susceptible, what one shall I, on the present occasion, select?" Having chosen a novel, first, and secondly a vivid effect, I

consider whether it can be best wrought by incident or tone—whether by ordinary incidents and peculiar tone or the converse, or by peculiarity both of incident and tone—afterward looking about me (or rather within) for such combinations of event, or tone, as shall best aid me in construction of the effect.

The kinds of effects Poe sought—horror, mystery, fear, loathing—were dependent not so much on real people in real situations as upon atmosphere. He placed his stories against a mysterious, often gothic, background. The setting of "The Black Cat" is not spelled out at the beginning, but there are "chambers" rather than rooms, and the narrator frequents "vile haunts" rather than bars. At the end, to intensify the effect, he introduces specific images: a cellar down steep stairs, a false chimney, a thick brick wall with damp plaster, the mark of the gallows on the cat's chest.

His language reinforces the supernaturalism and mystery. It is almost impossible to read the story rapidly—as, say, one can read Gogol's "The Overcoat" written at about the same time. Poe's rhythm is somber, steady, stately, and his sentences ("a more than fiendish malevolence, gin-nurtured, thrilled every fibre of my frame") are literary rather than colloquial. There is little humor in a Poe story and almost no irony.

Poe's work was much admired in Europe, as well as here. Baudelaire translated his fiction and Mallarmé his poems. Debussy attempted to write a symphony based on one of his stories. Elizabeth Barrett said of another story, "The certain thing in the tale in question is the power of the writer, and the faculty he has of making horrible improbabilities seem near and familiar."

Yet the violence and morbidity that so excited and horrified our forebears seems rather silly and artificial to a generation weaned on television atrocities and newspaper sensationalism. Even though his stories may not have the impact they once did, he himself must be given credit for his major contributions in the development not only of the horror story but of the detective story and science fiction, and indeed the techniques of the serious modern story. He used narrative voice—point of view, tone, distance—to limit and intensify the narrative and control the reader's responses.

Poe was born in 1809, was orphaned young, adopted, disinherited. He died at the age of forty on the eve of a second marriage. All his life he was plagued by poverty, gambling, alcoholism.

The Black Cat

For the most wild, yet most homely narrative which I am about to pen, I neither expect nor solicit belief. Mad indeed would I be to expect it, in a case where my very senses reject their own evidence. Yet, mad am I not—and very surely do I not dream. But to-morrow I die, and to-day I would unburthen my soul. My immediate purpose is to place before the world, plainly, succinctly, and without comment, a series of mere household events. In their consequences, these events have terrified—have tortured— have destroyed me. Yet I will not attempt to expound them. To me, they have presented little but Horror—to many they will seem less terrible than *baroques*. Hereafter, perhaps, some intellect may be found which will reduce my phantasm to the commonplace—some intellect more calm, more logical and far less excitable than my own, which will perceive, in the circumstances I detail with awe, nothing more than an ordinary succession of very natural causes and effects.

From my infancy I was noted for the docility and humanity of my disposition. My tenderness of heart was even so conspicuous as to make me the jest of my companions. I was especially fond of animals, and was indulged by my parents with a great variety of pets. With these I spent most of my time, and never was so happy as when feeding and caressing them. This peculiarity of character grew with my growth, and, in my manhood, I derived from it one of my principal sources of pleasure. To those who have cherished an affection for a faithful and sagacious dog, I need hardly be at the trouble of explaining the nature or the intensity of the gratification thus derivable. There is something in the unselfish and self-sacrificing love of a brute, which goes directly to the heart of him who has had frequent occasion to test the paltry friendship and gossamer fidelity of mere *Man*.

I married early, and was happy to find in my wife a disposition not uncongenial with my own. Observing my partiality for domestic pets, she lost no opportunity of procuring those of the most agreeable kind. We had birds, gold fish, a fine dog, rabbits, a small monkey, and *a cat*.

This latter was a remarkably large and beautiful animal, entirely black, and sagacious to an astonishing degree. In speaking of his intelligence, my wife, who at heart was not a little tinctured with superstition, made frequent allusion to the ancient popular notion, which regarded all black cats as witches in disguise. Not that she was ever *serious* upon this point—and I mention the matter at all for no better reason than that it happens, just now, to be remembered.

Pluto—this was the cat's name—was my favorite pet and playmate. I alone fed him, and he attended me wherever I went about the house. It was even with difficulty that I could prevent him from following me through the streets.

Our friendship lasted, in this manner, for several years, during which my general temperament and character—through the instrumentality of the Fiend Intemperance—had (I blush to confess it) experienced a radical alteration for the worse. I grew, day by day, more moody, more irritable, more regardless of the feelings of others. I suffered myself to use intemperate language to my wife. At length, I even offered her personal violence. My pets, of course, were made to feel the change in my disposition. I not only neglected, but ill-used them. For Pluto, however, I still retained sufficient regard to restrain me from maltreating him, as I made no scruple of maltreating the rabbits, the monkey, or even the dog, when by accident, or through affection, they came in my way. But my disease grew upon me—for what disease is like Alcohol!—and at length even Pluto, who was now becoming old, and consequently somewhat peevish—even Pluto began to experience the effects of my ill temper.

One night, returning home, much intoxicated, from one of my haunts about town, I fancied that the cat avoided my presence. I seized him; when, in his fright at my violence, he inflicted a slight wound upon my hand with his teeth. The fury of a demon instantly possessed me. I knew myself no longer. My original soul seemed, at once, to take its flight from my body; and a more than fiendish malevolence, gin-nurtured, thrilled every fibre of my frame. I took from my waistcoat-pocket a pen-knife, opened it, grasped the poor beast by the throat, and deliberately cut one of its eyes from the socket! I blush, I burn, I shudder, while I pen the damnable atrocity.

When reason returned with the morning—when I had slept off the fumes of the night's debauch—I experienced a sentiment half of horror, half of remorse, for the crime of which I had been guilty; but it was, at best, a feeble and equivocal feeling, and the soul remained untouched. I again plunged into excess, and soon drowned in wine all memory of the deed.

In the meantime the cat slowly recovered. The socket of the lost eye presented, it is true, a frightful appearance, but he no longer appeared to suffer any pain. He went about the house as usual, but, as might be expected, fled in extreme terror at my approach. I had so much of my old heart left, as to be at first grieved by this evident dislike on the part of a creature which had once so loved me. But this feeling soon gave place to irritation. And then came, as if to my final and irrevocable overthrow, the spirit of PERVERSENESS. Of this spirit philosophy takes no account. Yet I am not more sure that soul lives, than I am that perverseness is one of the primitive impulses of the human heart—one of the indivisible primary faculties, or sentiments, which give direction to the character of Man. Who has not, a hundred times, found himself committing a vile or a silly action, for no other reason than because he knows he should *not*? Have we not a perpetual inclination, in the teeth of our best judgment, to violate that which is *Law,* merely because we understand it to be such? This spirit of perverseness, I say, came to my final overthrow. It was this unfathomable longing of the soul *to vex itself*— to offer violence to its own nature—to do wrong for the wrong's sake only—that urged me to continue and finally consummate the injury I had inflicted upon the unoffending brute. One morning, in cold blood, I slipped a noose about his neck and hung it to the limb of a tree;—hung it with the tears streaming from my eyes, and with the bitterest remorse at my heart;—hung it *because* I knew that it had loved me, and *because* I felt it had given me no reason of offense;—hung it *because* I knew that in so doing I was committing a sin—a deadly sin that would so jeopardize my immortal soul as to place it—if such a thing were possible—even beyond the reach of the infinite mercy of the Most Merciful and Most Terrible God.

On the night of the day on which this cruel deed was done, I was aroused from sleep by the cry of fire. The curtains of my bed were in flames. The whole house was blazing. It was with great difficulty that my wife, a servant, and myself, made our escape from the conflagration. The destruction was complete. My entire wordly wealth was swallowed up, and I resigned myself thenceforward to despair.

I am above the weakness of seeking to establish a sequence of cause and effect, between the disaster and the atrocity. But I am detailing a chain of facts—and wish not to leave even a possible link imperfect. On the day succeeding the fire, I visited the ruins. The walls, with one exception, had fallen in. This exception was found in a compartment wall, not very thick, which stood about the middle of the house, and against which had rested the head of my bed. The plastering had here, in great measure, resisted the action of the fire—a fact which I attributed to its having been recently spread. About this wall a dense crowd were collected, and many persons seemed to be examining a particular portion of it with very minute and eager attention. The words "strange!" "singular!" and other similar expressions, excited my curiosity. I approached and saw, as if graven in *bas relief* upon the white surface, the figure of a gigantic *cat.* The impression was given with an accuracy truly marvellous. There was a rope about the animal's neck.

When I first beheld this apparition—for I could scarcely regard it as less—my wonder and my terror were extreme. But at length reflection came to my aid. The cat, I remembered, had been hung in a garden adjacent to the house. Upon the alarm of fire, this garden had been immediately filled by the crowd—by some one of whom the animal must have been cut from the tree and thrown, through an open window, into my chamber. This had probably been done with the view of arousing me from sleep. The falling of other walls had compressed the victim of my cruelty into the substance of the freshly-spread plaster; the lime of which, with the flames, and the *ammonia* from the carcass, had then accomplished the portraiture as I saw it.

Although I thus readily accounted to my reason, if not altogether to my conscience, for the startling fact just detailed, it did not the less fail to make a deep impression upon my fancy. For months I could not rid myself of the phantasm of the cat; and, during this period, there came back into my spirit a half-sentiment that seemed, but was not, remorse. I went so far as to regret the loss of the animal, and look about me, among the vile haunts which I now habitually frequented, for another pet of the same species, and of somewhat similar appearance, with which to supply its place.

One night as I sat, half stupified, in a den of more than infamy, my attention was suddenly drawn to some black object, reposing upon the head of one of the immense hogheads of Gin, or of Rum, which constituted the chief furniture of the apartment. I had been looking steadily at the top of this hogshead for some minutes, and what now caused me surprise was the fact that I had not sooner perceived the object thereupon. I approached it, and touched it with my hand. It was a black cat—a very large one— fully as large as Pluto, and closely resembling him in every respect but one. Pluto had not a white hair upon any portion of his body; but this cat had a large, although indefinite splotch of white, covering nearly the whole region of the breast.

Upon my touching him, he immediately arose, purred loudly, rubbed against my hand, and appeared delighted with my notice. This, then, was the very creature of which I was in search. I at once offered to purchase it of the landlord; but this person made no claim to it—knew nothing of it—had never seen it before.

I continued my caresses, and, when I prepared to go home, the animal evinced a disposition to accompany me. I permitted it to do so; occasionally stooping and patting it as I proceeded. When it reached the house it domesticated itself at once, and became immediately a great favorite with my wife.

For my own part, I soon found a dislike to it arising within me. This was just the reverse of what I had anticipated; but I know not how or why it was—its evident fondness for myself rather disgusted and annoyed. By slow degrees, these feelings of disgust and annoyance rose into the bitterness of hatred. I avoided the creature; a certain sense of shame, and the remembrance of my former deed of cruelty, preventing me from physically abusing it. I did not, for some weeks, strike, or otherwise violently ill use it; but gradually—very gradually—I came to look upon it with unutterable loathing, and to flee silently from its odious presence, as from the breath of a pestilence.

What added, no doubt, to my hatred of the beast, was the discovery, on the morning after I brought it home, that, like Pluto, it also had been deprived of one of its eyes. This circumstance, however, only endeared it to my wife, who, as I have already said, possessed, in a high degree, that humanity of feeling which had once been my distinguishing trait, and the source of many of my simplest and purest pleasures.

With my aversion to this cat, however, its partiality for myself seemed to increase. It followed my footsteps with a pertinacity which it would be difficult to make the reader comprehend. Whenever I sat, it would crouch beneath my chair, or spring upon my knees, covering me with its loathsome caresses. If I arose to walk it would get between my feet and thus nearly throw me down, or, fastening its long and sharp claws in my dress, clamber, in this manner, to my breast. At such times, although I longed to destroy it with a blow, I was yet withheld from so doing, partly by a memory of my former crime, but chiefly—let me confess it at once—by absolute *dread* of the beast.

This dread was not exactly a dread of physical evil—and yet I should be at a loss how otherwise to define it. I am almost ashamed to own—yes, even in this felon's cell, I am almost ashamed to own—that the terror and horror with which the animal inspired me, had been heightened by one of the merest chimæras it would be possible to conceive. My wife had called my attention, more than once, to the character of the mark of white hair, of which I have spoken, and which constituted the sole visible difference between the strange beast and the one I had destroyed. The reader will remember that this mark, although large, had been originally very indefinite; but, by slow degrees—degrees nearly imperceptible, and which for a long time my Reason struggled to reject as fanciful—it had, at length, assumed a rigorous distinctness of outline. It was now the representation of an object that I shudder to name—and for this, above all, I loathed, and dreaded, and would have rid myself of the monster *had I dared*—it was now, I say, the image of a hideous—ghastly thing—of the GAL-LOWS!—oh, mournful and terrible engine of Horror and of Crime—of Agony and of Death!

And now was I indeed wretched beyond the wretchedness of mere Humanity. And *a brute beast*—whose fellow I had contemptuously destroyed—*a brute beast* to work out for *me*—for me a man, fashioned in the image of the High God—so much of insufferable woe! Alas! neither by day nor by night knew I the blessing of Rest any more! During the former the creature left me no moment alone; and, in the latter, I started, hourly, from dreams of unutterable fear, to find the hot breath of *the thing* upon my face, and its vast weight—an incarnate Night-Mare that I had no power to shake off—incumbent eternally upon my *heart!*

Beneath the pressure of torments such as these, the feeble remnant of the good within me succumbed. Evil thoughts became my sole intimates—the darkest and most evil of thoughts. The moodiness of my usual temper increased to hatred of all things and of all mankind; while, from the sudden, frequent, and ungovernable outbursts of a fury to which I now blindly abandoned myself, my uncomplaining wife, alas! was the most usual and the most patient of sufferers.

One day she accompanied me, upon some household errand, into the cellar of the old building which our poverty compelled us to inhabit. The cat followed me down the steep stairs, and, nearly throwing me headlong, exasperated me to madness. Uplifting an axe, and forgetting, in my wrath, the childish dread which had hitherto stayed my hand, I aimed a blow at the animal which, of course, would have proved instantly fatal had it descended as I wished. But this blow was arrested by the hand of my wife. Goaded, by the interference, into a rage more than demoniacal, I withdrew my arm from her grasp and buried the axe in her brain. She fell dead upon the spot, without a groan.

This hideous murder accomplished, I sat myself forthwith, and with entire delib-eration, to the task of concealing the body. I knew that I could not remove it from the house, either by day or by night, without the risk of being observed by the neighbors. Many projects entered my mind. At one period I thought of cutting the corpse into minute fragments, and destroying them by fire. At another, I resolved to dig a grave for it in the floor of the cellar. Again, I deliberated about casting it in the well in the yard—about packing it in a box, as if merchandize, with the usual arrangements, and so getting a porter to take it from the house. Finally I hit upon what I considered a far better expedient than either of these. I determined to wall it up in the cellar—as the monks of the middle ages are recorded to have walled up their victims.

For a purpose such as this the cellar was well adapted. Its walls were loosely constructed, and had lately been plastered throughout with a rough plaster, which the dampness of the atmosphere had prevented from hardening. Moreover, in one of the walls was a projection, caused by a false chimney, or fireplace, that had been filled up, and made to resemble the rest of the cellar. I made no doubt that I could readily displace the bricks at this point, insert the corpse, and wall the whole up as before, so that no eye could detect anything suspicious.

And in this calculation I was not deceived. By means of a crow-bar I easily dislodged the bricks, and, having carefully deposited the body against the inner wall, I propped it in that position, while, with little trouble, I relaid the whole structure as it originally stood. Having procured mortar, sand, and hair, with every possible precaution, I prepared a plaster which could not be distinguished from the old, and with this I very carefully went over the new brick-work. When I had finished, I felt satisfied that all was right. The wall did not present the slightest appearance of having been disturbed. The rubbish on the floor was picked up with the minutest care. I looked around triumphantly, and said to myself—"Here at least, then, my labor has not been in vain."

My next step was to look for the beast which had been the cause of so much wretchedness; for I had, at length, firmly resolved to put it to death. Had I been able to meet with it, at the moment, there could have been no doubt of its fate; but it appeared that the crafty animal had been alarmed at the violence of my previous anger, and forebore to present itself in my present mood. It is impossible to describe, or to imagine, the deep, the blissful sense of relief which the absence of the detested creature occasioned in my bosom. It did not make its appearance during the night— and thus for one night at least, since its introduction into the house, I soundly and tranquilly slept; aye, *slept* even with the burden of murder upon my soul!

The second and third day passed, and still my tormentor came not. Once again I breathed as a freeman. The monster, in terror, had fled the premises forever! I should behold it no more! My happiness was supreme! The guilt of my dark deed disturbed me but little. Some few inquiries had been made, but these had been readily answered. Even a search had been instituted—but of course nothing was to be discovered. I looked upon my future felicity as secured.

Upon the fourth day of the assassination, a party of the police came, very unexpectedly, into the house, and proceeded again to make rigorous investigation of the premises. Secure, however, in the inscrutability of my place of concealment, I felt no embarrassment whatever. The officers bade me accompany them in their search. They left no nook or corner unexplored. At length, for the third or fourth time, they descended into the cellar. I quivered not in a muscle. My heart beat calmly as that of one who slumbers in innocence. I walked the cellar from end to end. I folded my arms upon my bosom, and roamed easily to and fro. The police were thoroughly satisfied and prepared to depart. The glee at my heart was too strong to be restrained. I burned to say if but one word, by way of triumph, and to render doubly sure their assurance of my guiltlessness.

"Gentlemen," I said at last, as the party ascended the steps, "I delight to have allayed your suspicions. I wish you all health, and a little more courtesy. By the bye, gentlemen, this—this is a very well constructed house." [In the rabid desire to say something easily, I scarcely knew what I uttered at all.]—"I may say an *excellently* well constructed house. These walls—are you going, gentlemen—these walls are solidly put together;" and here, through the mere phrenzy of bravado, I rapped heavily, with a cane which I held in my hand, upon that very portion of the brick-work behind which stood the corpse of the wife of my bosom.

But may God shield and deliver me from the fangs of the Arch-Fiend! No sooner had the reverberation of my blows sunk into silence, than I was answered by a voice from within the tomb!—by a cry, at first muffled and broken, like the sobbing of a child, and then quickly swelling into one long, loud, and continuous scream, utterly anomalous and inhuman—a howl—a wailing shriek, half of horror and half of triumph, such as might have arisen only out of hell, conjointly from the throats of the damned in their agony and of the demons that exult in the damnation.

Of my own thoughts it is folly to speak. Swooning, I staggered to the opposite wall. For one instant the party upon the stairs remained motionless, through extremity of terror and of awe. In the next, a dozen stout arms were toiling at the wall. It fell bodily. The corpse, already greatly decayed and clotted with gore, stood erect before the eyes of the spectators. Upon its head, with red extended mouth and solitary eye of fire, sat the hideous beast whose craft had seduced me into murder, and whose informing voice had consigned me to the hangman. I had walled the monster up within the tomb!

Nathaniel Hawthorne (1804–1864)

Hawthorne was born in Salem, Massachusetts, into a family which numbered among its ancestors one of the presiding judges at the infamous witchcraft trials in 1692. The family's Puritan roots were deep, and it is fair to say that in no other American writer of the nineteenth century do the religious mood and cultural heritage of colonial New England persist so centrally as they do in Hawthorne. Lamed at the age of seven, he spent his youth with books, developing a profound interest in early American history and otherwise saturating himself in the works of Spenser, Bunyan, and Milton. After graduation from Bowdoin College in 1825 (where on various occasions, with two or three classmates, Hawthorne donated sets of Dr. Johnson and Jonathan Swift to the library) he returned to Salem to write. A little over a decade was to pass before he won his first approving audience with the publication in 1837 of *Twice-Told Tales.* Hawthorne joined the Brook Farm experiment, a socialistic cooperative, in 1841, but left when he found that his writing was suffering. For the next seven or eight years he worked as a customs official and befriended other New England writers, among them Melville, who dedicated *Moby Dick* to him. Hawthorne's fame was established in 1850 with the publication of his masterpiece, *The Scarlet Letter,* our literature's first—and by many still regarded as greatest—symbolic novel. Thereafter Hawthorne wrote *The House of the Seven Gables* (1851), *The Blithedale Romance* (1852), and *The Marble Faun* (1860).

Like Poe, Hawthorne learned a certain amount from his reading of Gothic novels, and in his own way he worked just as assiduously as Poe in evoking and sustaining a dominant *atmosphere.* Unlike Poe, however, he did not concentrate on the single, startling or sensational, at times almost convulsive, *effect* as the be-all and end-all of his art. Most of his stories in fact take their rise from this or that anecdote he had picked up, from places he had visited, or from both usual and unusual incidents he had read or heard about. Near the beginning of "Wakefield" we are offered a clear enunciation of how the author's mind works, and of how it transforms—as though by invisible means—utterly unexceptional events into compelling fiction: "Thought has always its efficacy, and every striking incident its moral."

In the story that follows, Hawthorne tells us that he recollects a brief account from "some old magazine or newspaper" of a man who, for no evident reason, suddenly left his wife to reside in a lodging on the very next street to his own house. Though he had planned only a brief absence, the period stretches into twenty years. Why does Wakefield stay away so long? Because, as Hawthorne comments at the end, "by stepping aside for a moment, a man exposes himself to a fearful risk of losing his place forever. Like Wakefield, he may become, as it were, the Outcast of the Universe." Isolation born of whimsical eccentricity, but deepening into self-destruction, is fundamental to all of Hawthorne's major works. Nor was it remote from his own life, as we may tell from a letter written to Longfellow in 1837:

By some witchcraft or other—for I cannot assign any reasonable why and wherefore—I have been carried apart from the main current of life, and find it impossible to get back again . . . I have secluded myself from society; and yet I never meant any such thing, nor dreamed what sort of life I was going to lead. I have made a captive of myself and put me in a dungeon; and now I cannot find the key to let myself out . . . there is no fate in this world so horrible as to have no share in either its joys or sorrows. For the last ten years I have not lived, but only dreamed about living.

Wakefield

In some old magazine or newspaper I recollect a story, told as truth, of a man—let us call him Wakefield—who absented himself for a long time from his wife. The fact, thus abstractedly stated, is not very uncommon, nor—without a proper distinction of circumstances—to be condemned either as naughty or nonsensical. Howbeit, this, though far from the most aggravated, is perhaps the strangest, instance on record, of marital delinquency; and, moreover, as remarkable a freak as may be found in the whole list of human oddities. The wedded couple lived in London. The man, under pretence of going a journey, took lodgings in the next street to his own house, and there, unheard of by his wife or friends, and without the shadow of a reason for such self-banishment, dwelt upwards of twenty years. During that period, he beheld his home every day, and frequently the forlorn Mrs. Wakefield. And after so great a gap in his matrimonial felicity—when his death was reckoned certain, his estate settled, his name dismissed from memory, and his wife, long, long ago, resigned to her autumnal widowhood—he entered the door one evening, quietly, as from a day's absence, and became a loving spouse till death.

This outline is all that I remember. But the incident, though of the purest originality, unexampled, and probably never to be repeated, is one, I think, which appeals to the generous sympathies of mankind. We know, each for himself, that none of us would perpetrate such a folly, yet feel as if some other might. To my own contemplations, at least, it has often recurred, always exciting wonder, but with a sense that the story must be true, and a conception of its hero's character. Whenever any subject so forcibly affects the mind, time is well spent in thinking of it. If the reader choose, let him do his own meditation; or if he prefer to ramble with me through the twenty years of Wakefield's vagary, I bid him welcome; trusting that there will be a pervading spirit and a moral, even should we fail to find them, done up neatly, and condensed into the final sentence. Thought has always its efficacy, and every striking incident its moral.

What sort of a man was Wakefield? We are free to shape out our own idea, and call it by his name. He was now in the meridian of life; his matrimonial affections, never violent, were sobered into a calm, habitual sentiment; of all husbands, he was likely to be the most constant, because a certain sluggishness would keep his heart at rest, wherever it might be placed. He was intellectual, but not actively so; his mind occupied itself in long and lazy musings, that ended to no purpose, or had not vigor to attain it; his thoughts were seldom so energetic as to seize hold of words. Imagination, in the proper meaning of the term, made no part of Wakefield's gifts. With a cold but not depraved nor wandering heart, and a mind never feverish with riotous thoughts, nor perplexed with originality, who could have anticipated that our friend would entitle himself to a foremost place among the doers of eccentric deeds? Had his acquaintances been asked, who was the man in London the surest to perform nothing today which should be remembered on the morrow, they would have thought of Wakefield. Only the wife of his bosom might have hesitated. She, without having analyzed his character, was partly aware of a quiet selfishness, that had rusted into his inactive mind; of a peculiar sort of vanity, the most uneasy attribute about him; of a disposition to craft, which had seldom produced more positive effects than the keeping of petty secrets, hardly worth revealing; and, lastly, of what she called a little strangeness, sometimes, in the good man. This latter quality is indefinable, and perhaps nonexistent.

Let us now imagine Wakefield bidding adieu to his wife. It is the dusk of an October evening. His equipment is a drab great-coat, a hat covered with an oilcloth, top-boots, an umbrella in one hand and a small portmanteau in the other. He has informed Mrs. Wakefield that he is to take the night coach into the country. She would fain inquire the length of his journey, its object, and the probable time of his return; but, indulgent to his harmless love of mystery, interrogates him only by a look. He tells her not to expect him positively by the return coach, nor to be alarmed should he tarry three or four days; but, at all events, to look for him at supper on Friday evening. Wakefield himself, be it considered, has no suspicion of what is before him. He holds out his hand, she gives her own, and meets his parting kiss in the matter-of-course way of a ten years' matrimony; and forth goes the middle-aged Mr. Wakefield, almost resolved to perplex his good lady by a whole week's absence. After the door has closed behind him, she perceives it thrust partly open, and a vision of her husband's face, through the aperture, smiling on her, and gone in a moment. For the time, this little incident is dismissed without a thought. But, long afterwards, when she has been more years a widow than a wife, that smile recurs, and flickers across all her reminiscences of Wakefield's visage. In her many musings, she surrounds the original smile with a multitude of fantasies, which make it strange and awful: as, for instance, if she imagines him in a coffin, that parting look is frozen on his pale features; or, if she dreams of him in heaven, still his blessed spirit wears a quiet and crafty smile. Yet, for its sake, when all others have given him up for dead, she sometimes doubts whether she is a widow.

But our business is with the husband. We must hurry after him along the street, ere he lose his individuality, and melt into the great mass of London life. It would be vain searching for him there. Let us follow close at his heels, therefore, until, after several superfluous turns and doublings, we find him comfortably established by the fireside of a small apartment, previously bespoken. He is in the next street to his own, and at his journey's end. He can scarcely trust his good fortune, in having got thither unperceived—recollecting that, at one time, he was delayed by the throng, in the very focus of a lighted lantern; and, again, there were footsteps that seemed to tread behind his own, distinct from the multitudinous tramp around him; and, anon, he heard a voice shouting afar, and fancied that it called his name. Doubtless, a dozen busybodies had been watching him, and told his wife the whole affair. Poor Wakefield! Little knowest thou thine own insignificance in this great world! No mortal eye but mine has traced thee. Go quietly to thy bed, foolish man; and, on the morrow, if thou wilt be wise, get thee home to good Mrs. Wakefield, and tell her the truth. Remove not thyself, even for a little week, from thy place in her chaste bosom. Were she, for a single moment, to deem thee dead, or lost, or lastingly divided from her, thou wouldst be wofully conscious of a change in thy true wife forever after. It is perilous to make a chasm in human affections; not that they gape so long and wide—but so quickly close again!

Almost repenting of his frolic, or whatever it may be termed, Wakefield lies down betimes, and starting from his first nap, spreads forth his arms into the wide and solitary waste of the unaccustomed bed. "No,"—thinks he, gathering the bedclothes about him,—"*I* will not sleep alone another night."

In the morning he rises earlier than usual, and sets himself to consider what he really means to do. Such are his loose and rambling modes of thought that he has taken this very singular step with the consciousness of a purpose, indeed, but without being able to define it sufficiently for his own contemplation. The vagueness of the project, and the convulsive effort with which he plunges into the execution of it, are equally characteristic of a feeble-minded man. Wakefield sifts his ideas, however, as minutely as he may, and finds himself curious to know the progress of matters at home—how his exemplary wife will endure her widowhood of a week; and, briefly, how the little sphere of creatures and circumstances, in which he was a central object, will be affected by his removal. A morbid vanity, therefore, lies nearest the bottom of the affair. But, how is he to attain his ends? Not, certainly, by keeping close in this comfortable lodging, where, though he slept and awoke in the next street to his home, he is as effectually abroad as if the stage-coach had been whirling him away all night. Yet, should he reappear, the whole project is knocked in the head. His poor brains being hopelessly puzzled with this dilemma, he at length ventures out, partly resolving to cross the head of the street, and send one hasty glance towards his forsaken domicile. Habit—for he is a man of habits—takes him by the hand, and guides him, wholly unaware, to his own door, where, just at the critical moment, he is aroused by the scraping of his foot upon the step. Wakefield! whither are you going?

At that instant his fate was turning on the pivot. Little dreaming of the doom to which his first backward step devotes him, he hurries away, breathless with agitation hitherto unfelt, and hardly dares turn his head at the distant corner. Can it be that nobody caught sight of him? Will not the whole household—the decent Mrs. Wakefield, the smart maid servant, and the dirty little footboy—raise a hue and cry, through London streets, in pursuit of their fugitive lord and master? Wonderful escape! He gathers courage to pause and look homeward, but is perplexed with a sense of change about the familiar edifice, such as affects us all, when, after a separation of months or years, we again see some hill or lake, or work of art, with which we were friends of old. In ordinary cases, this indescribable impression is caused by the comparison and contrast between our imperfect reminiscences and the reality. In Wakefield, the magic of a single night has wrought a similar transformation, because, in that brief period, a great moral change has been effected. But this is a secret from himself. Before leaving the spot, he catches a far and momentary glimpse of his wife, passing athwart the front window, with her face turned towards the head of the street. The crafty nincompoop takes to his heels, scared with the idea that, among a thousand such atoms of mortality, her eye must have detected him. Right glad is his heart, though his brain be somewhat dizzy, when he finds himself by the coal fire of his lodgings.

So much for the commencement of this long whim-wham. After the initial conception, and the stirring up of the man's sluggish temperament to put it in practice, the whole matter evolves itself in a natural train. We may suppose him, as the result of deep deliberation, buying a new wig, of reddish hair, and selecting sundry garments, in a fashion unlike his customary suit of brown, from a Jew's old-clothes bag. It is accomplished. Wakefield is another man. The new system being now established, a retrograde movement to the old would be almost as difficult as the step that placed him in his unparalleled position. Furthermore, he is rendered obstinate by a sulkiness occasionally incident to his temper, and brought on at present by the inadequate sensation which he conceives to have been produced in the bosom of Mrs. Wakefield. He will not go back until she be frightened half to death. Well; twice or thrice has she passed before his sight, each time with a heavier step, a paler cheek, and more anxious brow; and in the third week of his non-appearance he detects a portent of evil entering the house, in the guise of an apothecary. Next day the knocker is muffled. Towards nightfall comes the chariot of a physician, and deposits its big-wigged and solemn burden at Wakefield's door, whence, after a quarter of an hour's visit, he emerges, perchance the herald of a funeral. Dear woman! Will she die? By this time, Wakefield is excited to something like energy of feeling, but still lingers away from his wife's bedside, pleading with his conscience that she must not be disturbed at such a juncture. If aught else restrains him, he does not know it. In the course of a few weeks she gradually recovers; the crisis is over; her heart is sad, perhaps, but quiet; and, let him return soon or late, it will never be feverish for him again. Such ideas glimmer through the mist of Wakefield's mind, and render him indistinctly conscious that an almost impassable gulf divides his hired apartment from his former home. "It is but in the next street!" he sometimes says. Fool! it is in another world. Hitherto, he has put off his return from one particular day to another; henceforward, he leaves the precise time undetermined. Not to-morrow—probably next week—pretty soon. Poor man! The dead have nearly as much chance of revisiting their earthly homes as the self-banished Wakefield.

Would that I had a folio to write, instead of an article of a dozen pages! Then might I exemplify how an influence beyond our control lays its strong hand on every deed which we do, and weaves its consequences into an iron tissue of necessity. Wakefield is spell-bound. We must leave him, for ten years or so, to haunt around his house, without once crossing the threshold, and to be faithful to his wife, with all the affection of which his heart is capable, while he is slowly fading out of hers. Long since, it must be remarked, he had lost the perception of singularity in his conduct.

Now for a scene! Amid the throng of a London street we distinguish a man, now waxing elderly, with few characteristics to attract careless observers, yet bearing, in his whole aspect, the handwriting of no common fate, for such as have the skill to read it. He is meagre; his low and narrow forehead is deeply wrinkled; his eyes, small and lustreless, sometimes wander apprehensively about him, but oftener seem to look inward. He bends his head, and moves with an indescribable obliquity of gait, as if unwilling to display his full front to the world. Watch him long enough to see what we have described, and you will allow that circumstances—which often produce remarkable men from nature's ordinary handiwork—have produced one such here. Next, leaving him to sidle along the footwalk, cast your eyes in the opposite direction, where a portly female, considerably in the wane of life, with a prayer-book in her hand, is proceeding to yonder church. She has the placid mien of settled widowhood. Her regrets have either died away, or have become so essential to her heart, that they would be poorly exchanged for joy. Just as the lean man and well-conditioned woman are passing, a slight obstruction occurs, and brings these two figures directly in contact. Their hands touch; the pressure of the crowd forces her bosom against his shoulder; they stand, face to face, staring into each other's eyes. After a ten years' separation, thus Wakefield meets his wife!

The throng eddies away, and carries them asunder. The sober widow, resuming her former pace, proceeds to church, but pauses in the portal, and throws a perplexed glance along the street. She passes in, however, opening her prayer-book as she goes. And the man! with so wild a face that busy and selfish London stands to gaze after him, he hurries to his lodgings, bolts the door, and throws himself upon the bed. The latent feelings of years break out; his feeble mind acquires a brief energy from their strength; all the miserable strangeness of his life is revealed to him at a glance: and he cries out, passionately, "Wakefield! Wakefield! You are mad!"

Perhaps he was so. The singularity of his situation must have so moulded him to himself, that, considered in regard to his fellow-creatures and the business of life, he could not be said to possess his right mind. He had contrived, or rather he had happened, to dissever himself from the world—to vanish—to give up his place and privileges with living men, without being admitted among the dead. The life of a hermit is nowise parallel to his. He was in the bustle of the city, as of old; but the crowd swept by and saw him not; he was, we may figuratively say, always beside his wife and at his hearth, yet must never feel the warmth of the one nor the affection of the other. It was Wakefield's unprecedented fate to retain his original share of human sympathies, and to be still involved in human interests, while he had lost his reciprocal influence on them. It would be a most curious speculation to trace out the effect of such circumstances on his heart and intellect, separately, and in unison. Yet, changed as he was, he would seldom be conscious of it, but deem himself the same man as ever; glimpses of the truth, indeed, would come, but only for the moment; and still he would keep saying, "I shall soon go back!"—nor reflect that he had been saying so for twenty years.

I conceive, also, that these twenty years would appear, in the retrospect, scarcely longer than the week to which Wakefield had at first limited his absence. He would look on the affair as no more than an interlude in the main business of his life. When, after a little while more, he should deem it time to reënter his parlor, his wife would ·

clap her hands for joy, on beholding the middle-aged Mr. Wakefield. Alas, what a mistake! Would Time but await the close of our favorite follies, we should be young men, all of us, and till Doomsday.

One evening, in the twentieth year since he vanished, Wakefield is taking his customary walk towards the dwelling which he still calls his own. It is a gusty night of autumn, with frequent showers that patter down upon the pavement, and are gone before a man can put up his umbrella. Pausing near the house, Wakefield discerns, through the parlor windows of the second floor, the red glow and the glimmer and fitful flash of a comfortable fire. On the ceiling appears a grotesque shadow of good Mrs. Wakefield. The cap, the nose and chin, and the broad waist, form an admirable caricature, which dances, moreover, with the up-flickering and down-sinking blaze, almost too merrily for the shade of an elderly widow. At this instant a shower chances to fall, and is driven, by the unmannerly gust, full into Wakefield's face and bosom. He is quite penetrated with its autumnal chill. Shall he stand, wet and shivering here, when his own hearth has a good fire to warm him, and his own wife will run to fetch the gray coat and small-clothes, which, doubtless, she has kept carefully in the closet of their bed chamber? No! Wakefield is no such fool. He ascends the steps—heavily!— for twenty years have stiffened his legs since he came down—but he knows it not. Stay, Wakefield! Would you go to the sole home that is left you? Then step into your grave! The door opens. As he passes in, we have a parting glimpse of his visage, and recognize the crafty smile, which was the precursor of the little joke that he has ever since been playing off at his wife's expense. How unmercifully has he quizzed the poor woman! Well, a good night's rest to Wakefield!

This happy event—supposing it to be such—could only have occurred at an unpremeditated moment. We will not follow our friend across the threshold. He has left us much food for thought, a portion of which shall lend its wisdom to a moral, and be shaped into a figure. Amid the seeming confusion of our mysterious world, individuals are so nicely adjusted to a system, and systems to one another and to a whole, that, by stepping aside for a moment, a man exposes himself to a fearful risk of losing his place forever. Like Wakefield, he may become, as it were, the Outcast of the Universe.

Ivan Turgenev (1818–1883)

According to Henry James, *The Hunter's Sketches* by Ivan Turgenev was to the freeing of the serfs in Russia what *Uncle Tom's Cabin* was to the emancipation of the slaves in the United States. Yet nothing could appear less propagandistic, less polemical, than Turgenev's book of stories, filled as it is with sensuous and poetic evocation of nature. Turgenev differs from Harriet Beecher Stowe, says James, by "having rather presented the case with an art too insidious for instant recognition, an art that stirred the depths more than the surface."

Turgenev's "insidious" art was perhaps as much a matter of self-preservation as of artistry. He was born in 1818, the son of rich landowners. Because he expressed an admiration for Gogol, who had been exiled after his satire *The Inspector General* had been performed, Turgenev was put under "house arrest." He came to know the serfs of his estate, and his natural sympathies and liberalism focused on their plight. He could not speak out directly for fear of further punishment, and so he wrote the indirect but effective *The Hunter's Sketches*. It is said that the Czar himself was influenced by it.

The book, from which the following story comes, is made up of a series of encounters the first-person narrator has on his hunting rounds. The stories have in common the general setting, narrative voice, and the peasants as subject matter, but are otherwise discrete. The narrator describes the hunt, the forest, the atmosphere in which he moves. Even in translation, the imagery is lyrical, vibrant, exquisitely physical:

> The trees blend into great, darkling masses; the first tiny stars emerge timorously in the indigo sky. All the birds are asleep. Only the redstarts and certain tiny woodpeckers keep whistling from time to time, drowsily. Finally they, too, have fallen quiet. One more time the sonorous voice of the pewit rang out overhead; a yellow thrush sadly sounded its call somewhere; a nightingale sent out its first choppy note.

The reader's senses are slowly submerged.

The plots of a Turgenev story are almost nil: the hunter arrives and departs; night falls and day breaks. These frames provide a feeling of action, but in fact the story is told indirectly and has little or nothing to do with the ostensible action. In "Ermolai and the Miller's Wife," the hunter and Ermolai seek shelter with the miller. The hunter remembers the miller's wife, Ermolai talks, the wife visits with them, they eat, they sleep. That is all. Yet the entire lives of Ermolai and the woman have emerged. By the end of the sketch the reader understands them, the injustices they have suffered, the patience with which they have endured. The sketches, says Henry James, "give the impression of life itself, and not of an arrangement."

Turgenev was the author of many novels, including the famous *Fathers and Sons* (1861) and *Smoke* (1867). He spent most of his adult life in Germany and France, and was rejected by many Russians—including Tolstoy and Dostoevsky—for being too "European." Actually he continued to care deeply about Russia and Russian literature, and from his deathbed he wrote to Tolstoy: "I write you expressly to tell you how happy I have been to be your contemporary, and to utter my last, my urgent prayer. Come back, my friend, to your literary labors." Turgenev died in France in 1883.

Ermolai and the Miller's Wife

IN THE EVENING Ermolai the hunter and I set out for a "night stand". . . . It's quite possible, however, that not all my readers know what a night stand is. Therefore hearken, gentlemen.

"Ermolai and the Miller's Wife" from *The Hunting Sketches*, by Ivan Turgenev, as translated by Bernard Guilbert Guerney. Copyright © 1962 by Bernard Guilbert Guerney. Reprinted by arrangement with The New American Library, Inc., New York.

A quarter of an hour before the setting of the sun, in the spring, you enter a grove with a gun but without a dog. You seek out a spot for yourself somewhere near the edge of the woods, look about you, examine the percussion cap on your gun, and exchange winks with your companion. The quarter of an hour has passed. The sun has set, but it's still light in the forest, the air is pure and clear, the birds are chattering away at a great rate, the young grass gleams with the joyous gleam of an emerald. You wait. The inner recesses of the forest grow darker by degrees; the ruby light of the evening glow glides slowly over the roots and trunks of the trees, rises higher, passes from the lower branches, as yet almost bare, to the motionless treetops that are now falling into slumber. See, the treetops themselves have grown dim; the rosy-cheeked sky is turning to indigo. The forest smell becomes stronger; there is a slight breath of warm dampness; the wind that had burst in so near to you dies away. The birds are falling asleep—not all of them at the same time, but each according to its kind: there, the chaffinches have fallen quiet; a few moments later the hedge sparrows do so; the siskins follow suit. It is growing darker in the forest, ever darker. The trees blend into great, darkling masses; the first tiny stars emerge timorously in the indigo sky. All the birds are asleep. Only the redstarts and certain tiny woodpeckers keep whistling from time to time, drowsily. Finally they, too, have fallen quiet. One more time the sonorous voice of the pewit rang out overhead; a yellow thrush sadly sounded its call somewhere; a nightingale sent out its first choppy note.

Your heart is languishing in expectancy, and suddenly—but it is only hunters who will understand me—suddenly in the deep quiet there resounds a peculiar sort of cawing and hissing, you hear the measured upsweep of agile wings, and a woodcock, its long nose gracefully tilted downward, flies smoothly out from behind a dark birch to encounter your shot.

There, that's what a "night stand" means.

And so, Ermolai and myself set out for a night stand—but, gentlemen, I crave your indulgence: I must first acquaint you with Ermolai.

Imagine a man of five and forty, tall, gaunt, with a long and thin nose, a narrow forehead, small gray eyes, hair all rumpled, and wide, mocking lips. This fellow walked about both winter and summer in a yellowish nankeen overcoat of a German cut, yet girded himself with a coachman's broad belt of leather; he wore blue Ukrainian trousers, so wide that they ballooned above his boot tops, and a karakul cap that had been presented to him in a lighthearted moment by a ruined landowner. He usually had two bags tied onto his belt: one in front, artfully twisted into two parts, one for gunpowder, the other for bird shot; the second bag, hanging behind, was for game; as for wadding, Ermolai always took it out of his seemingly inexhaustible cap. He could have easily bought himself a cartridge case and a gamebag for the money he made selling game, but the idea of making any such purchase did not once enter his head; and he went on loading his gun as he had always done, arousing amazement in all beholders by the art with which he avoided the risk of spilling shot and powder, or mixing the two. His gun was single-barreled, with a flintlock, endowed, furthermore, with an execrable habit of kicking, because of which Ermolai's right cheek was always plumper than his left. How he ever hit anything with that gun of his was something to stump even the cleverest man, yet hit the mark he did. He also had a setter by the name of Valetka—a most astonishing creature. Ermolai never fed it.

"I'm not going to bother feeding no hound," he argued. "Besides, a hound is a smart animal; it'll find what to eat for itself."

And, actually, although Valetka's exceeding gauntness struck even the indifferent passerby, he went on living just the same, and that for a long time and, despite his miserable situation, he never disappeared and evinced no desire to forsake his master. Only once, in the days of his youth, infatuated by love, had the hound happened to absent himself for a day or two, but this foolishness had soon left him.

Valetka's most remarkable peculiarity was his inconceivable indifference to everything in the world (if I were not talking about a dog, I would use the word "disillusionment"). He usually squatted with his stub of a tail tucked in under him, frowning, shuddering from time to time, and never smiled. (It's a known fact that dogs are capable of smiling, and even of smiling most charmingly.) He was extremely hideous, and there was never an idle house serf who let slip the chance of jeering venomously at Valetka's looks; all these jeers, however, and even blows, he bore with amazing *sang-froid*. He afforded special satisfaction to cooks, who would instantly drop their work and shouting and cursing, go for him whenever he, through a frailty not confined solely to dogs, thrust his starving snout within the half-open door of the kitchen, temptingly warm and full of heavenly smells.

When it came to hunting he was distinguished for his indefatigability and had a passable scent; however, if he chanced to catch up with a wounded rabbit he lost no time in devouring it with gusto, down to the smallest bone, somewhere in the cool shade under a green bush, at a respectable distance from Ermolai, who would be cursing him in all dialects, both known and unknown.

Ermolai belonged to one of my neighbors, a landowner of the old school. Landowners of the old school aren't fond of snipe and stick to domestic fowl. Only on extraordinary occasions, such as births, birthdays, and elections, will the cooks of the landowners of the old school tackle the preparation of these long-beaked birds and, becoming imbued with that fervor peculiar to the Russian when he hasn't the foggiest notion of what he's about, they think up such complicated fixings for the birds that the guests for the most part scrutinize the proffered viands with curiosity and great interest but can't somehow, bring themselves to partake thereof.

Ermolai was under orders to supply his master's kitchen monthly with two brace each of grouse and partridge but, on the whole, he was permitted to live where and how he liked. He had been rejected as a man unfit for any work, as "no account." Naturally, they didn't issue any gunpowder or bird shot to him, in keeping with the same principles on the strength of which he himself didn't feed his dog. Ermolai was a fellow of the oddest sort: as carefree as a bird, rather talkative, with an air of absent-mindedness and awkwardness, very fond of the bottle; he couldn't live too long in any one spot; he shuffled and waddled as he walked—and, shuffling and waddling, would put five and thirty miles behind him in a day. He went through the most diverse adventures: sleeping in swamps, up in the trees, on roofs, under bridges; more than once had he been locked up in attics, cellars, and barns, deprived of his gun, his dog, his most necessary garments; on occasion he had been beaten up, severely and protractedly—and, notwithstanding, after a time he'd come back home fully clothed, with his gun and his dog.

You couldn't call him a merry fellow, although he was almost always in fairly good spirits; on the whole he looked like a queer stick. Ermolai was fond of chinning a while with any good fellow, especially over a noggin—but not even that for long; he'd get up and be off.

"But where are you going, you devil? It's night out!"

"Why, I'm bound for Chaplino."

"And what would you be dragging yourself to Chaplino for? It's all of seven mile away—"

"Oh, I'm going to spend the night at a certain muzhik's place—Saphron, they call him."

"Come, spend the night here."

"No, I just can't."

And Ermolai was off with his Valetka, going out into the dark night, through bushes and washouts, yet, like as not that little muzhik[1] Saphron won't let him on to his place, even, and all the chances were he'd let Ermolai have it right in the neck: "Don't go 'round bothering honest folks, now!"

But then, no one could compare with Ermolai in the art of catching fish in the springtime, when the waters are at their highest, of getting crayfish out with his bare hands, of scenting out game, of luring quail, of training hawks, of snaring nightingales gifted with the "wood-sprite pipe," with the "cuckoo flight."[2] There was only one thing he didn't know how to do: train dogs. He hadn't patience enough for that.

He had a wife, too. He visited her once a week. She lived in a wretched, half-ruined little hut, getting along from hand to mouth, never knowing at night whether she would find food on the morrow and, in general, had to put up with a bitter lot. Ermolai, that carefree and good-natured man, treated her cruelly and roughly, assuming an awesome and harsh air in his house, and his poor wife knew not how she might please him, trembling at his mere look, buying liquor for him with her last coppers, and fawningly covering him with her own sheepskin coat when he, majestically sprawled out on the ledge atop the oven, would fall into titanic slumber. I myself had occasion to note, more than once, involuntary manifestations of a certain grim ferocity in him: I did not at all like the expression on his face whenever he finished off a wounded bird by biting through its throat.

However, Ermolai never remained home for more than a day, and when away from it he again became transformed into Ermolka, so nicknamed for threescore miles around, and as he at times called himself. The lowliest of house serfs felt himself superior to this vagabond—and for that very reason, perhaps, treated him amiably; as for the muzhiks, they at first took pleasure in cornering and catching him like a rabbit in a field, but later on they'd let him go with God's blessing and, having once learned what a queer stick he was, no longer harried him, even giving him bread and entering into conversation with him.

It was this very fellow whom I had taken on as my hunter, and it was with him that I set out for the night stand in the big grove of birches on the bank of the Ista.

Many Russian rivers have a resemblance to the Volga, in that they have one bank mountainous and the other meadowy; the Ista is like that, too. This small river winds along with exceeding whimsicality; it coils along like a snake, it won't flow straight for even a third of a mile, and there are spots, such as the top of a steep knoll, from which one can see a seven-mile stretch of this river with its dams, millponds, mills, truck patches surrounded by clumps of willows and luxuriant gardens. There's no end of fish in the Ista, especially bullheads (when the heat is at its worst, the muzhiks take them with their bare hands from around the underwater roots of the bushes). The tiny sandpipers whistle as they flit along the stony banks that are streaked with chill and crystal-clear springs; wild ducks swim out into the middle of

[1] A Russian peasant

[2] Admirers of the nightingale are familiar with these designations: they denote the best passages in the bird's song.—*Author.*

the ponds and look all about them warily; herons stand like sticks-in-the-mud in the shade, among the coves, under the cliffs.

The night stand lasted about an hour; we took two brace of woodcock and, wishing to try our luck again (for one can make a stand early in the morning as well) decided to sleep that night at the nearest mill. We left the grove, going down the knoll. The waves on the river rolled along, dark blue; the air was growing denser, weighed down with night moisture.

We knocked at the gate of the mill. The dogs in the yard broke into ecstatic barking.

"Who's there?" asked a hoarse and sleep-laden voice.

"A couple of hunters; let us in for the night."

There was no answer.

"We'll pay you."

"I'll go and tell the master. Stop your barking, damn your hides! There's no getting rid of you!"

We heard the hired man go into the hut; he came back to the gate shortly.

"No," said he, "the master's orders is not to let you in."

"Why not?"

"Well, he's afraid; you're hunters—first thing you know you'll set the mill on fire; just see what firearms you've got there!"

"Come, what sort of nonsense is that?"

"As it was, we had our mill burn down last year; we had some commission merchants stopping the night here, and I guess they must have set it on fire somehow."

"Come now, brother—are we to pass the night out in the open, then?"

"Do as you know best," and he went off, his boots clumping.

Ermolai wished him all sorts of unpleasant things.

"Let's go to the village," he suggested, at last, with a sigh. But it was well over a mile to the village.

"We're staying here for the night," I told him. "It's a warm night out; the miller will send some straw out to us if we pay him."

Ermolai agreed without demur; we fell to knocking on the gate again.

"Well, what are you after?" we heard the hired man's voice anew. "You were told you can't stay here."

We made clear to him what we wanted. He went to consult his master and came back with him. The wicket in the gate creaked, revealing the miller, a tall man with a fat face, the nape of his neck like a bull's, his belly round and big. He agreed to my suggestion. There was a small shed, open on all sides, a hundred paces from the mill. Straw was brought out there; the hired man set a samovar for us on the grass near the river and, squatting on his heels, began blowing zealously into its chimney. The charcoal embers, flaring up, cast a bright light on his young face. The miller hurried off to wake up his wife; he finally suggested that I myself might stay the night in his hut, but I preferred to remain in the open air.

The miller's wife brought us milk, eggs, potatoes, bread. In a short while the samovar came to a boil and we settled to our tea drinking. Vapors were rising from the river; there was no wind; corn crakes were calling all about us; faint sounds, caused by drops falling from the paddles of a water wheel, by water seeping through the uprights of the dam, came from around the mill wheels. We made a small fire. While Ermolai was roasting potatoes in the hot ashes I managed to have a nap. A low, restrained whispering awoke me. I raised my head: the miller's wife was sitting before the fire on an upturned tub and talking with my hunter. I had recognized her even before, by her dress, movements, and speech, as neither a country wife nor city dweller but a house serf. She looked about thirty; her gaunt and pale face still bore traces of a remarkable beauty—her eyes, great and sorrowing, had proved especially to my liking. She had propped her elbows on her knees and cupped her chin in her hands. Ermolai was sitting with his back to me and adding chips to the fire.

"There's a murrain in Zheltuhino again," the miller's wife was saying. "Both of Father Ivan's cows dropped from it. Lord have mercy upon us!"

"But what about your pigs?" Ermolai asked after a pause.

"Oh, they're alive!"

"You might make me a present of a little suckling pig, at least."

The miller's wife was silent for a while, then heaved a sigh: "Who's that with you?" she asked.

"One of the gentry—from Kostomarovsk." Ermolai tossed several fir branches on the fire; they at once began to crackle heartily; the thick white smoke billowed right into his face. "Why wouldn't your husband let us into the hut?"

"He's afraid."

"What a fat potbelly. . . . Arina Timotheievna, my dearest dear, bring me out a noggin of something to drink!"

The miller's wife got up and vanished in the murk. Ermolai began to hum:

"When I went to see my sweet
I wore the boots right off my feet—"

Arina returned with a small decanter and a tumbler. Ermolai raised himself a little, made the sign of the cross, and drank off a glass at one breath.

"I love the stuff!" he added. The miller's wife again seated herself on the tub. "Well now, Arina Timotheievna, you're still ailing, I guess?"

"I am that."

"How come?"

"My cough's killing me of nights."

"The master's fallen asleep, it looks like," Ermolai let drop after a short silence. "Don't you go to no doctor, Arina; it'll be worse for you if you do."

"I don't go to him, anyway."

"But you might drop in on me and stay a while."

Arina let her head drop.

"I'll chase my woman out—my wife, that is—in case you come," Ermolai went on. "I will, for sure."

"You'd better wake up the master, Ermolai Petrovich; see, the potatoes are baked."

"Aw, let him snooze," my loyal servant answered apathetically. "He's tuckered out from running around, so he's sleeping."

I began to turn in the hay. Ermolai got up and walked over to me.

"The potatoes are done, sir; come and eat, please."

I left the shed; the miller's wife got up from the tub and was about to leave; I spoke to her.

"Have you been renting this mill long?"

"The second year, beginning with Trinity."

"And where is your husband from?"

Arina failed to catch my question.

"Where does your husband hail from?" Ermolai repeated, raising his voice.

"From Belev. He's a Belev burgher."

"And are you from Belev too?"

"No; I'm a serf—or was, at least."

"Whose?"

"Squire Zverkov's. Now I'm free."

"What Zverkov is that?"

"Alexander Silych."

"Weren't you his wife's maid?"

"Why, how do you know? I was."

I looked at Arina with redoubled interest and sympathy. "I know your master," I went on.

"You do?" she responded in a low voice—and stopped short.

I must inform the reader why I had looked at Arina with such sympathy. During my stay in Petersburg I had chanced to make the acquaintance of Zverkov. He held a rather important post and enjoyed the reputation of a well-informed and businesslike person. He had a wife—plump, touchy, lachrymose, and malevolent, a most ordinary and depressing creature; he had a darling son as well, a real young master, spoiled and foolish. The appearance of Zverkov himself predisposed one but little in his favor; out of his broad, almost quadrangular face, mouse eyes peeped slyly and a nose, big and sharp and with distended nostrils, jutted forth; closely cropped gray hair bristled up over a wrinkled forehead; his thin lips were incessantly in motion and smiling mawkishly. Zverkov usually stood with his little feet wide apart and his chubby little hands thrust into his pockets.

One day he and I somehow chanced to share a carriage for a ride to the suburbs. We got into conversation. As a man of business and experience, Zverkov began to "set me right."

"Permit me to point out to you," he squeaked out at last, "that all you young people judge and explain all things offhand; you have but little knowledge of your fatherland; you are unfamiliar with Russia, gentlemen—that's what! All you ever do is read German books. There, for instance, you're now telling me this and that about . . . well, now, ahem . . . about house serfs. Very well, I'm not arguing; all that is very well, but you don't know them, you don't know what sort of people they are." Zverkov blew his nose loudly and took snuff. "Let me tell you, by the way, just one story, ever so brief—you may find it of interest." Zverkov cleared his throat. "I'm sure you know what my wife is; you'll agree it would be hard to find a kindlier woman. Her maids don't just live well, but simply have heaven on earth.

"However, my wife has laid down one rule for herself: not to keep any maids who are married. And really, that would never do; there are bound to be offspring and one thing or another—well, in that case, how is a maid to look after her mistress properly, to follow her mistress' habits? The maid is no longer interested in that; she's got other things on her mind. You must take human nature into consideration in judging such things.

"Well, sir, we were once passing through our village about . . . I wouldn't want to err in telling you how many years ago that was—about fifteen years, say. And what do we see at the village elder's house but a little girl, his daughter, the prettiest little thing;

there was something so ingratiating about her manners, actually. And so my wife says to me: 'Kokó,'—that's what she calls me, you understand—'let's take this little girl to Petersburg; I like her, Kokó.'—'Why, with pleasure,' I told her.

"The elder, naturally, bowed to our very feet; he could never have even expected such good fortune, you understand. Well, the little girl, being foolish, had a good cry. It actually was frightening at first, to be leaving her parental home—in general, there's nothing to wonder at about that. However, she soon became used to us; at first we placed her with the maids, training her, of course. Well, what do you think? The girl made astonishing progress; my wife grew simply mad about her, was gracious to her; finally, passing all the other girls by, she appointed her to be her personal maid, if you please!

"And one must give the girl her due; my wife had never yet had such a maid—absolutely not; she was obliging, modest, obedient, simply everything you could ask for. But then, it must be confessed, my wife did pamper her far too much: she dressed her excellently, gave her food from our own table, let her drink tea—oh, she indulged her in every imaginable way!

"And so she served my wife for ten years, or thereabouts. Suddenly, one fine morning—just imagine!—Arina (that's what they called her: Arina) entered my study unannounced and plumped down at my feet! That, I'll tell you frankly, is something I can't abide. A human being should never forget his or her dignity. 'What do you want?'—'Alexander Silych, my father, I'm asking a favor.'—'What favor?'—'Allow me to marry.'

"I confess to you I was amazed. 'Why, don't you know, you fool, that your mistress has no other maid?'—'I will go on serving my mistress as before.'—'Nonsense! Nonsense! Your mistress won't keep any married maids.'—'Melania can take my place.'—'I'll ask you not to argue!'—'Just as you will, master.'

"I confess I was simply bowled over. Nothing offends me as much—nothing offends me so powerfully, I venture to say—as ingratitude; that, I must inform you, is the sort of person I am. For I don't have to tell you what my wife is—you know that yourself: she's an angel incarnate, kind beyond words. You might think even the worst of villains would take pity on her.

"I chased Arina out. 'Guess she'll come to her senses,' I thought; one doesn't want to believe evil of human beings, to believe in their black ingratitude, you know.

"Well, what do you think? Half a year later she was pleased to come to me again with the same petition. At this, I confess, I chased her out with heartfelt anger, and threatened her, and promised to tell my wife. But, just imagine my amazement when, some time later, my wife came to me in tears, so agitated that I was actually frightened. 'What's happened?'—'Arina . . . You understand? I'm ashamed to say it.'—'It can't be! Who is it, then?'—'Petrushka the flunky!' I blew up. I don't like half measures—that's the sort of person I am! Petrushka wasn't to blame. One could punish him but, in my opinion, he wasn't to blame. Arina, though—well! Well, now . . . well, now, what's the use of saying anything more?

"Naturally, I immediately ordered her hair to be cropped, to dress her in coarse ticking, and to pack her off to the country. My wife was deprived of an excellent maid, but there was no help for it: one cannot, under any circumstances, tolerate irregularity in a household. It's best to lop off a diseased limb at once. There, there—judge for yourself; why, you know my wife—she's . . . she's . . . she's a downright angel! Why, she'd become attached to Arina, and Arina knew this and hadn't felt the least compunction. Eh? No, what do you say to that, eh? Oh, what's the use of arguing about this! In any case, there was nothing to be done. As for myself—for myself, personally—I was for a long time grieved, offended by the ingratitude of this girl. No matter what you may say, you should never look for any heart, for any sensibility among these people. Feed a wolf as you will, he will eye the forest still. It'll be a lesson to me in the future. However, I merely wished to prove to you—"

And Zverkov, without finishing what he had wanted to say, turned his head away and muffled himself more closely in his cape, manfully downing his involuntary agitation.

The reader by now probably understands why I had looked with such sympathy at Arina.

"Are you married to the miller long?" I asked her at last.

"Two years."

"Why, did your master give you permission to marry?"

"I was bought off."

"By whom?"

"Savelii Alexeievich."

"Who's that?"

"My husband. [Ermolai smiled to himself.] Why, did my master speak to you about me?" Arina added after a short silence.

I didn't know what answer to make to her question.

"Arina!" the miller began shouting in the distance. She got up and left.

"Is her husband a good man?" I asked Ermolai.

"So-so."

"And have they any children?"

"They had one child, but it died."

"Well, now, did she prove to the miller's liking—was that it? Did he pay a high price to buy her freedom?"

"That I couldn't say. She knows how to read and write; in their business, now, that comes in handy. So she must have proven to his liking."

"And have you known her a long time?"

"Yes, a long time. I used to go to her master's before. Their estate is no great ways from here."

"And do you know Petrushka the flunky?"

"Peter Vassilievich? Sure, I knew him."

"Where is he now?"

"Why, he was took a soldier."

We were silent for a while.

"She doesn't seem to be in good health. What's the matter with her?" I finally asked Ermolai.

"No, you couldn't call her healthy! . . . Well, I guess we'll have a good stand tomorrow. It wouldn't be a bad idea if you were to get some sleep now."

A flock of wild ducks swept by over our heads, whistling, and we heard them settling on the river not far from us. By now it had grown altogether dark and the air was becoming chill; a nightingale was sonorously trilling in a grove. We burrowed down in the hay and dozed off.

Herman Melville (1819–1891)

In the spring of 1851, struggling to finish *Moby Dick* even as he was seeing its early chapters through the press, Melville wrote Hawthorne: "The calm, the coolness, the silent grass-growing mood in which a man *ought* always to compose, —that, I fear, can seldom be mine. Dollars damn me. . . . What I feel most moved to write, that is banned,—it will not pay. Yet, altogether, write the *other* way I cannot." The *other* way had produced Melville's earlier novels of sea adventure (*Typee*, 1846; *Omoo*, 1847; *Redburn*, 1849; *White-Jacket*, 1850) and it had brought him popular success. Write again that other way he did not, and when *Moby Dick* appeared later in 1851, the public did not buy and the critics did not praise. The broad sweep of his prose style and the habits of a deeply metaphysical mind were mistaken by some for incoherence and even madness. With the publication of his next novel, *Pierre* (1852), an even more spectacular commercial failure, the reviewers turned into downright attackers.

With "Bartleby," Melville turned his hand to shorter fiction. It has been read by some critics—and the interpretation is persuasive—"as a parable having to do with Melville's fate as a writer":

> To begin with, the story *is* about a kind of writer, a "copyist" in a Wall Street lawyer's office. Furthermore, the copyist is a man who obstinately refuses to go on doing the sort of writing demanded of him. Under the circumstances there can be little doubt about the connection between Bartleby's dilemma and Melville's own. . . . "Bartleby" is not only about a writer who refuses to conform to the demands of society, but it is, more relevantly, about a writer who forsakes conventional modes because of an irresistible preoccupation with the most baffling philosophical questions.

In the above reading, Leo Marx asks us to think seriously about the subtitle, "A Story of Wall Street." The setting is clearly that of a commercial society, but the locale is not just Wall Street, New York: "As Melville describes the street it literally becomes a walled street. The walls are the controlling symbols of the story, and in fact it may be said that this is a parable of walls, the walls which hem in the meditative artist and for that matter every reflective man."

Suppose, on the other hand, that we did not have the letter to Hawthorne, that we knew nothing of Melville's professional literary career, that we had only "Bartleby." Who, we might be inclined to ask, is in fact the protagonist—the nameless narrator or the scrivener? Which one, as we later recall the story, stirs more vividly, more insistently in our memory? Is Bartleby's fate, the fate of a gray, semi-automaton, more moving than the graduated enlightenment and understanding—together with moments of love—that humanize the lawyer? For whom are we more happy—if we are happy for anyone—at the end of the tale? The effort to address questions such as these may help us to determine what we have a right, and perhaps what we have only a qualified right, to ask of both literature and biographical history.

Bartleby, the Scrivener: A Story of Wall Street

I am a rather elderly man. The nature of my avocations, for the last thirty years, has brought me into more than ordinary contact with what would seem an interesting and somewhat singular set of men, of whom, as yet, nothing, that I know of, has ever been written:—I mean the lawcopyists or scriveners. I have known very many of them, professionally and privately, and, if I pleased, could relate divers histories, at which good-natured gentlemen might smile, and sentimental souls might weep. But I waive the biographies of all other scriveners for a few passages in the life of Bartleby, who was a scrivener, the strangest I ever saw, or heard of. While, of other law-copyists, I might write the complete life, of Bartleby nothing of that sort can be done. I believe that no materials exist, for a full and satisfactory biography of this man. It is an irreparable loss to literature. Bartleby was one of those beings of whom nothing is ascertainable, except from the original sources, and, in his case, those are very small. What my own astonished eyes saw of Bartleby, *that* is all I know of him, except, indeed, one vague report, which will appear in the sequel.

Ere introducing the scrivener, as he first appeared to me, it is fit I make some mention of myself, my *employées,* my business, my chambers, and general surroundings; because some such description is indispensable to an adequate understanding of the chief character about to be presented.

Imprimis:[1] I am a man who, from his youth upwards, has been filled with a profound conviction that the easiest way of life is the best. Hence, though I belong to a profession proverbially energetic and nervous, even to turbulence, at times, yet nothing of that sort have I ever suffered to invade my peace. I am one of those unambitious lawyers who never addresses a jury, or in any way draws down public applause; but in the cool tranquillity of a snug retreat, do a snug business among rich men's bonds, and mortgages, and title-deeds. All who know me, consider me an eminently *safe* man. The late John Jacob Astor,[2] a personage little given to poetic enthusiasm, had no hesitation in pronouncing my first grand point to be prudence; my next, method. I do not speak it in vanity, but simply record the fact, that I was not unemployed in my profession by the late John Jacob Astor; a name which, I admit, I love to repeat; for it hath a rounded and orbicular sound to it, and rings like unto bullion. I will freely add, that I was not insensible to the late John Jacob Astor's good opinion.

Some time prior to the period at which this little history begins, my avocations had been largely increased. The good old office, now extinct in the State of New York, of a Master in Chancery,[3] had been conferred upon me. It was not a very arduous office, but very pleasantly remunerative. I seldom lose my temper; much more seldom indulge in dangerous indignation at wrongs and outrages; but I must be permitted to be rash here and declare, that I consider the sudden and violent abrogation of the office of Master in Chancery, by the new Constitution, as a—premature act; inasmuch as I had counted upon a life-lease of the profits, whereas I only received those of a few short years. But this is by the way.

My chambers were up stairs at No.—Wall Street. At one end they looked upon

---

[1] In the first place: a legal term.
[2] Astor (1763–1848) was at one time the richest man in the United States.
[3] The Court of Chancery in New York State was abolished in 1847.

the white wall of the interior of a spacious skylight shaft, penetrating the building from top to bottom.

This view might have been considered rather tame than otherwise, deficient in what landscape painters call "life." But, if so, the view from the other end of my chambers offered, at least, a contrast, if nothing more. In that direction my windows commanded an unobstructed view of a lofty brick wall, black by age and everlasting shade; which wall required no spyglass to bring out its lurking beauties, but, for the benefit of all near-sighted spectators, was pushed up to within ten feet of my window panes. Owing to the great height of the surrounding buildings, and my chambers being on the second floor, the interval between this wall and mine not a little resembled a huge square cistern.

At the period just preceding the advent of Bartleby, I had two persons as copyists in my employment, and a promising lad as an officeboy. First, Turkey; second, Nippers; third, Ginger Nut. These may seem names, the like of which are not usually found in the Directory. In truth, they were nicknames, mutually conferred upon each other by my three clerks, and were deemed expressive of their respective persons or characters. Turkey was a short, pursy Englishman of about my own age—that is, somewhere not far from sixty. In the morning, one might say, his face was a fine florid hue, but after twelve o'clock, meridian—his dinner hour—it blazed like a grate full of Christmas coals; and continued blazing—but, as it were, with a gradual wane—till 6 o'clock, P.M. or thereabouts, after which I saw no more of the proprietor of the face, which gaining its meridian with the sun, seemed to set with it, to rise, culminate, and decline the following day, with the like regularity and undiminished glory. There are many singular coincidences I have known in the course of my life, not the least among which was the fact, that exactly when Turkey displayed his fullest beams from his red and radiant countenance, just then, too, at that critical moment, began the daily period when I considered his business capacities as seriously disturbed for the remainder of the twenty-four hours. Not that he was absolutely idle, or adverse to business then; far from it. The difficulty was, he was apt to be altogether too energetic. There was a strange, inflamed, flurried, flighty recklessness of activity about him. He would be incautious in dipping his pen into his inkstand. All his blots upon my documents were dropped there after twelve o'clock, meridian. Indeed, not only would he be reckless and sadly given to making blots in the afternoon, but some days he went further, and was rather noisy. At such times, too, his face flamed with augmented blazonry, as if cannel coal had been heaped on anthracite.[4] He made an unpleasant racket with his chair; spilled his sand-box; in mending his pens, impatiently split them all to pieces, and threw them on the floor in a sudden passion; stood up and leaned over his table, boxing his papers about in a most indecorous manner, very sad to behold in an elderly man like him. Nevertheless, as he was in many ways a most valuable person to me, and all the time before twelve o'clock, meridian, was the quickest, steadiest creature, too, accomplishing a great deal of work in a style not easy to be matched—for these reasons, I was willing to overlook his eccentricities, though indeed, occasionally, I remonstrated with him. I did this very gently, however, because, though the civilest, nay, the blandest and most reverential of men in the morning, yet, in the afternoon he was disposed, upon provocation, to be slightly rash with his tongue, in fact, insolent. Now, valuing his morning services as I did, and resolved not to lose them—yet, at the same time, made uncomfortable by his inflamed ways

---

[4] Cannel burns brightly; anthracite shows almost no flame.

after twelve o'clock—and being a man of peace, unwilling by my admonitions to call forth unseemly retorts from him, I took upon me, one Saturday noon (he was always worse on Saturdays), to hint to him, very kindly, that, perhaps now that he was growing old, it might be well to abridge his labors; in short, he need not come to my chambers after twelve o'clock, but, dinner over, had best go home to his lodgings, and rest himself till tea-time. But no; he insisted upon his afternoon devotions. His countenance became intolerably fervid, as he oratorically assured me—gesticulating with a long ruler at the other end of the room—that if his services in the morning were useful, how indispensable, then, in the afternoon?

"With submission, sir," said Turkey, on this occasion, "I consider myself your right-hand man. In the morning I but marshal and deploy my columns; but in the afternoon I put myself at their head, and gallantly charge the foe, thus"—and he made a violent thrust with the ruler.

"But the blots, Turkey," intimated I.

"True; but, with submission, sir, behold these hairs! I am getting old. Surely, sir, a blot or two of a warm afternoon is not to be severely urged against gray hairs. Old age—even if it blot the page—is honorable. With submission, sir, we *both* are getting old."

This appeal to my fellow-feeling was hardly to be resisted. At all events, I saw that go he would not. So, I made up my mind to let him stay, resolving, nevertheless, to see to it, that during the afternoon he had to do with my less important papers.

Nippers, the second on my list, was a whiskered, sallow, and, upon the whole, rather piratical-looking young man, of about five and twenty. I always deemed him the victim of two evil powers—ambition and indigestion. The ambition was evinced by a certain impatience of the duties of a mere copyist, an unwarrantable usurpation of strictly professional affairs, such as the original drawing up of legal documents. The indigestion seemed betokened in an occasional nervous testiness and grinning irritability, causing the teeth to audibly grind together over mistakes committed in copying; unnecessary maledictions, hissed, rather than spoken, in the heat of business; and especially by a continual discontent with the height of the table where he worked. Though of a very ingenious mechanical turn, Nippers could never get this table to suit him. He put chips under it, blocks of various sorts, bits of pasteboard, and at last went so far as to attempt an exquisite adjustment by final pieces of folded blotting-paper. But no invention would answer. If, for the sake of easing his back, he brought the table lid at a sharp angle well up towards his chin, and wrote there like a man using the steep roof of a Dutch house for his desk, then he declared that it stopped the circulation in his arms. If now he lowered the table to his waistbands, and stooped over it in writing, then there was a sore aching in his back. In short, the truth of the matter was, Nippers knew not what he wanted. Or, if he wanted anything, it was to be rid of a scrivener's table altogether. Among the manifestations of his diseased ambition was a fondness he had for receiving visits from certain ambiguous-looking fellows in seedy coats, whom he called his clients. Indeed, I was aware that not only was he, at times, considerable of a ward-politician, but he occasionally did a little business at the Justices' courts, and was not unknown on the steps of the Tombs.[5] I have good reason to believe, however, that one individual who called upon him at my chambers, and who, with a grand air, he insisted was his client, was no other than a dun,[6] and the alleged

[5] A New York City prison.
[6] Bill collector.

title-deed, a bill. But with all his failings, and the annoyances he caused me, Nippers, like his compatriot Turkey, was a very useful man to me; wrote a neat, swift hand; and, when he chose, was not deficient in a gentlemanly sort of deportment. Added to this, he always dressed in a gentlemanly sort of way; and so, incidentally, reflected credit upon my chambers. Whereas, with respect to Turkey, I had much ado to keep him from being a reproach to me. His clothes were apt to look oily, and smell of eating-houses. He wore his pantaloons very loose and baggy in summer. His coats were execrable; his hat not to be handled. But while the hat was a thing of indifference to me, inasmuch as his natural civility and deference, as a dependent Englishman, always led him to doff it the moment he entered the room, yet his coat was another matter. Concerning his coats, I reasoned with him; but with no effect. The truth was, I suppose, that a man with so small an income, could not afford to sport such a lustrous face and a lustrous coat at one and the same time. As Nippers once observed, Turkey's money went chiefly for red ink. One winter day, I presented Turkey with a highly-respectable looking coat of my own—a padded gray coat, of a most comfortable warmth, and which buttoned straight up from the knee to the neck. I thought Turkey would appreciate the favor, and abate his rashness and obstreperousness of afternoons. But no; I verily believe that buttoning himself up in so downy and blanket-like a coat had a pernicious effect upon him—upon the same principle that too much oats are bad for horses. In fact, precisely as a rash, restive horse is said to feel his oats, so Turkey felt his coat. It made him insolent. He was a man whom prosperity harmed.

Though, concerning the self-indulgent habits of Turkey, I had my own private surmises, yet, touching Nippers, I was well persuaded that, whatever might be his faults in other respects, he was, at least, a temperate young man. But indeed, nature herself seemed to have been his vintner, and at his birth charged him so thoroughly with an irritable, brandy-like disposition, that all subsequent potations were needless. When I consider how, amid the stillness of my chambers, Nippers would sometimes impatiently rise from his seat, and stooping over his table, spread his arms wide apart, seize the whole desk, and move it, and jerk it, with a grim, grinding motion on the floor, as if the table were a perverse voluntary agent, intent on thwarting and vexing him, I plainly perceive that, for Nippers, brandy and water were altogether superfluous.

It was fortunate for me that, owing to its peculiar cause—indigestion—the irritability and consequent nervousness of Nippers, were mainly observable in the morning, while in the afternoon he was comparatively mild. So that, Turkey's paroxysms only coming on about twelve o'clock, I never had to do with their eccentricities at one time. Their fits relieved each other like guards. When Nippers' was on, Turkey's was off; and *vice versa*. This was a good natural arrangement under the circumstances.

Ginger Nut, the third on my list, was a lad, some twelve years old. His father was a carman,[7] ambitious of seeing his son on the bench instead of a cart, before he died. So he sent him to my office as student at law, errand boy, and cleaner and sweeper, at the rate of one dollar a week. He had a little desk to himself, but he did not use it much. Upon inspection, the drawer exhibited a great array of the shells of various sorts of nuts. Indeed, to this quick-witted youth the whole science of the law was contained in a nutshell. Not the least among the employments of Ginger Nut, as well as one which he discharged with the most alacrity, was his duty as cake and apple

---

[7] Wagon driver

purveyor for Turkey and Nippers. Copying law papers being proverbially a dry, husky sort of business, my two scriveners were fain to moisten their mouths very often with Spitzenbergs[8] to be had at the numerous stalls nigh the Custom House and Post Office. Also, they sent Ginger Nut very frequently for that peculiar cake—small, flat, round, and very spicy—after which he had been named by them. Of a cold morning when business was but dull, Turkey would gobble up scores of these cakes, as if they were mere wafers—indeed, they sell them at the rate of six or eight for a penny—the scrape of his pen blending with the crunching of the crisp particles in his mouth. Of all the fiery afternoon blunders and flurried rashnesses of Turkey, was his once moistening a ginger-cake between his lips, and clapping it on to a mortgage, for a seal. I came within an ace of dismissing him then. But he mollified me by making an oriental bow, and saying—

"With submission, sir, it was generous of me to find you in[9] stationery on my own account."

Now my original business—that of a conveyancer and title hunter, and drawer-up of recondite documents of all sorts—was considerably increased by receiving the Master's office. There was now great work for scriveners. Not only must I push the clerks already with me, but I must have additional help.

In answer to my advertisement, a motionless young man one morning stood upon my office threshold, the door being open, for it was summer. I can see that figure now—pallidly neat, pitiably respectable, incurably forlorn! It was Bartleby.

After a few words touching his qualifications, I engaged him, glad to have among my corps of copyists a man of so singularly sedate an aspect, which I thought might operate beneficially upon the flighty temper of Turkey, and the fiery one of Nippers.

I should have stated before that ground glass folding-doors divided my premises into two parts, one of which was occupied by my scriveners, the other by myself. According to my humor, I threw open these doors, or closed them. I resolved to assign Bartleby a corner by the folding-doors, but on my side of them, so as to have this quiet man within easy call, in case any trifling thing was to be done. I placed his desk close up to a small side-window in that part of the room, a window which originally had afforded a lateral view of certain grimy backyards and bricks, but which, owing to subsequent erections, commanded at present no view at all, though it gave some light. Within three feet of the panes was a wall, and the light came down from far above, between two lofty buildings, as from a very small opening in a dome. Still further to a satisfactory arrangement, I procured a high green folding screen, which might entirely isolate Bartleby from my sight, though not remove him from my voice. And thus, in a manner, privacy and society were conjoined.

At first, Bartleby did an extraordinary quantity of writing. As if long famishing for something to copy, he seemed to gorge himself on my documents. There was no pause for digestion. He ran a day and night line, copying by sunlight and by candle-light. I should have been quite delighted with his application, had he been cheerfully industrious. But he wrote on silently, palely, mechanically.

It is, of course, an indispensable part of a scrivener's business to verify the accuracy of his copy, word by word. Where there are two or more scriveners in an office, they assist each other in this examination, one reading from the copy, the other holding the original. It is a very dull, wearisome, and lethargic affair. I can readily imagine that, to some sanguine temperaments, it would be altogether intolerable. For example,

---

[8] Apples.
[9] Provide you with.

I cannot credit that the mettlesome poet, Byron, would have contentedly sat down with Bartleby to examine a law document of, say, five hundred pages, closely written in a crimpy hand.

Now and then, in the haste of business, it had been my habit to assist in comparing some brief document myself, calling Turkey or Nippers for this purpose. One object I had, in placing Bartleby so handy to me behind the screen, was, to avail myself on his services on such trivial occasions. It was on the third day, I think, of his being with me, and before any necessity had arisen for having his own writing examined, that, being much hurried to complete a small affair I had in hand, I abruptly called to Bartleby. In my haste and natural expectancy of instant compliance, I sat with my head bent over the original on my desk, and my right hand sideways, and somewhat nervously extended with the copy, so that, immediately upon emerging from his retreat, Bartleby might snatch it and proceed to business without the least delay.

In this very attitude did I sit when I called to him, rapidly stating what it was I wanted him to do—namely, to examine a small paper with me. Imagine my surprise, nay, my consternation, when without moving from his privacy, Bartleby, in a singularly mild, firm voice, replied, "I would prefer not to."

I sat awhile in perfect silence, rallying my stunned faculties. Immediately it occurred to me that my ears had deceived me, or Bartleby had entirely misunderstood my meaning. I repeated my request in the clearest tone I could assume: but in quite as clear a one came the previous reply, "I would prefer not to."

"Prefer not to," echoed I, rising in high excitement, and crossing the room with a stride. "What do you mean? Are you moon-struck? I want you to help me compare this sheet here—take it," and I thrust it towards him.

"I would prefer not to," said he.

I looked at him steadfastly. His face was leanly composed; his gray eye dimly calm. Not a wrinkle of agitation rippled him. Had there been the least uneasiness, anger, impatience or impertinence in his manner; in other words, had there been anything ordinarily human about him, doubtless I should have violently dismissed him from the premises. But as it was, I should have as soon thought of turning my pale plaster-of-paris bust of Cicero out-of-doors. I stood gazing at him awhile, as he went on with his own writing, and then reseated myself at my desk. This is very strange, thought I. What had one best do? But my business hurried me. I concluded to forget the matter for the present, reserving it for my future leisure. So, calling Nippers from the other room, the paper was speedily examined.

A few days after this, Bartleby concluded four lengthy documents, being quadruplicates of a week's testimony taken before me in my High Court of Chancery. It became necessary to examine them. It was an important suit, and great accuracy was imperative. Having all things arranged I called Turkey, Nippers and Ginger Nut from the next room, meaning to place the four copies in the hands of my four clerks, while I should read from the original. Accordingly, Turkey, Nippers and Ginger Nut had taken their seats in a row, each with his document in hand, when I called to Bartleby to join this interesting group.

"Bartleby! quick, I am waiting."

I heard a slow scrape of his chair legs on the uncarpeted floor, and soon he appeared standing at the entrance of his hermitage.

"What is wanted?" said he mildly.

"The copies, the copies," said I hurriedly. "We are going to examine them. There"—and I held towards him the fourth quadruplicate.

"I would prefer not to," he said, and gently disappeared behind the screen.

For a few moments I was turned into a pillar of salt, standing at the head of my seated column of clerks. Recovering myself, I advanced towards the screen, and demanded the reason for such extraordinary conduct.

"*Why* do you refuse?"

"I would prefer not to."

With any other man I should have flown outright into a dreadful passion, scorned all further words, and thrust him ignominiously from my presence. But there was something about Bartleby that not only strangely disarmed me, but in a wonderful manner touched and disconcerted me. I began to reason with him.

"These are your own copies we are about to examine. It is labor saving to you, because one examination will answer for your four papers. It is common usage. Every copyist is bound to help examine his copy. Is it not so? Will you not speak? Answer!"

"I prefer not to," he replied in a flute-like tone. It seemed to me that while I had been addressing him, he carefully revolved every statement that I made; fully comprehended the meaning; could not gainsay the irresistible conclusion; but, at the same time, some paramount consideration prevailed with him to reply as he did.

"You are decided, then, not to comply with my request—a request made according to common usage and common sense?"

He briefly gave me to understand, that on that point my judgment was sound. Yes: his decision was irreversible.

It is not seldom the case that, when a man is browbeaten in some unprecedented and violently unreasonable way, he begins to stagger in his own plainest faith. He begins, as it were, vaguely to surmise that, wonderful as it may be, all the justice and all the reason is on the other side. Accordingly, if any disinterested persons are present, he turns to them for some reinforcement for his own faltering mind.

"Turkey," said I, "what do you think of this? Am I not right?"

"With submission, sir," said Turkey, with his blandest tone, "I think that you are."

"Nippers," said I, "what do *you* think of it?"

"I think I should kick him out of the office."

(The reader of nice perceptions will here perceive that, it being morning, Turkey's answer is couched in polite and tranquil terms, but Nippers replies in ill-tempered ones. Or, to repeat a previous sentence, Nippers's ugly mood was on duty, and Turkey's off.)

"Ginger Nut," said I, willing to enlist the smallest suffrage in my behalf, "what do *you* think of it?"

"I think, sir, he's a little *luny*," replied Ginger Nut, with a grin.

"You hear what they say," said I, turning towards the screen, "come forth and do your duty."

But he vouchsafed no reply. I pondered a moment in sore perplexity. But once more business hurried me. I determined again to postpone the consideration of this dilemma to my future leisure. With a little trouble we made out to examine the papers without Bartleby, though at every page or two, Turkey deferentially dropped his opinion that this proceeding was quite out of the common; while Nippers, twitching in his chair with a dyspeptic nervousness, ground out between his set teeth occasional hissing maledictions against the stubborn oaf behind the screen. And for his (Nippers's) part, this was the first and the last time he would do another man's business without pay.

Meanwhile Bartleby sat in his hermitage, oblivious to everything but his own peculiar business there.

Some days passed, the scrivener being employed upon another lengthy work. His late remarkable conduct led me to regard his ways narrowly. I observed that he never went to dinner; indeed that he never went anywhere. As yet I had never of my personal knowledge known him to be outside of my office. He was a perpetual sentry in the corner. At about eleven o'clock though, in the morning, I noticed that Ginger Nut would advance toward the opening in Bartleby's screen, as if silently beckoned thither by a gesture invisible to me where I sat. The boy would then leave the office, jingling a few pence, and reappear with a handful of ginger-nuts which he delivered in the hermitage, receiving two of the cakes for his trouble.

He lives, then, on ginger-nuts, thought I; never eats a dinner, properly speaking; he must be a vegetarian, then, but no; he never eats even vegetables, he eats nothing but ginger-nuts. My mind then ran on in reveries concerning the probable effects upon the human constitution of living entirely on ginger-nuts. Ginger-nuts are so called because they contain ginger as one of their peculiar constituents, and the final flavoring one. Now, what was ginger? A hot, spicy thing. Was Bartleby hot and spicy? Not at all. Ginger, then, had no effect upon Bartleby. Probably he preferred it should have none.

Nothing so aggravates an earnest person as a passive resistance. If the individual so resisted be of a not inhumane temper, and the resisting one perfectly harmless in his passivity, then, in the better moods of the former, he will endeavor charitably to construe to his imagination what proves impossible to be solved by his judgment. Even so, for the most part, I regarded Bartleby and his ways. Poor fellow! thought I, he means no mischief; it is plain he intends no insolence; his aspect sufficiently evinces that his eccentricities are involuntary. He is useful to me. I can get along with him. If I turn him away, the chances are he will fall in with some less indulgent employer, and then he will be rudely treated, and perhaps driven forth miserably to starve. Yes. Here I can cheaply purchase a delicious self-approval. To befriend Bartleby; to humor him in his strange wilfulness, will cost me little or nothing, while I lay up in my soul what will eventually prove a sweet morsel for my conscience. But this mood was not invariable with me. The passiveness of Bartleby sometimes irritated me. I felt strangely goaded on to encounter him in new opposition, to elicit some angry spark from him answerable to my own. But indeed I might as well have essayed to strike fire with my knuckles against a bit of Windsor soap. But one afternoon the evil impulse in me mastered me, and the following little scene ensued:

"Bartleby," said I, "when those papers are all copied, I will compare them with you."

"I would prefer not to."

"How? Surely you do not mean to persist in that mulish vagary?"

No answer.

I threw open the folding-doors near by, and turning upon Turkey and Nippers, exclaimed in an excited manner—

"He says, a second time, he won't examine his papers. What do you think of it, Turkey?"

It was afternoon, be it remembered. Turkey sat glowing like a brass boiler, his bald head steaming, his hands reeling among his blotted papers.

"Think of it?" roared Turkey; "I think I'll just step behind his screen, and black his eyes for him!"

So saying, Turkey rose to his feet and threw his arms into a pugilistic position. He was hurrying away to make good his promise, when I detained him, alarmed at the effect of incautiously rousing Turkey's combativeness after dinner.

"Sit down, Turkey," said I, "and hear what Nippers has to say. What do you think of it, Nippers? Would I not be justified in immediately dismissing Bartleby?"

"Excuse me, that is for you to decide, sir. I think his conduct quite unusual, and indeed unjust, as regards Turkey and myself. But it may only be a passing whim."

"Ah," exclaimed I, "you have strangely changed your mind then—you speak very gently of him now."

"All beer," cried Turkey; "gentleness is effects of beer—Nippers and I dined together today. You see how gentle *I* am, sir. Shall I go and black his eyes?"

"You refer to Bartleby, I suppose. No, not today, Turkey," I replied; "pray, put up your fists."

I closed the doors, and again advanced towards Bartleby. I felt additional incentives tempting me to my fate. I burned to be rebelled against again. I remembered that Bartleby never left the office.

"Bartleby," said I, "Ginger Nut is away; just step round to the Post Office, won't you? (it was but a three minutes' walk,) and see if there is anything for me."

"I would prefer not to."

"You *will* not?"

"I *prefer* not."

I staggered to my desk, and sat there in a deep study. My blind inveteracy returned. Was there any other thing in which I could procure myself to be ignominiously repulsed by this lean, penniless wight?—my hired clerk? What added thing is there, perfectly reasonable, that he will be sure to refuse to do?

"Bartleby!"

No answer.

"Bartleby," in a louder tone.

No answer.

"Bartleby," I roared.

Like a very ghost, agreeably to the laws of magical invocation, at the third summons, he appeared at the entrance of his hermitage.

"Go to the next room, and tell Nippers to come to me."

"I prefer not to," he respectfully and slowly said, and mildly disappeared.

"Very good, Bartleby," said I, in a quiet sort of serenely severe self-possessed tone, intimating the unalterable purpose of some terrible retribution very close at hand. At the moment I half intended something of the kind. But upon the whole, as it was drawing towards my dinner-hour, I thought it best to put on my hat and walk home for the day, suffering much from perplexity and distress of mind.

Shall I acknowledge it? The conclusion of this whole business was, that it soon became a fixed fact of my chambers, that a pale young scrivener, by the name of Bartleby, had a desk there; that he copied for me at the usual rate of four cents a folio (one hundred words); but he was permanently exempt from examining the work done by him, that duty being transferred to Turkey and Nippers, out of compliment doubtless to their superior acuteness; moreover, said Bartleby was never on any account to be dispatched on the most trivial errand of any sort; and that even if entreated to take upon him such a matter, it was generally understood that he would "prefer not to"— in other words, that he would refuse point-blank.

As days passed on, I became considerably reconciled to Bartleby. His steadiness, his freedom from all dissipation, his incessant industry (except when he chose to throw himself into a standing revery behind his screen), his great stillness, his unalterableness of demeanor under all circumstances, made him a valuable acquisition. One prime thing was this—*he was always there*—first in the morning, continually through the day, and the last at night. I had a singular confidence in his honesty. I felt my most precious papers perfectly safe in his hands. Sometimes to be sure I could not, for the very soul of me, avoid falling into sudden spasmodic passions with him. For it was exceeding difficult to bear in mind all the time those strange peculiarities, privileges, and unheard of exemptions, forming the tacit stipulations on Bartleby's part under which he remained in my office. Now and then, in the eagerness of dispatching pressing business, I would inadvertently summon Bartleby, in a short, rapid tone, to put his finger, say, on the incipient tie of a bit of red tape with which I was about compressing some papers. Of course, from behind the screen the usual answer, "I prefer not to," was sure to come; and then, how could a human creature with the common infirmities of our nature, refrain from bitterly exclaiming upon such perverseness—such unreasonableness? However, every added repulse of this sort which I received only tended to lessen the probability of my repeating the inadvertence.

Here it must be said, that, according to the custom of most legal gentlemen occupying chambers in densely-populated law buildings, there were several keys to my door. One was kept by a woman residing in the attic, which person weekly scrubbed and daily swept and dusted my apartments. Another was kept by Turkey for convenience sake. The third I sometimes carried in my own pocket. The fourth I knew not who had.

Now, one Sunday morning I happened to go to Trinity Church, to hear a celebrated preacher, and finding myself rather early on the ground, I thought I would walk round to my chambers for a while. Luckily I had my key with me; but upon applying it to the lock, I found it resisted by something inserted from the inside. Quite surprised, I called out; when to my consternation a key was turned from within; and thrusting his lean visage at me, and holding the door ajar, the apparition of Bartleby appeared, in his shirt sleeves, and otherwise in a strangely tattered dishabille, saying quietly that he was sorry, but he was deeply engaged just then, and—preferred not admitting me at present. In a brief word or two, he moreover added, that perhaps I had better walk round the block two or three times, and by that time he would probably have concluded his affairs.

Now, the utterly unsurmised appearance of Bartleby, tenanting my law-chambers of a Sunday morning, with his cadaverously gentlemanly *nonchalance,* yet withal firm and self-possessed, had such a strange effect upon me, that incontinently I slunk away from my own door, and did as desired. But not without sundry twinges of impotent rebellion against the mild effrontery of this unaccountable scrivener. Indeed, it was his wonderful mildness, chiefly, which not only disarmed me, but unmanned me, as it were. For I consider that one, for the time, is sort of unmanned when he tranquilly permits his hired clerk to dictate to him, and order him away from his own premises. Furthermore, I was full of uneasiness as to what Bartleby could possibly be doing in my office in his shirt sleeves, and in an otherwise dismantled condition of a Sunday morning. Was anything amiss going on? Nay, that was out of the question. It was not to be thought of for a moment that Bartleby was an immoral person. But what could he be doing there?—copying? Nay again, whatever might be his eccentricities, Bartleby was an eminently decorous person. He would be the last man to sit down to his desk in any state approaching to nudity. Besides, it was Sunday; and there was something about Bartleby that forbade the supposition that he would by any secular occupation violate the proprieties of the day.

Nevertheless, my mind was not pacified; and full of a restless curiosity, at last I returned to the door. Without hindrance I inserted my key, opened it, and entered. Bartleby was not to be seen. I looked round anxiously, peeped behind his screen; but it was very plain that he was gone. Upon more closely examining the place, I surmised that for an indefinite period Bartleby must have ate, dressed, and slept in my office, and that too without plate, mirror, or bed. The cushioned seat of a rickety old sofa in one corner bore the faint impress of a lean, reclining form. Rolled away under his desk, I found a blanket under the empty grate, a blacking box [10] and brush; on a chair, a tin basin, with soap and a ragged towel; in a newspaper a few crumbs of ginger-nuts and a morsel of cheese. Yes, thought I, it is evident enough that Bartleby has been making his home here, keeping bachelor's hall all by himself. Immediately then the thought came sweeping across me, What miserable friendlessness and loneliness are here revealed! His poverty is great; but his solitude, how horrible! Think of it. Of a Sunday, Wall Street is deserted as Petra; [11] and every night of every day it is an emptiness. This building too, which of weekdays hums with industry and life, at nightfall echoes with sheer vacancy, and all through Sunday is forlorn. And here Bartleby makes his home; sole spectator of a solitude which he has seen all populous—a sort of innocent and transformed Marius brooding among the ruins of Carthage! [12]

For the first time in my life a feeling of overpowering stinging melancholy seized me. Before, I had never experienced aught but a not-unpleasing sadness. The bond of a common humanity now drew me irresistibly to gloom. A fraternal melancholy! For both I and Bartleby were sons of Adam. I remembered the bright silks and sparkling faces I had seen that day, in gala trim, swan-like sailing down the Mississippi of Broadway; and I contrasted them with the pallid copyist, and thought to myself, Ah, happiness courts the light, so we deem the world is gay; but misery hides aloof, so we deem that misery there is none. These sad fancyings—chimeras, doubtless, of a sick and silly brain—led on to other and more special thoughts, concerning the eccentricities of Bartleby. Presentiments of strange discoveries hovered round me. The scrivener's pale form appeared to me laid out, among uncaring strangers, in its shivering winding sheet.

Suddenly I was attracted by Bartleby's closed desk, the key in open sight left in the lock.

I mean no mischief, seek the gratification of no heartless curiosity, thought I; besides, the desk is mine, and its contents too, so I will make bold to look within. Everything was methodically arranged, the papers smoothly placed. The pigeonholes were deep, and removing the files of documents, I groped into their recesses. Presently I felt something there, and dragged it out. It was an old bandanna handkerchief, heavy and knotted. I opened it, and saw it was a savings' bank.

I now recalled all the quiet mysteries which I had noted in the man. I remembered that he never spoke but to answer; that though at intervals he had considerable time to himself, yet I had never seen him reading—no, not even a newspaper; that for

[10] Box of black shoe polish.

[11] Ancient city, long in ruins, in present state of Jordan. At one time it had been a major center of caravan routes and trade.

[12] Roman general and consul Gaius Marius (ca. 155-86 B.C.), having lost his power and exiled from Rome by Sulla in 88 B.C., brooded among the ruins of Carthage.

long periods he would stand looking out, at his pale window behind the screen, upon the dead brick wall; I was quite sure he never visited any refectory or eating house; while his pale face clearly indicated that he never drank beer like Turkey, or tea and coffee even, like other men; that he never went anywhere in particular that I could learn; never went out for a walk, unless indeed that was the case at present; that he had declined telling who he was, or whence he came, or whether he had any relatives in the world; that though so thin and pale, he never complained of ill health. And more than all, I remembered a certain unconscious air of pallid—how shall I call it?—of pallid haughtiness, say, or rather an austere reserve about him, which had positively awed me into my tame compliance with his eccentricities, when I had feared to ask him to do the slightest incidental thing for me, even though I might know, from his long-continued motionlessness, that behind his screen he must be standing in one of those dead-wall reveries of his.

Revolving all these things, and coupling them with the recently discovered fact, that he made my office his constant abiding place and home, and not forgetful of his morbid moodiness; revolving all these things, a prudential feeling began to steal over me. My first emotions had been those of pure melancholy and sincerest pity; but just in proportion as the forlornness of Bartleby grew and grew to my imagination, did that same melancholy merge into fear, that pity into repulsion. So true it is, and so terrible, too, that up to a certain point the thought or sight of misery enlists our best affections; but, in certain special cases, beyond that point it does not. They err who would assert that invariably this is owing to the inherent selfishness of the human heart. It rather proceeds from a certain hopelessness of remedying excessive and organic ill. To a sensitive being, pity is not seldom pain. And when at last it is perceived that such pity cannot lead to effectual succor, common sense bids the soul be rid of it. What I saw that morning persuaded me that the scrivener was the victim of innate and incurable disorder. I might give alms to his body; but his body did not pain him; it was his soul that suffered, and his soul I could not reach.

I did not accomplish the purpose of going to Trinity Church that morning. Somehow, the things I had seen disqualified me for the time from churchgoing. I walked homeward, thinking what I would do with Bartleby. Finally, I resolved upon this—I would put certain calm questions to him the next morning, touching his history, etc., and if he declined to answer them openly and unreservedly (and I supposed he would prefer not), then to give him a twenty-dollar bill over and above whatever I might owe him, and tell him his services were no longer required; but that if in any other way I could assist him, I would be happy to do so, especially if he desired to return to his native place, wherever that might be, I would willingly help to defray the expenses. Moreover, if, after reaching home, he found himself at any time in want of aid, a letter from him would be sure of a reply.

The next morning came.

"Bartleby," said I, gently calling to him behind his screen.

No reply.

"Bartleby," said I, in a still gentler tone, "come here; I am not going to ask you to do anything you would prefer not to do—I simply wish to speak to you."

Upon this he noiselessly slid into view.

"Will you tell me, Bartleby, where you were born?"

"I would prefer not to."

"Will you tell me *anything* about yourself?"

"I would prefer not to."

"But what reasonable objection can you have to speak to me? I feel friendly towards you."

He did not look at me while I spoke, but kept his glance fixed upon my bust of Cicero, which, as I then sat, was directly behind me, some six inches above my head.

"What is your answer, Bartleby?" said I, after waiting a considerable time for a reply, during which his countenance remained immovable, only there was the faintest conceivable tremor of the white attenuated mouth.

"At present I prefer to give no answer," he said, and retired into his hermitage.

It was rather weak in me I confess, but his manner, on this occasion, nettled me. Not only did there seem to lurk in it a certain calm disdain, but his perverseness seemed ungrateful, considering the undeniable good usage and indulgence he had received from me.

Again I sat ruminating what I should do. Mortified as I was at his behavior, and resolved as I had been to dismiss him when I entered my office, nevertheless I strangely felt something superstitious knocking at my heart, and forbidding me to carry out my purpose, and denouncing me for a villain if I dared to breathe one bitter word against this forlornest of mankind. At last, familiarly drawing my chair behind his screen, I sat down and said: "Bartleby, never mind then about revealing your history; but let me entreat you, as a friend, to comply as far as may be with the usages of this office. Say now, you will help to examine papers tomorrow or next day: in short, say now, that in a day or two you will begin to be a little reasonable:—say so, Bartleby."

"At present I would prefer not to be a little reasonable," was his mildly cadaverous reply.

Just then the folding-doors opened, and Nippers approached. He seemed suffering from an unusually bad night's rest, induced by severer indigestion than common. He overheard those final words of Bartleby.

"*Prefer not,* eh?" gritted Nippers—"I'd *prefer* him, if I were you, sir," addressing me—"I'd *prefer* him; I'd give him preferences, the stubborn mule! What is it, sir, pray, that he *prefers* not to do now?"

Bartleby moved not a limb.

"Mr. Nippers," said I, "I'd prefer that you would withdraw for the present."

Somehow, of late I had got into the way of involuntarily using this word "prefer" upon all sorts of not exactly suitable occasions. And I trembled to think that my contact with the scrivener had already and seriously affected me in a mental way. And what further and deeper aberration might it not yet produce? This apprehension had not been without efficacy in determining me to summary means.

As Nippers, looking very sour and sulky, was departing, Turkey blandly and deferentially approached.

"With submission, sir," said he, "yesterday I was thinking about Bartleby here, and I think that if he would but prefer to take a quart of good ale every day, it would do much towards mending him and enabling him to assist in examining his papers."

"So you have got the word, too," said I, slightly excited.

"With submission, what word, sir?" asked Turkey, respectfully crowding himself into the contracted space behind the screen, and by so doing, making me jostle the scrivener. "What word, sir?"

"I would prefer to be left alone here," said Bartleby, as if offended at being mobbed in his privacy.

"*That's* the word, Turkey," said I—"*that's* it."

"Oh, *prefer?* oh yes—queer word. I never use it myself. But, sir, as I was saying, if he would but prefer—"

"Turkey," interrupted I, "you will please withdraw."

"Oh certainly, sir, if you prefer that I should."

As he opened the folding-door to retire, Nippers at his desk caught a glimpse of me, and asked whether I would prefer to have a certain paper copied on blue paper or white. He did not in the least roguishly accent the word *prefer.* It was plain that it involuntarily rolled from his tongue. I thought to myself, surely I must get rid of a demented man, who already has in some degree turned the tongues, if not the heads of myself and clerks. But I thought it prudent not to break the dismission at once.

The next day I noticed that Bartleby did nothing but stand at his window in his dead-wall revery. Upon asking him why he did not write, he said that he had decided upon doing no more writing.

"Why, how now? what next?" exclaimed I, "do no more writing?"

"No more."

"And what is the reason?"

"Do you not see the reason for yourself," he indifferently replied.

I looked steadfastly at him, and perceived that his eyes looked dull and glazed. Instantly it occurred to me, that his unexampled diligence in copying by his dim window for the first few weeks of his stay with me might have temporarily impaired his vision.

I was touched. I said something in condolence with him. I hinted that of course he did wisely in abstaining from writing for a while; and urged him to embrace that opportunity of taking wholesome exercise in the open air. This, however, he did not do. A few days after this, my other clerks being absent, and being in a great hurry to dispatch certain letters by the mail, I thought that, having nothing else earthly to do, Bartleby would surely be less inflexible than usual, and carry these letters to the post office. But he blankly declined. So, much to my inconvenience, I went myself.

Still added days went by. Whether Bartleby's eyes improved or not, I could not say. To all appearance, I thought they did. But when I asked him if they did, he vouchsafed no answer. At all events, he would do no copying. At last, in reply to my urgings, he informed me that he had permanently given up copying.

"What!" exclaimed I; "suppose your eyes should get entirely well—better than ever before—would you not copy then?"

"I have given up copying," he answered, and slid aside.

He remained, as ever, a fixture in my chamber. Nay—if that were possible—he became still more of a fixture than before. What was to be done? He would do nothing in the office: why should he stay there? In plain fact, he had now become a millstone to me, not only useless as a necklace, but afflictive to bear. Yet I was sorry for him. I speak less than truth when I say that, on his own account, he occasioned me uneasiness. If he would but have named a single relative or friend, I would instantly have written, and urged their taking the poor fellow away to some convenient retreat. But he seemed alone, absolutely alone in the universe. A bit of wreck in the mid-Atlantic. At length, necessities connected with my business tyrannized over all other considerations. Decently as I could, I told Bartleby that in six days' time he must unconditionally leave the office. I wanted him to take measures, in the interval, for procuring some other abode. I offered to assist him in this endeavor, if he himself would but take the first step towards a removal. "And when you finally quit me, Bartleby," added I, "I shall see that you go not away entirely unprovided. Six days from this hour, remember."

At the expiration of that period, I peeped behind the screen, and lo! Bartleby was there.

I buttoned up my coat, balanced myself; advanced slowly towards him, touched his shoulder, and said, "The time has come; you must quit this place; I am sorry for you; here is money; but you must go."

"I would prefer not," he replied, with his back still towards me.

"You *must*."

He remained silent.

Now I had an unbounded confidence in this man's common honesty. He had frequently restored to me sixpences and shillings carelessly dropped upon the floor, for I am apt to be very reckless in such shirt-button affairs. The proceeding then which followed will not be deemed extraordinary.

"Bartleby," said I, "I owe you twelve dollars on account; here are thirty-two; the odd twenty are yours.—Will you take it?" and I handed the bills towards him.

But he made no notion.

"I will leave them here then," putting them under a weight on the table. Then taking my hat and cane and going to the door I tranquilly turned and added—"After you have removed your things from these offices, Bartleby, you will of course lock the door—since everyone is now gone for the day but you—and if you please, slip your key underneath the mat, so that I may have it in the morning. I shall not see you again; so good-bye to you. If hereafter in your new place of abode I can be of any service to you, do not fail to advise me by letter. Goodbye, Bartleby, and fare you well."

But he answered not a word; like the last column of some ruined temple, he remained standing mute and solitary in the middle of the otherwise deserted room.

As I walked home in a pensive mood, my vanity got the better of my pity. I could not but highly plume myself on my masterly management in getting rid of Bartleby. Masterly I call it, and such it must appear to any dispassionate thinker. The beauty of my procedure seemed to consist in its perfect quietness. There was no vulgar bullying, no bravado of any sort, no choleric hectoring, and striding to and fro across the apartment, jerking out vehement commands for Bartleby to bundle himself off with his beggarly traps.[13] Nothing of the kind. Without loudly bidding Bartleby depart—as an inferior genius might have done—I *assumed* the ground that depart he must; and upon the assumption built all I had to say. The more I thought over my procedure, the more I was charmed with it. Nevertheless, next morning, upon awakening, I had my doubts—I had somehow slept off the fumes of vanity. One of the coolest and wisest hours a man has is just after he awakes in the morning. My procedure seemed as sagacious as ever,—but only in theory. How it would prove in practice—there was the rub. It was truly a beautiful thought to have assumed Bartleby's departure; but, after all, that assumption was simply my own, and none of Bartleby's. The great point was, not whether I had assumed that he would quit me, but whether he would prefer to do so. He was more a man of preferences than assumptions.

After breakfast, I walked downtown, arguing the probabilities *pro* and *con.* One moment I thought it would prove a miserable failure, and Bartleby would be found all alive at my office as usual; the next moment it seemed certain that I should see his

---

[13] Personal belongings, luggage.

chair empty. And so I kept veering about. At the corner of Broadway and Canal Street, I saw quite an excited group of people standing in earnest conversation.

"I'll take odds he doesn't," said a voice as I passed.

"Doesn't go?—done!" said I, "put up your money."

I was instinctively putting my hand in my pocket to produce my own, when I remembered that this was an election day. The words I had overheard bore no reference to Bartleby, but to the success or nonsuccess of some candidate for the mayoralty. In my intent frame of mind, I had, as it were, imagined that all Broadway shared in my excitement, and were debating the same question with me. I passed on, very thankful that the uproar of the street screened my momentary absent-mindedness.

As I had intended, I was earlier than usual at my office door. I stood listening for a moment. All was still. He must be gone. I tried the knob. The door was locked. Yes, my procedure had worked to a charm; he indeed must be vanished. Yet a certain melancholy mixed with this: I was almost sorry for my brilliant success. I was fumbling under the door mat for the key, which Bartleby was to have left there for me, when accidentally my knee knocked against a panel, producing a summoning sound, and in response a voice came to me from within—"Not yet; I am occupied."

It was Bartleby.

I was thunderstruck. For an instant I stood like the man who, pipe in mouth, was killed one cloudless afternoon long ago in Virginia, by summer lightning; at his own warm open window he was killed, and remained leaning out there upon the dreamy afternoon, till some one touched him, when he fell.

"Not gone!" I murmured at last. But again obeying the wondrous ascendancy which the inscrutable scrivener had over me, and from which ascendancy, for all my chafing, I could not completely escape, I slowly went downstairs and out into the street, and while walking round the block, considered what I should next do in this unheard-of perplexity. Turn the man out by an actual thrusting I could not; to drive him away by calling him hard names would not do; calling in the police was an unpleasant idea; and yet, permit him to enjoy his cadaverous triumph over me—this, too, I could not think of. What was to be done? or, if nothing could be done, was there anything further that I could *assume* in the matter? Yes, as before I had prospectively assumed that Bartleby would depart, so now I might retrospectively assume that departed he was. In the legitimate carrying out of this assumption, I might enter my office in a great hurry, and pretending not to see Bartleby at all, walk straight against him as if he were air. Such a proceeding would in a singular degree have the appearance of a homethrust. It was hardly possible that Bartleby could withstand such an application of the doctrine of assumptions. But upon second thoughts the success of the plan seemed rather dubious. I resolved to argue the matter over with him again.

"Bartleby," said I, entering the office, with a quietly severe expression, "I am seriously displeased. I am pained, Bartleby. I had thought better of you. I had imagined you of such a gentlemanly organization, that in any delicate dilemma a slight hint would suffice—in short, an assumption. But it appears I am deceived. Why," I added, unaffectedly starting, "you have not even touched that money yet," pointing to it, just where I had left it the evening previous.

He answered nothing.

"Will you, or will you not, quit me?" I now demanded in a sudden passion, advancing close to him.

"I would prefer *not* to quit you," he replied gently emphasizing the *not.*

"What earthly right have you to stay here? Do you pay any rent? Do you pay my taxes? Or is this property yours?"

He answered nothing.

"Are you ready to go on and write now? Are your eyes recovered? Could you copy a small paper for me this morning? or help examine a few lines? or step round to the post office? In a word, will you do anything at all, to give a coloring to your refusal to depart the premises?"

He silently retired into his hermitage.

I was now in such a state of nervous resentment that I thought it but prudent to check myself at present from further demonstrations. Bartleby and I were alone. I remembered the tragedy of the unfortunate Adams and the still more unfortunate Colt[14] in the solitary office of the latter; and how poor Colt, being dreadfully incensed by Adams, and imprudently permitting himself to get wildly excited, was at unawares hurried into his fatal act—an act which certainly no man could possibly deplore more than the actor himself. Often it had occurred to me in my ponderings upon the subject, that had that altercation taken place in the public street, or at a private residence, it would not have terminated as it did. It was the circumstance of being alone in a solitary office, up stairs, of a building entirely unhallowed by humanizing domestic associations—an uncarpeted office, doubtless, of a dusty, haggard sort of appearance—this it must have been, which greatly helped to enhance the irritable desperation of the hapless Colt.

But when this old Adam of resentment rose in me and tempted me concerning Bartleby, I grappled him and threw him. How? Why, simply by recalling the divine injunction: "A new commandment give I unto you, that ye love one another." Yes, this it was that saved me. Aside from higher considerations, charity often operates as a vastly wise and prudent principle—a great safeguard to its possessor. Men have committed murder for jealousy's sake, and anger's sake, and hatred's sake, and selfishness's sake, and spiritual pride's sake; but no man that ever I heard of, ever committed a diabolical murder for sweet charity's sake. Mere self-interest, then, if no better motive can be enlisted, should, especially with high-tempered men, prompt all beings to charity and philanthropy. At any rate, upon the occasion in question, I strove to drown my exasperated feelings towards the scrivener by benevolently construing his conduct. Poor fellow, poor fellow! thought I, he don't mean anything; and besides, he has seen hard times, and ought to be indulged.

I endeavored also immediately to occupy myself, and at the same time to comfort my despondency. I tried to fancy that in the course of the morning, at such time as might prove agreeable to him, Bartleby, of his own free accord, would emerge from his hermitage, and take up some decided line of march in the direction of the door. But no. Half-past twelve o'clock came; Turkey began to glow in the face, overturn his inkstand, and become generally obstreperous; Nippers abated down into quietude and courtesy; Ginger Nut munched his noon apple; and Bartleby remained standing at his window in one of his profoundest dead-wall reveries. Will it be credited? Ought I to acknowledge it? That afternoon I left the office without saying one further word to him.

Some days now passed, during which, at leisure intervals I looked a little into

---

[14] Celebrated New York murder case in 1841. John C. Colt, brother of the famous gun manufacturer, killed Samuel Adams, a printer, with a heavy blow on the head.

"Edwards on the Will," and "Priestley on Necessity."[15] Under the circumstances, those books induced a salutary feeling. Gradually I slid into the persuasion that these troubles of mine touching the scrivener, had been all predestinated from eternity, and Bartleby was billeted upon me for some mysterious purpose of an all-wise Providence, which it was not for a mere mortal like me to fathom. Yes, Bartleby, stay there behind your screen, thought I; I shall persecute you no more; you are harmless and noiseless as any of these old chairs; in short, I never feel so private as when I know you are here. At last I see it, I feel it; I penetrate to the predestinated purpose of my life. I am content. Others may have loftier parts to enact; but my mission in this world, Bartleby, is to furnish you with office-room for such period as you may see fit to remain.

I believe that this wise and blessed frame of mind would have continued with me, had it not been for the unsolicited and uncharitable remarks obtruded upon me by my professional friends who visited the rooms. But thus it often is, that the constant friction of illiberal minds wears out at last the best resolves of the more generous. Though to be sure, when I reflected upon it, it was not strange that people entering my office should be struck by the peculiar aspect of the unaccountable Bartleby, and so be tempted to throw out some sinister observations concerning him. Sometimes an attorney having business with me, and calling at my office, and finding no one but the scrivener there, would undertake to obtain some sort of precise information from him touching my whereabouts; but without heeding his idle talk, Bartleby would remain standing immovable in the middle of the room. So after contemplating him in that position for a time, the attorney would depart, no wiser than he came.

Also, when a Reference[16] was going on, and the room full of lawyers and witnesses and business was driving fast, some deeply occupied legal gentleman present, seeing Bartleby wholly unemployed, would request him to run round to his (the legal gentleman's) office and fetch some papers for him. Thereupon, Bartleby would tranquilly decline, and yet remain idle as before. Then the lawyer would give a great stare, and turn to me. And what could I say? At last I was made aware that all through the circle of my professional acquaintance, a whisper of wonder was running round, having reference to the strange creature I kept at my office. This worried me very much. And as the idea came upon me of his possibly turning out a long-lived man, and keep occupying my chambers, and denying my authority; and perplexing my visitors; and scandalizing my professional reputation; and casting a general gloom over the premises; keeping soul and body together to the last upon his savings (for doubtless he spent but half a dime a day), and in the end perhaps outlive me, and claim possession of my office by right of his perpetual occupancy: as all these dark anticipations crowded upon me more and more, and my friends continually intruded their relentless remarks upon the apparition in my room; a great change was wrought in me. I resolved to gather all my faculties together, and forever rid me of this intolerable incubus.

Ere resolving any complicated project, however, adapted to this end, I first simply suggested to Bartleby the propriety of his permanent departure. In a calm and serious tone, I commended the idea to his careful and mature consideration. But having taken three days to meditate upon it, he appraised me that his original determination remained the same; in short, that he still preferred to abide with me.

[15] New England Theologian Jonathan Edwards (1703-1758) argued in *The Freedom of the Will* (1754) that the human will is not free, but subject. Joseph Priestley (1733-1803) was an English clergyman, scientist, and philosopher who also maintained the bondage of the will.

[16] Consultation or committee meeting.

What shall I do? I now said to myself, buttoning up my coat to the last button. What shall I do? what ought I to do? what does conscience say I *should* do with this man, or rather ghost. Rid myself of him, I must; go, he shall. But how? You will not thrust him, the poor, pale, passive mortal—you will not thrust such a helpless creature out of your door? you will not dishonor yourself by such cruelty? No, I will not, I cannot do that. Rather would I let him live and die here, and then mason up his remains in the wall. What then will you do? For all your coaxing, he will not budge. Bribes he leaves under your own paperweight on your table; in short, it is quite plain that he prefers to cling to you.

Then something severe, something unusual must be done. What! surely you will not have him collared by a constable, and commit his innocent pallor to the common jail? And upon what ground could you procure such a thing to be done?—a vagrant, is he? What! he a vagrant, a wanderer, who refuses to budge? It is because he will *not* be a vagrant then, that you seek to count him *as* a vagrant. That is too absurd. No visible means of support: there I have him. Wrong again: for indubitably he *does* support himself, and that is the only unanswerable proof that any man can show of his possessing the means so to do. No more then. Since he will not quit me, I must quit him. I will change my offices; I will move elsewhere; and give him fair notice, that if I find him on my new premises I will then proceed against him as a common trespasser.

Acting accordingly, next day I thus addressed him: "I find these chambers too far from the City Hall; the air is unwholesome. In a word, I propose to remove my offices next week, and shall no longer require your services. I tell you this now, in order that you may seek another place."

He made no reply, and nothing more was said.

On the appointed day I engaged carts and men, proceeded to my chambers, and having but little furniture, everything was removed in a few hours. Throughout, the scrivener remained standing behind the screen, which I directed to be removed the last thing. It was withdrawn; and being folded up like a huge folio, left him the motionless occupant of a naked room. I stood in the entry watching him a moment, while something from within me upbraided me.

I re-entered, with my hand in my pocket—and—and my heart in my mouth.

"Good-bye, Bartleby; I am going—good-bye, and God some way bless you; and take that," slipping something in his hand. But it dropped upon the floor, and then—strange to say—I tore myself from him whom I had so longed to be rid of.

Established in my new quarters, for a day or two I kept the door locked, and started at every footfall in the passages. When I returned to my rooms after any little absence, I would pause at the threshold for an instant, and attentively listen, ere applying my key. But these fears were needless. Bartleby never came nigh me.

I thought all was going well, when a perturbed-looking stranger visited me, inquiring whether I was the person who had recently occupied rooms at No.—Wall Street.

Full of forebodings, I replied that I was.

"Then sir," said the stranger, who proved a lawyer, "you are responsible for the man you left there. He refuses to do any copying; he refuses to do anything; he says he prefers not to; and he refuses to quit the premises."

"I am very sorry, sir," said I, with assumed tranquillity, but an inward tremor, "but, really, the man you allude to is nothing to me—he is no relation or apprentice of mine, that you should hold me responsible for him."

"In mercy's name, who is he?"

"I certainly cannot inform you. I know nothing about him. Formerly I employed him as a copyist; but he has done nothing for me now for some time past."

"I shall settle him then—good morning, sir."

Several days passed, and I heard nothing more, and though I often felt a charitable prompting to call at the place and see poor Bartleby, yet a certain squeamishness of I know not what withheld me.

All is over with him, by this time, thought I at last, when through another week no further intelligence reached me. But coming to my room the day after, I found several persons waiting at my door in a high state of nervous excitement.

"That's the man—here he comes," cried the foremost one, whom I recognized as the lawyer who had previously called upon me alone.

"You must take him away, sir, at once," cried a portly person among them, advancing upon me, and whom I knew to be the landlord of No.—Wall Street. "These gentlemen, my tenants, cannot stand it any longer; Mr. B ———" pointing to the lawyer, "has turned him out of his room, and he now persists in haunting the building generally, sitting upon the banisters of the stairs by day, and sleeping in the entry by night. Everybody is concerned; clients are leaving the offices; some fears are entertained of a mob; something you must do, and that without delay."

Aghast at this torrent, I fell back before it, and would fain have locked myself in my new quarters. In vain I persisted that Bartleby was nothing to me—no more than to anyone else. In vain—I was the last person known to have anything to do with him, and they held me to the terrible account. Fearful, then, of being exposed in the papers (as one person present obscurely threatened) I considered the matter, and at length said, that if the lawyer would give me a confidential interview with the scrivener, in his (the lawyer's) own room, I would that afternoon strive my best to rid them of the nuisance they complained of.

Going upstairs to my old haunt, there was Bartleby silently sitting upon the banister at the landing.

"What are you doing here, Bartleby?" said I.

"Sitting upon the banister," he mildly replied.

I motioned him into the lawyer's room, who then left us.

"Bartleby," said I, "are you aware that you are the cause of great tribulation to me, by persisting in occupying the entry after being dismissed from the office?"

No answer.

"Now one of two things must take place. Either you must do something, or something must be done to you. Now what sort of business would you like to engage in? Would you like to re-engage in copying for someone?"

"No; I would prefer not to make any change."

"Would you like a clerkship in a drygoods store?"

"There is too much confinement about that. No, I would not like a clerkship; but I am not particular."

"Too much confinement," I cried, "why you keep yourself confined all the time!"

"I would prefer not to take a clerkship," he rejoined, as if to settle that little item at once.

"How would a bartender's business suit you? There is no trying of eyesight in that."

"I would not like it at all; though, as I said before, I am not particular."

His unwonted wordiness inspirited me. I returned to the charge.

"Well, then, would you like to travel through the country collecting bills for the merchants? That would improve your health."

"No, I would prefer to be doing something else."

"How then would going as a companion to Europe, to entertain some young gentleman with your conversation,—how would that suit you?"

"Not at all. It does not strike me that there is anything definite about that. I like to be stationary. But I am not particular."

"Stationary you shall be then," I cried, now losing all patience, and for the first time in all my exasperating connection with him fairly flying into a passion. "If you do not go away from these premises before night, I shall feel bound—indeed I *am* bound—to—to—to quit the premises myself!" I rather absurdly concluded, knowing not with what possible threat to try to frighten his immobility into compliance. Despairing of all further efforts, I was precipitately leaving him, when a final thought occurred to me—one which had not been wholly unindulged before.

"Bartleby," said I, in the kindest tone I could assume under such exciting circumstances, "will you go home with me now—not to my office, but my dwelling—and remain there till we can conclude upon some convenient arrangement for you at our leisure? Come, let us start now, right away."

"No: at present I would prefer not to make any change at all."

I answered nothing; but, effectually dodging everyone by the suddenness and rapidity of my flight, rushed from the building, ran up Wall Street toward Broadway, and jumping into the first omnibus was soon removed from pursuit. As soon as tranquillity returned I distinctly perceived that I had now done all that I possibly could, both in respect to the demands of the landlord and his tenants, and with regard to my own desire and sense of duty, to benefit Bartleby, and shield him from rude persecution. I now strove to be entirely carefree and quiescent; and my conscience justified me in the attempt; though, indeed, it was not so successful as I could have wished. So fearful was I of being again hunted out by the incensed landlord and his exasperated tenants, that, surrendering my business to Nippers, for a few days, I drove about the upper part of the town and through the suburbs, in my rockaway; crossed over to Jersey City and Hoboken, and paid fugitive visits to Manhattanville and Astoria. In fact I almost lived in my rockaway for the time.

When again I entered my office, lo, a note from the landlord lay upon the desk. I opened it with trembling hands. It informed me that the writer had sent to the police, and had Bartleby removed to the Tombs as a vagrant. Moreover, since I knew more about him than anyone else, he wished me to appear at that place, and make a suitable statement of the facts. These tidings had a conflicting effect upon me. At first I was indignant; but at last almost approved. The landlord's energetic, summary disposition had led him to adopt a procedure which I do not think I would have decided upon myself; and yet, as a last resort, under such peculiar circumstances, it seemed the only plan.

As I afterwards learned, the poor scrivener, when told that he must be conducted to the Tombs, offered not the slightest obstacle, but in his pale unmoving way, silently acquiesced.

Some of the compassionate and curious bystanders joined the party; and headed by one of the constables arm in arm with Bartleby, the silent procession filed its way through all the noise, and heat, and joy of the roaring thoroughfares at noon.

The same day I received the note I went to the Tombs, or to speak more properly, the Halls of Justice. Seeking the right officer, I stated the purpose of my call, and was

informed that the individual I described was indeed within. I then assured the func-
tionary that Bartleby was a perfectly honest man, and greatly to be compassionated,
however unaccountably eccentric. I narrated all I knew, and closed by suggesting the
idea of letting him remain in as indulgent confinement as possible till something less
harsh might be done—though indeed I hardly knew what. At all events, if nothing else
could be decided upon, the alms-house must receive him. I then begged to have an
interview.

Being under no disgraceful charge, and quite serene and harmless in all his ways,
they had permitted him freely to wander about the prison, and especially in the in-
closed glass-platted yards thereof. And so I found him there, standing all alone in the
quietest of the yards, his face towards a high wall, while all around, from the narrow
slits of the jail windows, I thought I saw peering out upon him the eyes of murderers
and thieves.

"Bartleby!"

"I know you," he said, without looking round—"and I want nothing to say to
you."

"It was not I that brought you here, Bartleby," said I, keenly pained at his
implied suspicion. "And to you, this should not be so vile a place. Nothing reproachful
attaches to you by being here. And see, it is not so sad a place as one might think.
Look, there is the sky, and here is the grass."

"I know where I am," he replied, but would say nothing more, and so I left him.

As I entered the corridor again, a broad meat-like man, in an apron, accosted me,
and jerking his thumb over his shoulder said—"Is that your friend?"

"Yes."

"Does he want to starve? If he does, let him live on the prison fare, that's all."

"Who are you?" asked I, not knowing what to make of such an officially-speaking
person in such a place.

"I am the grub-man. Such gentlemen as have friends here, hire me to provide
them with something good to eat."

"Is this so?" said I, turning to the turnkey.

He said it was.

"Well then," said I, slipping some silver into the grub-man's hands (for so they
called him). "I want you to give particular attention to my friend there; let him have
the best dinner you can get. And you must be as polite to him as possible."

"Introduce me, will you?" said the grub-man, looking at me with an expression
which seemed to say he was all impatience for an opportunity to give a specimen of his
breeding.

Thinking it would prove of benefit to the scrivener, I acquiesced; and asking the
grub-man his name, went up with him to Bartleby.

"Bartleby, this is a friend; you will find him very useful to you."

"Your sarvant, sir, your sarvant," said the grub-man, making a low salutation
behind his apron. "Hope you find it pleasant here, sir—nice grounds—cool apartments—hope you'll stay with us some time—try to make it agreeable. What will you
have for dinner to-day?"

"I prefer not to dine today," said Bartleby, turning away. "It would disagree with
me; I am unused to dinners." So saying he slowly moved to the other side of the
inclosure, and took up a position fronting the dead-wall.

"How's this?" said the grub-man, addressing me with a stare of astonishment. "He's odd, ain't he?"

"I think he is a little deranged," said I, sadly.

"Deranged? deranged is it? Well now, upon my word, I thought that friend of yourn was a gentleman forger; they are always pale and genteel-like, them forgers. I can't help pity 'em—can't help it, sir. Did you know Monroe Edwards?" he added touchingly, and paused. Then, laying his hand piteously on my shoulder, sighed, "he died of consumption at Sing Sing. So you weren't acquainted with Monroe?"

"No, I was never socially acquainted with any forgers. But I cannot stop longer. Look to my friend yonder. You will not lose by it. I will see you again."

Some few days after this, I again obtained admission to the Tombs, and went through the corridors in quest of Bartleby; but without finding him.

"I saw him coming from his cell not long ago," said a turnkey, "maybe he's gone to loiter in the yards."

So I went in that direction.

"Are you looking for the silent man?" said another turnkey, passing me. "Yonder he lies—sleeping in the yard there. 'Tis not twenty minutes since I saw him lie down."

The yard was entirely quiet. It was not accessible to the common prisoners. The surrounding walls, of amazing thickness, kept off all sounds behind them. The Egyptian character of the masonry weighed upon me with its gloom. But a soft imprisoned turf grew under foot. The heart of the eternal pyramids, it seemed, wherein, by some strange magic, through the clefts, grass-seed, dropped by birds, had sprung.

Strangely huddled at the base of the wall, his knees drawn up, and lying by his side, his head touching the cold stones, I saw the wasted Bartleby. But nothing stirred. I paused; then went close up to him; stooped over, and saw that his dim eyes were open; otherwise he seemed profoundly sleeping. Something prompted me to touch him. I felt his hand, when a tingling shiver ran up my arm and down my spine to my feet.

The round face of the grub-man peered upon me now. "His dinner is ready. Won't he dine to-day, either? Or does he live without dining?"

"Lives without dining," said I, and closed the eyes.

"Eh!—He's asleep, ain't he?"

"With kings and counsellors,"[17] murmured I.

There would seem little need for proceeding further in this history. Imagination will readily supply the meager recital of poor Bartleby's interment. But, ere parting with the reader, let me say, that if this little narrative has sufficiently interested him, to awaken curiosity as to who Bartleby was, and what manner of life he led prior to the present narrator's making his acquaintance, I can only reply, that in such curiosity I fully share, but am wholly unable to gratify it. Yet here I hardly know whether I should divulge one little item of rumor, which came to my ear a few months after the scrivener's decease. Upon what basis it rested, I could never ascertain; and hence, how true it is I cannot now tell. But inasmuch as this vague report has not been without a certain suggestive interest to me, however sad, it may prove the same with others; and so I will briefly mention it. The report was this: that Bartleby had been a subordinate clerk in the Dead Letter Office at Washington, from which he had been suddenly

---

[17] See *Job* 3:13-14: " . . . then had I been at rest, With kings and counsellors of the earth, which built desolate places for themselves."

removed by a change in the administration. When I think over this rumor, I cannot adequately express the emotions which seize me. Dead letters! does it not sound like dead men? Conceive a man by nature and misfortune prone to a pallid hopelessness, can any business seem more fitted to heighten it than that of continually handling these dead letters, and assorting them for the flames? For by the cartload they are annually burned. Sometimes from out the folded paper the pale clerk takes a ring:— the finger it was meant for, perhaps, molders in the grave; a banknote sent in swiftest charity—he whom it would relieve, nor eats nor hungers any more; pardon for those who died despairing; hope for those who died unhoping; good tidings for those who died stifled by unrelieved calamities. On errands of life, these letters speed to death.

    Ah, Bartleby! Ah, humanity!

Gustave Flaubert (1821–1880)

Flaubert led a singularly uneventful life, except in a literary sense. As a result of a nervous seizure (then diagnosed as epilepsy) in 1844, he retired as a young man to the little Normandy town of Le Croisset and there lived almost as a hermit, devoting himself to writing. Being a man of means, he did not have to rush into print, and his friends dissuaded him from publishing his first efforts—which were in a romantic and semi-autobiographic vein, like his later-published *Salammbô* (1862) and *La Tentation de Saint-Antoine* (1874). They urged him to turn from romance to realism: to turn from fictionalizing a dim past and his own fantasies to the everyday, bourgeois life of a Normandy town. The result was *Madame Bovary* (1857), a novel that made him famous and infamous at once. Though Flaubert was bourgeois himself, he hated the commercialism, vulgarity, and prudery of his own class; and some members of that class saw in the book's realism only "a heap of manure," and sued him for immorality. But others, more discerning, hailed the book as a masterpiece, and it established Flaubert as a seminal influence on later writers. As the poet Alan Tate has said, Flaubert "created modern fiction." His attention to style, to *le mot juste,* to precisely observed detail, set a standard of perfection in fiction that permitted critics thereafter to think of the novel as an art form (as had not been the case before). Baudelaire, imaginatively reconstructing what went on in Flaubert's mind as he composed the book, wrote:

> We shall employ a style that is terse, vivid, subtle, and exact on a subject that is banal. We shall imprison the most burning and passionate feelings within the most commonplace intrigue. The most solemn utterances will come from the most imbecile mouths.

    These same effects are all apparent in the short novel "A Simple Heart," that appeared in *Trois Contes* in 1876. But, style apart, there is warmth and humanity here which the polished, perhaps too polished, *Madame Bovary* lacks. Though Flaubert was a furious anti-democrat and snob and could write (in a time of radical change), "I detest my fellow-beings and do not feel that I am their fellow at all," these feelings seem muted in the story. In the ancient serving-woman Félicité, whose life is almost as eventless as Flaubert's own, he finds a nobility beyond the reach of the corrupted middle classes. Yet even here, Flaubert holds Félicité at a great distance, as a specimen, an object to be pitied—which is to say he also holds himself at a great distance, detached: "the artist," he writes, "ought not to appear in his work any more than God in nature." Flaubert does not moralize, he lets the tale speak for itself; and in the emblem (see pp. 8, 22) of the parrot, literally the one bright spot in Félicité's gray and exploited life, we both enter the dignity of her suffering and transcend it—until at the end the bird has become for her (and for us) a religious symbol, almost literally a bird of paradise.

But if there is something self-effacing in Flaubert's furious perfectionism, there is also something nihilistic: "What seems beautiful to me," he writes, "what I should like to write, is a book about nothing, a book dependent on nothing external, which would be held together by the strength of its style, just as the earth, suspended in the void, depends on nothing external for its support. . . ." "A Simple Heart" is not that book, but it is interesting that this master of realism should come so close to voicing the credo of the anti-realists with which this collection ends. Flaubert to the last was a conflicted man, as seen in his effort to make his prose "as rhythmical as verse and as precise as the language of science." The "epilepsy" that visited him as a youth plagued him all his life; he died suddenly in 1880, apparently of a cerebral hemorrhage.

A Simple Heart

1

For half a century the women of Pont-l'Évêque envied Mme Aubain her maidservant Félicité.

In return for a hundred francs a year she did all the cooking and the housework, the sewing, the washing, and the ironing. She could bridle a horse, fatten poultry, and churn butter, and she remained faithful to her mistress, who was by no means an easy person to get on with.

Mme Aubain had married a young fellow who was goodlooking but badly-off, and who died at the beginning of 1809, leaving her with two small children and a pile of debts. She then sold all her property except for the farms of Toucques and Geffosses, which together brought in five thousand francs a year at the most, and left her house at Saint-Melaine for one behind the covered market which was cheaper to run and had belonged to her family.

This house had a slate roof and stood between an alley-way and a lane leading down to the river. Inside there were differences in level which were the cause of many a stumble. A narrow entrance-hall separated the kitchen from the parlour, where Mme Aubain sat all day long in a wicker easy-chair by the window. Eight mahogany chairs were lined up against the white-painted wainscoting, and under the barometer stood

From Gustave Flaubert, *Three Tales,* translated by Robert Baldick. Penguin Classics, 1961, pp. 17–56. Copyright © Robert Baldick, 1961. Reprinted by permission.

an old piano loaded with a pyramid of boxes and cartons. On either side of the chimney-piece, which was carved out of yellow marble in the Louis Quinze style, there was a tapestry-covered arm-chair, and in the middle was a clock designed to look like a temple of Vesta.[1] The whole room smelt a little musty, as the floor was on a lower level than the garden.

On the first floor was 'Madame's' bedroom—very spacious, with a patterned wallpaper of pale flowers and a portrait of 'Monsieur' dressed in what had once been the height of fashion. It opened into a smaller room in which there were two cots, without mattresses. Then came the drawing-room, which was always shut up and full of furniture covered with dust-sheets. Next there was a passage leading to the study, where books and papers filled the shelves of a book-case in three sections built round a big writing-table of dark wood. The two end panels were hidden under pen-and-ink drawings, landscapes in gouache, and etchings by Audran,[2] souvenirs of better days and bygone luxury. On the second floor a dormer window gave light to Félicité's room, which looked out over the fields.

Every day Félicité got up at dawn, so as not to miss Mass, and worked until evening without stopping. Then, once dinner was over, the plates and dishes put away, and the door bolted, she piled ashes on the log fire and went to sleep in front of the hearth, with her rosary in her hands. Nobody could be more stubborn when it came to haggling over prices, and as for cleanliness, the shine on her saucepans was the despair of all the other servants. Being of a thrifty nature, she ate slowly, picking up from the table the crumbs from her loaf of bread—a twelve pound loaf which was baked specially for her and lasted twenty days.

All the year round she wore a kerchief of printed calico fastened behind with a pin, a bonnet which covered her hair, grey stockings, a red skirt, and over her jacket a bibbed apron such as hospital nurses wear.

Her face was thin and her voice was sharp. At twenty-five she was often taken for forty; once she reached fifty, she stopped looking any age in particular. Always silent and upright and deliberate in her movements, she looked like a wooden doll driven by clock-work.

2

Like everyone else, she had had her love-story.

Her father, a mason, had been killed when he fell off some scaffolding. Then her mother died, and when her sisters went their separate ways, a farmer took her in, sending her, small as she was, to look after the cows out in the fields. She went about in rags, shivering with cold, used to lie flat on the ground to drink water out of the ponds, would be beaten for no reason at all, and was finally turned out of the house for stealing thirty sous, a theft of which she was innocent. She found work at another farm, looking after the poultry, and as she was liked by her employers the other servants were jealous of her.

One August evening—she was eighteen at the time—they took her off to the fête at Colleville. From the start she was dazed and bewildered by the noise of the fiddles,

---

[1] The Roman goddess of the hearth and the hearth fire. In her temple a fire was tended by the vestal virgins.

[2] Probably by Gérard or Jean Audran (1640-1703) (1667-1756), members of an illustrious family of French engravers.

the lamps in the trees, the medley of gaily coloured dresses, the gold crosses and lace, and the throng of people jigging up and down. She was standing shyly on one side when a smart young fellow, who had been leaning on the shaft of a cart, smoking his pipe, came up and asked her to dance. He treated her to cider, coffee, girdle-cake, and a silk neckerchief, and imagining that she knew what he was after, offered to see her home. At the edge of a field of oats, he pushed her roughly to the ground. Thoroughly frightened, she started screaming for help. He took to his heels.

Another night, on the road to Beaumont, she tried to get past a big, slow-moving waggon loaded with hay, and as she was squeezing by she recognized Théodore.

He greeted her quite calmly, saying that she must forgive him for the way he had behaved to her, as 'it was the drink that did it'.

She did not know what to say in reply and felt like running off.

Straight away he began talking about the crops and the notabilities of the commune, saying that his father had left Colleville for the farm at Les Écots, so that they were now neighbours.

'Ah!' she said.

He added that his family wanted to see him settle but that he was in no hurry and was waiting to find a wife to suit his fancy. She lowered her head. Then he asked her if she was thinking of getting married. She answered with a smile that it was mean of him to make fun of her.

'But I'm not making fun of you!' he said. 'I swear I'm not!'

He put his left arm round her waist, and she walked on supported by his embrace. Soon they slowed down. There was a gentle breeze blowing, the stars were shining, the huge load of hay was swaying about in front of them, and the four horses were raising clouds of dust as they shambled along. Then, without being told, they turned off to the right. He kissed her once more and she disappeared into the darkness.

The following week Théodore got her to grant him several rendezvous.

They would meet at the bottom of a farm-yard, behind a wall, under a solitary tree. She was not ignorant of life as young ladies are, for the animals had taught her a great deal; but her reason and an instinctive sense of honour prevented her from giving way. The resistance she put up inflamed Théodore's passion to such an extent that in order to satisfy it (or perhaps out of sheer naïvety) he proposed to her. At first she refused to believe him, but he swore that he was serious.

Soon afterwards he had a disturbing piece of news to tell her: the year before, his parents had paid a man to do his military service for him, but now he might be called up again any day, and the idea of going into the army frightened him. In Félicité's eyes this cowardice of his appeared to be a proof of his affection, and she loved him all the more for it. Every night she would steal out to meet him, and every night Théodore would plague her with his worries and entreaties.

In the end he said that he was going to the Prefecture himself to make inquiries, and that he would come and tell her how matters stood the following Sunday, between eleven and midnight.

At the appointed hour she hurried to meet her sweetheart, but found one of his friends waiting for her instead.

He told her that she would not see Théodore again. To make sure of avoiding conscription, he had married a very rich old woman, Mme Lehoussais of Toucques.

Her reaction was an outburst of frenzied grief. She threw herself on the ground, screaming and calling on God, and lay moaning all alone in the open until sunrise. Then she went back to the farm and announced her intention of leaving. At the end of the month, when she had received her wages, she wrapped her small belongings up in a kerchief and made her way to Pont-l'Évêque.

In front of the inn there, she sought information from a woman in a widow's bonnet, who, as it happened, was looking for a cook. The girl did not know much about cooking, but she seemed so willing and expected so little that finally Mme Aubain ended up by saying: 'Very well, I will take you on.'

A quarter of an hour later Félicité was installed in her house.

At first she lived there in a kind of fearful awe caused by 'the style of the house' and the memory of 'Monsieur' brooding over everything. Paul and Virginie, the boy aged seven and the girl barely four, seemed to her to be made of some precious substance. She used to carry them about pick-a-back, and when Mme Aubain told her not to keep on kissing them she was cut to the quick. All the same, she was happy now, for her pleasant surroundings had dispelled her grief.

On Thursdays, a few regular visitors came in to play Boston, and Félicité got the cards and the footwarmers ready beforehand. They always arrived punctually at eight, and left before the clock struck eleven.

Every Monday morning the second-hand dealer who lived down the alley put all his junk out on the pavement. Then the hum of voices began to fill the town, mingled with the neighing of horses, the bleating of lambs, the grunting of pigs, and the rattle of carts in the streets.

About midday, when the market was in full swing, a tall old peasant with a hooked nose and his cap on the back of his head would appear at the door. This was Robelin, the farmer from Geffosses. A little later, and Liébard, the farmer from Toucques, would arrive—a short, fat, red-faced fellow in a grey jacket and leather gaiters fitted with spurs.

Both men had hens or cheeses they wanted to sell to 'Madame'. But Félicité was up to all their tricks and invariably outwitted them, so that they went away full of respect for her.

From time to time Mme Aubain had a visit from an uncle of hers, the Marquis de Grémanville, who had been ruined by loose living and was now living at Falaise on his last remaining scrap of property. He always turned up at lunch-time, accompanied by a hideous poodle who dirtied all the furniture with its paws. However hard he tried to behave like a gentleman, even going so far as to raise his hat every time he mentioned 'my late father', the force of habit was usually too much for him, for he would start pouring himself one glass after another and telling bawdy stories. Félicité used to push him gently out of the house, saying politely: 'You've had quite enough, Monsieur de Grémanville. See you another time!' and shutting the door on him.

She used to open it with pleasure to M. Bourais, who was a retired solicitor. His white tie and his bald head, his frilled shirt-front and his ample brown frock-coat, the way he had of rounding his arm to take a pinch of snuff, and indeed everything about him made an overwhelming impression on her such as we feel when we meet some outstanding personality.

As he looked after 'Madame's' property, he used to shut himself up with her for hours in 'Monsieur's' study. He lived in dread of compromising his reputation, had a tremendous respect for the Bench, and laid claim to some knowledge of Latin.

To give the children a little painless instruction, he made them a present of a geography book with illustrations. These represented scenes in different parts of the world, such as cannibals wearing feather head-dresses, a monkey carrying off a young lady, Bedouins in the desert, a whale being harpooned, and so on.

Paul explained these pictures to Félicité, and that indeed was all the education she ever had. As for the children, they were taught by Guyot, a poor devil employed at the Town Hall, who was famous for his beautiful handwriting, and who had a habit of sharpening his penknife on his boots.

When the weather was fine the whole household used to set off early for a day on the Geffosses farm.

The farm-yard there was on a slope, with the house in the middle; and the sea, in the distance, looked like a streak of grey. Félicité would take some slices of cold meat out of her basket, and they would have their lunch in a room adjoining the dairy. It was all that remained of a country house which had fallen into ruin, and the wallpaper hung in shreds, fluttering in the draught. Mme Aubain used to sit with bowed head, absorbed in her memories, so that the children were afraid to talk. 'Why don't you run along and play?' she would say, and away they went.

Paul climbed up into the barn, caught birds, played ducks and drakes on the pond, or banged with a stick on the great casks, which sounded just like drums.

Virginie fed the rabbits, or scampered off to pick cornflowers, showing her little embroidered knickers as she ran.

One autumn evening they came home through the fields. The moon, which was in its first quarter, lit up part of the sky, and there was some mist floating like a scarf over the winding Toucques. The cattle, lying out in the middle of the pasture, looked peacefully at the four people walking by. In the third field a few got up and made a half circle in front of them.

'Don't be frightened!' said Félicité, and crooning softly, she stroked the back of the nearest animal. It turned about and the others did the same. But while they were crossing the next field they suddenly heard a dreadful bellowing. It came from a bull which had been hidden by the mist, and which now came towards the two women.

Mme Aubain started to run.

'No! No!' said Félicité. 'Not so fast!'

All the same they quickened their pace, hearing behind them a sound of heavy breathing which came nearer and nearer. The bull's hooves thudded like hammers on the turf, and they realized that it had broken into a gallop. Turning round, Félicité tore up some clods of earth and flung them at its eyes. It lowered its muzzle and thrust its horns forward, trembling with rage and bellowing horribly.

By now Mme Aubain had got to the end of the field with her two children and was frantically looking for a way over the high bank. Félicité was still backing away from the bull, hurling clods of turf which blinded it, and shouting: 'Hurry! Hurry!'

Mme Aubain got down into the ditch, pushed first Virginie and then Paul up the other side, fell once or twice trying to climb the bank, and finally managed it with a valiant effort.

. The bull had driven Félicité back against a gate, and its slaver was spurting into her face. In another second it would have gored her, but she just had time to slip between two of the bars, and the great beast halted in amazement.

This adventure was talked about at Pont-l'Évêque for a good many years, but Félicité never prided herself in the least on what she had done, as it never occurred to her that she had done anything heroic.

Virginie claimed all her attention, for the fright had affected the little girl's nerves, and M. Poupart, the doctor, recommended sea-bathing at Trouville.

In those days the resort had few visitors. Mme Aubain made inquiries, consulted Bourais, and got everything ready as though for a long journey.

Her luggage went off in Liébard's cart the day before she left. The next morning he brought along two horses, one of which had a woman's saddle with a velvet back, while the other carried a cloak rolled up to make a kind of seat on its crupper. Mme Aubain sat on this, with Liébard in front. Félicité looked after Virginie on the other horse, and Paul mounted M. Lechaptois's donkey, which he had lent them on condition they took great care of it.

The road was so bad that it took two hours to travel the five miles to Toucques. The horses sank into the mud up to their pasterns and had to jerk their hind-quarters to get out; often they stumbled in the ruts, or else they had to jump. In some places, Liébard's mare came to a sudden stop, and while he waited patiently for her to move off again, he talked about the people whose properties bordered the road, adding moral reflexions to each story. For instance, in the middle of Toucques, as they were passing underneath some windows set in a mass of nasturtiums, he shrugged his shoulders and said:

'There's a Madame Lehoussais lives here. Now instead of taking a young man, she . . .'

Félicité did not hear the rest, for the horses had broken into a trot and the donkey was galloping along. All three turned down a bridle-path, a gate swung open, a couple of boys appeared, and everyone dismounted in front of a manure-heap right outside the farm-house door.

Old Mother Liébard welcomed her mistress with every appearance of pleasure. She served up a sirloin of beef for lunch, with tripe and black pudding, a fricassee of chicken, sparkling cider, a fruit tart and brandy-plums, garnishing the whole meal with compliments to Madame, who seemed to be enjoying better health, to Mademoiselle, who had turned into a 'proper little beauty', and to Monsieur Paul, who had 'filled out a lot'. Nor did she forget their deceased grandparents, whom the Liébards had known personally, having been in the family's service for several generations.

Like its occupants, the farm had an air of antiquity. The ceiling-beams were worm-eaten, the walls black with smoke, and the window-panes grey with dust. There was an oak dresser laden with all sorts of odds and ends—jugs, plates, pewter bowls, wolf-traps, sheep-shears, and an enormous syringe which amused the children. In the three yards outside there was not a single tree without either mushrooms at its base or mistletoe in its branches. Several had been blown down and had taken root again in the middle; all of them were bent under the weight of their apples. The thatched roofs, which looked like brown velvet and varied in thickness, weathered the fiercest winds, but the cart-shed was tumbling down. Mme Aubain said that she would have it seen to, and ordered the animals to be reharnessed.

It took them another half-hour to reach Trouville. The little caravan dismounted to make their way along the Écores, a cliff jutting right out over the boats moored below; and three minutes later they got to the end of the quay and entered the courtyard of the Golden Lamb, the inn kept by Mère David.

After the first few days Virginie felt stronger, as a result of the change of air and the sea-bathing. Not having a costume, she went into the water in her chemise and her maid dressed her afterwards in a customs officer's hut which was used by the bathers.

In the afternoons they took the donkey and went off beyond the Roches-Noires, in the direction of Hennequeville. To begin with, the path went uphill between gentle slopes like the lawns in a park, and then came out on a plateau where pastureland and ploughed fields alternated. On either side there were holly-bushes standing out from the tangle of brambles, and here and there a big dead tree spread its zigzag branches against the blue sky.

They almost always rested in the same field, with Deauville on their left, Le Havre on their right, and the open sea in front. The water glittered in the sunshine, smooth as a mirror, and so still that the murmur it made was scarcely audible; unseen sparrows could be heard twittering, and the sky covered the whole scene with its huge canopy. Mme Aubain sat doing her needlework, Virginie plaited rushes beside her, Félicité gathered lavender, and Paul, feeling profoundly bored, longed to get up and go.

Sometimes they crossed the Toucques in a boat and hunted for shells. When the tide went out, sea-urchins, ormers,[3] and jelly-fish were left behind; and the children scampered around, snatching at the foam-flakes carried on the wind. The sleepy waves, breaking on the sand, spread themselves out along the shore. The beach stretched as far as the eye could see, bounded on the land side by the dunes which separated it from the Marais, a broad meadow in the shape of an arena. When they came back that way, Trouville, on the distant hillside, grew bigger at every step, and with its medley of oddly assorted houses seemed to blossom out in gay disorder.

On exceptionally hot days they stayed in their room. The sun shone in dazzling bars of light between the slats of the blind. There was not a sound to be heard in the village, and not a soul to be seen down in the street. Everything seemed more peaceful in the prevailing silence. In the distance caulkers were hammering away at the boats, and the smell of tar was wafted along by a sluggish breeze.

The principal amusement consisted in watching the fishingboats come in. As soon as they had passed the buoys, they started tacking. With their canvas partly lowered and their foresails blown out like balloons they glided through the splashing waves as far as the middle of the harbour, where they suddenly dropped anchor. Then each boat came alongside the quay, and the crew threw ashore their catch of quivering fish. A line of carts stood waiting, and women in cotton bonnets rushed forward to take the baskets and kiss their men.

One day one of these women spoke to Félicité, who came back to the inn soon after in a state of great excitement. She explained that she had found one of her sisters—and Nastasie Barette, now Leroux, made her appearance, with a baby at her breast, another child holding her right hand, and on her left a little sailor-boy, his arms akimbo and his cap over one ear.

Mme Aubain sent her off after a quarter of an hour. From then on they were forever hanging round the kitchen or loitering about when the family went for a walk, though the husband kept out of sight.

Félicité became quite attached to them. She bought them a blanket, several shirts, and a stove; and it was clear that they were bent on getting all they could out of her. This weakness of hers annoyed Mme Aubain, who in any event disliked the familiar way in which the nephew spoke to Paul. And so, as Virginie had started coughing and the good weather was over, she decided to go back to Pont-l'Évêque.

M. Bourais advised her on the choice of a school; Caen was considered the best, so it was there that Paul was sent. He said good-bye bravely, feeling really rather pleased to be going to a place where he would have friends of his own.

Mme Aubain resigned herself to the loss of her son, knowing that it was unavoidable. Virginie soon got used to it. Félicité missed the din he used to make, but she was

---

[3] From French *orielle de mer,* ear of the sea; an abalone shell.

given something new to do which served as a distraction: from Christmas onwards she had to take the little girl to catechism every day.

3

After genuflecting at the door, she walked up the centre aisle under the nave, opened the door of Mme Aubain's pew, sat down, and started looking about her.

The choir stalls were all occupied, with the boys on the right and the girls on the left, while the curé stood by the lectern. In one of the stained-glass windows in the apse the Holy Ghost looked down on the Virgin; another window showed her kneeling before the Infant Jesus; and behind the tabernacle there was a wood-carving of St. Michael slaying the dragon.

The priest began with a brief outline of sacred history. Listening to him, Félicité saw in imagination the Garden of Eden, the Flood, the Tower of Babel, cities burning, peoples dying, and idols being overthrown; and this dazzling vision left her with a great respect for the Almighty and profound fear of His wrath.

Then she wept as she listened to the story of the Passion. Why had they crucified Him, when He loved children, fed the multitudes, healed the blind, and had chosen out of humility to be born among the poor, on the litter of a stable? The sowing of the seed, the reaping of the harvest, the pressing of the grapes—all those familiar things of which the Gospels speak had their place in her life. God had sanctified them in passing, so that she loved the lambs more tenderly for love of the Lamb of God, and the doves for the sake of the Holy Ghost.

She found it difficult, however, to imagine what the Holy Ghost looked like, for it was not just a bird but a fire as well, and sometimes a breath. She wondered whether that was its light she had seen flitting about the edge of the marshes at night, whether that was its breath she had felt driving the clouds across the sky, whether that was its voice she had heard in the sweet music of the bells. And she sat in silent adoration, delighting in the coolness of the walls and the quiet of the church.

Of dogma she neither understood nor even tried to understand anything. The curé discoursed, the children repeated their lesson, and she finally dropped off to sleep, waking up suddenly at the sound of their sabots clattering across the flagstones as they left the church.

It was in this manner, simply by hearing it expounded, that she learnt her catechism, for her religious education had been neglected in her youth. From then on she copied all Virginie's observances, fasting when she did and going to confession with her. On the feast of Corpus Christi the two of them made an altar of repose together.

The preparations for Virginie's first communion caused her great anxiety. She worried over her shoes, her rosary, her missal, and her gloves. And how she trembled as she helped Mme Aubain to dress the child!

All through the Mass her heart was in her mouth. One side of the choir was hidden from her by M. Bourais, but directly opposite her she could see the flock of maidens, looking like a field of snow with their white crowns perched on top of their veils; and she recognized her little darling from a distance by her dainty neck and her rapt attitude. The bell tinkled. Every head bowed low, and there was a silence. Then, to the thunderous accompaniment of the organ, choir and congregation joined in singing the *Agnus Dei*. Next the boys' procession began, and after that the girls got up from their seats. Slowly, their hands joined in prayer, they went towards the brightly lit altar, knelt on the first step, received the Host one by one, and went back to their places in the same order. When it was Virginie's turn, Félicité leant forward to see her, and in one of those imaginative flights born of real affection, it seemed to her that she herself was in the child's place. Virginie's face became her own, Virginie's dress clothed her, Virginie's heart was beating in her breast; and as she closed her eyes and opened her mouth, she almost fainted away.

Early next morning she went to the sacristy and asked M. le Curé to give her communion. She received the sacrament with all due reverence, but did not feel the same rapture as she had the day before.

Mme Aubain wanted her daughter to possess every accomplishment, and since Guyot could not teach her English or music, she decided to send her as a boarder to the Ursuline Convent at Honfleur.

Virginie raised no objection, but Félicité went about sighing at Madame's lack of feeling. Then she thought that perhaps her mistress was right: such matters, after all, lay outside her province.

Finally the day arrived when an old waggonette stopped at their door, and a nun got down from it who had come to fetch Mademoiselle. Félicité hoisted the luggage up on top, gave the driver some parting instructions, and put six pots of jam, a dozen pears, and a bunch of violets in the boot.

At the last moment Virginie burst into a fit of sobbing. She threw her arms round her mother, who kissed her on the forehead, saying: 'Come now, be brave, be brave.' The step was pulled up and the carriage drove away.

Then Mme Aubain broke down, and that evening all her friends, M. and Mme Lormeau, Mme Lechaptois, the Rochefeuille sisters, M. de Houppeville, and Bourais, came in to console her.

To begin with she missed her daughter badly. But she had a letter from her three times a week, wrote back on the other days, walked round her garden, did a little reading, and thus contrived to fill the empty hours.

As for Félicité, she went into Virginie's room every morning from sheer force of habit and looked round it. It upset her not having to brush the child's hair any more, tie her bootlaces, or tuck her up in bed; and she missed seeing her sweet face all the time and holding her hand when they went out together. For want of something to do, she tried making lace, but her fingers were too clumsy and broke the threads. She could not settle to anything, lost her sleep, and, to use her own words, was 'eaten up inside'.

To 'occupy her mind', she asked if her nephew Victor might come and see her, and permission was granted.

He used to arrive after Mass on Sunday, his cheeks flushed, his chest bare, and smelling of the countryside through which he had come. She laid a place for him straight away, opposite hers, and they had lunch together. Eating as little as possible herself, in order to save the expense, she stuffed him so full of food that he fell asleep after the meal. When the first bell for vespers rang, she woke him up, brushed his trousers, tied his tie, and set off for church, leaning on his arm with all a mother's pride.

His parents always told him to get something out of her—a packet of brown sugar perhaps, some soap, or a little brandy, sometimes even money. He brought her his clothes to be mended, and she did the work gladly, thankful for anything that would force him to come again.

In August his father took him on a coasting trip. The children's holidays were just beginning, and it cheered her up to have them home again. But Paul was turning capricious and Virginie was getting too old to be addressed familiarly—a state of affairs which put a barrier of constraint between them.

Victor went to Morlaix, Dunkirk, and Brighton in turn, and brought her a present after each trip. The first time it was a box covered with shells, the second a coffee cup, the third a big gingerbread man. He was growing quite handsome, with his trim figure, his little moustache, his frank open eyes, and the little leather cap that he wore on the back of his head like a pilot. He kept her amused by telling her stories full of nautical jargon.

One Monday—it was the fourteenth of July 1819, a date she never forgot—Victor told her that he had signed on for an ocean voyage, and that on the Wednesday night he would be taking the Honfleur packet to join his schooner, which was due to sail shortly from Le Havre. He might be away, he said, for two years.

The prospect of such a long absence made Félicité extremely unhappy, and she felt she must bid him godspeed once more. So on the Wednesday evening, when Madame's dinner was over, she put on her clogs and swiftly covered the ten miles between Pont-l'Évêque and Honfleur.

When she arrived at the Calvary she turned right instead of left, got lost in the shipyards, and had to retrace her steps. Some people she spoke to advised her to hurry. She went right round the harbour, which was full of boats, constantly tripping over moorings. Then the ground fell away, rays of light criss-crossed in front of her, and for a moment, she thought she was going mad, for she could see horses up in the sky.

On the quayside more horses were neighing, frightened by the sea. A derrick was hoisting them into the air and dropping them into one of the boats, which was already crowded with passengers elbowing their way between barrels of cider, baskets of cheese, and sacks of grain. Hens were cackling and the captain swearing, while a cabin-boy stood leaning on the cats-head, completely indifferent to it all. Félicité, who had not recognized him, shouted: 'Victor!' and he raised his head. She rushed forward, but at that very moment the gangway was pulled ashore.

The packet moved out of the harbour with women singing as they hauled it along, its ribs creaking and heavy waves lashing its bows. The sail swung round, hiding everyone on board from view, and against the silvery, moonlit sea the boat appeared as a dark shape that grew ever fainter, until at last it vanished in the distance.

As Félicité was passing the Calvary, she felt a longing to commend to God's mercy all that she held most dear; and she stood there praying for a long time, her face bathed in tears, her eyes fixed upon the clouds. The town was asleep, except for the customs officers walking up and down. Water was pouring ceaselessly through the holes in the sluice-gate, making as much noise as a torrent. The clocks struck two.

The convent parlour would not be open before daybreak, and Madame would be annoyed if she were late; so, although she would have liked to give a kiss to the other child, she set off for home. The maids at the inn were just waking up as she got to Pont-l'Évêque.

So the poor lad was going to be tossed by the waves for months on end! His previous voyages had caused her no alarm. People came back from England and Brittany; but America, the Colonies, the Islands, were all so far away, somewhere at the other end of the world.

From then on Félicité thought of nothing but her nephew. On sunny days she hoped he was not too thirsty, and when there was a storm she was afraid he would be struck by lightning. Listening to the wind howling in the chimney or blowing slates off the roof, she saw him being buffeted by the very same storm, perched on the top of a broken mast, with his whole body bent backwards under a sheet of foam; or again—and these were reminiscences of the illustrated geography-book—he was being eaten by savages, captured by monkeys in the forest, or dying on a desert shore. But she never spoke of her worries.

Mme Aubain had worries of her own about her daughter. The good nuns said that she was an affectionate child, but very delicate. The slightest emotion upset her, and she had to give up playing the piano.

Her mother insisted on regular letters from the convent. One morning when the postman had not called, she lost patience and walked up and down the room, between her chair and the window. It was really extraordinary! Four days without any news!

Thinking her own example would comfort her, Félicité said:

'I've been six months, Madame, without news.'

'News of whom?'

The servant answered gently:

'Why—of my nephew.'

'Oh, your nephew!' And Mme Aubain started pacing up and down again, with a shrug of her shoulders that seemed to say: 'I wasn't thinking of him—and indeed, why should I? Who cares about a young, good-for-nothing cabin-boy? Whereas my daughter—why, just think!'

Although she had been brought up the hard way, Félicité was indignant with Madame, but she soon forgot. It struck her as perfectly natural to lose one's head where the little girl was concerned. For her, the two children were of equal importance; they were linked together in her heart by a single bond, and their destinies should be the same.

The chemist told her that Victor's ship had arrived at Havana: he had seen this piece of information in a newspaper.

Because of its association with cigars, she imagined Havana as a place where nobody did anything but smoke, and pictured Victor walking about among crowds of Negroes in a cloud of tobacco-smoke. Was it possible, she wondered, 'in case of need' to come back by land? And how far was it from Pont-l'Évêque? To find out she asked M. Bourais.

He reached for his atlas, and launched forth into an explanation of latitudes and longitudes, smiling like the pedant he was at Félicité's bewilderment. Finally he pointed with his pencil at a minute black dot inside a ragged oval patch, saying:

'There it is.'

She bent over the map, but the network of coloured lines meant nothing to her and only tired her eyes. So when Bourais asked her to tell him what was puzzling her, she begged him to show her the house where Victor was living. He threw up his hands, sneezed, and roared with laughter, delighted to come across such simplicity. And Félicité—whose intelligence was so limited that she probably expected to see an actual portrait of her nephew—could not make out why he was laughing.

It was a fortnight later that Liébard came into the kitchen at market-time, as he usually did, and handed her a letter from her brother-in-law. As neither of them could read, she turned to her mistress for help.

Mme Aubain, who was counting the stitches in her knitting, put it down and unsealed the letter. She gave a start, and, looking hard at Félicité, said quietly:

'They have some bad news for you . . . Your nephew . . .'

He was dead. That was all the letter had to say.

Félicité dropped on to a chair, leaning her head against the wall and closing her eyelids, which suddenly turned pink. Then, with her head bowed, her hands dangling, and her eyes set, she kept repeating:

'Poor little lad! Poor little lad!'

Liébard looked at her and sighed. Mme Aubain was trembling slightly. She suggested that she should go and see her sister at Trouville, but Félicité shook her head to indicate that there was no need for that.

There was a silence. Old Liébard thought it advisable to go.

Then Félicité said:

'It doesn't matter a bit, not to them it doesn't.'

Her head fell forward again, and from time to time she unconsciously picked up the knitting needles lying on the work table.

Some women went past carrying a tray full of dripping linen.

Catching sight of them through the window, she remembered her own washing; she had passed the lye through it the day before and today it needed rinsing. So she left the room.

Her board and tub were on the bank of the Toucques. She threw a pile of chemises down by the water's edge, rolled up her sleeves, and picked up her battledore. The lusty blows she gave with it could be heard in all the neighbouring gardens.

The fields were empty, the river rippling in the wind; at the bottom long weeds were waving to and fro, like the hair of corpses floating in the water. She held back her grief, and was very brave until the evening; but in her room she gave way to it completely, lying on her mattress with her face buried in the pillow and her fists pressed against her temples.

Long afterwards she learnt the circumstances of Victor's death from the captain of his ship. He had gone down with yellow fever, and they had bled him too much at the hospital. Four doctors had held him at once. He had died straight away, and the chief doctor had said:

'Good! There goes another!'

His parents had always treated him cruelly. She preferred not to see them again, and they made no advances, either because they had forgotten about her or out of the callousness of the poor.

Meanwhile Virginie was growing weaker. Difficulty in breathing, fits of coughing, protracted bouts of fever, and mottled patches on the cheekbones all indicated some deepseated complaint. M. Poupart had advised a stay in Provence. Mme Aubain decided to follow this suggestion, and, if it had not been for the weather at Pont-l'Évêque, she would have brought her daughter home at once.

She arranged with a jobmaster to drive her out to the convent every Tuesday. There was a terrace in the garden, overlooking the Seine, and there Virginie, leaning on her mother's arm, walked up and down over the fallen vineleaves. Sometimes, while she was looking at the sails in the distance, or at the long stretch of horizon from the Château de Tancarville to the lighthouses of Le Havre, the sun would break through the clouds and make her blink. Afterwards they would rest in the arbor. Her mother had secured a little cask of excellent Malaga, and, laughing at the idea of getting tipsy, Virginie used to drink a thimbleful, but no more.

Her strength revived. Autumn slipped by, and Félicité assured Mme Aubain that there was nothing to fear. But one evening, coming back from some errand in the neighbourhood, she found M. Poupart's gig standing at the door. He was in the hall, and Mme Aubain was tying on her bonnet.

'Give me my foot-warmer, purse, gloves. Quickly now!'

Virginie had pneumonia and was perhaps past recovery.

'Not yet!' said the doctor; and the two of them got into the carriage with snow-flakes swirling around them. Night was falling and it was very cold.

Félicité rushed into the church to light a candle, and then ran after the gig. She caught up with it an hour later, jumped lightly behind, and hung on to the fringe. But then a thought struck her: the courtyard had not been locked up, the burglars might get in. So she jumped down again.

At dawn the next day she went to the doctor's. He had come home and gone out again on his rounds. Then she waited at the inn, thinking that somebody who was a stranger to the district might call there with a letter. Finally, when it was twilight, she got into the coach for Lisieux.

The convent was at the bottom of a steep lane. When she was half-way down the hill, she heard a strange sound which she recognized as a death-bell tolling.

'It's for somebody else,' she thought, as she banged the door-knocker hard.

After a few minutes she heard the sound of shuffling feet, the door opened a little way, and a nun appeared.

The good sister said with an air of compunction that 'she had just passed away'. At that moment the bell of Saint-Léonard was tolled more vigorously than ever.

Félicité went up to the second floor. From the doorway of the room she could see Virginie lying on her back, her hands clapsed together, her mouth open, her head tilted back under a black crucifix that leant over her, her face whiter than the curtains that hung motionless on either side. Mme Aubain was clinging to the foot of the bed and sobbing desperately. The Mother Superior stood on the right. Three candlesticks on the chest of drawers added touches of red to the scene, and fog was whitening the windows. Some nuns led Mme Aubain away.

For two nights Félicité never left the dead girl. She said the same prayers over and over again, sprinkled holy water on the sheets, then sat down again to watch. At the end of her first vigil she noticed that the child's face had gone yellow, the lips were turning blue, the nose looked sharper, and the eyes were sunken. She kissed them several times, and would not have been particularly surprised if Virginie had opened them again: to minds like hers the supernatural is a simple matter. She laid her out, wrapped her in a shroud, put her in her coffin, placed a wreath on her, and spread out her hair. It was fair and amazingly long for her age. Félicité cut off a big lock, half of which she slipped into her bosom, resolving never to part with it.

The body was brought back to Pont-l'Évêque at the request of Mme Aubain, who followed the hearse in a closed carriage.

After the Requiem Mass, it took another three-quarters of an hour to reach the cemetery. Paul walked in front, sobbing. Then came M. Bourais, and after him the principal inhabitants of the town, the women all wearing long black veils, and Félicité. She was thinking about her nephew; and since she had been unable to pay him these last honours, she felt an added grief, just as if they were burying him with Virginie.

Mme Aubain's despair passed all bounds. First of all she rebelled against God, considering it unfair of Him to have taken her daughter from her—for she had never done any harm, and her conscience was quite clear. But was it? She ought to have taken Virginie to the south; other doctors would have saved her life. She blamed herself, wished she could have joined her daughter, and cried out in anguish in her dreams. One dream in particular obsessed her. Her husband, dressed like a sailor, came back from a long voyage, and told her amid tears that he had been ordered to take Virginie away—whereupon they put their heads together to discover somewhere to hide her.

One day she came in from the garden utterly distraught. A few minutes earlier— and she pointed to the spot—father and daughter had appeared to her, doing nothing, but simply looking at her.

For several months she stayed in her room in a kind of stupor. Félicité scolded her gently, telling her that she must take care of herself for her son's sake, and also in remembrance of 'her'.

'Her?' repeated Mme Aubain, as if she were waking from a sleep. 'Oh, yes, of course! You don't forget her, do you!' This was an allusion to the cemetery, where she herself was strictly forbidden to go.

Félicité went there every day. She would set out on the stroke of four, going past the houses, up the hill, and through the gate, until she came to Virginie's grave. There was a little column of pink marble with a tablet at its base, and a tiny garden enclosed by chains. The beds were hidden under a carpet of flowers. She watered their leaves and changed the sand, going down on her knees to fork the ground thoroughly. The result was that when Mme Aubain was able to come here, she experienced a feeling of relief, a kind of consolation.

Then the years slipped by, each one like the last, with nothing to vary the rhythm of the great festivals: Easter, the Assumption, All Saints' Day. Domestic events marked dates that later served as points of reference. Thus in 1825 a couple of glaziers whitewashed the hall; in 1827 a piece of the roof fell into the courtyard and nearly killed a man; and in the summer of 1828 it was Madame's turn to provide the bread for consecration. About this time Bourais went away in a mysterious fashion; and one by one the old acquaintances disappeared: Guyot, Liébard, Mme Lechaptois, Robelin, and Uncle Grémanville, who had been paralysed for a long time.

One night the driver of the mail-coach brought Pont-l'Évêque news of the July Revolution. A few days later a new sub-prefect was appointed. This was the Baron de Larsonnière, who had been a consul in America, and who brought with him, besides his wife, his sister-in-law and three young ladies who were almost grown-up. They were to be seen on their lawn, dressed in loose-fitting smocks; and they had a Negro servant and a parrot. They paid a call on Mme Aubain, who made a point of returning it. As soon as Félicité saw them coming, she would run and tell her mistress. But only one thing could really awaken her interest, and that was her son's letters.

He seemed to be incapable of following any career and spent all his time in taverns. She paid his debts, but he contracted new ones, and the sighs Mme Aubain heaved as she knitted by the window reached Félicité at her spinning wheel in the kitchen.

The two women used to walk up and down together beside the espalier, forever talking of Virginie and debating whether such and such a thing would have appealed to her, or what she would have said on such and such an occasion.

All her little belongings were in a cupboard in the children's bedroom. Mme Aubain went through them as seldom as possible. One summer day she resigned herself to doing so, and the moths were sent fluttering out of the cupboard.

Virginie's frocks hung in a row underneath a shelf containing three dolls, a few hoops, a set of toy furniture, and the wash-basin she had used. Besides the frocks, they took out her petticoats, her stockings and her handkerchiefs, and spread them out on the two beds before folding them up again. The sunlight streamed in on these pathetic objects, bringing out the stains and showing up the creases made by the child's movements. The air was warm, the sky was blue, a blackbird was singing, and everything seemed to be utterly at peace.

They found a little chestnut-coloured hat, made of plush with a long nap; but the moths had ruined it. Félicité asked if she might have it. The two women looked at each other and their eyes filled with tears. Then the mistress opened her arms, the maid threw herself into them, and they clasped each other in a warm embrace, satisfying their grief in a kiss which made them equal.

It was the first time that such a thing had happened, for Mme Aubain was not of a demonstrative nature. Félicité was as grateful as if she had received a great favour, and henceforth loved her mistress with dog-like devotion and religious veneration. Her heart grew softer as time went by.

When she heard the drums of a regiment coming down the street she stood at the door with a jug of cider and offered the soldiers a drink. She looked after the people who went down with cholera. She watched over the Polish refugees, and one of them actually expressed a desire to marry her. But they fell out, for when she came back from the Angelus one morning, she found that he had got into her kitchen and was calmly eating an oil-and-vinegar salad.

After the Poles it was Père Colmiche, an old man who was said to have committed fearful atrocities in '93. He lived by the river in a ruined pig-sty. The boys of the town used to peer at him through the cracks in the walls, and threw pebbles at him which landed on the litter where he lay, constantly shaken by fits of coughing. His hair was extremely long, his eyelids inflamed, and on one arm there was a swelling bigger than his head. Félicité brought him some linen, tried to clean out his filthy hovel, and even wondered if she could install him in the wash-house without annoying Madame. When the tumour had burst, she changed his dressings every day, brought him some cake now and then, and put him out in the sun on a truss of hay. The poor old fellow would thank her in a faint whisper, slavering and trembling all the while, fearful of losing her and stretching his hands out as soon as he saw her moving away.

He died, and she had a Mass said for the repose of his soul.

That same day a great piece of good fortune came her way. Just as she was serving dinner, Mme de Larsonnière's Negro appeared carrying the parrot in its cage, complete with perch, chain, and padlock. The Baroness had written a note informing Mme Aubain that her husband had been promoted to a Prefecture and they were leaving that evening; she begged her to accept the parrot as a keepsake and a token of her regard.

This bird had engrossed Félicité's thoughts for a long time, for it came from America, and that word reminded her of Victor. So she had asked the Negro all about it, and once she had even gone so far as to say:

'How pleased Madame would be if it were hers!'

The Negro had repeated this remark to his mistress, who, unable to take the parrot with her, was glad to get rid of it in this way.

4

His name was Loulou. His body was green, the tips of his wings were pink, his poll blue, and his breast golden.

Unfortunately he had a tiresome mania for biting his perch, and also used to pull his feathers out, scatter his droppings everywhere, and upset his bath water. He annoyed Mme Aubain, and so she gave him to Félicité for good.

Félicité started training him, and soon he could say: 'Nice boy! Your servant, sir! Hail, Mary!' He was put near the door, and several people who spoke to him said how strange it was that he did not answer to the name of Jacquot, as all parrots were called Jacquot. They likened him to a turkey or a block of wood, and every sneer cut Félicité to the quick. How odd, she thought, that Loulou should be so stubborn, refusing to talk whenever anyone looked at him!

For all that, he liked having people around him, because on Sundays, while the Rochefeuille sisters, M. Houppeville and some new friends—the apothecary Onfroy, M. Varin, and Captain Mathieu—were having their game of cards, he would beat on the window-panes with his wings and make such a din that it was impossible to hear oneself speak.

Bourais's face obviously struck him as terribly funny, for as soon as he saw it he was seized with uncontrollable laughter. His shrieks rang round the courtyard, the echo repeated them, and the neighbours came to their windows and started laughing too. To avoid being seen by the bird, M. Bourais used to creep along by the wall, hiding his face behind his hat, until he got to the river, and then come into the house from the garden. The looks he gave the parrot were far from tender.

Loulou had once been cuffed by the butcher's boy for poking his head into his basket; and since then he was always trying to give him a nip through his shirt. Fabu threatened to wring his neck, although he was not a cruel fellow, in spite of his tattooed arms and bushy whiskers. On the contrary, he rather liked the parrot, so much so indeed that in a spirit of jovial camaraderie he tried to teach him a few swear-words. Félicité, alarmed at this development, put the bird in the kitchen. His little chain was removed and he was allowed to wander all over the house.

Coming downstairs, he used to rest the curved part of his beak on each step and then raise first his right foot, then his left; and Félicité was afraid that this sort of gymnastic performance would make him giddy. He fell ill and could neither talk nor eat for there was a swelling under his tongue such as hens sometimes have. She cured him by pulling this pellicule[4] out with her finger-nails. One day M. Paul was silly enough to blow the smoke of his cigar at him; another time Mme Lormeau started teasing him with the end of her parasol, and he caught hold of the ferrule[5] with his beak. Finally he got lost.

Félicité had put him down on the grass in the fresh air, and left him there for a minute. When she came back, the parrot had gone. First of all she looked for him in the bushes, by the river and on the rooftops, paying no attention to her mistress's shouts of: 'Be careful, now! You must be mad!' Next she went over all the gardens in Pont-l'Évêque, stopping passersby and asking them: 'You don't happen to have seen my parrot by any chance?' Those who did not know him already were given a description of the bird. Suddenly she thought she could make out something green flying about behind the mills at the foot of the hill. But up on the hill there was nothing to be seen. A pedlar told her that he had come upon the parrot a short time before in Mère Simon's shop at Saint-Melaine. She ran all the way there, but no one knew what she was talking about. Finally she came back home, worn out, her shoes falling to pieces, and death in her heart. She was sitting beside Madame on the garden-seat and telling her what she had been doing, when she felt something light drop on her shoulder. It was Loulou! What he had been up to, no one could discover: perhaps he had just gone for a little walk round the town.

[4] Thin skin or membrane.
[5] Iron ring around the end of a staff.

Félicité was slow to recover from this fright, and indeed never really got over it.

As the result of a chill she had an attack of quinsy, and soon after that her ears were affected. Three years later she was deaf, and she spoke at the top of her voice, even in church. Although her sins could have been proclaimed over the length and breadth of the diocese without dishonour to her or offence to others, M. le Curé thought it advisable to hear her confession in the sacristy.

Imaginary buzzings in the head added to her troubles. Often her mistress would say: 'Heavens, how stupid you are!' and she would reply: 'Yes, Madame,' at the same time looking all around her for something.

The little circle of her ideas grew narrower and narrower, and the pealing of bells and the lowing of cattle went out of her life. Every living thing moved about in a ghostly silence. Only one sound reached her ears now, and that was the voice of the parrot.

As if to amuse her, he would reproduce the click-clack of the turn-spit, the shrill call of a man selling fish, and the noise of the saw at the joiner's across the way; and when the bell rang he would imitate Mme Aubain's 'Félicité! The door, the door!'

They held conversations with each other, he repeating *ad nauseam* the three phrases in his repertory, she replying with words which were just as disconnected but which came from the heart. In her isolation, Loulou was almost a son or a lover to her. He used to climb up her fingers, peck at her lips, and hang on to her shawl; and as she bent over him, wagging her head from side to side as nurses do, the great wings of her bonnet and the wings of the bird quivered in unison.

When clouds banked up in the sky and there was a rumbling of thunder, he would utter piercing cries, no doubt remembering the sudden downpours in his native forests. The sound of the rain falling roused him to frenzy. He would flap excitedly around, shoot up to the ceiling, knocking everything over, and fly out of the window to splash about in the garden. But he would soon come back to perch on one of the firedogs, hopping about to dry his feathers and showing tail and beak in turn.

One morning in the terrible winter of 1837, when she had put him in front of the fire because of the cold she found him dead in the middle of his cage, hanging head down with his claws caught in the bars. He had probably died of a stroke, but she thought he had been poisoned with parsley, and despite the absence of any proof, her suspicions fell on Fabu.

She wept so much that her mistress said to her: 'Why don't you have him stuffed?'

Félicité asked the chemist's advice, remembering that he had always been kind to the parrot. He wrote to Le Havre, and a man called Fellacher agreed to do the job. As parcels sometimes went astray on the mail-coach, she decided to take the parrot as far as Honfleur herself.

On either side of the road stretched an endless succession of apple-trees, all stripped of their leaves, and there was ice in the ditches. Dogs were barking around the farms; and Félicité, with her hands tucked under her mantlet, her little black sabots and her basket, walked briskly along the middle of the road.

She crossed the forest, passed Le Haut-Chêne, and got as far as Saint-Gatien.

Behind her, in a cloud of dust, and gathering speed as the horses galloped down-hill, a mail-coach swept along like a whirlwind. When he saw this woman making no attempt to get out of the way, the driver poked his head out above the hood, and he and the postilion shouted at her. His four horses could not be held in and galloped faster, the two leaders touching her as they went by. With a jerk of the reins the driver threw them to one side, and then, in a fury, he raised his long whip and gave her such a lash, from head to waist, that she fell flat on her back.

The first thing she did on regaining consciousness was to open her basket. Fortunately nothing had happened to Loulou. She felt her right cheek burning, and when she touched it her hand turned red; it was bleeding.

She sat down on a heap of stones and dabbed her face with her handkerchief. Then she ate a crust of bread which she had taken the precaution of putting in her basket, and tried to forget her wound by looking at the bird.

As she reached the top of the hill at Ecquemauville, she saw the lights of Honfleur twinkling in the darkness like a host of stars, and the shadowy expanse of the sea beyond. Then a sudden feeling of faintness made her stop; and the misery of her childhood, the disappointment of her first love, the departure of her nephew, and the death of Virginie all came back to her at once like the waves of a rising tide, and, welling up in her throat, choked her.

When she got to the boat she insisted on speaking to the captain, and without telling him what was in her parcel, asked him to take good care of it.

Fellacher kept the parrot a long time. Every week he promised it for the next; after six months he announced that a box had been sent off, and nothing more was heard of it. It looked as though Loulou would never come back, and Félicité told herself: 'They've stolen him for sure!'

At last he arrived—looking quite magnificent, perched on a branch screwed into a mahogany base, one foot in the air, his head cocked to one side, and biting a nut which the taxidermist, out of love of the grandiose, had gilded.

Félicité shut him up in her room.

This place, to which few people were ever admitted, contained such a quantity of religious bric-à-brac and miscellaneous oddments that it looked like a cross between a chapel and a bazaar.

A big wardrobe prevented the door from opening properly. Opposite the window that overlooked the garden was a little round one looking on to the courtyard. There was a table beside the bed, with a water-jug, a couple of combs, and a block of blue soap in a chipped plate. On the walls there were rosaries, medals, several pictures of the Virgin, and a holy-water stoup made out of a coconut. On the chest of drawers, which was draped with a cloth just like an altar, was the shell box Victor had given her, and also a watering-can and a ball, some copy-books, the illustrated geography book, and a pair of ankle-boots. And on the nail supporting the looking-glass, fastened by its ribbons, hung the little plush hat.

Félicité carried this form of veneration to such lengths that she even kept one of Monsieur's frock-coats. All the old rubbish Mme Aubain had no more use for, she carried off to her room. That was how there came to be artificial flowers along the edge of the chest of drawers, and a portrait of the Comte d'Artois in the window-recess.

With the aid of a wall-bracket, Loulou was installed on a chimney-breast that jutted out into the room. Every morning when she awoke, she saw him in the light of the dawn, and then she remembered the old days, and the smallest details of insignificant actions, not in sorrow but in absolute tranquillity.

Having no intercourse with anyone, she lived in the torpid state of a sleep-walker. The Corpus Christi processions roused her from this condition, for she would go round the neighbours collecting candlesticks and mats to decorate the altar of repose which they used to set up in the street.

In church she was forever gazing at the Holy Ghost, and one day she noticed that it had something of the parrot about it. This resemblance struck her as even more obvious in a colourprint depicting the baptism of Our Lord. With its red wings and its emerald-green body, it was the very image of Loulou.

She bought the print and hung it in the place of the Comte d'Artois, so that she could include them both in a single glance. They were linked together in her mind, the parrot being sanctified by this connexion with the Holy Ghost, which itself acquired new life and meaning in her eyes. God the Father could not have chosen a dove as a means of expressing Himself, since doves cannot talk, but rather one of Loulou's ancestors. And although Félicité used to say her prayers with her eyes on the picture, from time to time she would turn slightly towards the bird.

She wanted to join the Children of Mary, but Mme Aubain dissuaded her from doing so.

An important event now loomed up—Paul's wedding.

After starting as a lawyer's clerk, he had been in business, in the Customs, and in Inland Revenue, and had even begun trying to get into the Department of Woods and Forests, when, at the age of thirty-six, by some heaven-sent inspiration, he suddenly discovered his real vocation—in the Wills and Probate Department. There he proved so capable that one of the auditors had offered him his daughter in marriage and promised to use his influence on his behalf.

Paul, grown serious-minded, brought her to see his mother. She criticized the way things were done at Pont-l'Evêque, put on airs, and hurt Félicité's feelings. Mme Aubain was relieved to see her go.

The following week came news of M. Bourais's death in an inn in Lower Brittany. Rumours that he had committed suicide were confirmed, and doubts arose as to his honesty. Mme Aubain went over her accounts and was soon conversant with the full catalogue of his misdeeds—embezzlement of interest, secret sales of timber, forged receipts, etc. Besides all this, he was the father of an illegitimate child, and had had 'relations with a person at Dozulé'.

These infamies upset Mme Aubain greatly. In March 1853 she was afflicted with a pain in the chest; her tongue seemed to be covered with a film; leeches failed to make her breathing any easier; and on the ninth evening of her illness she died. She had just reached the age of seventy-two.

She was thought to be younger because of her brown hair, worn in bandeaux round her pale, pock-marked face. There were few friends to mourn her, for she had a haughty manner which put people off. Yet Félicité wept for her as servants rarely weep for their masters. That Madame should die before her upset her ideas, seemed to be contrary to the order of things, monstrous and unthinkable.

Ten days later—the time it took to travel hot-foot from Besançon—the heirs arrived. The daughter-in-law ransacked every drawer, picked out some pieces of furniture and sold the rest; and then back they went to the Wills and Probate Department.

Madame's arm-chair, her pedestal table, her foot-warmer, and the eight chairs had all gone. Yellow squares in the centre of the wall-panels showed where the pictures had hung. They had carried off the two cots with their mattresses, and no trace remained in the cupboard of all Virginie's things. Félicité climbed the stairs to her room, numbed with sadness.

The next day there was a notice on the door, and the apothecary shouted in her ear that the house was up for sale.

She swayed on her feet, and was obliged to sit down.

What distressed her most of all was the idea of leaving her room, which was so suitable for poor Loulou. Fixing an anguished look on him as she appealed to the Holy Ghost, she contracted the idolatrous habit of kneeling in front of the parrot to say her prayers. Sometimes the sun, as it came through the little window, caught his glass eye, so that it shot out a great luminous ray which sent her into ecstasies.

She had a pension of three hundred and eighty francs a year which her mistress had left her. The garden kept her in vegetables. As for clothes, she had enough to last her till the end of her days, and she saved on lighting by going to bed as soon as darkness fell.

She went out as little as possible, to avoid the second-hand dealer's shop where some of the old furniture was on display. Ever since her fit of giddiness, she had been dragging one leg; and as her strength was failing, Mère Simon, whose grocery business had come to grief, came in every morning to chop wood and pump water for her.

Her eyes grew weaker. The shutters were not opened any more. Years went by, and nobody rented the house and nobody bought it.

For fear of being evicted, Félicité never asked for any repairs to be done. The laths in the roof rotted, and all through one winter her bolster was wet. After Easter she began spitting blood.

When this happened Mère Simon called in a doctor. Félicité wanted to know what was the matter with her, but she was so deaf that only one word reached her: 'Pneumonia.' It was a word she knew, and she answered gently: 'Ah! like Madame', thinking it natural that she should follow in her mistress's footsteps.

The time to set up the altars of repose was drawing near.

The first altar was always at the foot of the hill, the second in front of the post office, the third about half-way up the street. There was some argument as to the siting of this one, and finally the women of the parish picked on Mme Aubain's courtyard.

The fever and the tightness of the chest grew worse. Félicité fretted over not doing anything for the altar. If only she could have something put on it! Then she thought of the parrot. The neighbours protested that it would not be seemly, but the curé gave his permission, and this made her so happy that she begged him to accept Loulou, the only thing of value she possessed, when she died.

From Tuesday to Saturday, the eve of Corpus Christi, she coughed more and more frequently. In the evening her face looked pinched and drawn, her lips stuck to her gums, and she started vomiting. At dawn the next day, feeling very low, she sent for a priest.

Three good women stood by her while she was given extreme unction. Then she said that she had to speak to Fabu.

He arrived in his Sunday best, very ill at ease in this funereal atmosphere.

'Forgive me,' she said, making an effort to stretch out her arm. 'I thought it was you who had killed him.'

What could she mean by such nonsense? To think that she had suspected a man like him of murder! He got very indignant and was obviously going to make a scene. 'Can't you see', they said, 'that she isn't in her right mind any more?'

From time to time Félicité would start talking to shadows. The women went away. Mère Simon had her lunch.

A little later she picked Loulou up and held him out to Félicité, saying:

'Come now, say good-bye to him.'

Although the parrot was not a corpse, the worms were eating him up. One of his wings was broken, and the stuffing was coming out of his stomach. But she was blind by now, and she kissed him on the forehead and pressed him against her cheek. Mère Simon took him away from her to put him on the altar.

5

The scents of summer came up from the meadows; there was a buzzing of flies; the sun was glittering in the river and warming the slates of the roof. Mère Simon had come back into the room and was gently nodding off to sleep.

The noise of church bells woke her up; the congregation was coming out from vespers. Félicité's delirium abated. Thinking of the procession, she could see it as clearly as if she had been following it.

All the school-children, the choristers, and the firemen were walking along the pavements, while advancing up the middle of the street came the church officer armed with his halberd, the beadle carrying a great cross, the schoolmaster keeping an eye on the boys, and the nun fussing over her little girls—three of the prettiest, looking like curly-headed angels, were throwing rose-petals into the air. Then came the deacon, with both arms outstretched, conducting the band, and a couple of censer-bearers who turned round at every step to face the Holy Sacrament, which the curé, wearing his splendid chasuble, was carrying under a canopy of poppy-red velvet held aloft by four churchwardens. A crowd of people surged along behind, between the white cloths covering the walls of the houses, and eventually they got to the bottom of the hill.

A cold sweat moistened Félicité's temples. Mère Simon sponged it up with a cloth, telling herself that one day she would have to go the same way.

The hum of the crowd increased in volume, was very loud for a moment, then faded away.

A fusillade shook the window-panes. It was the postilions[6] saluting the monstrance.[7] Félicité rolled her eyes and said as loud as she could: 'Is he all right?'—worrying about the parrot.

She entered into her death-agony. Her breath, coming ever faster, with a rattling sound, made her sides heave. Bubbles of froth appeared at the corners of her mouth, and her whole body trembled.

Soon the booming of the ophicleides,[8] the clear voices of the children, and the deep voices of the men could be heard near at hand. Now and then everything was quiet, and the tramping of feet, deadened by a carpet of flowers, sounded like a flock moving across pasture-land.

The clergy appeared in the courtyard. Mère Simon climbed on to a chair to reach the little round window, from which she had a full view of the altar below.

It was hung with green garlands and adorned with a flounce in English needle-point lace. In the middle was a little frame containing some relics, there were two orange-trees at the corners, and all the way along stood silver candlesticks and china vases holding sunflowers, lilies, peonies, foxgloves, and bunches of hydrangea. This pyramid of bright colours stretched from the first floor right down to the carpet which was spread out over the pavement. Some rare objects caught the eye: a silver-gilt sugar-basin wreathed in violets, some pendants of Alençon gems gleaming on a bed of moss, and two Chinese screens with landscape decorations. Loulou, hidden under roses, showed nothing but his blue poll, which looked like a plaque of lapis lazuli.

[6] Those who ride the left-hand horse of a two- or four-horse carriage.
[7] The showing of the consecrated Host.
[8] An early brass wind instrument.

The churchwardens, the choristers, and the children lined up along the three sides of the courtyard. The priest went slowly up the steps and placed his great shining gold sun on the lace altar-cloth. Everyone knelt down. There was a deep silence. And the censers, swinging at full tilt, slid up and down their chains.

A blue cloud of incense was wafted up into Félicité's room. She opened her nostrils wide and breathed it in with a mystical, sensuous fervour. Then she closed her eyes. Her lips smiled. Her heart-beats grew slower and slower, each a little fainter and gentler, like a fountain running dry, an echo fading away. And as she breathed her last, she thought she could see, in the opening heavens, a gigantic parrot hovering above her head.

Giovanni Verga (1840–1922)

Giovanni Verga was born in Sicily in 1840, the son of one of the oldest families on the island: his ancestors had come with Peter of Aragon in the thirteenth century. Not surprisingly, it was only when he returned to Sicily as a source for his fiction did he become an important writer of the nineteenth century. Of Sicily and Verga, D. H. Lawrence writes: "anyone who has known this land can never be quite free from the nostalgia for it, nor can he fail to fall under the spell of Verga's wonderful creation of it . . . ."

Verga went through a roundabout apprenticeship before arriving at his subject. He gave up the study of law for literature, and his first publication was a historical novel. His next works—written when he lived in Florence, the artistic capital of Italy at that time—were sentimental and melodramatic novels of passion, in the style of such French writers as Dumas *fils* and Octave Feuillet (who gave his name to the *feuilleton,* the part of a newspaper given to light fiction or general entertainment).

Moving northward to Milan, Verga turned his imagination south and began to write the Sicilian works which brought him fame. Best known are *Life in the Fields* (1880), containing both "The She-Wolf" and "Cavalleria Rusticana," which became the basis for Mascagni's opera of simple folk in 1890 and for *The House by the Medlar Tree* (1881) and *Little Novels of Sicily* (1883). Verga spent the last three decades of his life home in Sicily, silent and in seclusion. When he died in 1922 he was, in Lawrence's description, "proud in his privacy."

To match his strong Sicilian subject matter, Verga adopted the methods of naturalism, his particular approach becoming known as *verismo.* He has been compared to Flaubert and Zola. His kind of naturalism is based on meticulous observation of the physical ("She was tall, thin; she had the firm and vigorous breasts of the olive-skinned—and yet she was no longer young; she was pale, as if always plagued by malaria"). He appeals directly to the reader's senses ("In the immense fields, where you heard only the crackling flight of the grasshoppers, as the sun hammered down overhead"). His style is simple and straightforward, without flourishes of metaphor or sophisticated twists of irony. The reader is kept in close, and sensuous, contact with the materials of the story; despite his power of omniscience, the narrator stands aside. Even Verga's sympathy for the peasants is held down, surfacing only as the facts, the hard facts, of their lives ("weeding, hoeing, feeding the animals, pruning the vines, despite the northeast and levantine winds of January or the August sirocco, when the mules' heads drooped and the men slept face down along the wall, on the north side"). He trusts the power of his simple storytelling.

And well he should. D. H. Lawrence, who translated many of Verga's books, captures the quality of the work when he says, "He is *extraordinarily* good—peasant—quite modern—Homeric . . . ." For, in the hands of a writer who understands that overwhelming passions break forth from the simplest circumstances, "The She-Wolf" rises above pure naturalism. It provides the earthiness and simplicity of folktale, the passion of myth. The She-wolf is only an aging peasant who works the fields where she "gathered bundle after bundle, and sheaf after sheaf, never straightening for an instant, never raising the flask to her lips, just to remain at the heels of Nanni . . . ." But in her insatiable, destructive, reckless lust for her son-in-law, she is larger than life.

The She-Wolf

She was tall, thin; she had the firm and vigorous breasts of the olive-skinned—and yet she was no longer young; she was pale, as if always plagued by malaria, and in that pallor, two enormous eyes, and fresh red lips which devoured you.

In the village they called her the She-wolf, because she never had enough—of anything. The women made the sign of the cross when they saw her pass, alone as a wild bitch, prowling about suspiciously like a famished wolf; with her red lips she sucked the blood of their sons and husbands in a flash, and pulled them behind her skirt with a single glance of those devilish eyes, even if they were before the altar of Saint Agrippina. Fortunately, the She-wolf never went to church, not at Easter, not at Christmas, not to hear Mass, not for confession.—Father Angiolino of Saint Mary of Jesus, a true servant of God, had lost his soul on account of her.

Maricchia, a good girl, poor thing, cried in secret because she was the She-wolf's daughter, and no one would marry her, though, like every other girl in the village, she had her fine linen in a chest and her good land under the sun.

One day the She-wolf fell in love with a handsome young man who had just returned from the service and was mowing hay with her in the fields of the notary; and she fell in love in the strongest sense of the word, feeling the flesh afire beneath her clothes; and staring him in the eyes, she suffered the thirst one has in the hot hours of June, deep in the plain. But he went on mowing undisturbed, his nose bent over the swaths.

"What's wrong, Pina?" he would ask.

In the immense fields, where you heard only the crackling flight of the grasshoppers, as the sun hammered down overhead, the She-wolf gathered bundle after bundle, and sheaf after sheaf, never tiring, never straightening up for an instant, never raising

From Giovanni Verga, *The She Wolf and Other Stories*, translated by Giovanni Cecchetti. University of California Press, 1958. Originally published by the University of California Press; reprinted by permission of The Regents of the University of California.

the flask to her lips, just to remain at the heels of Nanni, who mowed and mowed and asked from time to time:

"What is it you want, Pina?"

One evening she told him, while the men were dozing on the threshing floor, tired after the long day, and the dogs were howling in the vast, dark countryside.

"It's you I want. You who're beautiful as the sun and sweet as honey. I want you!"

"And I want your daughter, instead, who's a maid," answered Nanni laughing.

The She-wolf thrust her hands into her hair, scratching her temples, without saying a word, and walked away. And she did not appear at the threshing floor any more. But she saw Nanni again in October, when they were making olive oil, for he was working near her house, and the creaking of the press kept her awake all night.

"Get the sack of olives," she said to her daughter, "and come with me."

Nanni was pushing olives under the millstone with a shovel, shouting "Ohee" to the mule, to keep it from stopping.

"You want my daughter Maricchia?" Pina asked him.

"What'll you give your daughter Maricchia?" answered Nanni.

"She has all her father's things, and I'll give her my house too; as for me, all I need is a little corner in the kitchen, enough for a straw mattress."

"If that's the way it is, we can talk about it at Christmas," said Nanni.

Nanni was all greasy and filthy, spattered with oil and fermented olives, and Maricchia didn't want him at any price. But her mother grabbed her by the hair before the fireplace, muttering between her teeth:

"If you don't take him, I'll kill you!"

The She-wolf was almost sick, and the people were saying that when the devil gets old he becomes a hermit. She no longer roamed here and there, no longer lingered at the doorway, with those bewitched eyes. Whenever she fixed them on his face, those eyes of hers, her son-in-law began to laugh and pulled out the scapular of the Virgin to cross himself. Maricchia stayed at home nursing the babies, and her mother went into the fields to work with the men, and just like a man too, weeding, hoeing, feeding the animals, pruning the vines, despite the northeast and levantine winds of January or the August sirocco, when the mules' heads drooped and the men slept face down along the wall, on the north side. "In those hours between nones and vespers when no good woman goes roving around,"[1] Pina was the only living soul to be seen wandering in the countryside, over the burning stones of the paths, through the scorched stubble of the immense fields that became lost in the suffocating heat, far, far away toward the foggy Etna, where the sky was heavy on the horizon.

"Wake-up!" said the She-wolf to Nanni, who was sleeping in the ditch, along the dusty hedge, his head on his arms. "Wake-up. I've brought you some wine to cool your throat."

Nanni opened his drowsy eyes wide, still half asleep, and finding her standing before him, pale, with her arrogant breasts and her cold-black eyes, he stretched out his hands gropingly.

[1] An old Sicilian proverb, which refers to the hours of the early afternoon, when the Sicilian countryside lies motionless under a scorching sun and no person would dare walk on the roads. Those hours are traditionally believed to be under the spell of malignant spirits. TRANSLATOR'S NOTE.

"No! no good woman goes roving around in the hours between nones and vespers!" sobbed Nanni, throwing his head back into the dry grass of the ditch, deep,
deep, his nails in his scalp. "Go away! go away! don't come to the threshing floor
again!"

The She-Wolf was going away, in fact, retying her superb tresses, her gaze bent
fixedly before her as she moved through the hot stubble, her eyes as black as coal.

But she came to the threshing floor again, and more than once, and Nanni did
not complain. On the contrary, when she was late, in the hours between nones and
vespers, he would go and wait for her at the top of the white, deserted path, with his
forehead bathed in sweat; and he would thrust his hands into his hair, and repeat
every time:

"Go away! go away! don't come to the threshing floor again!"

Maricchia cried night and day, and glared at her mother, her eyes burning with
tears and jealousy, like a young she-wolf herself, every time she saw her come, mute
and pale, from the fields.

"Vile, vile mother!" she said to her. "Vile mother!"

"Shut up!"

"Thief! Thief!"

"Shut up!"

"I'll go to the Sergeant, I will!"

"Go ahead!"

And she really did go, with her babies in her arms, fearing nothing, and without
shedding a tear, like a madwoman, because now she too loved that husband who had
been forced on her, greasy and filthy, spattered with oil and fermented olives.

The Sergeant sent for Nanni; he threatened him even with jail and the gallows.
Nanni began to sob and tear his hair; he didn't deny anything, he didn't try to clear
himself.

"It's the temptation!" he said. "It's the temptation of hell!"

He threw himself at the Sergeant's feet begging to be sent to jail.

"For God's sake, Sergeant, take me out of this hell! Have me killed, put me in
jail; don't let me see her again, never! never!"

"No!" answered the She-wolf instead, to the Sergeant. "I kept a little corner in
the kitchen to sleep in, when I gave him my house as dowry. It's my house. I don't
intend to leave it."

Shortly afterward, Nanni was kicked in the chest by a mule and was at the point
of death, but the priest refused to bring him the Sacrament if the She-wolf did not go
out of the house. The She-wolf left, and then her son-in-law could also prepare to leave
like a good Christian; he confessed and received communion with such signs of repen-
tance and contrition that all the neighbors and the curious wept before the dying
man's bed.—And it would have been better for him to die that day, before the devil
came back to tempt him again and creep into his body and soul, when he got well.

"Leave me alone!" he told the She-wolf. "For God's sake, leave me in peace! I've
seen death with my own eyes! Poor Maricchia is desperate. Now the whole town
knows about it! If I don't see you it's better for both of us . . ."

And he would have liked to gouge his eyes out not to see those of the She-wolf,
for whenever they peered into his, they made him lose his body and soul. He did not
know what to do to free himself from the spell. He paid for Masses for the souls in

purgatory and asked the priest and the Sergeant for help. At Easter he went to confession, and in penance he publicly licked more than four feet of pavement, crawling on the pebbles in front of the church—and then, as the She-wolf came to tempt him again:

"Listen!" he said to her. "Don't come to the threshing floor again; if you do, I swear to God, I'll kill you!"

"Kill me," answered the She-wolf. "I don't care; I can't stand it without you."

As he saw her from the distance, in the green wheat fields, Nanni stopped hoeing the vineyard, and went to pull the ax from the elm. The She-wolf saw him come, pale and wild-eyed, with the ax glistening in the sun, but she did not fall back a single step, did not lower her eyes; she continued toward him, her hands laden with red poppies, her black eyes devouring him.

"Ah! damn your soul!" stammered Nanni.

Thomas Hardy (1840-1928)

Hardy's fictional subjects are inseparable from his settings, most of which are based on that rural country around his native Dorsetshire that he called "Egdon Heath." But Hardy is no mere local colorist, touristing amid sentimental scenes. His sense of the land and its people is profoundly tragic; the forces of nature and human nature are often at fatal odds in his books, and Hardy—who was also a freethinker well versed in Schopenhauer, Darwin, John Stuart Mill, and other advanced Victorian writers—can with justice be called a pessimist. His characters often seem more archetypal than individual; and we know them first generically, through what they work at or in rather than (as Chekhov or James would show them) through the interactions of social life. Thus we meet Shepherd Fennel's wife in "The Three Strangers": "Shepherd Fennel had married well, his wife being a dairyman's daughter from a vale at a distance, who brought fifty guineas in her pocket—and kept them there, till they should be required for ministering to the needs of a coming family." Though Hardy wrote no historical novels, his characters, as Walter Allen says, "live in the additional dimension of history . . . peasants for the most part, they are close to an earth that has changed little over centuries. Most of them . . . seem to live in a timeless era in which actual historical events and persons have assumed the vagueness and largeness of myth."

Hardy perhaps comes closer than any modern writer in this collection to being a storyteller in the traditional sense. As Donald Davidson says, while he tried to write like a modern, "he thought, or artistically conceived, like a man of another century." "We story-tellers," Hardy said, "are all Ancient Mariners," and many of his tales are written—as Davidson pointed out—as an ancient balladmaker would write them were he to write prose. Hardy wished to be a poet (and his poetry today is highly esteemed), but in his own time his poems had small success. It was with novels like *Far from the Madding Crowd* (1874), the *Return of the Native* (1878), *The Mayor of Casterbridge* (1886), *Tess of the d'Urbervilles* (1891), *Jude the Obscure* (1894–95), and to a lesser extent with volumes of short fiction like *Wessex Tales* (1888), *A*

Group of Noble Dames (1890), and *Life's Little Ironies* (1894) that he made his reputation.

Though his tales, like his novels, tend to be uneven, and marred by all kinds of ham-handed plotting and writing, at their best they transcend their defects. A story is told that Hardy, when asked about his "technique," replied: "There isn't any technique about prose, is there? It just comes along of itself." That remark reveals an artist vastly different from Flaubert or James or Joyce, a provincial rather than a cosmopolite, but therein lies his great strength. He was a modern with a profound sense of the ageless and traditional, and of the "precipice in time" that separates the two. For example, Hardy describes the sense of *community* in Higher Crowstairs as something distinctly lacking in the modern world:

> Absolute confidence in each other's good opinion begat perfect ease, while the finishing stroke of manner, amounting to a truly princely serenity, was lent to the majority by the absence of any expression or trait denoting that they wished to get on in the world, enlarge their minds, or do any eclipsing thing whatever—which nowadays so generally nips the bloom and *bonhomie* of all except the two extremes of the social scale.

"The Three Strangers" is an almost classic example of a traditional folktale: plot is everything, characters exist for the action and not for their own sakes, description is no more than a setting for the action, and the whole turns on the moment of ironic discovery—what Aristotle called "peripety"—that brings about a change from one state of affairs to the opposite. The discovery here is that the fugitive sheepstealer was none other than the man who sat next to the hangman at the inn. It is little more than a joke, but hanging over it is the half-bitter sense that justice is as much a matter of chance as of divine purpose. It was what Hardy meant by "life's little ironies." Hardy lived to be eighty-eight, but in the last thirty years of his life, he wrote almost nothing but poetry.

The Three Strangers

Among the few features of agricultural England which retain an appearance but little modified by the lapse of centuries, may be reckoned the long, grassy and furzy downs, coombs, or ewe-leases, as they are called according to their kind, that fill a large area of certain counties in the south and south-west. If any mark of human occupation is met with hereon, it usually takes the form of the solitary cottage of some shepherd.

Fifty years ago such a lonely cottage stood on such a down, and may possibly be standing there now. In spite of its loneliness, however, the spot, by actual measurement, was not three miles from a county-town. Yet that affected it little. Three miles of irregular upland, during the long inimical seasons, with their sleets, snows, rains, and mists, afford withdrawing space enough to isolate a Timon or a Nebuchadnezzar; much less, in fair weather, to please that less repellent tribe, the poets, philosophers, artists, and others who "conceive and meditate of pleasant things."

"The Three Strangers" from *Wessex Tales* by Thomas Hardy. Reprinted by permission of the Trustees of the Hardy Estate and the Macmillan Company of Canada Limited.

Some old earthen camp or barrow, some clump of trees, at least some starved
fragment of ancient hedge is usually taken advantage of in the erection of these forlorn
dwellings. But, in the present case, such a kind of shelter had been disregarded. Higher
Crowstairs, as the house was called, stood quite detached and undefended. The only
reason for its precise situation seemed to be the crossing of two footpaths at right
angles hard by, which may have crossed there and thus for a good five hundred years.
Hence the house was exposed to the elements on all sides. But, though the wind up
here blew unmistakably when it did blow, and the rain hit hard whenever it fell, the
various weathers of the winter season were not quite so formidable on the down as
they were imagined to be by dwellers on low ground. The raw rimes were not so
pernicious as in the hollows, and the frosts were scarcely so severe. When the shepherd
and his family who tenanted the house were pitied for their sufferings from the exposure, they said that upon the whole they were less inconvenienced by "wuzzes and
flames" (hoarses and phlegms) than when they had lived by the stream of a snug
neighbouring valley.

The night of March 28, 182—, was precisely one of the nights that were wont to
call forth these expressions of commiseration. The level rainstorm smote walls, slopes,
and hedges like the clothyard shafts of Senlac and Crecy. Such sheep and outdoor
animals as had no shelter stood with their buttocks to the winds; while the tails of little
birds trying to roost on some scraggy thorn were blown inside-out like umbrellas. The
gable-end of the cottage was stained with wet, and the eavesdroppings flapped against
the wall. Yet never was commiseration for the shepherd more misplaced. For that
cheerful rustic was entertaining a large party in glorification of the christening of his
second girl.

The guests had arrived before the rain began to fall, and they were all now
assembled in the chief or living room of the dwelling. A glance into the apartment at
eight o'clock on this eventful evening would have resulted in the opinion that it was as
cosy and comfortable a nook as could be wished for in boisterous weather. The calling
of its inhabitant was proclaimed by a number of highly-polished sheep-crooks without
stems that were hung ornamentally over the fireplace, the curl of each shining crook
varying from the antiquated type engraved in the patriarchal pictures of old family
Bibles to the most approved fashion of the last local sheep-fair. The room was lighted
by half-a-dozen candles, having wicks only a trifle smaller than the grease which
enveloped them, in candlesticks that were never used but at high-days, holy-days, and
family feasts. The lights were scattered about the room, two of them standing on the
chimney-piece. This position of candles was in itself significant. Candles on the chimney-piece always meant a party.

On the hearth, in front of a back-brand to give substance, blazed a fire of thorns,
that crackled "like the laughter of the fool."

Nineteen persons were gathered here. Of these, five women, wearing gowns of
various bright hues, sat in chairs along the wall; girls shy and not shy filled the
window-bench; four men, including Charley Jake the hedge-carpenter, Elijah New the
parish-clerk, and John Pitcher, a neighbouring dairyman, the shepherd's father-in-law,
lolled in the settle; a young man and maid, who were blushing over tentative *pourpar-
lers* on a life-companionship, sat beneath the corner-cupboard; and an elderly engaged
man of fifty or upward moved restlessly about from spots where his betrothed was not
to the spot where she was. Enjoyment was pretty general, and so much the more
prevailed in being unhampered by conventional restrictions. Absolute confidence in
each other's good opinion begat perfect ease, while the finishing stroke of manner,

amounting to a truly princely serenity, was lent to the majority by the absence of any expression or trait denoting that they wished to get on in the world, enlarge their minds, or do any eclipsing thing whatever—which nowadays so generally nips the bloom and *bonhomie* of all except the two extremes of the social scale.

Shepherd Fennel had married well, his wife being a dairyman's daughter from a vale at a distance, who brought fifty guineas in her pocket—and kept them there, till they should be required for ministering to the needs of a coming family. This frugal woman had been somewhat exercised as to the character that should be given to the gathering. A sit-still party had its advantages; but an undisturbed position of ease in chairs and settles was apt to lead on the men to such an unconscionable deal of toping that they would sometimes fairly drink the house dry. A dancing-party was the alternative; but this, while avoiding the foregoing objection on the score of good drink, had a counterbalancing disadvantage in the matter of good victuals, the ravenous appetites engendered by the exercise causing immense havoc in the buttery. Shepherdess Fennel fell back upon the intermediate plan of mingling short dances with short periods of talk and singing, so as to hinder any ungovernable rage in either. But this scheme was entirely confined to her own gentle mind: the shepherd himself was in the mood to exhibit the most reckless phases of hospitality.

The fiddler was a boy of those parts, about twelve years of age, who had a wonderful dexterity in jigs and reels, though his fingers were so small and short as to necessitate a constant shifting for the high notes, from which he scrambled back to the first position with sounds not of unmixed purity of tone. At seven the shrill tweedle-dee of this youngster had begun, accompanied by a booming ground-bass from Elijah New, the parish-clerk, who had thoughtfully brought with him his favourite musical instrument, the serpent. Dancing was instantaneous, Mrs. Fennel privately enjoining the players on no account to let the dance exceed the length of a quarter of an hour.

But Elijah and the boy, in the excitement of their position, quite forgot the injunction. Moreover, Oliver Giles, a man of seventeen, one of the dancers, who was enamoured of his partner, a fair girl of thirty-three rolling years, had recklessly handed a new crown-piece to the musicians, as a bribe to keep going as long as they had muscle and wind. Mrs. Fennel, seeing the steam begin to generate on the countenances of her guests, crossed over and touched the fiddler's elbow and put her hand on the serpent's mouth. But they took no notice, and fearing she might lose her character of genial hostess if she were to interfere too markedly, she retired and sat down helpless. And so the dance whizzed on with cumulative fury, the performers moving in their planet-like courses, direct and retrograde, from apogee to perigee, till the hand of the well-kicked clock at the bottom of the room had travelled over the circumference of an hour.

While these cheerful events were in course of enactment within Fennel's pastoral dwelling, an incident having considerable bearing on the party had occurred in the gloomy night without. Mrs. Fennel's concern about the growing fierceness of the dance corresponded in point of time with the ascent of a human figure to the solitary hill of Higher Crowstairs from the direction of the distant town. This personage strode on through the rain without a pause, following the little-worn path which, further on in its course, skirted the shepherd's cottage.

It was nearly the time of full moon, and on this account, though the sky was lined with a uniform sheet of dripping cloud, ordinary objects out of doors were readily visible. The said wan light revealed the lonely pedestrian to be a man of supple frame; his gait suggested that he had somewhat passed the period of perfect and instinctive agility, though not so far as to be otherwise than rapid of motion when occasion required. At a rough guess, he might have been about forty years of age. He appeared tall, but a recruiting sergeant, or other person accustomed to the judging of men's heights by the eye, would have discerned that this was chiefly owing to his gauntness, and that he was not more than five-feet-eight or nine.

Notwithstanding the regularity of his tread, there was caution in it, as in that of one who mentally feels his way; and despite the fact that it was not a black coat nor a dark garment of any sort that he wore, there was something about him which suggested that he naturally belonged to the black-coated tribes of men. His clothes were of fustian, and his boots hobnailed, yet in his progress he showed not the mud-accustomed bearing of hobnailed and fustianed peasantry.

By the time that he had arrived abreast of the shepherd's premises the rain came down, or rather came along, with yet more determined violence. The outskirts of the little settlement partially broke the force of wind and rain, and this induced him to stand still. The most salient of the shepherd's domestic erections was an empty sty at the forward corner of his hedgeless garden, for in these latitudes the principle of masking the homelier features of your establishment by a conventional frontage was unknown. The traveller's eye was attracted to this small building by the pallid shine of the wet slates that covered it. He turned aside, and, finding it empty, stood under the pent-roof for shelter.

While he stood the boom of the serpent within the adjacent house, and the lesser strains of the fiddler, reached the spot as an accompaniment to the surging hiss of the flying rain on the sod, its louder beating on the cabbage-leaves of the garden, on the straw hackles of eight or ten beehives just discernible by the path, and its dripping from the eaves into a row of buckets and pans that had been placed under the walls of the cottage. For at Higher Crowstairs, as at all such elevated domiciles, the grand difficulty of housekeeping was an insufficiency of water; and a casual rainfall was utilized by turning out, as catchers, every utensil that the house contained. Some queer stories might be told of the contrivances for economy in suds and dishwaters that are absolutely necessitated in upland habitations during the droughts of summer. But at this season there were no such exigencies; a mere acceptance of what the skies bestowed was sufficient for an abundant store.

At last the notes of the serpent ceased and the house was silent. This cessation of activity aroused the solitary pedestrian from the reverie into which he had lapsed, and, emerging from the shed, with an apparently new intention, he walked up the path to the house-door. Arrived here, his first act was to kneel down on a large stone beside the row of vessels, and to drink a copious draught from one of them. Having quenched his thirst he rose and lifted his hand to knock, but paused with his eye upon the panel. Since the dark surface of the wood revealed absolutely nothing, it was evident that he must be mentally looking through the door, as if he wished to measure thereby all the possibilities that a house of this sort might include, and how they might bear upon the question of his entry.

In his indecision he turned and surveyed the scene around. Not a soul was anywhere visible. The garden-path stretched downward from his feet, gleaming like the track of a snail; the roof of the little well (mostly dry), the well-cover, the top rail of the garden-gate, were varnished with the same dull liquid glaze; while, far away in the vale, a faint whiteness of more than usual extent showed that the rivers were high in the meads. Beyond all this winked a few bleared lamplights through the beating drops—lights that denoted the situation of the county-town from which he had appeared to come. The absence of all notes of life in that direction seemed to clinch his intentions, and he knocked at the door.

Within, a desultory chat had taken the place of movement and musical sound. The hedge-carpenter was suggesting a song to the company, which nobody just then was inclined to undertake, so that the knock afforded a not unwelcome diversion.

"Walk in!" said the shepherd promptly.

The latch clicked upward, and out of the night our pedestrian appeared upon the door-mat. The shepherd arose, snuffed two of the nearest candles, and turned to look at him.

Their light disclosed that the stranger was dark in complexion and not unprepossessing as to feature. His hat, which for a moment he did not remove, hung low over his eyes, without concealing that they were large, open, and determined, moving with a flash rather than a glance round the room. He seemed pleased with his survey, and, baring his shaggy head, said, in a rich deep voice, "The rain is so heavy, friends, that I ask leave to come in and rest awhile."

"To be sure, stranger," said the shepherd. "And faith, you've been lucky in choosing your time, for we are having a bit of a fling for a glad cause—though, to be sure, a man could hardly wish that glad cause to happen more than once a year."

"Nor less," spoke up a woman. "For 'tis best to get your family over and done with, as soon as you can, so as to be all the earlier out of the fag o't."

"And what may be this glad cause?" asked the stranger.

"A birth and christening," said the shepherd.

The stranger hoped his host might not be made unhappy either by too many or too few of such episodes, and being invited by a gesture to a pull at the mug, he readily acquiesced. His manner, which, before entering, had been so dubious, was now altogether that of a careless and candid man.

"Late to be traipsing athwart this coomb—hey?" said the engaged man of fifty.

"Late it is, master, as you say.—I'll take a seat in the chimney-corner, if you have nothing to urge against it, ma'am; for I am a little moist on the side that was next the rain."

Mrs. Shepherd Fennel assented, and made room for the self-invited comer, who, having got completely inside the chimney-corner, stretched out his legs and his arms with the expansiveness of a person quite at home.

"Yes, I am rather cracked in the vamp," he said freely, seeing that the eyes of the shepherd's wife fell upon his boots, "and I am not well fitted either. I have had some rough times lately, and have been forced to pick up what I can get in the way of wearing, but I must find a suit better fit for working-days when I reach home."

"One of hereabouts?" she inquired.

"Not quite that—further up the country."

"I thought so. And so be I; and by your tongue you come from my neighbourhood."

"But you would hardly have heard of me," he said quickly. "My time would be long before yours, ma'am, you see."

This testimony to the youthfulness of his hostess had the effect of stopping her cross-examination.

"There is only one thing more wanted to make me happy," continued the newcomer. "And that is a little baccy, which I am sorry to say I am out of."

"I'll fill your pipe," said the shepherd.

"I must ask you to lend me a pipe likewise."

"A smoker, and no pipe about 'ee?"

"I have dropped it somewhere on the road."

The shepherd filled and handed him a new clay pipe, saying, as he did so, "Hand me your baccy-box—I'll fill that too, now I am about it."

The man went through the movement of searching his pockets.

"Lost that too?" said his entertainer, with some surprise.

"I am afraid so," said the man with some confusion. "Give it to me in a screw of paper." Lighting his pipe at the candle with a suction that drew the whole flame into the bowl, he resettled himself in the corner and bent his looks upon the faint steam from his damp legs, as if he wished to say no more.

Meanwhile, the general body of guests had been taking little notice of this visitor by reason of an absorbing discussion in which they were engaged with the band about a tune for the next dance. The matter being settled, they were about to stand up when an interruption came in the shape of another knock at the door.

At the sound of the same the man in the chimney-corner took up the poker and began stirring the brands as if doing it thoroughly were the one aim of his existence; and a second time the shepherd said, "Walk in!" In a moment another man stood upon the straw-woven door-mat. He too was a stranger.

This individual was one of a type radically different from the first. There was more of the commonplace in his manner, and a certain jovial cosmopolitanism sat upon his features. He was several years older than the first arrival, his hair being slightly frosted, his eyebrows bristly, and his whiskers cut back from his cheeks. His face was rather full and flabby, and yet it was not altogether a face without power. A few grog-blossoms marked the neighbourhood of his nose. He flung back his long drab greatcoat, revealing that beneath it he wore a suit of cinder-grey shade throughout, large heavy seals, of some metal or other that would take a polish, dangling from his fob as his only personal ornament. Shaking the water-drops from his low-crowned glazed hat, he said, "I must ask for a few minutes' shelter, comrades, or I shall be wetted to my skin before I get to Casterbridge."

"Make yourself at home, master," said the shepherd, perhaps a trifle less heartily than on the first occasion. Not that Fennel had the least tinge of niggardliness in his composition; but the room was far from large, spare chairs were not numerous, and damp companions were not altogether desirable at close quarters for the women and girls in their bright-coloured gowns.

However, the second comer, after taking off his greatcoat, and hanging his hat on a nail in one of the ceiling-beams as if he had been specially invited to put it there, advanced and sat down at the table. This had been pushed so closely into the chimney-corner, to give all available room to the dancers, that its inner edge grazed the elbow of the man who had ensconced himself by the fire; and thus the two strangers were brought into close companionship. They nodded to each other by way of breaking the ice of unacquaintance, and the first stranger handed his neighbour the family mug—a huge vessel of brown ware, having its upper edge worn away like a threshold by the rub of whole generations of thirsty lips that had gone the way of all flesh, and bearing the following inscription burnt upon its rotund side in yellow letters:—

THERE İS NO FUN
    UNTİLL İ CUM.

The other man, nothing loth, raised the mug to his lips, and drank on, and on, and on—till a curious blueness overspread the countenance of the shepherd's wife, who had regarded with no little surprise the first stranger's free offer to the second of what did not belong to him to dispense.

"I knew it!" said the toper to the shepherd with much satisfaction. "When I walked up your garden before coming in, and saw the hives all of a row, I said to myself, 'Where there's bees there's honey, and where there's honey there's mead.' But mead of such a truly comfortable sort as this I really didn't expect to meet in my older days." He took yet another pull at the mug, till it assumed an ominous elevation.

"Glad you enjoy it!" said the shepherd warmly.

"It is goodish mead," assented Mrs. Fennel, with an absence of enthusiasm which seemed to say that it was possible to buy praise for one's cellar at too heavy a price. "It is trouble enough to make—and really I hardly think we shall make any more. For honey sells well, and we ourselves can make shift with a drop o' small mead and metheglin for common use from the comb-washings."

"O, but you'll never have the heart!" reproachfully cried the stranger in cinder-grey, after taking up the mug a third time and setting it down empty. "I love mead, when 'tis old like this, as I love to go to church o' Sundays, or to relieve the needy any day of the week."

"Ha, ha, ha!" said the man in the chimney-corner, who, in spite of the taciturnity induced by the pipe of tobacco, could not or would not refrain from this slight testimony to his comrade's humour.

Now the old mead of those days, brewed of the purest first-year or maiden honey, four pounds to the gallon—with its due complement of white of eggs, cinnamon, ginger, cloves, mace, rosemary, yeast, and processes of working, bottling, and cellaring—tasted remarkably strong; but it did not taste so strong as it actually was. Hence, presently, the stranger in cinder-grey at the table, moved by its creeping influence, unbuttoned his waistcoat, threw himself back in his chair, spread his legs, and made his presence felt in various ways.

"Well, well, as I say," he resumed, "I am going to Casterbridge, and to Casterbridge I must go. I should have been almost there by this time; but the rain drove me into your dwelling, and I'm not sorry for it."

"You don't live in Casterbridge?" said the shepherd.

"Not as yet; though I shortly mean to move there."

"Going to set up in trade, perhaps?"

"No, no," said the shepherd's wife. "It is easy to see that the gentleman is rich, and don't want to work at anything."

The cinder-grey stranger paused, as if to consider whether he would accept that definition of himself. He presently rejected it by answering, "Rich is not quite the word for me, dame. I do work, and I must work. And even if I only get to Casterbridge by midnight I must begin work there at eight to-morrow morning. Yes, het or wet, blow or snow, famine or sword, my day's work to-morrow must be done."

"Poor man! Then, in spite o' seeming, you be worse off than we?" replied the shepherd's wife.

"'Tis the nature of my trade, men and maidens. 'Tis the nature of my trade more than my poverty. . . . But really and truly I must up and off, or I shan't get a lodging in the town." However, the speaker did not move, and directly added, "There's time for one more draught of friendship before I go; and I'd perform it at once if the mug were not dry."

"Here's a mug o' small," said Mrs. Fennel. "Small, we call it, though to be sure 'tis only the first wash o' the combs."

"No," said the stranger disdainfully. "I won't spoil your first kindness by partaking o' your second."

"Certainly not," broke in Fennel. "We don't increase and multiply every day, and I'll fill the mug again." He went away to the dark place under the stairs where the barrel stood. The shepherdess followed him.

"Why should you do this?" she said reproachfully, as soon as they were alone. "He's emptied it once, though it held enough for ten people; and now he's not contented wi' the small, but must needs call for more o' the strong! And a stranger unbeknown to any of us. For my part, I don't like the look o' the man at all."

"But he's in the house, my honey; and 'tis a wet night, and a christening. Daze it, what's a cup of mead more or less? There'll be plenty more next bee-burning."

"Very well—this time, then," she answered, looking wistfully at the barrel. "But what is the man's calling, and where is he one of, that he should come in and join us like this?"

"I don't know. I'll ask him again."

The catastrophe of having the mug drained dry at one pull by the stranger in cinder-grey was effectually guarded against this time by Mrs. Fennel. She poured out his allowance in a small cup, keeping the large one at a discreet distance from him. When he had tossed off his portion the shepherd renewed his inquiry about the stranger's occupation.

The latter did not immediately reply, and the man in the chimney-corner, with sudden demonstrativeness, said, "Anybody may know my trade—I'm a wheelwright."

"A very good trade for these parts," said the shepherd.

"And anybody may know mine—if they've the sense to find it out," said the stranger in cinder-grey.

"You may generally tell what a man is by his claws," observed the hedge-carpenter, looking at his own hands. "My fingers be as full of thorns as an old pin-cushion is of pins."

The hands of the man in the chimney-corner instinctively sought the shade, and he gazed into the fire as he resumed his pipe. The man at the table took up the hedge-carpenter's remark, and added smartly, "True; but the oddity of my trade is that, instead of setting a mark upon me, it sets a mark upon my customers."

No observation being offered by anybody in elucidation of this enigma, the shepherd's wife once more called for a song. The same obstacles presented themselves as at the former time—one had no voice, another had forgotten the first verse. The stranger at the table, whose soul had now risen to a good working temperature, relieved the difficulty by exclaiming that, to start the company, he would sing himself. Thrusting one thumb into the arm-hole of his waistcoat, he waved the other hand in the air, and, with an extemporizing gaze at the shining sheep-crooks above the mantelpiece, began:—

"O my trade it is the rarest one,
Simple shepherds all—
My trade is a sight to see;
For my customers I tie, and take them up on high,
And waft 'em to a far countree!"

The room was silent when he had finished the verse—with one exception, that of the man in the chimney-corner, who, at the singer's word, "Chorus!" joined him in a deep bass voice of musical relish—

"And waft 'em to a far countree!"

Oliver Giles, John Pitcher the dairyman, the parish-clerk, the engaged man of fifty, the row of young women against the wall, seemed lost in thought not of the gayest kind. The shepherd looked meditatively on the ground, the shepherdess gazed keenly at the singer, and with some suspicion; she was doubting whether this stranger were merely singing an old song from recollection, or was composing one there and then for the occasion. All were as perplexed at the obscure revelation as the guests at Belshazzar's Feast, except the man in the chimney-corner, who quietly said, "Second verse, stranger," and smoked on.

The singer thoroughly moistened himself from his lips inwards, and went on with the next stanza as requested:—

> "My tools are but common ones,
> Simple shepherds all—
> My tools are no sight to see:
> A little hempen string, and a post whereon to swing,
> Are implements enough for me!"

Shepherd Fennel glanced round. There was no longer any doubt that the stranger was answering his question rhythmically. The guests one and all started back with suppressed exclamations. The young woman engaged to the man of fifty fainted half-way, and would have proceeded, but finding him wanting in alacrity for catching her she sat down trembling.

"O, he's the ———!" whispered the people in the background, mentioning the name of an ominous public officer. "He's come to do it! 'Tis to be at Casterbridge jail to-morrow—the man for sheep-stealing—the poor clock-maker we heard of, who used to live away at Shottsford and had no work to do—Timothy Summers, whose family were a-starving, and so he went out of Shottsford by the high-road, and took a sheep in open daylight, defying the farmer and the farmer's wife and the farmer's lad, and every man jack among 'em. He" (and they nodded towards the stranger of the deadly trade) "is come from up the country to do it because there's not enough to do in his own county-town, and he's got the place here now our own county man's dead; he's going to live in the same cottage under the prison wall."

The stranger in cinder-grey took no notice of this whispered string of observations, but again wetted his lips. Seeing that his friend in the chimney-corner was the only one who reciprocated his joviality in any way, he held out his cup towards that appreciative comrade, who also held out his own. They clinked together, the eyes of the rest of the room hanging upon the singer's actions. He parted his lips for the third verse; but at that moment another knock was audible upon the door. This time the knock was faint and hesitating.

The company seemed scared; the shepherd looked with consternation towards the entrance, and it was with some effort that he resisted his alarmed wife's deprecatory glance, and uttered for the third time the welcoming words, "Walk in!"

The door was gently opened, and another man stood upon the mat. He, like those who had preceded him, was a stranger. This time it was a short, small personage, of fair complexion, and dressed in a decent suit of dark clothes.

"Can you tell me the way to ———?" he began: when, gazing around the room to observe the nature of the company amongst whom he had fallen, his eyes lighted on the stranger in cinder-grey. It was just at the instant when the latter, who had thrown his mind into his song with such a will that he scarcely heeded the interruption, silenced all whispers and inquiries by bursting into his third verse:

> "To-morrow is my working day,
> Simple shepherds all—
> To-morrow is a working day for me:
> For the farmer's sheep is slain, and the lad who did it ta'en,
> And on his soul may God ha' merc-y!"

The stranger in the chimney-corner, waving cups with the singer so heartily that his mead splashed over on the hearth, repeated in his bass voice as before:

> "And on his soul may God ha' merc-y!"

All this time the third stranger had been standing in the doorway. Finding now that he did not come forward or go on speaking, the guests particularly regarded him. They noticed to their surprise that he stood before them the picture of abject terror— his knees trembling, his hand shaking so violently that the door-latch by which he supported himself rattled audibly: his white lips were parted, and his eyes fixed on the merry officer of justice in the middle of the room. A moment more and he had turned, closed the door, and fled.

"What a man can it be?" said the shepherd.

The rest, between the awfulness of their late discovery and the odd conduct of this third visitor, looked as if they knew not what to think, and said nothing. Instinctively they withdrew further and further from the grim gentleman in their midst, whom some of them seemed to take for the Prince of Darkness himself, till they formed a remote circle, an empty space of floor being left between them and him—

> ". . . circulus, cujus centrum diabolus."

The room was so silent—though there were more than twenty people in it—that nothing could be heard but the patter of the rain against the window-shutters, accompanied by the occasional hiss of a stray drop that fell down the chimney into the fire, and the steady puffing of the man in the corner, who had now resumed his pipe of long clay.

The stillness was unexpectedly broken. The distant sound of a gun reverberated through the air—apparently from the direction of the county-town.

"Be jiggered!" cried the stranger who had sung the song, jumping up.

"What does that mean?" asked several.

"A prisoner escaped from the jail—that's what it means."

All listened. The sound was repeated, and none of them spoke but the man in the chimney-corner, who said quietly, "I've often been told that in this county they fire a gun at such times; but I never heard it till now."

"I wonder if it is *my* man?" murmured the personage in cinder-grey.

"Surely it is!" said the shepherd involuntarily. "And surely we've zeed him! That little man who looked in at the door by now, and quivered like a leaf when he zeed ye and heard your song!"

"His teeth chattered, and the breath went out of his body," said the dairyman.

"And his heart seemed to sink within him like a stone," said Oliver Giles.

"And he bolted as if he'd been shot at," said the hedge-carpenter.

"True—his teeth chattered, and his heart seemed to sink; and he bolted as if he'd been shot at," slowly summed up the man in the chimney-corner.

"I didn't notice it," remarked the hangman.

"We were all a-wondering what made him run off in such a fright," faltered one of the women against the wall, "and now 'tis explained!"

The firing of the alarm-gun went on at intervals, low and sullenly, and their suspicions became a certainty. The sinister gentleman in cinder-grey roused himself. "Is there a constable here?" he asked, in thick tones. "If so, let him step forward."

The engaged man of fifty stepped quavering out from the wall, his betrothed beginning to sob on the back of the chair.

"You are a sworn constable?"

"I be, sir."

"Then pursue the criminal at once, with assistance, and bring him back here. He can't have gone far."

"I will, sir, I will—when I've got my staff. I'll go home and get it, and come sharp here, and start in a body."

"Staff!—never mind your staff; the man'll be gone!"

"But I can't do nothing without my staff—can I, William, and John, and Charles Jake? No; for there's the king's royal crown a painted on en in yaller and gold, and the lion and the unicorn, so as when I raise en up and hit my prisoner, 'tis made a lawful blow thereby. I wouldn't 'tempt to take up a man without my staff—no, not I. If I hadn't the law to gie me courage, why, instead o' my taking up him he might take up me!"

"Now, I'm a king's man myself, and can give you authority enough for this," said the formidable officer in grey. "Now then, all of ye, be ready. Have ye any lanterns?"

"Yes—have ye any lanterns?—I demand it!" said the constable.

"And the rest of you able-bodied ———"

"Able-bodied men—yes—the rest of ye!" said the constable.

"Have you some good stout staves and pitchforks ———"

"Staves and pitchforks—in the name o' the law! And take 'em in yer hands and go in quest, and do as we in authority tell ye!"

Thus aroused, the men prepared to give chase. The evidence was, indeed, though circumstantial, so convincing, that but little argument was needed to show the shepherd's guests that after what they had seen it would look very much like connivance if they did not instantly pursue the unhappy third stranger, who could not as yet have gone more than a few hundred yards over such uneven country.

A shepherd is always well provided with lanterns; and, lighting these hastily, and with hurdle-staves in their hands, they poured out of the door, taking a direction along the crest of the hill, away from the town, the rain having fortunately a little abated.

Disturbed by the noise, or possibly by unpleasant dreams of her baptism, the child who had been christened began to cry heart-brokenly in the room overhead. These notes of grief came down through the chinks of the floor to the ears of the women below, who jumped up one by one, and seemed glad of the excuse to ascend and comfort the baby, for the incidents of the last half-hour greatly oppressed them. Thus in the space of two or three minutes the room on the ground-floor was deserted quite.

But it was not for long. Hardly had the sound of footsteps died away when a man returned round the corner of the house from the direction the pursuers had taken.

Peeping in at the door, and seeing nobody there, he entered leisurely. It was the stranger of the chimney-corner, who had gone out with the rest. The motive of his return was shown by his helping himself to a cut piece of skimmer-cake that lay on a ledge beside where he had sat, and which he had apparently forgotten to take with him. He also poured out half a cup more mead from the quantity that remained, ravenously eating and drinking these as he stood. He had not finished when another figure came in just as quietly—his friend in cinder-grey.

"O—you here?" said the latter, smiling. "I thought you had gone to help in the capture." And this speaker also revealed the object of his return by looking solicitously round for the fascinating mug of old mead.

"And I thought you had gone," said the other, continuing his skimmer-cake with some effort.

"Well, on second thoughts, I felt there were enough without me," said the first confidentially, "and such a night as it is, too. Besides, 'tis the business o' the Government to take care of its criminals—not mine."

"True; so it is. And I felt as you did, that there were enough without me."

"I don't want to break my limbs running over the humps and hollows of this wild country."

"Nor I neither, between you and me."

"These shepherd-people are used to it—simple-minded souls, you know, stirred up to anything in a moment. They'll have him ready for me before the morning, and no trouble to me at all."

"They'll have him, and we shall have saved ourselves all labour in the matter."

"True, true. Well, my way is to Casterbridge; and 'tis as much as my legs will do to take me that far. Going the same way?"

"No, I am sorry to say! I have to get home over there" (he nodded indefinitely to the right), "and I feel as you do, that it is quite enough for my legs to do before bedtime."

The other had by this time finished the mead in the mug, after which, shaking hands heartily at the door, and wishing each other well, they went their several ways.

In the meantime the company of pursuers had reached the end of the hog's-back elevation which dominated this part of the down. They had decided on no particular plan of action; and, finding that the man of the baleful trade was no longer in their company, they seemed quite unable to form any such plan now. They descended in all directions down the hill, and straightway several of the party fell into the snare set by Nature for all misguided midnight ramblers over this part of the cretaceous formation. The "lanchets," or flint slopes, which belted the escarpment at intervals of a dozen yards, took the less cautious ones unawares, and losing their footing on the rubbly steep they slid sharply downwards, the lanterns rolling from their hands to the bottom, and there lying on their sides till the horn was scorched through.

When they had again gathered themselves together, the shepherd, as the man knew the country best, took the lead, and guided them round these treacherous inclines. The lanterns, which seemed rather to dazzle their eyes and warn the fugitive than to assist them in the exploration, were extinguished, due silence was observed; and in this more rational order they plunged into the vale. It was a grassy, briery, moist defile, affording some shelter to any person who had sought it; but the party perambulated it in vain, and ascended on the other side. Here they wandered apart, and after an interval closed together again to report progress. At the second time of closing in they found themselves near a lonely ash, the single tree on this part of the coomb, probably sown there by a passing bird some fifty years before. And here, standing a little to one side of the trunk, as motionless as the trunk itself, appeared the man they were in quest of, his outline being well defined against the sky beyond. The band noiselessly drew up and faced him.

"Your money or your life!" said the constable sternly to the still figure.

"No, no," whispered John Pitcher. "'Tisn't our side ought to say that. That's the doctrine of vagabonds like him, and we be on the side of the law."

"Well, well," replied the constable impatiently; "I must say something, mustn't I? and if you had all the weight o' this undertaking upon your mind, perhaps you'd say the wrong thing too!—Prisoner at the bar, surrender, in the name of the Father—the Crown, I mane!"

The man under the tree seemed now to notice them for the first time, and giving them no opportunity whatever for exhibiting their courage, he strolled slowly towards them. He was, indeed, the little man, the third stranger; but his trepidation had in a great measure gone.

"Well, travellers," he said, "did I hear ye speak to me?"

"You did: you've got to come and be our prisoner at once!" said the constable. "We arrest 'ee on the charge of not biding in Casterbridge jail in a decent proper manner to be hung to-morrow morning. Neighbours, do your duty and seize the culpet!"

On hearing the charge the man seemed enlightened, and, saying not another word, resigned himself with preternatural civility to the search-party, who, with their staves in their hands, surrounded him on all sides, and marched him back towards the shepherd's cottage.

It was eleven o'clock by the time they arrived. The light shining from the open door, a sound of men's voices within, proclaimed to them as they approached the house that some new events had arisen in their absence. On entering they discovered the shepherd's living room to be invaded by two officers from Casterbridge jail, and a well-known magistrate who lived at the nearest country-seat, intelligence of the escape having become generally circulated.

"Gentlemen," said the constable, "I have brought back your man—not without risk and danger; but every one must do his duty! He is inside this circle of able-bodied persons, who have lent me useful aid, considering their ignorance of Crown work. Men, bring forward your prisoner!" And the third stranger was led to the light.

"Who is this?" said one of the officials.

"The man," said the constable.

"Certainly not," said the turnkey; and the first corroborated his statement.

"But how can it be otherwise?" asked the constable. "Or why was he so terrified at sight o' the singing instrument of the law who sat there?" Here he related the strange behaviour of the third stranger on entering the house during the hangman's song.

"Can't understand it," said the officer coolly. "All I know is that it is not the condemned man. He's quite a different character from this one; a gauntish fellow, with dark hair and eyes, rather good-looking, and with a musical bass voice that if you heard it once you'd never mistake as long as you lived."

"Why, souls—'twas the man in the chimney-corner!"

"Hey—what?" said the magistrate, coming forward after inquiring particulars from the shepherd in the background. "Haven't you got the man after all?"

"Well, sir, said the constable, "he's the man we were in search of, that's true; and yet he's not the man we were in search of. For the man we were in search of was not the man we wanted, sir, if you understand my every-day way; for 'twas the man in the chimney-corner!"

"A pretty kettle of fish altogether!" said the magistrate. "You had better start for the other man at once."

The prisoner now spoke for the first time. The mention of the man in the chimney-corner seemed to have moved him as nothing else could do. "Sir," he said, stepping forward to the magistrate, "take no more trouble about me. The time is come when I may as well speak. I have done nothing; my crime is that the condemned man is my brother. Early this afternoon I left home at Shottsford to tramp it all the way to Casterbridge jail to bid him farewell. I was benighted, and called here to rest and ask the way. When I opened the door I saw before me the very man, my brother, that I thought to see in the condemned cell at Casterbridge. He was in this chimney-corner; and jammed close to him, so that he could not have got out if he had tried, was the executioner who'd come to take his life, singing a song about it and not knowing that it was his victim who was close by, joining in to save appearances. My brother threw a glance of agony at me, and I knew he meant, 'Don't reveal what you see; my life depends on it.' I was so terror-struck that I could hardly stand, and, not knowing what I did, I turned and hurried away."

The narrator's manner and tone had the stamp of truth, and his story made a great impression on all around. "And do you know where your brother is at the present time?" asked the magistrate.

"I do not. I have never seen him since I closed this door."

"I can testify to that, for we've been between ye ever since," said the constable.

"Where does he think to fly to?—what is his occupation?"

"He's a watch-and-clock-maker, sir."

"'A said 'a was a wheelwright—a wicked rogue," said the constable.

"The wheels of clocks and watches he meant, no doubt," said Shepherd Fennel. "I thought his hands were palish for's trade."

"Well, it appears to me that nothing can be gained by retaining this poor man in custody," said the magistrate; "your business lies with the other, unquestionably."

And so the little man was released off-hand; but he looked nothing the less sad on that account, it being beyond the power of magistrate or constable to raze out the written troubles in his brain, for they concerned another whom he regarded with more solicitude than himself. When this was done, and the man had gone his way, the night was found to be so far advanced that it was deemed useless to renew the search before the next morning.

Next day, accordingly, the quest for the clever sheep-stealer became general and keen, to all appearance at least. But the intended punishment was cruelly disproportioned to the transgression, and the sympathy of a great many country-folk in that district was strongly on the side of the fugitive. Moreover, his marvellous coolness and daring in hob-and-nobbing with the hangman, under the unprecedented circumstances of the shepherd's party, won their admiration. So that it may be questioned if all those who ostensibly made themselves so busy in exploring woods and fields and lanes were quite so thorough when it came to the private examination of their own lofts and outhouses. Stories were afloat of a mysterious figure being occasionally seen in some old overgrown trackway or other, remote from turnpike roads; but when a search was instituted in any of these suspected quarters nobody was found. Thus the days and weeks passed without tidings.

In brief, the bass-voiced man of the chimney-corner was never recaptured. Some said that he went across the sea, others that he did not, but buried himself in the depths of a populous city. At any rate, the gentleman in cinder-grey never did his morning's work at Casterbridge, not met anywhere at all, for business purposes, the genial comrade with whom he had passed an hour of relaxation in the lonely house on the slope of the coomb.

The grass has long been green on the graves of Shepherd Fennel and his frugal wife; the guests who made up the christening party have mainly followed their entertainers to the tomb; the baby in whose honour they all had met is a matron in the sere and yellow leaf. But the arrival of the three strangers at the shepherd's that night, and the details connected therewith, is a story as well known as ever in the country about Higher Crowstairs.

Henry James (1843–1916)

Henry James was the great theoretician of fictional methods, and generations of young writers have gone to school to his essays, prefaces, letters, notebooks, criticism, as well as to his astonishing number of novels and tales. In "The Art of Fiction" he says that the source of fiction is not mere raw experience but "the power to guess the unseen from the seen, to trace the implication of things, to judge the whole piece by the pattern, the condition of feeling life in general so completely that you are well on your way to knowing any particular corner of it." He insisted, as had few of his predecessors, that fiction writing was a great art, that the aesthetic as well as the ethical element was of the highest importance.

"The Beast in the Jungle" illustrates at once James's importance in the development of fiction and the difficulty some readers may experience with him. He believed that the story ought to tell itself, that the writer should not comment or interfere with the characters or interpret their actions. Everything, he thought, must be rendered, dramatized. And yet his fiction is a monument to the inward, the subtle, the unseen. The practical world of politics and poverty, births, jobs, disease—which had so occupied earlier writers—with him must be inferred from his presentation of a subjective consciousness. Inwardness itself is the stage, the battlefield, where nuances of thought and feeling, gradations of decency and selfishness, play the leading parts. Joseph Conrad said,

> . . . the struggles Mr. James chronicles with such subtle and direct insight are, though only personal contests, desperate in their silence, none the less heroic . . . for the absence of shouted watchwords, clash of arms, and sound of trumpets.

To Conrad, he was "the historian of fine consciences."

James introduced the notion of a "central intelligence" (See Introduction, p. 14) through which all information is funneled to the reader. By means of the flow of this consciousness, the reader is privy to the important elements in the story. In *The Craft of Fiction*, Percy Lubbock describes the effect of James's method. "The world of silent thought," he says, "is thrown open, and instead of telling the reader what happened there, the novelist uses the look and behavior of thought as the vehicle by which the story is rendered. . . . The impulses and reactions of . . . mood are the players upon the new scene."

James's style matches the "fine consciences": carefully wrought, precisely qualified, sometimes opaque, sometimes radiant, always subtle and complex. Because he saw the human scene from all around, felt the effect of even the smallest perception, he was not comfortable in the short-story form with its demand for compression. He much preferred what he called "the beautiful and blest nouvelle," which is the form of "The Beast in the Jungle." The nouvelle moves at a stately pace over a period of time, and it gives full measure to the nuances James's prose is capable of. To some readers, James's style may seem precious, excessive, nearly impenetrable with its dashes and commas, its subordinate and coordinate clauses, its myriad qualifications. It is certainly easily parodied, as his contemporary Max Beerbohm demonstrated beautifully long ago. Yet other readers find that his language itself is exciting, arouses deep feeling and serves admirably his complex, deeply moral intentions.

The theme of "The Beast in the Jungle" is typically Jamesian: a man discovers, too late, that his egoism has caused him to miss the one passion of life he might have had. It is told in a fashion that provides rich, typically Jamesian, ironies. All that we know comes through the "central intelligence," John Marcher, and we accept him at his own value. But because of the language in which Marcher's perceptions are presented, we see him as foolish, selfish, unimaginative. And yet his humanity is so clearly and palpably rendered that our deepest sympathies are engaged: there but for the grace of God go I.

Although born in New York, James lived most of his life abroad and became a British subject in 1915. He died in 1916 at the age of seventy-three.

The Beast in the Jungle

What determined the speech that startled him in the course of their encounter scarcely matters, being probably but some words spoken by himself quite without intention— spoken as they lingered and slowly moved together after their renewal of acquaintance. He had been conveyed by friends an hour or two before to the house at which she was staying; the party of visitors at the other house, of whom he was one, and thanks to whom it was his theory, as always, that he was lost in the crowd, had been invited over to luncheon. There had been after luncheon much dispersal, all in the interest of the original move, a view of Weatherend itself and the fine things, intrinsic features, pictures, heirlooms, treasures of all the arts, that made the place almost famous; and the great rooms were so numerous that guests could wander at their will, hang back from the principal group and in cases where they took such matters with

"The Beast in the Jungle" is reprinted by permission of Charles Scribner's Sons from *The Novels and Tales of Henry James*, Vol. XVII. Copyright 1909 Charles Scribner's Sons.

the least seriousness give themselves up to mysterious appreciations and measurements. There were persons to be observed, singly or in couples, bending toward objects
in out-of-the-way corners with their hands on their knees and their heads nodding
quite as with the emphasis of an excited sense of smell. When they were two they
either mingled their sounds of ecstasy or melted into silences of even deeper import, so
that there were aspects of the occasion that gave it for Marcher much the air of the
"look round," previous to a sale highly advertised, that excites or quenches, as may be,
the dream of acquisition. The dream of acquisition at Weatherend would have had to
be wild indeed, and John Marcher found himself, among such suggestions, disconcerted almost equally by the presence of those who knew too much and by that of
those who knew nothing. The great rooms caused so much poetry and history to press
upon him that he needed some straying apart to feel in a proper relation with them,
though this impulse was not, as happened, like the gloating of some of his companions,
to be compared to the movements of a dog sniffing a cupboard. It had an issue
promptly enough in a direction that was not to have been calculated.

It led, briefly, in the course of the October afternoon, to his closer meeting with
May Bartram, whose face, a reminder, yet not quite a remembrance, as they sat much
separated at a very long table, had begun merely by troubling him rather pleasantly. It
affected him as the sequel of something of which he had lost the beginning. He knew
it, and for the time quite welcomed it, as a continuation, but didn't know what it
continued, which was an interest or an amusement the greater as he was also somehow
aware—yet without a direct sign from her—that the young woman herself hadn't lost
the thread. She hadn't lost it, but she wouldn't give it back to him, he saw, without
some putting forth of his hand for it; and he not only saw that, but saw several things
more, things odd enough in the light of the fact that at the moment some accident of
grouping brought them face to face he was still merely fumbling with the idea that any
contact between them in the past would have had no importance. If it had had no
importance he scarcely knew why his actual impression of her should so seem to have
so much; the answer to which, however, was that in such a life as they all appeared to
be leading for the moment one could but take things as they came. He was satisfied,
without in the least being able to say why, that this young lady might roughly have
ranked in the house as a poor relation; satisfied also that she was not there on a brief
visit, but was more or less a part of the establishment—almost a working, a remuner-
ated part. Didn't she enjoy at periods a protection that she paid for by helping, among
other services, to show the place and explain it, deal with the tiresome people, answer
questions about the dates of the building, the styles of the furniture, the authorship of
the pictures, the favourite haunts of the ghost? It wasn't that she looked as if you could
have given her shillings—it was impossible to look less so. Yet when she finally drifted
toward him, distinctly handsome, though ever so much older—older than when he had
seen her before—it might have been as an effect of her guessing that he had, within the
couple of hours, devoted more imagination to her than to all the others put together,
and had thereby penetrated to a kind of truth that the others were too stupid for. She
was there on harder terms than any one; she was there as a consequence of things
suffered, one way and another, in the interval of years; and she remembered him very
much as she was remembered—only a good deal better.

By the time they at last thus came to speech they were alone in one of the
rooms—remarkable for a fine portrait over the chimney-place—out of which their
friends had passed, and the charm of it was that even before they had spoken they had
practically arranged with each other to stay behind to talk. The charm, happily, was in

other things too—partly in there being scarce a spot at Weatherend without something
to stay behind for. It was in the way the autumn day looked into the high windows as
it waned; the way the red light, breaking at the close from under a low sombre sky,
reached out in a long shaft and played over old wainscots, old tapestry, old gold, old
colour. It was most of all perhaps in the way she came to him as if, since she had been
turned on to deal with the simpler sort, he might, should he choose to keep the whole
thing down, just take her mild attention for a part of her general business. As soon as
he heard her voice, however, the gap was filled up and the missing link supplied; the
slight irony he divined in her attitude lost its advantage. He almost jumped at it to get
there before her. "I met you years and years ago in Rome. I remember all about it."
She confessed to disappointment—she had been so sure he didn't; and to prove how
well he did he began to pour forth the particular recollections that popped up as he
called for them. Her face and her voice, all at his service now, worked the miracle—the
impression operating like the torch of a lamplighter who touches into flame, one by
one, a long row of gas-jets. Marcher flattered himself the illumination was brilliant, yet
he was really still more pleased on her showing him, with amusement, that in his haste
to make everything right he had got most things rather wrong. It hadn't been at
Rome—it had been at Naples; and it hadn't been eight years before—it had been
more nearly ten. She hadn't been, either, with her uncle and aunt, but with her mother
and her brother; in addition to which it was not with the Pembles *he* had been, but
with the Boyers, coming down in their company from Rome—a point on which she
insisted, a little to his confusion, and as to which she had her evidence in hand. The
Boyers she had known, but didn't know the Pembles, though she had heard of them,
and it was the people he was with who had made them acquainted. The incident of the
thunderstorm that had raged round them with such violence as to drive them for
refuge into an excavation—this incident had not occurred at the Palace of the Cæsars,
but at Pompeii, on an occasion when they had been present there at an important find.

He accepted her amendments, he enjoyed her corrections, though the moral of
them was, she pointed out, that he *really* didn't remember the least thing about her;
and he only felt it as a drawback that when all was made strictly historic there didn't
appear much of anything left. They lingered together still, she neglecting her office—
for from the moment he was so clever she had no proper right to him—and both
neglecting the house, just waiting as to see if a memory or two more wouldn't again
breathe on them. It hadn't taken them many minutes, after all, to put down on the
table, like the cards of a pack, those that constituted their respective hands; only what
came out was that the pack was unfortunately not perfect—that the past, invoked,
invited, encouraged, could give them, naturally, no more than it had. It had made
them anciently meet—her at twenty, him at twenty-five; but nothing was so strange,
they seemed to say to each other, as that, while so occupied, it hadn't done a little
more for them. They looked at each other as with the feeling of an occasion missed;
the present would have been so much better if the other, in the far distance, in the
foreign land, hadn't been so stupidly meagre. There weren't apparently, all counted,
more than a dozen little old things that had succeeded in coming to pass between
them; trivialities of youth, simplicities of freshness, stupidities of ignorance, small
possible germs, but too deeply buried—too deeply (didn't it seem?) to sprout after so
many years. Marcher could only feel he ought to have rendered her some service—
saved her from a capsized boat in the Bay or at least recovered her dressing-bag,
filched from her cab in the streets of Naples by a lazzarone with a stiletto. Or it would
have been nice if he could have been taken with fever all alone at his hotel, and she

could have come to look after him, to write to his people, to drive him out in convalescence. *Then* they would be in possession of the something or other that their actual show seemed to lack. It yet somehow presented itself, this show, as too good to be spoiled; so that they were reduced for a few minutes more to wondering a little helplessly why—since they seemed to know a certain number of the same people—their reunion had been so long averted. They didn't use that name for it, but their delay from minute to minute to join the others was a kind of confession that they didn't quite want it to be a failure. Their attempted supposition of reasons for their not having met but showed how little they knew of each other. There came in fact a moment when Marcher felt a positive pang. It was vain to pretend she was an old friend, for all the communities were wanting, in spite of which it was as an old friend that he saw she would have suited him. He had new ones enough—was surrounded with them for instance on the stage of the other house; as a new one he probably wouldn't have so much as noticed her. He would have liked to invent something, get her to make-believe with him that some passage of a romantic or critical kind *had* originally occurred. He was really almost reaching out in imagination—as against time—for something that would do, and saying to himself that if it didn't come this sketch of a fresh start would show for quite awkwardly bungled. They would separate, and now for no second or no third chance. They would have tried and not succeeded. Then it was, just at the turn, as he afterwards made it out to himself, that, everything else failing, she herself decided to take up the case and, as it were, save the situation. He felt as soon as she spoke that she had been consciously keeping back what she said and hoping to get on without it; a scruple in her that immensely touched him when, by the end of three or four minutes more, he was able to measure it. What she brought out, at any rate, quite cleared the air and supplied the link—the link it was so odd he should frivolously have managed to lose.

"You know you told me something I've never forgotten and that again and again has made me think of you since; it was that tremendously hot day when we went to Sorrento, across the bay, for the breeze. What I allude to was that you said to me, on the way back, as we sat under the awning of the boat enjoying the cool. Have you forgotten?"

He had forgotten and was even more surprised than ashamed. But the great thing was that he saw in this no vulgar reminder of any "sweet" speech. The vanity of women had long memories, but she was making no claim on him of a compliment or a mistake. With another woman, a totally different one, he might have feared the recall possibly even some imbecile "offer." So, in having to say that he had indeed forgotten, he was conscious rather of a loss than of a gain; he already saw an interest in the matter of her mention. "I try to think—but I give it up. Yet I remember the Sorrento day."

"I'm not very sure you do," May Bartram after a moment said; "and I'm not very sure I ought to want you to. It's dreadful to bring a person back at any time to what he was ten years before. If you've lived away from it," she smiled, "so much the better."

"Ah if *you* haven't why should I?" he asked.

"Lived away, you mean, from what I myself was?"

"From what *I* was. I was of course an ass," Marcher went on; "but I would rather know from you just the sort of ass I was than—from the moment you have something in your mind—not know anything."

Still, however, she hesitated. "But if you've completely ceased to be that sort—?"

"Why I can then all the more bear to know. Besides, perhaps I haven't."

"Perhaps. Yet if you haven't," she added, "I should suppose you'd remember. Not indeed that *I* in the least connect with my impression the invidious name you use. If I had only thought you foolish," she explained, "the thing I speak of wouldn't so have remained with me. It was about yourself." She waited as if it might come to him; but as, only meeting her eyes in wonder, he gave no sign, she burnt her ships. "Has it ever happened?"

Then it was that, while he continued to stare, a light broke for him and the blood slowly came to his face, which began to burn with recognition. "Do you mean I told you—?" But he faltered, lest what came to him shouldn't be right, lest he should only give himself away.

"It was something about yourself that it was natural one shouldn't forget—that is if one remembered you at all. That's why I ask you," she smiled, "if the thing you then spoke of has ever come to pass?"

Oh then he saw, but he was lost in wonder and found himself embarrassed. This, he also saw, made her sorry for him, as if her allusion had been a mistake. It took him but a moment, however, to feel it hadn't been, much as it had been a surprise. After the first little shock of it her knowledge on the contrary began, even if rather strangely, to taste sweet to him. She was the only other person in the world then who would have it, and she had had it all these years, while the fact of his having so breathed his secret had unaccountably faded from him. No wonder they couldn't have met as if nothing had happened. "I judge," he finally said, "that I know what you mean. Only I had strangely enough lost any sense of having taken you so far into my confidence."

"Is it because you've taken so many others as well?"

"I've taken nobody. Not a creature since then."

"So that I'm the only person who knows?"

"The only person in the world."

"Well," she quickly replied, "I myself have never spoken. I've never, never repeated of you what you told me." She looked at him so that he perfectly believed her. Their eyes met over it in such a way that he was without a doubt. "And I never will."

She spoke with an earnestness that, as if almost excessive, put him at ease about her possible derision. Somehow the whole question was a new luxury to him—that is from the moment she was in possession. If she didn't take the sarcastic view she clearly took the sympathetic, and that was what he had had, in all the long time, from no one whomsoever. What he felt was that he couldn't at present have begun to tell her, and yet could profit perhaps exquisitely by the accident of having done so of old. "Please don't then. We're just right as it is."

"Oh I am," she laughed, "if you are!" To which she added: "Then you do still feel in the same way?"

It was impossible he shouldn't take to himself that she was really interested, though it all kept coming as perfect surprise. He had thought of himself so long as abominably alone, and lo he wasn't alone a bit. He hadn't been, it appeared, for an hour—since those moments on the Sorrento boat. It was *she* who had been, he seemed to see as he looked at her—she who had been made so by the graceless fact of his lapse of fidelity. To tell her what he had told her—what had it been but to ask something of her? something that she had given, in her charity, without his having, by a remembrance, by a return of the spirit, failing another encounter, so much as thanked her. What he had asked of her had been simply at first not to laugh at him. She had beautifully not done so for ten years, and she was not doing so now. So he had endless gratitude to make up. Only for that he must see just how he had figured to her. "What, exactly, was the account I gave—?"

"Of the way you did feel? Well, it was very simple. You said you had had from your earliest time, as the deepest thing within you, the sense of being kept for something rare and strange, possibly prodigious and terrible, that was sooner or later to happen to you, that you had in your bones the foreboding and the conviction of, and that would perhaps overwhelm you."

"Do you call that very simple?" John Marcher asked.

She thought a moment. "It was perhaps because I seemed, as you spoke, to understand it."

"You do understand it?" he eagerly asked.

Again she kept her kind eyes on him. "You still have the belief?"

"Oh!" he exclaimed helplessly. There was too much to say.

"Whatever it's to be," she clearly made out, "it hasn't yet come."

He shook his head in complete surrender now. "It hasn't yet come. Only, you know, it isn't anything I'm to *do*, to achieve in the world, to be distinguished or admired for. I'm not such an ass as *that*. It would be much better, no doubt, if I were."

"It's to be something you're merely to suffer?"

"Well, say to wait for—to have to meet, to face, to see suddenly break out in my life; possibly destroying all further consciousness, possibly annihilating me; possibly, on the other hand, only altering everything, striking at the root of all my world and leaving me to the consequences, however they shape themselves."

She took this in, but the light in her eyes continued for him not to be that of mockery. "Isn't what you describe perhaps but the expectation—or at any rate the sense of danger, familiar to so many people—of falling in love?"

John Marcher wondered. "Did you ask me that before?"

"No—I wasn't so free-and-easy then. But it's what strikes me now."

"Of course," he said after a moment, "it strikes you. Of course it strikes *me*. Of course what's in store for me may be no more than that. The only thing is," he went on, "that I think if it had been that I should by this time know."

"Do you mean because you've *been* in love?" And then as he but looked at her in silence: "You've been in love, and it hasn't meant such a cataclysm, hasn't proved the great affair?"

"Here I am, you see. It hasn't been overwhelming."

"Then it hasn't been love," said May Bartram.

"Well, I at least thought it was. I took it for that—I've taken it till now. It was agreeable, it was delightful, it was miserable," he explained. "But it wasn't strange. It wasn't what *my* affair's to be."

"You want something all to yourself—something that nobody else knows or *has* known?"

"It isn't a question of what I 'want'—God knows I don't want anything. It's only a question of the apprehension that haunts me—that I live with day by day."

He said this so lucidly and consistently that he could see it further impose itself. If she hadn't been interested before she'd have been interested now. "Is it a sense of coming violence?"

Evidently now too again he liked to talk of it. "I don't think of it as—when it does come—necessarily violent. I only think of it as natural and as of course above all unmistakable. I think of it simply as *the* thing. *The* thing will of itself appear natural."

"Then how will it appear strange?"

Marcher bethought himself. "It won't—to *me*."

"To whom then?"

"Well," he replied, smiling at last, "say to you."

"Oh then I'm to be present?"

"Why you *are* present—since you know."

"I see." She turned it over. "But I mean at the catastrophe."

At this, for a minute, their lightness gave way to their gravity; it was as if the long look they exchanged held them together. "It will only depend on yourself—if you'll watch with me."

"Are you afraid?" she asked.

"Don't leave me *now*," he went on.

"Are you afraid?" she repeated.

"Do you think me simply out of my mind?" he pursued instead of answering. "Do I merely strike you as a harmless lunatic?"

"No," said May Bartram. "I understand you. I believe you."

"You mean you feel how my obsession—poor old thing!—may correspond to some possible reality?"

"To some possible reality."

"Then you *will* watch with me?"

She hesitated, then for the third time put her question. "Are you afraid?"

"Did I tell you I was—at Naples?"

"No, you said nothing about it."

"Then I don't know. And I should *like* to know," said John Marcher. "You'll tell me yourself whether you think so. If you'll watch with me you'll see."

"Very good then." They had been moving by this time across the room, and at the door, before passing out, they paused as for the full wind-up of their understanding. "I'll watch with you," said May Bartram.

2

The fact that she "knew"—knew and yet neither chaffed him nor betrayed him—had in a short time begun to constitute between them a goodly bond, which became more marked when, within the year that followed their afternoon at Weatherend, the opportunities for meeting multiplied. The event that thus promoted these occasions was the death of the ancient lady her great-aunt, under whose wing, since losing her mother, she had to such an extent found shelter, and who, though but the widowed mother of the new successor to the property, had succeeded—thanks to a high tone and a high temper—in not forfeiting the supreme position at the great house. The deposition of this personage arrived but with her death, which, followed by many changes, made in particular a difference for the young woman in whom Marcher's expert attention had recognised from the first a dependent with a pride that might ache though it didn't bristle. Nothing for a long time had made him easier than the thought that the aching must have been much soothed by Miss Bartram's now finding herself able to set up a small home in London. She had acquired property, to an amount that made that luxury just possible, under her aunt's extremely complicated will, and when the whole matter began to be straightened out, which indeed took time, she let him know that the happy issue was at last in view. He had seen her again before that day, both because she had more than once accompanied the ancient lady to town and because he had paid another visit to the friends who so conveniently made of Weatherend one of the charms of their own hospitality. These friends had taken him back there; he had achieved there again with Miss Bartram some quiet detachment; and he had in London succeeded in persuading her to more than one brief absence from her aunt. They went together, on these latter occasions, to the National Gallery and the South Kensington Museum, where, among vivid reminders, they talked of Italy at large—not now attempting to recover, as at first, the taste of their youth and their ignorance. That recovery, the first day at Weatherend, had served its purpose well, had given them quite enough; so that they were, to Marcher's sense, no longer hovering about the headwaters of their stream, but had felt their boat pushed sharply off and down the current.

They were literally afloat together; for our gentleman this was marked, quite as marked as that the fortunate cause of it was just the buried treasure of her knowledge. He had with his own hands dug up this little hoard, brought to light—that is to within reach of the dim day constituted by their discretions and privacies—the object of value the hiding-place of which he had, after putting it into the ground himself, so strangely, so long forgotten. The rare luck of his having again just stumbled on the spot made him indifferent to any other question; he would doubtless have devoted more time to the odd accident of his lapse of memory if he hadn't been moved to devote so much to the sweetness, the comfort, as he felt, for the future, that this accident itself had helped to keep fresh. It had never entered into his plan that any one should "know," and mainly for the reason that it wasn't in him to tell any one. That would have been impossible, for nothing but the amusement of a cold world would have waited on it. Since, however, a mysterious fate had opened his mouth betimes, in spite of him, he would count that a compensation and profit by it to the utmost. That the right person *should* know tempered the asperity of his secret more even than his shyness had permitted him to imagine; and May Bartram was clearly right, because—well, because there she was. Her knowledge simply settled it; he would have been sure enough by this time had she been wrong. There was that in his situation, no doubt, that disposed him too much to see her as a mere confidant, taking all her light for him from the fact—the fact only—of her interest in his predicament; from her mercy, sympathy, seriousness, her consent not to regard him as the funniest of the funny. Aware, in fine, that her price for him was just in her giving him this constant sense of his being admirably spared, he was careful to remember that she had also a life of her own, with things that might happen to *her,* things that in friendship one should likewise take account of. Something fairly remarkable came to pass with him, for that matter, in this connexion—something represented by a certain passage of his consciousness, in the suddenest way, from one extreme to the other.

He had thought himself, so long as nobody knew, the most disinterested person in the world, carrying his concentrated burden, his perpetual suspense, ever so quietly, holding his tongue about it, giving others no glimpse of it nor of its effect upon his life, asking of them no allowance and only making on his side all those that were asked. He hadn't disturbed people with the queerness of their having to know a haunted man, though he had had moments of rather special temptation on hearing them say they were forsooth "unsettled." If they were as unsettled as he was—he who had never been settled for an hour in his life—they would know what it meant. Yet it wasn't, all the same, for him to make them, and he listened to them civilly enough. This was why he had such good—though possibly such rather colourless—manners; this was why, above all, he could regard himself, in a greedy world, as decently—as in fact perhaps even a little sublimely—unselfish. Our point is accordingly that he valued this character quite sufficiently to measure his present danger of letting it lapse, against which he promised himself to be much on his guard. He was quite ready, none the less, to be selfish just a little, since surely no more charming occasion for it had come to him. "Just a little," in a word, was just as much as Miss Bartram, taking one day with another, would let him. He never would be in the least coercive, and would keep well before him the lines on which consideration for her—the very highest—ought to proceed. He would thoroughly establish the heads under which her affairs, her requirements, her peculiarities—he went so far as to give them the latitude of that name—would come into their intercourse. All this naturally was a sign of how much he took the intercourse itself for granted. There was nothing more to be done about *that*. It simply existed; had sprung into being with her first penetrating question to him in the autumn light there at Weatherend. The real form it should have taken on the basis that stood out large was the form of their marrying. But the devil in this was that the very basis itself put marrying out of the question. His conviction, his apprehension, his obsession, in short, wasn't a privilege he could invite a woman to share; and that consequence of it was precisely what was the matter with him. Something or other lay in wait for him, amid the twists and the turns of the months and the years, like a crouching beast in the jungle. It signified little whether the crouching beast were destined to slay him or to be slain. The definite point was the inevitable spring of the creature; and the definite lesson from that was that a man of feeling didn't cause himself to be accompanied by a lady on a tiger-hunt. Such was the image under which he had ended by figuring his life.

They had at first, none the less, in the scattered hours spent together, made no allusion to that view of it; which was a sign he was handsomely alert to give that he didn't expect, that he in fact didn't care, always to be talking about it. Such a feature in one's outlook was really like a hump on one's back. The differences it made every minute of the day existed quite independently of discussion. One discussed of course *like* a hunchback, for there was always, if nothing else, the hunchback face. That remained, and she was watching him; but people watched best, as a general thing, in silence, so that such would be predominantly the manner of their vigil. Yet he didn't want, at the same time, to be tense and solemn; tense and solemn was what he imagined he too much showed for with other people. The thing to be, with the one person who knew, was easy and natural—to make the reference rather than be seeming to avoid it, to avoid it rather than be seeming to make it, and to keep it, in any case, familiar, facetious even, rather than pedantic and portentous. Some such consideration as the latter was doubtless in his mind for instance when he wrote pleasantly to Miss Bartram that perhaps the great thing he had so long felt as in the lap of the gods was no more than this circumstance, which touched him so nearly, of her acquiring a house in London. It was the first allusion they had yet again made, needing any other hitherto so little; but when she replied, after having given him the news, that she was by no means satisfied with such a trifle as the climax to so special a suspense, she almost set him wondering if she hadn't even a larger conception of singularity for him than he had for himself. He was at all events destined to become aware little by little, as time went by, that she was all the while looking at his life, judging it, measuring it, in the light of the thing she knew, which grew to be at last, with the consecration of the years, never mentioned between them save as "the real truth" about him. That had always been his own form of reference to it, but she adopted the form so quietly that, looking back at the end of a period, he knew there was no moment at which it was traceable that she had, as he might say, got inside his idea, or exchanged the attitude of beautifully indulging for that of still more beautifully believing him.

It was always open to him to accuse her of seeing him but as the most harmless of maniacs, and this, in the long run—since it covered so much ground—was his easiest description of their friendship. He had a screw loose for her, but she liked him in spite of it and was practically, against the rest of the world, his kind wise keeper, unremunerated but fairly amused and, in the absence of other near ties, not disreputably occupied. The rest of the world of course thought him queer, but she, she only, knew how, and above all why, queer; which was precisely what enabled her to dispose the concealing veil in the right folds. She took his gaiety from him—since it had to pass with them for gaiety—as she took everything else; but she certainly so far justified by her unerring touch his finer sense of the degree to which he had ended by convincing her. *She* at least never spoke of the secret of his life except as "the real truth about you," and she had in fact a wonderful way of making it seem, as such, the secret of her own life too. That was in fine how he so constantly felt her as allowing for him; he couldn't on the whole call it anything else. He allowed for himself, but she, exactly, allowed still more; partly because, better placed for a sight of the matter, she traced his unhappy perversion through reaches of its course into which he could scarce follow it. He knew how he felt, but, besides knowing that, she knew how he *looked* as well; he knew each of the things of importance he was insidiously kept from doing, but she could add up the amount they made, understand how much, with a lighter weight on his spirit, he might have done, and thereby establish how, clever as he was, he fell short. Above all she was in the secret of the difference between the forms he went through—those of his little office under Government, those of caring for his modest patrimony, for his library, for his garden in the country, for the people in London whose invitations he accepted and repaid—and the detachment that reigned beneath them and that made of all behaviour, all that could in the least be called behaviour, a long act of dissimulation. What it had come to was that he wore a mask painted with the social simper, out of the eye-holes of which there looked eyes of an expression not in the least matching the other features. This the stupid world, even after years, had never more than half-discovered. It was only May Bartram who had, and she achieved, by an art indescribable, the feat of at once—or perhaps it was only alternately—meeting the eyes from in front and mingling her own vision, as from over his shoulder, with their peep through the apertures.

So while they grew older together she did watch with him, and so she let this association give shape and colour to her own existence. Beneath *her* forms as well detachment had learned to sit, and behaviour had become for her, in the social sense, a false account of herself. There was but one account of her that would have been true all the while and that she could give straight to nobody, least of all to John Marcher. Her whole attitude was a virtual statement, but the perception of that only seemed called to take its place for him as one of the many things necessarily crowded out of his consciousness. If she had moreover, like himself, to make sacrifices to their real truth, it was to be granted that her compensation might have affected her as more prompt and more natural. They had long periods, in this London time, during which, when they were together, a stranger might have listened to them without in the least pricking up his ears; on the other hand the real truth was equally liable at any moment to rise to the surface, and the auditor would then have wondered indeed what they were talking about. They had from an early hour made up their mind that society was, luckily, unintelligent, and the margin allowed them by this had fairly become one of their commonplaces. Yet there were still moments when the situation turned almost fresh—usually under the effect of some expression drawn from herself. Her expressions doubtless repeated themselves, but her intervals were generous. "What saves us, you know, is that we answer so completely to so usual an appearance: that of the man and woman whose friendship has become such a daily habit—or almost—as to be at last indispensable." That for instance was a remark she had frequently enough had occasion to make, though she had given it at different times different developments. What we are especially concerned with is the turn it happened to take from her one afternoon when he had come to see her in honour of her birthday. This anniversary had fallen on a Sunday, at a season of thick fog and general outward gloom; but he had brought her his customary offering, having known her now long enough to have established a hundred small traditions. It was one of his proofs to himself, the present he made her on her birthday, that he hadn't sunk into real selfishness. It was mostly nothing more than a small trinket, but it was always fine of its kind, and he was regularly careful to pay for it more than he thought he could afford. "Our habit saves you at least, don't you see? because it makes you, after all, for the vulgar, indistinguishable from other men. What's the most inveterate mark of men in general? Why the capacity to spend endless time with dull women—to spend it I won't say without being bored, but without minding that they are, without being driven off at a tangent by it; which comes to the same thing. I'm your dull woman, a part of the daily bread for which you pray at church. That covers your tracks more than anything."

"And what covers yours?" asked Marcher, whom his dull woman could mostly to this extent amuse. "I see of course what you mean by your saving me, in this way and that, so far as other people are concerned—I've seen it all along. Only what is it that saves *you*? I often think, you know, of that."

She looked as if she sometimes thought of that too, but rather in a different way. "Where other people, you mean, are concerned?"

"Well, you're really so in with me, you know—as a sort of result of my being so in with yourself. I mean of my having such an immense regard for you, being so tremendously mindful of all you've done for me. I sometimes ask myself if it's quite fair. Fair I mean to have so involved and—since one may say it—interested you. I almost feel as if you hadn't really had time to do anything else."

"Anything else but be interested?" she asked. "Ah what else does one ever want to be? If I've been 'watching' with you, as we long ago agreed I was to do, watching's always in itself an absorption."

"Oh certainly," John Marcher said, "if you hadn't had your curiosity—! Only doesn't it sometimes come to you as time goes on that your curiosity isn't being particularly repaid?"

May Bartram had a pause. "Do you ask that, by any chance, because you feel at all that yours isn't? I mean because you have to wait so long."

Oh he understood what she meant! "For the thing to happen that never does happen? For the beast to jump out? No, I'm just where I was about it. It isn't a matter as to which I can *choose,* I can decide for a change. It isn't one as to which there *can* be a change. It's in the lap of the gods. One's in the hands of one's law—there one is. As to the form the law will take, the way it will operate, that's its own affair."

"Yes," Miss Bartram replied; "of course one's fate's coming, of course it *has* come in its own form and its own way, all the while. Only, you know, the form and the way in your case were to have been—well, something so exceptional and, as one may say, so particularly *your* own."

Something in this made him look at her with suspicion. "You say 'were to *have* been,' as if in your heart you had begun to doubt."

"Oh!" she vaguely protested.

"As if you believed," he went on, "that nothing will now take place."

She shook her head slowly but rather inscrutably. "You're far from my thought."

He continued to look at her. "What then is the matter with you?"

"Well," she said after another wait, "the matter with me is simply that I'm more sure than ever my curiosity, as you call it, will be but too well repaid."

They were frankly grave now; he had got up from his seat, had turned once more about the little drawing-room to which, year after year, he brought his inevitable topic; in which he had, as he might have said, tasted their intimate community with every sauce, where every object was as familiar to him as the things of his own house and the very carpets were worn with his fitful walk very much as the desks in old counting-houses are worn by the elbows of generations of clerks. The generations of his nervous moods had been at work there, and the place was the written history of his whole middle life. Under the impression of what his friend had just said he knew himself, for some reason, more aware of these things; which made him, after a moment, stop again before her. "Is it possibly that you've grown afraid?"

"Afraid?" He thought, as she repeated the word, that his question had made her, a little, change colour; so that, lest he should have touched on a truth, he explained very kindly: "You remember that that was what you asked *me* long ago—that first day at Weatherend."

"Oh yes, and you told me you didn't know—that I was to see for myself. We've said little about it since, even in so long a time."

"Precisely," Marcher interposed—"quite as if it were too delicate a matter for us to make free with. Quite as if we might find, on pressure, that I *am* afraid. For then," he said, "we shouldn't, should we? quite know what to do."

She had for the time no answer to this question. "There have been days when I thought you were. Only, of course," she added, "there have been days when we have thought almost anything."

"Everything. Oh!" Marcher softly groaned as with a gasp, half-spent, at the face, more uncovered just then than it had been for a long while, of the imagination always with them. It had always had its incalculable moments of glaring out, quite as with the very eyes of the very Beast, and, used as he was to them, they could still draw from him the tribute of a sigh that rose from the depths of his being. All they had thought, first and last, rolled over him; the past seemed to have been reduced to mere barren speculation. This in fact was what the place had just struck him as so full of—the simplification of everything but the state of suspense. That remained only by seeming to hang in the void surrounding it. Even his original fear, if fear it had been, had lost itself in the desert. "I judge, however," he continued, "that you see I'm not afraid now."

"What I see, as I make it out, is that you've achieved something almost unprecedented in the way of getting used to danger. Living with it so long and so closely you've lost your sense of it; you know it's there, but you're indifferent, and you cease even, as of old, to have to whistle in the dark. Considering what the danger is," May Bartram wound up, "I'm bound to say I don't think your attitude could well be surpassed."

John Marcher faintly smiled. "It's heroic?"

"Certainly—call it that."

It was what he would have liked indeed to call it. "I *am* then a man of courage?"

"That's what you were to show me."

He still, however, wondered. "But doesn't the man of courage know what he's afraid of—or *not* afraid of? I don't know *that,* you see. I don't focus it. I can't name it. I only know I'm exposed."

"Yes, but exposed—how shall I say?—so directly. So intimately. That's surely enough."

"Enough to make you feel then—as what we may call the end and the upshot of our watch—that I'm not afraid?"

"You're not afraid. But it isn't," she said, "the end of our watch. That is it isn't the end of yours. You've everything still to see."

"Then why haven't *you?*" he asked. He had had, all along, to-day, the sense of her keeping something back, and he still had it. As this was his first impression of that it quite made a date. The case was the more marked as she didn't at first answer; which in turn made him go on. "You know something I don't." Then his voice, for that of a man of courage, trembled a little. "You know what's to happen." Her silence, with the face she showed, was almost a confession—it made him sure. "You know, and you're afraid to tell me. It's so bad that you're afraid I'll find out."

All this might be true, for she did look as if, unexpectedly to her, he had crossed some mystic line that she had secretly drawn round her. Yet she might, after all, not have worried; and the real climax was that he himself, at all events, needn't. "You'll never find out."

3

It was all to have made, none the less, as I have said, a date; which came out in the fact that again and again, even after long intervals, other things that passed between them wore in relation to this hour but the character of recalls and results. Its immediate effect had been indeed rather to lighten insistence—almost to provoke a reaction; as if their topic had dropped by its own weight and as if moreover, for that matter, Marcher had been visited by one of his occasional warnings against egotism. He had kept up, he felt, and very decently on the whole, his consciousness of the importance of not being selfish, and it was true that he had never sinned in that direction without promptly enough trying to press the scales the other way. He often repaired his fault, the season permitting, by inviting his friend to accompany him to the opera; and it not infrequently thus happened that, to show he didn't wish her to have but one sort of food for her mind, he was the cause of her appearing there with him a dozen nights in the month. It even happened that, seeing her home at such times, he occasionally went in with her to finish, as he called it, the evening, and, the better to make his point, sat down to the frugal but always careful little supper that awaited his pleasure. His point was made, he thought, by his not eternally insisting with her on himself; made for instance, at such hours, when it befell that, her piano at hand and each of them familiar with it, they went over passages of the opera together. It chanced to be on one of these occasions, however, that he reminded her of her not having answered a certain question he had put to her during the talk that had taken place between them on her last birthday. "What is it that saves *you?*"—saved her, he meant, from that appearance of variation from the usual human type. If he had practically escaped remark, as she pretended, by doing, in the most important particular, what most men do—find the answer to life in patching up an alliance of a sort with a woman no better than himself—how had she escaped it, and how could the alliance, such as it was, since they must suppose it had been more or less noticed, have failed to make her rather positively talked about?

"I never said," May Bartram replied, "that it hadn't made me a good deal talked about."

"Ah well then you're not 'saved.'"

"It hasn't been a question for me. If you've had your woman I've had," she said, "my man."

"And you mean that makes you all right?"

Oh it was always as if there were so much to say! "I don't know why it shouldn't make me—humanly, which is what we're speaking of—as right as it makes you."

"I see," Marcher returned. "'Humanly,' no doubt, as showing that you're living for something. Not, that is, just for me and my secret."

May Bartram smiled. "I don't pretend it exactly shows that I'm not living for you. It's my intimacy with you that's in question."

He laughed as he saw what she meant. "Yes, but since, as you say, I'm only, so far as people make out, ordinary, you're—aren't you?—no more than ordinary either. You help me to pass for a man like another. So if I *am*, as I understand you, you're not compromised. Is that it?"

She had another of her waits, but she spoke clearly enough. "That's it. It's all that concerns me—to help you to pass for a man like another."

He was careful to acknowledge the remark handsomely. "How kind, how beautiful, you are to me! How shall I ever repay you?"

She had her last grave pause, as if there might be a choice of ways. But she chose. "By going on as you are."

It was into this going on as he was that they relapsed, and really for so long a time that the day inevitably came for a further sounding of their depths. These depths, constantly bridged over by a structure firm enough in spite of its lightness and of its occasional oscillation in the somewhat vertiginous air, invited on occasion, in the interest of their nerves, a dropping of the plummet and a measurement of the abyss. A difference had been made moreover, once for all, by the fact that she had all the while not appeared to feel the need of rebutting his charge of an idea within her that she didn't dare to express—a charge uttered just before one of the fullest of their later discussions ended. It had come up for him then that she "knew" something and that what she knew was bad—too bad to tell him. When he had spoken of it as visibly so bad that she was afraid he might find it out, her reply had left the matter too equivocal to be let alone and yet, for Marcher's special sensibility, almost too formidable again to touch. He circled about it at a distance that alternately narrowed and widened and that still wasn't much affected by the consciousness in him that there was nothing she could "know," after all, any better than he did. She had no source of knowledge he hadn't equally—except of course that she might have finer nerves. That was what women had where they were interested; they made out things, where people were concerned, that the people often couldn't have made out for themselves. Their nerves, their sensibility, their imagination, were conductors and revealers, and the beauty of May Bartram was in particular that she had given herself so to his case. He felt in these days what, oddly enough, he had never felt before, the growth of a dread of losing her by some catastrophe—some catastrophe that yet wouldn't at all be *the* catastrophe: partly because she had almost of a sudden begun to strike him as more useful to him than ever yet, and partly by reason of an appearance of uncertainty in

her health, coincident and equally new. It was characteristic of the inner detachment
he had hitherto so successfully cultivated and to which our whole account of him is a
reference, it was characteristic that his complications, such as they were, had never yet
seemed so as at this crisis to thicken about him, even to the point of making him ask
himself if he were, by any chance, of a truth, within sight or sound, within touch or
reach, within the immediate jurisdiction, of the thing that waited.

When the day came, as come it had to, that his friend confessed to him her fear
of a deep disorder in her blood, he felt somehow the shadow of a change and the chill
of a shock. He immediately began to imagine aggravations and disasters, and above all
to think of her peril as the direct menace for himself of personal privation. This indeed
gave him one of those partial recoveries of equanimity that were agreeable to him—it
showed him that what was still first in his mind was the loss she herself might suffer.
"What if she should have to die before knowing, before seeing—?" It would have been
brutal, in the early stages of her trouble, to put that question to her; but it had
immediately sounded for him to his own concern, and the possibility was what most
made him sorry for her. If she did "know," moreover, in the sense of her having had
some—what should he think?—mystical irresistible light, this would make the matter
not better, but worse, inasmuch as her original adoption of his own curiosity had quite
become the basis of her life. She had been living to see what would *be* to be seen, and
it would quite lacerate her to have to give up before the accomplishment of the vision.
These reflexions, as I say, quickened his generosity; yet, make them as he might, he
saw himself, with the lapse of the period, more and more disconcerted. It lapsed for
him with a strange steady sweep, and the oddest oddity was that it gave him, independently of the threat of much inconvenience, almost the only positive surprise his
career, if career it could be called, had yet offered him. She kept the house as she had
never done; he had to go to her to see her—she could meet him nowhere now, though
there was scarce a corner of their loved old London in which she hadn't in the past, at
one time or another, done so; and he found her always seated by her fire in the deep
old-fashioned chair she was less and less able to leave. He had been struck one day,
after an absence exceeding his usual measure, with her suddenly looking much older to
him than he had ever thought of her being; then he recognized that the suddenness
was all on his side—he had just simply and suddenly noticed. She looked older because inevitably, after so many years, she *was* old, or almost; which was of course true
in still greater measure of her companion. If she was old, or almost, John Marcher
assuredly was, and yet it was her showing of the lesson, not his own, that brought the
truth home to him. His surprises began here; when once they had begun they multiplied; they came rather with a rush: it was as if, in the oddest way in the world, they
had all been kept back, sown in a thick cluster, for the late afternoon of life, the time
at which for people in general the unexpected has died out.

One of them was that he should have caught himself—for he *had* so done—*really*
wondering if the great accident would take form now as nothing more than his being
condemned to see this charming woman, this admirable friend, pass away from him.
He had never so unreservedly qualified her as while confronted in thought with such a
possibility; in spite of which there was small doubt for him that as an answer to his
long riddle the mere effacement of even so fine a feature of his situation would be an
abject anticlimax. It would represent, as connected with his past attitude, a drop of
dignity under the shadow of which his existence could only become the most grotesque
of failures. He had been far from holding it a failure—long as he had waited for the
appearance that was to make it a success. He had waited for quite another thing, not

for such a thing as that. The breath of his good faith came short, however, as he recognised how long he had waited, or how long at least his companion had. That she, at all events, might be recorded as having waited in vain—this affected him sharply, and all the more because of his at first having done little more than amuse himself with the idea. It grew more grave as the gravity of her condition grew, and the state of mind it produced in him, which he himself ended by watching as if it had been some definite disfigurement of his outer person, may pass for another of his surprises. This conjoined itself still with another, the really stupefying consciousness of a question that he would have allowed to shape itself had he dared. What did everything mean—what, that is, did *she* mean, she and her vain waiting and her probable death and the soundless admonition of it all—unless that, at this time of day, it was simply, it was overwhelmingly too late? He had never at any stage of his queer consciousness admitted the whisper of such a correction; he had never till within these last few months been so false to his conviction as not to hold that what was to come to him had time, whether *he* struck himself as having it or not. That at last, at last, he certainly hadn't it, to speak of, or had it but in the scantiest measure—such, soon enough, as things went with him, became the inference with which his old obsession had to reckon: and this it was not helped to do by the more and more confirmed appearance that the great vagueness casting the long shadow in which he had lived had, to attest itself, almost no margin left. Since it was in Time that he was to have met his fate, so it was in Time that his fate was to have acted; and as he waked up to the sense of no longer being young, which was exactly the sense of being stale, just as that, in turn, was the sense of being weak, he waked up to another matter beside. It all hung together; they were subject, he and the great vagueness, to an equal and indivisible law. When the possibilities themselves had accordingly turned stale, when the secret of the gods had grown faint, had perhaps even quite evaporated, that, and that only, was failure. It wouldn't have been failure to be bankrupt, dishonoured, pilloried, hanged; it was failure not to be anything. And so, in the dark valley into which his path had taken its unlooked-for twist, he wondered not a little as he groped. He didn't care what awful crash might overtake him, with what ignominy or what monstrosity he might yet be associated—since he wasn't after all too utterly old to suffer—if it would only be decently proportionate to the posture he had kept, all his life, in the threatened presence of it. He had but one desire left—that he shouldn't have been "sold."

4

Then it was that, one afternoon, while the spring of the year was young and new she met all in her own way his frankest betrayal of these alarms. He had gone in late to see her, but evening hadn't settled and she was presented to him in that long fresh light of waning April days which affects us often with a sadness sharper than the greyest hours of autumn. The week had been warm, the spring was supposed to have begun early, and May Bartram sat, for the first time in the year, without a fire; a fact that, to Marcher's sense, gave the scene of which she formed part a smooth and ultimate look, an air of knowing, in its immaculate order and cold meaningless cheer, that it would never see a fire again. Her own aspect—he could scarce have said why—intensified this note. Almost as white as wax, with the marks and signs in her face as numerous and as fine as if they had been etched by a needle, with soft white draperies relieved by a faded green scarf on the delicate tone of which the years had further refined, she was the picture of a serene and exquisite but impenetrable sphinx, whose head, or indeed all whose person, might have been powdered with silver. She was a sphinx, yet with her white petals and green fronds she might have been a lily too—only an artificial lily, wonderfully imitated and constantly kept, without dust or stain, though not exempt from a slight droop and a complexity of faint creases, under some clear glass bell. The perfection of household care, of high polish and finish, always reigned in her rooms, but they now looked most as if everything had been wound up, tucked in, put away, so that she might sit with folded hands and with nothing more to do. She was "out of it," to Marcher's vision; her work was over; she communicated with him as across some gulf or from some island of rest that she had already reached, and it made him feel strangely abandoned. Was it—or rather wasn't it—that if for so long she had been watching with him the answer to their question must have swum into her ken and taken on its name, so that her occupation was verily gone? He had as much as charged her with this in saying to her, many months before, that she even then knew something she was keeping from him. It was a point he had never since ventured to press, vaguely fearing as he did that it might become a difference, perhaps a disagreement, between them. He had in this later time turned nervous, which was what he in all the other years had never been; and the oddity was that his nervousness should have waited till he had begun to doubt, should have held off so long as he was sure. There was something, it seemed to him, that the wrong word would bring down on his head, something that would so at least ease off his tension. But he wanted not to speak the wrong word; that would make everything ugly. He wanted the knowledge he lacked to drop on him, if drop it could, by its own august weight. If she was to forsake him it was surely for her to take leave. This was why he didn't directly ask her again what she knew; but it was also why, approaching the matter from another side, he said to her in the course of his visit: "What do you regard as the very worst that at this time of day *can* happen to me?"

He had asked her that in the past often enough; they had, with the odd irregular rhythm of their intensities and avoidances, exchanged ideas about it and then had seen the ideas washed away by cool intervals, washed like figures traced in sea-sand. It had ever been the mark of their talk that the oldest allusions in it required but a little dismissal and reaction to come out again, sounding for the hour as new. She could thus at present meet his enquiry quite freshly and patiently. "Oh yes, I've repeatedly thought, only it always seemed to me of old that I couldn't quite make up my mind. I thought of dreadful things, between which it was difficult to choose; and so must you have done."

"Rather! I feel now as if I had scarce done anything else. I appear to myself to have spent my life in thinking of nothing *but* dreadful things. A great many of them I've at different times named to you, but there were others I couldn't name."

"They were too, too dreadful?"

"Too, too dreadful—some of them."

She looked at him a minute, and there came to him as he met it an inconsequent sense that her eyes, when one got their full clearness, were still as beautiful as they had been in youth, only beautiful with a strange cold light—a light that somehow was a part of the effect, if it wasn't rather a part of the cause, of the pale hard sweetness of the season and the hour. "And yet," she said at last, "there are horrors we've mentioned."

It deepened the strangeness to see her, as such a figure in such a picture, talk of "horrors," but she was to do in a few minutes something stranger yet—though even of

this he was to take the full measure but afterwards—and the note of it already trembled. It was, for the matter of that, one of the signs that her eyes were having again the
high flicker of their prime. He had to admit, however, what she said. "Oh yes, there
were times when we did go far." He caught himself in the act of speaking as if it all
were over. Well, he wished it were; and the consummation depended for him clearly
more and more on his friend.

But she had now a soft smile. "Oh far—!"

It was oddly ironic. "Do you mean you're prepared to go further?"

She was frail and ancient and charming as she continued to look at him, yet it
was rather as if she had lost the thread. "Do you consider that we went far?"

"Why I thought it the point you were just making—that we *had* looked most
things in the face."

"Including each other?" She still smiled. "But you're quite right. We've had
together great imaginations, often great fears; but some of them have been unspoken."

"Then the worst—we haven't faced that. I *could* face it, I believe, if I knew what
you think it. I feel," he explained, "as if I had lost my power to conceive such things."
And he wondered if he looked as blank as he sounded. "It's spent."

"Then why do you assume," she asked, "that mine isn't?"

"Because you've given me signs to the contrary. It isn't a question for you of
conceiving, imagining, comparing. It isn't a question now of choosing." At last he
came out with it. "You know something I don't. You've shown me that before."

These last words had affected her, he made out in a moment, exceedingly, and
she spoke with firmness. "I've shown you, my dear, nothing."

He shook his head. "You can't hide it."

"Oh, oh!" May Bartram sounded over what she couldn't hide. It was almost a
smothered groan.

"You admitted it months ago, when I spoke of it to you as of something you were
afraid I should find out. Your answer was that I couldn't, that I wouldn't, and I don't
pretend I have. But you had something therefore in mind, and I now see how it must
have been, how it still is, the possibility that, of all possibilities, has settled itself for
you as the worst. This," he went on, "is why I appeal to you. I'm only afraid of
ignorance to-day—I'm not afraid of knowledge." And then as for a while she said
nothing: "What makes me sure is that I see in your face and feel here, in this air and
amid these appearances, that you're out of it. You've done. You've had your experience. You leave me to my fate."

Well, she listened, motionless and white in her chair, as on a decision to be made,
so that her manner was fairly an avowal, though still, with a small fine inner stiffness,
an imperfect surrender. "It *would* be the worst," she finally let herself say. "I mean the
thing I've never said."

It hushed him a moment. "More monstrous than all the monstrosities we've
named?"

"More monstrous. Isn't that what you sufficiently express," she asked, "in calling
it the worst?"

Marcher thought. "Assuredly—if you mean, as I do, something that includes all
the loss and all the shame that are thinkable."

"It would if it *should* happen," said May Bartram. "What we're speaking of,
remember, is only my idea."

"It's your belief," Marcher returned. "That's enough for me. I feel your beliefs
are right. Therefore if, having this one, you give me no more light on it, you abandon
me."

"No, no!" she repeated. "I'm with you—don't you see?—still." And as to make it more vivid to him she rose from her chair—a movement she seldom risked in these days—and showed herself, all draped and all soft, in her fairness and slimness. "I haven't forsaken you."

It was really, in its effort against weakness, a generous assurance, and had the success of the impulse not, happily, been great, it would have touched him to pain more than to pleasure. But the cold charm in her eyes had spread, as she hovered before him, to all the rest of her person, so that it was for the minute almost a recovery of youth. He couldn't pity her for that; he could only take her as she showed—as capable even yet of helping him. It was as if, at the same time, her light might at any instant go out; wherefore he must make the most of it. There passed before him with intensity the three or four things he wanted most to know; but the question that came of itself to his lips really covered the others. "Then tell me if I shall consciously suffer."

She promptly shook her head. "Never!"

It confirmed the authority he imputed to her, and it produced on him an extraordinary effect. "Well, what's better than that? Do you call that the worst?"

"You think nothing is better?" she asked.

She seemed to mean something so special that he again sharply wondered, though still with the dawn of a prospect of relief. "Why not, if one doesn't *know*?" After which, as their eyes, over his question, met in a silence, the dawn deepened and something to his purpose came prodigiously out of her very face. His own, as he took it in, suddenly flushed to the forehead, and he gasped with the force of a perception to which, on the instant, everything fitted. The sound of his gasp filled the air; then he became articulate. "I see—if I don't suffer!"

In her own look, however, was doubt. "You see what?"

"Why what you mean—what you've always meant."

She again shook her head. "What I mean isn't what I've always meant. It's different."

"It's something new?"

She hung back from it a little. "Something new. It's not what you think. I see what you think."

His divination drew breath then; only her correction might be wrong. "It isn't that I *am* a blockhead?" he asked between faintness and grimness. "It isn't that it's all a mistake?"

"A mistake?" she pityingly echoed. *That* possibility, for her, he saw, would be monstrous; and if she guaranteed him the immunity from pain it would accordingly not be what she had in mind. "Oh no," she declared; "it's nothing of that sort. You've been right."

Yet he couldn't help asking himself if she weren't, thus pressed, speaking but to save him. It seemed to him he should be most in a hole if his history should prove all a platitude. "Are you telling me the truth, so that I shan't have been a bigger idiot than I can bear to know? I *haven't* lived with a vain imagination, in the most besotted illusion? I haven't waited but to see the door shut in my face?"

She shook her head again. "However the case stands *that* isn't the truth. Whatever the reality, it *is* a reality. The door isn't shut. The door's open," said May Bartram.

"Then something's to come?"

She waited once again, always with her cold sweet eyes on him. "It's never too late." She had, with her gliding step, diminished the distance between them, and she stood nearer to him, close to him, a minute, as if still charged with the unspoken. Her movement might have been for some finer emphasis on what she was at once hesitating and deciding to say. He had been standing by the chimney-piece, fireless and sparely adorned, a small perfect old French clock and two morsels of rosy Dresden constituting all its furniture; and her hand grasped the shelf while she kept him waiting, grasped it a little as for support and encouragement. She only kept him waiting, however; that is he only waited. It had become suddenly, from her movement and attitude, beautiful and vivid to him that she had something more to give him; her wasted face delicately shone with it—it glittered almost as with the white lustre of silver in her expression. She was right, incontestably, for what he saw in her face was the truth, and strangely, without consequence, while their talk of it as dreadful was still in the air, she appeared to present it as inordinately soft. This, prompting bewilderment, made him but gape the more gratefully for her revelation, so that they continued for some minutes silent, her face shining at him, her contact imponderably pressing, and his stare all kind but all expectant. The end, none the less, was that what he had expected failed to come to him. Something else took place instead, which seemed to consist at first in the mere closing of her eyes. She gave way at the same instant to a slow fine shudder, and though he remained staring—though he stared in fact but the harder—turned off and regained her chair. It was the end of what she had been intending, but it left him thinking only of that.

"Well, you don't say—?"

She had touched in her passage a bell near the chimney and had sunk back strangely pale. "I'm afraid I'm too ill."

"Too ill to tell me?" It sprang up sharp to him, and almost to his lips, the fear she might die without giving him light. He checked himself in time from so expressing his question, but she answered as if she had heard the words.

"Don't you know—now?"

"'Now'—?" She had spoken as if some difference had been made within the moment. But her maid, quickly obedient to her bell, was already with them. "I know nothing." And he was afterwards to say to himself that he must have spoken with odious impatience, such an impatience as to show that, supremely disconcerted, he washed his hands of the whole question.

"Oh!" said May Bartram.

"Are you in pain?" he asked as the woman went to her.

"No," said May Bartram.

Her maid, who had put an arm round her as if to take her to her room, fixed on him eyes that appealingly contradicted her; in spite of which, however, he showed once more his mystification. "What then has happened?"

She was once more, with her companion's help, on her feet, and, feeling withdrawal imposed on him, he had blankly found his hat and gloves and had reached the door. Yet he waited for her answer. "What *was* to," she said.

5

He came back the next day, but she was then unable to see him, and as it was literally the first time this had occurred in the long stretch of their acquaintance he turned away, defeated and sore, almost angry—or feeling at least that such a break in their custom was really the beginning of the end—and wandered alone with his thoughts, especially with the one he was least able to keep down. She was dying and he would lose her; she was dying and his life would end. He stopped in the Park, into which he had passed, and stared before him at his recurrent doubt. Away from her the doubt pressed again; in her presence he had believed her, but as he felt his forlornness he threw himself into the explanation that, nearest at hand, had most of a miserable warmth for him and least of a cold torment. She had deceived him to save him—to put him off with something in which he should be able to rest. What could the thing that was to happen to him be, after all, but just this thing that had begun to happen? Her dying, her death, his consequent solitude—*that* was what he had figured as the Beast in the Jungle, that was what had been in the lap of the gods. He had had her word for it as he left her—what else on earth could she have meant? It wasn't a thing of a monstrous order; not a fate rare and distinguished; not a stroke of fortune that over-whelmed and immortalised; it had only the stamp of the common doom. But poor Marcher at this hour judged the common doom sufficient. It would serve his turn, and even as the consummation of infinite waiting he would bend his pride to accept it. He sat down on a bench in the twilight. He hadn't been a fool. Something had *been*, as she had said, to come. Before he rose indeed it had quite struck him that the final fact really matched with the long avenue through which he had had to reach it. As sharing his suspense and as giving herself all, giving her life, to bring it to an end, she had come with him every step of the way. He had lived by her aid, and to leave her behind would be cruelly, damnably to miss her. What could be more overwhelming than that?

Well, he was to know within the week, for though she kept him a while at bay, left him restless and wretched during a series of days on each of which he asked about her only again to have to turn away, she ended his trial by receiving him where she had always received him. Yet she had been brought out at some hazard into the presence of so many of the things that were, consciously, vainly, half their past, and there was scant service left in the gentleness of her mere desire, all too visible, to check his obsession and wind up his long trouble. That was clearly what she wanted, the one thing more for her own peace while she could still put out her hand. He was so affected by her state that, once seated by her chair, he was moved to let everything go; it was she herself therefore who brought him back, took up again, before she dismissed him, her last word of the other time. She showed how she wished to leave their business in order. "I'm not sure you understood. You've nothing to wait for more. It *has* come."

Oh how he looked at her! "Really?"

"Really."

"The thing that, as you said, *was* to?"

"The thing that we began in our youth to watch for."

Face to face with her once more he believed her; it was a claim to which he had so abjectly little to oppose. "You mean that it has come as a positive definite occurrence, with a name and a date?"

"Positive. Definite. I don't know about the 'name,' but oh with a date!"

He found himself again too helplessly at sea. "But come in the night—come and passed me by?"

May Bartram had her strange faint smile. "Oh no, it hasn't passed you by!"

"But if I haven't been aware of it and it hasn't touched me—?"

"Ah your not being aware of it"—and she seemed to hesitate an instant to deal with this—"your not being aware of it is the strangeness *in* the strangeness. Its the wonder *of* the wonder." She spoke as with the softness almost of a sick child, yet now at last, at the end of all, with the perfect straightness of a sibyl. She visibly knew that she knew, and the effect on him was of something co-ordinate, in its high character, with the law that had ruled him. It was the true voice of the law; so on her lips would the law itself have sounded. "It *has* touched you," she went on. "It has done its office. It has made you all its own."

"So utterly without my knowing it?"

"So utterly without your knowing it." His hand, as he leaned to her, was on the arm of her chair, and, dimly smiling always now, she placed her own on it. "It's enough if *I* know it."

"Oh!" he confusedly breathed, as she herself of late so often had done.

"What I long ago said is true. You'll never know now, and I think you ought to be content. You've *had* it," said May Bartram.

"But had what?"

"Why what was to have marked you out. The proof of your law. It has acted. I'm too glad," she then bravely added, "to have been able to see what it's *not.*"

He continued to attach his eyes to her, and with the sense that it was all beyond him, and that *she* was too, he would still have sharply challenged her hadn't he so felt it an abuse of her weakness to do more than take devoutly what she gave him, take it hushed as to a revelation. If he did speak, it was out of the foreknowledge of his loneliness to come. "If you're glad of what it's 'not' it might then have been worse?"

She turned her eyes away, she looked straight before her; with which after a moment: "Well, you know our fears."

He wondered. "It's something then we never feared?"

On this slowly she turned to him. "Did we ever dream, with all our dreams, that we should sit and talk of it thus?"

He tried for a little to make out that they had; but it was as if their dreams, numberless enough, were in solution in some thick cold mist through which thought lost itself. "It might have been that we couldn't talk?"

"Well"—she did her best for him—"not from this side. This, you see," she said, "is the *other* side."

"I think," poor Marcher returned, "that all sides are the same to me." Then, however, as she gently shook her head in correction: "We mightn't, as it were, have got across—?"

"To where we are—no. We're *here*"—she made her weak emphasis.

"And much good does it do us!" was her friend's frank comment.

"It does us the good it can. It does us the good that *it* isn't here. It's past, It's behind," said May Bartram. "Before—" but her voice dropped.

He had got up, not to tire her, but it was hard to combat his yearning. She after all told him nothing but that his light had failed—which he knew well enough without her. "Before—?" he blankly echoed.

"Before, you see, it was always to *come.* That kept it present."

"Oh I don't care what comes now! Besides," Marcher added, "it seems to me I liked it better present, as you say, than I can like it absent with *your* absence."

"Oh mine!"—and her pale hands made light of it.

"With the absence of everything." He had a dreadful sense of standing there before her for—so far as anything but this proved, this bottomless drop was concerned—the last time of their life. It rested on him with a weight he felt he could scarce bear, and this weight it apparently was that still pressed out what remained in him of speakable protest. "I believe you; but I can't begin to pretend I understand. *Nothing,* for me, is past; nothing *will* pass till I pass myself, which I pray my stars may be as soon as possible. Say, however," he added, "that I've eaten my cake, as you contend, to the last crumb—how can the thing I've never felt at all be the thing I was marked out to feel?"

She met him perhaps less directly, but she met him unperturbed. "You take your 'feelings' for granted. You were to suffer your fate. That was not necessarily to know it."

"How in the world—when what is such knowledge but suffering?"

She looked up at him a while in silence. "No—you don't understand."

"I suffer," said John Marcher.

"Don't, don't!"

"How can I help at least *that*?"

"*Don't!*" May Bartram repeated.

She spoke it in a tone so special, in spite of her weakness, that he stared an instant—stared as if some light, hitherto hidden, had shimmered across his vision. Darkness again closed over it, but the gleam had already become for him an idea. "Because I haven't the right—?"

"Don't *know*—when you needn't," she mercifully urged. "You needn't—for we shouldn't."

"Shouldn't?" If he could but know what she meant!

"No—it's too much."

"Too much?" he still asked but, with a mystification that was the next moment of a sudden to give way. Her words, if they meant something, affected him in this light— the light also of her wasted face—as meaning *all,* and the sense of what knowledge had been for herself came over him with a rush which broke through into a question. "Is it of that then you're dying?"

She but watched him, gravely at first, as to see, with this, where he was, and she might have seen something or feared something that moved her sympathy. "I would live for you still—if I could." Her eyes closed for a little, as if, withdrawn into herself, she were for a last time trying. "But I can't!" she said as she raised them again to take leave of him.

She couldn't indeed, as but too promptly and sharply appeared, and he had no vision of her after this that was anything but darkness and doom. They had parted for ever in that strange talk; access to her chamber of pain, rigidly guarded, was almost wholly forbidden him; he was feeling now moreover, in the face of doctors, nurses, the two or three relatives attracted doubtless by the presumption of what she had to "leave," how few were the rights, as they were called in such cases, that he had to put forward, and how odd it might even seem that their intimacy shouldn't have given him more of them. The stupidest fourth cousin had more, even though she had been nothing in such a person's life. She had been a feature of features in *his,* for what else was it to have been so indispensable? Strange beyond saying were the ways of existence, baffling for him the anomaly of his lack, as he felt it to be, of producible claim. A woman might have been, as it were, everything to him, and it might yet present him in no connexion that any one seemed held to recognise. If this was the case in these closing weeks it was the case more sharply on the occasion of the last offices rendered, in the great grey London cemetery, to what had been mortal, to what had been precious, in his friend. The concourse at her grave was not numerous, but he saw himself treated as scarce more nearly concerned with it than if there had been a thousand others. He was in short from this moment face to face with the fact that he was to profit extraordinarily little by the interest May Bartram had taken in him. He couldn't quite have said what he expected, but he hadn't surely expected this approach to a double privation. Not only had her interest failed him, but he seemed to feel himself unattended—and for a reason he couldn't seize—by the distinction, the dignity, the propriety, if nothing else, of the man markedly bereaved. It was as if in the view of society he had not *been* markedly bereaved, as if there still failed some sign or proof of it, and as if none the less his character could never be affirmed nor the deficiency ever made up. There were moments as the weeks went by when he would have liked, by some almost aggressive act, to take his stand on the intimacy of his loss, in order that it *might* be questioned and his retort, to the relief of his spirit, so recorded; but the moments of an irritation more helpless followed fast on these, the moments during which, turning things over with a good conscience but with a bare horizon, he found himself wondering if he oughtn't to have begun, so to speak, further back.

He found himself wondering indeed at many things, and this last speculation had others to keep it company. What could he have done, after all, in her lifetime, without giving them both, as it were, away? He couldn't have made known she was watching him, for that would have published the superstition of the Beast. This was what closed his mouth now—now that the Jungle had been threshed to vacancy and that the Beast had stolen away. It sounded too foolish and too flat; the difference for him in this particular, the extinction in his life of the element of suspense, was such as in fact to surprise him. He could scarce have said what the effect resembled; the abrupt cessation, the positive prohibition, of music perhaps, more than anything else, in some place all adjusted and all accustomed to sonority and to attention. If he could at any rate have conceived lifting the veil from his image at some moment of the past (what had he done, after all, if not lift it to *her*?) so to do this to-day, to talk to people at large of the Jungle cleared and confide to them that he now felt it as safe, would have been not only to see them listen as to a goodwife's tale, but really to hear himself tell one. What it presently came to in truth was that poor Marcher waded through his beaten grass, where no life stirred, where no breath sounded, where no evil eye seemed to gleam from a possible lair, very much as if vaguely looking for the Beast, and still more as if acutely missing it. He walked about in an existence that had grown strangely more spacious, and, stopping fitfully in places where the undergrowth of life struck him as closer, asked himself yearningly, wondered secretly and sorely, if it would have lurked here or there. It would have at all events *sprung;* what was at least complete was his belief in the truth itself of the assurance given him. The change from his old sense to his new was absolute and final: what was to happen *had* so absolutely and finally happened that he was as little able to know a fear for his future as to know a hope; so absent in short was any question of anything still to come. He was to live entirely with the other question, that of his unidentified past, that of his having to see his fortune impenetrably muffled and masked.

The torment of this vision became then his occupation; he couldn't perhaps have consented to live but for the possibility of guessing. She had told him, his friend, not to guess; she had forbidden him, so far as he might, to know, and she had even in a sort denied the power in him to learn: which were so many things, precisely, to deprive him of rest. It wasn't that he wanted, he argued for fairness, that anything past and done should repeat itself; it was only that he shouldn't, as an anticlimax, have been taken sleeping so sound as not to be able to win back by an effort of thought the lost stuff of consciousness. He declared to himself at moments that he would either win it back or have done with consciousness for ever; he made this idea his one motive in fine, made it so much his passion that none other, to compare with it, seemed ever to have touched him. The lost stuff of consciousness became thus for him as a strayed or stolen child to an unappeasable father; he hunted it up and down very much as if he were knocking at doors and enquiring of the police. This was the spirit in which, inevitably, he set himself to travel; he started on a journey that was to be as long as he could make it; it danced before him that, as the other side of the globe couldn't possibly have less to say to him, it might, by a possibility of suggestion, have more. Before he quitted London, however, he made a pilgrimage to May Bartram's grave, took his way to it through the endless avenues of the grim suburban metropolis, sought it out in the wilderness of tombs, and, though he had come but for the renewal of the act of farewell, found himself, when he had at last stood by it, beguiled into long intensities. He stood for an hour, powerless to turn away and yet powerless to penetrate the darkness of death; fixing with his eyes her inscribed name and date, beating his fore-head against the fact of the secret they kept, drawing his breath, while he waited, as if some sense would in pity of him rise from the stones. He kneeled on the stones, however, in vain; they kept what they concealed; and if the face of the tomb did become a face for him it was because her two names became a pair of eyes that didn't know him. He gave them a last long look, but no palest light broke.

6

He stayed away, after this, for a year; he visited the depths of Asia, spending himself on scenes of romantic interest, of superlative sanctity; but what was present to him everywhere was that for a man who had known what *he* had known the world was vulgar and vain. The state of mind in which he had lived for so many years shone out to him, in reflexion, as a light that coloured and refined, a light beside which the glow of the East was garish, cheap and thin. The terrible truth was that he had lost—with everything else—a distinction as well; the things he saw couldn't help being common when he had become common to look at them. He was simply now one of them himself—he was in the dust, without a peg for the sense of difference; and there were hours when, before the temples of gods and the sepulchres of kings, his spirit turned for nobleness of association to the barely discriminated slab in the London suburb. That had become for him, and more intensely with time and distance, his one witness of a past glory. It was all that was left to him for proof or pride, yet the past glories of Pharaohs were nothing to him as he thought of it. Small wonder then that he came back to it on the morrow of his return. He was drawn there this time as irresistibly as the other, yet with a confidence, almost, that was doubtless the effect of the many months that had elapsed. He had lived, in spite of himself, into his change of feeling, and in wandering over the earth had wandered, as might be said, from the circumfer-ence to the centre of his desert. He had settled to his safety and accepted perforce his extinction; figuring to himself, with some colour, in the likeness of certain little old men he remembered to have seen, of whom, all meagre and wizened as they might look, it was related that they had in their time fought twenty duels or been loved by ten princesses. They indeed had been wondrous for others while he was but wondrous for himself; which, however, was exactly the cause of his haste to renew the wonder by getting back, as he might put it, into his own presence. That had quickened his steps and checked his delay. If his visit was prompt it was because he had been separated so long from the part of himself that alone he now valued.

It's accordingly not false to say that he reached his goal with a certain elation and stood there again with a certain assurance. The creature beneath the sod *knew* of his rare experience, so that, strangely now, the place had lost for him its mere blankness of expression. It met him in mildness—not, as before, in mockery; it wore for him the air of conscious greeting that we find, after absence, in things that have closely belonged to us and which seem to confess of themselves to the connexion. The plot of ground, the graven tablet, the tended flowers affected him so as belonging to him that he resembled for the hour a contented landlord reviewing a piece of property. Whatever had happened—well, had happened. He had not come back this time with the vanity of that question, his former worrying "What, *what*?" now practically so spent. Yet he would none the less never again so cut himself off from the spot; he would come back to it every month, for if he did nothing else by its aid he at least held up his head. It thus grew for him, in the oddest way, a positive resource; he carried out his idea of periodical returns, which took their place at last among the most inveterate of his habits. What it all amounted to, oddly enough, was that in his finally so simplified world this garden of death gave him the few square feet of earth on which he could still most live. It was as if, being nothing anywhere else for any one, nothing even for himself, he were just everything here, and if not for a crowd of witnesses or indeed for any witness but John Marcher, then by clear right of the register that he could scan like an open page. The open page was the tomb of his friend, and *there* were the facts of the past, there the truth of his life, there the backward reaches in which he could lose himself. He did this from time to time with such effect that he seemed to wander through the old years with his hand in the arm of a companion who was, in the most extraordinary manner, his other, his younger self; and to wander, which was more extraordinary yet, round and round a third presence—not wandering she, but stationary, still, whose eyes, turning with his revolution, never ceased to follow him, and whose seat was his point, so to speak, of orientation. Thus in short he settled to live—feeding all on the sense that he once *had* lived, and dependent on it not alone for a support but for an identity.

It sufficed him in its way for months and the year elapsed; it would doubtless even have carried him further but for an accident, superficially slight, which moved him, quite in another direction, with a force beyond any of his impressions of Egypt or of India. It was a thing of the merest chance—the turn, as he afterwards felt, of a hair, though he was indeed to live to believe that if light hadn't come to him in this particular fashion it would still have come in another. He was to live to believe this, I say, though he was not to live, I may not less definitely mention, to do much else. We allow him at any rate the benefit of the conviction, struggling up for him at the end, that, whatever might have happened or not happened, he would have come round of himself to the light. The incident of an autumn day had put the match to the train laid from of old by his misery. With the light before him he knew that even of late his ache had only been smothered. It was strangely drugged, but it throbbed; at the touch it began to bleed. And the touch, in the event, was the face of a fellow mortal. This face, one grey afternoon when the leaves were thick in the alleys, looked into Marcher's own, at the cemetery, with an expression like the cut of a blade. He felt it, that is, so deep down that he winced at the steady thrust. The person who so mutely assaulted him was a figure he had noticed, on reaching his own goal, absorbed by a grave a short distance away, a grave apparently fresh, so that the emotion of the visitor would probably match it for frankness. This fact alone forbade further attention, though during the time he stayed he remained vaguely conscious of his neighbour, a middle-aged man apparently, in mourning, whose bowed back, among the clustered monuments and mortuary yews, was constantly presented. Marcher's theory that these were elements in contact with which he himself revived, had suffered, on this occasion, it may be granted, a marked, an excessive check. The autumn day was dire for him as none had recently been, and he rested with a heaviness he had not yet known on the low stone table that bore May Bartram's name. He rested without power to move, as if some spring in him, some spell vouchsafed, had suddenly been broken for ever. If he could have done that moment as he wanted he would simply have stretched himself on the slab that was ready to take him, treating it as a place prepared to receive his last sleep. What in all the wide world had he now to keep awake for? He stared before him with the question, and it was then that, as one of the cemetery walks passed near him, he caught the shock of the face.

His neighbour at the other grave had withdrawn, as he himself, with force enough in him, would have done by now, and was advancing along the path on his way to one of the gates. This brought him close, and his pace was slow, so that—and all the more as there was a kind of hunger on his look—the two men were for a minute directly confronted. Marcher knew him at once for one of the deeply stricken—a perception so sharp that nothing else in the picture comparatively lived, neither his dress, his age, nor his presumable character and class; nothing lived but the deep ravage of the features he showed. He *showed* them—that was the point; he was moved, as he passed, by some impulse that was either a signal for sympathy or, more possibly, a challenge to an opposed sorrow. He might already have been aware of our friend, might at some previous hour have noticed in him the smooth habit of the scene, with which the state of his own senses so scantly consorted, and might thereby have been stirred as by an overt discord. What Marcher was at all events conscious of was in the first place that the image of scarred passion presented to him was conscious too—of something that profaned the air; and in the second that, roused, startled, shocked, he was yet the next moment looking after it, as it went, with envy. The most extraordinary thing that had happened to him—though he had given that name to other matters as well—took place, after his immediate vague stare, as a consequence of this impression. The stranger passed, but the raw glare of his grief remained, making our friend wonder in pity what wrong, what wound it expressed, what injury not to be healed. What had the man *had,* to make him by the loss of it so bleed and yet live?

Something—and this reached him with a pang—that *he,* John Marcher, hadn't; the proof of which was precisely John Marcher's arid end. No passion had ever touched him, for this was what passion meant; he had survived and maundered and pined, but where had been *his* deep ravage? The extraordinary thing we speak of was the sudden rush of the result of this question. The sight that had just met his eyes named to him, as in letters of quick flame, something he had utterly, insanely missed, and what he had missed made these things a train of fire, made them mark themselves in an anguish of inward throbs. He had seen *outside* of his life, not learned it within, the way a woman was mourned when she had been loved for herself: such was the force of his conviction of the meaning of the stranger's face, which still flared for him as a smoky torch. It hadn't come to him, the knowledge, on the wings of experience; it had brushed him, jostled him, upset him, with the disrespect of chance, the insolence of accident. Now that the illumination had begun, however, it blazed to the zenith, and what he presently stood there gazing at was the sounded void of his life. He gazed, he drew breath, in pain; he turned in his dismay, and, turning, he had before him in sharper incision than ever the open page of his story. The name on the table smote him as the passage of his neighbour had done, and what it said to him, full in the face, was that *she* was what he had missed. This was the awful thought, the answer to all the past, the vision at the dread clearness of which he grew as cold as the stone beneath him. Everything fell together, confessed, explained, overwhelmed; leaving him most of all stupefied at the blindness he had cherished. The fate he had been marked for he had met with a vengeance—he had emptied the cup to the lees; he had been the man of his time, *the* man, to whom nothing on earth was to have happened. That was the rare stroke—that was his visitation. So he saw it, as we say, in pale horror, while the pieces fitted and fitted. So *she* had seen it while he didn't, and so she served at this hour to drive the truth home. It was the truth, vivid and monstrous, that all the while he had waited the wait was itself his portion. This the companion of his vigil had at a given moment made out, and she had then offered him the chance to baffle his doom. One's doom, however, was never baffled, and on the day she told him his own had come down she had seen him but stupidly stare at the escape she offered him.

The escape would have been to love her; then, *then* he would have lived. *She* had lived—who could say now with what passion?—since she had loved him for himself; whereas he had never thought of her (ah how it hugely glared at him!) but in the chill of his egotism and the light of her use. Her spoken words came back to him—the chain stretched and stretched. The Beast had lurked indeed, and the Beast, at its hour, had sprung; it had sprung in that twilight of the cold April when, pale, ill, wasted, but all beautiful, and perhaps even then recoverable, she had risen from her chair to stand before him and let him imaginably guess. It had sprung as he didn't guess; it had sprung as she hopelessly turned from him, and the mark, by the time he left her, had fallen where it *was* to fall. He had justified his fear and achieved his fate; he had failed, with the last exactitude, of all he was to fail of; and a moan now rose to his lips as he remembered she had prayed he mightn't know. This horror of waking—*this* was knowledge, knowledge under the breath of which the very tears in his eyes seemed to freeze. Through them, none the less, he tried to fix it and hold it; he kept it there before him so that he might feel the pain. That at least, belated and bitter, had something of the taste of life. But the bitterness suddenly sickened him, and it was as if, horribly, he saw, in the truth, in the cruelty of his image, what had been appointed and done. He saw the Jungle of his life and saw the lurking Beast; then, while he looked, perceived it, as by a stir of the air, rise, huge and hideous, for the leap that was to settle him. His eyes darkened—it was close; and, instinctively turning, in his hallucination, to avoid it, he flung himself, face down, on the tomb.

Guy de Maupassant (1850–1893)

Guy de Maupassant was born in Normandy in 1850, the son of a well-to-do stock-broker. Gustave Flaubert was a family friend and called the young Maupassant "my disciple." "For seven years," says Maupassant of this relationship, "I wrote verses, short stories, longer stories, even a wretched play. Nothing survived. The master read everything. Then, the following Sunday at lunch, developed his criticisms." Flaubert taught him to write so that the reader will know "by means of a single word, wherein one cab-horse does not resemble the fifty others ahead of it. . . ." Exact description, *le mot juste,* became the outstanding quality of Maupassant's work.

Through Flaubert, the young writer met such great literary men of Europe as James and Turgenev—but most important was Émile Zola. In 1880, the Zola circle of naturalists published a volume of stories on the Franco-Prussian War, which had been a humiliating disaster for France; Maupassant's contribution "Boule de Suif"—a devastating picture of bourgeois hypocrisy—was almost unanimously hailed as the book's prize.

Maupassant's stories move swiftly, directly and dramatically toward their point of illumination (see Introduction, pp. 8–9). His narrative line is compact and elegant, avoiding the disgressiveness and excessive explanation of many earlier writers. Under his influence, compression became the hallmark of the short story. He renders a character in a gesture ("Monsieur Dufour, shaken by violent hiccoughs, had unbuttoned his waistcoat and the top button of his trousers"), a social class in a picture (the family driving out from Paris in a two-wheeled milkman's cart), a whole life in a scene (the old grandmother chasing the strange cat, "showering it in vain with affectionate pet names").

In a critical essay, Henry James says, "As a commentator, Maupassant is slightly common, while as an artist he is wonderfully rare. . . . His [instrument of art] is that of the senses, and it is through them alone, or almost alone, that life appeals to him; it is almost alone by their help that he . . . produces brilliant works." His was no mean talent: he is unsurpassed in his ability to render sense impressions. The opening passages of "A Country Outing" provide a vivid scene as the cart, with the reader, moves toward the country: "Here and there, tall factory chimneys sprang out of the barren soil, the only vegetation in those putrid fields across which the light spring breezes spread the aroma of kerosene and soot mixed with another smell, even less alluring." And sounds: the nightingale "was singing full-throatedly. It emitted trills and warbles, then let out great vibrating sounds that filled the air and seemed to fade somewhere beyond the horizon." And feelings: the girl "abandoned herself to the gentle sensation of gliding over the water. . . . A vague need for sensuous pleasure, a fermentation of the blood, ran through her flesh. . . ."

Maupassant has been compared, usually to his detriment, to his slightly younger contemporary Anton Chekhov. They are perhaps equally responsible for technical advances that moved the short story toward greater intensity through compression. Both had a wide range of characters and subjects. Their difference is in their relation to their characters. Chekhov views his characters—even so rigid and cold a one as Vierochka—with a sympathetic irony. But, except for the young girl in whom he expresses a wholly sexual interest, Maupassant views his characters from an ironic distance. The mother with her fat thighs, the father with his dull egotism, the boy, the grandmother—all are dealt with at arm's length and rather coldly. Maupassant had immense technical skill, but he shared some of Flaubert's contempt for his fellow humans.

Although he died at the age of forty-three of paresis, he had written enough to fill thirty volumes, including over three-hundred stories.

A Country Outing

For five months they had been talking of having lunch outside Paris on the saint's day of Madame Dufour, whose first name was Pétronille. And since they had been waiting impatiently for this outing for a long time, they got up very early that morning.

Monsieur Dufour had borrowed the milkman's cart, which he drove himself. The two-wheeled cart was quite presentable; its top was supported by four iron rods with curtains attached to them—curtains that were rolled up now, the better to admire the landscape. Only the curtain in the rear had been left loose, and it was flapping like a flag.

The wife, sitting next to her husband, had blossomed forth in an extraordinary, cherry-colored silk dress. Behind them, on two chairs, sat the old grandmother and a young girl, and one could also see the yellow thatch of a young fellow who, since there was nothing for him to sit on, had sprawled out in the bottom of the cart so that only his head showed.

When they had driven down the Champs Elysées and passed the fortifications at the Porte Maillot, the party began to admire the countryside.

When they reached the Neuilly Bridge, Monsieur Dufour announced: "Here we are, in the country at last," and at this signal, his wife became very emotional about nature.

When they reached the traffic circle of Courbevoie, they were filled with admiration at the vast expanse of the horizon. To the right, at a distance, lay Argenteuil with its church tower standing out; above it appeared the Sannois hills and the Orgemont mill. To the left, the aqueduct of Marly was outlined against the pale morning sky and, farther away, one could also see the high ground of Saint Germain; directly ahead of them, at the end of a chain of hills, the upturned earth indicated the site of the new fort of Cormeilles. And very, very far away, at an impressive distance, they caught a glimpse of the dark green line of the forest.

The sun began to scorch their faces and the dust kept getting into their eyes as, on either side of the road, a barren, dirty, stinking countryside unfolded. One would have thought it had been ravaged by a leprosy that had attacked even the houses, for the skeletons of gutted and abandoned dwellings and of huts that hadn't been finished because the builders couldn't be paid showed nothing to the world but four roofless walls.

Here and there, tall factory chimneys sprang out of the barren soil, the only vegetation in those putrid fields across which the light spring breezes spread the aroma of kerosene and soot mixed with another smell, even less alluring.

Finally they crossed the Seine for a second time, giving rein to their delight as they rolled over the bridge. The river was bursting with light—a haze rose from it, drawn up by the sun. A sweet feeling of peace came over them and they felt refreshed as they breathed a cleaner air that was no longer filled with the black smoke of the factories and stenches from the refuse dumps.

A man who passed by told them the name of the place: Bezons.

"A Country Outing" from *Boule de Suif and Selected Stories* by Guy de Maupassant, as translated by Andrew R. MacAndrew. Copyright © 1964 by Andrew R. MacAndrew. Reprinted by arrangement with The New American Library, Inc., New York, New York.

The carriage stopped and Monsieur Dufour started to read an inviting sign posted over an eating-place: "Restaurant Poulin, Fish Stews and Fish Fries, Dining Rooms for Private Parties, Garden and Swings."

"Well, what do you say, Madame Dufour—does this suit you? Will you finally make up your mind?"

Madame Dufour read the sign in her turn, after which she examined the house at length.

It was a white country inn, standing by the side of the road. Through the open door one could see the shining zinc of the counter at which two workers dressed in their Sunday best were standing.

Finally Madame Dufour decided:

"Yes, it looks all right," she said; "besides, there's the view."

The cart rolled onto the spacious grounds planted with large trees that extended behind the inn and that were only separated from the Seine by the towpath.

They got out. The husband jumped down first and opened his arms to receive his wife. The footboard, supported by two iron brackets, was very low, so that to reach it, Madame Dufour had to uncover a leg whose erstwhile slenderness was vanishing under the invasion of flesh coming down from her thighs.

Monsieur Dufour, already aroused by the countryside, quickly pinched her calf and then, catching her under the arms, deposited her heavily on the ground as if she were a huge package.

She patted her silk dress with the palms of her hands to shake the dust off it, and began to examine the place she had come to.

She was a woman of thirty-six or so, well fleshed, blooming, and pleasant to look at. She breathed painfully, held in the stranglehold of her corset, and the pressure of that contraption squeezed the quivering mass of her over-abundant bosom right up to her double chin.

Then came the young girl who, placing her hand on her father's shoulder, jumped down lightly without any further help. The yellow-haired boy had climbed down by himself, using the spokes of the wheel, and now helped Monsieur Dufour to unload the grandmother.

After that they unharnessed the horse and tied it to a tree, letting the cart fall on its nose with the two shafts on the ground. The men removed their coats, washed their hands in a bucket of water, and then joined the ladies who were already installed on the swings.

Mademoiselle Dufour was trying to swing herself by standing up on the board, but couldn't manage to give herself a sufficiently vigorous send-off. She was a handsome girl between eighteen and twenty, one of those women who, met in the street, fill a man with a sudden, whipping desire and leave the vague disturbance and agitation of the senses with him until he goes to sleep. Tall, slender at the waist, broad at the hip, she had a very dark complexion and very black hair. Her dress clearly revealed the full curves of her flesh, further accentuated by the movement of her hips as she tried to set the swing going. Her arms were stretched upward as she held on to the ropes above her head so that her breast bulged smoothly at each push she gave. Her hat, carried away by a gust of wind, had fallen behind her. Finally the swing set into motion, revealing her legs, which were quite slender, up to the knee with each swing; and throwing into the faces of the two men who were laughingly watching her the gossamer of her skirts, headier than wine vapors.

Sitting on the other swing, Madame Dufour kept moaning constantly and monotonously:

"Come over here and push me, Cyprien; come, Cyprien, give me a push."

Finally he went over to her. Rolling up the sleeves of his shirt as though he were going to start on a heavy job, he made a tremendous effort and set his wife into motion.

Grasping the ropes tightly, she held her legs out straight to avoid the ground and was delighted by the feeling of dizziness the rhythmic motion of the swing gave her. Her shaken body quivered like a jelly in a dish. But as the motion of the swing increased, she became dizzy and frightened. At each descent she let out a piercing scream that attracted the urchins of the neighborhood, so that she vaguely saw in front of her a row of mischievous faces peering over the garden hedge and distorted in a variety of ways by their laughter.

A maidservant came out from the inn and they ordered lunch.

"A fish fry from the Seine, a sautéed rabbit, a salad, and dessert," Madame Dufour spelled out with an important air.

"Bring two liters of ordinary wine and a bottle of Bordeaux," her husband said.

And their daughter added:

"We'll have our meal on the grass."

The grandmother had been seized by a feeling of tenderness at the sight of the inn's cat and had been chasing it for ten minutes, showering it in vain with affectionate pet names. The animal, although probably secretly flattered by these attentions, remained constantly close at hand without ever allowing her to get hold of it; it walked quietly around the trees, rubbing itself against them with its tail in the air and emitting little purrs of satisfaction.

"Look at that!" the blond young man cried suddenly. He had been ferreting around the grounds. "What swell boats!"

They went to have a look. Two splendid skiffs, fine and worked like costly pieces of furniture, hung in a little wooden boathouse. The boats rested side by side like two tall young maidens, stretched out in all their slender length, evoking a desire to glide over the water on gentle evenings or on bright summer mornings, to slip along past the flower-covered banks where the trees dip their branches in the water, where the eternally shivering reeds tremble and from which the lively kingfishers take off like blue streaks of lightning.

The entire family admired them reverently.

"They sure are beautiful," Monsieur Dufour repeated, examining them like a connoisseur. He had done his share of rowing when he was young, he told the others. Indeed, when he was pulling on those things—and he pretended to be pulling on oars—he didn't care a hoot for the rest of the world. He had, in his time, outraced many of those Englishmen at Joinville. . . . Then he made a few puns about the word *dames,* as oarsmen call oarlocks, saying that rowing men never went out without their *dames,* and for good reason. He got all excited as he spoke and insisted on betting that, with a boat like one of these, he could easily go fifteen miles in an hour, and without even hurrying.

"It's ready," the servant announced, appearing in the doorway.

They hurried off to eat, but they found that the spot Madame Dufour had mentally picked out as the best for their lunch was already occupied. Two young men were having their lunch there. They were obviously the owners of the boats, for they were dressed as oarsmen.

They were reclining—almost stretched out—in their chairs. Their faces were blackened by the sun and their chests were covered by the thin, white cotton jerseys from which their bare arms, as powerful as blacksmiths', emerged. They were two solid fellows, very powerfully muscled, but displaying in all their movements that graceful looseness of limb which is acquired through exercise and which is so different from the deformation produced in the worker by the repetition of the same painful effort again and again.

They exchanged a quick smile when they saw the mother and a look when they saw the daughter.

"Let's give them our place," one of the young men said; "that way we'll make their acquaintance."

The other immediately got up and, holding his half-black, half-red cap in his hand, gallantly offered the ladies the only spot in the garden unreached by the sun. His offer was accepted after a chorus of protestations and then, so that they would feel more as if they were in the country, the family installed themselves on the grass, scorning table and chairs.

The young men carried their plates a few steps away and resumed their lunch. Their bare arms, which they showed off constantly, disturbed the girl somewhat and she even turned her head away and pretended not to notice them, while Madame Dufour, bolder and impelled by a feminine curiosity that was perhaps really desire, kept looking at them constantly, probably comparing them to the concealed ugliness of her husband.

She was sitting on the grass with her legs bent and crossed tailor-fashion, and she kept wriggling constantly on the pretext that ants had got under her clothes somewhere. Monsieur Dufour, soured by the presence of the two strangers and by their amiability, was looking for a comfortable position, which he couldn't find. As to the young man with yellow hair, he was silently tucking away food like an ogre.

"What wonderful weather, monsieur," big Madame Dufour said to one of the oarsmen, trying to be amiable because they had so gallantly yielded their place.

"Oh yes, ma'am," the man replied. "Do you often come out of town?"

"Well, only once or twice a year, to breathe some fresh air. And what about you, monsieur?"

"I come out here every evening and spend the night."

"Oh, that must be ever so nice!"

"It certainly is, ma'am."

And he expanded poetically on his daily life in a way that awakened in the hearts of these shopkeepers, deprived of grass and hungry for a walk across the fields, that silly love of nature which haunts such people throughout the year as they stand behind the counters of their shops.

Moved, the girl raised her eyes and glanced at the oarsman. Then Monsieur Dufour spoke for the first time.

"That's the real life," he said, and turning to his wife: "Could you eat a bit more of this rabbit, dearie?"

"No thank you, my dear," she said and again turned toward the two young men. She indicated their bare arms and asked: "Aren't you ever cold like that?"

They laughed and proceeded to shock the family with tales of their prodigious feats of endurance, of going swimming while they were in a sweat, of long rows through night and fog. And as they spoke, they kept thumping their chests to emphasize each word with the sound it made.

"Ah, you sure look sturdy!" Monsieur Dufour said.

He no longer held forth about the times he had inflicted those wallopings on the English oarsmen.

The girl examined them out of the corner of her eye. The yellow-haired young clerk, whose wine had gone down the wrong way, started to choke and cough, splattering the cherry-colored dress of his lady employer, who angrily demanded some water with which to wash off the stains.

In the meantime, it was growing terribly hot. The sparkling river seemed to radiate waves of heat and the wine fumes mounted to their heads.

Monsieur Dufour, shaken by violent hiccoughs, had unbuttoned his waistcoat and the top button of his trousers. His wife, feeling suffocated, was gradually unhooking her dress. Their clerk was gaily shaking his shock of yellow hair and kept filling his glass. The grandmother, feeling a little tipsy, sat stiffly, looking very dignified.

As to the young girl, she remained impassive, except that a faint sparkle appeared in her eyes and the dark skin of her cheeks turned rather pink.

The coffee finished them off completely. They decided to sing, each singing his own couplet while the others applauded frantically. Then, with some difficulty, they got up. While the two women, rather dizzy, stood there getting their breath, the two men, who were quite drunk, tried to perform some acrobatic exercises.

Heavy, flabby, their faces congested, they hung limply on the rings, quite unable to pull themselves up, while their shirts constantly threatened to escape from their trousers and wave in the wind like flags.

The oarsmen, who had put their boats into the water, now came up and politely offered to take the ladies for a row on the river.

"May I, dear? Please!" Madame Dufour cried.

Her husband stared at her drunkenly, without understanding.

Then one of the oarsmen, holding two fishing rods in his hand, walked over to him. The hope of catching a gudgeon flashed through his head. That shopkeeper's dream lit up his mournful stare. He gave his sanction to everything and installed himself in the shade under the bridge, his feet hanging over the water. The yellow-haired clerk sat down beside him and immediately fell asleep.

One of the oarsmen sacrificed himself and took the mother.

"To the little wood on the Île-aux-Anglais!" he called out, rowing away.

The other skiff proceeded at a slower pace. The man at the oars was staring so hard at his companion that he couldn't concentrate on anything else. A certain emotion had taken hold of him and was sapping his strength.

The girl, sitting on the coxswain's seat, abandoned herself to the gentle sensation of gliding over the water. She felt the ability to think deserting her; her limbs felt supremely relaxed; she was as free of herself as if permeated by total intoxication. She had turned very red and her breath came short. Dizziness caused by the wine and amplified by the heat waves shimmering around her made all the trees along the bank seem to bow to her in salutation. A vague need for sensuous pleasure, a fermentation of the blood, ran through her flesh which was excited by the ardors of the day; she was also stirred by this tête-à-tête on the water in the midst of a countryside emptied by the blazing sky, with this young man who thought her beautiful—whose eye caressed her skin and whose desire was as penetrating as the sun.

Their inability to speak further increased their emotion and they kept looking at the water around them. Then making an effort, he asked her name.

"Henriette," she said.

"Ah, really? Mine's Henri."

The sound of their own voices had a calming effect upon them and they became interested in the river bank. The other skiff had stopped there and seemed to be waiting for them. The other oarsman called out to them:

"We'll join you in the woods. We're going to Robinson's now because Madame is thirsty."

He leaned heavily on his oars and moved off so quickly that in no time he was out of sight.

In the meantime a continuous roar that they had vaguely discerned before was rapidly growing nearer to them. The river itself seemed to tremble as if the deadened sound was emerging from its depths.

"What's that noise?" she inquired.

It was the water falling from the dam that cut the river in two at the tip of the island. He was becoming entangled in this explanation when, through the roar of the cascade, they were struck by a bird's song that seemed to come from very far off.

"Imagine that!" he said. "The nightingales are singing during the day now. The hens must be hatching."

A nightingale! She had never heard nightingales sing. The thought of hearing one now aroused tender, poetic notions in her heart.

A nightingale! That invisible witness of love-trysts invoked by Juliet on her balcony; that heavenly music bestowed upon humans to accompany their kisses; that eternal inspiration of all the languorous romances that open up an azure ideal to the poor little hearts of young girls trembling with emotion!

So she was going to hear a nightingale.

"Don't let's make any noise," her companion said. "We could go ashore by the wood and sit down quite close to it."

The skiff seemed to be gliding on ice. The tree-lined bank was so low that their eyes seemed to plunge into the depth of the wood. They stopped. The skiff was tied up. Henriette leaned on Henri's arm and they made their way among the branches.

"Bend down," he said.

She did so and they made their way through an inextricable tangle of creepers, leaves, and reeds, into a shelter that had to be known to be found and that the young man laughingly called his "private study."

Immediately above their heads the bird was singing full-throatedly. It emitted trills and warbles, then let out great vibrating sounds that filled the air and seemed to fade somewhere beyond the horizon, rolling off along the river and flying away over the meadows, through the blazing silence that weighed on the countryside.

They didn't speak for fear of frightening the bird and making it fly away. They sat next to each other and slowly Henri's arm slipped round Henriette's waist, exerting a gentle pressure. Without anger, she took that bold hand and pushed it farther away from her. And she did so whenever he brought his hand closer. She felt no embarrassment whatever at his caress, as if it were quite natural. And she pushed it off most naturally too.

Lost in a sort of ecstasy, she listened to the bird. She was filled with infinite desires, with sudden tender impulses, with revelations of superhuman poetry, and with such a softening of the nerves and heart that she began to cry without knowing why.

The young man pressed her against him, but now she didn't push him away, didn't even think of doing so.

Suddenly the nightingale fell silent. A distant voice called:

"Henriette!"

"Don't answer," her companion whispered, "or you'll scare away the bird."

She hadn't even thought of answering.

For some time they remained sitting there like that. Madame Dufour must also have been sitting somewhere, for from time to time, they would hear the shrill little cries of the big lady whom the other oarsman must have been fondling.

The girl, still crying, was filled with delightful sensations, her skin hot and prickled all over by an unfamiliar tingling. Henri's head was on her shoulder.

Suddenly he kissed her on the lips. She drew back, furious, and to avoid him, threw herself down on her back. But he threw himself on top of her, covering her with his entire body. He had to pursue that fleeting mouth for a long time before he caught it and welded it to his. Then maddened by a formidable desire, she responded to his kiss, pressing him against her breast. All her resistance collapsed as if crushed by a weight too heavy for it.

Everything around them was quiet. The bird resumed his song. It burst out at first in three strident notes that seemed an appeal for love, then after a moment's silence, it again sang in a weakened tone, in very slow trills.

A soft breeze slipped by, causing the leaves to murmur, and from beneath the tangle of branches came two ardent sighs which blended with the song of the nightingale and the gentle breath of the wood.

Drunkenness seemed to overcome the bird, and its voice, gradually gaining in momentum like a fire flaring up or like a mounting passion, seemed to accompany the crackling of kisses under the tree. Then, the delirium in its throat was let loose in complete abandon. It went through long, drawn-out swoons, great melodious spasms.

Now and then it would stop to rest, threading out only two or three light sounds that ended suddenly on a strident note. Or else it would go off at a mad pace, with gushing scales, with shudders and jerks—a sort of fierce, furious hymn of love followed by cries of triumph.

But then the bird fell silent, hearing below it a moan so deep that one might have taken it for a soul taking leave of this world. The sound lasted for a while and then culminated in a sob.

They were both quite pale as they left their green bed. The sky seemed to them to have become overcast; to their eyes, the glowing sun had been extinguished; they were aware of their loneliness and of the silence around them. They walked quickly, side by side, without touching each other, without talking, for they seemed to have become irreconcilable enemies—as if disgust had sprung up between their bodies and hatred between their spirits.

Occasionally Henriette would call: "Mamma!"

There was a stir beneath a bush. Henri thought he saw a white underskirt quickly pulled over a thick calf. Then the huge lady emerged, a bit embarrassed and even redder than before, her eyes aglow and her stormy bosom perhaps a bit too close to her companion. As for him, he must have witnessed some rather funny things, for his face was furrowed by an irrepressible hilarity that kept bursting out despite all his efforts.

Madame Dufour took his arm affectionately and they returned to the boats. Henri, who was walking in front next to the girl, thought at one point that he heard a hard kiss that was intended to be noiseless.

Finally they returned to Bezons.

Monsieur Dufour, now sober, was impatient. The blond clerk was having a bite to eat before leaving the inn. The cart, already harnessed, was waiting for them in the courtyard. The grandmother was already in her seat, very worried that they might be overtaken by darkness before reaching Paris, for the countryside was none too safe.

Hands were shaken and the Dufour family left.

"So long!" the oarsmen shouted, and received a sigh and a tear in reply.

Two months later, passing along the Rue des Martyrs, Henri saw a sign over a door which read: "Dufour—Hardware Merchant." He went in.

The big lady was displaying her rotundity across the counter. They recognized each other right away. After a thousand polite remarks, he inquired:

"And how's Mademoiselle Henriette?"

"She's fine, thank you. In fact, she got married."

"Ah . . ." he said, seized by emotion. "And whom did she marry?"

"The young man who was with us then, you know. . . . He'll be the one to take over the business."

"Yes, yes, I remember very well. . . ."

He started to leave, feeling very sad without knowing why. Madame Dufour called him back.

"And how is your friend?" she asked shyly.

"He's fine."

"Please give him our best and tell him to drop in on us whenever he comes by." She turned very red and added: "Tell him I'd like him to do that very much."

"I certainly will tell him. Good-bye."

"No. . . . See you very soon!"

A year later, on a very sultry summer Sunday, every detail of the adventure he had always remembered came back to Henri; the recollection was so vivid and he felt such nostalgia that he returned all alone to his "private study" in the little wood.

As he crept in, he received a shock. She was there. She was sitting on the grass looking very sad, while next to her, still in his shirt sleeves, the yellow-haired young man was stretched out asleep. He had given himself entirely to his sleep, like an animal.

She turned very pale when she saw Henri and he thought she was about to faint. But then they started to talk quite naturally, as if nothing had ever happened between them.

As he was telling her that he often came to this place on Sundays to rest and to relive many past memories, she looked lengthily into his eyes.

"Me," she said, "I think of it every night."

"Well, dear," her husband mumbled, yawning, "I guess it's time we were on our way back."

Anton Chekhov (1860–1904)

For many critics, Anton Chekhov is *the* master of the short-story form. Beginning with comic potboilers to help support his family while he was a medical student, he wrote over six hundred stories, many among the finest ever done. Only when he discovered, in 1886, that his work was highly regarded in St. Petersburg did he begin to take himself seriously as a writer. Even so, he called medicine his wife, literature his mistress.

To the editor who first encouraged him, Chekhov—the son of a slave who failed as a shopkeeper—wrote an appealing self-portrait:

> Write a story, do, about a young man, the son of a serf, a former grocery boy, a choir singer, a high school pupil and university student, brought up to respect rank, to kiss the hands of priests, to truckle to the ideas of others—a young man who expressed thanks for every piece of bread, who was whipped many times, who went without galoshes to do his tutoring, who used his fists, tortured animals, was fond of dining with rich relatives, was a hypocrite in his dealings with God and men, needlessly, solely out of a realization of his own insignificance—write how this young man squeezes the slave out of himself, drop by drop, and how, on awaking one fine morning, he feels that the blood coursing through his veins is no longer that of a slave but that of a real human being.

Chekhov was immensely influential in the development of the short story, affecting both its form and subject matter. Rather than writing of immense crises, he writes of small sins and common misfortunes: self-deceit, lack of consideration, wounded vanity, disappointed hopes, failed human connections. Even when his subject matter is potentially overwhelming—like the death of the son in "Heartache"—he resists the grand emotions, keeps the tragedy within a human range. His characters come from all walks of life: landowners, peasants, shopkeepers, doctors, teachers, foolish men and foolish women, and neglected children. He views each of them not as a cog in a social wheel but as an individual.

His technique is disarmingly simple. Relatively plotless, his stories have no resounding upbeat ending. He introduces a character or two, gives a little background, shifts to the people themselves, and allows them to move around, talk, interact. Little happens: a woman declares her love and is disappointed; a cabbie talks to his horse; a *ménage à trois* is quietly agreed to. As H. E. Bates says, there is "no grandiose staying of the scene."

The reader is apt to feel a little uncomfortable at the end of a Chekhov story. Justice has hardly triumphed just because the cuckolded husband accepts the lover, or because a rejecting young man realizes his loss. The good is not amply served by the horse who merely stands still for the poor cabbie. In fact, each of Chekhov's stories in this book seems simply to die away at the end.

Yet something has happened. A situation is clarified or a character is revealed. A tension is relaxed, a rough edge worn smooth, a hidden self has surfaced. And it is right, the truth has been served. We have been with the people, have understood them in their complexity and venality, have better understood ourselves. Virginia

Woolf said that "as we read these little stories about nothing at all, the horizon widens; the soul gains an astonishing sense of freedom."

Although never successful in writing a novel, Chekhov became one of the greatest playwrights of the modern age. His most frequently produced plays are *The Sea Gull* (1896), *Uncle Vanya* (1897), *The Cherry Orchard* (1904), and *The Three Sisters* (1900), which has been called the finest play since Shakespeare. Like his stories, his plays emphasize the everyday moments that define his characters.

Ninochka: A Love Story

The door opened quietly and my good friend Pavel Sergeyevich Vikhlyenev entered. Although a young man, he was sickly, old-looking, and, in general—with his round shoulders, long nose, and gaunt features—unattractive. But, on the other hand, his face was so bland, soft, and undefined that every time you looked at it you experienced a strange desire to get hold of it with your five fingers and to feel, as it were, the doughy soft-heartedness and warmth of my friend. Like all bookish people, he was quiet, diffident, and shy; besides which, at this time he was paler than usual, and for some reason violently agitated.

"What's the matter with you?" I asked, glancing at his white face and faintly trembling lips. "Are you sick, or has there been another misunderstanding with your wife? You don't look yourself."

After hesitating for a moment Vikhlyenev coughed slightly, then with a gesture of despair said "Yes . . . with Ninochka again. I've been so miserable I couldn't sleep all night, and, as you see, I'm barely alive. Damn it all! Other people don't let things get them down; they take injury, loss, or pain lightly. But it requires a mere trifle to depress and upset me."

"But what happened?"

"A trifle—a little domestic drama. But I'll tell you the whole story, if you like. Yesterday my Ninochka did not go out. She took it into her head to spend an evening with me and stayed at home. I was, of course, overjoyed. She usually goes out to a meeting somewhere at night, and since that's the only time I'm at home, you can imagine how I was . . . well . . . I was overjoyed. But then, you have never been married, so you don't know how cozy and warm it feels when you come home from work to find the woman you live for . . . . Ah!"

Vikhlyenev made an inventory of the charms of married life. Then he wiped the perspiration from his forehead, and continued. "Ninochka thought she'd like to spend an evening with me. Well, you know how I am—dull, heavy, and far from clever. It's not much fun to be with me; I'm forever at my drafting board or my soil filters; I never play, or dance, or joke. And you must admit that Ninochka is pleasure-loving. Youth has its rights, don't you think so? Well, I began by showing her various little things, photographs and one thing and another, told her some stories, and then I suddenly remembered that I had some old letters in my desk, among them some that

"Ninochka: A Love Story" from *Anton Chekhov: Selected Stories,* as translated by Ann Dunnigan. Copyright © 1960 by Ann Dunnigan. Reprinted by arrangement with The New American Library, Inc., New York.

were very funny. In my student days I had friends who wrote devilishly clever letters: you read them and you split your guts laughing! I pulled these letters out of the desk and commenced reading them to Ninochka. I read her one, then another, than a third, and suddenly—the whole thing broke down! In one letter she came across the phrase: 'Katya sends her regards.' To a jealous wife such a phrase is like a sharp knife, and my Ninochka—an Othello in petticoats! The questions rained down on my unfortunate head: Who is this Katya? And how? And why? I explained to her that she was in some way a kind of first love, something out of my young student life, my salad days, to which it was impossible to attach any significance whatsoever. Every youth, I told her, has his Katya; it would be impossible not to—but my Ninochka wouldn't listen. She imagined—God knows what!—and started to cry. After the tears, hysterics. 'You're vile, filthy,' she screamed. 'You hid your past from me! You probably have some kind of a Katya even now, and you're hiding it from me!' I tried and I tried to reassure her, but to no avail. Masculine logic never convinced a woman. In the end I begged her forgiveness—on my knees. I crawled, and where did it get me? She went to bed in hysterics—she in the bedroom and I on the sofa in my study. This morning she was pouting, wouldn't look at me, and spoke to me as though I were a stranger. She threatens to move to her mother's, and she probably will—I know her!"

"Hm-m. Not a very pleasant story."

"Women are incomprehensible to me! Granting that Ninochka is young, pure, fastidious, and can't help being shocked by something so earthy—is that so hard to forgive? I may be guilty, but I begged her forgiveness—I crawled on my knees! I even, if you must know, wept!"

"Yes, women are a great riddle."

"My dear friend, you have a strong influence over Ninochka. She respects you; she sees in you an authority. Please, go and see her. Exert your influence, and make her understand how wrong she is. I am suffering, my friend. If this goes on one more day I won't be able to endure it. Go—be a friend!"

"But do you think that would be . . . proper?"

"Why not? You and she have been friends almost since childhood. She trusts you. As a friend, please go!"

Vikhlyenev's tearful pleading touched me. I dressed and went to see his wife. I found Ninochka engaged in her favorite occupation: she was sitting on the sofa, one leg crossed over the other, blinking her beautiful eyes and doing nothing. When I came in she jumped up and ran to me; then she glanced round, quietly closed the door, and, with the lightness of a feather, clung to my neck. (You must not think, dear reader, that this is a misprint. For a year now, I had been sharing with Vikhlyenev his conjugal obligations.)

"What deviltry have you thought up now?" I asked Ninochka, seating her beside me.

"What do you mean?"

"Again you have managed to torment your better half. He came to see me today and told me all about it."

"Oh—that! So he found someone to complain to!"

"What actually happened?"

"Oh, not much. I was bored last night . . . and got angry because I had no place to go, so, out of spite, I started nagging him about his Katya. I cried simply from boredom—and how can I explain that to him?"

"But you know, my darling, that's cruel and inhuman. He's so nervous, and yet you plague him with your scenes."

"Oh, that's nothing. He loves it when I act jealous. And there's no better blind than fictitious jealousy. But let's drop it. I don't like it when you start talking about my milksop; I'm fed up with him! Let's have tea."

"Well, in any case, stop tormenting him. You know, he's pathetic: he describes his happiness and his faith in your love so frankly and sincerely that it makes one uncomfortable. Do control yourself somehow; show him some affection; lie! One word from you and he's in seventh heaven."

Ninochka frowned and pouted, but a little later when Vikhlyenev came in and timidly looked into my face, she gaily and affectionately smiled at him.

"You're just in time for tea!" she said to him. "How clever of you, my pet, never to be late. Lemon or cream for you?"

Vikhlyenev, not expecting such a welcome, was moved; he kissed his wife's hand warmly, and embraced me. This embrace was so absurd and so untimely that both Ninochka and I blushed.

"Blessed are the peacemakers!" clucked the happy husband. "You've made her listen to reason; and why? Because you're a man of the world; you mingle in society, and you know all the fine points of a woman's heart! Ha! Ha! Ha! I'm a clumsy ox; when one word is needed, I say ten; when I should kiss her hand or something, I start to find fault! Ha! Ha!"

After tea Vikhlyenev led me into his study, buttonholed me, and mumbled, "I don't know how to thank you, my dear friend. Believe me, I suffered; I was tortured; and now I am so happy—I'm simply overwhelmed! And this isn't the first time that you've pulled me out of a terrible situation. My dear friend—now, don't refuse me— I have here a little something. . . . It's just a little model locomotive that I made myself; I got a medal for it at the exposition. Take it as a token of my gratitude . . . my friendship. Do me this favor!"

Naturally, I refused in every possible way, but Vikhlyenev was insistent and, like it or not, I had to accept his precious gift.

Days, weeks, months passed. Sooner or later the ugly truth was bound to be revealed to him in all its enormity. When, by accident, he did find out, he turned frightfully pale, sat down on the sofa, and stared dully at the ceiling without saying a word. A heartache has to express itself in some kind of movement, and he began to turn from side to side on the sofa in an agonizing way. Even these movements were circumscribed by his milksop nature.

A week later, somewhat recovered from the shock of this news, he came to see me. We were both embarrassed and avoided looking at each other. I began to spout some sort of nonsense about free love, marital selfishness, submission to fate.

"It wasn't about that—" he interrupted meekly, "all that I understand perfectly. In matters of the heart, no one is guilty. What concerns me is the other side of the business . . . the purely practical. You see, I don't know life at all, and where the actual arrangements . . . the social conventions are concerned, I'm a real greenhorn. So, help me, my friend! Tell me, what is Ninochka supposed to do now? Should she go on living with me, or do you think it would be better if she moved in with you?"

Having deliberated briefly, we left it at this: Ninochka would continue to live at Vikhlyenev's; I would go to see her whenever I liked, and he would take the corner room, which formerly had been the storeroom, for himself. This room was rather dark and damp, and the entrance to it was through the kitchen, but, on the other hand, he could perfectly well shut himself up in it and not be a nuisance to anyone.

Heartache

"To whom shall I tell my sorrow?"[1]

Evening twilight. Large flakes of wet snow are circling lazily about the street lamps which have just been lighted, settling in a thin soft layer on roofs, horses' backs, peoples' shoulders, caps. Iona Potapov, the cabby, is all white like a ghost. As hunched as a living body can be, he sits on the box without stirring. If a whole snowdrift were to fall on him, even then, perhaps, he would not find it necessary to shake it off. His nag, too, is white and motionless. Her immobility, the angularity of her shape, and the sticklike straightness of her legs make her look like a penny gingerbread horse. She is probably lost in thought. Anyone who has been torn away from the plow, from the familiar gray scenes, and cast into this whirlpool full of monstrous lights, of ceaseless uproar and hurrying people, cannot help thinking.

Iona and his nag have not budged for a long time. They had driven out of the yard before dinnertime and haven't had a single fare yet. But now evening dusk is descending upon the city. The pale light of the street lamps changes to a vivid color and the bustle of the street grows louder.

"Sleigh to the Vyborg District!" Iona hears. "Sleigh!"

Iona starts, and through his snow-plastered eyelashes sees an officer in a military overcoat with a hood.

"To the Vyborg District!" repeats the officer. "Are you asleep, eh? To the Vyborg District!"

As a sign of assent Iona gives a tug at the reins, which sends layers of snow flying from the horse's back and from his own shoulders. The officer gets into the sleigh. The driver clucks to the horse, cranes his neck like a swan, rises in his seat and, more from habit than necessity, flourishes his whip. The nag, too, stretches her neck, crooks her sticklike legs and irresolutely sets off.

"Where are you barging in, damn you?" Iona is promptly assailed by shouts from the massive dark wavering to and fro before him. "Where the devil are you going? Keep to the right!"

"Don't you know how to drive? Keep to the right," says the officer with vexation.

A coachman driving a private carriage swears at him; a pedestrian who was crossing the street and brushed against the nag's nose with his shoulder, looks at him angrily and shakes the snow off his sleeve. Iona fidgets on the box as if sitting on needles and pins, thrusts out his elbows and rolls his eyes like a madman, as though he did not know where he was or why he was there.

"What rascals they all are," the officer jokes. "They are doing their best to knock into you or be trampled by the horse. It's a conspiracy."

[1] From an old Russian folksong.

From *The Portable Chekhov*, edited by Avrahm Yarmolinsky. Copyright 1947, © 1968 by The Viking Press, Inc. All rights reserved. Reprinted by permission of The Viking Press, Inc. (1968)

Iona looks at his fare and moves his lips. He wants to say something, but the only sound that comes out is a wheeze.

"What is it?" asks the officer.

Iona twists his mouth into a smile, strains his throat and croaks hoarsely: "My son, sir . . . er, my son died this week."

"H'm, what did he die of?"

Iona turns his whole body around to his fare and says, "Who can tell? It must have been a fever. He lay in the hospital only three days and then he died. . . . It is God's will."

"Get over, you devil!" comes out of the dark. "Have you gone blind, you old dog? Keep your eyes peeled!"

"Go on, go on," says the officer. "We shan't get there until tomorrow at this rate. Give her the whip!"

The driver cranes his neck again, rises in his seat, and with heavy grace swings his whip. Then he looks around at the officer several times, but the latter keeps his eyes closed and is apparently indisposed to listen. Letting his fare off in the Vyborg District, Iona stops by a teahouse and again sits motionless and hunched on the box. Again the wet snow paints him and his nag white. One hour passes, another . . .

Three young men, two tall and lanky, one short and hunchbacked, come along swearing at each other and loudly pound the pavement with their galoshes.

"Cabby, to the Police Bridge!" the hunchback shouts in a cracked voice. "The three of us . . . twenty kopecks!"

Iona tugs at the reins and clucks to his horse. Twenty kopecks is not fair, but his mind is not on that. Whether it is a ruble or five kopecks, it is all one to him now, so long as he has a fare. . . . The three young men, jostling each other and using foul language, go up to the sleigh and all three try to sit down at once. They start arguing about which two are to sit and who shall be the one to stand. After a long ill-tempered and abusive altercation, they decide that the hunchback must stand up because he is the shortest.

"Well, get going," says the hunchback in his cracked voice, taking up his station and breathing down Iona's neck. "On your way! What a cap you've got, brother! You won't find a worse one in all Petersburg—"

"Hee, hee . . . hee, hee . . ." Iona giggles, "as you say—"

"Well, then, 'as you say,' drive on. Are you going to crawl like this all the way, eh? D'you want to get it in the neck?"

"My head is splitting," says one of the tall ones. "At the Dukmasov's yesterday, Vaska and I killed four bottles of cognac between us."

"I don't get it, why lie?" says the other tall one angrily. "He is lying like a trouper."

"Strike me dead, it's the truth!"

"It is about as true as that a louse sneezes."

"Hee, hee," giggles Iona. "The gentlemen are feeling good!"

"Faugh, the devil take you!" cries the hunchback indignantly. "Will you get a move on, you old pest, or won't you? Is that the way to drive? Give her a crack of the whip! Giddap, devil! Giddap! Let her feel it!"

Iona feels the hunchback's wriggling body and quivering voice behind his back. He hears abuse addressed to him, sees people, and the feeling of loneliness begins little by little to lift from his heart. The hunchback swears till he chokes on an elaborate three-decker oath and is overcome by cough. The tall youths begin discussing a certain

Nadezhda Petrovna. Iona looks round at them. When at last there is a lull in the conversation for which he has been waiting, he turns around and says: "This week . . . er . . . my son died."

"We shall all die," says the hunchback, with a sigh wiping his lips after his coughing fit. "Come, drive on, drive on. Gentlemen, I simply cannot stand this pace! When will he get us there?"

"Well, you give him a little encouragement. Biff him in the neck!"

"Do you hear, you old pest? I'll give it to you in the neck. If one stands on ceremony with fellows like you, one may as well walk. Do you hear, you old serpent? Or don't you give a damn what we say?"

And Iona hears rather than feels the thud of a blow on his neck.

"Hee, hee," he laughs. "The gentlemen are feeling good. God give you health!"

"Cabby, are you married?" asks one of the tall ones.

"Me? Hee, hee! The gentlemen are feeling good. The only wife for me now is the damp earth . . . Hee, haw, haw! The grave, that is! . . . Here my son is dead and me alive . . . It is a queer thing, death comes in at the wrong door . . . It don't come for me, it comes for my son. . . ."

And Iona turns round to tell them how his son died, but at that point the hunchback gives a sigh of relief and announces that, thank God, they have arrived at last. Having received his twenty kopecks, for a long while Iona stares after the revelers, who disappear into a dark entrance. Again he is alone and once more silence envelops him. The grief which has been allayed for a brief space comes back again and wrenches his heart more cruelly than ever. There is a look of anxiety and torment in Iona's eyes as they wander restlessly over the crowds moving to and fro on both sides of the street. Isn't there someone among those thousands who will listen to him? But the crowds hurry past, heedless of him and his grief. His grief is immense, boundless. If his heart were to burst and his grief to pour out, it seems that it would flood the whole world, and yet no one sees it. It has found a place for itself in such an insignificant shell that no one can see it in broad daylight.

Iona notices a doorkeeper with a bag and makes up his mind to speak to him.

"What time will it be, friend?" he asks.

"Past nine. What have you stopped here for? On your way!"

Iona drives a few steps away, hunches up and surrenders himself to his grief. He feels it is useless to turn to people. But before five minutes are over, he draws himself up, shakes his head as though stabbed by a sharp pain and tugs at the reins . . . He can bear it no longer.

"Back to the yard!" he thinks. "To the yard!"

And his nag, as though she knew his thoughts, starts out at a trot. An hour and a half later, Iona is sitting beside a large dirty stove. On the stove, on the floor, on benches are men snoring. The air is stuffy and foul. Iona looks at the sleeping figures, scratches himself and regrets that he has come home so early.

"I haven't earned enough to pay for the oats," he reflects. "That's what's wrong with me. A man that knows his job . . . who has enough to eat and has enough for his horse don't need to fret."

In one of the corners a young driver gets up, hawks sleepily and reaches for the water bucket.

"Thirsty?" Iona asks him.

"Guess so."

"H'm, may it do you good, but my son is dead, brother . . . did you hear? This week in the hospital. . . . What a business!"

Iona looks to see the effect of his words, but he notices none. The young man has drawn his cover over his head and is already asleep. The old man sighs and scratches himself. Just as the young man was thirsty for water so he thirsts for talk. It will soon be a week since his son died and he hasn't talked to anybody about him properly. He ought to be able to talk about it, taking his time, sensibly. He ought to tell how his son was taken ill, how he suffered, what he said before he died, how he died. . . . He ought to describe the funeral, and how he went to the hospital to fetch his son's clothes. His daughter Anisya is still in the country. . . . And he would like to talk about her too. Yes, he has plenty to talk about now. And his listener should gasp and moan and keen. . . . It would be even better to talk to women. Though they are foolish, two words will make them blubber.

"I must go out and have a look at the horse," Iona thinks. "There will be time enough for sleep. You will have enough sleep, no fear. . . ."

He gets dressed and goes into the stable where his horse is standing. He thinks about oats, hay, the weather. When he is alone, he dares not think of his son. It is possible to talk about him with someone, but to think of him when one is alone, to evoke his image is unbearably painful.

"You chewing?" Iona asks his mare seeing her shining eyes. "There, chew away, chew away. . . . If we haven't earned enough for oats, we'll eat hay. . . . Yes. . . . I've grown too old to drive. My son had ought to be driving, not me. . . . He was a real cabby. . . . He had ought to have lived. . . ."

Iona is silent for a space and then goes on: "That's how it is, old girl. . . . Kuzma Ionych is gone. . . . Departed this life. . . . He went and died to no purpose. . . . Now let's say you had a little colt, and you were that little colt's own mother. And suddenly, let's say, that same little colt departed this life. . . . You'd be sorry, wouldn't you?"

The nag chews, listens and breathes on her master's hands. Iona is carried away and tells her everything.

Vierochka

Ivan Alexeyevich Ogniov well remembers the August evening when he opened noisily the glazed hall door and went out on to the terrace. He wore a light cloak and a wide-brimmed straw hat—the very hat which now, beside his top-boots, lies in the dust underneath his bed. He remembers that he carried a heavy package of books and manuscripts, and that in his free hand was a stout stick.

In the doorway, holding up a lamp, stood his host, Kuznetzov, aged and bald-headed, with his long grey beard, and his cotton jacket, white as snow. And Kuznetzov smiled benevolently and nodded his head.

"Good-bye, old friend!" cried Ogniov.

Kuznetzov laid the lamp on the hall table, and followed Ogniov to the terrace. The narrow shadows of the two men swept down the steps, and, crossing the flower-

From *The Stories of Anton Chekhov*, edited by Robert N. Linscott. Copyright 1932 and renewed 1960 by Modern Library, Inc. Reprinted by Permission of Random House, Inc.

beds, swayed, and came to a stop with the heads silhouetted against the lime-trees.

"Good-bye, and yet once more, thank you, old friend," said Ogniov. "Thanks for your heartiness, your kindness, your love. . . . Never . . . never in my whole life shall I forget your goodness. . . . You have been so kind . . . and your daughter has been so kind . . . all of you have been so kind, so gay, so hearty. . . . So good, indeed, that I cannot express my gratitude."

Under stress of feeling, under influence of the parting glass, Ogniov's voice sounded like a seminarist's, and his feeling showed not only in his words but in the nervous twitching of eyes and shoulders. And Kuznetzov, touched also by emotion and wine, bent over the young man and kissed him.

"I have grown as used to you as if I were your dog," continued Ogniov. "I have been with you day after day. I have spent the night at your house a dozen times, and drunk so much of your liqueurs that it frightens me to think of it. . . . But, most of all, Gavriil Petrovich, I thank you for your co-operation and help. Without you, I should have been worrying over my statistics till October. But I will put in my preface: 'It is my duty to express to M. Kuznetzov, President of the N. District Zemstvo Executive, my gratitude for his kind assistance.' Statistics have a brilliant future! Give my deepest regards to Vera Gaviilovna! And tell the doctors, the two magistrates, and your secretary that I shall never forget their kindness. . . . And now, old friend, let us embrace and kiss for the last time!"

Ogniov again kissed the old man. When he reached the last step, he turned his head and said—

"I wonder shall we ever meet again."

"God knows," answered Kuznetzov. "Probably never."

"I fear so. Nothing will lure you to Petersburg, and it is not likely that I shall ever return to these parts. Good-bye!"

"But leave your books," called Kuznetzov after him. "Why carry such a weight? My man will bring them to-morrow."

But Ogniov, who had not heard him, walked quickly away. Warmed with wine, his heart was full at the same time of sorrow and joy. He walked forward reflecting how often in life we meet such kindly men and women, how sad it is that they leave but memories behind. It is as on a journey. The traveller sees on the flat horizon the outline of a crane; the weak wind bears its plaintive cry; yet in a moment it is gone; and strain his eyes as he may towards the blue distance, he sees no bird, and hears no sound. So in the affairs of men, faces and voices tremble a moment before us, and slip away into the gone-before, leaving behind them nothing but the vain records of memory. Having been every day at hearty Kuznetzov's house since he arrived that spring at N., Ogniov had come to know and love as kinsmen the old man, his daughter, their servants. He knew every spot in the old house, the cosy terrace, the turns in the garden paths, the trees outlined against garden and bathing-box. And now in a few seconds when he had passed the wicket-gate, all these would be memories, void for evermore of real significance. A year—two years—would pass, and all these kindly images, dulled beyond restoring, would recur only in memory as the shapeless impressions of a dream.

"In life," thought Ogniov, as he approached the gate, "there is nothing better than men. Nothing!"

It was warm and still. The whole world smelt of heliotropes, mignonette, and tobacco-plants which had not yet shed their blooms. Around shrubs and tree-trunks flowed a sea of thin, moonlight-soaked mist; and—what long remained in Ogniov's memory—wisps of vapour, white as ghosts, floated with motion imperceptibly slow across the garden path. Near the moon, shining high in heaven, swam transparent patches of cloud. The whole world, it seemed, was built of coal-black shadows and wandering wisps of white; and, to Ogniov, it seemed as if he were looking not at Nature, but at a decorated scene, as if clumsy pyrotechnists, illuminating the garden with white Bengal fire, had flooded the air with a sea of snowy smoke.

As Ogniov approached the wicket-gate a black shadow moved from the low palisade and came to meet him.

"Vera Gavriilovna," he exclaimed joyfully. "You here! After I had looked for you everywhere to say good-bye! . . . Good-bye, I am going."

"So early—it is barely eleven o'clock."

"But late for me. I have a five-verst walk, and I must pack up to-night. I leave early to-morrow. . . ."

Before Ogniov stood Kuznetzov's daughter, twenty-one-year-old Vera, whom he had seen so often, pensive and carelessly-dressed and interesting. Day-dreaming girls who spend whole days lying down in desultory reading, who suffer from tedium and melancholy, usually dress without care. But if Nature has given them taste and the instinct of beauty, this negligence in dress has often a charm of its own. And, indeed, Ogniov, recalling the vision of pretty Vera, cannot imagine her without a loose jacket, hanging in folds away from her waist, without untidy curls on her forehead, without the red, shaggy-tasselled shawl which all day long lay in the hall among the men's caps, or on the chest in the dining-room, where the old cat used it unceremoniously as bed. The shawl and the creased jacket seemed to express the easy-going indolence of a sedentary life. But perhaps it was because Ogniov liked Vera, that every button and fold exhaled to him goodness and poetry, something foreign to women insincere, void of the instinct of beauty, and cold. . . . And Vera, too, had a good figure, regular features, and pretty wavy hair. To Ogniov, who knew few women, she seemed beautiful.

"I am going away," he said again, bidding her good-bye at the wicket-gate. "Think well of me! And thanks for everything!"

And again twitching his shoulders, and speaking in the sing-song seminarist's voice which he had used to the old man, he thanked Vera for her hospitality, her kindness, her heartiness.

"I wrote about you to my mother in every letter," he said. "If all men were like you and your father, life on earth would be paradise. Every one in your house is the same. So simple, so hearty, so sincere. . . ."

"Where are you going?"

"First to my mother, in Oriol. I shall spend two days there. Then to St. Petersburg to work."

"And then?"

"Then? I shall work all winter, and in spring go somewhere in the country to collect material. Well . . . be happy, live a hundred years, and think well of me! This is the last time we meet."

Ogniov bowed his head and kissed Vierochka's hand, then in silent confusion straightened his cloak, rearranged his package of books, and said—

"What a thick mist to-night!"

"Yes. Have you not forgotten anything?"

"Nothing . . . I think."

For a moment Ogniov stood silently. Then he turned awkwardly to the gate and went out of the garden.

"Wait! Let me go with you as far as the wood," said Vera, running after him.

They followed the road. Trees no longer obscured the view, and they could see the sky, and the country far ahead. Through breaks in the veil of semi-transparent smoke, the world exposed its fairness; the white mist lay unevenly around bushes and hayricks, or wandered in tiny cloudlets, clinging to the surface as if not to cut off the view. The road could be seen all the way to the wood, and in the ditches beside it rose little bushes which trapped and hindered the vagabond mist wisps. Half a verst away rose a dark belt of forest.

"Why has she come? I shall have to see her home," Ogniov asked himself. But looking at Vera's profile, he smiled kindly, and said—

"I hate going away in weather like this. This evening is quite romantic, what with the moonlight, the silence . . . and all the honours! Do you know what, Vera Gavriilovna? I am now twenty-nine years old, yet have never had a single romance! In all my life so far, not one! So of trysts, paths of signs, and kisses, I know only by hearsay. It is abnormal. Sitting in my own room in town, I never notice the void. But here in the open air I somehow feel it . . . strongly . . . it is almost annoying."

"But what is the cause?"

"I can't say. Perhaps it is because so far I have never had time, perhaps simply because I have never yet met a woman who . . . But I have few friends, and seldom go anywhere."

They walked three hundred yards in silence. As Ogniov looked at Vera's shawl and uncovered head, he recalled the past spring and summer days, when far from his grey St. Petersburg rooms, caressed by kindly Nature and by kindly friends, pursuing his much-loved work, he had seen slip by, uncounted, sunset after dawn, day after day, nor noticed how, foreshadowing summer's end, the nightingale first, the quail, and then the corncrake ceased their songs. Time had passed unseen; and that, he supposed, meant that life had spun out pleasantly and without jar. He recalled how at the end of April he had arrived at N., a poor man, unused to society; and expected nothing but tedium, solitude, and contempt for statistics—which in his opinion took a high place among the useful sciences. He remembered the April evening of his arrival at the inn of Old-Believer Riabukhin, where for twenty kopecks a day he was given a bright, clean room, with only one restriction, that he should smoke out of doors. He remembered how he had rested a few hours, and, asking for the address of the President of the Zemstvo Executive, had set out on foot to Gavriil Petrovich's house; how he had tramped through four versts of rich meadows and young plantations; how high under a veil of cloud trembled a lark, filling the world with silver sounds, while above the green pastures, with a stolid, pompous flapping of wings, the rooks flew up and down.

"Is it possible?" Ogniov asked himself, "that they breathe this air every day, or is it perfumed only this evening in honour of me?"

He remembered how, expecting a dry, business-like reception, he had entered Kuznetzov's study timidly, with averted face, and shyly stroked his beard. And how the old man contracted his brows, and failed utterly to understand what this young man with his statistics wanted with the Zemstvo Executive. But as he began to understand what statistics really mean, and how they are collected, Gavriil Petrovich woke up, smiled, and with infantile curiosity began to examine his visitor's note-books. . . . And on the evening of the same day, Ogniov sat at Kuznetzov's supper-table, grew tipsy on strong liqueurs, and, watching the placid faces and lazy gestures of his new acquaintances, felt spreading through his whole body that sweet, drowsy indolence of one who, wanting to continue his sleep, stretches himself and smiles. And his new-found friends looked at him lovingly, asked were his father and mother alive, how much he earned a month, and whether he often went to the theatre.

Ogniov recalled the long drives through the cantons, the picnics, the fishing parties, the trip to the convent when the Mother Superior presented each visitor with a bead-purse; he recalled the endless, heated, truly Russian arguments in which the disputants, banging their fists on the table, misunderstood and interrupted without knowing what they meant to say, wandered from the subject, and after arguing fiercely a couple of hours, exclaimed with a laugh, "The devil knows what this dispute is about. We began about health, and are now arguing about rest in the grave!"

"Do you remember when you and I rode to Shestovo with the doctor?" asked Ogniov as they drew near to the wood. "We met a lunatic. I gave him five kopecks, and he crossed himself thrice, and threw the money in my face. What hosts of impressions I carry away—if fused in a compact mass, I should have a big ingot of gold! I never understood why clever, sensitive men crowd into big cities instead of living in the country. Is there more space and truth on the Nevsky, and in the big damp houses? My house, for instance, which is packed from top to bottom with artists, students, and journalists, always seems to me to embody an absurd prejudice."

Some twenty paces from the wood the road crossed a narrow bridge with posts at the corners. During their spring walks, this bridge was a stopping place for the Kuznetzovs and their visitors. Thence they could draw echoes from the wood, and watch the road as it vanished in a black drive.

"We are at the bridge," said Ogniov. "You must return."

Vera stopped, and drew a deep breath.

"Let us sit down for a minute," she said, seating herself on a pillar. "When we say good-bye to friends we always sit down here."

Ogniov sat beside her on his parcel of books, and continued to speak. Vera breathed heavily, and looked straight into the distance, so that he could not see her face.

"Perhaps some day, in ten years' time, we'll meet somewhere again," he said. "Things will be different. You will be the honoured mother of a family, and I the author of a respectable, useless book of statistics, fat as forty albums put together. . . . To-night, the present counts, it absorbs and agitates us. But ten years hence we shall remember neither the date nor the month, nor even the year, when we sat on this bridge together for the last time. You, of course, will be changed. You will change."

"What?"

"I ask you just now. . . ."

"I did not hear."

Only now did Ogniov notice the change that had come over Vera. She was pale and breathless; her hands and lips trembled; and instead of the usual single lock of hair falling on her forehead, there were two. She did her best to mask her agitation and avoid looking him in the face; and to help in this, she first straightened her collar as if it were cutting her neck, and then drew the red shawl from one side to the other.

"You are cold, I am afraid," began Ogniov. "You must not sit in the mist. Let me see you home."

Vera did not answer.

"What is the matter?" resumed Ogniov. "You do not answer my questions. You are ill?"

Vera pressed her hand firmly to her cheek, and suddenly drew it away.

"It is too awful," she whispered, with a look of intense agony. "Too awful!"

"What is too awful?" asked Ogniov, shrugging his shoulders, and making no effort to conceal his surprise. "What is the matter?"

Still breathing heavily and twitching her shoulders, Vera turned away from him, and after looking a moment at the sky, began—

"I have to speak to you, Ivan Alekseyevich. . . ."

"I am listening."

"I know it will seem strange to you . . . you will be astonished, but I do not care. . . ."

Ogniov again shrugged his shoulders and prepared to listen.

"It is this . . . ," began Vera, averting her eyes, and twirling the shawl-tassel in her fingers. "You see, this is . . . that is what I wanted to say. . . . It will seem absurd to you . . . and stupid . . . but I cannot bear it!"

Vera's words, half smothered in incoherent stammerings, were suddenly interrupted by tears. She hid her face in the shawl, and wept bitterly. Ogniov, confused and stupefied, coughed, and, having no idea what to say or do, looked helplessly around. He was unused to tears, and Vera's breakdown seemed to make his own eyes water.

"Come, come!" he stammered helplessly. "Vera Gavriilovna? What does this mean? Are you ill? Some one has annoyed you? Tell me what it is . . . and perhaps I can help you."

And when, in a last attempt to console her, he drew her hands cautiously from her face, she smiled at him through her tears, and said—

"I . . . I love you!"

The words, simple and ordinary, were spoken in a simple and ordinary voice. But Ogniov, covered with intense confusion, turned his face away.

His confusion was followed by fright. The atmosphere of mournfulness, warmth, and sentiment inspired by liqueurs and leave-takings, suddenly made way for a sharp, unpleasant feeling of awkwardness. Feeling that his whole soul had been turned inside out, he looked shyly at Vera; and she, having avowed her love, and cast for ever away her woman's enhancing inaccessibility, seemed smaller, simpler, meaner.

"What does it all mean?" he asked himself in terror. "And then . . . do I love her . . . or not?—that is the problem."

But she, now that the hardest, painfulest part was ended, breathed easily and freely. She rose from her seat, and, looking straight into Ogniov's eyes, spoke quickly, warmly, without constraint.

Those who have been overtaken by sudden terror seldom remember details, and Ogniov to-day recalls not one of Vera's words. He remembers only their import and the emotions they brought forth. He remembers her voice, which seemed to come from a strangled throat, a voice hoarse with emotion, and the magic passion and harmony in its intonations. Crying, smiling, scattering tear-drops from her eyes, she confessed that since the first days of their friendship she had been won by his originality, his intellect, his kind, clever eyes, and by the aims and aspirations of his life. That she loved him devoutly, passionately, madly; that in summer when she went from the garden into the house, and saw his coat in the hall, or heard his voice, her heart thrilled with a presage of intense joy; that his most trivial jokes had made her laugh; that every figure in his note-books exhaled to her wisdom and majesty; that even his cane standing in the hall had seemed to her lovelier than the trees.

The wood, the patches of mist, even the black roadside ditches were charmed, it seemed, as they listened. But Ogniov's heart felt only estrangement and pain. Avowing her love, Vera was entrancingly fair; her words were noble and impassioned. But Ogniov felt not the pleasure or vital joy which he himself yearned for, but only sympathy with Vera, and pain that a fellow-creature should suffer so for his sake. Heaven only knows why it was so! But whether the cause was book-learned reason, or merely that impregnable objectivity which forbids some men to live as men, the ecstasy and passion of Vera seemed to him affected and unreal. Yet even while he felt this, something whispered that, in the light of Nature and personal happiness, that which he listened to then was a thousand times more vital than all his books, his statistics, his eternal verities. And he was angry, and reproached himself, though he had no idea wherein he was at fault.

What increased his confusion was that he knew he must reply. An answer was inevitable. To say to Vera plainly "I do not love you!" he had not the strength. But he could not say "I do," for with all his searchings he could not find in his heart a single spark.

And he listened silently while she said that she could know no greater happiness than to see him, to follow him, to go with him wheresoever he might go, to be his wife and helper . . . and that if he abandoned her she would die of grief.

"I cannot stay here," she exclaimed, wringing her hands. "I have come to detest this house, and this wood, and this air. I am tired of this changeless restfulness and aimless life; I can stand no longer our colourless, pale people, as like one another as two drops of water! They are genial and kind . . . because they are contented, because they have never suffered and never struggled. But I can stand it no more. . . . I want to go to the big grey houses, where people suffer, embittered by labour and need. . . ."

And all this seemed to Ogniov affected and unreal. When Vera ceased to speak he was still without an answer. But silence was impossible, and he stammered out—

"I . . . Vera Gavriilovna . . . I am very grateful to you, although I feel that I deserve no such . . . such feelings. In the second place, as an honest man, I must say that . . . happiness is based on mutuality . . . that is, when both parties . . . when they love equally."

Ogniov suddenly felt ashamed of his stammering speech, and was silent. He felt that his expression was guilty, stupid, and dull, and that his face was strained and drawn out. And Vera, it seemed, could read the truth in his looks, for she paled, looked at him with terror, and averted her eyes.

"You will forgive me," stammered Ogniov, feeling the silence past bearing. "I respect you so very, very much that . . . that I am sorry . . ."

Vera suddenly turned away, and walked rapidly towards the house. Ogniov followed her.

"No, there is no need!" she said, waving her hand. "Do not come! I will go alone. . . ."

"But still . . . I must see you home."

All that Ogniov had said, even his last words, seemed to him flat and hateful. The feeling increased with each step. He raged at himself and, clenching his fists, cursed his coldness and awkwardness with women. In a last vain effort to stir his own feelings he looked at Vera's pretty figure, at her hair, at the imprints of her little feet on the dusty road. He remembered her words and her tears. But all this filled him only with pain, and left his feelings dead.

"Yes. . . . A man cannot force himself to love!" he reasoned, and at the same time thought, "When shall I ever love except by force? I am nearly thirty. Better than Vierochka among women I have never met . . . and never shall meet. Oh, accursed old age! Old age at thirty!"

Vera walked before him, each moment quickening her step. Her face was bowed to the ground, and she did not look round once. It seemed to Ogniov that she had suddenly grown slighter and that her shoulders were narrower.

"I can imagine her feelings," he said to himself. "Shame . . . and such pain as to make her wish for death! . . . And in her words there was life and poetry, and meaning enough to have melted a stone! But I . . . I am senseless and blind."

"Listen, Vera Gavriilovna." This cry burst from him against his will. "You must not think that I . . . that I . . ."

Ogniov hesitated and said nothing more. At the wicket-gate Vera turned, looked at him for an instant, and, wrapping her shawl tightly around her shoulders, walked quickly up the path.

Ogniov remained alone. He turned back to the wood, and walked slowly, stopping now and then and looking towards the gate. His movements expressed doubt of himself. He searched the road for the imprints of Vierochka's feet. He refused to credit that one whom he liked so much had avowed to him her love, and that he had awkwardly, boorishly scorned her. For the first time in life he realised how little one's actions depend from mere goodwill; and he felt as feels every honourable, kindly man who, despite his intentions, has caused his nearest and dearest unmeant and unmerited suffering.

His conscience stung him. When Vierochka vanished in the garden he felt that he had lost something very dear which he would never find again. With Vera, it seemed to him, a part of his youth had passed away, and he knew that the precious moments he had let slip away without profit would never return.

When he reached the bridge he stopped in thought, and sought the cause of his unnatural coldness. That it lay not outside himself, but within, he saw clearly. And he frankly confessed that this was not the rational calmness boasted by clever men, not the coldness of inflated egoism, but simply impotence of soul, dull insensibility to all that is beautiful, old age before its day—the fruit, perhaps, of his training, his grim struggle for bread, his friendless, bachelor life.

He walked slowly, as if against his own will, from the bridge to the wood. There where on a pall of impenetrable black the moonlight shone in jagged patches he remained alone with his thoughts; and he passionately longed to regain all that he had lost.

And Ogniov remembers that he returned to the house. Goading himself forward with memories of what had passed, straining his imagination to paint Vera's face, he walked quickly as far as the garden. From road and garden the mist had melted away, and a bright, newly washed moon looked down from an unflecked sky; the east alone frowned with clouds. Ogniov remembers his cautious steps, the black windows, the drowsy scent of heliotropes and mignonette. He remembers how old friend Karpo, wagging genially his tail, came up and snuffed at his hand. But no other living thing did he see. He remembers how he walked twice around the house, stood awhile before the black window of Vera's room; and abandoning his quest with a sigh returned to the road.

An hour later he was back in town; and, weary, broken, leaning his body and hot face against the gate, knocked at the inn. In the distance barked a sleepy dog; and the night watchman at the church beat an iron shield.

"Still gadding about at night!" grumbled the Old-Believer, as in a long, woman's night-dress he opened the door. "What do you gain by it? It would be better for you if you stayed at home and prayed to God!"

When he entered his room Ogniov threw himself upon the bed, and long gazed steadily at the fire. At last he rose, shood his head, and began to pack his trunk.

Rudyard Kipling (1865–1936)

Between 1886 and 1902, with those early poems and stories celebrating imperialism and the White Man's Burden, Kipling achieved an enormous popularity with British readers. Songs and poems like "Gunga Din" and "The Road to Mandalay" were on all patriotic lips, and such books as *Plain Tales from the Hills* (1888), *Soldiers Three* (1888), *The Jungle Book* (1894), *Kim* (1901), and the *Just-So Stories* (1902) won him a popular following with young and old alike. But after the Boer War (1889–1902) many Englishmen lost their stomach for imperialism and their taste for the author who had done so much to fan the fires of music-hall jingoism and notions that strong nations had the right to dominate "the lesser breeds without the law."

> Take up the White Man's Burden—
>   Send forth the best ye breed—
> Go bind your sons to exile
>   To serve your captive's need. . . .

Consequently, liberal critics, almost to the present, have scorned the name of Kipling; his name has been virtually synonymous with racism, jingoism, imperialism, militarism—"isms" that have over the past half century tended to get a bad press among people of conscience. Such critics, however, tended to remember Kipling's coarseness and brutality and to forget his humor, his virtuosity with dialect and verse, and—more hidden—a strain of something like tenderness running through much of his work. It was the critic Edmund Wilson in an essay called "The Kipling That Nobody Read" (1941) who first called attention to this other Kipling. Wilson discusses the story "Baa, Baa, Black Sheep" and part of *The Light That Failed* (1891) where Kipling, under slight fictional disguise, recounts the pitiable events of his childhood. At the age of six, with his sister of four, Kipling was sent from his Bombay home to England, to board in the family of a woman who was, in Wilson's words, "a religious tyrant in the worst English tradition of Dickens and Samuel Butler." This cruel exile lasted six years, and its sufferings included a nervous breakdown (with partial blindness), hallucinations, and beatings so frequent that when at last his mother arrived and bent over to kiss her son, he instinctively raised his arm as if to ward off a blow. But Kipling denied himself the indulgence of self-pity; instead, he developed a code of masochistic acceptance that, in both his life and his fiction, justified such suffering in the name of the "Law"—the same "Law" that not only made the white races superior but that required their indenture "to serve [their] captive's need." Morality with Kipling, as Noel Annan says, is "an entirely social product": what is important is not justice for the individual (including himself) but an understanding of how the "Law" operates on individuals. The highest virtue was the ability to endure; the worst evil, "introspection and self-pity."

These values permeate "The Wish House" (1924), a late tale that W. W. Robson calls "the most remarkable story Kipling ever wrote." The two old women, one dying of cancer and the other going blind, talk to each other in the rich local dialect, while their shoddy suburban house is shaken by passing pleasure busses. The cruel realism of their lives is pitilessly drawn, yet the story is also a wish-fulfilling fantasy that has as its unifying force an act of incredible compassion. Grace Ashcroft has a "superstition" that, by wishing, she can take on herself "everythin' bad that's in store for my man, 'Arry Mockler, for love's sake"—even though her man has treated her shamefully. She believes she has taken Harry's cancer into her own body, thus making him unbeknownst "take his good from her." T. S. Eliot has called this story "hard and obscure," but he liked it. Certainly it is a love story—or rather a story of love—that is ground directly out of Kipling's sense of life.

The Wish House

The new Church Visitor[1] had just left after a twenty minutes' call. During that time, Mrs. Ashcroft had used such English as an elderly, experienced, and pensioned cook should, who had seen life in London. She was the readier, therefore, to slip back into easy, ancient Sussex ("t"s softening to "d"s as one warmed) when the 'bus brought Mrs. Fettley from thirty miles away for a visit, that pleasant March Saturday. The two had been friends since childhood; but, of late, destiny had separated their meetings by long intervals.

Much was to be said, and many ends, loose since last time, to be ravelled up on both sides, before Mrs. Fettley, with her bag of quilt-patches, took the couch beneath the window commanding the garden, and the football-ground in the valley below.

"Most folk got out at Bush Tye for the match there," she explained, "so there weren't no one for me to cushion agin, the last five mile. An' she *do* just-about bounce ye."

"You've took no hurt," said her hostess. "You don't brittle by agein', Liz."

Mrs. Fettley chuckled and made to match a couple of patches to her liking. "No, or I'd ha' broke twenty year back. You can't ever mind when I was so's to be called round, can ye?"

Mrs. Ashcroft shook her head slowly—she never hurried—and went on stitching a sack-cloth lining into a list-bound rush tool-basket. Mrs. Fettley laid out more patches in the Spring light through the geraniums on the window-sill, and they were silent awhile.

"What like's this new Visitor o' yourn?" Mrs. Fettley inquired with a nod towards the door. Being very short-sighted, she had, on her entrance, almost bumped into the lady.

[1] A church lady who volunteers to visit the sick.

"The Wish House" copyright 1924 by Rudyard Kipling from *Debits and Credits* by Rudyard Kipling. Reprinted by permission of Mrs. George Bambridge and Doubleday & Company, Inc.

Mrs. Ashcroft suspended the big packing-needle judicially on high, ere she stabbed home. "Settin' aside she don't bring much news with her yet, I dunno as I've anythin' special agin her."

"Ourn, at Keyneslade," said Mrs. Fettley, "she's full o' words an' pity, but she don't stay for answers. Ye can get on with your thoughts while she clacks."

"This 'un don't clack. She's aimin' to be one o' those High Church nuns, like."

"Ourn's married, but, by what they say, she've made no great gains of it . . ." Mrs. Fettley threw up her sharp chin. "Lord! How they dam' cherubim do shake the very bones o' the place!"

The tile-sided cottage trembled at the passage of two specially chartered forty-seat charabancs on their way to the Bush Tye match; a regular Saturday "shopping" 'bus, for the county's capital, fumed behind them; while, from one of the crowded inns, a fourth car backed out to join the procession, and held up the stream of through pleasure-traffic.

"You're as free-tongued as ever, Liz," Mrs. Ashcroft observed.

"Only when I'm with you. Otherwhiles, I'm Granny—three times over. I lay that basket's for one o' your gran'chiller—ain't it?"

"'Tis for Arthur—my Jane's eldest."

"But he ain't workin' nowheres, is he?"

"No. 'Tis a picnic-basket."

"You're let off light. My Willie, he's allus at me for money for them aireated wash-poles folk puts up in their gardens to draw the music from Lunnon, like. An' I give it 'im—pore fool me!"

"An' he forgets to give you the promise-kiss after, don't he?" Mrs. Ashcroft's heavy smile seemed to strike inwards.

"He do. 'No odds 'twixt boys now an' forty year back. 'Take all an' give naught—an' we to put up with it! Pore fool we! Three shillin' at a time Willie'll ask me for!"

"They don't make nothin' o' money these days," Mrs. Ashcroft said.

"An' on'y last week," the other went on, "me daughter, she ordered a quarter pound suet at the butchers's; an' she sent it back to'um to be chopped. She said she couldn't bother with choppin' it."

"I lay he charged her, then"

"I lay he did. She told me there was a whisk-drive that afternoon at the Institute, an' she couldn't bother to do the choppin'."

"Tck!"

Mrs. Ashcroft put the last firm touches to the basket-lining. She had scarcely finished when her sixteen-year-old grandson, a maiden of the moment in attendance, hurried up the garden-path shouting to know if the thing were ready, snatched it, and made off without acknowledgment. Mrs. Fettley peered at him closely.

"They're goin' picnickin' somewheres," Mrs. Ashcroft explained.

"Ah," said the other, with narrowed eyes. "I lay *he* won't show much mercy to any he comes across, either. Now 'oo the dooce do he remind me of, all of a sudden?"

"They must look arter theirselves—'same as we did." Mrs. Ashcroft began to set out the tea.

"No denyin' *you* could, Gracie," said Mrs. Fettley.

"What's in your head now?"

"Dunno . . . But it come over me, sudden-like—about dat woman from Rye—I've slipped the name—Barnsley, wadn't it?"

"Batten—Polly Batten, you're thinkin' of."

"That's it—Polly Batten. That day she had it in for you with a hay-fork—'time we was all hayin' at Smalldene—for stealin' her man."

"But you heered me tell her she had my leave to keep him?" Mrs. Ashcroft's voice and smile were smoother than ever.

"I did—an' we was all looking that she'd prod the fork spang through your breastes when you said it."

"No-oo. She'd never go beyond bounds—Polly. She shruck too much for reel doin's."[2]

"Allus seem to *me*," Mrs. Fettley said after a pause, "that a man 'twixt two fightin' women is the foolishest thing on earth. 'Like a dog bein' called two ways."

"Mebbe. But what set ye off on those times, Liz?"

"That boy's fashion o'carryin' his head an' arms. I haven't rightly looked at him since he's growed. Your Jane never showed it, but—*him!* Why, 'tis Jim Batten and his tricks come to life again! . . . Eh?"

"Mebbe. There's some that would ha' made it out so—bein' barren-like, themselves."

"Oho! Ah well! Dearie, dearie me, now! . . . An' Jim Batten's been dead this———"

"Seven and twenty years," Mrs. Ashcroft answered briefly. "Won't ye draw up, Liz?"

Mrs. Fettley drew up to buttered toast, currant bread, stewed tea, bitter as leather, some home-preserved pears, and a cold boiled pig's tail to help down the muffins. She paid all the proper compliments.

"Yes. I dunno as I've ever owed me belly much," said Mrs. Ashcroft thoughtfully. "We only go through this world once."

"But don't it lay heavy on ye, sometimes?" her guest suggested.

"Nurse says I'm a sight liker to die o' me indigestion than me leg." For Mrs. Ashcroft had a long-standing ulcer on her shin, which needed regular care from the Village Nurse, who boasted (or others did, for her) that she had dressed it one hundred and three times already during her term of office.

"An' you that *was* so able, too! It's all come on ye before your full time, like. *I*'ve watched ye goin'." Mrs. Fettley spoke with real affection.

"Somethin's bound to find ye sometime. I've me 'eart left me still," Mrs. Ashcroft returned.

"You was always big-hearted enough for three. That's somethin' to look back on at the day's eend."

"I reckon you've *your* back-lookin's, too," was Mrs. Ashcroft's answer.

"You know it. But I don't think much regardin' such matters excep' when I'm along with you, Gra'. 'Takes two sticks to make a fire."

Mrs. Fettley stared, with jaw half-dropped, at the grocer's bright calendar on the wall. The cottage shook again to the roar of the motor-traffic, and the crowded football-ground below the garden roared almost as loudly; for the village was well set to its Saturday leisure.

Mrs. Fettley had spoken very precisely for some time without interruption, before she wiped her eyes. "And," she concluded, "they read 'is death-notice to me, out o' the paper last month. O' course it wadn't any o' *my* becomin' concerns—let be I 'adn't set eyes on him for so long. O' course *I* couldn't say nor show nothin'. Nor I've no rightful

---

[2] i.e; shrank into herself, was too timid.

call to go to Eastbourne to see 'is grave, either. I've been schemin' to slip over there by the 'bus some day; but they'd ask questions at 'ome past endurance. So I 'aven't even *that* to stay me."

"But you've 'ad your satisfaction?"

"Godd! Yess! Those four years 'e was workin' on the rail near us. An' the other drivers they gave him a brave funeral, too."

"Then you've naught to cast-up about. 'Nother cup o' tea?"

The light and air had changed a little with the sun's descent, and the two elderly ladies closed the kitchen-door against chill. A couple of jays squealed and skirmished through the undraped apple-trees in the garden. This time, the word was with Mrs. Ashcroft, her elbows on the tea-table, and her sick leg propped on a stool. . . .

"Well I never! But what did your 'usband say to that?" Mrs. Fettley asked, when the deep-toned recital halted.

"'E said I might go where I pleased for all of 'im. But seein' 'e was bedrid, I said I'd 'tend 'im out. 'E knowed I wouldn't take no advantage of 'im in that state. 'E lasted eight or nine weeks. Then he was took with a seizure-like; an' laid stone-still for days. Then 'e propped 'imself up abed an' says: 'You pray no man'll ever deal with you like you've dealed with some.' 'An' you?' I says, for *you* know, Liz, what a rover 'e was. 'It cuts both ways,' says 'e, 'but *I*'m death-wise, an' I can see what's comin' to you.' He died a-Sunday an' was buried a-Thursday . . . An' yet I'd set a heap by him—one time or—did I ever?"

"You never told me that before," Mrs. Fettley ventured.

"I'm payin' ye for what ye told me just now. Him bein' dead, I wrote up, sayin' I was free for good, to that Mrs. Marshall in Lunnon—which gave me my first place as kitchen-maid—Lord, how long ago! She was well pleased, for they two was both gettin' on, an' I knowed their ways. You remember, Liz, I used to go to 'em in service between whiles, for years—when we wanted money, or—or my 'usband was away—on occasion."

"'E *did* get that six months at Chichester, didn't 'e?" Mrs. Fettley whispered. "We never rightly won to the bottom of it."

"E'd ha' got more, but the man didn't die."

"'None o' your doin's, was it, Gra'?"

"No! 'Twas the woman's husband this time. An' so, my man bein' dead, I went back to them Marshalls, as cook, to get me legs under a gentleman's table again, and be called with a handle to me name. That was the year you shifted to Portsmouth."

"Cosham," Mrs. Fettley corrected. "There was a middlin' lot o' new buildin' bein' done there. My man went first, an' got the room, an' I follered."

"Well, then, I was a year-abouts in Lunnon, all at a breath, like, four meals a day an' livin' easy. Then, 'long towards autumn, they two went travellin', like, to France; keepin' me on, for they couldn't do without me. I put the house to rights for the caretaker, an' then I slipped down 'ere to me sister Bessie—me wages in me pockets, an' all 'ands glad to be'old of me."

"That would be when I was at Cosham," said Mrs. Fettley.

"*You* know, Liz, there wasn't no cheap-dog pride to folk, those days, no more than there was cinemas nor whisk-drives. Man or woman 'ud lay hold o' any job that promised a shillin' to the backside of it, didn't they? I was all peaked up after Lunnon, an' I thought the fresh airs 'ud serve me. So I took on at Smalldene, obligin' with a hand at the early potato-liftin', stubbin' hens³, an' such-like. They'd ha' mocked me sore in my kitchen in Lunnon, to see me in men's boots, an' me petticoats all shorted."

"Did it bring ye any good?" Mrs. Fettley asked.

"'Twadn't for that I went. You know, 's'well's me, that na'un happens to ye till it *'as* 'appened. Your mind don't warn ye before'and of the road ye've took, till you're at the far eend ot it. We've only a backwent view of our proceedin's."

"'Oo was it?"

" 'Arry Mockler." Mrs. Ashcroft's face puckered to the pain of her sick leg. Mrs. Fettley gasped. "'Arry? Bert Mockler's son! An' *I* never guessed!"

Mrs. Ashcroft nodded. "An' I told myself—*an'* I beleft it—that I wanted field-work."

"What did ye get out of it?"

"The usuals. Everythin' at first—worse than naught after. I had signs an' warn-ings a-plenty, but I took no heed of 'em. For we was burnin' rubbish one day, just when we'd come to know how 'twas with—with both of us. 'Twas early in the year for burnin', an' I said so. 'No!' says he. 'The sooner dat old stuff's off an' done with,' 'e says, 'the better.' 'Is face was harder'n rocks when he spoke. Then it come over me that I'd found me master, which I 'adn't ever before. I'd allus owned 'em, like."

"Yes! Yes! They're yourn or you're theirn," the other sighed. "I like the right way best."

"I didn't. But 'Arry did . . . 'Long then, it come time for me to go back to Lunnon. I couldn't. I clean couldn't! So, I took an' tipped a dollop o' scaldin' water out o' the copper one Monday mornin' over me left 'and and arm. Dat stayed me where I was for another fortnight."

"Was it worth it?" said Mrs. Fettley, looking at the silvery scar on the wrinkled fore-arm.

Mrs. Ashcroft nodded. "An' after that, we two made it up 'twixt us so's 'e could come to Lunnon for a job in a liv'ry-stable not far from me. 'E got it. *I* 'tended to that. There wadn't no talk nowhere. His own mother never suspicioned how 'twas. He just slipped up to Lunnon, an' there we abode that winter, not 'alf a mile 'tother from each."

"Ye paid 'is fare an' all, though"; Mrs. Fettley spoke convincedly.

Again Mrs. Ashcroft nodded. "Dere wadn't much I didn't do for him. 'E was me master, an'—O God, help us!—we'd laugh over it walkin' together after dark in them paved streets, an' me corns fair wrenchin' in me boots! I'd never been like that before. Ner he! Ner he!"

Mrs. Fettley clucked sympathetically.

"An' when did ye come to the eend?" she asked.

"When 'e paid it all back again, every penny. Then I knowed, but I wouldn't *suffer* meself to know. 'You've been mortal kind to me,' he says. 'Kind!' I said. "Twixt *us?*' But 'e kep' all on tellin' me 'ow kind I'd been an' 'e'd never forget it all his days. I held it from off o' me for three evenin's, because I would *not* believe. Then 'e talked about not bein' satisfied with 'is job in the stables, an' the men there puttin' tricks on 'im, an' all they lies which a man tells when 'e's leavin' ye. I heard 'im out, neither 'elpin' nor 'inderin'. At the last, I took off a liddle brooch which he'd give me an' I

---

³ Picking pinfeathers.

says: 'Dat'll do. *I* ain't askin' na'un.' An' I turned me round an' walked off to me own sufferin's. 'E didn't make 'em worse. 'E didn't come nor write after that. 'E slipped off 'ere back 'ome to 'is mother again."

"An' 'ow often did ye look for 'en to come back?" Mrs. Fettley demanded mercilessly.

"More'n once—more'n once! Goin' over the streets we'd used, I thought de very pave-stones 'ud shruck our under me feet."

"Yes," said Mrs. Fettley. "I dunno but dat don't 'urt as much as aught else. An' dat was all ye got?"

"No. 'Twadn't. That's the curious part, if you'll believe it, Liz."

"I do. I lay you're further off lyin' now than in all your life, Gra'."

"I am . . . An' I suffered, like I'd not wish my most arrantest enemies to. God's Own Name! I went through the hoop that spring! One part of it was headaches which I'd never known all me days before. Think o' *me* with an 'eddick! But I come to be grateful for 'em. They kep' me from thinkin' . . ."

"'Tis like a tooth," Mrs. Fettley commented. "It must rage an' rugg till it tortures itself quiet on ye; an' then—then there's na'un left."

"*I* got enough lef' to last me all *my* days on earth. It come about through our charwoman's liddle girl—Sophy Ellis was 'er name—all eyes an' elbers an' hunger. I used to give 'er vittles. Otherwhiles, I took no special notice of 'er, an' a sight less, o' course, when me trouble about 'Arry was on me. But—you know how liddle maids first feel it sometimes—she come to be crazy-fond o' me, pawin' an' cuddlin' all whiles; an' I 'adn't the 'eart to beat 'er off . . . One afternoon, early in spring 'twas, 'er mother 'ad sent 'er round to scutchel up what vittles she could off of us. I was settin' by the fire, me apern over my head, half-mad with the 'eddick, when she slips in. I reckin I was middlin' short with 'er. 'Lor'!' she says. 'Is *that* all? I'll take it off you in two-twos!' I told her not to lay a finger on me, for I thought she'd want to stroke my forehead; an'—I ain't that make. 'I won't tech ye,' she says, an' slips out again. She 'adn't been gone ten minutes 'fore me old 'eddick took off quick as bein' kicked. So I went about my work. Prasin'ly, Sophy comes back, an' creeps into my chair quiet as a mouse. 'Er eyes was deep in 'er 'ead an' 'er face all drawed. I asked 'er what 'ad 'appened. 'Nothin',' she says. 'On'y *I*'ve got it now.' 'Got what?' I says. 'Your 'eddick,' she says, all hoarse an' sticky-lipped. 'I've took it on me.' 'Nonsense,' I says, 'it went of itself when you was out. Lay still an' I'll make ye a cup o' tea.' ''Twon't do no good,' she says, ''til your time's up. 'Ow long do *your* 'eddicks last?' 'Don't talk silly,' I says, 'or I'll send for the Doctor.' It looked to me like she might be hatchin' de measles. 'Oh, Mrs. Ashcroft,' she says, stretchin' out 'er liddle thin arms. 'I *do* love ye.' There wasn't any holdin' agin that. I took 'er into me lap an' made much of 'er. 'Is it truly gone?' she says. 'Yes,' I says, 'an' if 'twas you took it away, I'm truly grateful.' ''Twas me,' she says, layin' 'er cheek to mine. 'No one but me knows how.' An' then she said she'd changed me 'eddick for me at a Wish 'Ouse."

"Whatt?" Mrs. Fettley spoke sharply.

"A Wish House. No! *I* 'adn't 'eard o' such things, either. I couldn't get it straight at first, but, puttin' all together, I made out that a Wish 'Ouse 'ad to be a house which 'ad stood unlet an' empty long enough for Some One, like, to come an' in'abit there. She said, a liddle girl that she'd played with in the livery-stables where 'Arry worked 'ad told 'er so. She said the girl 'ad belonged in a caravan that laid up, o' winters, in Lunnon. Gipsy, I judge."

"Ooh! There's no sayin' what Gippos know, but *I've* never 'eard of a Wish 'Ouse, an' I know—some things," said Mrs. Fettley.

"Sophy said there was a Wish 'Ouse in Wadloes Road—just a few streets off, on the way to our green-grocer's. All you 'ad to do, she said, was to ring the bell an' wish your wish through the slit o' the letter-box. I asked 'er if the fairies give it 'er? 'Don't ye know,' she says, 'there's no fairies in a Wish 'Ouse? There's only a Token.'"

"Goo' Lord A'mighty! Where did she come by *that* word?" cried Mrs. Fettley; for a Token is a wraith of the dead or, worse still, of the living.

"The caravan-girl 'ad told 'er, she said. Well, Liz, it troubled me to 'ear 'er, an' lyin' in me arms she must ha' felt it. 'That's very kind o' you,' I says, holdin' 'er tight, 'to wish me 'eddick away. But why didn't ye ask somethin' nice for yourself?' 'You can't do that,' she says. 'All you'll get at a Wish 'Ouse is leave to take some one else's trouble. I've took Ma's 'eadaches, when she's been kind to me; but this is the first time I've been able to do aught for you. Oh, Mrs. Ashcroft, I *do* just-about love you.' An' she goes on all like that. Liz, I tell you my 'air e'en a'most stood on end to 'ear 'er. I asked 'er what like a Token was. 'I dunno,' she says, 'but after you've ringed the bell, you'll 'ear it run up from the basement, to the front door. Then say your wish,' she says, 'an' go away.' 'The Token don't open de door to ye, then?' I says. 'Oh, no,' she says. 'You on'y 'ear gigglin', like, be'ind the front door. Then you say you'll take the trouble off of 'oo ever 'tis you've chose for your love; an' ye'll get it,' she says. I didn't ask no more—she was too 'ot an' fevered. I made much of 'er till it come time to light de gas, an' a liddle after that, 'er 'eddick—mine, I suppose—took off, an' she got down an' played with the cat."

"Well, I never!" said Mrs. Fettley. "Did—did ye foller it up, anyways?"

"She askt me to, but I wouldn't 'ave no such dealin's with a child."

"What *did* ye do, then?"

"'Sat in me own room 'stid o' the kitchen when me 'eddicks come on. But it lay at de back o' me mind."

"'Twould. Did she tell ye more, ever?"

"No. Besides what the Gippo girl 'ad told 'er, she knew naught, 'cept that the charm worked. An', next after that—in May 'twas—I suffered the summer out in Lunnon. 'Twas hot an' windy for weeks, an' the streets stinkin' o' dried 'orse-dung blowin' from side to side an' lyin' level with the kerb. We don't get that nowadays. I 'ad my 'ol'day just before hoppin',[4] an' come down 'ere to stay with Bessie again. She noticed I'd lost flesh, an' was all poochy under the eyes."

"Did ye see 'Arry?"

Mrs. Ashcroft nodded. "The fourth—no, the fifth day. Wednesday 'twas. I knowed 'e was workin' at Smalldene again. I asked 'is mother in the street, bold as brass. She 'adn't room to say much, for Bessie—you know 'er tongue—was talkin' full-clack. But that Wednesday, I was walkin' with one o' Bessie's chillern hangin' on me skirts, at de back o' Chanter's Tot. Prasin'ly, I felt 'e was be'ind me on the footpath, an' I knowed by 'is tread 'e'd changed 'is nature. I slowed, an' I heard 'im slow. Then I fussed a piece with the child, to force him past me, like. So 'e 'ad to come past. 'E just says 'Good-evenin',' and goes on, tryin' to pull 'isself together."

"Drunk, was he?" Mrs. Fettley asked.

"Never! S'runk an' wizen; 'is clothes 'angin on 'im like bags, an' the back of 'is neck whiter'n chalk. 'Twas all I could do not to oppen my arms an' cry after him. But

---

[4] Hop-picking.

I swallered me spittle till I was back 'ome again an' the chillern abed. Then I says to Bessie, after supper, 'What in de world's come to 'Arry Mockler?' Bessie told me 'e'd been a-Hospital for two months, 'long o' cuttin' 'is foot wid a spade, muckin' out the old pond at Smalldene. There was poison in de dirt, an' it rooshed up 'is leg, like, an' come out all over him. 'E 'adn't been back to 'is job—carterin' at Smalldene—more'n a fortnight. She told me the Doctor said he'd go off, likely, with the November frostes; an' 'is mother 'ad told 'er that 'e didn't rightly eat nor sleep, an' sweated 'imself into pools, no odds 'ow chill 'e lay. An' spit terrible o' mornin's. 'Dearie me,' I says, 'But, mebbe hoppin' 'll set 'im right again,' an' I licked me thread-point an' I fetched me needle's eye up to it an' I threads me needle under de lamp, steady as rocks. An' dat night (me bed was in de wash-house) I cried an' I cried. An' *you* know, Liz—for you've been with me in my throes—it takes summat to make me cry."

"Yes; but chile-bearin' is on'y just pain," said Mrs. Fettley.

"I come round by cock-crow, an' dabbed cold tea on me eyes to take away the signs. Long towards nex' evenin'—I was settin' out to lay some flowers on me 'usband's grave, for the look 'o the thing—I met 'Arry over against where the War Memorial is now. 'E was comin' back from 'is 'orses, so 'e couldn't *not* see me. I looked 'im all over, an' ''Arry,' I says twix' me teeth, 'come back an' rest-up in Lunnon.' 'I won't take it,' he says, 'for I can give ye naught.' 'I don't ask it,' I says. 'By God's Own Name, I don't ask na'un! On'y come up an' see a Lunnon doctor.' 'E lifts 'is two 'eavy eyes at me: ''Tis past that, Gra',' 'e says. 'I've but a few months left.' ' 'Arry!' I says. '*My* man!' I says. I couldn't say no more. 'Twas all up in me throat. 'Thank ye kindly, Gra',' 'e says (but 'e never says 'my woman'), an' 'e went on up-street an' 'is mother— Oh, damn 'er!—she was watchin' for 'im, an' she shut de door be'ind 'im."

Mrs. Fettley stretched an arm across the table, and made to finger Mrs. Ashcroft's sleeve at the wrist, but the other moved it out of reach.

"So I went on to the churchyard with my flowers, an' I remembered my 'usband's warnin' that night he spoke. 'E *was* death-wise, an' it 'ad 'appened as 'e said. But as I was settin' down de jam-pot on the grave-mound, it come over me there was one thing I *could* do for 'Arry. Doctor or no Doctor, I thought I'd make a trial of it. So I did. Nex' mornin', a bill came down from our Lunnon green-grocer. Mrs. Marshall, she'd lef' me petty cash for suchlike—o' course—but I tole Bess 'twas for me to come an' open the 'ouse. So I went up, afternoon train."

"An'—but I know you 'adn't—'adn't you no fear?"

"What for?" There was nothin' front o' me but my own shame an' God's croolty. I couldn't ever get 'Arry—'ow *could* I? I knowed it must go on burnin' till it burned me out."

"Aie!" said Mrs. Fettley, reaching for the wrist again, and this time Mrs. Ashcroft permitted it.

"Yit 'twas a comfort to know I could try *this* for 'im. So I went an' I paid the green-grocer's bill, an' put 'is receipt in me hand-bag, an' then I stepped round to Mrs. Ellis—our char—an' got the 'ouse keys an' opened the 'ouse. First I made me bed to come back to (God's Own Name! Me bed to lie upon!). Nex' I made me a cup o' tea an' sat down in the kitchen thinkin', till 'long towards dusk. Terrible close, 'twas. Then I dressed me an' went out with the receipt in me 'and-bag, feignin' to study it for an address, like. Fourteen, Wadloes Road, was the place—a liddle basement-kitchen 'ouse, in a row of twenty-thirty such, an' tiddy strips o' walled garden in front—the paint off the front doors, an' na'un done to na'un since ever so long. There wasn't 'ardly no one in the streets 'cept the cats. *'Twas* 'ot, too! I turned into the gate bold as

brass; up de steps I went an' I ringed the front-door bell. She pealed loud, like it do in
an empty house. When she'd all ceased, I 'eard a cheer, like, pushed back on de floor
o' the kitchen. Then I 'eard feet on de kitchen-stairs, like it might ha' been a heavy
woman in slippers. They come up to de stairhead, acrost the hall—I 'eard the bare
boards creak under 'em—an' at de front door dey stopped. I stooped me to the letter-
box slit, an' I says: 'Let me take everythin' bad that's in store for my man, 'Arry
Mockler, for love's sake.' Then, whatever it was t'other side de door let its breath out,
like, as if it 'ad been holdin' it for to 'ear better.''

"Nothin' was *said* to ye?" Mrs. Fettley demanded.

"Na'un. She just breathed out—a sor of *A-ah*, like. Then the steps went back an'
down-stairs to the kitchen—all draggy—an' I heard the cheer drawed up again."

"An' you abode on de doorstep, throughout all, Gra'?"

Mrs. Ashcroft nodded.

"Then I went away, an' a man passin' says to me: 'Didn't you know that house
was empty?' 'No,' I says. 'I must ha' been give the wrong number.' An' I went back to
our 'ouse, an' I went to bed; for I was fair flogged out. 'Twas too 'ot to sleep more'n
snatches, so I walked me about, lyin' down betweens, till crack o' dawn. Then I went
to the kitchen to make me a cup o' tea, an' I hitted meself just above the ankle on an
old roastin'-jack o' mine that Mrs. Ellis had moved out from the corner, her last
cleanin'. An' so—nex' after that—I waited till the Marshalls come back o' their holiday."

"Alone there? I'd ha' thought you'd 'ad enough of empty houses," said Mrs.
Fettley, horrified.

"Oh, Mrs. Ellis an' Sophy was runnin' in an' out soon's I was back, an' 'twixt us
we cleaned de house again top-to-bottom. There's allus a hand's turn more to do in
every house. An' that's 'ow 'twas with me that autumn an' winter, in Lunnon."

"Then na'un hap—overtook ye for your doin's?"

Mrs. Ashcroft smiled. "No. Not then. 'Long in November I sent Bessie ten shillin's."

"You was allus free-'anded," Mrs. Fettley interrupted.

"An' I got what I paid for, with the rest o' the news. She said the hoppin' 'ad set
'im up wonderful. 'E'd 'ad six weeks of it, and now 'e was back again carterin' at
Smalldene. No odds to me *'ow* it 'ad 'appened—'slong's it *'ad*. But I dunno as my ten
shillin's eased me much. 'Arry bein' *dead*, like, 'e'd ha' been mine, till Judgment. 'Arry
bein' alive, 'e'd like as not pick up with some woman middlin' quick. I raged over that.
Come spring, I 'ad somethin' else to rage for. I'd growed a nasty little weepin' boil,
like, on me shin, just above the boot-top, that wouldn't heal no shape. It made me sick
to look at it, for I'm clean-fleshed by nature. Chop me all over with a spade, an' I'd
heal like turf. Then Mrs. Marshall she set 'er own doctor at me. 'E said I ought to ha'
come to him at first go-off, 'stead o' drawin' all manner o' dyed stockin's over it for
months. 'E said I'd stood up too much to me work, for it was settin' very close atop of
a big swelled vein, like, behither the small o' me ankle. 'Slow come, slow go,' 'e says.
'Lay your leg up on high an' rest it,' he says, 'an' 'twill ease off. Don't let it close up too
soon. You've got a very fine leg, Mrs. Ashcroft,' 'e says. An' he put wet dressin's on it."

"'E done right." Mrs. Fettley spoke firmly. "Wet dressin's to wet wounds. They
draw de humours, same's a lamp-wick draws de oil."

"That's true. An' Mrs. Marshall was allus at me to make me set down more, an'
dat nigh healed it up. An' then after a while they packed me off down to Bessie's to

finish the cure; for I ain't the sort to sit down when I ought to stand up. You was back in the village then, Liz."

"I was. I was, but—never did I guess!"

"I didn't desire ye to." Mrs. Ashcroft smiled. "I saw 'Arry once or twice in de street, wonnerful fleshed up an' restored back. Then, one day I didn't see 'im, an' 'is mother told me one of 'is 'orses 'ad lashed out an' caught 'im on the 'ip. So 'e was abed an' middlin' painful. An' Bessie, she says to his mother, 'twas a pity 'Arry 'adn't a woman of 'is own to take the nursin' off 'er. And the old lady *was* mad! She told us that 'Arry 'ad never looked after any woman in 'is born days, an' as long as she was atop the mowlds, she'd contrive for 'im till 'er two 'ands dropped off. So I knowed she'd do watch-dog for me, 'thout askin' for bones."

Mrs. Fettley rocked with small laughter.

"That day," Mrs. Ashcroft went on, "I'd stood on me feet nigh all the time, watchin' the doctor go in an' out; for they thought it might be 'is ribs, too. That made my boil break again, issuin' an' weepin'. But it turned out 'twadn't ribs at all, an' 'Arry 'ad a good night. When I heard that nex' mornin', I says to meself, 'I won't lay two an' two together *yit*. I'll keep me leg down a week, an' see what comes of it.' It didn't hurt me that day, to speak of—'seemed more to draw the strength out o' me like—an' 'Arry 'ad another good night. That made me persevere; but I didn't dare lay two an' two together till the week-end, an' then, 'Arry come forth e'en a'most 'imself again—na'un hurt outside ner in of him. I nigh fell on me knees in de wash-house when Bessie was up-street. 'I've got ye now, my man,' I says, 'You'll take your good from me 'thout knowin' it till my life's end. O God send me long to live for 'Arry's sake!' I says. An' I dunno that didn't still me ragin's."

"For good?" Mrs. Fettley asked.

"They come back, plenty times, but, let be how 'twould, I knowed I was doin' for 'im. I *knowed* it. I took an' worked me pains on an' off, like regulatin' my own range, till I learned to 'ave 'em at my commandments. An' that was funny, too. There was times, Liz, when my trouble 'ud all s'rink an' dry up, like. First, I used to try an' fetch it on again; bein' fearful to leave 'Arry alone too long for anythin' to lay 'old of. Prasin'ly I come to see that was a sign he'd do all right awhile, an' so I saved myself."

" 'Ow long for?" Mrs. Fettley asked, with deepest interest.

"I've gone de better part of a year onct or twice with na'un more to show than the liddle weepin' core of it, like. *All* s'rinked up an' dried off. Then he'd inflame up—for a warnin'—an' I'd suffer it. When I couldn't no more—an' I *'ad* to keep on goin' with my Lunnon work—I'd lay me leg high on a cheer till it eased. Not too quick. I knowed by the feel of it, those times, dat 'Arry was in need. Then I'd send another five shillin's to Bess, or somethin' for the chillern, to find out if, mebbe, 'e'd took any hurt through my neglects. 'Twas *so!* Year in, year out, I worked it dat way, Liz, an' 'e got 'is good from me 'thout knowin'—for years and years."

"But what did *you* get out of it, Gra'?" Mrs. Fettley almost wailed. "Did ye see 'im reg'lar?"

"Times—when I was 'ere on me 'ol'days. An' more, now that I'm 'ere for good. But 'e's never looked at me, ner any other woman 'cept 'is mother. 'Ow I used to watch an' listen! So did she."

"Years an' years!" Mrs. Fettley repeated. "An' where's 'e workin' at now?"

"Oh, 'e's give up carterin' quite a while. He's workin' for one o' them big trac-torisin' firms—ploughin' sometimes, an' sometimes off with lorries—fur as Wales, I've 'eard. He comes 'ome to 'is mother 'tween whiles; but I don't set eyes on him now, fer weeks on end. No odds! 'Is job keeps 'im from continuin' in one stay anywheres."

"But—just for de sake o' sayin' somethin'—s'pose 'Arry *did* get married?" said Mrs. Fettley.

Mrs. Ashcroft drew her breath sharply between her still even and natural teeth. "*Dat* ain't been required of me," she answered. "I reckon my pains 'ull be counted agin that. Don't *you,* Liz?"

"It ought to be, dearie. It ought to be."

"It *do* 'urt sometimes. You shall see it when Nurse comes. She thinks I don't know it's turned."

Mrs. Fettley understood. Human nature seldom walks up to the word "cancer."

"Be ye certain sure, Gra'?" she asked.

"I was sure of it when old Mr. Marshall 'ad me up to 'is study an' spoke a long piece about my faithful service. I've obliged 'em on an' off for a goodish time, but not enough for a pension. But they give me a weekly 'lowance for life. I knew what *that* sinnified—as long as three years ago."

"Dat don't *prove* it, Gra'."

"To give fifteen bob a week to a woman 'oo'd live twenty year in the course o' nature? It *do!*"

"You're mistook! You're mistook!" Mrs. Fettley insisted.

"Liz, there's *no* mistakin' when the edges are all heaped up, like—same as a collar. You'll see it. An' I laid out Dora Wickwood, too. *She* 'ad it under the arm-pit, like."

Mrs. Fettley considered awhile, and bowed her head in finality.

"'Ow long d'you reckon 'twill allow ye, countin' from now, dearie?"

"Slow come, slow go. But if I don't set eyes on ye 'fore next hoppin', this'll be good-bye, Liz."

"Dunno as I'll be able to manage by then—not 'thout I have a liddle dog to lead me. For de chillern, dey won't be troubled, an'—O Gra'!—I'm blindin' up—I'm blindin' up!"

"Oh, *dat* was why you didn't more'n finger with your quilt-patches all this while! I was wonderin' . . . But the pain *do* count, don't ye think, Liz? The pain *do* count to keep 'Arry—where I want 'im. Say it can't be wasted, like."

"I'm sure of it—sure of it, dearie. You'll 'ave your reward."

"I don't want no more'n this—*if* de pain is taken into de reckonin'."

"'Twill be—'twill be, Gra'."

There was a knock on the door.

"That's Nurse. She's before 'er time," said Mrs. Ashcroft. "Open to 'er."

The young lady entered briskly, all the bottles in her bag clicking. "Evenin', Mrs. Ashcroft," she began. "I've come raound a little earlier than usual because of the Institute dance to-na-ite. You won't ma-ind, will you?"

"Oh, no. Me dancin' days are over." Mrs. Ashcroft was the self-contained domestic at once. "My old friend, Mrs. Fettley 'ere, has been settin' talkin' with me a while."

"I hope she 'asn't been fatiguing you?" said the Nurse a little frostily.

"Quite the contrary. It 'as been a pleasure. Only—only—just at the end I felt a bit—a bit flogged out, like."

"Yes, yes." The Nurse was on her knees already, with the washes to hand. "When old ladies get together they talk a deal too much, I've noticed."

"Mebbe we do," said Mrs. Fettley, rising, "So, now, I'll make myself scarce."

"Look at it first, though," said Mrs. Ashcroft feebly. "I'd like ye to look at it."

Mrs. Fettley looked, and shivered. Then she leaned over, and kissed Mrs. Ashcroft once on the waxy yellow forehead, and again on the faded grey eyes.

"It *do* count, don't it—de pain?" The lips that still kept trace of their original moulding hardly more than breathed the words.

Mrs. Fettley kissed them and moved towards the door.

Stephen Crane (1871–1900)

Stephen Crane could be thought of as a funnel through which the forces of nineteenth-century literature entered the American twentieth century. He was at once a naturalist, a realist, an impressionist, and a symbolist. And though he died before the age of twenty-nine in 1900, he is a towering figure in American fiction. His influence went to both technique and subject matter. He was, said his contemporary H. G. Wells, "the first expression of the opening mind of a new period."

Maggie: A Girl of the Streets (1892) was the first American novel to use the techniques of naturalism derived from Flaubert and Zola. Its fearless portrayal of American society and its sympathy for the underside of our culture were shocking at the time, and despite the support of established writers like William Dean Howells and Hamlin Garland, Crane had a hard time giving away copies of the book. *The Red Badge of Courage* (1895), written in the realist tradition of his befrienders, made more of a splash, especially in England. Although Crane claimed to believe that personal experience was the basis for literature, this work was pure invention: Crane was born six years after the end of the Civil War which it depicted so movingly.

"The Open Boat" was indeed based on personal experience. As a correspondent in search of adventure, Crane had been shipwrecked off Cuba, and in his story he attempted faithfully to render the experience. Yet despite its historical basis and its colloquial, even breezy, language, this story must be read symbolically. The sea and the little craft and the men working together are symbols of Crane's beliefs about the harsh indifferent universe, and man's indomitable will, and the spiritual brotherhood of survivors. These symbols are as important in this story as the white whale in *Moby Dick*.

Crane had a sharp eye for the exact detail that could convey a whole scene and its meaning. He describes the little boat on the sea: "As the boat bounced from the top of each wave the wind tore through the hair of the hatless men, and as the craft plopped her stern down again the spray splashed past them." He describes the cook: "His sleeves were rolled over his fat forearms, and the two flaps of his unbottoned vest dangled as he bent to bail out the boat." Though pictorial and precise, his prose can without awkwardness present the weight of meaning, psychological and philosophical, that underlies the concrete details: "The injured captain, lying in the bow, was at this time buried in that profound dejection and indiffer-

ence which comes, temporarily at least, to even the bravest and most enduring. . . ."
These passages illustrate two of the advantages of the omniscient point-of-view
(See Introduction, p. 12): a distance sufficient to allow perspective on more than
one character, and a chance for authorial comment without destroying the mood of
the story.

Many critics have called attention to the story's magnificent opening lines
which rivet the reader's attention so tightly to the perilous situation. The closing
line, too, deserves attention. It seems to release the story from its specific and
confining moorings and allow it to ascend into universal significance. What this last
line expresses, of course, is the hope and ambition of Crane, and of all writers and
artists:

> When it came night, the white waves paced to and fro in the moonlight, and
> the wind brought the sound of the great sea's voice to the men on the shore,
> and they felt that they could then be interpreters.

The Open Boat

A TALE INTENDED TO BE AFTER THE FACT. BEING THE EXPERIENCE OF FOUR MEN FROM THE SUNK STEAMER *COMMODORE*.

None of them knew the color of the sky. Their eyes glanced level, and were fastened
upon the waves that swept toward them. These waves were of the hue of slate, save for
the tops, which were of foaming white, and all of the men knew the colors of the sea.
The horizon narrowed and widened, and dipped and rose, and at all times its edge was
jagged with waves that seemed thrust up in points like rocks. Many a man ought to
have a bathtub larger than the boat which here rode upon the sea. These waves were
most wrongfully and barbarously abrupt and tall, and each froth-top was a problem in
small-boat navigation.

The cook squatted in the bottom and looked with both eyes at the six inches of
gunwale which separated him from the ocean. His sleeves were rolled over his fat
forearms, and the two flaps of his unbuttoned vest dangled as he bent to bail out the
boat. Often he said: "Gawd! That was a narrow clip." As he remarked it he invariably
gazed eastward over the broken sea.

The oiler, steering with one of the two oars in the boat, sometimes raised himself
suddenly to keep clear of water that swirled in over the stern. It was a thin little oar
and it seemed often ready to snap.

The correspondent, pulling at the other oar, watched the waves and wondered
why he was there.

The injured captain, lying in the bow, was at this time buried in that profound
dejection and indifference which comes, temporarily at least, to even the bravest and
most enduring when, willy nilly, the firm fails, the army loses, the ship goes down. The
mind of the master of a vessel is rooted deep in the timbers of her, though he command for a day or a decade, and this captain had on him the stern impression of a
scene in the greys of dawn of seven turned faces, and later a stump of a top-mast with

a white ball on it that slashed to and fro at the waves, went low and lower, and down. Thereafter there was something strange in his voice. Although steady, it was deep with mourning, and of a quality beyond oration or tears.

"Keep 'er a little more south, Billie," said he.

"'A little more south,' sir," said the oiler in the stern.

A seat in this boat was not unlike the seat upon a bucking broncho, and by the same token, a broncho is not much smaller. The craft pranced and reared, and plunged like an animal. As each wave came, and she rose for it, she seemed like a horse making at a fence outrageously high. The manner of her scramble over these walls of water is a mystic thing, and, moreover, at the top of them were ordinarily these problems in white water, the foam racing down from the summit of each wave, requiring a new leap, and a leap from the air. Then, after scornfully bumping a crest, she would slide, and race, and splash down a long incline, and arrive bobbing and nodding in front of the next menace.

A singular disadvantage of the sea lies in the fact that after successfully surmounting one wave you discover that there is another behind it just as important and just as nervously anxious to do something effective in the way of swamping boats. In a ten-foot dinghy one can get an idea of the resources of the sea in the line of waves that is not probable to the average experience which is never at sea in a dinghy. As each slatey wall of water approached, it shut all else from the view of the men in the boat, and it was not difficult to imagine that this particular wave was the final outburst of the ocean, the last effort of the grim water. There was a terrible grace in the move of the waves, and they came in silence, save for the snarling of the crests.

In the wan light, the faces of the men must have been grey. Their eyes must have glinted in strange ways as they gazed steadily astern. Viewed from a balcony, the whole thing would doubtless have been weirdly picturesque. But the men in the boat had no time to see it, and if they had had leisure there were other things to occupy their minds. The sun swung steadily up the sky, and they knew it was broad day because the color of the sea changed from slate to emerald-green, streaked with amber lights, and the foam was like tumbling snow. The process of the breaking day was unknown to them. They were aware only of this effect upon the color of the waves that rolled toward them.

In disjointed sentences the cook and the correspondent argued as to the difference between a life-saving station and a house of refuge. The cook had said: "There's a house of refuge just north of the Mosquito Inlet Light, and as soon as they see us, they'll come off in their boat and pick us up."

"As soon as who see us?" said the correspondent.

"The crew," said the cook.

"Houses of refuge don't have crews," said the correspondent. "As I understand them, they are only places where clothes and grub are stored for the benefit of shipwrecked people. They don't carry crews."

"Oh, yes, they do," said the cook.

"No, they don't," said the correspondent.

"Well, we're not there yet, anyhow," said the oiler, in the stern.

"Well," said the cook, "perhaps it's not a house of refuge that I'm thinking of as being near Mosquito Inlet Light. Perhaps it's a life-saving station."

"We're not there yet," said the oiler, in the stern.

2

As the boat bounced from the top of each wave, the wind tore through the hair of the hatless men, and as the craft plopped her stern down again the spray splashed past them. The crest of each of these waves was a hill, from the top of which the men surveyed, for a moment, a broad tumultuous expanse, shining and wind-riven. It was probably splendid. It was probably glorious, this play of the free sea, wild with lights of emerald and white and amber.

"Bully good thing it's an on-shore wind," said the cook. "If not, where would we be? Wouldn't have a show."

"That's right," said the correspondent.

The busy oiler nodded his assent.

Then the captain, in the bow, chuckled in a way that expressed humor, contempt, tragedy, all in one. "Do you think we've got much of a show now, boys?" said he.

Whereupon the three were silent, save for a trifle of hemming and hawing. To express any particular optimism at this time they felt to be childish and stupid, but they all doubtless possessed this sense of the situation in their mind. A young man thinks doggedly at such times. On the other hand, the ethics of their condition was decidely against any open suggestion of hopelessness. So they were silent.

"Oh, well," said the captain, soothing his children, "we'll get ashore all right."

But there was that in his tone which made them think, so the oiler quoth: "Yes! If this wind holds!"

The cook was bailing: "Yes! If we don't catch hell in the surf."

Canton flannel gulls flew near and far. Sometimes they sat down on the sea, near patches of brown seaweed that rolled on the waves with a movement like carpets on a line in a gale. The birds sat comfortably in groups, and they were envied by some in the dinghy, for the wrath of the sea was no more to them than it was to a covey of prairie chickens a thousand miles inland. Often they came very close and stared at the men with black bead-like eyes. At these times they were uncanny and sinister in their unblinking scrutiny, and the men hooted angrily at them, telling them to be gone. One came, and evidently decided to alight on the top of the captain's head. The bird flew parallel to the boat and did not circle, but made short sidelong jumps in the air in chicken-fashion. His black eyes were wistfully fixed upon the captain's head. "Ugly brute," said the oiler to the bird. "You look as if you were made with a jack-knife." The cook and the correspondent swore darkly at the creature. The captain naturally wished to knock it away with the end of the heavy painter; but he did not dare do it, because anything resembling an emphatic gesture would have capsized this freighted boat, and so with his open hand, the captain gently and carefully waved the gull away. After it had been discouraged from the pursuit the captain breathed easier on account of his hair, and others breathed easier because the bird struck their minds at this time as being somehow grewsome and ominous.

In the meantime the oiler and the correspondent rowed. And also they rowed.

They sat together in the same seat, and each rowed an oar. Then the oiler took both oars; then the correspondent took both oars; then the oiler; then the correspondent. They rowed and they rowed. The very ticklish part of the business was when the time came for the reclining one in the stern to take his turn at the oars. By the very last star of truth, it is easier to steal eggs from under a hen than it was to change seats in the dinghy. First the man in the stern slid his hand along the thwart and moved with care, as if he were of Sèvres. Then the man in the rowing seat slid his hand along the other thwart. It was all done with the most extraordinary care. As the two sidled past each other, the whole party kept watchful eyes on the coming wave, and the captain cried: "Look out now! Steady there!"

The brown mats of seaweed that appeared from time to time were like islands, bits of earth. They were traveling, apparently, neither one way nor the other. They were, to all intents, stationary. They informed the men in the boat that it was making progress slowly toward the land.

The captain, rearing cautiously in the bow, after the dinghy soared on a great swell, said that he had seen the lighthouse at Mosquito Inlet. Presently the cook remarked that he had seen it. The correspondent was at the oars then and for some reason he too wished to look at the lighthouse, but his back was toward the far shore and the waves were important, and for some time he could not seize an opportunity to turn his head. But at last there came a wave more gentle than the others, and when at the crest of it he swiftly scoured the western horizon.

"See it?" said the captain.

"No," said the correspondent slowly, "I didn't see anything."

"Look again," said the captain. He pointed. "It's exactly in that direction."

At the top of another wave, the correspondent did as he was bid, and this time his eyes chanced on a small still thing on the edge of the swaying horizon. It was precisely like the point of a pin. It took an anxious eye to find a lighthouse so tiny.

"Think we'll make it, captain?"

"If this wind holds and the boat don't swamp, we can't do much else," said the captain.

The little boat, lifted by each towering sea, and splashed viciously by the crests, made progress that in the absence of seaweed was not apparent to those in her. She seemed just a wee thing wallowing, miraculously top-up, at the mercy of five oceans. Occasionally, a great spread of water, like white flames, swarmed into her.

"Bail her, cook," said the captain serenely.

"All right, captain," said the cheerful cook.

3

It would be difficult to describe the subtle brotherhood of men that was here established on the seas. No one said that it was so. No one mentioned it. But it dwelt in the boat, and each man felt it warm him. They were a captain, an oiler, a cook, and a correspondent, and they were friends, friends in a more curiously iron-bound degree than may be common. The hurt captain, lying against the water-jar in the bow, spoke always in a low voice and calmly, but he could never command a more ready and swiftly obedient crew than the motley three of the dinghy. It was more than a mere recognition of what was best for the common safety. There was surely in it a quality that was personal and heartfelt. And after this devotion to the commander of the boat there was this comradeship that the correspondent, for instance, who had been taught to be cynical of men, knew even at the time was the best experience of his life. But no one said that it was so. No one mentioned it.

"I wish we had a sail," remarked the captain, "We might try my overcoat on the end of an oar and give you two boys a chance to rest." So the cook and the correspondent held the mast and spread wide the overcoat. The oiler steered, and the little boat made good way with her new rig. Sometimes the oiler had to scull sharply to keep a sea from breaking into the boat, but otherwise sailing was a success.

Meanwhile the lighthouse had been growing slowly larger. It had now almost assumed color, and appeared like a little grey shadow on the sky. The man at the oars could not be prevented from turning his head rather often to try for a glimpse of this little grey shadow.

At last, from the top of each wave the men in the tossing boat could see land. Even as the lighthouse was an upright shadow on the sky, this land seemed but a long black shadow on the sea. It certainly was thinner than paper. "We must be about opposite New Smyrna," said the cook, who had coasted this shore often in schooners. "Captain, by the way, I believe they abandoned that life-saving station there about a year ago."

"Did they?" said the captain.

The wind slowly died away. The cook and the correspondent were not now obliged to slave in order to hold high the oar. But the waves continued their old impetuous swooping at the dinghy, and the little craft, no longer under way, struggled woundily over them. The oiler or the correspondent took the oars again.

Shipwrecks are *à propos* of nothing. If men could only train for them and have them occur when the men had reached pink condition, there would be less drowning at sea. Of the four in the dinghy none had slept any time worth mentioning for two days and two nights previous to embarking in the dinghy, and in the excitement of clambering about the deck of a foundering ship they had also forgotten to eat heartily.

For these reasons, and for others, neither the oiler nor the correspondent was fond of rowing at this time. The correspondent wondered ingenuously how in the name of all that was sane could there be people who thought it amusing to row a boat. It was not an amusement; it was a diabolical punishment, and even a genius of mental aberrations could never conclude that it was anything but a horror to the muscles and a crime against the back. He mentioned to the boat in general how the amusement of rowing struck him, and the weary-faced oiler smiled in full sympathy. Previously to the foundering, by the way, the oiler had worked double-watch in the engine-room of the ship.

"Take her easy, now, boys," said the captain. "Don't spend yourselves. If we have to run a surf you'll need all your strength, because we'll sure have to swim for it. Take your time."

Slowly the land arose from the sea. From a black line it became a line of black and a line of white, trees and sand. Finally, the captain said that he could make out a house on the shore. "That's the house of refuge, sure," said the cook. "They'll see us before long, and come out after us."

The distant lighthouse reared high. "The keeper ought to be able to make us out now, if he's looking through a glass," said the captain. "He'll notify the life-saving people."

"None of those other boats could have got ashore to give word of the wreck," said the oiler, in a low voice. "Else the lifeboat would be out hunting us."

Slowly and beautifully the land loomed out of the sea. The wind came again. It had veered from the north-east to the south-east. Finally, a new sound struck the ears of the men in the boat. It was the low thunder of the surf on the shore. "We'll never be able to make the lighthouse now," said the captain. "Swing her head a little more north, Billie," said he.

"A little more north,' sir," said the oiler.

Whereupon the little boat turned her nose once more down the wind, and all but the oarsman watched the shore grow. Under the influence of this expansion doubt and direful apprehension was leaving the minds of the men. The management of the boat was still most absorbing, but it could not prevent a quiet cheerfulness. In an hour, perhaps, they would be ashore.

Their backbones had become thoroughly used to balancing in the boat, and they now rode this wild colt of a dinghy like circus men. The correspondent thought that he had been drenched to the skin, but happening to feel in the top pocket of his coat, he found therein eight cigars. Four of them were soaked with sea-water; four were perfectly scathless. After a search, somebody produced three dry matches, and thereupon the four waifs rode impudently in their little boat, and with an assurance of an impending rescue shining in their eyes, puffed at the big cigars and judged well and ill of all men. Everybody took a drink of water.

4

"Cook," remarked the captain, "there don't seem to be any signs of life about your house of refuge."

"No," replied the cook. "Funny they don't see us!"

A broad stretch of lowly coast lay before the eyes of the men. It was of dunes topped with dark vegetation. The roar of the surf was plain, and sometimes they could see the white lip of a wave as it spun up the beach. A tiny house was blocked out black upon the sky. Southward, the slim lighthouse lifted its little grey length.

Tide, wind, and waves were swinging the dinghy northward. "Funny they don't see us," said the men.

The surf's roar was here dulled, but its tone was, nevertheless, thunderous and mighty. As the boat swam over the great rollers, the men sat listening to this roar. "We'll swamp sure," said everybody.

It is fair to say here that there was not a life-saving station within twenty miles in either direction, but the men did not know this fact, and in consequence they made dark and opprobrious remarks concerning the eyesight of the nation's life-savers. Four scowling men sat in the dinghy and surpassed records in the invention of epithets.

"Funny they don't see us."

The lightheartedness of a former time had completely faded. To their sharpened minds it was easy to conjure pictures of all kinds of incompetency and blindness and, indeed, cowardice. There was the shore of the populous land, and it was bitter and bitter to them that from it came no sign.

"Well," said the captain, ultimately, "I suppose we'll have to make a try for ourselves. If we stay out here too long, we'll none of us have strength left to swim after the boat swamps."

And so the oiler, who was at the oars, turned the boat straight for the shore. There was a sudden tightening of muscle. There was some thinking.

"If we don't all get ashore—" said the captain. "If we don't all get ashore, I suppose you fellows know where to send news of my finish?"

They then briefly exchanged some addresses and admonitions. As for the reflections of the men, there was a great deal of rage in them. Perchance they might be formulated thus: "If I am going to be drowned—if I am going to be drowned—if I am going to be drowned, why in the name of the seven mad gods who rule the sea, was I allowed to come thus far and contemplate sand and trees? Was I brought here merely to have my nose dragged away as I was about to nibble the sacred cheese of life? It is preposterous. If this old ninny-woman, Fate, cannot do better than this, she should be deprived of the management of men's fortunes. She is an old hen who knows not her intention. If she has decided to drown me, why did she not do it in the beginning and save me all this trouble? The whole affair is absurd. . . . But no, she cannot mean to drown me. She dare not drown me. She cannot drown me. Not after all this work." Afterward the man might have had an impulse to shake his fist at the clouds: "Just you drown me, now, and then hear what I call you!"

The billows that came at this time were more formidable. They seemed always just about to break and roll over the little boat in a turmoil of foam. There was a preparatory and long growl in the speech of them. No mind unused to the sea would have concluded that the dinghy could ascend these sheer heights in time. The shore was still afar. The oiler was a wily surfman. "Boys," he said swiftly, "she won't live three minutes more, and we're too far out to swim. Shall I take her to sea again, captain?"

"Yes! Go ahead!" said the captain.

This oiler, by a series of quick miracles, and fast and steady oarsmanship, turned the boat in the middle of the surf and took her safely to sea again.

There was a considerable silence as the boat bumped over the furrowed sea to deeper water. Then somebody in gloom spoke. "Well, anyhow, they must have seen us from the shore by now."

The gulls went in slanting flight up the wind toward the grey desolate east. A squall, marked by dingy clouds, and clouds, brick-red, like smoke from a burning building, appeared from the south-east.

"What do you think of those life-saving people? Ain't they peaches?"

"Funny they haven't seen us."

"Maybe they think we're out here for sport! Maybe they think we're fishin'. Maybe they think we're damned fools."

It was a long afternoon. A changed tide tried to force them southward, but the wind and wave said northward. Far ahead, where coast-line, sea, and sky formed their mighty angle, there were little dots which seemed to indicate a city on the shore.

"St. Augustine?"

The captain shook his head. "Too near Mosquito Inlet."

And the oiler rowed, and then the correspondent rowed. Then the oiler rowed. It was a weary business. The human back can become the seat of more aches and pains than are registered in books for the composite anatomy of a regiment. It is a limited area, but it can become the theatre of innumerable muscular conflicts, tangles, wrenches, knots, and other comforts.

"Did you ever like to row, Billie?" asked the correspondent.

"No," said the oiler. "Hang it!"

When one exchanged the rowing-seat for a place in the bottom of the boat, he suffered a bodily depression that caused him to be careless of everything save an obligation to wiggle one finger. There was cold sea-water swashing to and fro in the boat, and he lay in it. His head, pillowed on a thwart, was within an inch of the swirl of a wave crest, and sometimes a particularly obstreperous sea came in-board and drenched him once more. But these matters did not annoy him. It is almost certain that if the boat had capsized he would have tumbled comfortably out upon the ocean as if he felt sure that it was a great soft mattress.

"Look! There's a man on the shore!"

"Where?"

"There! See 'im? See 'im?"

"Yes, sure! He's walking along."

"Now he's stopped. Look! He's facing us!"

"He's waving at us!"

"So he is! By thunder!"

"Ah, now we're all right! Now we're all right! There'll be a boat out here for us in half-an-hour.

"He's going on. He's running. He's going up to that house there."

The remote beach seemed lower than the sea, and it required a searching glance to discern the little black figure. The captain saw a floating stick and they rowed to it. A bath-towel was by some weird chance in the boat, and, tying this on the stick, the captain waved it. The oarsman did not dare turn his head, so he was obliged to ask questions.

"What's he doing now?"

"He's standing still again. He's looking, I think. . . . There he goes again. Toward the house. . . . Now he's stopped again."

"Is he waving at us?"

"No, not now! He was, though."

"Look! There comes another man!"

"He's running."

"Look at him go, would you."

"Why, he's on a bicycle. Now he's met the other man. They're both waving at us. Look!"

"There comes something up the beach."

"What the devil is that thing?"

"Why it looks like a boat."

"Why, certainly it's a boat."

"No, it's on wheels."

"Yes, so it is. Well, that must be the life-boat. They drag them along shore on a wagon."

"That's the life-boat, sure."

"No, by———, it's—it's an omnibus."

"I tell you it's a life-boat."

"It is not! It's an omnibus. I can see it plain. See? One of these big hotel omnibuses."

"By thunder, you're right. It's an omnibus, sure as fate. What do you suppose they are doing with an omnibus? Maybe they are going around collecting the life-crew, hey?"

"That's it, likely. Look! There's a fellow waving a little black flag. He's standing on the steps of the omnibus. There come those other two fellows. Now they're all talking together. Look at the fellow with the flag. Maybe he ain't waving it."

"That ain't a flag, is it? That's his coat. Why, certainly, that's his coat."

"So it is. It's his coat. He's taken it off and is waving it around his head. But would you look at him swing it."

"Oh, say, there isn't any life-saving station there. That's just a winter resort hotel omnibus that has brought over some of the boarders to see us drown."

"What's that idiot with the coat mean? What's he signaling, anyhow?"

"It looks as if he were trying to tell us to go north. There must be a life-saving station up there."

"No! He thinks we're fishing. Just giving us a merry hand. See? Ah, there, Willie!"

"Well, I wish I could make something out of those signals. What do you suppose he means?"

"He don't mean anything. He's just playing."

"Well, if he'd just signal us to try the surf again, or to go to sea and wait, or go north, or go south, or go to hell—there would be some reason in it. But look at him. He just stands there and keeps his coat revolving like a wheel. The ass!"

"There come more people."

"Now there's quite a mob. Look! Isn't that a boat?"

"Where? Oh, I see where you mean. No, that's no boat."

"That fellow is still waving his coat."

"He must think we like to see him do that. Why don't he quit it? It don't mean anything."

"I don't know. I think he is trying to make us go north. It must be that there's a life-saving station there somewhere."

"Say, he ain't tired yet. Look at 'im wave."

"Wonder how long he can keep that up. He's been revolving his coat ever since he caught sight of us. He's an idiot. Why aren't they getting men to bring a boat out? A fishing boat—one of those big yawls—could come out here all right. Why don't he do something?"

"Oh, it's all right, now."

"They'll have a boat out here for us in less than no time, now that they've seen us."

A faint yellow tone came into the sky over the low land. The shadows on the sea slowly deepened. The wind bore coldness with it, and the men began to shiver.

"Holy smoke!" said one, allowing his voice to express his impious mood, "if we keep on monkeying out here! If we've got to flounder out here all night!"

"Oh, we'll never have to stay here all night! Don't you worry. They've seen us now, and it won't be long before they'll come chasing out after us."

The shore grew dusky. The man waving a coat blended gradually into this gloom, and it swallowed in the same manner the omnibus and the group of people. The spray, when it dashed uproariously over the side, made the voyagers shrink and swear like men who were being branded.

"I'd like to catch the chump who waved the coat. I feel like soaking him one, just for luck."

"Why? What did he do?"

"Oh, nothing, but then he seemed so damned cheerful."

In the meantime the oiler rowed, and then the correspondent rowed, and then the oiler rowed. Grey-faced and bowed forward, they mechanically, turn by turn, plied the leaden oars. The form of the lighthouse had vanished from the southern horizon, but finally a pale star appeared, just lifting from the sea. The streaked saffron in the west passed before the all-merging darkness, and the sea to the east was black. The land had vanished, and was expressed only by the low and drear thunder of the surf.

"If I am going to be drowned—if I am going to be drowned—if I am going to be drowned, why, in the name of the seven mad gods who rule the sea, was I allowed to come thus far and contemplate sand and trees? Was I brought here merely to have my nose dragged away as I was about to nibble the sacred cheese of life?"

The patient captain, drooped over the water-jar, was sometimes obliged to speak to the oarsman.

"Keep her head up! Keep her head up!"

"Keep her head up, sir." The voices were weary and low.

This was surely a quiet evening. All save the oarsman lay heavily and listlessly in the boat's bottom. As for him, his eyes were just capable of noting the tall black waves that swept forward in a most sinister silence, save for an occasional subdued growl of a crest.

The cook's head was on a thwart, and he looked without interest at the water under his nose. He was deep in other scenes. Finally he spoke. "Billie," he murmured, dreamfully, "what kind of pie do you like best?"

5

"Pie," said the oiler and the correspondent, agitatedly. "Don't talk about those things, blast you!"

"Well," said the cook, "I was just thinking about ham sandwiches and—"

A night on the sea in an open boat is a long night. As darkness settled finally, the shine of the light, lifting from the sea in the south, changed to full gold. On the northern horizon a new light appeared, a small bluish gleam on the edge of the waters. These two lights were the furniture of the world. Otherwise there was nothing but waves.

Two men huddled in the stern, and distances were so magnificent in the dinghy that the rower was enabled to keep his feet partly warmed by thrusting them under his companions. Their legs indeed extended far under the rowing-seat until they touched the feet of the captain forward. Sometimes, despite the efforts of the tired oarsman, a wave came piling into the boat, an icy wave of the night, and the chilling water soaked them anew. They would twist their bodies for a moment and groan, and sleep the dead sleep once more, while the water in the boat gurgled about them as the craft rocked.

The plan of the oiler and the correspondent was for one to row until he lost the ability, and then arouse the other from his sea-water couch in the bottom of the boat.

The oiler plied the oars until his head drooped forward, and the overpowering sleep blinded him. And he rowed yet afterward. Then he touched a man in the bottom of the boat, and called his name. "Will you spell me for a little while?" he said, meekly.

"Sure, Billie," said the correspondent, awakening and dragging himself to a sitting position. They exchanged places carefully, and the oiler, cuddling down in the sea-water at the cook's side, seemed to go to sleep instantly.

The particular violence of the sea had ceased. The waves came without snarling. The obligation of the man at the oars was to keep the boat headed so that the tilt of the rollers would not capsize her, and to preserve her from filling when the crests rushed past. The black waves were silent and hard to be seen in the darkness. Often one was almost upon the boat before the oarsman was aware.

In a low voice the correspondent addressed the captain. He was not sure that the captain was awake, although this iron man seemed to be always awake. "Captain, shall I keep her making for that light north, sir?"

The same steady voice answered him. "Yes. Keep it about two points off the port bow."

The cook had tied a life-belt around himself in order to get even the warmth which this clumsy cork contrivance could donate, and he seemed almost stove-like when a rower, whose teeth invariably chattered wildly as soon as he ceased his labor, dropped down to sleep.

The correspondent, as he rowed, looked down at the two men sleeping under-foot. The cook's arm was around the oiler's shoulders, and, with their fragmentary clothing and haggard faces, they were the babes of the sea, a grotesque rendering of the old babes in the wood.

Later he must have grown stupid at his work, for suddenly there was a growling of water, and a crest came with a roar and a swash into the boat, and it was a wonder that it did not set the cook afloat in his life-belt. The cook continued to sleep, but the oiler sat up, blinking his eyes and shaking with the new cold.

"Oh, I'm awful sorry, Billie," said the correspondent contritely.

"That's all right, old boy," said the oiler, and lay down again and was asleep.

Presently it seemed that even the captain dozed, and the correspondent thought that he was the one man afloat on all the oceans. The wind had a voice as it came over the waves, and it was sadder than the end.

There was a long, loud swishing astern of the boat, and a gleaming trail of phosphorescence, like blue flame, was furrowed on the black waters. It might have been made by a monstrous knife.

Then there came a stillness, while the correspondent breathed with open mouth and looked at the sea.

Suddenly there was another swish and another long flash of bluish light, and this time it was alongside the boat, and might almost have been reached with an oar. The correspondent saw an enormous fin speed like a shadow through the water, hurling the crystalline spray and leaving the long glowing trail.

The correspondent looked over his shoulder at the captain. His face was hidden, and he seemed to be asleep. He looked at the babes of the sea. They certainly were asleep. So, being bereft of sympathy, he leaned a little way to one side and swore softly in to the sea.

But the thing did not then leave the vicinity of the boat. Ahead or astern, on one side or the other, at intervals long or short, fled the long sparkling streak, and there was to be heard the whirroo of the dark fin. The speed and power of the thing was greatly to be admired. It cut the water like a gigantic and keen projectile.

The presence of this biding thing did not affect the man with the same horror that it would if he had been a picnicker. He simply looked at the sea dully and swore in an undertone.

Nevertheless, it is true that he did not wish to be alone, He wished one of his companions to awaken by chance and keep him company with it. But the captain hung motionless over the water-jar, and the oiler and the cook in the bottom of the boat were plunged in slumber.

6

"If I am going to be drowned—if I am going to be drowned—if I am going to be drowned, why, in the name of the seven mad gods who rule the sea, was I allowed to come thus far and contemplate sand and trees?"

During this dismal night, it may be remarked that a man would conclude that it was really the intention of the seven mad gods to drown him, despite the abominable injustice of it. For it was certainly an abominable injustice to drown a man who had worked so hard, so hard. The man felt it would be a crime most unnatural. Other people had drowned at sea since galleys swarmed with painted sails, but still—

When it occurs to a man that nature does not regard hum as important, and that she feels she would not maim the universe by disposing of him, he at first wishes to throw bricks at the temple, and he hates deeply the fact that there are no brick and no temples. Any visible expression of nature would surely be pelleted with his jeers.

Then, if there be no tangible thing to hoot he feels, perhaps, the desire to confront a personification and indulge in pleas, bowed to one knee, and with hands supplicant, saying: "Yes, but I love myself."

A high cold star on a winter's night is the word he feels that she says to him. Thereafter he knows the pathos of his situation.

The men in the dinghy had not discussed these matters, but each had, no doubt, reflected upon them in silence and according to his mind. There was seldom any expression upon their faces save the general one of complete weariness. Speech was devoted to the business of the boat.

To chime the notes of his emotion, a verse mysteriously entered the correspondent's head. He had even forgotten that he had forgotten this verse, but it suddenly was in his mind.

"A soldier of the Legion lay dying in Algiers.
There was a lack of woman's nursing, there was dearth of woman's tears;
But a comrade stood beside him, and he took that comrade's hand,
And he said: 'I shall never see my own, my native land.'"

In his childhood, the correspondent had been made acquainted with the fact that a soldier of the Legion lay dying in Algiers, but he had never regarded the fact as important. Myriads of his school-fellows had informed him of the soldier's plight, but the dinning had naturally ended by making him perfectly indifferent. He had never considered it his affair that a soldier of the Legion lay dying in Algiers, nor had it appeared to him as a matter for sorrow. It was less to him than the breaking of a pencil's point.

Now, however, it quaintly came to him as a human, living thing. It was no longer merely a picture of a few throes in the breast of a poet, meanwhile drinking tea and warming his feet at the grate; it was an actuality—stern, mournful, and fine.

The correspondent plainly saw the soldier. He lay on the sand with his feet out straight and still. While his pale left hand was upon his chest in an attempt to thwart the going of life, the blood came between his fingers. In the far Algerian distance, a city of low square forms was set against a sky that was faint with the last sunset hues. The correspondent, plying the oars and dreaming of the slow and slower movements of the lips of the soldier, was moved by a profound and perfectly impersonal comprehension. He was sorry for the soldier of the Legion who lay dying in Algiers.

The thing which had followed the boat and waited had evidently grown bored at the delay. There was no longer to be heard the slash of the cut-water, and there was no longer the flame of the long trail. The light in the north still glimmered, but it was apparently no nearer to the boat. Sometimes the boom of the surf rang in the correspondent's ears, and he turned the craft seaward then and rowed harder. Southward, some one had evidently built a watch-fire on the beach. It was too low and too far to be seen, but it made a shimmering, roseate reflection upon the bluff back of it, and this could be discerned from the boat. The wind came stronger, and sometimes a wave suddenly raged out like a mountain-cat, and there was to be seen the sheen and sparkle of a broken crest.

The captain, in the bow, moved on his water-jar and sat erect. "Pretty long night," he observed to the correspondent. He looked at the shore, "Those life-saving people take their time."

"Did you see that shark playing around?"

"Yes, I saw him. He was a big fellow, all right."

"Wish I had known you were awake."

Later the correspondent spoke into the bottom of the boat.

"Billie!" There was a slow and gradual disentanglement. "Billie, will you spell me?" "Sure," said the oiler.

As soon as the correspondent touched the cold comfortable sea-water in the bottom of the boat, and had huddled close to the cook's lifebelt he was deep in sleep, despite the fact that his teeth played all the popular airs. This sleep was so good to him that it was but a moment before he heard a voice call his name in a tone that demonstrated the last stages of exhaustion. "Will you spell me?"

"Sure, Billie."

The light in the north had mysteriously vanished, but the correspondent took his course from the wide-awake captain.

Later in the night they took the boat further out to sea, and the captain directed the cook to take one oar at the stern and keep the boat facing the seas. He was to call out if he should hear the thunder of the surf. This plan enabled the oiler and the correspondent to get respite together. "We'll give those boys a chance to get into shape again," said the captain. They curled down and, after a few preliminary chatterings and trembles, slept once more the dead sleep. Neither knew they had bequeathed to the cook the company of another shark, or perhaps the same shark.

As the boat caroused on the waves, spray occasionally bumped over the side and gave them a fresh soaking, but this had no power to break their repose. The ominous slash of the wind and the water affected them as it would have affected mummies.

"Boys," said the cook, with the notes of every reluctance in his voice, "she's drifted in pretty close. I guess one of you had better take her to sea again." The correspondent, aroused, heard the crash of the toppled crests.

As he was rowing, the captain gave him some whisky-and-water, and this steadied the chills out of him. "If I ever get ashore and anybody shows me even a photograph of an oar—"

At last there was a short conversation.

"Billie. . . . Billie, will you spell me?"

"Sure," said the oiler.

7

When the correspondent again opened his eyes, the sea and the sky were each of the grey hue of the dawning. Later, carmine and gold was painted upon the waters. The morning appeared finally, in its splendor, with a sky of pure blue, and the sunlight flamed on the tips of the waves.

On the distant dunes were set many little black cottages, and a tall white windmill reared above them. No man, nor dog, nor bicycle appeared on the beach. The cottages might have formed a deserted village.

The voyagers scanned the shore. A conference was held in the boat. "Well," said the captain, "if no help is coming we might better try a run through the surf right away. If we stay out here much longer we will be too weak to do anything for ourselves at all." The others silently acquiesced in this reasoning. The boat was headed for the beach. The correspondent wondered if none ever ascended the tall wind-tower, and if then they never looked seaward. This tower was a giant, standing with its back to the plight of the ants. It represented in a degree, to the correspondent, the serenity of nature amid the struggles of the individual—nature in the wind, and nature in the vision of men. She did not seem cruel to him then, nor beneficent, nor treacherous, nor wise. But she was indifferent, flatly indifferent. It is, perhaps, plausible that a man in this situation, impressed with the unconcern of the universe, should see the innumerable flaws of his life, and have them taste wickedly in his mind and wish for another chance. A distinction between right and wrong seems absurdly clear to him, then, in this new ignorance of the grave-edge, and he understands that if he were given another opportunity he would mend his conduct and his words, and be better and brighter during an introduction or at a tea.

"Now, boys," said the captain, "she is going to swamp, sure. All we can do is to work her in as far as possible, and then when she swamps, pile out and scramble for the beach. Keep cool now, and don't jump until she swamps sure."

The oiler took the oars. Over his shoulders he scanned the surf. "Captain," he said, "I think I'd better bring her about, and keep her head-on to the seas and back her in."

"All right, Billie," said the captain. "Back her in." The oiler swung the boat then and, seated in the stern, the cook and the correspondent were obliged to look over their shoulders to contemplate the lonely and indifferent shore.

The monstrous in-shore rollers heaved the boat high until the men were again enabled to see the white sheets of water scudding up the slanted beach. "We won't get in very close," said the captain. Each time a man could wrest his attention from the rollers, he turned his glance toward the shore, and in the expression of the eyes during this contemplation there was a singular quality. The correspondent, observing the others, knew that they were not afraid, but the full meaning of their glances was shrouded.

As for himself, he was too tired to grapple fundamentally with the fact. He tried to coerce his mind into thinking of it, but the mind was dominated at this time by the muscles, and the muscles said they did not care. It merely occurred to him that if he should drown it would be a shame.

There were no hurried words, no pallor, no plain agitation. The men simply looked at the shore. "Now, remember to get well clear of the boat when you jump," said the captain.

Seaward the crest of a roller suddenly fell with a thunderous crash, and the long white comber came roaring down upon the boat.

"Steady now," said the captain. The men were silent. They turned their eyes from the shore to the comber and waited. The boat slid up the incline, leaped at the furious top, bounced over it, and swung down the long back of the wave. Some water had been shipped and the cook bailed it out.

But the next crest crashed also. The tumbling, boiling flood of white water caught the boat and whirled it almost perpendicular. Water swarmed in from all sides. The correspondent had his hands on the gunwale at this time, and when the water entered at that place he swiftly withdrew his fingers, as if he objected to wetting them.

The little boat, drunken with this weight of water, reeled and snuggled deeper into the sea.

"Bail her out, cook! Bail her out," said the captain.

"All right, captain," said the cook.

"Now, boys, the next one will do for us, sure," said the oiler. "Mind to jump clear of the boat."

The third wave moved forward, huge, furious, implacable. It fairly swallowed the dinghy, and almost simultaneously the men tumbled into the sea. A piece of lifebelt had lain in the bottom of the boat, and as the correspondent went overboard he held this to his chest with his left hand.

The January water was icy, and he reflected immediately that it was colder than he had expected to find it on the coast of Florida. This appeared to his dazed mind as a fact important enough to be noted at the time. The coldness of the water was sad; it was tragic. This fact was somehow so mixed and confused with his opinion of his own situation that it seemed almost a proper reason for tears. The water was cold.

When he came to the surface he was conscious of little but the noisy water. Afterward he saw his companions in the sea. The oiler was ahead in the race. He was swimming strongly and rapidly. Off to the correspondent's left, the cook's great white and corked back bulged out of the water, and in the rear the captain was hanging with his one good hand to the keel of the overturned dinghy.

There is a certain immovable quality to a shore, and the correspondent wondered at it amid the confusion of the sea.

It seemed also very attractive, but the correspondent knew that it was a long journey, and he paddled leisurely. The piece of life-preserver lay under him, and sometimes he whirled down the incline of a wave as if he were on a hand-sled.

But finally he arrived at a place in the sea where travel was beset with difficulty. He did not pause swimming to inquire what manner of current had caught him, but there his progress ceased. The shore was set before him like a bit of scenery on a stage, and he looked at it and understood with his eyes each detail of it.

As the cook passed, much further to the left, the captain was calling to him, "Turn over on your back, cook! Turn over on your back and use the oar."

"All right, sir." The cook turned on his back, and, paddling with an oar, went ahead as if he were a canoe.

Presently the boat also passed to the left of the correspondent with the captain clinging with one hand to the keel. He would have appeared like a man raising himself to look over a board fence, if it were not for the extraordinary gymnastics of the boat. The correspondent marvelled that the captain could still hold to it.

They passed on, nearer to shore—the oiler, the cook, the captain—and following them went the water-jar, bouncing gaily over the seas.

The correspondent remained in the grip of this strange new enemy—a current. The shore, with its white slope of sand and its green bluff, topped with little silent cottages, was spread like a picture before him. It was very near to him then, but he was impressed as one who in a gallery looks at a scene from Brittany or Holland.

He thought: "I am going to drown? Can it be possible? Can it be possible? Can it be possible?" Perhaps an individual must consider his own death to be the final phenomenon of nature.

But later a wave perhaps whirled him out of this small, deadly current, for he found suddenly that he could again make progress toward the shore. Later still, he was aware that the captain, clinging with one hand to the keel of the dinghy, had his face turned away from the shore and toward him, and was calling his name. "Come to the boat! Come to the boat!"

In his struggle to reach the captain and the boat, he reflected that when one gets properly wearied, drowning must really be a comfortable arrangement, a cessation of hostilities accompanied by a large degree of relief, and he was glad of it, for the main thing in his mind for some moments had been horror of the temporary agony. He did not wish to be hurt.

Presently he saw a man running along the shore. He was undressing with most remarkable speed. Coat, trousers, shirt, everything flew magically off him.

"Come to the boat," called the captain.

"All right, captain." As the correspondent paddled, he saw the captain let himself down to bottom and leave the boat. Then the correspondent performed his one little marvel of the voyage. A large wave caught him and flung him with ease and supreme speed completely over the boat and far beyond it. It struck him even then as an event in gymnastics, and a true miracle of the sea. An over-turned boat in the surf is not a plaything to a swimming man.

The correspondent arrived in water that reached only to his waist, but his condition did not enable him to stand for more than a moment. Each wave knocked him into a heap, and the under-tow pulled at him.

Then he saw the man who had been running and undressing, and undressing and running, come bounding into the water. He dragged ashore the cook, and then waded towards the captain, but the captain waved him away, and sent him to the correspondent. He was naked, naked as a tree in winter, but a halo was about his head, and he shone like a saint. He gave a strong pull, and a long drag, and a bully heave at the correspondent's hand. The correspondent, schooled in the minor formulæ, said: "Thanks, old man." But suddenly the man cried: "What's that?" He pointed a swift finger. The correspondent said: "Go."

In the shallows, face downward, lay the oiler. His forehead touched sand that was periodically, between each wave, clear of the sea.

The correspondent did not know all that transpired afterward. When he achieved safe ground he fell, striking the sand with each particular part of his body. It was as if he had dropped from a roof, but the thud was grateful to him.

It seems that instantly the beach was populated with men with blankets, clothes, and flasks, and women with coffeepots and all the remedies sacred to their minds. The welcome of the land to the men from the sea was warm and generous, but a still and dripping shape was carried slowly up the beach, and the land's welcome for it could only be the different and sinister hospitality of the grave.

When it came night, the white waves paced to and fro in the moonlight, and the wind brought the sound of the great sea's voice to the men on shore, and they felt that they could then be interpreters.

Part Three

The Golden Age

Thomas Mann (1875–1955)

Thomas Mann has been compared with Marcel Proust and James Joyce in literary achievement and influence. He is one of the towering intellects of the modern age. His interests range from the Bible to twelve-tone music, from medicine to mythology, from artistic consciousness to fascism, from history to science to psychoanalysis. His writing displays a prodigious scholarship.

For Mann, mental aberration and genius lie close together; often, he seemed to believe, the artistic urge is based on an affinity with death. In *The Magic Mountain* (1926), for which Mann received the Nobel Prize for Literature in 1929, these themes are explored with subtlety and drama. Hans Castorp, a young bourgeois, visits his cousin at a tuberculosis sanitarium and—seduced by the heightened sentience and sensuality of the diseased—stays seven years. He becomes the battleground of opposing intellectual and artistic forces of various people at the sanitarium. Finally, when World War I breaks out, he leaves the mountain; but he is no longer the stolid bourgeois: through his experience he has achieved a new sensibility and a complex fulfillment.

In *Joseph and His Brothers,* a tetralogy which occupied Mann from 1926 to 1943, the themes are further developed through use of biblical stories. Mann sees

Joseph as both the genius with the power to interpret dreams and a practical man who saves his family.

Although in his early work Mann seemed to accept the authoritarian aspect of German culture, he was intensely anti-Nazi and became a self-exile in 1933. In 1948, *Doctor Faustus* appeared. It is a modern version of the Faust legend: Adrian Leverkühn, a composer, bargains away to the Devil his capacity for human love in exchange for genius. Although primarily an embodiment of Mann's views of the connection between the creativity and the destructiveness of genius, Leverkühn symbolizes the demonic forces in German life.

The English translations of his short stories were collected as *Stories of Three Decades* (1935), which contains the three great novellas as well: *Tonio Kröger, Death in Venice, Mario and the Magician.* The themes of the novels pervade the shorter work. For instance, Johannes, the title character of "Little Herr Friedemann," like Mann the son of an upper-middle-class bourgeois family, is deformed for life as a result of an injury when a baby. He builds an orderly existence for himself, rejects the hope for romantic love, and cultivates the aesthetic side of life. When his mother dies, "He cherished this grief, he gave himself up to it as one gives oneself to a great joy. . . ." He accepts his loneliness, his difference. But when he misinterprets the intentions of a new lady in town, and then is humiliated, he "feels a disgust, perhaps of himself, which filled him with a thirst to destroy himself. . . ."

Mann's was not essentially a short-story skill. He insisted upon the full complexity of scenes and situations which interested him. It is not enough for the reader to know that Johannes is deformed: Mann tells us that the nurse who dropped him had been drinking methylated spirit. The complexity often has a strong intellectual aspect, for Mann was a believer in the power of ideas and theories to shape human behavior. Thus, in discussing the development of Johannes' aesthetic proclivities, he writes, "And that we need to be taught how to enjoy, yes, that our education is always and only equal to our capacity for enjoyment—he knew that too, and he trained himself."

One must not be satisfied with the surface of the drama in a work by Thomas Mann. The reader will find beneath the surface the play of a complex idea, perhaps an esoteric theory, a myth clothed in modern dress, a philosophic argument.

Mann was born in Lübeck, Germany, in the year 1875 and died in Zürich in 1955.

Little Herr Friedemann

It was the nurse's fault. When they first suspected, Frau Consul Friedemann had spoken to her very gravely about the need of controlling her weakness. But what good did that do? Or the glass of red wine which she got daily besides the beer which was needed for the milk? For they suddenly discovered that she even sank so low as to drink the methylated spirit which was kept for the spirit lamp. Before they could send her away and get someone to take her place, the mischief was done. One day the mother and sisters came home to find that little Johannes, then about a month old,

From *Stories of Three Decades*, by Thomas Mann, translated by H. T. Lowe-Porter. Copyright 1936 and renewed 1964 by Alfred A. Knopf, Inc. Reprinted by permission of the publisher.

had fallen from the couch and lay on the floor, uttering an appallingly faint little cry, while the nurse stood beside him quite stupefied.

The doctor came and with firm, gentle hands tested the little creature's contracted and twitching limbs. He made a very serious face. The three girls stood sobbing in a corner and the Frau Consul in the anguish of her heart prayed aloud.

The poor mother, just before the child's birth, had already suffered a crushing blow: her husband, the Dutch Consul, had been snatched away from her by sudden and violent illness, and now she was too broken to cherish any hope that little Johannes would be spared to her. But by the second day the doctor had given her hand an encouraging squeeze and told her that all immediate danger was over. There was no longer any sign that the brain was affected. The facial expression was altered, it had lost the fixed and staring look. . . . Of course, they must see how things went on—and hope for the best, hope for the best.

The grey gabled house in which Johannes Friedemann grew up stood by the north gate of the little old commercial city. The front door led into a large flag-paved entry, out of which a stair with a white wooden balustrade led up into the second storey. The faded wall-paper in the living-room had a landscape pattern, and straight-backed chairs and sofas in dark-red plush stood round the heavy mahogany table.

Often in his childhood Johannes sat here at the window, which always had a fine showing of flowers, on a small footstool at his mother's feet, listening to some fairy-tale she told him, gazing at her smooth grey head, her mild and gentle face, and breathing in the faint scent she exhaled. She showed him the picture of his father, a kindly man with grey side-whiskers—he was now in heaven, she said, and awaiting them there.

Behind the house was a small garden where in summer they spent much of their time, despite the smell of burnt sugar which came over from the refinery close by. There was a gnarled old walnut tree in whose shade little Johannes would sit, on a low wooden stool, cracking walnuts, while Frau Friedemann and her three daughters, now grown women, took refuge from the sun under a grey canvas tent. The mother's gaze often strayed from her embroidery to look with sad and loving eyes at her child.

He was not beautiful, little Johannes, as he crouched on his stool industriously cracking his nuts. In fact, he was a strange sight, with his pigeon breast, humped back, and disproportionately long arms. But his hands and feet were delicately formed, he had soft red-brown eyes like a doe's, a sensitive mouth, and fine, light-brown hair. His head, had it not sat so deep between his shoulders, might almost have been called pretty.

When he was seven he went to school, where time passed swiftly and uniformly. He walked every day, with the strut deformed people often have, past the quaint gabled houses and shops to the old schoolhouse with the vaulted arcades. When he had done his preparation he would read in his books with the lovely title-page illustrations in colour, or else work in the garden, while his sisters kept house for their invalid mother. They went out too, for they belonged to the best society of the town; but unfortunately they had not married, for they had not much money nor any looks to recommend them.

Johannes too was now and then invited out by his schoolmates, but it is not likely that he enjoyed it. He could not take part in their games, and they were always embarrassed in his company, so there was no feeling of good fellowship.

There came a time when he began to hear certain matters talked about, in the courtyard at school. He listened wide-eyed and large-eared, quite silent, to his companions' raving over this or that little girl. Such things, though they entirely engrossed the attention of these others, were not, he felt, for him; they belonged in the same category as the ball games and gymnastics. At times he felt a little sad. But at length he had become quite used to standing on one side and not taking part.

But after all it came about—when he was sixteen—that he felt suddenly drawn to a girl of his own age. She was the sister of a classmate of his, a blonde, hilarious hoyden, and he met her when calling at her brother's house. He felt strangely embarrassed in her neighbourhood; she too was embarrassed and treated him with such artificial cordiality that it made him sad.

One summer afternoon as he was walking by himself on the wall outside the town, he heard a whispering behind a jasmine bush and peeped cautiously through the branches. There she sat on a bench beside a long-legged, red-haired youth of his acquaintance. They had their arms about each other and he was imprinting on her lips a kiss, which she returned amid giggles. Johannes looked, turned round, and went softly away.

His head was sunk deeper than ever between his shoulders, his hands trembled, and a sharp pain shot upwards from his chest to his throat. But he choked it down, straightening himself as well as he could. "Good," said he to himself. "That is over. Never again will I let myself in for any of it. To the others it brings joy and happiness, for me it can only mean sadness and pain. I am done with it. For me that is all over. Never again."

The resolution did him good. He had renounced, renounced forever. He went home, took up a book, or else played on his violin, which despite his deformed chest he had learned to do.

At seventeen Johannes left school to go into business, like everybody else he knew. He was apprenticed to the big lumber firm of Herr Schlievogt down on the river-bank. They were kind and considerate, he on his side was responsive and friendly, time passed with peaceful regularity. But in his twenty-first year his mother died, after a lingering illness.

This was a sore blow for Johannes Friedemann, and the pain of it endured. He cherished this grief, he gave himself up to it as one gives oneself to a great joy, he fed it with a thousand childhood memories; it was the first important event in his life and he made the most of it.

Is not life in and for itself a good, regardless of whether we may call its content "happiness"? Johannes Friedemann felt that it was so, and he loved life. He, who had renounced the greatest joy it can bring us, taught himself with infinite, incredible care to take pleasure in what it had still to offer. A walk in the springtime in the parks surrounding the town; the fragrance of a flower; the song of a bird—might not one feel grateful for such things as these?

And that we need to be taught how to enjoy, yes, that our education is always and only equal to our capacity for enjoyment—he knew that too, and he trained himself. Music he loved, and attended all the concerts that were given in the town. He came to play the violin not so badly himself, no matter what a figure of fun he made when he did it; and took delight in every beautiful soft tone he succeeded in producing. Also, by much reading he came in time to possess a literary taste the like of which did not exist in the place. He kept up with the new books, even the foreign ones; he knew how to savour the seductive rhythm of a lyric or the ultimate flavour of a subtly told tale—yes, one might almost call him a connoisseur.

He learned to understand that to everything belongs its own enjoyment and that it is absurd to distinguish between an experience which is "happy" and one which is not. With a right good will he accepted each emotion as it came, each mood, whether sad or gay. Even he cherished the unfulfilled desires, the longings. He loved them for their own sakes and told himself that with fulfilment the best of them would be past. The vague, sweet, painful yearning and hope of quiet spring evenings—are they not richer in joy than all the fruition the summer can bring? Yes, he was a connoisseur, our little Herr Friedemann.

But of course they did not know that, the people whom he met on the street, who bowed to him with the kindly, compassionate air he knew so well. They could not know that this unhappy cripple, strutting comically along in his light overcoat and shiny top hat—strange to say, he was a little vain—they could not know how tenderly he loved the mild flow of his life, charged with no great emotions, it is true, but full of a quiet and tranquil happiness which was his own creation.

But Herr Friedemann's great preference, his real passion, was for the theatre. He possessed a dramatic sense which was unusually strong; at a telling theatrical effect or the catastrophe of a tragedy his whole small frame would shake with emotion. He had his regular seat in the first row of boxes at the opera-house; was an assiduous frequenter and often took his sisters with him. Since their mother's death they kept house for their brother in the old home which they all owned together.

It was a pity they were unmarried still; but with the decline of hope had come resignation—Friederike, the eldest, was seventeen years further on than Herr Friedemann. She and her sister Henriette were over-tall and thin, whereas Pfiffi, the youngest, was too short and stout. She had a funny way, too, of shaking herself as she talked, and water came in the corners of her mouth.

Little Herr Friedemann did not trouble himself overmuch about his three sisters. But they stuck together loyally and were always of one mind. Whenever an engagement was announced in their circle they with one voice said how very gratifying that was.

Their brother continued to live with them even after he became independent, as he did by leaving Herr Schlievogt's firm and going into business for himself, in an agency of sorts, which was no great tax on his time. His offices were in a couple of rooms on the ground floor of the house so that at mealtimes he had but the pair of stairs to mount—for he suffered now and then from asthma.

His thirtieth birthday fell on a fine warm June day, and after dinner he sat out in the grey canvas tent, with a new head-rest embroidered by Henriette. He had a good cigar in his mouth and a good book in his hand. But sometimes he would put the latter down to listen to the sparrows chirping blithely in the old nut tree and look at the clean gravel path leading up to the house between lawns bright with summer flowers.

Little Herr Friedemann wore no beard, and his face had scarcely changed at all, save that the features were slightly sharper. He wore his fine light-brown hair parted on one side.

Once, as he let the book fall on his knee and looked up into the sunny blue sky, he said to himself: "Well, so that is thirty years. Perhaps there may be ten or even twenty more, God knows. They will mount up without a sound or a stir and pass by like those that are gone; and I look forward to them with peace in my heart."

Now, it happened in July of the same year that a new appointment to the office of District Commandant had set the whole town talking. The stout and jolly gentleman who had for many years occupied the post had been very popular in social circles and they saw him go with great regret. It was in compliance with goodness knows what regulations that Herr von Rinnlingen and no other was sent hither from the capital.

In any case the exchange was not such a bad one. The new Commandant was married but childless. He rented a spacious villa in the southern suburbs of the city and seemed to intend to set up an establishment. There was a report that he was very rich—which received confirmation in the fact that he brought with him four servants, five riding and carriage horses, a landau and a light hunting-cart.

Soon after their arrival the husband and wife left cards on all the best society, and their names were on every tongue. But it was not Herr von Rinnlingen, it was his wife who was the centre of interest. All the men were dazed, for the moment too dazed to pass judgment; but their wives were quite prompt and definite in the view that Gerda von Rinnlingen was not their sort.

"Of course, she comes from the metropolis, her ways would naturally be different," Frau Hagenström, the lawyer's wife, said, in conversation with Henriette Friedemann. "She smokes, and she rides. That is of course. But it is her manners—they are not only free, they are positively brusque, or even worse. You see, no one could call her ugly, one might even say she is pretty; but she has not a trace of feminine charm in her looks or gestures or her laugh—they completely lack everything that makes a man fall in love with a woman. She is not a flirt—and goodness knows I would be the last to disparage her for that. But it is strange to see so young a woman—she is only twenty-four—so entirely wanting in natural charm. I am not expressing myself very well, my dear, but I know what I mean. All the men were simply bewildered. In a few weeks, you will see, they will be disgusted."

"Well," Fräulein Friedemann said, "she certainly has everything she wants."

"Yes," cried Frau Hagenström, "look at her husband! And how does she treat him? You ought to see it—you will see it! I would be the first to approve of a married woman behaving with a certain reserve towards the other sex. But how does she behave to her own husband? She has a way of fixing him with an ice-cold stare and saying 'My dear friend!' with a pitying expression that drives me mad. For when you look at him—upright, correct, gallant, a brilliant officer and a splendidly preserved man of forty! They have been married four years, my dear."

Herr Friedemann was first vouchsafed a glimpse of Frau von Rinnlingen in the main street of the town, among all the rows of shops, at midday, when he was coming from the Bourse, where he had done a little bidding.

He was strolling along beside Herr Stephens, looking tiny and important, as usual. Herr Stephens was in the wholesale trade, a huge stocky man with round side-whiskers and bushy eyebrows. Both of them wore top hats; their overcoats were unbuttoned on account of the heat. They tapped their canes along the pavement and talked of the political situation; but half-way down the street Stephens suddenly said:

"Deuce take it if there isn't the Rinnlingen driving along."

"Good," answered Herr Friedemann in his high, rather sharp voice, looking expectantly ahead. "Because I have never yet set eyes on her. And here we have the yellow cart we hear so much about."

It was in fact the hunting-cart which Frau von Rinnlingen was herself driving today with a pair of thoroughbreds; a groom sat behind her, with folded arms. She wore a loose beige coat and skirt and a small round straw hat with a brown leather band, beneath which her well-waved red-blond hair, a good, thick crop, was drawn into a knot at the nape of her neck. Her face was oval, with a dead-white skin and faint bluish shadows lurking under the close-set eyes. Her nose was short but well-shaped, with a becoming little saddle of freckles; whether her mouth was as good or no could not be told, for she kept it in continual motion, sucking the lower and biting the upper lip.

Herr Stephens, as the cart came abreast of them, greeted her with a great show of deference; little Herr Friedemann lifted his hat too and looked at her with wide-eyed attention. She lowered her whip, nodded slightly, and drove slowly past, looking at the houses and shop-windows.

After a few paces Herr Stephens said:

"She has been taking a drive and was on her way home."

Little Herr Friedemann made no answer, but stared before him at the pavement. Presently he started, looked at his companion, and asked: "What did you say?"

And Herr Stephens repeated his acute remark.

Three days after that Johannes Friedemann came home at midday from his usual walk. Dinner was at half past twelve, and he would spend the interval in his office at the right of the entrance door. But the maid came across the entry and told him that there were visitors.

"In my office?" he asked.

"No, upstairs with the mistresses."

"Who are they?"

"Herr and Frau Colonel von Rinnlingen."

"Ah," said Johannes Friedemann. "Then I will—"

And he mounted the stairs. He crossed the lobby and laid his hand on the knob of the high white door leading into the "landscape room." And then he drew back, turned round, and slowly returned as he had come. And spoke to himself, for there was no one else there, and said: "No, better not."

He went into his office, sat down at his desk, and took up the paper. But after a little he dropped it again and sat looking to one side out of the window. Thus he sat until the maid came to say that luncheon was ready; then he went up into the dining-room where his sisters were already waiting, and sat down in his chair, in which there were three music-books.

As she ladled the soup Henriette said:

"Johannes, do you know who were here?"

"Well?" he asked.

"The new Commandant and his wife."

"Indeed? That was friendly of them."

"Yes," said Pfiffi, a little water coming in the corners of her mouth. "I found them both very agreeable."

"And we must lose no time in returning the call," said Friederike. "I suggest that we go next Sunday, the day after tomorrow."

"Sunday," Henriette and Pfiffi said.

"You will go with us, Johannes?" asked Friederike.

"Of course he will," said Pfiffi, and gave herself a little shake. Herr Friedemann had not heard her at all; he was eating his soup, with a hushed and troubled air. It was as though he were listening to some strange noise he heard.

Next evening *Lohengrin* was being given at the opera, and everybody in society was present. The small auditorium was crowded, humming with voices and smelling of gas and perfumery. And every eye-glass in the stalls was directed towards box thirteen, next to the stage; for this was the first appearance of Herr and Frau von Rinnlingen and one could give them a good looking-over.

When little Herr Friedemann, in flawless dress clothes and glistening white pigeon-breasted shirt-front, entered his box, which was number thirteen, he started back at the door, making a gesture with his hand towards his brow. His nostrils dilated feverishly. Then he took his seat, which was next to Frau von Rinnlingen's.

She contemplated him for a little while, with her under lip stuck out; then she turned to exchange a few words with her husband, a tall, broad-shouldered gentleman with a brown, good-natured face and turned-up moustaches.

When the overture began and Frau von Rinnlingen leaned over the balustrade Herr Friedemann gave her a quick, searching side glance. She wore a light-coloured evening frock, the only one in the theatre which was slightly low in the neck. Her sleeves were full and her white gloves came up to her elbows. Her figure was statelier than it had looked under the loose coat; her full bosom slowly rose and fell and the knot of red-blonde hair hung low and heavy at the nape of her neck.

Herr Friedemann was pale, much paler than usual, and little beads of perspiration stood on his brow beneath the smoothly parted brown hair. He could see Frau von Rinnlingen's left arm, which lay upon the balustrade. She had taken off her glove and the rounded, dead-white arm and ringless hand, both of them shot with pale blue veins, were directly under his eye—he could not help seeing them.

The fiddles sang, the trombones crashed, Telramund was slain, general jubilation reigned in the orchestra, and little Herr Friedemann sat there motionless and pallid, his head drawn in between his shoulders, his forefinger to his lips and one hand thrust into the opening of his waistcoat.

As the curtain fell, Frau von Rinnlingen got up to leave the box with her husband. Johannes Friedemann saw her without looking, wiped his handkerchief across his brow, then rose suddenly and went as far as the door into the foyer, where he turned, came back to his chair, and sat down in the same posture as before.

When the bell rang and his neighbours re-entered the box he felt Frau von Rinnlingen's eyes upon him, so that finally against his will he raised his head. As their eyes met, hers did not swerve aside; she continued to gaze without embarrassment until he himself, deeply humiliated, was forced to look away. He turned a shade paler and felt a strange, sweet pang of anger and scorn. The music began again.

Towards the end of the act Frau von Rinnlingen chanced to drop her fan; it fell at Herr Friedemann's feet. They both stooped at the same time, but she reached it first and gave a little mocking smile as she said: "Thank you."

Their heads were quite close together and just for a second he got the warm scent of her breast. His face was drawn, his whole body twitched, and his heart thumped so horribly that he lost his breath. He sat without moving for half a minute, then he pushed back his chair, got up quietly, and went out.

He crossed the lobby, pursued by the music; got his top hat from the cloak-room, his light overcoat and his stick, went down the stairs and out of doors.

It was a warm, still evening. In the gas-lit street the gabled houses towered towards a sky where stars were softly beaming. The pavement echoed the steps of a few passers-by. Someone spoke to him, but he heard and saw nothing; his head was bowed and his deformed chest shook with the violence of his breathing. Now and then he murmured to himself:

"My God, my God!"

He was gazing horror-struck within himself, beholding the havoc which had been wrought with his tenderly cherished, scrupulously managed feelings. Suddenly he was quite overpowered by the strength of his tortured longing. Giddy and drunken he leaned against a lamp-post and his quivering lips uttered the one word: "Gerda!"

The stillness was complete. Far and wide not a soul was to be seen. Little Herr Friedemann pulled himself together and went on, up the street in which the opera-house stood and which ran steeply down to the river, then along the main street northwards to his home.

How she had looked at him! She had forced him, actually, to cast down his eyes! She had humiliated him with her glance. But was she not a woman and he a man? And those strange brown eyes of hers—had they not positively glittered with unholy joy?

Again he felt the same surge of sensual, impotent hatred mount up in him; then he relived the moment when her head had touched his, when he had breathed in the fragrance of her body—and for the second time he halted, bent his deformed torso backwards, drew in the air through clenched teeth, and murmured helplessly, desperately, uncontrollably:

"My God, my God!"

Then went on again, slowly, mechanically, through the heavy evening air, through the empty echoing streets until he stood before his own house. He paused a minute in the entry, breathing the cool, dank inside air; then he went into his office.

He sat down at his desk by the open window and stared straight ahead of him at a large yellow rose which somebody had set there in a glass of water. He took it up and smelt it with his eyes closed, then put it down with a gesture of weary sadness. No, no. That was all over. What was even that fragrance to him now? What any of all those things that up to now had been the well-springs of his joy?

He turned away and gazed into the quiet street. At intervals steps passed and the sound died away. The stars stood still and glittered. He felt so weak, so utterly tired to death. His head was quite vacant, and suddenly his despair began to melt into a gentle, pervading melancholy. A few lines of a poem flickered through his head, he heard the *Lohengrin* music in his ears, he saw Frau von Rinnlingen's face and her round white arm on the red velvet—then he fell into a heavy fever-burdened sleep.

Often he was near waking, but feared to do so and managed to sink back into forgetfulness again. But when it had grown quite light, he opened his eyes and looked round him with a wide and painful gaze. He remembered everything, it was as though the anguish had never been intermitted by sleep.

His head was heavy and his eyes burned. But when he had washed up and bathed his head with cologne he felt better and sat down in his place by the still open window. It was early, perhaps only five o'clock. Now and then a baker's boy passed; otherwise there was no one to be seen. In the opposite house the blinds were down. But birds were twittering and the sky was luminously blue. A wonderfully beautiful Sunday morning.

A feeling of comfort and confidence came over little Herr Friedemann. Why had he been distressing himself? Was not everything just as it had been? The attack of yesterday had been a bad one. Granted. But it should be the last. It was not too late, he could still escape destruction. He must avoid every occasion of a fresh seizure; he felt sure he could do this. He felt the strength to conquer and suppress his weakness.

It struck half past seven and Friederike came in with the coffee, setting it on the round table in front of the leather sofa against the rear wall.

"Good morning, Johannes," said she; "here is your breakfast."

"Thanks," said little Herr Friedemann. And then: "Dear Friederike, I am sorry, but you will have to pay your call without me, I do not feel well enough to go. I have slept badly and have a headache—in short, I must ask you—"

"What a pity!" answered Friederike. "You must go another time. But you do look ill. Shall I lend you my menthol pencil?"

"Thanks," said Herr Friedemann. "It will pass." And Friederike went out.

Standing at the table he slowly drank his coffee and ate a croissant. He felt satisfied with himself and proud of his firmness. When he had finished he sat down again by the open window, with a cigar. The food had done him good and he felt happy and hopeful. He took a book and sat reading and smoking and blinking into the sunlight.

Morning had fully come, wagons rattled past, there were many voices and the sound of the bells on passing trams. With and among it all was woven the twittering and chirping; there was a radiant blue sky, a soft mild air.

At ten o'clock he heard his sisters cross the entry; the front door creaked, and he idly noticed that they passed his window. An hour went by. He felt more and more happy.

A sort of hubris mounted in him. What a heavenly air—and how the birds were singing! He felt like taking a little walk. Then suddenly, without any transition, yet accompanied by a terror namelessly sweet came the thought: "Suppose I were to go to her!" And suppressing, as though by actual muscular effort, every warning voice within him, he added with blissful resolution: "I will go to her!"

He changed into his Sunday clothes, took his top hat and his stick, and hurried with quickened breath through the town and into the southern suburbs. Without looking at a soul he kept raising and dropping his head with each eager step, completely rapt in his exalted state until he arrived at the avenue of chestnut trees and the red brick villa with the name of Commandant von Rinnlingen on the gate-post.

But here he was seized by a tremor, his heart throbbed and pounded in his breast. He went across the vestibule and rang at the inside door. The die was cast, there was no retreating now. "Come what come may," thought he, and felt the stillness of death within him.

The door suddenly opened and the maid came towards him across the vestibule; she took his card and hurried away up the red-carpeted stair. Herr Friedemann gazed fixedly at the bright colour until she came back and said that her mistress would like him to come up.

He put down his stick beside the door leading into the salon and stole a look at himself in the glass. His face was pale, the eyes red, his hair was sticking to his brow, the hand that held his top hat kept on shaking.

The maid opened the door and he went in. He found himself in a rather large, half-darkened room, with drawn curtains. At his right was a piano, and about the round table in the centre stood several arm-chairs covered in brown silk. The sofa stood along the left-hand wall, with a landscape painting in a heavy gilt frame hanging above it. The wall-paper too was dark in tone. There was an alcove filled with potted palms.

A minute passed, then Frau von Rinnlingen opened the portières on the right and approached him noiselessly over the thick brown carpet. She wore a simply cut frock of red and black plaid. A ray of light, with motes dancing in it, streamed from the alcove and fell upon her heavy red hair so that it shone like gold. She kept her strange eyes fixed upon him with a searching gaze and as usual stuck out her under lip.

"Good morning, Frau Commandant," began little Herr Friedemann, and looked up at her, for he came only as high as her chest. "I wished to pay you my respects too. When my sisters did so I was unfortunately out . . . I regretted sincerely . . ."

He had no idea at all what else he should say; and there she stood and gazed ruthlessly at him as though she would force him to go on. The blood rushed to his head. "She sees through me," he thought, "she will torture and despise me. Her eyes keep flickering. . . ."

But at last she said, in a very high, clear voice:

"It is kind of you to have come. I have also been sorry not to see you before. Will you please sit down?"

She took her seat close beside him, leaned back, and put her arm along the arm of the chair. He sat bent over, holding his hat between his knees. She went on:

"Did you know that your sisters were here a quarter of an hour ago? They told me you were ill."

"Yes," he answered, "I did not feel well enough to go out, I thought I should not be able to. That is why I am late."

"You do not look very well even now," said she tranquilly, not shifting her gaze. "You are pale and your eyes are inflamed. You are not very strong, perhaps?"

"Oh," said Herr Friedemann, stammering, "I've not much to complain of, as a rule."

"I am ailing a good deal too," she went on, still not turning her eyes from him, "but nobody notices it. I am nervous, and sometimes I have the strangest feelings."

She paused, lowered her chin to her breast, and looked up expectantly at him. He made no reply, simply sat with his dreamy gaze directed upon her. How strangely she spoke, and how her clear and thrilling voice affected him! His heart beat more quietly and he felt as though he were in a dream. She began again:

"I am not wrong in thinking that you left the opera last night before it was over?"

"Yes, madam."

"I was sorry to see that. You listened like a music-lover—though the performance was only tolerable. You are fond of music, I am sure. Do you play the piano?"

"I play the violin, a little," said Herr Friedemann. "That is, really not very much—"

"You play the violin?" she asked, and looked past him consideringly. "But we might play together," she suddenly said. "I can accompany a little. It would be a pleasure to find somebody here—would you come?"

"I am quite at your service—with pleasure," said he, stiffly. He was still as though in a dream. A pause ensued. Then suddenly her expression changed. He saw it alter for one of cruel, though hardly perceptible mockery, and again she fixed him with that same searching, uncannily flickering gaze. His face burned, he knew not where to turn; drawing his head down between his shoulders he stared confusedly at the carpet, while there shot through him once more that strangely sweet and torturing sense of impotent rage.

He made a desperate effort and raised his eyes. She was looking over his head at the door. With the utmost difficulty he fetched out a few words:

"And you are so far not too dissatisfied with your stay in our city?"

"Oh, no," said Frau Rinnlingen indifferently. "No, certainly not; why should I not be satisfied? To be sure, I feel a little hampered, as though everybody's eyes were upon me, but—oh, before I forget it," she went on quickly, "we are entertaining a few people next week, a small, informal company. A little music, perhaps, and conversation. . . . There is a charming garden at the back, it runs down to the river. You and your sisters will be receiving an invitation in due course, but perhaps I may ask you now to give us the pleasure of your company?"

Herr Friedeman was just expressing his gratitude for the invitation when the door-knob was seized energetically from without and the Commandant entered. They both rose and Frau von Rinnlingen introduced the two men to each other. Her husband bowed to them both with equal courtesy. His bronze face glistened with the heat.

He drew off his gloves, addressing Herr Freidemann in a powerful, rather sharp-edged voice. The latter looked up at him with large vacant eyes and had the feeling that he would presently be clapped benevolently on the shoulder. Heels together, inclining from the waist, the Commandant turned to his wife and asked, in a much gentler tone:

"Have you asked Herr Friedemann if he will give us the pleasure of his company at our little party, my love? If you are willing I should like to fix the date for next week and I hope that the weather will remain fine so that we can enjoy ourselves in the garden."

"Just as you say," answered Frau von Rinnlingen, and gazed past him.

Two minutes later Herr Friedemann got up to go. At the door he turned and bowed to her once more, meeting her expressionless gaze still fixed upon him.

He went away, but he did not go back to the town; unconsciously he struck into a path that led away from the avenue towards the old ruined fort by the river, among well-kept lawns and shady avenues with benches.

He walked quickly and absently, with bent head. He felt intolerably hot, as though aware of flames leaping and sinking within him, and his head throbbed with fatigue.

It was as though her gaze still rested on him—not vacantly as it had at the end, but with that flickering cruelty which went with the strange still way she spoke. Did it give her pleasure to put him beside himself, to see him helpless? Looking through and through him like that, could she not feel a little pity?

He had gone along the river-bank under the moss-grown wall; he sat down on a bench within a half-circle of blossoming jasmine. The sweet, heavy scent was all about him, the sun brooded upon the dimpling water.

He was weary, he was worn out; and yet within him all was tumult and anguish. Were it not better to take one last look and then to go down into that quiet water; after a brief struggle to be free and safe and at peace? Ah, peace, peace—that was what he wanted! Not peace in an empty and soundless void, but a gentle, sunlit peace, full of good, of tranquil thoughts.

All his tender love of life thrilled through him in that moment, all his profound yearning for his vanished "happiness." But then he looked about him into the silent, endlessly indifferent peace of nature, saw how the river went its own way in the sun, how the grasses quivered and the flowers stood up where they blossomed, only to fade and to be blown away; saw how all that was bent submissively to the will of life; and there came over him all at once that sense of acquaintance and understanding with the inevitable which can make those who know it superior to the blows of fate.

He remembered the afternoon of his thirtieth birthday and the peaceful happiness with which he, untroubled by fears or hopes, had looked forward to what was left of his life. He had seen no light and no shadow there, only a mild twilight radiance gently declining into the dark. With what a calm and superior smile had he contemplated the years still to come—how long ago was that?

Then this woman had come, she had to come, it was his fate that she should, for she herself was his fate and she alone. He had known it from the first moment. She had come—and though he had tried his best to defend his peace, her coming had roused in him all those forces which from his youth up he had sought to suppress, feeling, as he did, that they spelled torture and destruction. They had seized upon him with frightful, irresistible power and flung him to the earth.

They were his destruction, well he knew it. But why struggle, then, and why torture himself? Let everything take its course. He would go his appointed way, closing his eyes before the yawning void, bowing to his fate, bowing to the overwhelming, anguishingly sweet, irresistible power.

The water glittered, the jasmine gave out its strong, pungent scent, the birds chattered in the tree-tops that gave glimpses among them of a heavy, velvety-blue sky. Little hump-backed Herr Friedemann sat long upon his bench; he sat bent over, holding his head in his hands.

Everybody agreed that the Rinnlingens entertained very well. Some thirty guests sat in the spacious dining-room, at the long, prettily decorated table, and the butler and two hired waiters were already handing round the ices. Dishes clattered, glasses rang, there was a warm aroma of food and perfumes. Here were comfortable merchants with their wives and daughters; most of the officers of the garrison; a few professional men, lawyers and the popular old family doctor—in short, all the best society.

A nephew of the Commandant, on a visit, a student of mathematics, sat deep in conversation with Fräulein Hagenström, whose place was directly opposite Herr Friedemann's, at the lower end of the table. Johannes Friedemann sat there on a rich velvet cushion, beside the unbeautiful wife of the Colonial Director and not far off Frau von Rinnlingen, who had been escorted to table by Consul Stephens. It was astonishing, the change which had taken place in little Herr Friedemann in these few days. Perhaps the incandescent lighting in the room was partly to blame; but his cheeks looked sunken, he made a more crippled impression even than usual, and his inflamed eyes, with their dark rings, glowed with an inexpressibly tragic light. He drank a great deal of wine and now and then addressed a remark to his neighbour.

Frau von Rinnlingen had not so far spoken to him at all; but now she leaned over and called out:

"I have been expecting you in vain these days, you and your fiddle."

He looked vacantly at her for a while before he replied. She wore a light-coloured frock with a low neck that left the white throat bare; a Maréchal Niel rose in full bloom was fastened in her shining hair. Her cheeks were a little flushed, but the same bluish shadows lurked in the corners of her eyes.

Herr Friedemann looked at his plate and forced himself to make some sort of reply; after which the school superintendent's wife asked him if he did not love Beethoven and he had to answer that too. But at this point the Commandant, sitting at the head of the table, caught his wife's eye, tapped on his glass and said:

"Ladies and gentlemen, I suggest that we drink our coffee in the next room. It must be fairly decent out in the garden too, and whoever wants a little fresh air, I am for him."

Lieutenant von Deidesheim made a tactful little joke to cover the ensuing pause, and the table rose in the midst of laughter. Herr Friedemann and his partner were among the last to quit the room; he escorted her through the "old German" smoking-room to the dim and pleasant living-room, where he took his leave.

He was dressed with great care: his evening clothes were irreproachable, his shirt was dazzlingly white, his slender, well-shaped feet were encased in patent-leather pumps, which now and then betrayed the fact that he wore red silk stockings.

He looked out into the corridor and saw a good many people descending the steps into the garden. But he took up a position at the door of the smoking-room, with his cigar and coffee, where he could see into the living-room.

Some of the men stood talking in this room, and at the right of the door a little knot had formed round a small table, the centre of which was the mathematics student, who was eagerly talking. He had made the assertion that one could draw through a given point more than one parallel to a straight line; Frau Hagenström had cried that this was impossible, and he had gone on to prove it so conclusively that his hearers were constrained to behave as though they understood.

At the rear of the room, on the sofa beside the red-shaded lamp, Gerda von Rinnlingen sat in conversation with young Fräulein Stephens. She leaned back among the yellow silk cushions with one knee slung over the other, slowly smoking a cigarette, breathing out the smoke through her nose and sticking out her lower lip. Fräulein Stephens sat stiff as a graven image beside her, answering her questions with an assiduous smile.

Nobody was looking at little Herr Freidemann, so nobody saw that his large eyes were constantly directed upon Frau von Rinnlingen. He sat rather droopingly and looked at her. There was no passion in his gaze nor scarcely any pain. But there was something dull and heavy there, a dead weight of impotent, involuntary adoration.

Some ten minutes went by. Then as though she had been secretly watching him the whole time, Frau von Rinnlingen approached and paused in front of him. He got up as he heard her say:

"Would you care to go into the garden with me, Herr Friedemann?"

He answered:

"With pleasure, madam."

"You have never seen our garden?" she asked him as they went down the steps. "It is fairly large. I hope that there are not too many people in it; I should like to get a breath of fresh air. I got a headache during supper; perhaps the red wine was too strong for me. Let us go this way." They passed through a glass door, the vestibule, and a cool little courtyard, whence they gained the open air by descending a couple more steps.

The scent of all the flower-beds rose into the wonderful, warm, starry night. The garden lay in full moonlight and the guests were strolling up and down the white gravel paths, smoking and talking as they went. A group had gathered round the old fountain, where the much-loved old doctor was making them laugh by sailing paper boats.

With a little nod Frau von Rinnlingen passed them by, and pointed ahead of her, where the fragrant and well-cared-for garden blended into the deeper park.

"Shall we go down this middle path?" asked she. At the beginning of it stood two low, squat obelisks.

In the vista at the end of the chestnut alley they could see the river shining green and bright in the moonlight. All about them was darkness and coolness. Here and there side paths branched off, all of them probably curving down to the river. For a long time there was not a sound.

"Down by the water," she said, "there is a pretty spot where I often sit. We could stop and talk a little. See the stars glittering here and there through the trees."

He did not answer, gazing, as they approached it, at the river's shimmering green surface. You could see the other bank and the park along the city wall. They left the alley and came out on the grassy slope down to the river, and she said:

"Here is our place, a little to the right, and there is no one there."

The bench stood facing the water, some six paces away, with its back to the trees. It was warmer here in the open. Crickets chirped among the grass, which at the river's edge gave way to sparse reeds. The moonlit water gave off a soft light.

For a while they both looked in silence. Then he heard her voice; it thrilled him to recognize the same low, gentle, pensive tone of a week ago, which now as then moved him so strangely:

"How long have you had your infirmity, Herr Friedemann? Were you born so?"

He swallowed before he replied, for his throat felt as though he were choking. Then he said, politely and gently:

"No, *gnädige Frau.* It comes from their having let me fall, when I was an infant."

"And how old are you now?" she asked again.

"Thirty years old."

"Thirty years old," she repeated. "And these thirty years were not happy ones?"

Little Herr Friedemann shook his head, his lips quivered.

"No," he said, "that was all lies and my imagination."

"Then you have thought that you were happy?" she asked.

"I have tried to be," he replied, and she responded:

"That was brave of you."

A minute passed. The crickets chirped and behind them the boughs rustled lightly.

"I understand a good deal about unhappiness," she told him. "These summer nights by the water are the best thing for it."

He made no direct answer, but gestured feebly across the water, at the opposite bank, lying peaceful in the darkness.

"I was sitting over there not long ago," he said.

"When you came from me?" she asked. He only nodded.

Then suddenly he started up from his seat, trembling all over; he sobbed and gave vent to a sound, a wail which yet seemed like a release from strain, and sank slowly to the ground before her. He had touched her hand with his as it lay beside him on the bench, and clung to it now, seizing the other as he knelt before her, this little cripple, trembling and shuddering; he buried his face in her lap and stammered between his gasps in a voice which was scarcely human:

"You know, you understand . . . let me . . . I can no longer . . . my God, oh, my God!"

She did not repulse him, neither did she bend her face towards him. She sat erect, leaning a little away, and her close-set eyes, wherein the liquid shimmer of the water seemed to be mirrored, stared beyond him into space.

Then she gave him an abrupt push and uttered a short, scornful laugh. She tore her hands from his burning fingers, clutched his arm, and flung him sidewise upon the ground. Then she sprang up and vanished down the wooded avenue.

He lay there with his face in the grass, stunned, unmanned, shudders coursing swiftly through his frame. He pulled himself together, got up somehow, took two steps, and fell again, close to the water. What were his sensations at this moment? Perhaps he was feeling that same luxury of hate which he had felt before when she had humiliated him with her glance, degenerated now, when he lay before her on the ground and she had treated him like a dog, into an insane rage which must at all costs find expression even against himself—a disgust, perhaps of himself, which filled him with a thirst to destroy himself, to tear himself to pieces, to blot himself utterly out.

On his belly he dragged his body a little further, lifted its upper part, and let it fall into the water. He did not raise his head nor move his legs, which still lay on the bank.

The crickets stopped chirping a moment at the noise of the little splash. Then they went on as before, the boughs lightly rustled, and down the long alley came the faint sound of laughter.

Sherwood Anderson (1876–1941)

When Henry James, commenting on Turgenev's *The Hunter's Sketches,* said that they "give the impression of life itself, and not of an arrangement," he could as easily have been speaking of Sherwood Anderson. Maxwell Geismar, Anderson's editor, wrote on the "apparent formlessness" of his stories, of "the sudden, shifting associations of thought and feeling which come, apparently at the writer's whim, and actually by the most meticulous use of detail." Each of those comments may serve as a guide to the special quality of Anderson's art. What we get is an arrangement, seemingly unarranged, of carefully selected, realistic detail (see Introduction, p. 22). Though he employs only a limited number of sensory brush-strokes in what may seem "artless," often fragmentary, clusters, Anderson nevertheless conveys indelibly the impression made upon his backward-looking narrator by the experiences he observes. Those impressions, those observations, become ours.

All of Anderson's best writing deals with the soil, sidewalks, and people of small-town Midwestern America. He was himself born in Camden, Ohio, and, much like the narrator of "The Egg," spent his youth drifting with his family from town to town. Following an irregular, interrupted education, he went to Chicago as a laborer. Then came brief service in the Spanish-American War, after which he returned to the Midwest, first as an advertising writer, then as a paint manufacturer in

Elyria, Ohio. Though he prospered financially, he (by his own account) felt choked spiritually, and in 1913 he returned to Chicago, walking out on both his business and the first of what were to be four wives. The so-called Chicago "little renaissance" brought him in touch with a number of newly emerging voices in American letters, notably Dreiser, Lindsay, Masters, and Sandburg (nearly all of whom, like Anderson, experienced their first literary achievement and acclaim in middle age). With their encouragement—however expert—he managed to publish three utterly unsuccessful novels. But in the year 1919, when Anderson was forty-three, there appeared *Winesburg, Ohio,* a group of interrelated stories that explore with compassion and psychological acuity the loneliness and frustration of small-town lives. The book won him international recognition and is usually regarded as his masterpiece, though many readers argue that certain stories in *The Triumph of the Egg* (1921), from which the following selection is taken, excel anything in the earlier collection. In his later years he edited newspapers in Virginia and wrote articles about American industrial conditions. He died in Panama in 1941.

In "The Egg" Anderson joins to his delineation of physical and psychological misfits a withering denunciation—if naively set forth—of the bitch goddess: "Something happened to the two people. They became ambitious. The American passion for getting up in the world took possession of them." The story is told from the point of view, and through the eyes, of a child. But things are managed with such skill that we never forget we are seeing things in a way the grown man *remembers* having seen them. For example, in the climactic episode both child and mother are awakened by the father's roar from downstairs. A door slams, the father arrives upstairs with a deranged look, egg in hand, and collapses in tears beside his wife in bed. The narrator tells us he cannot remember what his mother said, nor can he recall what his father's explanation was. He remembers only his own grief and fright. Already, even though as readers we are still in that bedroom, we are simultaneously aware of the narrator as adult, sensing the distance between now and then. The transition now is violent: "As to what happened downstairs," even though we have just been told it is gone from memory: "For some unexplainable reason I know the story as well as though I had been a witness to my father's discomfiture." And he proceeds to recite, in minutest detail, the entire grotesque downstairs sequence that occurred. Enigmatic? Absurd? Illogical? Crazy? The narrator has only this to offer: "One in time gets to know many unexplainable things."

The Egg

My father was, I am sure, intended by nature to be a cheerful, kindly man. Until he was thirty-four years old he worked as a farm-hand for a man named Thomas Butterworth whose place lay near the town of Bidwell, Ohio. He had then a horse of his own and on Saturday evenings drove into town to spend a few hours in social intercourse with other farm-hands. In town he drank several glasses of beer and stood about in Ben Head's saloon—crowded on Saturday evenings with visiting farm-hands. Songs

From Sherwood Anderson, *The Triumph of the Egg.* Copyright 1920 by Eleanor Copenhaver Anderson. Renewed. Reprinted by permission of Harold Ober Associates, Incorporated.

were sung and glasses thumped on the bar. At ten o'clock father drove home along a lonely country road, made his horse comfortable for the night and himself went to bed, quite happy in his position in life. He had at that time no notion of trying to rise in the world.

It was in the spring of his thirty-fifth year that father married my mother, then a country school-teacher, and in the following spring I came wriggling and crying into the world. Something happened to the two people. They became ambitious. The American passion for getting up in the world took possession of them.

It may have been that mother was responsible. Being a school-teacher she had no doubt read books and magazines. She had, I presume, read of how Garfield, Lincoln, and other Americans rose from poverty to fame and greatness and as I lay beside her—in the days of her lying-in—she may have dreamed that I would some day rule men and cities. At any rate she induced father to give up his place as a farm-hand, sell his horse and embark on an independent enterprise of his own. She was a tall silent woman with a long nose and troubled grey eyes. For herself she wanted nothing. For father and myself she was incurably ambitious.

The first venture into which the two people went turned out badly. They rented ten acres of poor stony land on Grigg's Road, eight miles from Bidwell, and launched into chicken raising. I grew into boyhood on the place and got my first impressions of life there. From the beginning they were impressions of disaster and if, in my turn, I am a gloomy man inclined to see the darker side of life, I attribute it to the fact that what should have been for me the happy joyous days of childhood were spent on a chicken farm.

One unversed in such matters can have no notion of the many and tragic things that can happen to a chicken. It is born out of an egg, lives for a few weeks as a tiny fluffy thing such as you will see pictured on Easter cards, then becomes hideously naked, eats quantities of corn and meal bought by the sweat of your father's brow, gets diseases called pip, cholera, and other names, stands looking with stupid eyes at the sun, becomes sick and dies. A few hens and now and then a rooster, intended to serve God's mysterious ends, struggle through to maturity. The hens lay eggs out of which come other chickens and the dreadful cycle is thus made complete. It is all unbelievably complex. Most philosophers must have been raised on chicken farms. One hopes for so much from a chicken and is so dreadfully disillusioned. Small chickens, just setting out on the journey of life, look so bright and alert and they are in fact so dreadfully stupid. They are so much like people they mix one up in one's judgments of life. If disease does not kill them they wait until your expectations are thoroughly aroused and then walk under the wheels of a wagon—to go squashed and dead back to their maker. Vermin infest their youth, and fortunes must be spent for curative powders. In later life I have seen how a literature has been built up on the subject of fortunes to be made out of the raising of chickens. It is intended to be read by the gods who have just eaten of the tree of the knowledge of good and evil. It is a hopeful literature and declares that much may be done by simple ambitious people who own a few hens. Do not be led astray by it. It was not written for you. Go hunt for gold on the frozen hills of Alaska, put your faith in the honesty of a politician, believe if you will that the world is daily growing better and that good will triumph over evil, but do not read and believe the literature that is written concerning the hen. It was not written for you.

I, however, digress. My tale does not primarily concern itself with the hen. If correctly told it will centre on the egg. For ten years my father and mother struggled to make our chicken farm pay and then they gave up that struggle and began another. They moved into the town of Bidwell, Ohio and embarked in the restaurant business. After ten years of worry with incubators that did not hatch, and with tiny—and in their own way lovely—balls of fluff that passed on into semi-naked pullethood and from that into dead henhood, we threw all aside and packing our belongings on a wagon drove down Grigg's Road toward Bidwell, a tiny caravan of hope looking for a new place from which to start on our upward journey through life.

We must have been a sad looking lot, not, I fancy, unlike refugees fleeing from a battlefield. Mother and I walked in the road. The wagon that contained our goods had been borrowed for the day from Mr. Albert Griggs, a neighbor. Out of its sides stuck the legs of cheap chairs and at the back of the pile of beds, tables, and boxes filled with kitchen utensils was a crate of live chickens, and on top of that the baby carriage in which I had been wheeled about in my infancy. Why we stuck to the baby carriage I don't know. It was unlikely other children would be born and the wheels were broken. People who have few possessions cling tightly to those they have. That is one of the facts that make life so discouraging.

Father rode on top of the wagon. He was then a bald-headed man of forty-five, a little fat and from long association with mother and the chickens he had become habitually silent and discouraged. All during our ten years on the chicken farm he had worked as a laborer on neighboring farms and most of the money he had earned had been spent for remedies to cure chicken diseases, on Wilmer's White Wonder Cholera Cure or Professor Bidlow's Egg Producer or some other preparations that mother found advertised in the poultry papers. There were two little patches of hair on father's head just above his ears. I remember that as a child I used to sit looking at him when he had gone to sleep in a chair before the stove on Sunday afternoons in the winter. I had at that time already begun to read books and have notions of my own and the bald path that led over the top of his head was, I fancied, something like a broad road, such a road as Ceasar might have made on which to lead his legions out of Rome and into the wonders of an unknown world. The tufts of hair that grew above father's ears were, I thought, like forests. I fell into a half-sleeping, half-waking state and dreamed I was a tiny thing going along the road into a far beautiful place where there were no chicken farms and where life was a happy eggless affair.

One might write a book concerning our flight from the chicken farm into town. Mother and I walked the entire eight miles—she to be sure that nothing fell from the wagon and I to see the wonder of the world. On the seat of the wagon beside father was his greatest treasure. I will tell you of that.

On a chicken farm where hundreds and even thousands of chickens come out of eggs surprising things sometimes happen. Grotesques are born out of eggs as out of people. The accident does not often occur—perhaps once in a thousand births. A chicken is, you see, born that has four legs, two pairs of wings, two heads or what not. The things do not live. They go quickly back to the hand of their maker that has for a moment trembled. The fact that the poor little things could not live was one of the tragedies of life to father. He had some sort of notion that if he could but bring into henhood or roosterhood a five-legged hen or a two-headed rooster his fortune would be made. He dreamed of taking the wonder about to county fairs and of growing rich by exhibiting it to other farm-hands.

At any rate he saved all the little monstrous things that had been born on our chicken farm. They were preserved in alcohol and put each in its own glass bottle. These he had carefully put into a box and on our journey into town it was carried on the wagon seat beside him. He drove the horses with one hand and with the other clung to the box. When we got to our destination the box was taken down at once and the bottles removed. All during our days as keepers of a restaurant in the town of Bidwell, Ohio, the grotesques in their little glass bottles sat on a shelf back of the counter. Mother sometimes protested but father was a rock on the subject of his treasure. The grotesques were, he declared, valuable. People, he said, liked to look at strange and wonderful things.

Did I say that we embarked in the restaurant business in the town of Bidwell, Ohio? I exaggerated a little. The town itself lay at the foot of a low hill and on the shore of a small river. The railroad did not run through the town and the station was a mile away to the north at a place called Pickleville. There had been a cider mill and pickle factory at the station, but before the time of our coming they had both gone out of business. In the morning and in the evening busses came down to the station along a road called Turner's Pike from the hotel on the main street of Bidwell. Our going to the out of the way place to embark in the restaurant business was mother's idea. She talked of it for a year and then one day went off and rented an empty store building opposite the railroad station. It was her idea that the restaurant would be profitable. Travelling men, she said, would be always waiting around to take trains out of town and town people would come to the station to await incoming trains. They would come to the restaurant to buy pieces of pie and drink coffee. Now that I am older I know that she had another motive in going. She was ambitious for me. She wanted me to rise in the world, to get into a town school and become a man of the towns.

At Pickleville father and mother worked hard as they always had done. At first there was the necessity of putting our place into shape to be a restaurant. That took a month. Father built a shelf on which he put tins of vegetables. He painted a sign on which he put his name in large red letters. Below his name was the sharp command— "EAT HERE"—that was so seldom obeyed. A show case was bought and filled with cigars and tobacco. Mother scrubbed the floor and the walls of the room. I went to school in the town and was glad to be away from the farm and from the presence of the discouraged, sad-looking chickens. Still I was not very joyous. In the evening I walked home from school along Turner's Pike and remembered the children I had seen playing in the town school yard. A troop of little girls had gone hopping about and singing. I tried that. Down along the frozen road I went hopping solemnly on one leg. "Hippity Hop To The Barber Shop," I sang shrilly. Then I stopped and looked doubtfully about. I was afraid of being seen in my gay mood. It must have seemed to me that I was doing a thing that should not be done by one who, like myself, had been raised on a chicken farm where death was a daily visitor.

Mother decided that our restaurant should remain open at night. At ten in the evening a passenger train went north past our door followed by a local freight. The freight crew had switching to do in Pickleville and when the work was done they came to our restaurant for hot coffee and food. Sometimes one of them ordered a fried egg. In the morning at four they returned north-bound and again visited us. A little trade began to grow up. Mother slept at night and during the day tended the restaurant and fed our boarders while father slept. He slept in the same bed mother had occupied during the night and I went off to the town of Bidwell and to school. During the long nights, while mother and I slept, father cooked meats that were to go into sandwiches for the lunch baskets of our boarders. Then an idea in regard to getting up in the world came into his head. The American spirit took hold of him. He also became ambitious.

In the long nights when there was little to do father had time to think. That was his undoing. He decided that he had in the past been an unsuccessful man because he had not been cheerful enough and that in the future he would adopt a cheerful outlook on life. In the early morning he came upstairs and got into bed with mother. She woke and the two talked. From my bed in the corner I listened.

It was father's idea that both he and mother should try to entertain the people who came to eat at our restaurant. I cannot now remember his words, but he gave the impression of one about to become in some obscure way a kind of public entertainer. When people, particularly young people from the town of Bidwell, came into our place, as on very rare occasions they did, bright entertaining conversation was to be made. From father's words I gathered that something of the jolly inn-keeper effect was to be sought. Mother must have been doubtful from the first, but she said nothing discouraging. It was father's notion that a passion for the company of himself and mother would spring up in the breasts of the younger people of the town of Bidwell. In the evening bright happy groups would come singing down Turner's Pike. They would troop shouting with joy and laughter into our place. There would be song and festivity. I do not mean to give the impression that father spoke so elaborately of the matter. He was as I have said an uncommunicative man. "They want some place to go. I tell you they want some place to go," he said over and over. That was as far as he got. My own imagination has filled in the blanks.

For two or three weeks this notion of father's invaded our house. We did not talk much, but in our daily lives tried earnestly to make smiles take the place of glum looks. Mother smiled at the boarders and I, catching the infection, smiled at our cat. Father became a little feverish in his anxiety to please. There was no doubt, lurking some-where in him, a touch of the spirit of the showman. He did not waste much of his ammunition on the railroad men he served at night but seemed to be waiting for a young man or woman from Bidwell to come in to show what he could do. On the counter in the restaurant there was a wire basket kept always filled with eggs, and it must have been before his eyes when the idea of being entertaining was born in his brain. There was something pre-natal about the way eggs kept themselves connected with the development of his idea. At any rate an egg ruined his new impulse in life. Late one night I was awakened by a roar of anger coming from father's throat. Both mother and I sat upright in our beds. With trembling hands she lighted a lamp that stood on a table by her head. Downstairs the front door of our restaurant went shut with a bang and in a few minutes father tramped up the stairs. He held an egg in his hand and his hand trembled as though he were having a chill. There was a half insane light in his eyes. As he stood glaring at us I was sure he intended throwing the egg at either mother or me. Then he laid it gently on the table beside the lamp and dropped on his knees beside mother's bed. He began to cry like a boy and I, carried away by his grief, cried with him. The two of us filled the little upstairs room with our wailing voices. It is ridiculous, but of the picture we made I can remember only the fact that mother's hand continually stroked the bald patch that ran across the top of his head. I have forgotten what mother said to him and how she induced him to tell her of what had happened downstairs. His explanation also has gone out of my mind. I remember only my own grief and fright and the shiny path over father's head glowing in the lamp light as he knelt by the bed.

As to what happened downstairs. For some unexplainable reason I know the story as well as though I had been a witness to my father's discomfiture. One in time gets to know many unexplainable things. On that evening young Joe Kane, son of a merchant of Bidwell, came to Pickleville to meet his father, who was expected on the ten o'clock evening train from the South. The train was three hours late and Joe came into our place to loaf about and to wait for its arrival. The local freight train came in and the freight crew were fed. Joe was left alone in the restaurant with father.

From the moment he came into our place the Bidwell young man must have been puzzled by my father's actions. It was his notion that father was angry at him for hanging around. He noticed that the restaurant keeper was apparently disturbed by his presence and he thought of going out. However, it began to rain and he did not fancy the long walk to town and back. He bought a five-cent cigar and ordered a cup of coffee. He had a newspaper in his pocket and took it out and began to read. "I'm waiting for the evening train. It's late," he said apologetically.

For a long time father, whom Joe Kane had never seen before, remained silently gazing at his visitor. He was no doubt suffering an attack of stage fright. As so often happens in life he had thought so much and so often of the situation that now confronted him that he was somewhat nervous in its presence.

For one thing, he did not know what to do with his hands. He thrust one of them nervously over the counter and shook hands with Joe Kane. "How-de-do," he said. Joe Kane put his newspaper down and stared at him. Father's eyes lighted on the basket of eggs that sat on the counter and he began to talk. "Well," he began hesitatingly, "well, you have heard of Christopher Columbus, eh?" He seemed to be angry. "That Christopher Columbus was a cheat," he declared emphatically. "He talked of making an egg stand on its end. He talked, he did and then he went and broke the end of the egg."

My father seemed to his visitor to be beside himself at the duplicity of Christopher Columbus. He muttered and swore. He declared it was wrong to teach children that Christopher Columbus was a great man when, after all, he cheated at the critical moment. He had declared he would make an egg stand on end and then when his bluff had been called he had done a trick. Still grumbling at Columbus, father took an egg from the basket on the counter and began to walk up and down. He rolled the egg between the palms of his hands. He smiled genially. He began to mumble words regarding the effect to be produced on an egg by the electricity that comes out of the human body. He declared that without breaking its shell and by virtue of rolling it back and forth in his hands he could stand the egg on its end. He explained that the warmth of his hands and the gentle rolling movement he gave the egg created a new centre of gravity, and Joe Kane was mildly interested. "I have handled thousands of eggs," father said. "No one knows more about eggs than I do."

He stood the egg on the counter and it fell on its side. He tried the trick again and again, each time rolling the egg between the palms of his hands and saying the words regarding the wonders of electricity and the laws of gravity. When after a half hour's effort he did succeed in making the egg stand for a moment he looked up to find that his visitor was no longer watching. By the time he had succeeded in calling Joe Kane's attention to the success of his effort the egg had again rolled over and lay on its side.

Afire with the showman's passion and at the same time a good deal disconcerted by the failure of his first effort, father now took the bottles containing the poultry monstrosities down from their place on the shelf and began to show them to his visitor. "How would you like to have seven legs and two heads like this fellow?" he asked, exhibiting the most remarkable of his treasures. A cheerful smile played over his face. He reached over the counter and tried to slap Joe Kane on the shoulder as he had seen men do in Ben Head's saloon when he was a young farmhand and drove to town on Saturday evenings. His visitor was made a little ill by the sight of the body of the terribly deformed bird floating in the alcohol in the bottle and got up to go. Coming from behind the counter father took hold of the young man's arm and led him back to his seat. He grew a little angry and for a moment had to turn his face away and force himself to smile. Then he put the bottles back on the shelf. In an outburst of generosity he fairly compelled Joe Kane to have a fresh cup of coffee and another cigar at his expense. Then he took a pan and filling it with vinegar, taken from a jug that sat beneath the counter, he declared himself about to do a new trick. "I will heat this egg in this pan of vinegar," he said. "Then I will put it through the neck of a bottle without breaking the shell. When the egg is inside the bottle it will resume its normal shape and the shell will become hard again. Then I will give the bottle with the egg in it to you. You can take it about with you wherever you go. People will want to know how you got the egg in the bottle. Don't tell them. Keep them guessing. This is the way to have fun with this trick."

Father grinned and winked at his visitor. Joe Kane decided that the man who confronted him was mildly insane but harmless. He drank the cup of coffee that had been given him and began to read his paper again. When the egg had been heated in vinegar father carried it on a spoon to the counter and going into a back room got an empty bottle. He was angry because his visitor did not watch him as he began to do his trick, but nevertheless went cheerfully to work. For a long time he struggled, trying to get the egg to go through the neck of the bottle. He put the pan of vinegar back on the stove, intending to reheat the egg, then picked it up and burned his fingers. After a second bath in the hot vinegar the shell of the egg had been softened a little but not enough for his purpose. He worked and worked and a spirit of desperate determination took possession of him. When he thought that at last the trick was about to be consummated the delayed train came in at the station and Joe Kane started to go nonchalantly out at the door. Father made a last desperate effort to conquer the egg and make it do the things that would establish his reputation as one who knew how to entertain guests who came into his restaurant. He worried the egg. He attempted to be somewhat rough with it. He swore and the sweat stood out on his forehead. The egg broke under his hand. When the contents spurted over his clothes, Joe Kane, who had stopped at the door, turned and laughed.

A roar of anger rose from my father's throat. He danced and shouted a string of inarticulate words. Grabbing another egg from the basket on the counter, he threw it, just missing the head of the young man as he dodged through the door and escaped.

Father came upstairs to mother and me with an egg in his hand. I do not know what he intended to do. I imagine he had some idea of destroying it, of destroying all eggs, and that he intended to let mother and me see him begin. When, however, he got into the presence of mother something happened to him. He laid the egg gently on the table and dropped on his knees by the bed as I have already explained. He later decided to close the restaurant for the night and to come upstairs and get into bed. When he did so he blew out the light and after much muttered conversation both he and mother went to sleep. I suppose I went to sleep also, but my sleep was troubled. I awoke at dawn and for a long time looked at the egg that lay on the table. I wondered why eggs had to be and why from the egg came the hen who again laid the egg. The question got into my blood. It has stayed there, I imagine, because I am the son of my father. At any rate, the problem remains unsolved in my mind. And that, I conclude, is but another evidence of the complete and final triumph of the egg—at least as far as my family is concerned.

E. M. Forster (1879–1970)

E. M. Forster, a fringe member of the so-called "Bloomsbury Group," is best known for his novels, *Where Angels Fear to Tread* (1905), *The Longest Journey* (1907), *A Room With a View* (1908), *Howards End* (1910), and *A Passage to India* (1924), but he has also had a tremendous influence—particularly on a post-World War II generation—with his short stories and his two volumes of essays, *Abinger Harvest* (1936) and *Two Cheers for Democracy* (1951). He is honored not only as a fiction writer but as a liberal humanist, as a believer in "personal relations" in an age of bigness, monopoly, and totalitarianism, where the individual counts for less and less. One of his radical statements in his essay "What I Believe" is: "If I had to choose between betraying my country and betraying my friend, I hope I should have the guts to betray my country." He believes in democracy because it allows free speech, but he does not idealize it—hence, he gives it only two cheers, not three. Chief honors go to the individual and to art, which respects the individual. Actually, Forster believes in aristocracy rather than the common man, but it is an aristocracy of character rather than of class, an aristocracy of "the sensitive, the considerate, and the plucky."

Like D. H. Lawrence, Forster hates everything that regiments the spirit ("The more highly public life is organised the lower does its morality sink"), and he laments deeply the defilement of nature by industrialism: "I am glad to have known our countryside before its roads were too dangerous to walk on and its rivers too dirty to bathe in, before its butterflies and wild flowers were decimated by arsenical spray, before Shakespeare's Avon frothed with detergents and the fish floated belly-up in the Cam."

Since his death in 1970, two important posthumous volumes have appeared: *Maurice* (written in 1913 but suppressed because of its homosexual theme) and *The Life To Come* (1972), containing mainly hitherto unpublished stories. Forster's earlier stories, appearing in *The Celestial Omnibus* (1911) and *The Eternal Moment* (1928), were all fantasies, full of—in his words—"all beings who inhabit the lower air, the shallow water, and the smaller hills, all Fauns and Dryads and slips of the memory, all verbal coincidences, Pans and puns. . . ." But light as these stories are, they are also exercises in criticism, delivering comeuppance to those stuffy guardians of Late Victorian conventions that Forster suffered under as a boy. The unpublished stories do the same, but they go further, dealing in large part with that forbidden subject—homosexuality—which throughout most of Forster's life had to be carefully hidden. Inferior, by and large, to the published stories, they all have the Forster touch, the casual, witty manner that, upon close examination, is a carrier of great wisdom and serious moral purpose.

"The Rock" is a slight piece, probably written in 1906, and it is one of those early stories that earned him a rejection slip. Yet, as Forster says, it came to him in a moment of "inspiration," and its composition was a process of "sitting down on the theme as if it were an anthill." The story is little more than an exemplum (see p.

35) without the sermon, or rather an implicit testing of the Christian exhortation "Go and sell that thou hast, and give to the poor" (Matt. 19:21). The hero does this, and is hated for it. What went wrong? Was the fault in the hero or in the text? The question is left open, and the reader must answer; but Forster has here translated into fiction one of his deepest moral concerns: how to convert the matters of the spirit into earthly coin. "Only Connect" is the epigraph of his novel *Howards End,* and the problems of connection between lower and upper class, between the seen and the unseen, between the worldly and the spiritual, constitute the essential dialectic of this story as well.

The Rock

We had been talking for some time, and she was so full of kindness and of insight that at last I ventured to ask about her husband.

"Did you ever question him? I hope so," she added, seeing that I hesitated.

"I went down to see him last month. We went for a sail."

"Did he charge you anything?"

"I did pay him a little."

"And I suppose you talked to the people?"

"The excitement is over. They resent him no longer. They—I won't say understand, for nobody could understand. But they have accepted him."

"I hoped for that," she said gravely. "They are simple and manly again, and he will be one of them. You saw the rock?"

"Oh yes. He showed me the rock."

On the north coast of Cornwall there is a promontory, high and fantastic, stretching for a half mile into the sea. In places it is crowned with broad boulders, in places its backbone is so narrow that one can see the water on either side, foaming against precipices that are polished black. Great moors are behind it, full of cairns and stone circles and the chimneys of deserted mines. Nearer at hand lies the farmers' country, a fertile strip that follows the indentations of the cliff. And close under the promontory itself is a little fishing village, so that many types of civilization, fruitful and fruitless, can be encompassed in a single gaze.

The rock of which she was speaking is hidden from all of them, for it lies very low in the water. It is some two hundred yards from the extreme point and resembles a square brown desk, with a slope towards the land. A wave will break on the high part, seethe down the slope, and then be merged in the surrounding blue, to break yet again at the foot of the promontory. One day, during their holidays, he sailed too near this rock, capsized, and was washed up onto it. There he lay, face downwards, with the rising tide frothing over him. She was up on the headland, and ran to the village for help. A boat put out at once. They rowed manfully—they were splendid fellows—and they reached him just as his hands relaxed and he was sliding head foremost into death. So much is known to all of us, and it was the crisis of his life. But in a story about his life, it is not the crisis.

Reprinted in the United States with permission of the W. W. Norton & Company, Inc. From *The Life to Come and Other Short Stories* by E. M. Forster. Copyright © 1972 by The Provost and Scholars of King's College, Cambridge. Reprinted in Canada with permission of the Macmillan Company of Canada Limited. From *The Life to Come and Other Stories* by E. M. Forster. Copyright © 1972 by the Trustees of the late E. M. Forster.

She began to speak, but waited a moment for the maid to clear away the tea. In the waning light her room seemed gentle and gray, and there hung about it an odour (I do not write "*the* odour") of Roman Catholicism, which is assuredly among the gracious things of the world. It was the room of a woman who had found time to be good to herself as well as to others; who had brought forth fruit, spiritual and temporal; who had borne a mysterious tragedy not only with patience but actually with joy.

"When he got to land," she said, "he would not even shake hands with them. He kept on saying, 'I don't know what to do. I can't think. I shall come to you again,' and they replied, 'Oh, that'll be all right, sir.' You can imagine the scene, and it was not till the evening that I realized his difficulty. You—how much would you give for your life?"

I stared blankly.

"I hope that you will never have to decide. May you always have your life as a right. Most of us do. But now and then a life is saved—as one might save a vase from breaking—and then the proprietor must think what is it worth."

"Is there not a tariff for rescues?" said I, inclined to be irritable and dense.

"In calm weather—it was quite calm and they did not run the slightest danger— the tariff appears to be fifteen shillings a rescuer. For two pounds five my husband could have been clear of all obligation. We neither of us felt two pounds five enough. Next morning we left, full of promises. I think they still believed in us, but I am not sure."

She paused, and I ventured to say: "But a sum that was great to *them*—that was the point. The question is purely practical."

"So all our friends said. One suggested a hundred pounds, another the present of a new boat, another that, every Christmas, I should knit each man a comforter. You see, there are no such things as purely practical questions. Every question springs straight out of the infinite, and until you acknowledge that you will never answer it."

"Then what did *you* suggest?"

"I suggested that I should settle that bill myself, and never show him the receipt. But he refused and, I think, rightly. Nor do I know what I should have done."

"But what did those three men want?" I persisted. "You cannot drive me from it: that's the point."

"They would have accepted anything: they were in want of nothing. Until we tourists came they were happy and independent. We taught them the craving for money—money obtained by rowing half a mile upon the tranquil sea. The minister, with whom we corresponded, implored us to be quick. He said that the whole village was anxious and greedy, and that the men were posing as heroes. And there were we, finding the world more glorious every day, the air more delicate, music sweeter, birds, sky, the sun—everything transfigured because he had been saved. And our love—we had been married five years, but now it never seemed to have been love before. Can you tell me what these things are worth?"

I was silent. I told myself that this was fluid, unsubstantial stuff. But in my heart I knew that she and all that she said was a rock in the tideway.

"For a time he was merely interested. He was amused at the problem, and the sensations it aroused in him. But at last he only cared for the solution. He found it one evening in this little room, when a sunset, more glorious than today's, was flaming under the wych-elm. He asked me, as I ask you, what such things were worth, and gave the answer: 'Nothing; and nothing is my reward to the men who saved me.' I said: 'It is the only possible reward. But they will never understand it.' 'I shall make them understand it in time,' he told me, 'for my gift of nothing shall be all that I have in the world.'"

Again the story becomes common property. He sold up his goods—everything—every cherished trifle that he had—and gave the value of them to the poor. Some money was settled on her, and that he could not touch, but he gave away the rest. Then he went down to that village penniless and asked for charity from his rescuers.

His sufferings had been terrible. He drew out all their disappointment and pettiness and cruelty; she covered her face when she spoke of it. I was glad to tell her that this had passed: they had come to treat him as an idiot and then as a good fellow, and now he was working for one of them. As I moved from her room I said, "No one but you will ever understand it." But her eyes filled with tears and she cried: "Don't—don't praise me for that. For if I had not understood, he might be with us now."

This conversation taught me that some of us can meet reality on this side of the grave. I do not envy them. Such adventures may profit the disembodied soul, but as long as I have flesh and blood I pray that my grossness preserve me. Our lower nature had its dreams. Mine is of a certain farm, windy but fruitful, halfway between the deserted moorland and the uninhabitable sea. Hither, at rare intervals, she should descend and he ascend, to shatter their spiritual communion by one caress.

James Joyce (1882–1941)

After half a century of controversy, during which he was thought by turns to be obscene and obscure, James Joyce has achieved his place as one of the giants of the modern age. His output was small: two volumes of verse, a play, fifteen short stories, three novels, a few critical pieces. Yet he is unsurpassed in achievement, perhaps unmatched in influence upon the development of present-day fiction.

James Augustine Aloysius Joyce was born in Ireland in 1882 to a genteel family on the downward slope of respectability. The two great influences on him were the Catholic faith of his mother and the nationalism of his father. In 1912 he departed Ireland never to return, but he never wrote of anything else. And though he renounced his faith, he replied when asked if he had found a substitute, "I have lost my faith, I have not lost my mind."

His growth as an artist charted the course of twentieth-century fiction. *Dubliners* (1914), a collection of stories, was written in the tradition of naturalism. "My intention," he wrote his publisher,

> was to write a chapter of the moral history of my country and I chose Dublin for the scene because that city seemed to me the centre of paralysis. . . . I have written it for the most part in a style of scrupulous meanness and with the conviction that he is a very bold man who dares to alter in the presentment, still more to deform, whatever he has seen and heard.

A Portrait of the Artist as a Young Man (1916) chronicles the early life of Stephen Dedalus. It is lyrical and impressionistic in its imagery. Notable is the growing complexity and sophistication of the language as Stephen matures in the book.

Ulysses (1922) covers a day, June 16, 1904, in the lives of Stephen Dedalus, Leopold Bloom, and Molly Bloom. The book is realistic, yet richly symbolic and lyrical. Katherine Mansfield said, "I can't get over the feeling of wet linoleum and unemptied pails and far worse horrors in the house of his mind." T. S. Eliot was more prophetic: "I hold this book to be the most important expression which the present age has found; it is a book to which we are all indebted, and from which none of us can escape."

Finnegans Wake (1939) is raucous and erudite, a coarse comedy and an encyclopedia of religion, a descent into the unconscious and a history of civilization. For the casual reader, it may seem gibberish; for some critics, it is the highest achievement of the human imagination in our century.

Joyce was not accepted by a wide public during his lifetime. He supported his family by giving language lessons and doing office tasks. He died, nearly blind, in 1941.

Joyce's stories combine seemingly disparate elements: poetic mysticism and naturalistic technique; pictorial exactness and deep concern for sound and cadence; a scrupulous meanness and a pervasive sympathy. By "scrupulous meanness," Joyce apparently meant that his prose would faithfully mirror his subject matter: Mrs. Mercer, for example, was "an old garrulous woman, a pawnbroker's widow, who collected used stamps for some pious purpose." The word *garrulous* at least borders on the onomatopoeic, and the very sounds, bland and indefinite, of "some pious purpose" expose the emptiness of the woman's efforts.

"Araby" depicts a highly significant experience in Joyce's youth, but it is no simple *rite de passage.* The young boy carries a heavy burden through the story: Catholicism, his family, Irish culture, his own love of mystery, his growing sexuality, his desire for freedom. Because the story is so rich with symbol and allusion (he bears his love as a chalice "through a throng of foes," the silence of the bazaar is like a "church after a service,") "Araby" profoundly rewards a second, slow, careful reading. Even at the end of the first reading, the reader will share with the boy the tremendously lyrical though painful epiphany that marks his self-knowledge.

Araby

North Richmond street, being blind, was a quiet street except at the hour when the Christian Brothers' School set the boys free. An uninhabited house of two stories stood at the blind end, detached from its neighbors in a square ground. The other houses of the street, conscious of decent lives within them, gazed at one another with brown imperturbable faces.

The former tenant of our house, a priest, had died in the back drawing room. Air, musty from having been long enclosed, hung in all the rooms, and the waste room behind the kitchen was littered with old useless papers. Among these I found a few paper-covered books, the pages of which were curled and damp: *The Abbot,* by Walter Scott, *The Devout Communicant,* and *The Memoirs of Vidocq.* I like the last best be-

From *Dubliners* by James Joyce. Originally published by B. W. Huebsch, Inc. in 1916. Copyright © 1967 by the Estate of James Joyce. All rights reserved. Reprinted by permission of The Viking Press, Inc.

cause its leaves were yellow. The wild garden behind the house contained a central apple tree and a few straggling bushes under one of which I found the late tenant's rusty bicycle pump. He had been a very charitable priest; in his will he left all his money to institutions and the furniture of his house to his sister.

When the short days of winter came dusk fell before we had well eaten our dinners. When we met in the street the houses had grown somber. The space of sky above us was the color of everchanging violet and towards it the lamps of the street lifted their feeble lanterns. The cold air stung us and we played till our bodies glowed. Our shouts echoed in the silent street. The career of our play brought us through the dark muddy lanes behind the houses where we ran the gauntlet of the rough tribes from the cottages, to the back doors of the dark dripping gardens where odors arose from the ashpits, to the dark odorous stables where a coachman smoothed and combed the horse or shook music from the buckled harness. When we returned to the street, light from the kitchen windows had filled the areas. If my uncle was seen turning the corner we hid in the shadow until we had seen him safely housed. Or if Mangan's sister came out on the doorstep to call her brother in to his tea we watched her from our shadow peer up and down the street. We waited to see whether she would remain or go in and, if she remained, we left our shadow and walked up to Mangan's steps resignedly. She was waiting for us, her figure defined by the light from the half-opened door. Her brother always teased her before he obeyed and I stood by the railings looking at her. Her dress swung as she moved her body and the soft rope of her hair tossed from side to side.

Every morning I lay on the floor in the front parlor watching her door. The blind was pulled down to within an inch of the sash so that I could not be seen. When she came out on the doorstep my heart leaped. I ran to the hall, seized my books and followed her. I kept her brown figure always in my eye and, when we came near the point at which our ways diverged, I quickened my pace and passed her. This happened morning after morning. I had never spoken to her, except for a few casual words, and yet her name was like a summons to all my foolish blood.

Her image accompanied me even in places the most hostile to romance. On Saturday evenings when my aunt went marketing I had to go to carry some of the parcels. We walked through the flaring streets, jostled by drunken men and bargaining women, amid the curses of laborers, the shrill litanies of shop boys who stood on guard by the barrels of pigs' cheeks, the nasal chanting of street singers, who sang a *come-all-you* about O'Donovan Rossa, or a ballad about the troubles in our native land. These noises converged in a single sensation of life for me: I imagined that I bore my chalice safely through a throng of foes. Her name sprang to my lips at moments in strange prayers and praises which I myself did not understand. My eyes were often full of tears (I could not tell why) and at times a flood from my heart seemed to pour itself out into my bosom. I thought little of the future. I did not know whether I would ever speak to her or not or, if I spoke to her, how I could tell her of my confused adoration. But my body was like a harp and her words and gestures were like fingers running upon the wires.

One evening I went into the back drawing room in which the priest had died. It was a dark rainy evening and there was no sound in the house. Through one of the broken panes I heard the rain impinge upon the earth, the fine incessant needles of water playing in the sodden beds. Some distant lamp or lighted window gleamed below me. I was thankful that I could see so little. All my senses seemed to desire to veil themselves and, feeling that I was about to slip from them, I pressed the palms of my hands together until they trembled, murmuring: *"O love! O love!"* many times.

At last she spoke to me. When she addressed the first words to me I was so confused that I did not know what to answer. She asked me was I going to *Araby.* I forgot whether I answered yes or no. It would be a splendid bazaar, she said; she would love to go.

"And why can't you?" I asked.

While she spoke she turned a silver bracelet round and round her wrist. She could not go, she said, because there would be a retreat that week in her convent. Her brother and two other boys were fighting for their caps and I was alone at the railings. She held one of the spikes, bowing her head towards me. The light from the lamp opposite our door caught the white curve of her neck, lit up her hair that rested there and, falling, lit up the hand upon the railing. It fell over one side of her dress and caught the white border of a petticoat, just visible as she stood at ease.

"It's well for you," she said.

"If I go," I said, "I will bring you something."

What innumerable follies laid waste my waking and sleeping thoughts after that evening! I wished to annihilate the tedious intervening days. I chafed against the work of school. At night in my bedroom and by day in the classroom her image came between me and the page I strove to read. The syllables of the word *Araby* were called to me through the silence in which my soul luxuriated and cast an Eastern exchantment over me. I asked for leave to go to the bazaar on Saturday night. My aunt was surprised and hoped it was not some Freemason affair. I answered few questions in class. I watched my master's face pass from amiability to sternness; he hoped I was not beginning to idle. I could not call my wandering thoughts together. I had hardly any patience with the serious work of life which, now that it stood between me and my desire, seemed to me child's play, ugly monotonous child's play.

On Saturday morning I reminded my uncle that I wished to go to the bazaar in the evening. He was fussing at the hall stand, looking for the hat brush, and answered me curtly:

"Yes, boy, I know."

As he was in the hall I could not go into the front parlor and lie at the window. I left the house in bad humor and walked slowly towards the school. The air was pitilessly raw and already my heart misgave me.

When I came home to dinner my uncle had not yet been home. Still it was early. I sat staring at the clock for some time and, when its ticking began to irritate me, I left the room. I mounted the staircase and gained the upper part of the house. The high cold empty gloomy rooms liberated me and I went from room to room singing. From the front window I saw my companions playing below in the street. Their cries reached me weakened and indistinct and, leaning my forehead against the cool glass, I looked over at the dark house where she lived. I may have stood there for an hour, seeing nothing but the brown-clad figure cast by my imagination, touched discreetly by the lamplight at the curved neck, at the hand upon the railings and at the border below the dress.

When I came downstairs again I found Mrs. Mercer sitting at the fire. She was an old garrulous woman, a pawnbroker's widow, who collected used stamps for some pious purpose. I had to endure the gossip of the tea table. My meal was prolonged beyond an hour and still my uncle did not come. Mrs. Mercer stood up to go: she was sorry she couldn't wait any longer, but it was after eight o'clock and she did not like to be out late, as the night air was bad for her. When she had gone I began to walk up and down the room, clenching my fists. My aunt said:

"I'm afraid you may put off your bazaar for this night of Our Lord."

At nine o'clock I heard my uncle's latchkey in the hall door. I heard him talking to himself and heard the hall stand rocking when it had received the weight of his overcoat. I could interpret these signs. When he was midway through his dinner I asked him to give me the money to go to the bazaar. He had forgotten.

"The people are in bed and after their first sleep now," he said.

I did not smile. My aunt said to him energetically:

"Can't you give him the money and let him go? You've kept him late enough as it is."

My uncle said he was very sorry he had forgotten. He said he believed in the old saying: "All work and no play makes Jack a dull boy." He asked me where I was going and, when I had told him a second time he asked me did I know *The Arab's Farewell to His Steed.* When I left the kitchen he was about to recite the opening lines of the piece to my aunt.

I held a florin tightly in my hand as I strode down Buckingham Street towards the station. The sight of the streets thronged with buyers and glaring with gas recalled to me the purpose of my journey. I took my seat in a third-class carriage of a deserted train. After an intolerable delay the train moved out of the station slowly. It crept onward among ruinous houses and over the twinkling river. At Westland Row Station a crowd of people pressed to the carriage doors; but the porters moved them back, saying that it was a special train for the bazaar. I remained alone in the bare carriage. In a few minutes the train drew up beside an improvised wooden platform. I passed out on to the road and saw by the lighted dial of a clock that it was ten minutes to ten. In front of me was a large building which displayed the magical name.

I could not find any sixpenny entrance and, fearing that the bazaar would be closed, I passed in quickly through a turnstile, handing a shilling to a weary-looking man. I found myself in a big hall girded at half its height by a gallery. Nearly all the stalls were closed and the greater part of the hall was in darkness. I recognized a silence like that which pervades a church after a service. I walked into the center of the bazaar timidly. A few people were gathered about the stalls which were still open. Before a curtain, over which the words *Café Chantant* were written in colored lamps, two men were counting money on a salver. I listened to the fall of the coins.

Remembering with difficulty why I had come I went over to one of the stalls and examined porcelain vases and flowered tea sets. At the door of the stall a young lady was talking and laughing with two young gentlemen. I remarked their English accents and listened vaguely to their conversation.

"O, I never said such a thing!"

"O, but you did!"

"O, but I didn't."

"Didn't she say that?"

"Yes. I heard her."

"O, there's a . . . fib!"

Observing me, the young lady came over and asked me did I wish to buy anything. The tone of her voice was not encouraging; she seemed to have spoken to me out of a sense of duty. I looked humbly at the great jars that stood like eastern guards at either side of the dark entrance to the stall and murmured:

"No, thank you."

The young lady changed the position of one of the vases and went back to the two young men. They began to talk of the same subject. Once or twice the young lady glanced at me over her shoulder.

I lingered before her stall, though I knew my stay was useless, to make my interest in her wares seem the more real. Then I turned away slowly and walked down the middle of the bazaar. I allowed the two pennies to fall against the sixpense in my pocket. I heard a voice call from one end of the gallery that the light was out. The upper part of the hall was completely dark.

Gazing up into the darkness I saw myself as a creature driven and derided by vanity; and my eyes burned with anguish and anger.

Virginia Woolf (1882–1941)

Virginia Woolf, like E. M. Forster a member of the so-called "Bloomsbury Group," began her serious career as a writer with the appearance in 1915 of her first novel, *The Voyage Out,* which had taken her seven years to write. It is a more or less conventional novel, but in the works that followed—notably *Jacob's Room* (1922), *Mrs. Dalloway* (1925), *To the Lighthouse* (1927), *The Waves* (1931), and *Between the Acts* (1941)—Virginia Woolf developed more and more radical techniques for rendering her sense of "life" and "reality." In the essay "Mr. Bennett and Mrs. Brown" she expressed her profound dissatisfaction with the "reality" of the fictional world of naturalistic writers like John Galsworthy, H. G. Wells, and Arnold Bennett. "Life is not," she says elsewhere, "a series of gig-lamps symmetrically arranged; life is a luminous halo, a semi-transparent envelope surrounding us from the beginning of consciousness to the end." To penetrate this envelope, to render "life itself," one must capture "the stream of thought, of consciousness" which is its subjective vehicle. In pursuit of this end, Woolf eliminated more and more externals, seeking a fictional structure that would be "miraculously habitable without the help of walls, staircases, or partitions"—an effort that caused her good friend and critic E. M. Forster to wonder whether she hadn't gone too far: "She does not tell a story or weave a plot, and—can she create character?" A character in her first novel says, "I want to write a novel about Silence, about the things people don't say," and by the time of her penultimate novel, *The Waves,* she has very nearly succeeded. The ambition expressed in her *Writer's Dairy* of eliminating "all waste, deadness, superfluity" and "to give the moment whole; whatever it includes" is close to realization. Gone are story and plot, dialogue, and characterization (as it is usually conceived); instead we have the flow of the six characters' thoughts and feelings, presented as a kind of reverie. One cannot in this space describe the excitement and beauty of Virginia Woolf's writing: but writing was her very life, and in a very real sense her stay against madness and death.

"The Mark on the Wall" is as unconventional a "story" as *The Waves* is a "novel," but it beautifully illustrates her technique. The narrator (clearly Woolf her-

self) remembers a mark on the wall. What was it? At the end we learn what it was—
and that, so to speak, is the "plot." But the plot is not the point, just as the satisfying
of such curiosity is not the point of life. The point is that the mark becomes the
focus of a whole series of free associations, ranging from Shakespeare to women's
rights, but all returning to those fundamental questions of Woolf's art—the nature of
"reality" and of "life itself." "If I should get up . . . and ascertain that the mark on the
wall is really . . . the head of a . . . nail . . . what should I gain? Knowledge? . . . And
what is knowledge?" She plays with the epistomological question. And life? "Why, if
one wants to compare life to anything, one must liken it to being blown through the
Tube at fifty miles an hour—landing at the other end without a single hairpin in
one's hair. Shot out at the feet of God entirely naked!" But such marks, like the
grain of sand around which the oyster builds a pearl, were the nuclei of Woolf's art,
and her perilous tie to order and sanity. In 1941 she committed suicide by drowning
in the River Ouse. As the story tells us, "One by one the fibres snap beneath the
immense cold pressure of the earth. . . ."

The Mark on the Wall

Perhaps it was the middle of January in the present year that I first looked up and saw
the mark on the wall. In order to fix a date it is necessary to remember what one saw.
So now I think of the fire; the steady film of yellow light upon the page of my book;
the three chrysanthemums in the round glass bowl on the mantelpiece. Yes, it must
have been the winter time, and we had just finished our tea, for I remember that I was
smoking a cigarette when I looked up and saw the mark on the wall for the first time.
I looked up through the smoke of my cigarette and my eye lodged for a moment upon
the burning coals, and that old fancy of the crimson flag flapping from the castle tower
came into my mind, and I thought of the cavalcade of red knights riding up the side of
the black rock. Rather to my relief the sight of the mark interrupted the fancy, for it is
an old fancy, an automatic fancy, made as a child perhaps. The mark was a small
round mark, black upon the white wall, about six or seven inches above the mantelpiece.
      How readily our thoughts swarm upon a new object, lifting it a little way, as ants
carry a blade of straw so feverishly, and then leave it. . . . If that mark was made by a
nail, it can't have been for a picture, it must have been for a miniature—the miniature
of a lady with white powdered curls, powder-dusted cheeks, and lips like red carna-
tions. A fraud of course, for the people who had this house before us would have
chosen pictures in that way—an old picture for an old room. That is the sort of people
they were—very interesting people, and I think of them so often, in such queer places,
because one will never see them again, never know what happened next. They wanted
to leave this house because they wanted to change their style of furniture, so he said,
and he was in process of saying that in his opinion art should have ideas behind it
when we were torn asunder, as one is torn from the old lady about to pour out tea and
the young man about to hit the tennis ball in the back garden of the suburban villa as
one rushes past in the train.

"The Mark on the Wall," from *A Haunted House and Other Stories,* by Virginia Woolf, copyright, 1944,
1972 by Harcourt Brace Jovanovich, Inc.

But for that mark, I'm not sure about it; I don't believe it was made by a nail after all; it's too big, too round, for that. I might get up, but if I got up and looked at it, ten to one I shouldn't be able to say for certain; because once a thing's done, no one ever knows how it happened. Oh! dear me, the mystery of life; the inaccuracy of thought! The ignorance of humanity! To show how very little control of our possessions we have—what an accidental affair this living is after all our civilization—let me just count over a few of the things lost in one lifetime, beginning, for that seems always the most mysterious of losses—what cat would gnaw, what rat would nibble—three pale blue canisters of book-binding tools? Then there were the bird cages, the iron hoops, the steel skates, the Queen Anne coal-scuttle, the bagatelle board, the hand organ—all gone, and jewels, too. Opals and emeralds, they lie about the roots of turnips. What a scraping paring affair it is to be sure! The wonder is that I've any clothes on my back, that I sit surrounded by solid furniture at this moment. Why, if one wants to compare life to anything, one must liken it to being blown through the Tube at fifty miles an hour—landing at the other end without a single hairpin in one's hair! Shot out at the feet of God entirely naked! Tumbling head over heels in the asphodel meadows like brown paper parcels pitched down a shoot in the post office! With one's hair flying back like the tail of a race-horse. Yes, that seems to express the rapidity of life, the perpetual waste and repair; all so casual, all so haphazard. . . .

But after life. The slow pulling down of thick green stalks so that the cup of the flower, as it turns over, deluges one with purple and red light. Why, after all, should one not be born there as one is born here, helpless, speechless, unable to focus one's eyesight, groping at the roots of the grass, at the toes of the Giants? As for saying which are trees, and which are men and women, or whether there are such things, that one won't be in a condition to do for fifty years or so. There will be nothing but spaces of light and dark, intersected by thick stalks, and rather higher up perhaps, rose-shaped blots of an indistinct colour—dim pinks and blues—which will, as time goes on, become more definite, become—I don't know what. . . .

And yet that mark on the wall is not a hole at all. It may even be caused by some round black substance, such as a small rose leaf, left over from the summer, and I, not being a very vigilant housekeeper—look at the dust on the mantelpiece, for example, the dust which, so they say, buried Troy three times over, only fragments of pots utterly refusing annihilation, as one can believe.

The tree outside the window taps very gently on the pane. . . . I want to think quietly, calmly, spaciously, never to be interruped, never to have to rise from my chair, to slip easily from one thing to another, without any sense of hostility, or obstacle. I want to sink deeper and deeper, away from the surface, with its hard separate facts. To steady myself, let me catch hold of the first idea that passes . . . Shakespeare. . . . Well, he will do as well as another. A man who sat himself solidly in an arm-chair, and looked into the fire, so—A shower of ideas fell perpetually from some very high Heaven down through his mind. He leant his forehead on his hand, and people, looking in through the open door—for this scene is supposed to take place on a summer's evening—But how dull this is, this historical fiction! It doesn't interest me at all. I wish I could hit upon a pleasant track of thought, a track indirectly reflecting credit upon myself, for those are the pleasantest thoughts, and very frequent even in the minds of modest mouse-coloured people, who believe genuinely that they dislike to hear their own praises. They are not thoughts directly praising oneself; that is the beauty of them; they are thoughts like this:

"And then I came into the room. They were discussing botany. I said how I'd seen a flower growing on a dust heap on the site of an old house in Kingsway. The seed, I said, must have been sown in the reign of Charles the First. What flowers grew in the reign of Charles the First?" I asked—(But I don't remember the answer.) Tall flowers with purple tassels to them perhaps. And so it goes on. All the time I'm dressing up the figure of myself in my own mind, lovingly, stealthily, not openly adoring it, for if I did that, I should catch myself out, and stretch my hand at once for a book in self-protection. Indeed, it is curious how instinctively one protects the image of oneself from idolatry or any other handling that could make it ridiculous, or too unlike the original to be believed in any longer. Or is it not so very curious after all? It is a matter of great importance. Suppose the looking-glass smashes, the image disappears, and the romantic figure with the green of forest depths all about it is there no longer, but only that shell of a person which is seen by other people—what an airless, shallow, bald, prominent world it becomes! A world not to be lived in. As we face each other in omnibuses and underground railways we are looking into the mirror; that accounts for the vagueness, the gleam of glassiness, in our eyes. And the novelists in future will realize more and more the importance of these reflections, for of course there is not one reflection but an almost infinite number; those are the depths they will explore, those the phantoms they will pursue, leaving the description of reality more and more out of their stories, taking a knowledge of it for granted, as the Greeks did and Shakespeare perhaps—but these generalizations are very worthless. The military sound of the word is enough. It recalls leading articles, cabinet ministers—a whole class of things indeed which, as a child, one thought the thing itself, the standard thing, the real thing, from which one could not depart save at the risk of nameless damnation. Generalizations bring back somehow Sunday in London, Sunday afternoon walks, Sunday luncheons, and also ways of speaking of the dead, clothes, and habits—like the habit of sitting all together in one room until a certain hour, although nobody liked it. There was a rule for everything. The rule for tablecloths at that particular period was that they should be made of tapestry with little yellow compartments marked upon them, such as you may see in photographs of the carpets in the corridors of the royal palaces. Tablecloths of a different kind were not real tablecloths. How shocking, and yet how wonderful it was to discover that these real things, Sunday luncheons, Sunday walks, country houses, and tablecloths were not entirely real, were indeed half phantoms, and the damnation which visited the disbeliever in them was only a sense of illegitimate freedom. What now takes the place of those things I wonder, those real standard things? Men perhaps, should you be a woman; the masculine point of view which governs our lives, which sets the standard, which establishes Whitaker's Table of Precedency,[1] which has become, I suppose, since the war, half a phantom to many men and women, which soon, one may hope, will be laughed into the dustbin where the phantoms go, the mahogany sideboards and the Landseer prints, Gods and Devils, Hell and so forth, leaving us all with an intoxicating sense of illegitimate freedom—if freedom exists. . . .

In certain lights that mark on the wall seems actually to project from the wall. Nor is it entirely circular. I cannot be sure, but it seems to cast a perceptible shadow, suggesting that if I ran my finger down that strip of the wall it would, at a certain point, mount and descend a small tumulus, a smooth tumulus like those barrows on the South Downs which are, they say, either tombs or camps. Of the two I should

---

[1] A table listing the rank order of the British aristocracy and notables in *Whitaker's Almanak,* (est. 1868), an annual publication like the *World Almanac* in The United States.

prefer them to be tombs, desiring melancholy like most English people, and finding it natural at the end of a walk to think of the bones stretched beneath the turf. . . . There must be some book about it. Some antiquary must have dug up those bones and given them a name. . . . What sort of a man is an antiquary, I wonder? Retired Colonels for the most part, I daresay, leading parties of aged labourers to the top here, examining clods of earth and stone, and getting into correspondence with the neighbouring clergy, which, being opened at breakfast time, gives them a feeling of importance, and the comparison of arrow-heads necessitates cross-country journeys to the county towns, an agreeable necessity both to them and to their elderly wives, who wish to make plum jam or to clean out the study, and have every reason for keeping that great question of the camp or the tomb in perpetual suspension, while the Colonel himself feels agreeably philosophic in accumulating evidence on both sides of the question. It is true that he does finally incline to believe in the camp; and, being opposed, indites a pamphlet which he is about to read at the quarterly meeting of the local society when a stroke lays him low, and his last conscious thoughts are not of wife or child, but of the camp and that arrow-head there, which is now in the case at the local museum, together with the foot of a Chinese murderess, a handful of Elizabethan nails, a great many Tudor clay pipes, a piece of Roman pottery, and the wineglass that Nelson drank out of—proving I really don't know what.

No, no, nothing is proved, nothing is known. And if I were to get up at this very moment and ascertain that the mark on the wall is really—what shall we say?—the head of a gigantic old nail, driven in two hundred years ago, which has now, owing to the patient attrition of many generations of housemaids, revealed its head above the coat of paint, and is taking its first view of modern life in the sight of a white-walled fire-lit room, what should I gain?—Knowledge? Matter for further speculation? I can think sitting still as well as standing up. And what is knowledge? What are our learned men save the descendants of witches and hermits who crouched in caves and in woods brewing herbs, interrogating shrew-mice and writing down the language of the stars? And the less we honour them as our superstitions dwindle and our respect for beauty and health of mind increases. . . . Yes, one could imagine a very pleasant world. A quiet, spacious world, with the flowers so red and blue in the open fields. A world without professors or specialists or house-keepers with the profiles of policemen, a world which one could slice with one's thought as a fish slices the water with his fin, grazing the stems of the water-lilies, hanging suspended over nests of white sea eggs. . . . How peaceful it is down here, rooted in the centre of the world and gazing up through the grey waters, with their sudden gleams of light, and their reflections—if it were not for Whitaker's Almanack—if it were not for the Table of Precedency!

I must jump up and see for myself what that mark on the wall really is—a nail, a rose-leaf, a crack in the wood?

Here is nature once more at her old game of self-preservation. This train of thought, she perceives, is threatening mere waste of energy, even some collision with reality, for who will ever be able to lift a finger against Whitaker's Table of Precedency? The Archbishop of Canterbury is followed by the Lord High Chancellor; the Lord High Chancellor is followed by the Archbishop of York. Everybody follows somebody, such is the philosophy of Whitaker; and the great thing is to know who follows whom. Whitaker knows, and let that, so Nature counsels, comfort you, instead of enraging you; and if you can't be comforted, if you must shatter this hour of peace, think of the mark on the wall.

I understand Nature's game—her prompting to take action as a way of ending any thought that threatens to excite or to pain. Hence, I suppose, comes our slight contempt for men of action—men, we assume, who don't think. Still, there's no harm in putting a full stop to one's disagreeable thoughts by looking at a mark on the wall.

Indeed, now that I have fixed my eyes upon it, I feel that I have grasped a plank in the sea; I feel a satisfying sense of reality which at once turns the two Archbishops and the Lord High Chancellor to the shadows of shades. Here is something definite, something real. Thus, waking from a midnight dream of horror, one hastily turns on the light and lies quiescent, worshipping the chest of drawers, worshipping solidity, worshipping reality, worshipping the impersonal world which is a proof of some existence other than ours. That is what one wants to be sure of. . . . Wood is a pleasant thing to think about. It comes from a tree; and trees grow, and we don't know how they grow. For years and years they grow, without paying any attention to us, in meadows, in forests, and by the side of rivers—all things one likes to think about. The cows swish their tails beneath them on hot afternoons; they paint rivers so green that when a moorhen dives one expects to see its feathers all green when it comes up again. I like to think of the fish balanced against the stream like flags blown out; and of water-beetles slowly raising domes of mud upon the bed of the river. I like to think of the tree itself: first of the close dry sensation of being wood; then the grinding of the storm; then the slow, delicious ooze of sap; I like to think of it, too, on winter's nights standing in the empty field with all leaves close-furled, nothing tender exposed to the iron bullets of the moon, a naked mast upon an earth that goes tumbling, tumbling, all night long. The song of birds must sound very loud and strange in June; and how cold the feet of insects must feel upon it, as they make laborious progresses up the creases of the bark, or sun themselves upon the thin green awning of the leaves, and look straight in front of them with diamond-cut red eyes. . . . One by one the fibres snap beneath the immense cold pressure of the earth, then the last storm comes and, falling, the highest branches drive deep into the ground again. Even so, life isn't done with; there are a million patient, watchful lives still for a tree, all over the world, in bedrooms, in ships, on the pavement, lining rooms, where men and women sit after tea, smoking cigarettes. It is full of peaceful thoughts, happy thoughts, this tree. I should like to take each one separately—but something is getting in the way. . . . Where was I? What has it all been about? A tree? A river? The Downs? Whitaker's Almanack? The fields of asphodel? I can't remember a thing. Everything's moving, falling, slipping, vanishing. . . . There is a vast upheaval of matter. Someone is standing over me and saying:

"I'm going out to buy a newspaper."

"Yes?"

"Though it's no good buying newspapers. . . . Nothing ever happens. Curse this war; God damn this war! . . . All the same, I don't see why we should have a snail on our wall."

Ah, the mark on the wall! It was a snail.

D. H. Lawrence (1885–1930)

D. H. Lawrence was born in England's coal-mining country, the son of a miner. His father was a black-bearded, irreligious, heavy drinking man who spoke the rough Nottinghamshire dialect; his mother was a "refined" chapel-goer who had been a schoolteacher and spoke the King's English. Between these two there developed deep tensions, and *Sons and Lovers* (1913), Lawrence's first important novel, is the unforgettable story of how a mother sought to *possess* her son, and how this possessiveness corrupted his sexual relations with other women. At her death Lawrence said to Jessie Chambers, with whom he had sought a "spiritual" relationship: "I've *loved* her, like a lover. That's why I could never love you." This oedipal conflict appears in many guises in Lawrence's later novels, in *The Rainbow* (1915), *Women in Love* (1920), and *Lady Chatterley's Lover* (1928), to name but a few. Again and again, we see characters struggling to relate to others and at the same time struggling to break free; and part of the struggle is often the individual's difficulty in sorting out the male and female, the earthy and the refined, the intellectual and the passional, the homo- and the hetero-sexual sides of his being. The ideal was, as Lawrence expressed it in *Women in Love,* a "star-equilibrium," in which two beings are held each to each by forces of attraction, but never fusing, never losing their individuality. The ideal was more easily stated than demonstrated, however, and his short stories (which many think constitute his best work) render these struggles in a protean variety of ways.

Lawrence saw the modern world as anathema to love; he saw its ugliness, its mechanization, its economics of greed as invading human personality and impairing that *flow* of life, that wholeness, which can only occur when the "dark self" of the unconscious and the "knowing self" of the conscious are in relation with each other. "My great religion," he wrote in 1913, "is a belief in the blood, the flesh, as being wiser than the intellect." That faith in the "blood" led Lawrence into some strange corners (including a kind of flirtation with fascism), but what he wanted essentially was wholeness, an end to the alienation and disintegration brought on by the "hopeless squalor of industrialism, the huge cemetery of human hopes."

"The Blind Man" is quintessential Lawrence. Isabel Pervin is feeling the burden of intimacy with her war-maimed husband, "a terrible joy to her, and a terrible burden." Maurice's blindness is symbolic of those dark depths of the unconscious where one encounters the awful paradox of love: its richness but also its anonymity. Bertie Reid, the undersexed intellectual, provides a "way out"—the superficial relief she needs. The triangle of Isabel, Maurice, and Bertie is a rearrangement of the triangle Lawrence grew up in: Maurice perhaps reflects his father, Bertie a male version of Jessie Chambers, and Isabel Lawrence himself, torn between two kinds of love. But what is memorable about the story is its passion, the combination of its power and its tenderness: Maurice, feeling alone and "tortured in the shattered chaos of his own blood," finds a solution when he reaches out of his darkness and touches Bertie, who shrinks in revulsion. Bertie, alienated from his own "dark self," is terror-struck at the idea of a physical encounter. There is no solution—this kind of adjustment must go on and on—but a kind of equilibrium and a kind of poetic justice are achieved.

Lawrence led a tempestuous and nomadic life, traveling with his wife Frieda through Europe and to the American Southwest and Mexico. He died of tuberculosis in southern France in 1930.

The Blind Man

Isabel Pervin was listening for two sounds—for the sound of wheels on the drive outside and for the noise of her husband's footsteps in the hall. Her dearest and oldest friend, a man who seemed almost indispensable to her living, would drive up in the rainy dusk of the closing November day. The trap had gone to fetch him from the station. And her husband, who had been blinded in Flanders, and who had a disfiguring mark on his brow, would be coming in from the out-houses.

He had been home for a year now. He was totally blind. Yet they had been very happy. The Grange was Maurice's own place. The back was a farmstead, and the Wernhams, who occupied the rear premises, acted as farmers. Isabel lived with her husband in the handsome rooms in front. She and he had been almost entirely alone together since he was wounded. They talked and sang and read together in a wonderful and unspeakable intimacy. Then she reviewed books for a Scottish newspaper, carrying on her old interest, and he occupied himself a good deal with the farm. Sightless, he could still discuss everything with Wernham, and he could also do a good deal of work about the place—menial work, it is true, but it gave him satisfaction. He milked the cows, carried in the pails, turned the separator, attended to the pigs and horses. Life was still very full and strangely serene for the blind man, peaceful with the almost incomprehensible peace of immediate contact in darkness. With his wife he had a whole world, rich and real and invisible.

They were newly and remotely happy. He did not even regret the loss of his sight in these times of dark, palpable joy. A certain exultance swelled his soul.

But as time wore on, sometimes the rich glamour would leave them. Sometimes, after months of this intensity, a sense of burden overcame Isabel, a weariness, a terrible *ennui,* in that silent house approached between a colonnade of tall-shafted pines. Then she felt she would go mad, for she could not bear it. And sometimes he had devastating fits of depression, which seemed to lay waste his whole being. It was worse than depression—a black misery, when his own life was a torture to him, and when his presence was unbearable to his wife. The dread went down to the roots of her soul as these black days recurred. In a kind of panic she tried to wrap herself up still further in her husband. She forced the old spontaneous cheerfulness and joy to continue. But the effort it cost her was almost too much. She knew she could not keep it up. She felt she would scream with the strain, and would give anything, anything, to escape. She longed to possess her husband utterly; it gave her inordinate joy to have him entirely to herself. And yet, when again he was gone in a black and massive misery, she could not bear him, she could not bear herself; she wished she could be snatched away off the earth altogether, anything rather than live at this cost.

Dazed, she schemed for a way out. She invited friends, she tried to give him some further connection with the outer world. But it was no good. After all their joy and suffering, after their dark, great year of blindness and solitude and unspeakable nearness, other people seemed to them both shallow, rattling, rather impertinent. Shallow prattle seemed presumptuous. He became impatient and irritated, she was wearied. And so they lapsed into their solitude again. For they preferred it.

From *The Complete Short Stories of D. H. Lawrence.* Copyright 1922 by Thomas B. Seltzer, copyright renewed 1950 by Frieda Lawrence. All rights reserved. Reprinted by permission of the Viking Press, Inc.

But now, in a few weeks' time, her second baby would be born. The first had died, an infant, when her husband first went out to France. She looked with joy and relief to the coming of the second. It would be her salvation. But also she felt some anxiety. She was thirty years old, her husband was a year younger. They both wanted the child very much. Yet she could not help feeling afraid. She had her husband on her hands, a terrible joy to her, and a terrifying burden. The child would occupy her love and attention. And then, what of Maurice? What would he do? If only she could feel that he, too, would be at peace and happy when the child came! She did so want to luxuriate in a rich, physical satisfaction of maternity. But the man, what would he do? How could she provide for him, how avert those shattering black moods of his, which destroyed them both?

She sighed with fear. But at this time Bertie Reid wrote to Isabel. He was her old friend, a second or third cousin, a Scotchman, as she was a Scotchwoman. They had been brought up near to one another, and all her life he had been her friend, like a brother, but better than her own brothers. She loved him—though not in the marrying sense. There was a sort of kinship between them, an affinity. They understood one another instinctively. But Isabel would never have thought of marrying Bertie. It would have seemed like marrying in her own family.

Bertie was a barrister and a man of letters, a Scotchman of the intellectual type, quick, ironical, sentimental, and on his knees before the woman he adored but did not want to marry. Maurice Pervin was different. He came of a good old country family— the Grange was not a very great distance from Oxford. He was passionate, sensitive, perhaps over-sensitive, wincing—a big fellow with heavy limbs and a forehead that flushed painfully. For his mind was slow, as if drugged by the strong provincial blood that beat in his veins. He was very sensitive to his own mental slowness, his feelings being quick and acute. So that he was just the opposite to Bertie, whose mind was much quicker than his emotions, which were not so very fine.

From the first the two men did not like each other. Isabel felt that they *ought* to get on together. But they did not. She felt that if only each could have the clue to the other there would be such a rare understanding between them. It did not come off, however. Bertie adopted a slightly ironical attitude, very offensive to Maurice, who returned the Scotch irony with English resentment, a resentment which deepened sometimes into stupid hatred.

This was a little puzzling to Isabel. However, she accepted it in the course of things. Men were made freakish and unreasonable. Therefore, when Maurice was going out to France for the second time, she felt that, for her husband's sake, she must discontinue her friendship with Bertie. She wrote to the barrister to this effect. Bertram Reid simply replied that in this, as in all other matters, he must obey her wishes, if these were indeed her wishes.

For nearly two years nothing had passed between the two friends. Isabel rather gloried in the fact; she had no compunction. She had one great article of faith, which was, that husband and wife should be so important to one another, that the rest of the world simply did not count. She and Maurice were husband and wife. They loved one another. They would have children. Then let everybody and everything else fade into insignificance outside this connubial felicity. She professed herself quite happy and ready to receive Maurice's friends. She was happy and ready: the happy wife, the ready woman in possession. Without knowing why, the friends retired abashed, and came no more. Maurice, of course, took as much satisfaction in this connubial absorption as Isabel did.

He shared in Isabel's literary activities, she cultivated a real interest in agriculture and cattle-raising. For she, being at heart perhaps an emotional enthusiast, always cultivated the practical side of life, and prided herself on her mastery of practical affairs. Thus the husband and wife had spent the five years of their married life. The last had been one of blindness and unspeakable intimacy. And now Isabel felt a great indifference coming over her, a sort of lethargy. She wanted to be allowed to bear her child in peace, to nod by the fire and drift vaguely, physically, from day to day. Maurice was like an ominous thunder-cloud. She had to keep waking up to remember him.

When a little note came from Bertie, asking if he was to put up a tombstone to their dead friendship, and speaking of the real pain he felt on account of her husband's loss of sight, she felt a pang, a fluttering agitation of reawakening. And she read the letter to Maurice.

"Ask him to come down," he said.

"Ask Bertie to come here!" she re-echoed.

"Yes—if he wants to."

Isabel paused for a few moments.

"I know he wants to—he'd only be too glad," she replied. "But what about you, Maurice? How would you like it?"

"I should like it."

"Well—in that case —— But I thought you didn't care for him ——"

"Oh, I don't know. I might think differently of him now," the blind man replied. It was rather abstruse to Isabel.

"Well, dear," she said, "if you're quite sure ——"

"I'm sure enough. Let him come," said Maurice.

So Bertie was coming, coming this evening, in the November rain and darkness. Isabel was agitated, racked with her old restlessness and indecision. She had always suffered from this pain of doubt, just an agonising sense of uncertainty. It had begun to pass off, in the lethargy of maternity. Now it returned, and she resented it. She struggled as usual to maintain her calm, composed, friendly bearing, a sort of mask she wore over all her body.

A woman had lighted a tall lamp beside the table, and spread the cloth. The long dining-room was dim, with its elegant but rather severe pieces of old furniture. Only the round table glowed softly under the light. It had a rich, beautiful effect. The white cloth glistened and dropped its heavy, pointed lace corners almost to the carpet, the china was old and handsome, creamy-yellow, with a blotched pattern of harsh red and deep blue, the cups large and bell-shaped, the teapot gallant. Isabel looked at it with superficial appreciation.

Her nerves were hurting her. She looked automatically again at the high, uncurtained windows. In the last dusk she could just perceive outside a huge fir-tree swaying its boughs: it was as if she thought it rather than saw it. The rain came flying on the window panes. Ah, why had she no peace? These two men, why did they tear at her? Why did they not come—why was there this suspense?

She sat in a lassitude that was really suspense and irritation. Maurice, at least, might come in—there was nothing to keep him out. She rose to her feet. Catching sight of her reflection in a mirror, she glanced at herself with a slight smile of recognition, as if she were an old friend to herself. Her face was oval and calm, her nose a little arched. Her neck made a beautiful line down to her shoulder. With hair knotted loosely behind, she had something of a warm, maternal look. Thinking this of herself, she arched her eyebrows and her rather heavy eyelids, with a little flicker of a smile, and for a moment her grey eyes looked amused and wicked, a little sardonic, out of her transfigured Madonna face.

Then, resuming her air of womanly patience—she was really fatally self-determined—she went with a little jerk towards the door. Her eyes were slightly reddened.

She passed down the wide hall, and through a door at the end. Then she was in the farm premises. The scent of dairy, and of farm-kitchen, and of farm-yard and of leather almost overcame her: but particularly the scent of dairy. They had been scalding out the pans. The flagged passage in front of her was dark, puddled and wet. Light came out from the open kitchen door. She went forward and stood in the doorway. The farm-people were at tea, seated at a little distance from her, round a long, narrow table, in the centre of which stood a white lamp. Ruddy faces, ruddy hands holding food, red mouths working, heads bent over the tea-cups: men, land-girls, boys: it was tea-time, feeding-time. Some faces caught sight of her. Mrs. Wernham, going round behind the chairs with a large black teapot, halting slightly in her walk, was not aware of her for a moment. Then she turned suddenly.

"Oh, is it Madam!" she exlaimed. "Come in, then, come in! We're at tea." And she dragged forward a chair.

"No, I won't come in," said Isabel. "I'm afraid I interrupt your meal."

"No—no—not likely, Madam, not likely."

"Hasn't Mr. Pervin come in, do you know?"

"I'm sure I couldn't say! Missed him, have you, Madam?"

"No, I only wanted him to come in," laughed Isabel, as if shyly.

"Wanted him, did ye? Get up, boy—get up, now ——"

Mrs. Wernham knocked one of the boys on the shoulder. He began to scrape to his feet, chewing largely.

"I believe he's in top stable," said another face from the table.

"Ah! No, don't get up. I'm going myself," said Isabel.

"Don't you go out of a dirty night like this. Let the lad go. Get along wi' ye, boy," said Mrs. Wernham.

"No, no," said Isabel, with a decision that was always obeyed. "Go on with your tea, Tom. I'd like to go across to the stable, Mrs. Wernham."

"Did ever you hear tell!" exclaimed the woman.

"Isn't the trap late?" asked Isabel.

"Why, no," said Mrs. Wernham, peering into the distance at the tall, dim clock. "No, Madam—we can give it another quarter or twenty minutes yet, good—yes, every bit of a quarter."

"Ah! It seems late when darkness falls so early," said Isabel.

"It do, that it do. Bother the days, that they draw in so," answered Mrs. Wernham. "Proper miserable!"

"They are," said Isabel, withdrawing.

She pulled on her overshoes, wrapped a large tartan shawl around her, put on a man's felt hat, and ventured out along the causeways of the first yard. It was very dark. The wind was roaring in the great elms behind the outhouses. When she came to the second yard the darkness seemed deeper. She was unsure of her footing. She wished she had brought a lantern. Rain blew against her. Half she liked it, half she felt unwilling to battle.

She reached at last the just visible door of the stable. There was no sign of a light anywhere. Opening the upper half, she looked in: into a simple well of darkness. The smell of horses, and ammonia, and of warmth was startling to her, in that full night. She listened with all her ears, but could hear nothing save the night, and the stirring of a horse.

"Maurice!" she called, softly and musically, though she was afraid. "Maurice—are you there?"

Nothing came from the darkness. She knew the rain and wind blew in upon the horses, the hot animal life. Feeling it wrong, she entered the stable, and drew the lower half of the door shut, holding the upper part close. She did not stir, because she was aware of the presence of the dark hind-quarters of the horses, though she could not see them, and she was afraid. Something wild stirred in her heart.

She listened intensely. Then she heard a small noise in the distance—far away, it seemed—the chink of a pan, and a man's voice speaking a brief word. It would be Maurice, in the other part of the stable. She stood motionless, waiting for him to come through the partition door. The horses were so terrifyingly near to her, in the invisible.

The loud jarring of the inner door-latch made her start; the door was opened. She could hear and feel her husband entering and invisibly passing among the horses near to her, darkness as they were, actively intermingled. The rather low sound of his voice as he spoke to the horses came velvety to her nerves. How near he was, and how invisible! The darkness seemed to be in a strange swirl of violent life, just upon her. She turned giddy.

Her presence of mind made her call, quietly and musically:

"Maurice! Maurice—dea-ar!"

"Yes," he answered. "Isabel?"

She saw nothing, and the sound of his voice seemed to touch her.

"Hello!" she answered cheerfully, straining her eyes to see him. He was still busy, attending to the horses near her, but she saw only darkness. It made her almost desperate.

"Won't you come in, dear?" she said.

"Yes, I'm coming. Just half a minute. *Stand over—now!* Trap's not come, has it?"

"Not yet," said Isabel.

His voice was pleasant and ordinary, but it had a slight suggestion of the stable to her. She wished he would come away. Whilst he was so utterly invisible, she was afraid of him.

"How's the time?" he asked.

"Not yet six," she replied. She disliked to answer into the dark. Presently he came very near to her, and she retreated out of doors.

"The weather blows in here," he said, coming steadily forward, feeling for the doors. She shrank away. At last she could dimly see him.

"Bertie won't have much of a drive," he said, as he closed the doors.

"He won't indeed!" said Isabel calmly, watching the dark shape at the door.

"Give me your arm, dear," she said.

She pressed his arm close to her, as she went. But she longed to see him, to look at him. She was nervous. He walked erect, with face rather lifted, but with a curious tentative movement of his powerful, muscular legs. She could feel the clever, careful, strong contact of his feet with the earth, as she balanced against him. For a moment he was a tower of darkness to her, as if he rose out of the earth.

In the house-passage he wavered, and went cautiously, with a curious look of silence about him as he felt for the bench. Then he sat down heavily. He was a man with rather sloping shoulders, but with heavy limbs, powerful legs that seemed to know the earth. His head was small, usually carried high and light. As he bent down to unfasten his gaiters and boots he did not look blind. His hair was brown and crisp, his hands were large, reddish, intelligent, the veins stood out in the wrists; and his thighs and knees seemed massive. When he stood up his face and neck were surcharged with blood, the veins stood out on his temples. She did not look at his blindness.

Isabel was always glad when they had passed through the dividing door into their own regions of repose and beauty. She was a little afraid of him, out there in the animal grossness of the back. His bearing also changed, as he smelt the familiar indefinable odour that pervaded his wife's surroundings, a delicate, refined scent, very faintly spicy. Perhaps it came from the pot-pourri bowls.

He stood at the foot of the stairs, arrested, listening. She watched him, and her heart sickened. He seemed to be listening to fate.

"He's not here yet," he said. "I'll go up and change."

"Maurice," she said, "you're not wishing he wouldn't come, are you?"

"I couldn't quite say," he answered. "I feel myself rather on the *qui vive.*"

"I can see you are," she answered. And she reached up and kissed his cheek. She saw his mouth relax into a slow smile.

"What are you laughing at?" she said, roguishly.

"You consoling me," he answered.

"Nay," she answered. "Why should I console you? You know we love each other—you know *how* married we are! What does anything else matter?"

"Nothing at all, my dear."

He felt for her face, and touched it, smiling.

"*You're* all right, aren't you?" he asked, anxiously.

"I'm wonderfully all right, love," she answered. "It's you I am a little troubled about, at times."

"Why me?" he said, touching her cheeks delicately with the tips of his fingers. The touch had an almost hypnotising effect on her.

He went away upstairs. She saw him mount into the darkness, unseeing and unchanging. He did not know that the lamps on the upper corridor were unlighted. He went on into the darkness with unchanging step. She heard him in the bath-room.

Pervin moved about almost unconsciously in his familiar surroundings, dark though everything was. He seemed to know the presence of objects before he touched them. It was a pleasure to him to rock thus through a world of things, carried on the flood in a sort of blood-prescience. He did not think much or trouble much. So long as he kept this sheer immediacy of blood-contact with the substantial world he was happy, he wanted no intervention of visual consciousness. In this state there was a certain rich positivity, bordering sometimes on rapture. Life seemed to move in him like a tide lapping, lapping, and advancing, enveloping all things darkly. It was a pleasure to stretch forth the hand and meet the unseen object, clasp it, and possess it in pure contact. He did not try to remember, to visualise. He did not want to. The new way of consciousness substituted itself in him.

The rich suffusion of this state generally kept him happy, reaching its culmination in the consuming passion for his wife. But at times the flow would seem to be checked and thrown back. Then it would beat inside him like a tangled sea, and he was tortured in the shattered chaos of his own blood. He grew to dread this arrest, this throw-back, this chaos inside himself, when he seemed merely at the mercy of his own powerful and conflicting elements. How to get some measure of control or surety, this was the question. And when the question rose maddening in him, he would clench his fists as if he would *compel* the whole universe to submit to him. But it was in vain. He could not even compel himself.

To-night, however, he was still serene, though little tremors of unreasonable exasperation ran through him. He had to handle the razor very carefully, as he shaved, for it was not at one with him, he was afraid of it. His hearing also was too much sharpened. He heard the woman lighting the lamps on the corridor, and attending to the fire in the visitors' room. And then, as he went to his room, he heard the trap arrive. Then came Isabel's voice, lifted and calling, like a bell ringing:

"Is it you, Bertie? Have you come?"

And a man's voice answered out of the wind:

"Hello, Isabel: There you are."

"Have you had a miserable drive? I'm so sorry we couldn't send a closed carriage. I can't see you at all, you know."

"I'm coming. No, I liked the drive—it was like Perthshire. Well, how are you? You're looking fit as ever, as far as I can see."

"Oh, yes," said Isabel. "I'm wonderfully well. How are you? Rather thin, I think ——"

"Worked to death—everybody's old cry. But I'm all right, Ciss. How's Pervin?—isn't he here?"

"Oh, yes, he's upstairs changing. Yes, he's awfully well. Take off your wet things; I'll send them to be dried."

"And how are you both, in spirits? He doesn't fret?"

"No—no, not at all. No, on the contrary, really. We've been wonderfully happy, incredibly. It's more than I can understand—so wonderful: the nearness, and the peace——"

"Ah! Well, that's awfully good news ——"

They moved away. Pervin heard no more. But a childish sense of desolation had come over him, as he heard their brisk voices. He seemed shut out—like a child that is left out. He was aimless and excluded, he did not know what to do with himself. The helpless desolation came over him. He fumbled nervously as he dressed himself, in a state almost of childishness. He disliked the Scotch accent in Bertie's speech, and the slight response it found on Isabel's tongue. He disliked the slight purr of complacency in the Scottish speech. He disliked intensely the glib way in which Isabel spoke of their happiness and nearness. It made him recoil. He was fretful and beside himself like a child, he had almost a childish nostalgia to be included in the life circle. And at the same time he was a man, dark and powerful and infuriated by his own weakness. By some fatal flaw, he could not be by himself, he had to depend on the support of another. And this very dependence enraged him. He hated Bertie Reid, and at the same time he knew the hatred was nonsense, he knew it was the outcome of his own weakness.

He went downstairs. Isabel was alone in the dining-room. She watched him enter, head erect, his feet tentative. He looked so strong-blooded and healthy, and, at the same time, cancelled. Cancelled—that was the word that flew across her mind. Perhaps it was his scar suggested it.

"You heard Bertie come, Maurice?" she said.

"Yes—isn't he here?"

"He's in his room. He looks very thin and worn."

"I suppose he works himself to death."

A woman came in with a tray—and after a few minutes Bertie came down. He was a little dark man, with a very big forehead, thin, wispy hair, and sad, large eyes. His expression was inordinately sad—almost funny. He had odd, short legs.

Isabel watched him hesitate under the door, and glance nervously at her husband. Pervin heard him and turned.

"Here you are, now," said Isabel. "Come, let us eat."

Bertie went across to Maurice.

"How are you, Pervin?" he said, as he advanced.

The blind man stuck his hand out into space, and Bertie took it.

"Very fit. Glad you've come," said Maurice.

Isabel glanced at them, and glanced away, as if she could not bear to see them.

"Come," she said. "Come to table. Aren't you both awfully hungry? I am, tremendously."

"I'm afraid you waited for me," said Bertie, as they sat down.

Maurice had a curious monolithic way of sitting in a chair, erect and distant. Isabel's heart always beat when she caught sight of him thus.

"No," she replied to Bertie. "We're very little later than usual. We're having a sort of high tea, not dinner. Do you mind? It gives us such a nice long evening, uninterrupted."

"I like it," said Bertie.

Maurice was feeling, with curious little movements, almost like a cat kneading her bed, for his plate, his knife and fork, his napkin. He was getting the whole geography of his cover into his consciousness. He sat erect and inscrutable, remote-seeming. Bertie watched the static figure of the blind man, the delicate tactile discernment of the large, ruddy hands, and the curious mindless silence of the brow, above the scar. With difficulty he looked away, and without knowing what he did, picked up a little crystal bowl of violets from the table, and held them to his nose.

"They are sweet-scented," he said. "Where do they come from?"

"From the garden—under the windows," said Isabel.

"So late in the year—and so fragrant! Do you remember the violets under Aunt Bell's south wall?"

The two friends looked at each other and exchanged a smile, Isabel's eyes lighting up.

"Don't I?" she replied. "*Wasn't* she queer!"

"A curious old girl," laughed Bertie. "There's a streak of freakishness in the family, Isabel."

"Ah—but not in you and me, Bertie," said Isabel. "Give them to Maurice, will you?" she added, as Bertie was putting down the flowers. "Have you smelled the violets, dear? Do!—they are so scented."

Maurice held out his hand, and Bertie placed the tiny bowl against his large, warm-looking fingers. Maurice's hand closed over the thin white fingers of the barrister. Bertie carefully extricated himself. Then the two watched the blind man smelling the violets. He bent his head and seemed to be thinking. Isabel waited.

"Aren't they sweet, Maurice?" she said at last, anxiously.

"Very," he said. And he held out the bowl. Bertie took it. Both he and Isabel were a little afraid, and deeply disturbed.

The meal continued. Isabel and Bertie chatted spasmodically. The blind man was silent. He touched his food repeatedly, with quick, delicate touches of his knifepoint, then cut irregular bits. He could not bear to be helped. Both Isabel and Bertie suffered: Isabel wondered why. She did not suffer when she was alone with Maurice, Bertie made her conscious of a strangeness.

After the meal the three drew their chairs to the fire, and sat down to talk. The decanters were put on a table near at hand. Isabel knocked the logs on the fire, and clouds of brilliant sparks went up the chimney. Bertie noticed a slight weariness in her bearing.

"You will be glad when your child comes now, Isabel?" he said.

She looked up to him with a quick wan smile.

"Yes, I shall be glad," she answered. "It begins to seem long. Yes, I shall be very glad. So will you, Maurice, won't you?" she added.

"Yes, I shall," replied her husband.

"We are both looking forward so much to having it," she said.

"Yes, of course," said Bertie.

He was a bachelor, three or four years older than Isabel. He lived in beautiful rooms overlooking the river, guarded by a faithful Scottish man-servant. And he had his friends among the fair sex—not lovers, friends. So long as he could avoid any danger of courtship or marriage, he adored a few good women with constant and unfailing homage, and he was chivalrously fond of quite a number. But if they seemed to encroach on him, he withdrew and detested them.

Isabel knew him very well, knew his beautiful constancy, and kindness, also his incurable weakness, which made him unable ever to enter into close contact of any sort. He was ashamed of himself, because he could not marry, could not approach women physically. He wanted to do so. But he could not. At the centre of him he was afraid, helplessly and even brutally afraid. He had given up hope, had ceased to expect any more that he could escape his own weakness. Hence he was a brilliant and successful barrister, also a *littérateur* of high repute, a rich man, and a great social success. At the centre he felt himself neuter, nothing.

Isabel knew him well. She despised him even while she admired him. She looked at his sad face, his little short legs, and felt contempt of him. She looked at his dark grey eyes, with their uncanny, almost childlike intuition, and she loved him. He understood amazingly—but she had no fear of his understanding. As a man she patronised him.

And she turned to the impassive, silent figure of her husband. He sat leaning back, with folded arms, and face a little uptilted. His knees were straight and massive. She sighed, picked up the poker, and again began to prod the fire, to rouse the clouds of soft brilliant sparks.

"Isabel tells me," Bertie began suddenly, "that you have not suffered unbearably from the loss of sight."

Maurice straightened himself to attend, but kept his arms folded.

"No, he said, "not unbearably. Now and again one struggles against it, you know. But there are compensations."

"They say it is much worse to be stone deaf," said Isabel.

"I believe it is," said Bertie. "Are there compensations?" he added, to Maurice.

"Yes. You cease to bother about a great many things." Again Maurice stretched his figure, stretched the strong muscles of his back, and leaned backwards, with uplifted face.

"And that is a relief," said Bertie. "But what is there in place of the bothering? What replaces the activity?"

There was a pause. At length the blind man replied, as out of a negligent, unattentive thinking:

"Oh, I don't know. There's a good deal when you're not active."

"Is there?" said Bertie. "What, exactly? It always seems to me that when there is no thought and no action, there is nothing."

Again Maurice was slow in replying.

"There is something," he replied. "I couldn't tell you what it is."

And the talk lapsed once more, Isabel and Bertie chatting gossip and reminiscence, the blind man silent.

At length Maurice rose restlessly, a big, obtrusive figure. He felt tight and hampered. He wanted to go away.

"Do you mind," he said, "if I go and speak to Wernham?"

"No—go along, dear," said Isabel.

And he went out. A silence came over the two friends. At length Bertie said:

"Nevertheless, it is a great deprivation, Cissie."

"It is, Bertie. I know it is."

"Something lacking all the time," said Bertie.

"Yes, I know. And yet—and yet—Maurice is right. There is something else, something *there*, which you never knew was there, and which you can't express."

"What is there?" asked Bertie.

"I don't know—it's awfully hard to define it—but something strong and immediate. There's something strange in Maurice's presence—indefinable—but I couldn't do without it. I agree that it seems to put one's mind to sleep. But when we're alone I miss nothing; it seems awfully rich, almost splendid, you know."

"I'm afraid I don't follow," said Bertie.

They talked desultorily. The wind blew loudly outside, rain chattered on the window-panes, making a sharp drum-sound, because of the closed, mellow-golden shutters inside. The logs burned slowly, with hot, almost invisible small flames. Bertie seemed uneasy, there were dark circles round his eyes. Isabel, rich with her approaching maternity, leaned looking into the fire. Her hair curled in odd, loose strands, very pleasing to the man. But she had a curious feeling of old woe in her heart, old, timeless night-woe.

"I suppose we're all deficient somewhere," said Bertie.

"I suppose so," said Isabel wearily.

"Damned, sooner or later."

"I don't know," she said, rousing herself. "I feel quite all right, you know. The child coming seems to make me indifferent to everything, just placid. I can't feel that there's anything to trouble about, you know."

"A good thing, I should say," he replied slowly.

"Well, there it is. I suppose it's just Nature. If only I felt I needn't trouble about Maurice, I should be perfectly content ——"

"But you feel you must trouble about him?"

"Well—I don't know ——" She even resented this much effort.

The night passed slowly. Isabel looked at the clock. "I say," she said. "It's nearly ten o'clock. Where can Maurice be? I'm sure they're all in bed at the back. Excuse me a moment."

She went out, returning almost immediately.

"It's all shut up and in darkness," she said. "I wonder where he is. He must have gone out to the farm ——"

Bertie looked at her.

"I suppose he'll come in," he said.

"I suppose so," she said. "But it's unusual for him to be out now."

"Would you like me to go out and see?"

"Well—if you wouldn't mind. I'd go, but ——" She did not want to make the physical effort.

Bertie put on an old overcoat and took a lantern. He went out from the side door. He shrank from the wet and roaring night. Such weather had a nervous effect on him: too much moisture everywhere made him feel almost imbecile. Unwilling, he went through it all. A dog barked violently at him. He peered in all the buildings. At last, as he opened the upper door of a sort of intermediate barn, he heard a grinding noise, and looking in, holding up his lantern, saw Maurice, in his shirt-sleeves, standing listening, holding the handle of a turnip-pulper. He had been pulping sweet roots, a pile of which lay dimly heaped in a corner behind him.

"That you, Wernham?" said Maurice, listening.

"No, it's me," said Bertie.

A large, half-wild grey cat was rubbing at Maurice's leg. The blind man stooped to rub its sides. Bertie watched the scene, then unconsciously entered and shut the door behind him. He was in a high sort of barn-place, from which, right and left, ran off the corridors in front of the stalled cattle. He watched the slow, stooping motion of the other man, as he caressed the great cat.

Maurice straightened himself.

"You came to look for me?" he said.

"Isabel was a little uneasy," said Bertie.

"I'll come in. I like messing about doing these jobs." The cat had reared her sinister, feline length against his leg, clawing at his thigh affectionately. He lifted her claws out of his flesh.

"I hope I'm not in your way at all at the Grange here," said Bertie, rather shy and stiff.

"My way? No, not a bit. I'm glad Isabel has somebody to talk to. I'm afraid it's I who am in the way. I know I'm not very lively company. Isabel's all right, don't you think? She's not unhappy, is she?"

"I don't think so."

"What does she say?"

"She says she's very content—only a little troubled about you."

"Why me?"

"Perhaps afraid that you might brood," said Bertie, cautiously.

"She needn't be afraid of that." He continued to caress the flattened grey head of the cat with his fingers. "What I am a bit afraid of," he resumed, "is that she'll find me a dead weight, always alone with me down here."

"I don't think you need think that," said Bertie, though this was what he feared himself.

"I don't know," said Maurice. "Sometimes I feel it isn't fair that she's saddled with me." Then he dropped his voice curiously. "I say," he asked, secretly struggling, "is my face much disfigured? Do you mind telling me?"

"There is the scar," said Bertie, wondering. "Yes, it is a disfigurement. But more pitiable than shocking."

"A pretty bad scar, though," said Maurice.

"Oh, yes."

There was a pause.

"Sometimes I feel I am horrible," said Maurice, in a low voice, talking as if to himself. And Bertie actually felt a quiver of horror.

"That's nonsense," he said.

Maurice again straightened himself, leaving the cat.

"There's no telling," he said. Then again, in an odd tone, he added: "I don't really know you, do I?"

"Probably not," said Bertie.

"Do you mind if I touch you?"

The lawyer shrank away instinctively. And yet, out of very philanthropy, he said, in a small voice: "Not at all."

But he suffered as the blind man stretched out a strong, naked hand to him. Maurice accidentally knocked off Bertie's hat.

"I thought you were taller," he said, starting. Then he laid his hand on Bertie Reid's head, closing the dome of the skull in a soft, firm grasp, gathering it, as it were; then, shifting his grasp and softly closing again, with a fine, close pressure, till he had covered the skull and the face of the smaller man, tracing the brows, and touching the full, closed eyes, touching the small nose and the nostrils, the rough, short moustache, the mouth, the rather strong chin. The hand of the blind man grasped the shoulder, the arm, the hand of the other man. He seemed to take him, in the soft, travelling grasp.

"You seem young," he said quietly, at last.

The lawyer stood almost annihilated, unable to answer.

"Your head seems tender, as if you were young," Maurice repeated. "So do your hands. Touch my eyes, will you?—touch my scar."

Now Bertie quivered with revulsion. Yet he was under the power of the blind man, as if hypnotised. He lifted his hand, and laid the fingers on the scar, on the scarred eyes. Maurice suddenly covered them with his own hand, pressed the fingers of the other man upon his disfigured eye-sockets, trembling in every fibre, and rocking slightly, slowly, from side to side. He remained thus for a minute or more, whilst Bertie stood as if in a swoon, unconscious, imprisoned.

Then suddenly Maurice removed the hand of the other man from his brow, and stood holding it in his own.

"Oh my God," he said, "we shall know each other now, shan't we? We shall know each other now."

Bertie could not answer. He gazed mute and terror-struck, overcome by his own weakness. He knew he could not answer. He had an unreasonable fear, lest the other man should suddenly destroy him. Whereas Maurice was actually filled with hot, poignant love, the passion of friendship. Perhaps it was this very passion of friendship which Bertie shrank from most.

"We're all right together now, aren't we?" said Maurice. "It's all right now, as long as we live, so far as we're concerned?"

"Yes," said Bertie, trying by any means to escape.

Maurice stood with head lifted, as if listening. The new delicate fulfilment of mortal friendship had come as a revelation and surprise to him, something exquisite and unhoped-for. He seemed to be listening to hear if it were real.

Then he turned for his coat.

"Come," he said, "we'll go to Isabel."

Bertie took the lantern and opened the door. The cat disappeared. The two men went in silence along the causeways. Isabel, as they came, thought their footsteps sounded strange. She looked up pathetically and anxiously for their entrance. There seemed a curious elation about Maurice. Bertie was haggard, with sunken eyes.

"What is it?" she asked.

"We've become friends," said Maurice, standing with his feet apart, like a strange colossus.

"Friends!" re-echoed Isabel. And she looked again at Bertie. He met her eyes with a furtive, haggard look; his eyes were as if glazed with misery.

"I'm so glad," she said, in sheer perplexity.

"Yes," said Maurice.

He was indeed so glad. Isabel took his hand with both hers, and held it fast.

"You'll be happier now, dear," she said.

But she was watching Bertie. She knew that he had one desire—to escape from this intimacy, this friendship, which had been thrust upon him. He could not bear it that he had been touched by the blind man, his insane reserve broken in. He was like a mollusc whose shell is broken.

Katherine Mansfield (1888–1923)

Like several other important short-story writers (Chekhov, Maupassant, Poe), Katherine Mansfield died quite young. After an ultra-Bohemian life, she succumbed to tuberculosis in 1923. Her reputation as a writer rests upon forty-two short stories, a volume of critical pieces, a group of revealing letters, and a remarkable journal.

Born Kathleen Beauchamp, daughter of a well-to-do New Zealand banker, Mansfield went to England as a schoolgirl of fifteen, and except for a visit the next year, she never went home again. Yet some of her best stories take place in the New Zealand of her childhood. As an adult, she was always an alien, an outsider. She traveled in Europe, lived in England, Germany, Italy, died in France, stayed on the fringes of groups like Bloomsbury or the mystics among whom she spent her last days at Fontainebleau. Her friends were Bohemians and artists. Gudrun in Lawrence's *Women in Love* and Beatrice Gilray in Aldous Huxley's *Point Counterpoint* seem to be modeled after her. She and Virginia Woolf were uneasy friends. ("She's done for!" Woolf said upon reading one of Mansfield's stories.) The great relationship of her adult life was with John Middleton Murry, whom she married in 1918. After her death, Murry edited her letters and journals and did much to promote the cult of Katherine Mansfield as the doomed artist who lived to the hilt all the time.

Mansfield read Chekhov in German translation before his work appeared in English, and he was the great influence on her development as a writer. At least five of her stories are closely modeled after stories by him. Like Chekhov, Mansfield uses small moments to reveal large significance in the lives of people, and, like him, she develops the irony inherent in so many human situations.

But she must be credited with her own substantial contributions to the development of the short story, its language and its structure. Under her influence the language of the genre became more lyrical and expressive. She does not merely denote or describe the feelings and thoughts of her characters, she recreates them. Her language closely tracks their sensitivity, perception, intensity; in short, the slang, the cadence, the phrasing reproduce the personality of the character. This technique at its best draws the reader very close to the emotional center of the story, so that the writer, the reader, and the protagonist all seem to be occupying the same space and experiencing the same emotions.

Because, true romantic that she was, she cared so much about intensity of feeling, Mansfield attempted to remove all that did not directly contribute to the emotional impact. She concentrated the presentation of plot into a brief time span covering only the most dramatic moments (See Introduction pp. 6–7). Time past, present, and future all seem to be occurring now in the mind of the protagonist. The whole weight of a life—or of a marriage—is compressed in a moment.

Her main characters are usually extremely vulnerable to experience and their own emotions. By focusing so exclusively on their heightened sensibility, Mansfield sometimes seems to oversimplify her people and the human story. Occasionally her stories carry into sentimentality. "Marriage a la Mode" is saved from this fate finally by the somewhat disconcerting but effectively ironic shift to Isabel's point of view at the end.

Marriage À La Mode

On his way to the station William remembered with a fresh pang of disappointment that he was taking nothing down to the kiddies. Poor little chaps! It was hard lines on them. Their first words always were as they ran to greet him, "What have you got for me, daddy?" and he had nothing. He would have to buy them some sweets at the station. But that was what he had done for the past four Saturdays; their faces had fallen last time when they saw the same old boxes produced again.

And Paddy had said, "I had red ribbing on mine *bee*-fore!"

And Johnny had said, "It's always pink on mine. I hate pink."

But what was William to do? The affair wasn't so easily settled. In the old days, of course, he would have taken a taxi off to a decent toyshop and chosen them something in five minutes. But nowadays they had Russian toys, French toys, Serbian toys—toys from God knows where. It was over a year since Isabel had scrapped the old donkeys and engines and so on because they were so "dreadfully sentimental" and "so appallingly bad for the babies' sense of form."

"It's so important," the new Isabel had explained, "that they should like the right things from the very beginning. It saves so much time later on. Really, if the poor pets have to spend their infant years staring at these horrors, one can imagine them growing up and asking to be taken to the Royal Academy."

And she spoke as though a visit to the Royal Academy was certain immediate death to any one. . . .

Copyright 1922 by Alfred A. Knopf, Inc. and renewed 1950 by John Middleton Murry: Reprinted from *The Short Stories of Katherine* Mansfield, by permission of the publisher.

"Well, I don't know," said William slowly. "When I was their age I used to go to bed hugging an old towel with a knot in it."

The new Isabel looked at him, her eyes narrowed, her lips apart.

"*Dear* William! I'm sure you did!" She laughed in the new way.

Sweets it would have to be, however, thought William gloomily, fishing in his pocket for change for the taxi-man. And he saw the kiddies handing the boxes round—they were awfully generous little chaps—while Isabel's precious friends didn't hesitate to help themselves. . . .

What about fruit? William hovered before a stall just inside the station. What about a melon each? Would they have to share that, too? Or a pineapple for Pad, and a melon for Johnny? Isabel's friends could hardly go sneaking up to the nursery at the children's meal-times. All the same, as he bought the melon William had a horrible vision of one of Isabel's young poets lapping up a slice, for some reason, behind the nursery door.

With his two very awkward parcels he strode off to his train. The platform was crowded, the train was in. Doors banged open and shut. There came such a loud hissing from the engine that people looked dazed as they scurried to and fro. William made straight for a first-class smoker, stowed away his suit-case and parcels, and taking a huge wad of papers out of his inner pocket, he flung down in the corner and began to read.

"Our client moreover is positive. . . . We are inclined to reconsider . . . in the event of—" Ah, that was better. William pressed back his flattened hair and stretched his legs across the carriage floor. The familiar dull gnawing in his breast quietened down. "With regard to our decision—" He took out a blue pencil and scored a paragraph slowly.

Two men came in, stepped across him, and made for the farther corner. A young fellow swung his golf clubs into the rack and sat down opposite. The train gave a gentle lurch, they were off. William glanced up and saw the hot, bright station slipping away. A red-faced girl raced along by the carriages, there was something strained and almost desperate in the way she waved and called. "Hysterical!" thought William dully. Then a greasy, black-faced workman at the end of the platform grinned at the passing train. And William thought, "A filthy life!" and went back to his papers.

When he looked up again there were fields, and beasts standing for shelter under the dark trees. A wide river, with naked children splashing in the shallows, glided into sight and was gone again. The sky shone pale, and one bird drifted high like a dark fleck in a jewel.

"We have examined our client's correspondence files. . . ." The last sentence he had read echoed in his mind. "We have examined . . ." William hung on to that sentence, but it was no good; it snapped in the middle, and the fields, the sky, the sailing bird, the water, all said, "Isabel." The same thing happened every Saturday afternoon. When he was on his way to meet Isabel there began those countless imaginary meetings. She was at the station, standing just a little apart from everybody else; she was sitting in the open taxi outside; she was at the garden gate; walking across the parched grass; at the door, or just inside the hall.

And her clear, light voice said, "It's William," or "Hillo, William!" or "So William has come!" He touched her cool hand, her cool cheek.

The exquisite freshness of Isabel! When he had been a little boy, it was his delight to run into the garden after a shower of rain and shake the rose-bush over him. Isabel was that rose-bush, petal-soft, sparkling and cool. And he was still that little boy. But there was no running into the garden now, no laughing and shaking. The dull, persistent gnawing in his breast started again. He drew up his legs, tossed the papers aside, and shut his eyes.

"What is it, Isabel? What is it?" he said tenderly. They were in their bedroom in the new house. Isabel sat on a painted stool before the dressing table that was strewn with little black and green boxes.

"What is what, William?" And she bent forward, and her fine light hair fell over her cheeks.

"Ah, you know!" He stood in the middle of the strange room and he felt a stranger. At that Isabel wheeled round quickly and faced him.

"Oh, William!" she cried imploringly, and she held up the hair-brush: "Please! Please don't be so dreadfully stuffy and—tragic. You're always saying or looking or hinting that I've changed. Just because I've got to know really congenial people, and go about more, and am frightfully keen on—on everything, you behave as though I'd—" Isabel tossed back her hair and laughed—"killed our love or something. It's so awfully absurd"—she bit her lip—"and it's so maddening, William. Even this new house and the servants you grudge me."

"Isabel!"

"Yes, yes, it's true in a way," said Isabel quickly. "You think they are another bad sign. Oh, I know you do. I feel it," she said softly, "every time you come up the stairs. But we couldn't have gone on living in that other poky little hole, William. Be practical, at least! Why, there wasn't enough room for the babies even."

No, it was true. Every morning when he came back from chambers it was to find the babies with Isabel in the back drawing-room. They were having rides on the leopard skin thrown over the sofa back, or they were playing shops with Isabel's desk for a counter, or Pad was sitting on the hearthrug rowing away for dear life with a little brass fire shovel, while Johnny shot at pirates with the tongs. Every evening they each had a pick-a-back up the narrow stairs to their fat old Nanny.

Yes, he supposed it was a poky little house. A little white house with blue curtains and a window-box of petunias. William met their friends at the door with "Seen our petunias? Pretty terrific for London, don't you think?"

But the imbecile thing, the absolutely extraordinary thing was that he hadn't the slightest idea that Isabel wasn't as happy as he. God, what blindness! He hadn't the remotest notion in those days that she really hated that inconvenient little house, that she thought the fat Nanny was ruining the babies, that she was desperately lonely, pining for new people and new music and pictures and so on. If they hadn't gone to that studio party at Moira Morrison's—if Moira Morrison hadn't said as they were leaving. "I'm going to rescue your wife, selfish man. She's like an exquisite little Titania"—if Isabel hadn't gone with Moira to Paris—if—if . . .

The train stopped at another station. Bettingford. Good heavens! They'd be there in ten minutes. William stuffed the papers back into his pockets; the young man opposite had long since disappeared. Now the other two got out. The late afternoon sun shone on women in cotton frocks and little sunburnt, barefoot children. It blazed on a silky yellow flower with coarse leaves which sprawled over a bank of rock. The air ruffling through the window smelled of the sea. Had Isabel the same crowd with her this week-end, wondered William?

And he remembered the holidays they used to have, the four of them, with a little farm girl, Rose, to look after the babies. Isabel wore a jersey and her hair in a plait; she looked about fourteen. Lord! how his nose used to peel! And the amount they ate,

and the amount they slept in that immense feather bed with their feet locked together.
. . . William couldn't help a grim smile as he thought of Isabel's horror if she knew the
full extent of his sentimentality.

"Hillo, William!" She was at the station after all, standing just as he had imagined, apart from the others, and—William's heart leapt—she was alone.

"Hallo, Isabel!" William stared. He thought she looked so beautiful that he had
to say something, "You look very cool."

"Do I?" said Isabel. "I don't feel very cool. Come along, your horrid old train is
late. The taxi's outside." She put her hand lightly on his arm as they passed the ticket
collector. "We've all come to meet you," she said. "But we've left Bobby Kane at the
sweet shop, to be called for."

"Oh!" said William. It was all he could say for the moment.

There in the glare waited the taxi, with Bill Hunt and Dennis Green sprawling on
one side, their hats tilted over their faces, while on the other, Moira Morrison, in a
bonnet like a huge strawberry, jumped up and down.

"No ice! No ice! No ice!" she shouted gaily.

And Dennis chimed in from under his hat. "*Only* to be had from the fishmon-
ger's."

And Bill Hunt, emerging, added, "With *whole* fish in it."

"Oh, what a bore!" wailed Isabel. And she explained to William how they had
been chasing round the town for ice while she waited for him. "Simply everything is
running down the steep cliffs into the sea, beginning with the butter."

"We shall have to anoint ourselves with the butter," said Dennis. "May thy head,
William, lack not ointment."

"Look here," said William, "how are we going to sit? I'd better get up by the
driver."

"No, Bobby Kane's by the driver," said Isabel. "You're to sit between Moira and
me." The taxi started. "What have you got in those mysterious parcels?"

"De-cap-it-ated heads!" said Bill Hunt, shuddering beneath his hat.

"Oh, fruit!" Isabel sounded very pleased. "Wise William! A melon and a pineapple. How too nice!"

"No, wait a bit," said William, smiling. But he really was anxious. "I brought
them down for the kiddies."

"Oh, my dear!" Isabel laughed, and slipped her hand through his arm. "They'd
be rolling in agonies if they were to eat them. No"—she patted his hand—"you must
bring them something next time. I refuse to part with my pineapple."

"Cruel Isabel! Do let me smell it!" said Moira. She flung her arms across William
appealingly. "Oh!" The strawberry bonnet fell forward: she sounded quite faint.

"A Lady in Love with a Pineapple," said Dennis, as the taxi drew up before a
little shop with a striped blind. Out came Bobby Kane, his arms full of little packets.

"I do hope they'll be good. I've chosen them because of the colours. There are
some round things which really look too divine. And just look at this nougat," he cried
ecstatically, "just look at it! It's a perfect little ballet."

But at that moment the shopman appeared. "Oh, I forgot. They're none of them
paid for," said Bobby, looking frightened. Isabel gave the shopman a note, and Bobby
was radiant again. "Hallo, William! I'm sitting by the driver." And bareheaded, all in
white, with his sleeves rolled up to the shoulders, he leapt into his place. "Avanti!" he
cried. . . .

After tea the others went off to bathe, while William stayed and made his peace with the kiddies. But Johnny and Paddy were asleep, the rose-red glow had paled, bats were flying, and still the bathers had not returned. As William wandered downstairs, the maid crossed the hall carrying a lamp. He followed her into the sitting-room. It was a long room, coloured yellow. On the wall opposite William some one had painted a young man, over life-size, with very wobbly legs, offering a wide-eyed daisy to a young woman who had one very short arm and one very long, thin one. Over the chairs and sofa there hung strips of black material, covered with big splashes like broken eggs, and everywhere one looked there seemed to be an ash-tray full of cigarette ends. William sat down in one of the arm-chairs. Nowadays, when one felt with one hand down the sides, it wasn't to come upon a sheep with three legs or a cow that had lost one horn, or a very fat dove out of the Noah's Ark. One fished up yet another little paper-covered book of smudged-looking poems. . . . He thought of the wad of papers in his pocket, but he was too hungry and tired to read. The door was open; sounds came from the kitchen. The servants were talking as if they were alone in the house. Suddenly there came a loud screech of laughter and an equally loud "Sh!" They had remembered him. William got up and went through the French windows into the garden, and as he stood there in the shadow he heard the bathers coming up the sandy road; their voices rang through the quiet.

"I think it's up to Moira to use her little arts and wiles."

A tragic moan from Moira.

"We ought to have a gramophone for the week-ends that played 'The Maid of the Mountains.'"

"Oh no! Oh no!" cried Isabel's voice. "That's not fair to William. Be nice to him, my children! He's only staying until to-morrow evening."

"Leave him to me," cried Bobby Kane. "I'm awfully good at looking after people."

The gate swung open and shut. William moved on the terrace; they had seen him. "Hallo, William!" and Bobby Kane, flapping his towel, began to leap and pirouette on the parched lawn. "Pity you didn't come, William. The water was divine. And we all went to a little pub afterwards and had sloe gin."

The others had reached the house. "I say, Isabel," called Bobby, "would you like me to wear my Nijinsky dress to-night?"

"No," said Isabel, "nobody's going to dress. We're all starving. William's starving, too. Come along, *mes amis,* let's begin with sardines."

"I've found the sardines," said Moira, and she ran into the hall, holding a box high in the air.

"A Lady with a Box of Sardines," said Dennis gravely.

"Well, William, and how's London?" asked Bill Hunt, drawing the cork out of a bottle of whisky.

"Oh, London's not much changed," answered William.

"Good old London," said Bobby, very hearty, spearing a sardine.

But a moment later William was forgotten. Moira Morrison began wondering what colour one's legs really were under water.

"Mine are the palest, palest mushroom colour."

Bill and Dennis ate enormously. And Isabel filled glasses, and changed plates, and found matches, smiling blissfully. At one moment she said, "I do wish, Bill, you'd paint it."

"Paint what?" said Bill loudly, stuffing his mouth with bread.

"Us," said Isabel, "round the table. It would be so fascinating in twenty years' time."

Bill screwed up his eyes and chewed. "Light's wrong," he said rudely, "far too much yellow"; and went on eating. And that seemed to charm Isabel, too.

But after supper they were all so tired they could do nothing but yawn until it was late enough to go to bed. . . .

It was not until William was waiting for his taxi the next afternoon that he found himself alone with Isabel. When he brought his suit-case down into the hall, Isabel left the others and went over to him. She stooped down and picked up the suit-case. "What a weight!" she said, and she gave a little awkward laugh. "Let me carry it! To the gate."

"No, why should you" said William. "Of course not. Give it to me."

"Oh, please do let me," said Isabel. "I want to, really." They walked together silently. William felt there was nothing to say now.

"There," said Isabel triumphantly, setting the suit-case down, and she looked anxiously along the sandy road. "I hardly seem to have seen you this time," she said breathlessly. "It's so short, isn't it? I feel you've only just come. Next time—" The taxi came into sight. "I hope they look after you properly in London. I'm so sorry the babies have been out all day, but Miss Neil had arranged it. They'll hate missing you. Poor William, going back to London." The taxi turned. "Good-bye!" She gave him a little hurried kiss; she was gone.

Fields, trees, hedges streamed by. They shook through the empty, blind-looking little town, ground up the steep pull to the station.

The train was in. William made straight for a first-class smoker, flung back into the corner, but this time he let the papers alone. He folded his arms against the dull, persistent gnawing, and began in his mind to write a letter to Isabel.

The post was late as usual. They sat outside the house in long chairs under coloured parasols. Only Bobby Kane lay on the turf at Isabel's feet. It was dull, stifling; the day drooped like a flag.

"Do you think there will be Mondays in Heaven?" asked Bobby childishly.

And Dennis murmured, "Heaven will be one long Monday."

But Isabel couldn't help wondering what had happened to the salmon they had for supper last night. She had meant to have fish mayonnaise for lunch and now . . .

Moira was asleep. Sleeping was her latest discovery. "It's *so* wonderful. One simply shuts one's eyes, that's all. It's *so* delicious."

When the old ruddy postman came beating along the sandy road on his tricycle one felt the handlebars ought to have been oars.

Bill Hunt put down his book. "Letters," he said complacently, and they all waited. But, heartless postman—O malignant world! There was only one, a fat one for Isabel. Not even a paper.

"And mine's only from William," said Isabel mournfully.

"From William—already?"

"He's sending you back your marriage lines as a gentle reminder."

"Does everybody have marriage lines? I thought they were only for servants."

"Pages and pages! Look at her! A Lady reading a Letter," said Dennis.

My darling, precious Isabel. Pages and pages there were. As Isabel read on her feeling of astonishment changed to a stifled feeling. What on earth had induced William . . . ? How extraordinary it was. . . . What could have made him . . . ? She felt confused, more and more excited, even frightened. It was just like William. Was it? It was absurd, of course, it must be absurd, ridiculous. "Ha, ha, ha! Oh dear!" What was she to do? Isabel flung back in her chair and laughed till she couldn't stop laughing.

"Do, do tell us," said the others. "You must tell us."

"I'm longing to," gurgled Isabel. She sat up, gathered the letter, and waved it at them. "Gather round," she said. "Listen, it's too marvellous. A love-letter!"

"A love-letter! But how divine!" *Darling, precious Isabel.* But she had hardly begun before their laughter interrupted her.

"Go on, Isabel, it's perfect."

"It's the most marvellous find."

"Oh, do go on, Isabel!"

God forbid, my darling, that I should be a drag on your happiness.

'Oh! oh! oh!"

"Sh! sh! sh!"

And Isabel went on. When she reached the end they were hysterical: Bobby rolled on the turf and almost sobbed.

"You must let me have it just as it is, entire, for my new book," said Dennis firmly. "I shall give it a whole chapter."

"Oh, Isabel," moaned Moira, "that wonderful bit about holding you in his arms!"

"I always thought those letters in divorce cases were made up. But they pale before this."

"Let me hold it. Let me read it, mine own self," said Bobby Kane.

But, to their surprise, Isabel crushed the letter in her hand. She was laughing no longer. She glanced quickly at them all; she looked exhausted. "No, not just now. Not just now," she stammered.

And before they could recover she had run into the house, through the hall, up the stairs into her bedroom. Down she sat on the side of the bed. "How vile, odious, abominable, vulgar," muttered Isabel. She pressed her eyes with her knuckles and rocked to and fro. And again she saw them, but not four, more like forty, laughing, sneering, jeering, stretching out their hands while she read them William's letter. Oh, what a loathsome thing to have done. How could she have done it! *God forbid, my darling, that I should be a drag on your happiness.* William! Isabel pressed her face into the pillow. But she felt that even the grave bedroom knew her for what she was, shallow, tinkling, vain. . . .

Presently from the garden below there came voices.

"Isabel, we're all going for a bathe. Do come!"

"Come, thou wife of William!"

"Call her once before you go, call once yet!"

Isabel sat up. Now was the moment, now she must decide. Would she go with them, or stay here and write to William. Which, which should it be? "I must make up my mind." Oh, but how could there be any question? Of course she would stay here and write.

"Titania!" piped Moira.

"Isa-bel?"

No, it was too difficult. "I'll—I'll go with them, and write to William later. Some other time. Later. Not now. But I shall *certainly* write," thought Isabel hurriedly.

And, laughing in the new way, she ran down the stairs.

Conrad Aiken (1889-1973)

Until his death in August 1973, Conrad Aiken had enjoyed a long and distinguished career as poet, critic, and writer of fiction. He began his undergraduate studies in 1908 with a freshman class which included T. S. Eliot (whom Aiken nicknamed *tsetse*), Van Wyck Brooks, John Reed, and Robert Benchley. During his senior year at Harvard he was placed on probation for poor class attendance; indignant, he took off for Europe. Six months later he returned and completed his degree in June 1912. Between 1916 and 1922 he wrote poetry and fiction, as well as serving actively as a reviewer-critic for the *Dial, The New Republic,* and various London journals. Except for one brief stint in 1927-28 as tutor in English at Harvard, Aiken seems to have functioned throughout his long and productive career wholly as a professional writer and editor. While his work brought him many honors—Pulitzer Prize (1930), Library of Congress Chair of Poetry (1950), National Book Award (1954), Bollingen Prize (1956)—he was always thought to be somewhat outside the main currents of American literary fashion.

Behind any and all of the externals of Aiken's life and career lay a shattering experience of boyhood. At age eleven and a half, in the year 1900, he heard two pistol shots and discovered that his father had killed his mother and himself. Here is how Aiken writes of that terrible event years later in his autobiographical *Ushant* (1952):

> He was retaining all this, and re-enacting it, even to the final scene of all: when, after the desultory early-morning quarrel, came the half-stifled scream, and then the sound of his father's voice counting three, and the two loud pistol-shots; and he had tiptoed into the dark room, where the two bodies lay motionless, and apart, and finding them dead, *found himself possessed of them forever.*

We may only guess what the long-term effects of that profound wound were to be. Much of Aiken's criticism is Freudian, and Freudian psychoanalysis did become important to him. Enlargement of consciousness, human relationships, individual isolation—all these are central themes and tensions in his poems, novels, and stories. But any full study of his work will reveal that he went beyond Freudianism. As Henry A. Murray, psychoanalyst and close friend, put it: "Aiken allowed the Freudian dragon to swallow him, and then, after a sufficient sojourn in its maw, cut his way out to a new freedom."

"Silent Snow, Secret Snow" belongs to a gathering of Aiken's short stories published in 1934 under the title *Among the Lost People.* Other stories in the collection set forth configurations of separation and isolation (the lonely child, the lonely old man), but none more dramatically than this one. Among all those lost people of the volume, no one gets lost so sheerly, so completely, so *purely* as does Paul. Some readers take the snow as representing death or a metaphoric means to death. And yet Paul's final condition suggests a living death. The action commences in the preliminary stages of schizophrenia and moves through stages of intensification to the final and permanent withdrawal from an irrecoverable objective reality—Paul's end being not death, but a state of ultimate, autistic catatonia. The ending of Aiken's story brings to mind the end of Ibsen's play *Ghosts,* where Oswald, suffering the final ravages of syphilis, sits motionless, staring at an eclipsing sun, going blind and mad all at once.

Whatever their final interpretation, readers have uniformly regarded this as Aiken's most powerful tale. We are led into the center of the story gradually, but with a kind of relentless suspense that will not let us go. Part of Aiken's technique is to arouse within us the expectation that the snow stands for, or contains, some deeper meaning or reality that will eventually be revealed, perhaps in some kind of confrontation scene, in which we will share recognition with Paul (or his parents) of what they come to recognize. But it doesn't happen; we never get beyond the snow itself, "whose meanings remain secret." One of the most judicious commentaries on the story is that of Frederick J. Hoffman:

> The narrative consistently stays within the boy's mind, moving with it toward his destruction, never suggesting or stating reasons or trying to probe "psychologically" into the boy's injured spirit. It is a psychic scene of remarkable purity; the adult world stays always dimly at the fringe of the boy's awareness and of his sense of his relationship. What has caused the aberration is never revealed, but his desire to withdraw from human communication is faithfully followed to its ultimate, total rejection of the family and submission to the vision.

Silent Snow, Secret Snow

Just why it should have happened, or why it should have happened just when it did, he could not, of course, possibly have said; nor perhaps could it even have occurred to him to ask. The thing was above all a secret, something to be preciously concealed from Mother and Father; and to that very fact it owed an enormous part of its deliciousness. It was like a peculiarly beautiful trinket to be carried unmentioned in one's trouser-pocket—a rare stamp, an old coin, a few tiny gold links found trodden out of shape on the path in the park, a pebble of carnelian,[1] a sea shell distinguishable from all others by an unusual spot or stripe—and, as if it were any one of these, he carried around with him everywhere a warm and persistent and increasingly beautiful sense of possession. Nor was it only a sense of possession—it was also a sense of protection. It was as if, in some delightful way, his secret gave him a fortress, a wall behind which he could retreat into heavenly seclusion. This was almost the first thing he had noticed about it—apart from the oddness of the thing itself—and it was this that now again, for the fiftieth time, occurred to him, as he sat in the little schoolroom. It was the half hour for geography. Miss Buell was revolving with one finger, slowly, a huge terrestrial globe which had been placed on her desk. The green and yellow continents passed and repassed, questions were asked and answered, and now the little girl in front of him, Deirdre, who had a funny little constellation of freckles on the back of her neck, exactly like the Big Dipper, was standing up and telling Miss Buell that the equator was the line that ran around the middle.

---

[1] A reddish quartz, used in jewelry.

From Conrad Aiken, *The Collected Stories of Conrad Aiken.* Copyright © 1922, 1923, 1924, 1925, 1927, 1928, 1929, 1930, 1931, 1932, 1933, 1934, 1935, 1941–1950, 1952, 1953, 1955, 1956, 1957, 1958–1959, 1960. Reprinted by permission of Thomas Y. Crowell Co., Inc.

Miss Buell's face, which was old and grayish and kindly, with gray stiff curls beside the cheeks, and eyes that swam very brightly, like little minnows, behind thick glasses, wrinkled itself into a complication of amusements.

"Ah! I see. The earth is wearing a belt, or a sash. Or someone drew a line round it!"

"Oh, no—not that—I mean—"

In the general laughter, he did not share, or only a very little. He was thinking about the Arctic and Antarctic regions, which of course, on the globe, were white. Miss Buell was now telling them about the tropics, the jungles, the steamy heat of equatorial swamps, where the birds and butterflies, and even the snakes, were like living jewels. As he listened to these things, he was already, with a pleasant sense of half-effort, putting his secret between himself and the words. Was it really an effort at all? For effort implied something voluntary, and perhaps even something one did not especially want; whereas this was distinctly pleasant, and came almost of its own accord. All he needed to do was to think of that morning, the first one, and then of all the others—

But it was all so absurdly simple! It had amounted to so little. It was nothing, just an idea—and just why it should have become so wonderful, so permanent, was a mystery—a very pleasant one, to be sure, but also, in an amusing way, foolish. However, without ceasing to listen to Miss Buell, who had now moved up to the north temperate zone, he deliberately invited his memory of the first morning. It was only a moment or two after he had waked up—or perhaps the moment itself. But was there, to be exact, an exact moment? Was one awake all at once? Or was it gradual? Anyway, it was after he had stretched a lazy hand up towards the headrail, and yawned, and then relaxed again among his warm covers, all the more grateful on a December morning, that the thing had happened. Suddenly, for no reason, he had thought of the postman, he remembered the postman. Perhaps there was nothing so odd in that. After all, he heard the postman almost every morning in his life—his heavy boots could be heard clumping round the corner at the top of the little cobbled hill-street, and then, progressively nearer, progressively louder, the double knock at each door, the crossings and re-crossings of the street, till finally the clumsy steps came stumbling across to the very door, and the tremendous knock came which shook the house itself.

(Miss Buell was saying "Vast wheat-growing areas in North America and Siberia."

Deirdre had for the moment placed her left hand across the back of her neck.)

But on this particular morning, the first morning, as he lay there with his eyes closed, he had for some reason *waited* for the postman. He wanted to hear him come round the corner. And that was precisely the joke—he never did. He never came. He never had come—*round the corner*—again. For when at last the steps *were* heard, they had already, he was quite sure, come a little down the hill, to the first house; and even so, the steps were curiously different—they were softer, they had a new secrecy about them, they were muffled and indistinct; and while the rhythm of them was the same, it now said a new thing—it said peace, it said remoteness, it said cold, it said sleep. And he had understood the situation at once—nothing could have seemed simpler—there had been snow in the night, such as all winter he had been longing for; and it was this which had rendered the postman's first footsteps inaudible, and the later ones faint. Of course! How lovely! And even now it must be snowing—it was going to be a snowy day—the long white ragged lines were drifting and sifting across the street, across the faces of the old houses, whispering and hushing, making little triangles of white in the corners between cobblestones, seething a little when the wind blew them over the ground to a drifted corner; and so it would be all day, getting deeper and deeper and silenter and silenter.

(Miss Buell was saying "Land of perpetual snow.")

All this time, of course (while he lay in bed), he had kept his eyes closed, listening to the nearer progress of the postman, the muffled footsteps thumping and slipping on the snow-sheathed cobbles; and all the other sounds—the double knocks, a frosty far-off voice or two, a bell ringing thinly and softly as if under a sheet of ice—had the same slightly abstracted quality, as if removed by one degree from actuality—as if everything in the world had been insulated by snow. But when at last, pleased, he opened his eyes, and turned them towards the window, to see for himself this long-desired and now so clearly imagined miracle—what he saw instead was brilliant sunlight on a roof; and when, astonished, he jumped out of bed and stared down into the street, expecting to see the cobbles obliterated by the snow, he saw nothing but the bare bright cobbles themselves.

Queer, the effect this extraordinary surprise had had upon him—all the following morning he had kept with him a sense as of snow falling about him, a secret screen of new snow between himself and the world. If he had not dreamed such a thing—and how could he have dreamed it while awake?—how else could one explain it? In any case, the delusion had been so vivid as to affect his entire behavior. He could not now remember whether it was on the first or the second morning—or was it even the third?—that his mother had drawn attention to some oddness in his manner.

"But my darling"—she had said at the breakfast table—"what has come over you? You don't seem to be listening. . . ."

And how often that very thing had happened since!

(Miss Buell was now asking if anyone knew the difference between the North Pole and the Magnetic Pole. Deirdre was holding up her flickering brown hand, and he could see the four white dimples that marked the knuckles.)

Perhaps it hadn't been either the second or third morning—or even the fourth or fifth. How could he be sure? How could he be sure just when the delicious *progress* had become clear? Just when it had really *begun?* The intervals weren't very precise. . . . All he now knew was, that at some point or other—perhaps the second day, perhaps the sixth—he had noticed that the presence of the snow was a little more insistent, the sound of it clearer; and, conversely, the sound of the postman's footsteps more indistinct. Not only could he not hear the steps come round the corner, he could not even hear them at the first house. It was below the first house that he heard them; and then, a few days later, it was below the second house that he heard them; and a few days later again, below the third. Gradually, gradually, the snow was becoming heavier, the sound of its seething louder, the cobblestones more and more muffled. When he found, each morning, on going to the window, after the ritual of listening, that the roofs and cobbles were as bare as ever, it made no difference. This was, after all, only what he had expected. It was even what pleased him, what rewarded him: the thing was his own, belonged to no one else. No one else knew about it, not even his mother and father. There, outside, were the bare cobbles; and here, inside, was the snow. Snow growing heavier each day, muffling the world, hiding the ugly, and deadening increasingly—above all—the steps of the postman.

"But my darling"—she had said at the luncheon table—"what has come over you? You don't seem to listen when people speak to you. That's the third time I've asked you to pass your plate. . . ."

How was one to explain this to Mother? or to Father? There was, of course, nothing to be done about it: nothing. All one could do was to laugh embarrassedly, pretend to be a little ashamed, apologize, and take a sudden and somewhat disingenuous interest in what was being done or said. The cat had stayed out all night. He had a curious swelling on his left cheek—perhaps somebody had kicked him, or a stone had struck him. Mrs. Kempton was or was not coming to tea. The house was going to be house cleaned, or "turned out," on Wednesday instead of Friday. A new lamp was provided for his evening work—perhaps it was eyestrain which accounted for this new and so peculiar vagueness of his—Mother was looking at him with amusement as she said this, but with something else as well. A new lamp? A new lamp. Yes Mother, No Mother, Yes Mother. School is going very well. The geometry is very easy. The history is very dull. The geography is very interesting—particularly when it takes one to the North Pole. Why the North Pole? Oh, well, it would be fun to be an explorer. Another Peary or Scott or Shackleton. And then abruptly he found his interest in the talk at an end, stared at the pudding on his plate, listened, waited, and began once more—ah, how heavenly, too, the first beginnings—to hear or feel—for could he actually hear it?—the silent snow, the secret snow.

(Miss Buell was telling them about the search for the Northwest Passage, about Hendrik Hudson, the Half Moon.)

This had been, indeed, the only distressing feature of the new experience: the fact that it so increasingly had brought him into a kind of mute misunderstanding, or even conflict, with his father and mother. It was as if he were trying to lead a double life. On the one hand he had to be Paul Hasleman, and keep up the appearance of being that person—dress, wash, and answer intelligently when spoken to—; on the other, he had to explore this new world which had been opened to him. Nor could there be the slightest doubt—not the slightest—that the new world was the profounder and more wonderful of the two. It was irresistible. It was miraculous. Its beauty was simply beyond anything—beyond speech as beyond thought—utterly incommunicable. But how then, between the two worlds, of which he was thus constantly aware, was he to keep a balance? One must get up, one must go to breakfast, one must talk with Mother, go to school, do one's lessons—and, in all this, try not to appear too much of a fool. But if all the while one was also trying to extract the full deliciousness of another and quite separate existence, one which could not easily (if at all) be spoken of—how was one to manage? How was one to explain? Would it be safe to explain? Would it be absurd? Would it merely mean that he would get into some obscure kind of trouble?

These thoughts came and went, came and went, as softly and secretly as the snow; they were not precisely a disturbance, perhaps they were even a pleasure; he liked to have them; their presence was something almost palpable, something he could stroke with his hand, without closing his eyes, and without ceasing to see Miss Buell and the schoolroom and the globe and the freckles on Deirdre's neck; nevertheless he did in a sense cease to see, or to see the obvious external world, and substituted for this vision the vision of snow, the sound of snow, and the slow, almost soundless, approach of the postman. Yesterday, it had been only at the sixth house that the postman had become audible; the snow was much deeper now, it was falling more swiftly and heavily, the sound of its seething was more distinct, more soothing, more persistent. And this morning, it had been—as nearly as he could figure—just above the seventh house—perhaps only a step or two above: at most, he had heard two or three footsteps before the knock had sounded. . . . And with each such narrowing of the sphere, each nearer approach of the limit at which the postman was first audible, it was odd how sharply was increased the amount of illusion which had to be carried into the ordinary business of daily life. Each day it was harder to get out of bed, to go to the window, to look out at the—as always—perfectly empty and snowless street. Each day it was more difficult to go through the perfunctory motions of greeting Mother and Father at breakfast, to reply to their questions, to put his books together and go to school. And at school, how extraordinarily hard to conduct with success simultaneously the public life and the life that was secret. There were times when he longed—positively ached— to tell everyone about it—to burst out with it—only to be checked almost at once by a far-off feeling as of some faint absurdity which was inherent in it—but *was* it absurd?—and more importantly by a sense of mysterious power in his very secrecy. Yes: it must be kept secret. That, more and more, became clear. At whatever cost to himself, whatever pain to others—

(Miss Buell looked straight at him, smiling, and said, "Perhaps we'll ask Paul. I'm sure Paul will come out of his day-dream long enough to be able to tell us. Won't you, Paul?" He rose slowly from his chair, resting one hand on the brightly varnished desk, and deliberately stared through the snow towards the blackboard. It was an effort, but it was amusing to make it. "Yes," he said slowly, "it was what we now call the Hudson River. This he thought to be the Northwest Passage. He was disappointed." He sat down again, and as he did so Deirdre half turned in her chair and gave him a shy smile, of approval and admiration.)

At whatever pain to others.

This part of it was very puzzling, very puzzling. Mother was very nice, and so was Father. Yes, that was all true enough. He wanted to be nice to them, to tell them everything—and yet, was it really wrong of him to want to have a secret place of his own?

At bedtime, the night before, Mother had said, "If this goes on, my lad, we'll have to see a doctor, we will! We can't have our boy—" But what was it she had said? "Live in another world"? "Live so far away"? The word "far" had been in it, he was sure, and then Mother had taken up a magazine again and laughed a little, but with an expression which wasn't mirthful. He had felt sorry for her. . . .

The bell rang for dismissal. The sound came to him through long curved parallels of falling snow. He saw Deirdre rise, and had himself risen almost as soon—but not quite as soon—as she.

2

On the walk homeward, which was timeless, it pleased him to see through the accompaniment, or counterpoint, of snow, the items of mere externality on his way. There were many kinds of bricks in the sidewalks, and laid in many kinds of pattern. The garden walls too were various, some of wooden palings, some of plaster, some of stone. Twigs of bushes leaned over the walls; the little hard green winter-buds of lilac, on gray stems, sheathed and fat; other branches very thin and fine and black and desiccated. Dirty sparrows huddled in the bushes, as dull in color as dead fruit left in leafless trees. A single starling creaked on a weather vane. In the gutter, beside a drain, was a scrap of torn and dirty newspaper, caught in a little delta of filth: the word ECZEMA appeared in large capitals, and below it was a letter from Mrs. Amelia D. Cravath, 2100 Pine Street, Fort Worth, Texas, to the effect that after being a sufferer for years she had been cured by Caley's Ointment. In the little delta, beside the fan-shaped and deeply runneled continent of brown mud, were lost twigs, descended from their parent trees, dead matches, a rusty horse-chestnut burr, a small concentration of sparkling gravel on the lip of the sewer, a fragment of eggshell, a streak of yellow sawdust which had been wet and was now dry and congealed, a brown pebble, and a broken feather. Further on was a cement sidewalk, ruled into geometrical parallel-ograms, with a brass inlay at one end commemorating the contractors who had laid it, and, halfway across, an irregular and random series of dog-tracks, immortalized in synthetic stone. He knew these well, and always stepped on them; to cover the little hollows with his own foot had always been a queer pleasure; today he did it once more, but perfunctorily and detachedly, all the while thinking of something else. That was a dog, a long time ago, who had made a mistake and walked on the cement while it was still wet. He had probably wagged his tail, but that hadn't been recorded. Now, Paul Hasleman, aged twelve, on his way home from school, crossed the same river, which in the meantime had frozen into rock. Homeward through the snow, the snow falling in bright sunshine. Homeward?

Then came the gateway with the two posts surmounted by egg-shaped stones which had been cunningly balanced on their ends, as if by Columbus, and mortared in the very act of balance: a source of perpetual wonder. On the brick wall just beyond, the letter H had been stenciled, presumably for some purpose. H? H.

The green hydrant, with a little green-painted chain attached to the brass screw-cap.

The elm tree, with the great gray wound in the bark, kidney-shaped, into which he always put his hand—to feel the cold but living wood. The injury, he had been sure, was due to the gnawings of a tethered horse. But now it deserved only a passing palm, a merely tolerant eye. There were more important things. Miracles. Beyond the thoughts of trees, mere elms. Beyond the thoughts of sidewalks, mere stone, mere brick, mere cement. Beyond the thoughts even of his own shoes, which trod these sidewalks obediently, bearing a burden—far above—of elaborate mystery. He watched them. They were not very well polished; he had neglected them, for a very good reason: they were one of the many parts of the increasing difficulty of the daily return to daily life, the morning struggle. To get up, having at last opened one's eyes, to go to the window, and discover no snow, to wash, to dress, to descend the curving stairs to breakfast—

At whatever pain to others, nevertheless, one must persevere in severance, since the incommunicability of the experience demanded it. It was desirable of course to be kind to Mother and Father, especially as they seemed to be worried, but it was also desirable to be resolute. If they should decide—as appeared likely—to consult the doctor, Doctor Howells, and have Paul inspected, his heart listened to through a kind of dictaphone, his lungs, his stomach—well, that was all right. He would go through with it. He would give them answer for question, too—perhaps such answers as they hadn't expected? No. That would never do. For the secret world must, at all costs, be preserved.

The bird-house in the apple-tree was empty—it was the wrong time of year for wrens. The little round black door had lost its pleasure. The wrens were enjoying other houses, other nests, remoter trees. But this too was a notion which he only vaguely and grazingly entertained—as if, for the moment, he merely touched an edge of it; there was something further on, which was already assuming a sharper importance; some-thing which already teased at the corners of his eyes, teasing also at the corner of his mind. It was funny to think that he so wanted this, so awaited it—and yet found himself enjoying this momentary dalliance with the bird-house, as if for a quite deliberate postponement and enhancement of the approaching pleasure. He was aware of his delay, of his smiling and detached and now almost uncomprehending gaze at the little bird-house; he knew what he was going to look at next: it was his own little cobbled hill-street, his own house, the little river at the bottom of the hill, the grocer's shop with the cardboard man in the window—and now, thinking of all this, he turned his head, still smiling, and looking quickly right and left through the snow-laden sunlight.

And the mist of snow, as he had foreseen, was still on it—a ghost of snow falling in the bright sunlight, softly and steadily floating and turning and pausing, soundlessly meeting the snow that covered, as with a transparent mirage, the bare bright cobbles. He loved it—he stood still and loved it. Its beauty was paralyzing—beyond all words, all experience, all dream. No fairy-story he had ever read could be compared with it—none had ever given him this extraordinary combination of ethereal loveliness with a something else, unnameable, which was just faintly and deliciously terrifying. What was this thing? As he thought of it, he looked upward toward his own bedroom window, which was open—and it was as if he looked straight into the room and saw himself lying half awake in his bed. There he was—at this very instant he was still perhaps actually there—more truly there than standing here at the edge of the cobbled hill-street, with one hand lifted to shade his eyes against the snow-sun. Had he indeed ever left his room, in all this time? since that very first morning? Was the whole progress still being enacted there, was it still the same morning, and himself not yet wholly awake? And even now, had the postman not yet come round the corner? . . .

This idea amused him, and automatically, as he thought of it, he turned his head and looked toward the top of the hill. There was, of course, nothing there—nothing and no one. The street was empty and quiet. And all the more because of its emptiness it occurred to him to count the houses—a thing which, oddly enough, he hadn't before thought of doing. Of course, he had known there weren't many—many, that is, on his own side of the street, which were the ones that figured in the postman's progress—but nevertheless it came to him as something of a shock to find that there were precisely *six,* above his own house—his own house was the seventh.

Six!

Astonished, he looked at his own house—looked at the door, on which was the number thirteen—and then realized that the whole thing was exactly and logically and absurdly what he ought to have known. Just the same, the realization gave him abruptly, and even a little frighteningly, a sense of hurry. He was being hurried—he was being rushed. For—he knit his brows—he couldn't be mistaken—it was just above the *seventh* house, his *own* house, that the postman had first been audible this very morning. But in that case—in that case—did it mean that tomorrow he would hear nothing? The knock he had heard must have been the knock of their own door. Did it mean—and this was an idea which gave him a really extraordinary feeling of surprise—that he would never hear the postman again?—that tomorrow morning the postman would already have passed the house, in a snow by then so deep as to render his footsteps completely inaudible? That he would have made his approach down the snow-filled street so soundlessly, so secretly, that he, Paul Hasleman, there lying in bed, would not have waked in time, or, waking, would have heard nothing?

But how could that be? Unless even the knocker should be muffled in the snow—frozen tight, perhaps? . . . But in that case—

A vague feeling of disappointment came over him; a vague sadness, as if he felt himself deprived of something which he had long looked forward to, something much prized. After all this, all this beautiful progress, the slow delicious advance of the postman through the silent and secret snow, the knock creeping closer each day, and the footsteps nearer, the audible compass of the world thus daily narrowed, narrowed, narrowed, as the snow soothingly and beautifully encroached and deepened, after all this, was he to be defrauded of the one thing he had so wanted—to be able to count, as it were, the last two or three solemn footsteps, as they finally approached his own door? Was it all going to happen, at the end, so suddenly? or indeed, had it already happened? with no slow and subtle gradations of menace, in which he could luxuriate?

He gazed upward again, toward his own window which flashed in the sun: and this time almost with a feeling that it would be better if he *were* still in bed, in that room; for in that case this must still be the first morning, and there would be six more mornings to come—or, for that matter, seven or eight or nine—how could he be sure?—or even more.

3

After supper, the inquisition began. He stood before the doctor, under the lamp, and submitted silently to the usual thumpings and tappings.

"Now will you please say 'Ah!'?"

"Ah!"

"Now again please, if you don't mind."

"Ah."

"Say it slowly and hold it if you can—"

"Ah-h-h-h-h-h—"

"Good."

How silly all this was. As if it had anything to do with his throat! Or his heart or lungs!

Relaxing his mouth, of which the corners, after all this absurd stretching, felt uncomfortable, he avoided the doctor's eyes, and stared towards the fireplace, past his mother's feet (in gray slippers) which projected from the green chair, and his father's feet (in brown slippers) which stood neatly side by side on the hearth rug.

"Hm. There is certainly nothing wrong there . . ."

He felt the doctor's eyes fixed upon him, and, as if merely to be polite, returned the look, but with a feeling of justifiable evasiveness.

"Now, young man, tell me,—do you feel all right?"

"Yes, sir, quite all right."

"No headaches? No dizziness?"

"No, I don't think so."

"Let me see. Let's get a book, if you don't mind—yes, thank you, that will do splendidly—and now, Paul, if you'll just read it, holding it as you would normally hold it—"

He took the book and read:

"And another praise have I to tell for this the city our mother, the gift of a great god, a glory of the land most high; the might of horses, the might of young horses, the might of the sea. . . . For thou, son of Cronus, our lord Poseidon, hast throned herein this pride, since in these roads first thou didst show forth the curb that cures the rage of steeds. And the shapely oar, apt to men's hands, hath a wonderous speed on the brine, following the hundred-footed Nereids. . . . O land that art praised above all lands, now is it for thee to make those bright praises seen in deeds."

He stopped, tentatively, and lowered the heavy book.

"No—as I thought—there is certainly no superficial sign of eyestrain."

Silence thronged the room, and he was aware of the focused scrutiny of the three people who confronted him. . . .

"We could have his eyes examined—but I believe it is something else."

"What could it be?" This was his father's voice.

"It's only this curious absent-minded—" This was his mother's voice.

In the presence of the doctor, they both seemed irritatingly apologetic.

"I believe it is something else. Now, Paul—I would like very much to ask you a question or two. You will answer them, won't you—you know I'm an old, old friend of yours, eh? That's right! . . ."

His back was thumped twice by the doctor's fat fist—then the doctor was grinning at him with false amiability, while with one finger-nail he was scratching the top button of his waistcoat. Beyond the doctor's shoulder was the fire, the fingers of flame making light prestidigitation against the sooty fireback, the soft sound of their random flutter the only sound.

"I would like to know—is there anything that worries you?"

The doctor was again smiling, his eyelids low against the little black pupils, in each of which was a tiny white bead of light. Why answer him? Why answer him at all? "At whatever pain to others"—but it was all a nuisance, this necessity for resistance, this necessity for attention: it was as if one had been stood up on a brilliantly lighted stage, under a great round blaze of spotlight; as if one were merely a trained seal, or a performing dog, or a fish, dipped out of an aquarium and held up by the tail. It would serve them right if he were merely to bark or growl. And meanwhile, to miss these last few precious hours, these hours of which every minute was more beautiful than the last, more menacing—? He still looked, as if from a great distance, at the beads of light in the doctor's eyes, at the fixed false smile, and then, beyond, once more at his mother's slippers, his father's slippers, the soft flutter of the fire. Even here, even amongst these hostile presences, and in this arranged light, he could see the snow, he could hear it—it was in the corners of the room, where the shadow was deepest, under the sofa, behind the half-opened door which led to the dining room. It was gentler here, softer, its seethe the quietest of whispers, as if, in deference to a drawing room, it had quite deliberately put on its "manners"; it kept itself out of sight, obliterated itself, but distinctly with an air of saying, "Ah, but just wait! Wait till we are alone together! Then I will begin to tell you something new! Something white! something cold! something sleepy! something of cease, and peace, and the long bright curve of space! Tell them to go away. Banish them. Refuse to speak. Leave them, go upstairs to your room, turn out the light and get into bed—I will go with you, I will be waiting for you, I will tell you a better story than Little Kay of the Skates, or The Snow Ghost—I will surround your bed, I will close the windows, pile a deep drift against the door, so that none will ever again be able to enter. Speak to them! . . ." It seemed as if the little hissing voice came from a slow white spiral of falling flakes in the corner by the front window—but he could not be sure. He felt himself smiling, then, and said to the doctor, but without looking at him, looking beyond him still—

"Oh, no, I think not—"

"But are you sure, my boy?"

His father's voice came softly and coldly then—the familiar voice of silken warning. . . .

"You needn't answer at once, Paul—remember we're trying to help you—think it over and be quite sure, won't you?"

He felt himself smiling again, at the notion of being quite sure. What a joke! As if he weren't so sure that reassurance was no longer necessary, and all this cross-examination a ridiculous farce, a grotesque parody! What could they know about it? These gross intelligences, these humdrum minds so bound to the usual, the ordinary? Impossible to tell them about it! Why, even now, even now, with the proof so abundant, so formidable, so imminent, so appallingly present here in this very room, could they believe it?—could even his mother believe it? No—it was only too plain that if anything were said about it, the merest hint given, they would be incredulous—they would laugh—they would say "Absurd!"—think things about him which weren't true. . . .

"Why no, I'm not worried—why should I be?"

He looked then straight at the doctor's low-lidded eyes, looked from one of them to the other, from one bead of light to the other, and gave a little laugh.

The doctor seemed to be disconcerted by this. He drew back in his chair, resting a fat white hand on either knee. The smile faded slowly from his face.

"Well, Paul!" he said, and paused gravely, "I'm afraid you don't take this quite seriously enough. I think you perhaps don't quite realize—don't quite realize—" He took a deep quick breath, and turned, as if helpless, at a loss for words, to the others. But Mother and Father were both silent—no help was forthcoming.

"You must surely know, be aware, that you have not been quite yourself, of late? Don't you know that? . . ."

It was amusing to watch the doctor's renewed attempt at a smile, a queer disorganized look, as of confidential embarrassment.

"I feel all right, sir," he said, and again gave the little laugh.

"And we're trying to help you." The doctor's tone sharpened.

"Yes, sir, I know. But why? I'm all right. I'm just *thinking*, that's all."

His mother made a quick movement forward, resting a hand on the back of the doctor's chair.

"Thinking?" she said. "But my dear, about what?"

This was a direct challenge—and would have to be directly met. But before he met it, he looked again into the corner by the door, as if for reassurance. He smiled again at what he saw, at what he heard. The little spiral was still there, still softly whirling, like the ghost of a white kitten chasing the ghost of a white tail, and making as it did so the faintest of whispers. It was all right! If only he could remain firm, everything was going to be all right.

"Oh, about anything, about nothing.—*you* know the way you do!"

"You mean—day-dreaming?"

"Oh, no—thinking!"

"But thinking about *what?*"

"Anything."

He laughed a third time—but this time, happening to glance upward towards his mother's face, he was appalled at the effect his laughter seemed to have upon her. Her mouth had opened in an expression of horror. . . . This was too bad! Unfortunate! He had known it would cause pain, of course—but he hadn't expected it to be quite so bad as this. Perhaps—perhaps if he just gave them a tiny gleaming hint—?

"About the snow," he said.

"What on earth!" This was his father's voice. The brown slippers came a step nearer on the hearth-rug.

"But my dear, what do you mean!" This was his mother's voice.

The doctor merely stared.

"Just *snow,* that's all. I like to think about it."

"Tell us about it, my boy."

"But that's all it is. There's nothing to tell. *You* know what snow is."

This he said almost angrily, for he felt that they were trying to corner him. He turned sideways so as no longer to face the doctor, and the better to see the inch of blackness between the window-sill and the lowered curtains,—the cold inch of beckoning and delicious night. At once he felt better, more assured.

"Mother—can I go to bed, now, please? I've got a headache."

"But I thought you said—"

"It's just come. It's all these questions—! Can I, Mother?"

"You can go as soon as the doctor has finished."

"Don't you think this thing ought to be gone into thoroughly, and *now?*" This was Father's voice. The brown slippers again came a step nearer, the voice was the well-known "punishment" voice, resonant and cruel.

"Oh, what's the use, Norman—"

Quite suddenly, everyone was silent. And without precisely facing them, nevertheless he was aware that all three of them were watching him with an extraordinary intensity—staring hard at him—as if he had done something monstrous, or was himself some kind of monster. He could hear the soft irregular flutter of the flames; the cluck-click-cluck-click of the clock; far and faint, two sudden spurts of laughter from the kitchen, as quickly cut off as begun; a murmur of water in the pipes; and then, the silence seemed to deepen, to spread out, to become worldlong and worldwide, to become timeless and shapeless, and to center inevitably and rightly, with a slow and sleepy but enormous concentration of all power, on the beginning of a new sound. What this new sound was going to be, he knew perfectly well. It might begin with a hiss, but it would end with a roar—there was no time to lose—he must escape. It mustn't happen here—

Without another word, he turned and ran up the stairs.

4

Not a moment too soon. The darkness was coming in long white waves. A prolonged sibilance filled the night—a great seamless seethe of wild influence went abruptly across it—a cold low humming shook the windows. He shut the door and flung off his clothes in the dark. The bare black floor was like a little raft tossed in waves in snow, almost overwhelmed, washed under whitely, up again, smothered in curled billows of feather. The snow was laughing: it spoke from all sides at once: it pressed closer to him as he ran and jumped exulting into his bed.

"Listen to us!" it said. "Listen! We have come to tell you the story we told you about. You remember? Lie down. Shut your eyes, now—you will no longer see much—in this white darkness who could see, or want to see? We will take the place of everything. . . . Listen—"

A beautiful varying dance of snow began at the front of the room, came forward and then retreated, flattened out toward the floor, then rose fountain-like to the ceiling, swayed, recruited itself from a new stream of flakes which poured laughing in through the humming window, advanced again, lifted long white arms. It said peace, it said remoteness, it said cold—it said—

But then a gash of horrible light fell brutally across the room from the opening door—the snow drew back hissing—something alien had come into the room—something hostile. This thing rushed at him, clutched at him, shook him—and he was not merely horrified, he was filled with such a loathing as he had never known. What was this? this cruel disturbance? this act of anger and hate? It was as if he had to reach up a hand toward another world for any understanding of it—an effort of which he was only barely capable. But of that other world he still remembered just enough to know the exorcising words. They tore themselves from his other life suddenly—

"Mother! Mother! Go away! I hate you!"

And with that effort, everything was solved, everything became all right: the seamless hiss advanced once more, the long white wavering lines rose and fell like enormous whispering sea-waves, the whisper becoming louder, the laughter more numerous.

"Listen!" it said. "We'll tell you the last, the most beautiful and secret story— shut your eyes—it is a very small story—a story that gets smaller and smaller—it comes inward instead of opening like a flower—it is a flower becoming a seed—a little cold seed—do you hear? We are leaning closer to you—"

The hiss was now becoming a roar—the whole world was a vast moving screen of snow—but even now it said peace, it said remoteness, it said cold, it said sleep.

Katherine Anne Porter (1890–   )

Katherine Anne Porter was born in Texas in 1890 to a prominent Catholic family. Her first marriage was at sixteen, her first divorce at nineteen. Two more of each followed. She traveled extensively, lived in many foreign and American cities, settled at last in a suburb of Washington, D.C. She writes, "I am the grandchild of a lost War, and I have blood-knowledge of what life can be in a defeated country on the bare bones of privation." Many of her stories are set in the South of her childhood, and almost all of them deal with loss and reconciliation.

Although critics and other writers have rated her work among the best, she did not achieve general popularity until her only novel, *Ship of Fools,* was published in 1962. It was a best seller of mammoth proportions and was made into a film.

"My whole attempt," she says, in discussing her work

has been to discover and understand human motives, human feelings, to make a distillation of what human relations and experiences my mind has been able to absorb. I have never known an uninteresting human being, and I have never known two alike.

A writer, she says, begins with

first a theme, and then a point of view, a certain knowledge of human nature and strong feelings about it, and style—that is to say, his own special way of telling a thing that makes it precisely his own and no one else's.

Porter's style is not so instantly recognizable as, say, Faulkner's or Hemingway's. But her range is tremendous. Sometimes naïve, sometimes sophisticated, or ironic, sardonic, anguished, or remote, objective, her style seems to follow theme and subject matter. But always her language is beautifully exact, pictorial, rhythmically balanced. She is not afraid of adjectives and rich imagery. The first sentence of the second paragraph of "The Grave" illustrates her skill. The reader's imagination moves from the abstract ("family cemetery") to a slightly more concrete image ("pleasant, small, neglected garden") to a carefully chosen and precisely qualified description of objects in the garden. At the end of the sentence, the reader is submerged in the "uncropped sweet-smelling wild grass." Each noun and adjective brings the reader deeper into the story.

This sentence also contains the themes of the story, the intermingling of sweetness and death and corruption. It places the reader, metaphorically and literally, in the middle of the world where the story takes place. The themes are developed as much through language as through plot. After a graceful, stately opening, the language adjusts to the coarser sensibilities of the children ("scratching," "scooped," "leaped"). When Miranda puts on the ring, the subordinate theme of women and men is introduced, and the language reflects the difference between the children. Paul talks of "get[ting] your bird" and "bulls-eyes" while Miranda has "vague stirrings of desire for luxury," a sensual image which reinforces her emerging awareness of herself. When the experience with the rabbits emphasizes the dominant theme of death and corruption, the language reflects the changed sensibility of Miranda.

The epiphany is borne to Miranda, and the reader, not alone by memory of the rabbits aroused by the little sugar figures but by the vision of her brother "standing in the blazing sunshine, again twelve years old, a pleased sober smile in his eyes, turning the silver dove over and over in his hands." More by means of the sounds and the imagery than by what could be paraphrased as meaning, the reader understands that Miranda has become reconciled with the "mingled sweetness and corruption" of her life.

The Grave

The grandfather, dead for more than thirty years, had been twice disturbed in his long repose by the constancy and possessiveness of his widow. She removed his bones first to Louisiana and then to Texas as if she had set out to find her own burial place, knowing well she would never return to the places she had left. In Texas she set up a small cemetery in a corner of her first farm, and as the family connection grew, and oddments of relations came over from Kentucky to settle, it contained at last about twenty graves. After the grandmother's death, part of her land was to be sold for the benefit of certain of her children, and the cemetery happened to lie in the part set aside for sale. It was necessary to take up the bodies and bury them again in the family plot

Katherine Anne Porter "The Grave," from *The Leaning Tower and Other Stories*, copyright, 1944, 1972 by Katherine Anne Porter. Reprinted by permission of Harcourt Brace Jovanovich, Inc.

in the big new public cemetery, where the grandmother had been buried. At last her husband was to lie beside her for eternity, as she had planned.

The family cemetery had been a pleasant small neglected garden of tangled rose bushes and ragged cedar trees and cypress, the simple flat stones rising out of uncropped sweet-smelling wild grass. The graves were lying open and empty one burning day when Miranda and her brother Paul, who often went together to hunt rabbits and doves, propped their twenty-two Winchester rifles carefully against the rail fence, climbed over and explored among the graves. She was nine years old and he was twelve.

They peered into the pits all shaped alike with such purposeful accuracy, and looking at each other with pleased adventurous eyes, they said in solemn tones: "These were graves!" trying by words to shape a special, suitable emotion in their minds, but they felt nothing except an agreeable thrill of wonder: they were seeing a new sight, doing something they had not done before. In them both there was also a small disappointment at the entire commonplaceness of the actual spectacle. Even if it had once contained a coffin for years upon years, when the coffin was gone a grave was just a hole in the ground. Miranda leaped into the pit that had held her grandfather's bones. Scratching around aimlessly and pleasurably as any young animal, she scooped up a lump of earth and weighted it in her palm. It had a pleasantly sweet, corrupt smell, being mixed with cedar needles and small leaves, and as the crumbs fell apart, she saw a silver dove no larger than a hazel nut, with spread wings and a neat fan-shaped tail. The breast had a deep round hollow in it. Turning it up to the fierce sunlight, she saw that the inside of the hollow was cut in little whorls. She scrambled out, over the pile of loose earth that had fallen back into one end of the grave, calling to Paul that she had found something, he must guess what . . . His head appeared smiling over the rim of another grave. He waved a closed hand at her. "I've got something too!" They ran to compare treasures, making a game of it, so many guesses each, all wrong, and a final showdown with opened plams. Paul had found a thin wide gold ring carved with intricate flowers and leaves. Miranda was smitten at sight of the ring and wished to have it. Paul seemed more impressed by the dove. They made a trade, with some little bickering. After he had got the dove in his hand, Paul said, "Don't you know what this is? This is a screw head for a *coffin!* . . . I'll bet nobody else in the world has one like this!"

Miranda glanced at it without covetousness. She had the gold ring on her thumb; it fitted perfectly. "Maybe we ought to go now," she said, "maybe one of the niggers 'll see us and tell somebody." They knew the land had been sold, the cemetery was no longer theirs, and they felt like trespassers. They climbed back over the fence, slung their rifles loosely under their arms—they had been shooting at targets with various kinds of firearms since they were seven years old—and set out to look for the rabbits and doves or whatever small game might happen along. On these expeditions Miranda always followed at Paul's heels along the path, obeying instructions about handling her gun when going through fences; learning how to stand it up properly so it would not slip and fire unexpectedly; how to wait her time for a shot and not just bang away in the air without looking, spoiling shots for Paul, who really could hit things if given a chance. Now and then, in her excitement at seeing birds whizz up suddenly before her face, or a rabbit leap across her very toes, she lost her head, and almost without sighting she flung her rifle up and pulled the trigger. She hardly ever hit any sort of mark. She had no proper sense of hunting at all. Her brother would be often completely disgusted with her. "You don't care whether you get your bird or not," he said. "That's no way to hunt." Miranda could not understand his indignation. She had seen him smash his hat and yell with fury when he had missed his aim. "What I like about shooting," said Miranda, with exasperating inconsequence, "is pulling the trigger and hearing the noise."

"Then, by golly," said Paul, "whyn't you go back to the range and shoot at bulls-eyes?"

"I'd just as soon," said Miranda, "only like this, we walk around more."

"Well, you just stay behind and stop spoiling my shots," said Paul, who, when he made a kill, wanted to be certain he had made it. Miranda, who alone brought down a bird once in twenty rounds, always claimed as her own any game they got when they fired at the same moment. It was tiresome and unfair and her brother was sick of it.

"Now, the first dove we see, or the first rabbit, is mine," he told her. "And the next will be yours. Remember that and don't get smarty."

"What about snakes?" asked Miranda idly. "Can I have the first snake?"

Waving her thumb gently and watching her gold ring glitter, Miranda lost interest in shooting. She was wearing her summer roughing outfit: dark blue overalls, a light blue shirt, a hired-man's straw hat, and thick brown sandals. Her brother had the same outfit except his was a sober hickory-nut color. Ordinarily Miranda preferred her overalls to any other dress, though it was making rather a scandal in the countryside, for the year was 1903, and in the back country the law of female decorum had teeth in it. Her father had been criticized for letting his girls dress like boys and go careering around astride barebacked horses. Big sister Maria, the really independent and fearless one, in spite of her rather affected ways, rode at a dead run with only a rope knotted around her horse's nose. It was said the motherless family was running down, with the Grandmother no longer there to hold it together. It was known that she had discriminated against her son Harry in her will, and that he was in straits about money. Some of his old neighbors reflected with vicious satisfaction that now he would probably not be so stiffnecked, nor have any more high-stepping horses either. Miranda knew this, though she could not say how. She had met along the road old women of the kind who smoked corn-cob pipes, who had treated her grandmother with most sincere respect. They slanted their gummy old eyes side-ways at the granddaughter and said, "Ain't you ashamed of yoself, Missy? It's aginst the Scriptures to dress like that. Whut yo Pappy thinkin about?" Miranda, with her powerful social sense, which was like a fine set of antennae radiating from every pore of her skin, would feel ashamed because she knew well it was rude and ill-bred to shock anybody, even bad-tempered old crones, though she had faith in her father's judgment and was perfectly comfortable in the clothes. Her father had said, "They're just what you need, and they'll save your dresses for school . . ." This sounded quite simple and natural to her. She had been brought up in rigorous economy. Wastefulness was vulgar. It was also a sin. These were truths; she had heard them repeated many times and never once disputed.

Now the ring, shining with the serene purity of fine gold on her rather grubby thumb, turned her feelings against her overalls and sockless feet, toes sticking through the thick brown leather straps. She wanted to go back to the farmhouse, take a good cold bath, dust herself with plenty of Maria's violet talcum powder—provided Maria was not present to object, of course—put on the thinnest, most becoming dress she owned, with a big sash, and sit in a wicker chair under the trees . . . These things were not all she wanted, of course; she had vague stirrings of desire for luxury and a grand way of living which could not take precise form in her imagination but were founded on family legend of past wealth and leisure. These immediate comforts were what she could have, and she wanted them at once. She lagged rather far behind Paul, and once she thought of just turning back without a word and going home. She stopped, thinking that Paul would never do that to her, and so she would have to tell him. When a rabbit leaped, she let Paul have it without dispute. He killed it with one shot.

When she came up with him, he was already kneeling, examining the wound, the rabbit trailing from his hands. "Right through the head," he said complacently, as if he had aimed for it. He took out his sharp, competent bowie knife and started to skin the body. He did it very cleanly and quickly. Uncle Jimbilly knew how to prepare the skins so that Miranda always had fur coats for her dolls, for though she never cared much for her dolls she liked seeing them in fur coats. The children knelt facing each other over the dead animal. Miranda watched admiringly while her brother stripped the skin away as if he were taking off a glove. The flayed flesh emerged dark scarlet, sleek, firm; Miranda with thumb and finger felt the long fine muscles with the silvery flat strips binding them to the joints. Brother lifted the oddly bloated belly. "Look," he said, in a low amazed voice. "It was going to have young ones."

Very carefully he slit the thin flesh from the center ribs to the flanks, and a scarlet bag appeared. He slit again and pulled the bag open, and there lay a bundle of tiny rabbits, each wrapped in a thin scarlet veil. The brother pulled these off and there they were, dark gray, their sleek wet down lying in minute even ripples, like a baby's head just washed, their unbelievably small delicate ears folded close, their little blind faces almost featureless.

Miranda said, "Oh, I want to *see*," under her breath. She looked and looked—excited but not frightened, for she was accustomed to the sight of animals killed in hunting—filled with pity and astonishment and a kind of shocked delight in the wonderful little creatures for their own sakes, they were so pretty. She touched one of them ever so carefully, "Ah, there's blood running over them," she said and began to tremble without knowing why. Yet she wanted most deeply to see and to know. Having seen, she felt at once as if she had known all along. The very memory of her former ignorance faded, she had always known just this. No one had ever told her anything outright, she had been rather unobservant of the animal life around her because she was so accustomed to animals. They seemed simply disorderly and unaccountably rude in their habits, but altogether natural and not very interesting. Her brother had spoken as if he had known about everything all along. He may have seen all this before. He had never said a word to her, but she knew now a part at least of what he knew. She understood a little of the secret, formless intuitions in her own mind and body, which had been clearing up, taking form, so gradually and so steadily she had not realized that she was learning what she had to know. Paul said cautiously, as if he were talking about something forbidden: "They were just about ready to be born." His voice dropped on the last word. "I know," said Miranda, "like kittens. I know, like babies." She was quietly and terribly agitated, standing again with her rifle under her arm, looking down at the bloody heap. "I don't want the skin," she said, "I won't have it." Paul buried the young rabbits again in their mother's body, wrapped the skin around her, carried her to a clump of sage bushes, and hid her away. He came out again at once and said to Miranda, with an eager friendliness, a confidential tone quite unusual in him, as if he were taking her into an important secret on equal terms: "Listen now. Now you listen to me, and don't ever forget. Don't you ever tell a living soul that you saw this. Don't tell a soul. Don't tell Dad because I'll get into trouble.

He'll say I'm leading you into things you ought not to do. He's always saying that. So now don't you go and forget and blab out sometime the way you're always doing . . . Now, that's a secret. Don't you tell."

Miranda never told, she did not even wish to tell anybody. She thought about the whole worrisome affair with confused unhappiness for a few days. Then it sank quietly into her mind and was heaped over by accumulated thousands of impressions, for nearly twenty years. One day she was picking her path among the puddles and crushed refuse of a market street in a strange city of a strange country, when without warning, plain and clear in its true colors as if she looked through a frame upon a scene that had not stirred nor changed since the moment it happened, the episode of that far-off day leaped from its burial place before her mind's eye. She was so reasonlessly horrified she halted suddenly staring, the scene before her eyes dimmed by the vision back of them. An Indian vendor had held up before her a tray of dyed sugar sweets, in the shapes of all kinds of small creatures: birds, baby chicks, baby rabbits, lambs, baby pigs. They were in gay colors and smelled of vanilla, maybe. . . . It was a very hot day and the smell in the market, with its piles of raw flesh and wilting flowers, was like the mingled sweetness and corruption she had smelled that other day in the empty cemetery at home: the day she had remembered always until now vaguely as the time she and her brother had found treasure in the opened graves. Instantly upon this thought the dreadful vision faded, and she saw clearly her brother, whose childhood face she had forgotten, standing again in the blazing sunshine, again twelve years old, a pleased sober smile in his eyes, turning the silver dove over and over in his hands.

Isaac Babel (1894-1941)

Contradiction and anomaly marked the life of Isaac Babel. A Jew, he glorified his people's age-old enemy, the Cossacks. A scholar, he romanticized violence. An intellectual, he exalted the military. To celebrate the Red Army, he wrote stories of it that were heavy with irony. His accounts of violence are written with elegance; his scenes of disorder are painted with precision. One of the few authentic voices of the Russian Revolution, by the 1930s he had become, in his words, "the past master of silence." To serve the Party, he withdrew from literature. A Communist loyalist, he died in a Russian concentration camp. His output was small: some fifty stories. His achievement was enormous: he is perhaps the greatest short-storywriter since Anton Chekhov.

Babel was born in Odessa in 1894, the son of a Jewish warehousekeeper. In 1916 he met Gorki: "I owe everything to this meeting, and to this day I speak the name of Alexei Maximovich with love and reverence." Gorki told him to get experience before trying to write. The next seven years, Babel spent as a Red Army soldier, a production supervisor, and a journalist.

His literary career began in earnest in 1924 with the publication of half a dozen stories. By 1925, he was a celebrity, the rage of Moscow. Although his wife, mother, and sister emigrated, Babel apparently believed that his talent could not flourish outside Russia. But with the advent of Stalin and the increased demand for conformity, Babel's output declined precipitately. When Gorki died in 1936, Babel lost his great friend and protector, and over the next few years his existence grew more precarious. He was arrested in 1939 and was seen no more. The official date of his death was given as March 17, 1941. The final irony was the revocation, in 1954, by the Supreme Court of the USSR of the sentence imposed on Babel.

At the heart of Babel's fiction is the conflict between violence and compassion. The violence is often romanticized, as in "My First Goose," and the compassion is often ironic, as in "The Sin of Jesus." His stories are usually quite short and pungent. Even in translation the language is subtle and rich in imagery. He keeps exposition to a minimum: drama is all. There is almost always a host of lively energetic characters cavorting through his scenes in amusing, telling, sometimes frightening or touching ways.

In "My First Goose" a Jewish intellectual cruelly destroys a goose in order to win acceptance from the Cossacks. The first-person narrator never expresses judgment of the violent Cossack way of life; yet the changing tone of metaphors in the story prepares the reader to recognize, in the epiphany (see p. 10), the divided heart of the narrator.

There are some elements of humor in that grim, violent story. In "The Sin of Jesus," humor is the vital force and is established in the first paragraph. The reader knows from the first he will be entertained (see Introduction, p. 15). But in the second paragraph a new note is presented: Arina is helpless, foolish, mistreated. When Seryoga "took off his belt and beat her like a hero," the terrible tension is established and the reader uneasily shifts from hilarity to horror. And when Arina asks Jesus Christ for help, the full complexity of Babel's intention is revealed. From then on the story veers from farce to realism to naturalism and almost to myth, but its tone is always compassionate toward poor foolish Arina, who is, even in her relations with Jesus Christ, more sinned against than sinning. In such a brief space, and in so amused a tone, Babel has managed to do full justice to Arina's humanity, and in the end it is not Arina we scorn, but rather the cruelty of the world and of fate.

My First Goose

Savitsky, Commander of the VI Division, rose when he saw me, and I wondered at the beauty of his giant's body. He rose, the purple of his riding breeches and the crimson of his little tilted cap and the decorations stuck on his chest cleaving the hut as a standard cleaves the sky. A smell of scent and the sickly sweet freshness of soap emanated from him. His long legs were like girls sheathed to the neck in shining riding boots.

He smiled at me, struck his riding whip on the table, and drew toward him an order that the Chief of Staff had just finished dictating. It was an order for Ivan Chesnokov to advance on Chugunov-Dobryvodka with the regiment entrusted to him, to make contact with the enemy and destroy the same.

"For which destruction," the Commander began to write, smearing the whole sheet, "I make this same Chesnokov entirely responsible, up to and including the supreme penalty, and will if necessary strike him down on the spot; which you, Chesnokov, who have been working with me at the front for some months now, cannot doubt."

From Isaac Babel, *The Collected Stories,* translated by Walter Morison. Copyright © 1955 by S. G. Phillips, Inc. Reprinted by permission of S. G. Phillips, Inc.

The Commander signed the order with a flourish, tossed it to his orderlies and turned upon me gray eyes that danced with merriment.

I handed him a paper with my appointment to the Staff of the Division.

"Put it down in the Order of the Day," said the Commander. "Put him down for every satisfaction save the front one. Can you read and write?"

"Yes, I can read and write," I replied, envying the flower and iron of that youthfulness. "I graduated in law from St. Petersburg University."

"Oh, are you one of those grinds?" he laughed. "Specs on your nose, too! What a nasty little object! They've sent you along without making any enquiries; and this is a hot place for specs. Think you'll get on with us?"

The quartermaster carried my trunk on his shoulder. Before us stretched the village street. The dying sun, round and yellow as a pumpkin, was giving up its roseate ghost to the skies.

We went up to a hut painted over with garlands. The quartermaster stopped, and said suddenly, with a guilty smile:

"Nuisance with specs. Can't do anything to stop it, either. Not a life for the brainy type here. But you go and mess up a lady, and a good lady too, and you'll have the boys patting you on the back."

He hesitated, my little trunk on his shoulder; then he came quite close to me, only to dart away again despairingly and run to the nearest yard. Cossacks were sitting there, shaving one another.

"Here, you soldiers," said the quartermaster, setting my little trunk down on the ground. "Comrade Savitsky's orders are that you're to take this chap in your billets, so no nonsense about it, because the chap's been through a lot in the learning line."

The quartermaster, purple in the face, left us without looking back. I raised my hand to my cap and saluted the Cossacks. A lad with long straight flaxen hair and the handsome face of the Ryazan Cossacks[1] went over to my little trunk and tossed it out at the gate. Then he turned his back on me and with remarkable skill emitted a series of shameful noises.

"To your guns—number double-zero!" an older Cossack shouted at him, and burst out laughing. "Running fire!"

His guileless art exhausted, the lad made off. Then, crawling over the ground, I began to gather together the manuscripts and tattered garments that had fallen out of the trunk. I gathered them up and carried them to the other end of the yard. Near the hut, on a brick stove, stood a cauldron in which pork was cooking. The steam that rose from it was like the far-off smoke of home in the village, and it mingled hunger with desperate loneliness in my head. Then I covered my little broken trunk with hay, turning it into a pillow, and lay down on the ground to read in *Pravda* Lenin's speech at the Second Congress of the Comintern. The sun fell upon me from behind the toothed hillocks, the Cossacks trod on my feet, the lad made fun of me untiringly, the beloved lines came toward me along a thorny path and could not reach me. Then I put aside the paper and went out to the landlady, who was spinning on the porch.

"Landlady," I said, "I've got to eat."

The old woman raised to me the diffused whites of her purblind eyes and lowered them again.

"Comrade," she said, after a pause, "what with all this going on, I want to go and hang myself."

[1] Noted cavalrymen from southern Russia.

"Christ!" I muttered, and pushed the old woman in the chest with my fist. "You don't suppose I'm going to go into explanations with you, do you?"

And turning around I saw somebody's sword lying within reach. A severe-looking goose was waddling about the yard, inoffensively preening its feathers. I overtook it and pressed it to the ground. Its head cracked beneath my boot, cracked and emptied itself. The white neck lay stretched out in the dung, the wings twitched.

"Christ!" I said, digging into the goose with my sword. "Go and cook it for me, landlady."

Her blind eyes and glasses glistening, the old woman picked up the slaughtered bird, wrapped it in her apron, and started to bear it off toward the kitchen.

"Comrade," she said to me, after a while, "I want to go and hang myself." And she closed the door behind her.

The Cossacks in the yard were already sitting around their cauldron. They sat motionless, stiff as heathen priests at a sacrifice, and had not looked at the goose.

"The lad's all right," one of them said, winking and scooping up the cabbage soup with his spoon.

The Cossacks commenced their supper with all the elegance and restraint of peasants who respect one another. And I wiped the sword with sand, went out at the gate, and came in again, depressed. Already the moon hung above the yard like a cheap earring.

"Hey, you," suddenly said Surovkov, an older Cossack. "Sit down and feed with us till your goose is done."

He produced a spare spoon from his boot and handed it to me. We supped up the cabbage soup they had made, and ate the pork.

"What's in the newspaper?" asked the flaxen-haired lad, making room for me.

"Lenin writes in the paper," I said, pulling out *Pravda*. "Lenin writes that there's a shortage of everything."

And loudly, like a triumphant man hard of hearing, I read Lenin's speech out to the Cossacks.

Evening wrapped about me the quickening moisture of its twilight sheets; evening laid a mother's hand upon my burning forehead. I read on and rejoiced, spying out exultingly the secret curve of Lenin's straight line.

"Truth tickles everyone's nostrils," said Surovkov, when I had come to the end. "The question is, how's it to be pulled from the heap. But he goes and strikes at it straight off like a hen pecking at a grain!"

This remark about Lenin was made by Surovkov, platoon commander of the Staff Squadron; after which we lay down to sleep in the hayloft. We slept, all six of us, beneath a wooden roof that let in the stars, warming one another, our legs intermingled. I dreamed: and in my dreams saw women. But my heart, stained with bloodshed, grated and brimmed over.

The Sin of Jesus

Arina was a servant at the hotel. She lived next to the main staircase, while Seryoga, the janitor's helper, lived over the back stairs. Between them there was shame. On Palm Sunday Arina gave Seryoga a present—twins. Water flows, stars shine, a man

From Isaac Babel, *The Collected Stories,* translated by Walter Morison. Copyright © 1955 by S. G. Phillips, Inc. Reprinted by permission from the publisher.

lusts, and soon Arina was big again, her sixth month was rolling by—they're slippery, a woman's months. And now Seryoga must go into the army. There's a mess for you!

So Arina goes and says: "No sense, Seryoga. There's no sense in my waiting for you. For four years we'll be parted, and in four years, whichever way you look at it, I'll be sure to bring two or three more into this world. It's like walking around with your skirt turned up, working at the hotel. Whoever stops here, he's your master, let him be a Jew, let him be anybody at all. By the time you come home, my insides will be no good any more. I'll be a used-up woman, no match for you."

"That's so," Seryoga nodded.

"There's many that want me. Trofimych the contractor—but he's no gentleman. And Isai Abramych, the warden of Nikolo-Svyatsky Church, a feeble old man, but anyway I'm sick to the stomach of your murderous strength. I tell you this now, I say it like I would at confession, I've got the wind plain knocked out of me. I'll spill my load in three months, then I'll take the baby to the orphanage and marry the old man."

When Seryoga heard this, he took off his belt and beat her like a hero, right on the belly.

"Look out there," Arina says to him, "go soft on the belly. It's your stuffing, no one else's."

There was no end to the beating, no end to the man's tears and the woman's blood, but that is neither here nor there.

Then the woman came to Jesus Christ.

"So on and so forth," she says, "Lord Jesus, I am the woman from the Hotel Madrid and Louvre, the one on Tverskaya Street. Working at the hotel, it's just like going around with your skirt up. Just let a man stop there, and he's your lord and master, let him be a Jew, let him be anyone at all. There is another slave of yours walking the earth, the janitor's helper, Seryoga. Last year on Palm Sunday I bore him twins."

And so she described it all to the Lord.

"And what if Seryoga were not to go into the army after all?" the Saviour suggested.

"Try and get away with it—not with the policeman around. He'll drag him off as sure as daylight."

"Oh yes, the policeman," the Lord bowed His head, "I never thought of him. Then perhaps you ought to live in purity for a while?"

"For four years?" the woman cried. "To hear you talk, all people should deny their animal nature. That's just your old ways all over again. And where will the increase come from? No, you'd better give me some sensible advice."

The Lord's cheeks turned scarlet, the woman's words had touched a tender spot. But He said nothing. You cannot kiss your own ear—even God knows that.

"I'll tell you what, God's servant, glorious sinner, maiden Arina," the Lord proclaimed in all His glory, "I have a little angel here in heaven, hanging around uselessly. His name is Alfred. Lately he's gotten out of hand altogether, keeps crying and nagging all the time: 'What have you done to me, Lord? Why do you turn me into an angel in my twentieth year, and me a hale young fellow?' So I'll give you Alfred the angel as a husband for four years. He'll be your prayer, he'll be your protection, and he'll be your solace. And as for offspring, you've nothing to worry about—you can't bear a duckling from him, let alone a baby, for there's a lot of fun in him, but no seriousness."

"That's just what I need," the maid Arina wept gratefully. "Their seriousness takes me to the doorstep of the grave three times every two years."

"You'll have a sweet respite, God's child Arina. May your prayer be light as a song. Amen."

And so it was decided. Alfred was brought in—a frail young fellow, delicate, two wings fluttering behind his pale-blue shoulders, rippling with rosy light like two doves playing in heaven. Arina threw her hefty arms about him, weeping out of tenderness, out of her woman's soft heart.

"Alfred, my soul, my consolation, my bridegroom . . ."

In parting, the Lord gave her strict instructions to take off the angel's wings every night before he went to bed. His wings were attached to hinges, like a door, and every night she was to take them off and wrap them in a clean sheet, because they were brittle, his wings, and could snap as he tossed in bed—for what were they made of but the sighs of babes, no more than that.

For the last time the Lord blessed the union, while the choir of bishops, called in for the occasion, rendered thunderous praises. No food was served, not a crumb—that wasn't the style in heaven—and then Arina and Alfred, their arms about each other, ran down a silken ladder, straight back to earth. They came to Petrovka, the street where nothing but the best is sold. The woman would do right by her Alfred for he, if one might say so, not only lacked socks, but was altogether as natural as when his mother bore him. And she bought him patent-leather half-boots, checked jersey trousers, a fine hunting jacket, and an electric-blue vest.

"The rest," she says, "we'll find at home."

That day Arina begged off from work. Seryoga came and raised a fuss, but she did not even come out to him, only said from behind her locked door:

"Sergey Nifantyich, I am at present a-washing my feet and beg you to retire without further noise."

He went away without a word—the angel's power was already beginning to manifest itself!

In the evening Arina set out a supper fit for a merchant—the woman had devilish vanity! A half-pint of vodka, wine on the side, a Danube herring with potatoes, a samovar of tea. When Alfred had partaken of all these earthly blessings, he keeled over in a dead sleep. Quick as a wink, Arina lifted off his wings from the hinges, packed them away, and carried him to bed in her arms.

There it lies, the snowy wonder on the eiderdown pillows of her tattered, sinful bed, sending forth a heavenly radiance: moon-silver shafts of light pass and repass, alternate with red ones, float across the floor, sway over his shining feet. Arina weeps and rejoices, sings and prays. Arina, thou hast been granted a happiness unheard of on this battered earth. Blessed are thou among women!

They had drunk the vodka to the last drop, and now it took effect. As soon as they fell asleep, she went and rolled over on top of Alfred with her hot, six-months-big belly. Not enough for her to sleep with an angel, not enough that nobody beside her spat at the wall, snored and snorted—that wasn't enough for the clumsy, ravening slut. No, she had to warm her belly too, her burning belly big with Seryoga's lust. And so she smothered him in her fuddled sleep, smothered him like a week-old babe in the midst of her rejoicing, crushed him under her bloated weight, and he gave up the ghost, and his wings, wrapped in her sheet, wept pale tears.

Dawn came—and all the trees bowed low to the ground. In distant northern forests each fir tree turned into a priest, each fir tree bent its knees in silent worship.

Once more the woman stands before the Lord's throne. She is broad in the shoulders, mighty, the young corpse drooping in her huge red arms.

"Behold, Lord . . ."

But here the gentle heart of Jesus could endure no more, and He cursed the woman in His anger:

"As it is on earth, so shall it be with you, Arina, from this day on."

"How is it then, Lord?" the woman replied in a scarcely audible voice. "Was it I who made my body heavy, was it I that brewed vodka on earth, was it I that created a woman's soul, stupid and lonely?"

"I don't wish to be bothered with you," exclaimed the Lord Jesus. "You've smothered my angel, you filthy scum."

And Arina was thrown back to earth on a putrid wind, straight down to Tverskaya Street, to the Hotel Madrid and Louvre, where she was doomed to spend her days. And once there, the sky was the limit. Seryoga was carousing, drinking away his last days, seeing as he was a recruit. The contractor Trofimych, just come from Kolomna, took one look at Arina, hefty and red-cheeked: "Oh, you cute little belly," he said, and so on and so forth.

Isai Abramych, the old codger, heard about this cute little belly, and he was right there too, wheezing toothlessly:

"I cannot wed you lawfully," he said, "after all that happened. However, I can lie with you the same as anyone."

The old man ought to be lying in cold mother earth instead of thinking of such things, but no, he too must take his turn at spitting into her soul. It was as though they had all slipped the chain—kitchen-boys, merchants, foreigners. A fellow in trade—he likes to have his fun.

And that is the end of my tale.

Before she was laid up, for three months had rolled by in the meantime, Arina went out into the back yard, behind the janitor's rooms, raised her monstrous belly to the silken sky, and said stupidly:

"See, Lord, what a belly! They hammer at it like peas falling in a colander. And what sense there's in it I just can't see. But I've had enough."

With His tears Jesus laved Arina when He heard these words. The Saviour fell on His knees before her.

"Forgive me, little Arina. Forgive your sinful God for all He has done to you . . ."

But Arina shook her head and would not listen.

"There's no forgiveness for you, Jesus Christ," she said. "No forgiveness, and never will be."

James Thurber (1894–1961)

Born in Columbus, Ohio, Thurber grew up in a family which was, by his own account, addicted to absurdity, and the events of his childhood furnished him with material for some of his funniest sketches. Unfortunately, the comedy of his youth was interrupted by an eye injury that eventually blinded him. He entered Ohio State University in 1913 but took the next year off to read books not included in his course of study. Refused by the army because of his poor eyesight, he served in the State Department during the First World War, returning to college after his discharge. In 1927, following several years as a reporter for newspapers in New York and Paris, he became a writer for the newly founded *The New Yorker.* The development of that magazine's unique tone and style was in considerable part Thurber's work.

The books that followed, such as *My Life and Hard Times* (1933), *The Cream of Thurber* (1939), *My World—and Welcome to It* (1942), and *The Thurber Carnival* (1942), firmly established his fame as a brilliant humorist and illustrator of great genius. He is probably as well known for his witty drawings as for his essays and stories. While he resisted the label of cartoonist, he was equally uncomfortable with the designation of artist. Of his drawings he once wrote:

> My drawings sometimes seem to have reached completion by some other route than the common one of intent. They have been described as pre-intentionalist, meaning that they were finished before the ideas for them had occurred to me. I shall not argue the point.

In all of his essays and fictions, Thurber's predominant theme and subject is man menaced by the complicated civilization he has himself created. He writes infinite variations on the ways in which ordinary mortals who, asking of life only that things not get in their way, are constantly attacked and battered about by the inanities of experience. When his protagonists risk the heroic act or gesture, they are invariably, as Richard C. Tobias says, "squelched by dogs, psychologists, women, shower faucets and overcoats." Things are always closing in. (See Introduction, p. 7.)

Among modern American short-story writers included in this collection, the following regularly turn up in the larger, omnibus anthologies of American literature: Hemingway, Faulkner, Anderson, Updike, Wright, and Malamud. Thurber has not been so fortunate. And yet to omit him from any representative gathering of twentieth-century American literature in all of its forms would seem the equivalent of leaving the olive out of a martini. In a review during the 1930s Malcolm Cowley did a demolition job on one of Thurber's books because it did not—by Cowley's lights—treat serious subjects seriously. And another critic, Otto Friedrich, charged Thurber with the sin of indulging in trivia. Thurber's response to this kind of criticism was characteristic:

> Trivia Mundi has always been as dear and as necessary to me as her bigger and more glamorous sister, Gloria. They have both long and amicably inhabited a phrase of Coleridge's, "All things both great and small," and I like to think of them taking turns at shooting albatrosses and playing the bassoon.

Had Chaucer been alive to hear Matthew Arnold's refusal to admit him to the ranks of truly great writers because he lacked "high seriousness," he could not have replied more happily. Thurber's vision and achievement are those of the great comic writer in any generation. He is aware that comedy and tragedy are akin, that comedy can tell us much about the human condition that tragedy cannot. And so he dissects human experience for the sake of laughter, never allowing us to forget as we laugh the simultaneous presence of pain and uncertainty.

The Secret Life of Walter Mitty

"We're going through!" The Commander's voice was like thin ice breaking. He wore his full-dress uniform, with the heavily braided white cap pulled down rakishly over one cold gray eye. "We can't make it, sir. It's spoiling for a hurricane, if you ask me." "I'm not asking you, Lieutenant Berg," said the Commander. "Throw on the power lights! Rev her up to 8,500! We're going through!" The pounding of the cylinders increased: ta-pocketa-pocketa-pocketa-*pocketa-pocketa*. The Commander stared at the ice forming on the pilot window. He walked over and twisted a row of complicated dials. "Switch on No. 8 auxiliary!" he shouted. "Switch on No. 8 auxiliary!" repeated Lieutenant Berg. "Full strength in No. 3 turret!" shouted the Commander. "Full strength in No. 3 turret!" The crew, bending to their various tasks in the huge, hurtling eight-engined Navy hydroplane, looked at each other and grinned. "The Old Man'll get us through," they said to one another. "The Old Man ain't afraid of Hell!" . . .

"Not so fast! You're driving too fast!" said Mrs. Mitty. "What are you driving so fast for?"

"Hmm?" said Walter Mitty. He looked at his wife, in the seat beside him, with shocked astonishment. She seemed grossly unfamiliar, like a strange woman who had yelled at him in a crowd. "You were up to fifty-five," she said. "You know I don't like to go more than forty. You were up to fifty-five." Walter Mitty drove on toward Waterbury in silence, the roaring of the SN202 through the worst storm in twenty years of Navy flying fading in the remote, intimate airways of his mind. "You're tensed up again," said Mrs. Mitty. "It's one of your days. I wish you'd let Dr. Renshaw look you over."

Walter Mitty stopped the car in front of the building where his wife went to have her hair done. "Remember to get those overshoes while I'm having my hair done," she said. "I don't need overshoes," said Mitty. She put her mirror back into her bag. "We've been all through that," she said, getting out of the car. "You're not a young man any longer." He raced the engine a little. "Why don't you wear your gloves? Have you lost your gloves?" Walter Mitty reached in a pocket and brought out the gloves. He put them on, but after she had turned and gone into the building and he had driven on to a red light, he took them off again. "Pick it up, brother!" snapped a cop as the light changed, and Mitty hastily pulled on his gloves and lurched ahead. He drove around the streets aimlessly for a time, and then he drove past the hospital on his way to the parking lot.

. . . "It's the millionaire banker, Wellington McMillan" said the pretty nurse. "Yes?" said Walter Mitty, removing his gloves slowly. "Who has the case?" "Dr. Renshaw and Dr. Benbow, but there are two specialists here, Dr. Remington from New York and Mr. Pritchard-Mitford from London. He flew over." A door opened down a long, cool corridor and Dr. Renshaw came out. He looked distraught and haggard. "Hello, Mitty," he said. "We're having the devil's own time with McMillan, the millionaire banker and close personal friend of Roosevelt. Obstreosis of the ductal tract. Tertiary. Wish you'd take a look at him." "Glad to," said Mitty.

Copyright © 1942 James Thurber. Copyright © 1970 Helen W. Thurber and Rosemary Thurber Sauers. From *My World—And Welcome To It*, published by Harcourt Brace Jovanovich. Originally printed in *The New Yorker*.

In the operating room there were whispered introductions: "Dr. Remington, Dr. Mitty. Mr. Pritchard-Mitford, Dr. Mitty." "I've read your book on streptothricosis," said Pritchard-Mitford, shaking hands. "A brilliant performance, sir." "Thank you," said Walter Mitty. "Didn't know you were in the States, Mitty," grumbled Remington. "Coals to Newcastle, bringing Mitford and me here for a tertiary." "You are very kind," said Mitty. A huge, complicated machine, connected to the operating table, with many tubes and wires, began at this moment to go pocketa-pocketa-pocketa. "The new anesthetizer is giving way!" shouted an interne. "There is no one in the East who knows how to fix it!" "Quiet, man!" said Mitty, in a low, cool voice. He sprang to the machine, which was now going pocketa-pocketa-queep-pocketa-queep. He began fingering delicately a row of glistening dials. "Give me a fountain pen!" he snapped. Someone handed him a fountain pen. He pulled a faulty piston out of the machine and inserted the pen in its place. "That will hold for ten minutes," he said. "Get on with the operation." A nurse hurried over and whispered to Renshaw, and Mitty saw the man turn pale. "Coreopsis has set in," said Renshaw nervously. "If you would take over, Mitty?" Mitty looked at him and at the craven figure of Benbow, who drank, and at the grave, uncertain faces of the two great specialists. "If you wish," he said. They slipped a white gown on him; he adjusted a mask and drew on thin gloves; nurses handed him shining. . . .

"Back it up, Mac! Look out for that Buick!" Walter Mitty jammed on the brakes. "Wrong lane, Mac," said the parking-lot attendant, looking at Mitty closely. "Gee. Yeh," muttered Mitty. He began cautiously to back out of the lane marked "Exit Only." "Leave her sit there," said the attendant. "I'll put her away." Mitty got out of the car. "Hey, better leave the key." "Oh," said Mitty, handing the man the ignition key. The attendant vaulted into the car, backed it up with insolent skill, and put it where it belonged.

They're so damn cocky, thought Walter Mitty, walking along Main Street; they think they know everything. Once he had tried to take his chains off, outside New Milford, and he had got them wound around the axles. A man had had to come out in a wrecking car and unwind them, a young, grinning garageman. Since then Mrs. Mitty always made him drive to a garage to have the chains taken off. The next time, he thought, I'll wear my right arm in a sling; they won't grin at me then. I'll have my right arm in a sling and they'll see I couldn't possibly take the chains off myself. He kicked at the slush on the sidewalk. "Overshoes," he said to himself, and he began looking for a shoe store.

When he came out into the street again, with the overshoes in a box under his arm, Walter Mitty began to wonder what the other thing was his wife had told him to get. She had told him twice, before they set out from their house for Waterbury. In a way he hated these weekly trips to town—he was always getting something wrong. Kleenex, he thought, Squibb's, razor blades? No. Toothpaste, toothbrush, bicarbonate, carborundum, initiative and referendum? He gave it up. But she would remember it. "Where's the what's-its-name?" she would ask. "Don't tell me you forgot the what's-its-name?" A newsboy went by shouting something about the Waterbury trial.

. . . "Perhaps this will refresh your memory." The District Attorney suddenly thrust a heavy automatic at the quiet figure on the witness stand. "Have you ever seen this before?" Walter Mitty took the gun and examined it expertly. "This is my Webley-Vickers 50.80," he said calmly. An excited buzz ran around the courtroom. The judge rapped for order. "You are a crack shot with any sort of firearms, I believe?" said the District Attorney, insinuatingly. "Objection!" shouted Mitty's attorney. "We have shown that the defendant could not have fired the shot. We have shown that he wore his right arm in a sling on the night of the fourteenth of July." Walter Mitty raised his hand briefly and the bickering attorneys were stilled. "With any known make of gun," he said evenly, "I could have killed Gregory Fitzhurst at three hundred feet *with my left hand.*" Pandemonium broke loose in the courtroom. A woman's scream rose above the bedlam and suddenly a lovely, dark-haired girl was in Walter Mitty's arms. The District Attorney struck at her savagely. Without rising from his chair, Mitty let the man have it on the point of the chin. "You miserable cur!" . . .

"Puppy biscuit," said Walter Mitty. He stopped walking and the buildings of Waterbury rose up out of the misty courtroom and surrounded him again. A woman who was passing laughed. "He said 'Puppy biscuit,'" she said to her companion. "That man said 'Puppy biscuit' to himself." Walter Mitty hurried on. He went into an A & P, not the first one he came to but a smaller one farther up the street. "I want some biscuit for small, young dogs," he said to the clerk. "Any special brand, sir?" The greatest pistol shot in the world thought a moment. "It says 'Puppies Bark for It' on the box," said Walter Mitty.

His wife would be through at the hairdresser's in fifteen minutes, Mitty saw in looking at his watch, unless they had trouble drying it; sometimes they had trouble drying it. She didn't like to get to the hotel first; she would want him to be there waiting for her as usual. He found a big leather chair in the lobby, facing a window, and he put the overshoes and the puppy biscuit on the floor beside it. He picked up an old copy of *Liberty* and sank down into the chair. "Can Germany Conquer the World Through the Air?" Walter Mitty looked at the pictures of bombing planes and of ruined streets.

. . . "The cannonading has got the wind up in young Raleigh, sir," said the sergeant. Captain Mitty looked up at him through tousled hair. "Get him to bed," he said wearily. "With the others. I'll fly alone." "But you can't, sir," said the sergeant anxiously. "It takes two men to handle that bomber and the Archies are pounding hell out of the air. Von Richtman's circus is between here and Saulier." "Somebody's got to get that ammunition dump," said Mitty. "I'm going over. Spot of brandy?" He poured a drink for the sergeant and one for himself. War thundered and whined around the dugout and battered at the door. There was a rending of wood and splinters flew through the room. "A bit of a near thing," said Captain Mitty carelessly. "The box barrage is closing in," said the sergeant. "We only live once, Sergeant," said Mitty, with his faint, fleeting smile. "Or do we?" He poured another brandy and tossed it off. "I never see a man could hold his brandy like you, sir," said the sergeant. "Begging your pardon, sir." Captain Mitty stood up and strapped on his huge Webley-Vickers automatic. "It's forty kilometers through hell, sir," said the sergeant. Mitty finished one last brandy. "After all," he said softly, "what isn't?" The pounding of the cannon increased; there was the rat-tat-tatting of machine guns, and from somewhere came the menacing pocketa-pocketa-pocketa of the new flame-throwers. Walter Mitty walked to the door of the dugout humming "Auprès de Ma Blonde." He turned and waved to the sergeant. "Cheerio!" he said. . . .

Something struck his shoulder. "I've been looking all over this hotel for you," said Mrs. Mitty. "Why do you have to hide in this old chair? How did you expect me to find you?" "Things close in," said Walter Mitty vaguely. "What?" Mrs. Mitty said. "Did you get the what's-its-name? The puppy biscuit? What's in the box?" "Overshoes," said Mitty. "Couldn't you have put them on in the store?" "I was thinking," said Walter Mitty. "Does it ever occur to you that I am sometimes thinking?" She looked at him. "I'm going to take your temperature when I get you home," she said.

They went out through the revolving doors that made a faintly derisive whistling sound when you pushed them. It was two blocks to the parking lot. At the drugstore on the corner she said, "Wait here for me. I forgot something. I won't be a minute." She was more than a minute. Walter Mitty lighted a cigarette. It began to rain, rain with sleet in it. He stood up against the wall of the drugstore, smoking. . . . He put his shoulders back and his heels together. "To hell with the handkerchief," said Walter Mitty scornfully. He took one last drag on his cigarette and snapped it away. Then, with that faint, fleeting smile playing about his lips, he faced the firing squad; erect and motionless, proud and disdainful, Walter Mitty the Undefeated, inscrutable to the last.

William Faulkner (1897–1962)

William Faulkner was born in Mississippi in 1897. He was never an expatriate as were many of his writing contemporaries, notably Hemingway and Fitzgerald. He spent almost all his life in Oxford, the site of the University of Mississippi. He says, "I discovered that my own little postage stamp of native soil was worth writing about and that I would never live long enough to exhaust it." The fruit of this discovery is a self-contained world of fiction:

> "Jefferson, Yoknapatawpha Co., Mississippi
> Area, 2400 Square Miles—Population, Whites, 6298; Negroes, 9313
> William Faulkner, Sole Owner & Proprietor."

A map of this mythical place appears at the end of *Absalom, Absalom!* (1936). From book to book, story to story, Faulkner fills in the background, rivers, and cross-roads, businesses and homesteads. He provides a rich legend of Indian beginnings and early times of white settlement, slavery, and the Civil War, and the struggle for the soul of the modern South. This world is one of the great constructs of the human imagination.

His primary intention as a writer, however, was not to create a fictionalized social history, as did, say, Balzac in his *La Comédie Humaine.* "I have been writing all the time," Faulkner says, "about honor, truth, pity, consideration, the capacity to endure well grief and misfortune and injustice and then endure again." This theme was restated in his eloquent address upon receiving the Nobel Prize for Literature in 1949. Few writers can match him in the largeness of his themes and his passionate commitment to them. Isaac Rosenfeld says that Faulkner "would certainly be a homiletic writer were it not for the fact that he is pointing up no trite morality."

There is no trite morality in "Barn Burning." The opposing forces struggling for the soul of Sarty Snopes are not simple Good and Evil, but complex mixtures of both. For Faulkner, the white house and the pale rug, the collar and cravat and the magnificent horse, are the outward signs of the inward grace of men like Major de Spain, who believe in honor and duty and order. But they are also signs, as Faulkner knew, of living off the sweat of others. In contrast and conflict is Abner Snopes, poor white. Sarty remarks "the absolutely undeviating course which his father held and saw the stiff foot come squarely down in a pile of fresh droppings where a horse had stood in the drive and which his father could have avoided by a simple change of stride." And so we behold Abner: proud, relentless, uncompromising, crude, malicious. Sarty is torn between loyalty to this man and his admiration for "People whose lives are a part of this peace and dignity."

In "Barn Burning" his profound understanding of the human condition and his passion to render the opposing forces as well as the inner life of Sarty seem to burst the bounds of the story. Faulkner starts the story with what almost amounts to a preamble, when Abner was on trial; he changes point of view, leaves the mind of Sarty to comment on that mind, has Sarty look back from years hence; he even corrects for the reader's sake the boy's misapprehensions about his father's war service. Perhaps it is the pressure to do justice to the rich social context out of which his fiction rose and at the same time to illuminate such large motifs that made the short story less congenial than the novel to Faulkner. Yet who can complain of such riches?

Faulkner was the author of many volumes of poems, stories, and novels. The novels considered most significant are *The Sound and the Fury* (1929), *Light in August* (1932), and *Absalom, Absalom!* (1936). He died in 1962 in Oxford, Mississippi, estranged, because of his moderate views on civil rights, from the people of the postage stamp he had made immortal.

Barn Burning

The store in which the Justice of the Peace's court was sitting smelled of cheese. The boy, crouched on his nail keg at the back of the crowded room, knew he smelled cheese, and more: from where he sat he could see the ranked shelves close-packed with the solid, squat, dynamic shapes of tin cans whose labels his stomach read, not from the lettering which meant nothing to his mind but from the scarlet devils and the silver curve of fish—this, the cheese which he knew he smelled and the hermetic meat which his intestines believed he smelled coming in intermittent gusts momentary and brief between the other constant one, the smell and sense just a little of fear because mostly of despair and grief, the old fierce pull of blood. He could not see the table where the Justice sat and before which his father and his father's enemy (*our enemy* he thought in that despair; *ourn! mine and hisn both! He's my father!*) stood, but he could hear them, the two of them that is, because his father had said no word yet:

"But what proof have you, Mr. Harris?"

"I told you. The hog got into my corn. I caught it up and sent it back to him. He had no fence that would hold it. I told him so, warned him. The next time I put the hog in my pen. When he came to get it I gave him enough wire to patch up his pen. The next time I put the hog up and kept it. I rode down to his house and saw the wire I gave him still rolled on to the spool in his yard. I told him he could have the hog when he paid me a dollar pound fee. That evening a nigger came with the dollar and

Copyright 1939 and renewed 1967 by Estelle Faulkner and Jill Faulkner Summers. Reprinted from *Collected Stories of William Faulkner,* by permission of Random House, Inc.

got the hog. He was a strange nigger. He said, 'He say to tell you wood and hay kin
burn.' I said, 'What?' 'That whut he say to tell you,' the nigger said. 'Wood and hay
kin burn.' That night my barn burned. I got the stock out but I lost the barn."

"Where is the nigger? Have you got him?"

"He was a strange nigger, I tell you. I don't know what became of him."

"But that's not proof. Don't you see that's not proof?"

"Get that boy up here. He knows." For a moment the boy thought too that the
man meant his older brother until Harris said, "Not him. The little one. The boy,"
and, crouching, small for his age, small and wiry like his father, in patched and faded
jeans even too small for him, with straight, uncombed, brown hair and eyes gray and
wild as storm scud, he saw the men between himself and the table part and become a
lane of grim faces, at the end of which he saw the Justice, a shabby, collarless, graying
man in spectacles, beckoning him. He felt no floor under his bare feet; he seemed to
walk beneath the palpable weight of the grim turning faces. His father, stiff in his
black Sunday coat donned not for the trial but for the moving, did not even look at
him. *He aims for me to lie,* he thought, again with that frantic grief and despair. *And I
will have to do hit.*

"What's your name, boy?" the Justice said.

"Colonel Sartoris Snopes," the boy whispered.

"Hey?" the Justice said. "Talk louder. Colonel Sartoris? I reckon anybody named
for Colonel Sartoris in this country can't help but tell the truth, can they?" The boy
said nothing. *Enemy! Enemy!* he thought; for a moment he could not even see, could
not see that the Justice's face was kindly nor discern that his voice was troubled when
he spoke to the man named Harris: "Do you want me to question this boy?" But he
could hear, and during those subsequent long seconds while there was absolutely no
sound in the crowded little room save that of quiet and intent breathing it was as if he
had swung outward at the end of a grape vine, over a ravine, and at the top of the
swing had been caught in a prolonged instant of mesmerized gravity, weightless in
time.

"No!" Harris said violently, explosively. "Damnation! Send him out of here!"
Now time, the fluid world, rushed beneath him again, the voices coming to him again
through the smell of cheese and sealed meat, the fear and despair and the old grief of
blood:

"This case is closed. I can't find against you, Snopes, but I can give you advice.
Leave this country and don't come back to it."

His father spoke for the first time, his voice cold and harsh, level, without emphasis: "I aim to. I don't figure to stay in a country among people who . . ." he said
something unprintable and vile, addressed to no one.

"That'll do," the Justice said. "Take your wagon and get out of this country
before dark. Case dismissed."

His father turned, and he followed the stiff black coat, the wiry figure walking a
little stiffly from where a Confederate provost's man's musket ball had taken him in
the heel on a stolen horse thirty years ago, followed the two backs now, since his older
brother had appeared from somewhere in the crowd, no taller than the father but
thicker, chewing tobacco steadily, between the two lines of grim-faced men and out of
the store and across the worn gallery and down the sagging steps and among the dogs
and half-grown boys in the mild May dust, where as he passed a voice hissed:

"Barn burner!"

Again he could not see, whirling; there was a face in a red haze, moonlike, bigger than the full moon, the owner of it half again his size, he leaping in the red haze toward the face, feeling no blow, feeling no shock when his head struck the earth, scrabbling up and leaping again, feeling no blow this time either and tasting no blood, scrabbling up to see the other boy in full flight and himself already leaping into pursuit as his father's hand jerked him back, the harsh, cold voice speaking above him: "Go get in the wagon."

It stood in a grove of locusts and mulberries across the road. His two hulking sisters in their Sunday dresses and his mother and her sister in calico and sunbonnets were already in it, sitting on and among the sorry residue of the dozen and more movings which even the boy could remember—the battered stove, the broken beds and chairs, the clock inlaid with mother-of-pearl, which would not run, stopped at some fourteen minutes past two o'clock of a dead and forgotten day and time, which had been his mother's dowry. She was crying, though when she saw him she drew her sleeve across her face and began to descend from the wagon. "Get back," the father said.

"He's hurt. I got to get some water and wash his . . ."

"Get back in the wagon," his father said. He got in too, over the tail-gate. His father mounted to the seat where the older brother already sat and struck the gaunt mules two savage blows with the peeled willow, but without heat. It was not even sadistic; it was exactly that same quality which in later years would cause his descendants to over-run the engine before putting a motor car into motion, striking and reining back in the same movement. The wagon went on, the store with its quiet crowd of grimly watching men dropped behind; a curve in the road hid it. *Forever* he thought. *Maybe he's done satisfied now, now that he has* . . . stopping himself, not to say it aloud even to himself. His mother's hand touched his shoulder.

"Does hit hurt?" she said.

"Naw," he said. "Hit don't hurt. Lemme be."

"Can't you wipe some of the blood off before hit dries?"

"I'll wash to-night," he said. "Lemme be, I tell you."

The wagon went on. He did not know where they were going. None of them ever did or ever asked, because it was always somewhere, always a house of sorts waiting for them a day or two days or even three days away. Likely his father had already arranged to make a crop on another farm before he . . . Again he had to stop himself. He (the father) always did. There was something about his wolflike independence and even courage when the advantage was at least neutral which impressed strangers, as if they got from his latent ravening ferocity not so much a sense of dependability as a feeling that his ferocious conviction in the rightness of his own actions would be of advantage to all whose interest lay with his.

That night they camped, in a grove of oaks and beeches where a spring ran. The nights were still cool and they had a fire against it, of a rail lifted from a nearby fence and cut into lengths—a small fire, neat, niggard almost, a shrewd fire; such fires were his father's habit and custom always, even in freezing weather. Older, the boy might have remarked this and wondered why not a big one; why should not a man who had not only seen the waste and extravagance of war, but who had in his blood an inherent voracious prodigality with material not his own, have burned everything in sight? Then he might have gone a step farther and thought that that was the reason: that niggard blaze was the living fruit of nights passed during those four years in the woods hiding from all men, blue or gray, with his strings of horses (captured horses, he called them). And older still, he might have divined the true reason: that the element of fire spoke to some deep mainspring of his father's being, as the element of steel or of powder spoke to other men, as the one weapon for the preservation of integrity, else breath were not worth the breathing, and hence to be regarded with respect and used with discretion.

But he did not think this now and he had seen those same niggard blazes all his life. He merely ate his supper beside it and was already half asleep over his iron plate when his father called him, and once more he followed the stiff back, the stiff and ruthless limp, up the slope and on to the starlit road where, turning, he could see his father against the stars but without face or depth—a shape black, flat, and bloodless as though cut from tin in the iron folds of the frockcoat which had not been made for him, the voice harsh like tin and without heat like tin:

"You were fixing to tell them. You would have told him." He didn't answer. His father struck him with the flat of his hand on the side of the head, hard but without heat, exactly as he had struck the two mules at the store, exactly as he would strike either of them with any stick in order to kill a horse fly, his voice still without heat or anger: "You're getting to be a man. You got to learn. You got to learn to stick to your own blood or you ain't going to have any blood to stick to you. Do you think either of them, any man there this morning, would? Don't you know all they wanted was a chance to get at me because they knew I had them beat? Eh?" Later, twenty years later, he was to tell himself, "If I had said they wanted only truth, justice, he would have hit me again." But now he said nothing. He was not crying. He just stood there. "Answer me," his father said.

"Yes," he whispered. His father turned.

"Get on to bed. We'll be there tomorrow."

To-morrow they were there. In the early afternoon the wagon stopped before a paintless two-room house identical almost with the dozen others it had stopped before even in the boy's ten years, and again, as on the other dozen occasions, his mother and aunt got down and began to unload the wagon, although his two sisters and his father and brother had not moved.

"Likely hit ain't fitten for hawgs," one of the sisters said.

"Nevertheless, fit it will and you'll hog it and like it," his father said. "Get out of them chairs and help your Ma unload."

The two sisters got down, big, bovine, in a flutter of cheap ribbons; one of them drew from the jumbled wagon bed a battered lantern, the other a worn broom. His father handed the reins to the older son and began to climb stiffly over the wheel. "When they get unloaded, take the team to the barn and feed them." Then he said, and at first the boy thought he was still speaking to his brother: "Come with me."

"Me?" he said.

"Yes," his father said. "You."

"Abner," his mother said. His father paused and looked back—the harsh level stare beneath the shaggy, graying, irascible brows.

"I reckon I'll have a word with the man that aims to begin to-morrow owning me body and soul for the next eight months."

They went back up the road. A week ago—or before last night, that is—he would have asked where they were going, but not now. His father had struck him before last night but never before had he paused afterward to explain why; it was as if the blow and the following calm, outrageous voice still rang, repercussed, divulging nothing to him save the terrible handicap of being young, the light weight of his few years, just heavy enough to prevent his soaring free of the world as it seemed to be ordered but not heavy enough to keep him footed solid in it, to resist it and try to change the course of its events.

Presently he could see the grove of oaks and cedars and the other flowering trees and shrubs where the house would be, though not the house yet. They walked beside a fence massed with honeysuckle and Cherokee roses and came to a gate swinging open between two brick pillars, and now, beyond a sweep of drive, he saw the house for the first time and at that instant he forgot his father and the terror and despair both, and even when he remembered his father again (who had not stopped) the terror and despair did not return. Because, for all the twelve movings, they had sojourned until now in a poor country, a land of small farms and fields and houses, and he had never seen a house like this before. *Hit's big as a courthouse* he thought quietly, with a surge of peace and joy whose reason he could not have thought into words, being too young for that: *They are safe from him. People whose lives are a part of this peace and dignity are beyond his touch, he no more to them than a buzzing wasp: capable of stinging for a little moment but that's all; the spell of this peace and dignity rendering even the barns and stable and cribs which belong to it impervious to the puny flames he might contrive* . . . this, the peace and joy, ebbing for an instant as he looked again at the stiff black back, the stiff and implacable limp of the figure which was not dwarfed by the house, for the reason that it had never looked big anywhere and which now, against the serene columned backdrop, had more than ever that impervious quality of something cut ruthlessly from tin, depthless, as though, sidewise to the sun, it would cast no shadow. Watching him, the boy remarked the absolutely undeviating course which his father held and saw the stiff foot come squarely down in a pile of fresh droppings where a horse had stood in the drive and which his father could have avoided by a simple change of stride. But it ebbed only for a moment, though he could not have thought this into words either, walking on in the spell of the house, which he could even want but without envy, without sorrow, certainly never with that ravening and jealous rage which unknown to him walked in the ironlike black coat before him: *Maybe he will feel it too. Maybe it will even change him now from what maybe he couldn't help but be.*

They crossed the portico. Now he could hear his father's stiff foot as it came down on the boards with clocklike finality, a sound out of all proportion to the displacement of the body it bore and which was not dwarfed either by the white door before it, as though it had attained to a sort of vicious and ravening minimum not to be dwarfed by anything—the flat, wide, black hat, the formal coat of broadcloth which had once been black but which had now that friction-glazed greenish cast of the bodies of old house flies, the lifted sleeve which was too large, the lifted hand like a curled claw. The door opened so promptly that the boy knew the Negro must have been watching them all the time, an old man with neat grizzled hair, in a linen jacket, who stood barring the door with his body, saying, "Wipe yo foots, white man, fo you come in here. Major ain't home nohow."

"Get out of my way, nigger," his father said, without heat too, flinging the door back and the Negro also and entering, his hat still on his head. And now the boy saw the prints of the stiff foot on the doorjamb and saw them appear on the pale rug behind the machinelike deliberation of the foot which seemed to bear (or transmit) twice the weight which the body compassed. The Negro was shouting "Miss Lula! Miss Lula!" somewhere behind them, then the boy, deluged as though by a warm wave by a suave turn of carpeted stair and a pendant glitter of chandeliers and a mute gleam of gold frames, heard the swift feet and saw her too, a lady—perhaps he had never seen her like before either—in a gray, smooth gown with lace at the throat and an apron tied at the waist and the sleeves turned back, wiping cake or biscuit dough from her hands with a towel as she came up the hall, looking not at his father at all but at the tracks on the blond rug with an expression of incredulous amazement.

"I tried," the Negro cried. "I tole him to . . ."

"Will you please go away?" she said in a shaking voice. "Major de Spain is not at home. Will you please go away?"

His father had not spoken again. He did not speak again. He did not even look at her. He just stood stiff in the center of the rug, in his hat, the shaggy iron-gray brows twitching slightly above the pebble-colored eyes as he appeared to examine the house with brief deliberation. Then with the same deliberation he turned; the boy watched him pivot on the good leg and saw the stiff foot drag round the arc of the turning, leaving a final long and fading smear. His father never looked at it, he never once looked down at the rug. The Negro held the door. It closed behind them, upon the hysteric and indistinguishable woman-wail. His father stopped at the top of the steps and scraped his boot clean on the edge of it. At the gate he stopped again. He stood for a moment, planted stiffly on the stiff foot, looking back at the house. "Pretty and white, ain't it?" he said. "That's sweat. Nigger sweat. Maybe it ain't white enough yet to suit him. Maybe he wants to mix some white sweat with it."

Two hours later the boy was chopping wood behind the house within which his mother and aunt and the two sisters (the mother and aunt, not the two girls, he knew that; even at this distance and muffled by walls the flat loud voices of the two girls emanated an incorrigible idle inertia) were setting up the stove to prepare a meal, when he heard the hooves and saw the linen-clad man on a fine sorrel mare, whom he recognized even before he saw the rolled rug in front of the Negro youth following on a fat bay carriage horse—a suffused, angry face vanishing, still at full gallop, beyond the corner of the house where his father and brother were sitting in the two tilted chairs; and a moment later, almost before he could have put the axe down, he heard the hooves again and watched the sorrel mare go back out of the yard, already galloping again. Then his father began to shout one of the sisters' names, who presently emerged backward from the kitchen door dragging the rolled rug along the ground by one end while the other sister walked behind it.

"If you ain't going to tote, go on and set up the wash pot," the first said.

"You, Sarty!" the second shouted. "Set up the wash pot!" His father appeared at the door, framed against that shabbiness, as he had been against that other bland perfection, impervious to either, the mother's anxious face at his shoulder.

"Go on," the father said. "Pick it up." The two sisters stooped, broad, lethargic; stooping, they presented an incredible expanse of pale cloth and a flutter of tawdry ribbons.

"If I thought enough of a rug to have to git hit all the way from France I wouldn't keep hit where folks coming in would have to tromp on hit," the first said. They raised the rug.

"Abner," the mother said. "Let me do it."

"You go back and git dinner," his father said. "I'll tend to this."

From the woodpile through the rest of the afternoon the boy watched them, the rug spread flat in the dust beside the bubbling wash-pot, the two sisters stooping over it with that profound and lethargic reluctance, while the father stood over them in turn, implacable and grim, driving them though never raising his voice again. He could smell the harsh homemade lye they were using; he saw his mother come to the door once and look toward them with an expression not anxious now but very like despair; he saw his father turn, and he fell to with the axe and saw from the corner of his eye his father raise from the ground a flattish fragment of field stone and examine it and return to the pot, and this time his mother actually spoke: "Abner. Abner. Please don't. Please, Abner."

Then he was done too. It was dusk; the whippoorwills had already begun. He could smell coffee from the room where they would presently eat the cold food remaining from the mid-afternoon meal, though when he entered the house he realized they were having coffee again probably because there was a fire on the hearth, before which the rug now lay spread over the backs of the two chairs. The tracks of his father's foot were gone. Where they had been were now long, water-cloudy scoriations resembling the sporadic course of a lilliputian mowing machine.

It still hung there while they ate the cold food and then went to bed, scattered without order or claim up and down the two rooms, his mother in one bed, where his father would later lie, the older brother in the other, himself, the aunt, and the two sisters on pallets on the floor. But his father was not in bed yet. The last thing the boy remembered was the depthless, harsh silhouette of the hat and coat bending over the rug and it seemed to him that he had not even closed his eyes when the silhouette was standing over him, the fire almost dead behind it, the stiff foot prodding him awake. "Catch up the mule," his father said.

When he returned with the mule his father was standing in the black door, the rolled rug over his shoulder. "Ain't you going to ride?" he said.

"No. Give me your foot."

He bent his knee into his father's hand, the wiry, surprising power flowed smoothly, rising, he rising with it, on to the mule's bare back (they had owned a saddle once; the boy could remember it though not when or where) and with the same effortlessness his father swung the rug up in front of him. Now in the starlight they retraced the afternoon's path, up the dusty road rife with honeysuckle, through the gate and up the black tunnel of the drive to the lightless house, where he sat on the mule and felt the rough warp of the rug drag across his thighs and vanish.

"Don't you want me to help?" he whispered. His father did not answer and now he heard again that stiff foot striking the hollow portico with that wooden and clock-like deliberation, that outrageous overstatement of the weight it carried. The rug, hunched, not flung (the boy could tell that even in the darkness) from his father's shoulder struck the angle of wall and floor with a sound unbelievably loud, thunderous, then the foot again, unhurried and enormous; a light came on in the house and the boy sat, tense, breathing steadily and quietly and just a little fast, though the foot itself did not increase its beat at all, descending the steps now; now the boy could see him.

"Don't you want to ride now?" he whispered. "We kin both ride now," the light within the house altering now, flaring up and sinking. *He's coming down the stairs now,* he thought. He had already ridden the mule up beside the horse block; presently his father was up behind him and he doubled the reins over and slashed the mule across the neck, but before the animal could begin to trot the hard, thin arm came round him, the hard, knotted hand jerking the mule back to a walk.

In the first red rays of the sun they were in the lot, putting plow gear on the mules. This time the sorrel mare was in the lot before he heard it at all, the rider collarless and even bareheaded, trembling, speaking in a shaking voice as the woman in the house had done. His father merely looking up once before stooping again to the hame he was buckling, so that the man on the mare spoke to his stooping back:

"You must realize you have ruined that rug. Wasn't there anybody here, any of your women . . ." he ceased, shaking, the boy watching him, the older brother leaning now in the stable door, chewing, blinking slowly and steadily at nothing apparently. "It cost a hundred dollars. But you never had a hundred dollars. You never will. So I'm going to charge you twenty bushels of corn against your crop. I'll add it in your contract and when you come to the commissary you can sign it. That won't keep Mrs. de Spain quiet but maybe it will teach you to wipe your feet off before you enter her house again."

Then he was gone. The boy looked at his father, who still had not spoken or even looked up again, who was now adjusting the logger-head in the hame.

"Pap," he said. His father looked at him—the inscrutable face, the shaggy brows beneath which the gray eyes glinted coldly. Suddenly the boy went toward him, fast, stopping as suddenly. "You done the best you could!" he cried. "If he wanted hit done different why didn't he wait and tell you how? He won't git no twenty bushels! He won't git none! We'll gether hit and hide hit! I kin watch . . ."

"Did you put the cutter back in that straight stock like I told you?"

"No, sir," he said.

"Then go do it."

That was Wednesday. During the rest of that week he worked steadily, at what was within his scope and some which was beyond it, with an industry that did not need to be driven nor even commanded twice; he had this from his mother, with the difference that some at least of what he did he liked to do, such as splitting wood with the half-size axe which his mother and aunt had earned, or saved money somehow, to present him with at Christmas. In company with the two older women (and on one afternoon, even one of the sisters), he built pens for the shoat and the cow which were a part of his father's contract with the landlord, and one afternoon, his father being absent, gone somewhere on one of the mules, he went to the field.

They were running a middle buster now, his brother holding the plow straight while he handled the reins, and walking beside the straining mule, the rich black soil shearing cool and damp against his bare ankles, he thought *Maybe this is the end of it. Maybe even that twenty bushels that seems hard to have to pay for just a rug will be a cheap price for him to stop forever and always from being what he used to be;* thinking, dreaming now, so that his brother had to speak sharply to him to mind the mule: *Maybe he even won't collect the twenty bushels. Maybe it will all add up and balance and vanish—corn, rug, fire; the terror and grief, the being pulled two ways like between two teams of horses—gone, done with for ever and ever.*

Then it was Saturday; he looked up from beneath the mule he was harnessing and saw his father in the black coat and hat. "Not that," his father said. "The wagon gear." And then, two hours later, sitting in the wagon bed behind his father and brother on the seat, the wagon accomplished a final curve, and he saw the weathered paintless store with its tattered tobacco- and patent-medicine posters and the tethered wagons and saddle animals below the gallery. He mounted the gnawed steps behind his father and brother, and there again was the lane of quiet, watching faces for the three of them to walk through. He saw the man in spectacles sitting at the plank table and he did not need to be told this was a Justice of the Peace; he sent one glare of fierce, exultant, partisan defiance at the man in collar and cravat now, whom he had seen but twice before in his life, and that on a galloping horse, who now wore on his face an expression not of rage but of amazed unbelief which the boy could not have known was at the incredible circumstance of being sued by one of his own tenants, and came and stood against his father and cried at the Justice: "He ain't done it! He ain't burnt . . ."

"Go back to the wagon," his father said.

"Burnt?" the Justice said. "Do I understand this rug was burned too?"

"Does anybody here claim it was?" his father said. "Go back to the wagon." But he did not, he merely retreated to the rear of the room, crowded as that other had been, but not to sit down this time, instead, to stand pressing among the motionless bodies, listening to the voices:

"And you claim twenty bushels of corn is too high for the damage you did to the rug?"

"He brought the rug to me and said he wanted the tracks washed out of it. I washed the tracks out and took the rug back to him."

"But you didn't carry the rug back to him in the same condition it was in before you made the tracks on it."

His father did not answer, and now for perhaps half a minute there was no sound at all save that of breathing, the faint, steady suspiration of complete and intent listening.

"You decline to answer that, Mr. Snopes?" Again his father did not answer. "I'm going to find against you, Mr. Snopes. I'm going to find that you were responsible for the injury to Major de Spain's rug and hold you liable for it. But twenty bushels of corn seems a little high for a man in your circumstances to have to pay. Major de Spain claims it cost a hundred dollars. October corn will be worth about fifty cents. I figure that if Major de Spain can stand a ninety-five dollar loss on something he paid cash for, you can stand a five-dollar loss you haven't earned yet. I hold you in damages to Major de Spain to the amount of ten bushels of corn over and above your contract with him, to be paid to him out of your crop at gathering time. Court adjourned."

It had taken no time hardly, the morning was but half begun. He thought they would return home and perhaps back to the field, since they were late, far behind all other farmers. But instead his father passed on behind the wagon, merely indicating with his hand for the older brother to follow with it, and crossed the road toward the blacksmith shop opposite, pressing on after his father, overtaking him, speaking, whispering up at the harsh, calm face beneath the weathered hat: "He won't git no ten bushels neither. He won't git one. We'll . . ." until his father glanced for an instant down at him, the face absolutely calm, the grizzled eyebrows tangled above the cold eyes, the voice almost pleasant, almost gentle:

"You think so? Well, we'll wait till October anyway."

The matter of the wagon—the setting of a spoke or two and the tightening of the tires—did not take long either, the business of the tires accomplished by driving the wagon into the spring branch behind the shop and letting it stand there, the mules nuzzling into the water from time to time, and the boy on the seat with the idle reins, looking up the slope and through the sooty tunnel of the shed where the slow hammer rang and where his father sat on an upended cypress bolt, easily, either talking or listening, still sitting there when the boy brought the dripping wagon up out of the branch and halted it before the door.

"Take them on to the shade and hitch," his father said. He did so and returned. His father and the smith and a third man squatting on his heels inside the door were talking, about crops and animals; the boy, squatting too in the ammoniac dust and hoof-parings and scales of rust, heard his father tell a long and unhurried story out of the time before the birth of the older brother even when he had been a professional horsetrader. And then his father came up beside him where he stood before a tattered last year's circus poster on the other side of the store, gazing rapt and quiet at the scarlet horses, the incredible poisings and convolutions of tulle and tights and the painted leers of comedians, and said, "It's time to eat."

But not at home. Squatting beside his brother against the front wall, he watched his father emerge from the store and produce from a paper sack a segment of cheese and divide it carefully and deliberately into three with his pocket knife and produce crackers from the same sack. They all three squatted on the gallery and ate, slowly, without talking; then in the store again, they drank from a tin dipper tepid water smelling of the cedar bucket and of living beech trees. And still they did not go home. It was a horse lot this time, a tall rail fence upon and along which men stood and sat and out of which one by one horses were led, to be walked and trotted and then cantered back and forth along the road while the slow swapping and buying went on and the sun began to slant westward, they—the three of them—watching and listening, the older brother with his muddy eyes and his steady, inevitable tobacco, the father commenting now and then on certain of the animals, to no one in particular.

It was after sundown when they reached home. They ate supper by lamplight, then, sitting on the doorstep, the boy watched the night fully accomplish, listening to the whippoorwills and the frogs, when he heard his mother's voice: "Abner! No! No! Oh, God. Oh, God. Abner!" and he rose, whirled, and saw the altered light through the door where a candle stub now burned in a bottle neck on the table and his father, still in the hat and coat, at once formal and burlesque as though dressed carefully for some shabby and ceremonial violence, emptying the reservoir of the lamp back into the five-gallon kerosene can from which it had been filled, while the mother tugged at his arm until he shifted the lamp to the other hand and flung her back, not savagely or viciously, just hard, into the wall, her hands flung out against the wall for balance, her mouth open and in her face the same quality of hopeless despair as had been in her voice. Then his father saw him standing in the door.

"Go to the barn and get that can of oil we were oiling the wagon with," he said. The boy did not move. Then he could speak.

"What . . ." he cried. "What are you . . ."

"Go get that oil," his father said. "Go."

Then he was moving, running, outside the house, toward the stable: this the old habit, the old blood which he had not been permitted to choose for himself, which had been bequeathed him willy nilly and which had run for so long (and who knew where, battening on what of outrage and savagery and lust) before it came to him. *I could keep on,* he thought. *I could run on and on and never look back, never need to see his face again. Only I can't. I can't,* the rusted can in his hand now, the liquid splashing in it as he ran back to the house and into it, into the sound of his mother's weeping in the next room, and handed the can to his father.

"Ain't you going to even send a nigger?" he cried. "At least you sent a nigger before!"

This time his father didn't strike him. The hand came even faster than the blow had, the same hand which had set the can on the table with almost excruciating care flashing from the can toward him too quick for him to follow it, gripping him by the back of his shirt and on to tiptoe before he had seen it quit the can, the face stooping at him in breathless and frozen ferocity, the cold, dead voice speaking over him to the older brother who leaned against the table, chewing with that steady, curious, sidewise motion of cows:

"Empty the can into the big one and go on. I'll catch up with you."

"Better tie him up to the bedpost," the brother said.

"Do like I told you," the father said. Then the boy was moving, his bunched shirt and the hard, bony hand between his shoulder-blades, his toes just touching the floor, across the room and into the other one, past the sisters sitting with spread heavy thighs in the two chairs over the cold hearth, and to where his mother and aunt sat side by side on the bed, the aunt's arms about his mother's shoulders.

"Hold him," the father said. The aunt made a startled movement. "Not you," the father said. "Lennie. Take hold of him. I want to see you do it." His mother took him by the wrist. "You'll hold him better than that. If he gets loose don't you know what he is going to do? He will go up yonder." He jerked his head toward the road. "Maybe I'd better tie him."

"I'll hold him," his mother whispered.

"See you do then." Then his father was gone, the stiff foot heavy and measured upon the boards, ceasing at last.

Then he began to struggle. His mother caught him in both arms, he jerking and wrenching at them. He would be stronger in the end, he knew that. But he had no time to wait for it. "Lemme go!" he cried. "I don't want to have to hit you!"

"Let him go!" the aunt said. "If he don't go, before God, I am going up there myself!"

"Don't you see I can't?" his mother cried. "Sarty! Sarty! No! No! Help me, Lizzie!"

Then he was free. His aunt grasped at him but it was too late. He whirled, running, his mother stumbled forward on to her knees behind him, crying to the nearer sister: "Catch him, Net! Catch him!" But that was too late too, the sister (the sisters were twins, born at the same time, yet either of them now gave the impression of being, encompassing as much living meat and volume and weight as any other two of the family) not yet having begun to rise from the chair, her head, face, alone merely turned, presenting to him in the flying instant an astonishing expanse of young female features untroubled by any surprise even, wearing only an expression of bovine interest. Then he was out of the room, out of the house, in the mild dust of the starlit road and the heavy rifeness of honeysuckle, the pale ribbon unspooling with terrific slowness under his running feet, reaching the gate at last and turning in, running, his heart and lungs drumming, on up the drive toward the lighted house, the lighted door. He did not knock, he burst in, sobbing for breath, incapable for the moment of speech; he saw the astonished face of the Negro in the linen jacket without knowing when the Negro had appeared.

"De Spain!" he cried, panted. "Where's . . ." then he saw the white man too emerging from a white door down the hall. "Barn!" he cried. "Barn!"

"What?" the white man said. "Barn?"

"Yes!" the boy cried. "Barn!"

"Catch him!" the white man shouted.

But it was too late this time too. The Negro grasped his shirt, but the entire sleeve, rotten with washing, carried away, and he was out that door too and in the drive again, and had actually never ceased to run even while he was screaming into the white man's face.

Behind him the white man was shouting, "My horse! Fetch my horse!" and he thought for an instant of cutting across the park and climbing the fence into the road, but he did not know the park nor how high the vine-massed fence might be and he dared not risk it. So he ran on down the drive, blood and breath roaring; presently he was in the road again though he could not see it. He could not hear either: the galloping mare was almost upon him before he heard her, and even then he held his course, as if the very urgency of his wild grief and need must in a moment more find him wings, waiting until the ultimate instant to hurl himself aside and into the weed-choked roadside ditch as the horse thundered past and on, for an instant in furious silhouette against the stars, the tranquil early summer night sky which, even before the shape of the horse and rider vanished, stained abruptly and violently upward: a long, swirling roar incredible and soundless, blotting the stars, and he springing up and into the road again, running again, knowing it was too late yet still running even after he heard the shot and, an instant later, two shots, pausing now without knowing he had ceased to run, crying "Pap! Pap!", running again before he knew he had begun to run, stumbling, tripping over something and scrabbling up again without ceasing to run, looking backward over his shoulder at the glare as he got up, running on among the invisible trees, panting, sobbing, "Father! Father!"

At midnight he was sitting on the crest of a hill. He did not know it was midnight and he did not know how far he had come. But there was no glare behind him now and he sat now, his back toward what he had called home for four days anyhow, his face toward the dark woods which he would enter when breath was strong again, small, shaking steadily in the chill darkness, hugging himself into the remainder of his thin, rotten shirt, the grief and despair now no longer terror and fear but just grief and despair. *Father. My father,* he thought. "He was brave!" He cried suddenly, aloud but not loud, no more than a whisper: "He was! He was in the war! He was in Colonel Sartoris' cav'ry!" not knowing that his father had gone to that war a private in the fine old European sense, wearing no uniform, admitting the authority of and giving fidelity to no man or army or flag, going to war as Malbrouck himself did: for booty—it meant nothing and less than nothing to him if it were enemy booty or his own.

The slow constellations wheeled on. It would be dawn and then sun-up after a while and he would be hungry. But that would be to-morrow and now he was only cold, and walking would cure that. His breathing was easier now and he decided to get up and go on, and then he found that he had been asleep because he knew it was almost dawn, the night almost over. He could tell that from the whippoorwills. They were everywhere now among the dark trees below him, constant and inflectioned and ceaseless, so that, as the instant for giving over to the day birds drew nearer and nearer, there was no interval at all between them. He got up. He was a little stiff, but walking would cure that too as it would the cold, and soon there would be the sun. He went on down the hill, toward the dark woods within which the liquid silver voices of the birds called unceasing—the rapid and urgent beating of the urgent and quiring heart of the late spring night. He did not look back.

Ernest Hemingway (1899–1961)

The stories of Ernest Hemingway are at once an expression of disillusionment bordering on nihilism and a celebration of the ethic of courage or, as he put it, "grace under pressure." His style is closely parallel to his theme: terse, spare, somber, stripped of the verbiage and stylistic "elegance" he disliked in much turn-of-the-century writing. His prose is marked by an understatement that may seem to suggest lack of adequate feeling, yet its very terseness arouses a great emotional response from many readers. Both in his technical development and in his tone and themes, he has exercised an immense influence on American fiction.

Although he was himself a man of action and celebrated protagonists who had experienced physically dangerous situations—war, the hunt, violent sports—his stories are not particularly action-packed or heavily plotted. As in the story which follows, dialogue is often the whole of the action, and he has been justly admired for its power and realism. A Hemingway story can beautifully demonstrate that what people in fiction say to each other is what they do to each other. (See Introduction, p. 13.) "Hills Like White Elephants" takes place almost entirely within quotation marks. Practically all we know of the characters we learn through what they say. The man through speech slowly manipulates the girl toward the operation. "I wouldn't have you do it if you didn't want to," he says. "But I know it's perfectly simple." His frequent repetition of the word "perfectly" defines his insincerity. And, after the girl acquiesces, he begins to manipulate himself out of responsibility until the girl says she'll scream; because she says that, we learn that she is not completely swayed by him.

In the spaces outside quotation marks, Hemingway builds not so much with verbs as with nouns, and he almost totally eschews adjectives and qualifiers. Though his descriptive passages are short and infrequent, they count heavily in two ways. First, the setting can create the atmosphere, the mood, of the story, and can serve as a kind of Greek chorus. In the following story, the controlling symbols come from the scene and the scenery: the hills, the river, the little crossroads station leading anywhere, nowhere, the barren fields that connote the barrenness of the lives. Description also provides a sense of movement, as Hemingway directs the eye of the reader's imagination from object to object, "panning" as a movie does. The opening paragraph illustrates this technique. The reader has the feeling that the story is moving.

Hemingway was born in Oak Park, Illinois, in 1899. He became an ambulance driver in the First World War and was wounded while serving on the Italian Front. This experience formed the basis for many of his stories and for his most popular novel, A Farewell To Arms (1929). After the war, dissatisfied with life in America, he went to Paris as correspondent for the Toronto Star. He lived most of his life in Europe and Cuba.

Hemingway's work was greatly influenced by Stephen Crane and Joseph Conrad in theme—the test, the ordeal—and by Sherwood Anderson and Gertrude Stein in his use of simple, colloquial language. According to Frank O'Connor, he learned from Joyce the power of repeating key words in order to build a reader's mood.

Besides his short stories, which have been acclaimed as among the very best in the world, his novels The Sun Also Rises (1926) and The Old Man and the Sea

(1952) brought him the highest critical praise. When he won the Nobel Prize for Literature in 1954, he was cited for his "powerful, style-making mastery of the art of modern narration." He died of a self-inflicted gunshot wound in 1961.

Hills Like White Elephants

The hills across the valley of the Ebro were long and white. On this side there was no shade and no trees and the station was between two lines of rails in the sun. Close against the side of the station there was the warm shadow of the building and a curtain, made of strings of bamboo beads, hung across the open door into the bar, to keep out flies. The American and the girl with him sat at a table in the shade, outside the building. It was very hot and the express from Barcelona would come in forty minutes. It stopped at this junction for two minutes and went on to Madrid.

"What should we drink?" the girl asked. She had taken off her hat and put it on the table.

"It's pretty hot," the man said.

"Let's drink beer."

"Dos cervezas," the man said into the curtain.

"Big ones?" a woman asked from the doorway.

"Yes. Two big ones."

The woman brought two glasses of beer and two felt pads. She put the felt pads and the beer glasses on the table and looked at the man and the girl. The girl was looking off at the line of hills. They were white in the sun and the country was brown and dry.

"They look like white elephants," she said.

"I've never seen one," the man drank his beer.

"No, you wouldn't have."

"I might have," the man said. "Just because you say I wouldn't have doesn't prove anything."

The girl looked at the bead curtain. "They've painted something on it," she said. "What does it say?"

"Anis del Toro. It's a drink."

"Could we try it?"

The man called "Listen" through the curtain. The woman came out from the bar.

"Four reales."

"We want two Anis del Toro."

"With water?"

"Do you want it with water?"

"I don't know," the girl said. "Is it good with water?"

"It's all right."

"You want them with water?" asked the woman.

From *Hills Like White Elephants*. Reprinted with the permission of Charles Scribner's Sons from *Men Without Women* by Ernest Hemingway. Copyright 1927 Charles Scribner's Sons; renewal copyright © 1955 Ernest Hemingway. First published in 1927.

"Yes, with water."

"It tastes like licorice," the girl said and put the glass down.

"That's the way with everything."

"Yes," said the girl. "Everything tastes of licorice. Especially all the things you've waited so long for, like absinthe."

"Oh, cut it out."

"You started it," the girl said. "I was being amused. I was having a fine time."

"Well, let's try to have a fine time."

"All right. I was trying. I said the mountains looked like white elephants. Wasn't that bright?"

"That was bright."

"I wanted to try this new drink. That's all we do, isn't it—look at things and try new drinks?"

"I guess so."

The girl looked across at the hills.

"They're lovely hills," she said. "They don't really look like white elephants. I just meant the coloring of their skin through the trees."

"Should we have another drink?"

"All right."

The warm wind blew the bead curtain against the table.

"The beer's nice and cool," the man said.

"It's lovely," the girl said.

"It's really an awfully simple operation, Jig," the man said. "It's not really an operation at all."

The girl looked at the ground the table legs rested on.

"I know you wouldn't mind it, Jig. It's really not anything. It's just to let the air in."

The girl did not say anything.

"I'll go with you and I'll stay with you all the time. They just let the air in and then it's all perfectly natural."

"Then what will we do afterward?"

"We'll be fine afterward. Just like we were before."

"What makes you think so?"

"That's the only thing that bothers us. It's the only thing that's made us unhappy."

The girl looked at the bead curtain, put her hand out and took hold of two of the strings of beads.

"And you think then we'll be all right and be happy."

"I know we will. You don't have to be afraid. I've known lots of people that have done it."

"So have I," said the girl. "And afterward they were all so happy."

"Well," the man said, "if you don't want to you don't have to. I wouldn't have you do it if you didn't want to. But I know it's perfectly simple."

"And you really want to?"

"I think it's the best thing to do. But I don't want you to do it if you don't really want to."

"And if I do it you'll be happy and things will be like they were and you'll love me?"

"I love you now. You know I love you."

"I know. But if I do it, then it will be nice again if I say things are like white elephants, and you'll like it?"

"I'll love it. I love it now but I just can't think about it. You know how I get when I worry."

"If I do it you won't ever worry?"

"I won't worry about that because it's perfectly simple."

"Then I'll do it. Because I don't care about me."

"What do you mean?"

"I don't care about me."

"Well, I care about you."

"Oh, yes. But I don't care about me. And I'll do it and then everything will be fine."

"I don't want you to do it if you feel that way."

The girl stood up and walked to the end of the station. Across, on the other side, were fields of grain and trees along the banks of the Ebro. Far away, beyond the river, were mountains. The shadow of a cloud moved across the field of grain and she saw the river through the trees.

"And we could have all this," she said. "And we could have everything and every day we make it more impossible."

"What did you say?"

"I said we could have everything."

"We can have everything."

"No, we can't."

"We can have the whole world."

"No, we can't."

"We can go everywhere."

"No, we can't. It isn't ours any more."

"It's ours."

"No, it isn't. And once they take it away, you never get it back."

"But they haven't taken it away."

"We'll wait and see."

"Come on back in the shade," he said. "You mustn't feel that way."

"I don't feel any way," the girl said. "I just know things."

"I don't want you to do anything that you don't want to do———"

"Nor that isn't good for me," she said. "I know. Could we have another beer?"

"All right. But you've got to realize———"

"I realize," the girl said. "Can't we maybe stop talking?"

They sat down at the table and the girl looked across at the hills on the dry side of the valley and the man looked at her and at the table.

"You've got to realize," he said, "that I don't want you to do it if you don't want to. I'm perfectly willing to go through with it if it means anything to you."

"Doesn't it mean anything to you? We could get along."

"Of course it does. But I don't want anybody but you. I don't want any one else. And I know it's perfectly simple."

"Yes, you know it's perfectly simple."

"It's all right for you to say that, but I do know it."

"Would you do something for me now?"

"I'd do anything for you."

"Would you please please please please please please please stop talking?"

He did not say anything but looked at the bags against the wall of the station. There were labels on them from all the hotels where they had spent nights.

"But I don't want you to," he said, "I don't care anything about it."

"I'll scream," said the girl.

The woman came out through the curtains with two glasses of beer and put them down on the damp felt pads. "The train comes in five minutes," she said.

"What did she say?" asked the girl.

"That the train is coming in five minutes."

The girl smiled brightly at the woman, to thank her.

"I'd better take the bags over to the other side of the station," the man said. She smiled at him.

"All right. Then come back and we'll finish the beer."

He picked up the two heavy bags and carried them around the station to the other tracks. He looked up the tracks but could not see the train. Coming back, he walked through the barroom, where people waiting for the train were drinking. He drank an Anis at the bar and looked at the people. They were all waiting reasonably for the train. He went out through the bead curtain. She was sitting at the table and smiled at him.

"Do you feel better?" he asked.

"I feel fine," she said. "There's nothing wrong with me. I feel fine."

Part Four

The Contemporary Scene

Richard Wright (1908–1960)

Richard Wright was perhaps the most significant and influential black writer of the 1930s and 1940s. By opening up black ghetto experience to serious fictional treatment, he helped arouse a somnolent American conscience. Of Wright's great early novel, Irving Howe wrote, "The day *Native Son* appeared, American culture was changed forever. No matter how much qualifying the book might need, it made impossible a repetition of the old lies. In all its crudeness, melodrama and claustrophobia of vision, Richard Wright's novel brought out into the open, as no one ever had before, the hatred, fear and violence that have crippled and may yet destroy our culture."

Born in Mississippi in 1908, Wright was the grandson of a slave, the son of a sharecropper who deserted his family. Despite the fact that his mother had been a teacher, his schooling was intermittent at best, caught on the run between family disasters. Yet he was a voracious reader, and when he went to Chicago in 1928 he could hold his own with the intellectual radicals who became his friends. He joined the Communist Party, and his writing—largely polemical at this point—began to appear regularly in Communist publications. But he began to chafe under the party discipline and to question the purity of its motives, and in 1944 he resigned his membership.

Wright's most important work, *Native Son* (1940), was an instant success. It is the story of Bigger Thomas, product of the Chicago ghetto, a murderer, surely one of the first anti-heroes in American fiction. Many readers were deeply affected by the unusual glimpse it provided of the underside of black society. Wright's black predecessors had often so idealized black culture and relationships that an ignorant reader might wonder if segregation was really evil. Wright changed that, exposed honestly the effects of repression and poverty. The technique of naturalism which he used in his work was common to proletarian writers and social realists in the 1930s, but he achieved particularly deep and lasting effects. He did not view his subjects from a distance or through a microscope. Bigger—and Dave in "The Man Who Was Almost a Man"—are not examples or symbols or representatives of a remote social order. Their experience was his experience, for he had lived in the same circumstances. Thus he combined the authenticity of honest observation with the deeper authenticity of personal experience. His work, didactic though it may be, is passionately felt.

Wright's novels and stories are valuable not only as a portrayal of the black society he knew so well, but as the forerunner of a new motif in American fiction. No wonder that when he moved permanently to France in 1947 he found kinship with French existentialists: Bigger and Dave are in a real sense existential anti-heroes. They seek to realize themselves by escaping to freedom from a harsh, oppressive environment. For Bigger, the escape ends inexorably in his execution, for he has become the outlaw, guilty of a useless murder. After reading "The Man Who Was Almost a Man," we can have little more hope for Dave, whose passion for the gun—representing his chance to escape from being just a "boy," that is, young, black, inferior—has already started him toward violence.

Wright died in Paris in 1960. Black writers he had befriended and inspired—Ellison, Himes, Baldwin—have built on his accomplishment, and black experience is now an integral part of the mainstream of American fiction.

The Man Who Was Almost a Man

Dave struck out across the fields, looking homeward through paling light. Whut's the usa talkin wid em niggers in the field? Anyhow, his mother was putting supper on the table. Them niggers can't understan nothing. One of these days he was going to get a gun and practice shooting, then they can't talk to him as though he were a little boy. He slowed, looking at the ground. Shucks, Ah ain scareda them even ef they are biggern me! Aw, Ah know whut Ahma do. . . . Ahm going by ol Joe's sto n git that Sears Roebuck catlog n look at them guns. Mabbe Ma will lemme buy one when she gits mah pay from ol man Hawkins. Ahma beg her t gimme some money. Ahm ol ernough to hava gun. Ahm seventeen. Almos a man. He strode, feeling his long, loose-jointed limbs. Shucks, a man oughta hava little gun aftah he done worked hard all day. . . .

He came in sight of Joe's store. A yellow lantern glowed on the front porch. He mounted steps and went through the screen door, hearing it bang behind him. There

From Richard Wright, *Eight men.* Copyright © Thomas Y. Crowell Company, Inc., 1961, 1940. Reprinted by permission of Thomas Y. Crowell Company, Inc.

was a strong smell of coal oil and mackerel fish. He felt very confident until he saw fat Joe walk in through the rear door, then his courage began to ooze.

"Howdy, Dave! Whutcha want?"

"How yuh, Mistah Joe? Aw, Ah don wanna buy nothing. Ah jus wanted t see ef yuhd lemme look at tha ol catlog erwhile."

"Sure! You wanna see it here?"

"Nawsuh. Ah wans t take it home wid me. Ahll bring it back termorrow when Ah come in from the fiels."

"You plannin on buyin something?"

"Yessuh."

"Your ma letting you have your own money now?"

"Shucks. Mistah Joe, Ahm gittin t be a man like anybody else!"

Joe laughed and wiped his greasy white face with a red bandanna.

"Whut you plannin on buyin?"

Dave looked at the floor, scratched his head, scratched his thigh, and smiled. Then he looked up shyly.

"Ahll tell yuh, Mistah Joe, ef yuh promise yuh won't tell."

"I promise."

"Waal, Ahma buy a gun."

"A gun? Whut you want with a gun?"

"Ah wanna keep it."

"You ain't nothing but a boy. You don't need a gun."

"Aw, lemme have the catlog, Mistah Joe. Ahll bring it back."

Joe walked through the rear door. Dave was elated. He looked around at barrels of sugar and flour. He heard Joe coming back. He craned his neck to see if he were bringing the book. Yeah, he's got it! Gawddog, he's got it!

"Here, but be sure you bring it back. It's the only one I got."

"Sho, Mistah Joe."

"Say, if you wanna buy a gun, why don't you buy one from me? I gotta gun to sell."

"Will it shoot?"

"Sure it'll shoot."

"Whut kind is it?"

"Oh, it's kinda old. . . . A lefthand Wheeler. A pistol. A big one."

"Is it got bullets in it?"

"It's loaded."

"Kin Ah see it?"

"Where's your money?"

"Whut yuh wan fer it?"

"I'll let you have it for two dollars."

"Just two dollahs? Shucks, Ah could buy tha when Ah git mah pay."

"I'll have it here when you want it."

"Awright, suh. Ah be in fer it."

He went through the door, hearing it slam again behind him. Ahma git some money from Ma n buy me a gun! Only two dollahs! He tucked the thick catalogue under his arm and hurried.

"Where yuh been, boy?" His mother held a steaming dish of black-eyed peas.

"Aw, Ma, Ah jus stopped down the road t talk wid th boys."

"Yuh know bettah than t keep suppah waitin."

He sat down, resting the catalogue on the edge of the table.

"Yuh git up from there and git to the well n wash yosef! Ah ain feedin no hogs in mah house!"

She grabbed his shoulder and pushed him. He stumbled out of the room, then came back to get the catalogue.

"Whut this?"

"Aw, Ma, it's jusa catlog."

"Who yuh git it from?"

"From Joe, down at the sto."

"Waal, thas good. We kin use it around the house."

"Naw, Ma." He grabbed for it. "Gimme mah catlog, Ma."

She held onto it and glared at him.

"Quit hollerin at me! Whut's wrong wid yuh? Yuh crazy?"

"But Ma, please. It ain mine! It's Joe's! He tol me t bring it back t im termorrow."

She gave up the book. He stumbled down the back steps, hugging the thick book under his arm. When he had splashed water on his face and hands, he groped back to the kitchen and fumbled in a corner for the towel. He bumped into a chair; it clattered to the floor. The catalogue sprawled at his feet. When he had dried his eyes, he snatched up the book and held it again under his arm. His mother stood watching him.

"Now, ef yuh gonna acka fool over that ol book, Ahll take it n burn it up."

"Naw, Ma, please."

"Waal, set down n be still!"

He sat down and drew the oil lamp close. He thumbed page after page, unaware of the food his mother set on the table. His father came in. Then his small brother.

"Whutcha got there, Dave?" his father asked.

"Jusa catlog," he answered, not looking up.

"Yawh, here they is!" His eyes glowed at blue and black revolvers. He glanced up, feeling sudden guilt. His father was watching him. He eased the book under the table and rested it on his knees. After the blessing was asked, he ate. He scooped up peas and swallowed fat meat without chewing. Buttermilk helped to wash it down. He did not want to mention money before his father. He would do much better by cornering his mother when she was alone. He looked at his father uneasily out of the edge of his eye.

"Boy, how come yuh don quit foolin wid tha book n eat yo suppah."

"Yessuh."

"How yuh n ol man Hawkins gittin erlong?"

"Suh?"

"Can't yuh hear. Why don yuh listen? Ah ast yuh how wuz yuh n ol man Hawkins gittin erlong?"

"Oh, swell, Pa. Ah plows mo lan than anybody over there."

"Waal, yuh oughta keep yo min on whut yuh doin."

"Yessuh."

He poured his plate full of molasses and sopped at it slowly with a chunk of cornbread. When all but his mother had left the kitchen he still sat and looked again at the guns in the catalogue. Lawd, ef Ah only had the pretty one! He could almost feel the slickness of the weapon with his fingers. If he had a gun like that he would polish it and keep it shining so it would never rust. N Ahd keep it loaded, by Gawd!

"Ma?"

"Hunh?"

"Ol man Hawkins give yuh mah money yit?"

"Yeah, but ain no usa yuh thinkin bout thowin nona it erway. Ahm keepin tha money sos yuh kin have cloes t go to school this winter."

He rose and went to her side with the open catalogue in his palms. She was washing dishes, her head bent low over a pan. Shyly he raised the open book. When he spoke his voice was husky, faint.

"Ma, Gawd knows Ah wans one of these."

"One of whut?" she asked, not raising her eyes.

"One of these," he said again, not daring even to point. She glanced up at the page, then at him with wide eyes.

"Nigger, is yuh gone plum crazy?"

"Aw, Ma—"

"Git outta here! Don't yuh talk t me bout no gun! Yuh a fool!"

"Ma, Ah kin buy one fer two dollahs."

"Not ef Ah knows it yuh ain!"

"But yuh promised me one—"

"Ah don care whut Ah promised! Yuh ain nothing but a boy yit!"

"Ma, ef yuh lemme buy one Ahll never ast yuh fer nothing no mo."

"Ah tol yuh t git outta here! Yuh ain gonna toucha penny of tha money fer no gun! Thas how come Ah has Mistah Hawkins pay yo wages t me, cause Ah knows yuh ain got no sense."

"But Ma, we needa gun. Pa ain got no gun. We needa gun in the house. Yuh kin never tell whut might happen."

"Now don yuh try to maka fool outta me, boy! Ef we did hava gun yuh wouldn't have it!"

He laid the catalogue down and slipped his arm around her waist. "Aw, Ma, Ah done worked hard alla summer n ain ast yuh fer nothing, is Ah, now?"

"Thas whut yuh spose t do!"

"But Ma. Ah wants a gun. Yuh kin lemme have two dollahs outa mah money. Please Ma. I kin give it to Pa. . . . Please, Ma! Ah loves yuh, Ma."

When she spoke her voice came soft and low.

"What yuh wan wida gun, Dave? Yuh don need no gun. Yuhll git in trouble. N ef yo Pa jus thought Ah letyuh have money t buy a gun he'd hava fit."

"Ahll hide it, Ma. It ain but two dollahs."

"Lawd, chil, whuts wrong wid yuh?"

"Ain nothing wrong, Ma. Ahm almos a man now. Ah wants a gun."

"Who gonna sell yuh a gun?"

"Ol Joe at the sto."

"N it don cos but two dollahs?"

"Thas all, Ma. Just two dollahs. Please, Ma."

She was stacking the plates away; her hands moved slowly, reflectively. Dave kept an anxious silence. Finally she turned to him.

"Ahll let yuh git the gun ef yuh promise me one thing."

"Whuts tha, Ma?"

"Yuh bring it straight back t me, yuh hear? It'll be fer Pa."

"Yessum! Lemme go now, Ma."

She stooped, turned slightly to one side, raised the hem of her dress, rolled down the top of her stocking, and came up with a slender wad of bills.

"Here," she said. "Lawd knows yuh don need no gun. But yer Pa does. Yuh bring it right back t me, yuh hear. Ahma put it up. Now ef yuh don, Ahma have yuh Pa lick yuh so hard yuh won ferget it."

"Yessum."

He took the money, ran down the steps, and across the yard.

"Dave! Yuuuuuuh Daaaaaave!"

He heard, but he was not going to stop now. "Naw, Lawd!"

The first movement he made the following morning was to reach under his pillow for the gun. In the gray light of dawn he held it loosely, feeling a sense of power. Could killa man wida gun like this. Kill anybody, black or white. And if he were holding this gun in his hand nobody could run over him; they would have to respect him. It was a big gun, with a long barrel and a heavy handle. He raised and lowered it in his hand, marveling at its weight.

He had not come straight home with it as his mother had asked; instead he had stayed out in the fields, holding the weapon in his hand, aiming it now and then at some imaginary foe. But he had not fired it; he had been afraid that his father might hear. Also he was not sure he knew how to fire it.

To avoid surrendering the pistol he had not come into the house until he knew that all were asleep. When his mother had tiptoed to his bedside late that night and demanded the gun, he had first played 'possum; then he had told her that the gun was hidden outdoors, that he would bring it to her in the morning. Now he lay turning it slowly in his hands. He broke it, took out the cartridges, felt them, and then put them back.

He slid out of bed, got a long strip of old flannel from a trunk, wrapped the gun in it, and tied it to his naked thigh while it was still loaded. He did not go in to breakfast. Even though it was not yet daylight, he started for Jim Hawkins's plantation. Just as the sun was rising he reached the barns where the mules and plows were kept.

"Hey! That you, Dave?"

He turned. Jim Hawkins stood eyeing him suspiciously.

"What're yuh doing here so early?"

"Ah didn't know Ah wuz gittin up so early, Mistah Hawkins. Ah wuz fixing t hitch up ol Jenny n take her t the fiels."

"Good. Since you're here so early, how about plowing that stretch down by the woods?"

"Suits me, Mistah Hawkins."

"O.K. Go to it!"

He hitched Jenny to a plow and started across the fields. Hot dog! This was just what he wanted. If he could get down by the woods, he could shoot his gun and nobody would hear. He walked behind the plow, hearing the traces creaking, feeling the gun tied tight to his thigh.

When he reached the woods, he plowed two whole rows before he decided to take out the gun. Finally he stopped, looked in all directions, then untied the gun and held it in his hand. He turned to the mule and smiled.

"Know whut this is, Jenny? Naw, yuh wouldn't know! Yuhs jus a ol mule! Anyhow, this is a gun, n it kin shoot, by Gawd!"

He held the gun at arm's length. Whut t hell, Ahma shoot this thing! He looked at Jenny again.

"Lissen here, Jenny! When Ah pull this ol trigger Ah don wan yuh t run n acka fool now."

Jenny stood with head down, her short ears pricked straight. Dave walked off about twenty feet, held the gun far out from him, at arms' length, and turned his head. Hell, he told himself, Ah ain afraid. The gun felt loose in his fingers; he waved it wildly for a moment. Then he shut his eyes and tightened his forefinger. Bloom! The report half-deafened him and he thought his right hand was torn from his arm. He heard Jenny whinnying and galloping over the field, and he found himself on his knees squeezing his fingers hard between his legs. His hand was numb; he jammed it into his mouth, trying to warm it, trying to stop the pain. The gun lay at his feet. He did not quite know what had happened. He stood up and stared at the gun as though it were a living thing. He gritted his teeth and kicked the gun. Yuh almos broke mah arm! He turned to look for Jenny; she was far over the fields, tossing her head and kicking wildly.

"Hol on there, ol mule!"

When he caught up with her she stood trembling, walling her big white eyes at him. The plow was far away; the traces had broken. Then Dave stopped short, looking, not believing. Jenny was bleeding. Her left side was red and wet with blood. He went closer. Lawd, have mercy! Wondah did Ah shoot this mule? He grabbed for Jenny's mane. She flinched, snorted, whirled, tossing her head.

"Hol on now! Hol on."

Then he saw the hole in Jenny's side, right between the ribs. It was round, wet, red. A crimson stream streaked down the front leg, flowing fast. Good Gawd! Ah wuzn't shootin at tha mule. He felt panic. He knew he had to stop that blood, or Jenny would bleed to death. He had never seen so much blood in all his life. He chased the mule for half a mile, trying to catch her. Finally she stopped, breathing hard, stumpy tail half arched. He caught her mane and led her back to where the plow and gun lay. Then he stooped and grabbed handfuls of damp black earth and tried to plug the bullet hole. Jenny shuddered, whinnied, and broke from him.

"Hol on! Hol on now!"

He tried to plug it again, but blood came anyhow. His fingers were hot and sticky. He rubbed dirt into his palms, trying to dry them. Then again he attempted to plug the bullet hole, but Jenny shied away, kicking her heels high. He stood helpless. He had to do something. He ran at Jenny; she dodged him. He watched a red stream of blood flow down Jenny's leg and form a bright pool at her feet.

"Jenny . . . Jenny . . ." he called weakly.

His lips trembled! She's bleeding t death! He looked in the direction of home, wanting to go back, wanting to get help. But he saw the pistol lying in the damp black clay. He had a queer feeling that if he only did something, this would not be; Jenny would not be there bleeding to death.

When he went to her this time, she did not move. She stood with sleepy, dreamy eyes; and when he touched her she gave a low-pitched whinny and knelt to the ground, her front knees slopping in blood.

"Jenny . . . Jenny . . ." he whispered.

For a long time she held her neck erect; then her head sank, slowly. Her ribs swelled with a mighty heave and she went over.

Dave's stomach felt empty, very empty. He picked up the gun and held it gingerly between his thumb and forefinger. He buried it at the foot of a tree. He took a stick and tried to cover the pool of blood with dirt—but what was the use? There was Jenny lying with her mouth open and her eyes walled and glassy. He could not tell Jim Hawkins he had shot his mule. But he had to tell him something. Yeah, Ahll tell em Jenny started gittin wil n fell on the joint of the plow. . . . But that would hardly happen to a mule. He walked across the field slowly, head down.

It was sunset. Two of Jim Hawkins's men were over near the edge of the woods digging a hole in which to bury Jenny. Dave was surrounded by a knot of people; all of them were looking down at the dead mule.

"I don't see how in the world it happened," said Jim Hawkins for the tenth time.

The crowd parted and Dave's mother, father, and small brother pushed into the center.

"Where Dave?" his mother called.

"There he is," said Jim Hawkins.

His mother grabbed him.

"Whut happened, Dave? Whut yuh done?"

"Nothing."

"C'mon, boy, talk," his father said.

Dave took a deep breath and told the story he knew nobody believed.

"Waal," he drawled. "Ah brung ol Jenny down here sos Ah could do mah plow-in. Ah plowed bout two rows, just like yuh see." He stopped and pointed at the long rows of upturned earth. "Then something musta been wrong wid ol Jenny. She wouldn't ack right a-tall. She started snortin n kickin her heels. Ah tried to hol her, but she pulled erway, rearin n goin on. Then when the point of the plow was stickin up in the air, she swung erroun n twisted herself back on it. . . . She stuck herself n started t bleed. N fo Ah could do anything, she wuz dead."

"Did you ever hear of anything like that in all your life?" asked Jim Hawkins.

There were white and black standing in the crowd. They murmured. Dave's mother came close to him and looked hard into his face.

"Tell the truth, Dave," she said.

"Looks like a bullet hole ter me," said one man.

"Dave, whut yuh do wid the gun?" his mother asked.

The crowd surged in, looking at him. He jammed his hands into his pockets, shook his head slowly from left to right, and backed away. His eyes were wide and painful.

"Did he hava gun?" asked Jim Hawkins.

"By Gawd, Ah tol yuh tha wuz a gunwound," said a man, slapping his thigh.

His father caught his shoulders and shook him till his teeth rattled.

"Tell whut happened, yuh rascal! Tell whut . . ."

Dave looked at Jenny's stiff legs and began to cry.

"Whut yuh do wid tha gun?" his mother asked.

"Come on and tell the truth," said Hawkins. "Ain't nobody going to hurt you. . . ."

His mother crowded close to him.

"Did yuh shoot tha mule, Dave?"

Dave cried, seeing blurred white and black faces.

"Ahh ddinnt gggo tt sshoooot hher. . . . Ah ssswear off Gawd Ahh ddint. . . . Ah wuz a-tryin t sssee ef the ol gggun would sshoot—"

"Where yuh git the gun from?" his father asked.

"Ah got it from Joe, at the sto."

"Where yuh git the money?"

"Ma give it t me."

"He kept worryin me, Bob. . . . Ah had t. . . . Ah tol im t bring the gun right back t me. . . . It was fer yuh, the gun."

"But how yuh happen to shoot that mule?" asked Jim Hawkins.

"Ah wuznt shootin at the mule, Mistah Hawkins. The gun jumped when Ah pulled the trigger . . . N for Ah knowed anything Jenny wuz there a-bleedin."

Somebody in the crowd laughed. Jim Hawkins walked close to Dave and looked into his face.

"Well, looks like you have bought you a mule, Dave."

"Ah swear for Gawd, Ah didn't go t kill the mule, Mistah Hawkins!"

"But you killed her!"

All the crowd was laughing now. They stood on tiptoe and poked heads over one another's shoulders.

"Well, boy, looks like yuh done bought a dead mule! Hahaha!"

"Ain tha ershame."

"Hohohohoho."

Dave stood, head down, twisting his feet in the dirt.

"Well, you needn't worry about it, Bob," said Jim Hawkins to Dave's father. "Just let the boy keep on working and pay me two dollars a month."

"Whut yuh wan fer yo mule, Mistah Hawkins?"

Jim Hawkins screwed up his eyes.

"Fifty dollars."

"Whut yuh do wid tha gun?" Dave's father demanded.

Dave said nothing.

"Yuh wan me t take a tree lim n beat yuh till yuh talk!"

"Nawsuh!"

"Whut yuh do wid it?"

"Ah thowed it erway."

"Where?"

"Ah . . . Ah thowed it in the creek."

"Waal, c mon home. N firs thing in the mawnin git to tha creek n fin tha gun."

"Yessuh."

"Whut yuh pay fer it?"

"Two dollahs."

"Take tha gun n git yo money back n carry it t Mistah Hawkins, yuh hear? N don fergit Ahma lam you black bottom good fer this! Now march yosef on home, suh!"

Dave turned and walked slowly. He heard people laughing. Dave glared, his eyes welling with tears. Hot anger bubbled in him. Then he swallowed and stumbled on.

That night Dave did not sleep. He was glad that he had gotten out of killing the mule so easily, but he was hurt. Something hot seemed to turn over inside him each time he remembered how they had laughed. He tossed on his bed, feeling his hard pillow. N Pa says he's gonna beat me. . . . He remembered other beatings, and his back quivered. Naw, naw, Ah sho don wan im t beat me tha way no mo. . . . Dam em all! Nobody ever gave him anything. All he did was work. They treat me lika mule. . . . N then they beat me. . . . He gritted his teeth. N Ma had t tell on me.

Well, if he had to, he would take old man Hawkins that two dollars. But that meant selling the gun. And he wanted to keep that gun. Fifty dollahs fer a dead mule.

He turned over, thinking how he had fired the gun. He had an itch to fire it again. Ef other men kin shoota gun, by Gawd, Ah kin! He was still listening. Mebbe they all sleepin now. . . . The house was still. He heard the soft breathing of his brother. Yes, now! He would go down an get that gun and see if he could fire it! He eased out of bed and slipped into overalls.

The moon was bright. He ran almost all the way to the edge of the woods. He stumbled over the ground, looking for the spot where he had buried the gun. Yeah, here it is. Like a hungry dog scratching for a bone he pawed it up. He puffed his black cheeks and blew dirt from the trigger and barrel. He broke it and found four cartridges unshot. He looked around; the fields were filled with silence and moonlight. He clutched the gun stiff and hard in his fingers. But as soon as he wanted to pull the trigger, he shut his eyes and turned his head. Naw, Ah can't shoot wid mah eyes closed n mah head turned. With effort he held his eyes open; then he squeezed. Blooooom! He was stiff, not breathing. The gun was still in his hands. Dammit, he'd done it! He fired again. Blooooom! He smiled. Blooooom! Blooooom! Click, click. There! It was empty. If anybody could shoot a gun, he could. He put the gun into his hip pocket and started across the fields.

When he reached the top of a ridge he stood straight and proud in the moonlight, looking at Jim Hawkins's big white house, feeling the gun sagging in his pocket. Lawd, ef Ah had jus one mo bullet Ahd taka shot at tha house. Ahd like t scare ol man Hawkins jussa little. . . . Jussa enough t let im know Dave Sanders is a man.

To his left the road curved, running to the tracks of the Illinois Central. He jerked his head, listening. From far off came a faint hoooof-hoooof; hoooof-hoooof; hoooof-hoooof. . . . That's number eight. He took a swift look at Jim Hawkins's white house; he thought of Pa, of Ma, of his little brother, and the boys. He thought of the dead mule and heard hooof-hooof; hooof-hooof; hooof-hooof. . . . He stood rigid. Two dollahs a mont. Les see now . . . Tha means itll take bout two years. Shucks! Ahll be dam! He started down the road, toward the tracks. Yeah, here she comes! He stood beside the track and held himself stiffly. Here she comes, erroun the ben. . . . C mon, yuh slow poke! C mon! He had his hand on his gun; something quivered in his stomach. Then the train thundered past, the gray and brown boxcars rumbling and clinking. He gripped the gun tightly; then he jerked his hand out of his pocket. Ah betcha Bill wouldn't do it! Ah betcha. . . . The cars slid past, steel grinding upon steel. Ahm riding yuh ternight so hep me Gawd! He was hot all over. He hesitated just a moment; then he grabbed, pulled atop of a car, and lay flat. He felt his pocket; the gun was still there. Ahead the long rails were glinting in moonlight, stretching away, away to somewhere, somewhere where he could be a man. . . .

Eudora Welty (1909–   )

Eudora Welty, who makes her home in Jackson, Mississippi, is one of the leading writers in the so-called "Southern Renascence" (which includes William Faulkner, Robert Penn Warren, John Crowe Ransom, Flannery O'Connor, and others), and belongs firmly in that tradition beginning with Chekhov and extending through Henry James and Katherine Anne Porter. Her interest is not primarily in plot or action, but in the effect of action on character—on the motions of experience that occur in the inner life. Unlike James or Woolf, she does not use stream of consciousness in tapping the inner life, but instead depends on an exquisite manipulation of detail, mood, and accent. As Ruth Vande Kieft says, in comparing Welty with those in the

Chekhovian tradition: "They invest with maximum significance each detail, each small piece of dialogue, narration or description; and they endow each metaphor with an emotional resonance comparable to that of poetic metaphor." The lyric intensity of her stories gives them that unity that Poe called for (see Introduction, pp. 5–6), and to hear Eudora Welty read aloud (several of her stories are on records) is a unique delight.

Though she was born in Jackson, she is in some ways less "Southern" than the other Renascence writers, less preoccupied with the tragic courses of Southern history—slavery, the Civil War, industrialism, the land, the race problem; her subject is the plight of the individual and, as Vande Kieft says, "the general hostility of life to man's fulfillment." She makes "what one might call an attempt to escape from the South," writes Isaac Rosenfeld, but this is an escape from great public issues, not from the land or its people. Early in her career as "Junior Publicity Agent" for the WPA, a job that required her to travel about the state of Mississippi interviewing people, taking pictures, and writing newspaper copy, she developed a keen eye for detail that so enriches her art. That was but one of many part-time jobs she held in those Depression years (1930 to 1936)—in advertising, radio scriptwriting, public relations—following her graduation from the University of Wisconsin and a year's study of advertising at Columbia. Welty has remembered these early experiences in her recent *One Time, One Place: Mississippi in the Depression* (1971).

Her first story appeared in *Manuscript* in 1936 and her first volume of stories, *A Curtain of Green* (with a generous introduction by Katherine Anne Porter), in 1941. Stories and novels since have included *Delta Wedding* (1946), *The Golden Apples* (1949), *The Ponder Heart* (1954), *The Bride of Innisfallen and Other Stories* (1955), and—her most recent novel—*The Optimist's Daughter* (1972).

"A Worn Path" is perhaps Eudora Welty's classic story. Without raising her voice or any social banner—and without abandoning her rich sense of humor (which here in no way demeans her serious subject)—she presents in the lonely walk of Old Phoenix along the Natchez Trace to get free medicine for her sick grandson something of the quintessence of all suffering and all oppression. "Out of my way, all you foxes, owls, beetles, jack rabbits, coons, and wild animals! . . . Keep out from under these feet, little bobwhites. . . . Keep the big wild hogs out of my path. . . . I got a long way." She is almost at one with the animals; defenseless, she endures—yet there is no suggestion of sentimentality here, just as there is none of bitterness. Of all the stories heard by black children in a Jackson Freedom School in 1964, this was their favorite. Here, in this exploited ex-slave, rendered by Welty with such tenderness and love, was their own dear mother; here with no political issues raised, was the call for justice they best understood.

A Worn Path

It was December—a bright frozen day in the early morning. Far out in the country there was an old Negro woman with her head tied in a red rag, coming along a path through the pinewoods. Her name was Phoenix Jackson. She was very old and small and she walked slowly in the dark pine shadows, moving a little from side to side in

"A Worn Path" copyright 1941, 1969, by Eudora Welty. Reprinted from her volume *A Curtain of Green* by permission of Harcourt Brace Jovanovich, Inc.

her steps, with the balanced heaviness and lightness of a pendulum in a grandfather clock. She carried a thin, small cane made from an umbrella, and with this she kept tapping the frozen earth in front of her. This made a grave and persistent noise in the still air, that seemed meditative like the chirping of a solitary little bird.

She wore a dark striped dress reaching down to her shoe tops, and an equally long apron of bleached sugar sacks, with a full pocket: all neat and tidy, but every time she took a step she might have fallen over her shoe-laces, which dragged from her unlaced shoes. She looked straight ahead. Her eyes were blue with age. Her skin had a pattern all its own of numberless branching wrinkles and as though a whole little tree stood in the middle of her forehead, but a golden color ran underneath, and the two knobs of her cheeks were illuminated by a yellow burning under the dark. Under the red rag her hair came down on her neck in the frailest of ringlets, still black, and with an odor like copper.

Now and then there was a quivering in the thicket. Old Phoenix said, "Out of my way, all you foxes, owls, beetles, jack rabbits, coons, and wild animals! . . . Keep out from under these feet, little bob-whites. . . . Keep the big wild hogs out of my path. Don't let none of those come running my direction. I got a long way." Under her small black-freckled hand her cane, limber as a buggy whip, would switch at the brush as if to rouse up any hiding things.

On she went. The woods were deep and still. The sun made the pine needles almost too bright to look at, up where the wind rocked. The cones dropped as light as feathers. Down in the hollow was the mourning dove—it was not too late for him.

The path ran up a hill. "Seem like there is chains about my feet, time I get this far," she said, in the voice of argument old people keep to use with themselves. "Something always take a hold of me on this hill—pleads I should stay."

After she got to the top she turned and gave a full, severe look behind her where she had come. "Up through pines," she said at length. "Now down through oaks."

Her eyes opened their widest, and she started down gently. But before she got to the bottom of the hill a bush caught her dress.

Her fingers were busy and intent, but her skirts were full and long, so that before she could pull them free in one place they were caught in another. It was not possible to allow the dress to tear. "I in the thorny bush," she said. "Thorns, you doing your appointed work. Never want to let folks pass—no sir. Old eyes thought you was a pretty little *green* bush."

Finally, trembling all over, she stood free, and after a moment dared to stoop for her cane.

"Sun so high!" she cried, leaning back and looking, while the thick tears went over her eyes. "The time getting all gone here."

At the foot of this hill was a place where a log was laid across the creek.

"Now comes the trial," said Phoenix.

Putting her right foot out, she mounted the log and shut her eyes. Lifting her skirt, levelling her cane fiercely before her, like a festival figure in some parade, she began to march across. Then she opened her eyes and she was safe on the other side.

"I wasn't as old as I thought," she said.

But she sat down to rest. She spread her skirts on the bank around her and folded her hands over her knees. Up above her was a tree in a pearly cloud of mistletoe. She did not dare to close her eyes, and when a little boy brought her a little plate with a slice of marble-cake on it she spoke to him. "That would be acceptable," she said. But when she went to take it there was just her own hand in the air.

So she left that tree, and had to go through a barbed-wire fence. There she had to creep and crawl, spreading her knees and stretching her fingers like a baby trying to climb the steps. But she talked loudly to herself: she could not let her dress be torn now, so late in the day, and she could not pay for having her arm or her leg sawed off if she got caught fast where she was.

At last she was safe through the fence and risen up out in the clearing. Big dead trees, like black men with one arm, were standing in the purple stalks of the withered cotton field. There sat a buzzard.

"Who you watching?"

In the furrow she made her way along.

"Glad this not the season for bulls," she said, looking sideways, "and the good Lord made his snakes to curl up and sleep in the winter. A pleasure I don't see no two-headed snake coming around that tree, where it come once. It took a while to get by him, back in the summer."

She passed through the old cotton and went into a field of dead corn. It whispered and shook and was taller than her head. "Through the maze now," she said, for there was no path.

Then there was something tall, black, and skinny there, moving before her.

At first she took it for a man. It could have been a man dancing in the field. But she stood still and listened, and it did not make a sound. It was as silent as a ghost.

"Ghost," she said sharply, "who be you the ghost of? For I have heard of nary death close by."

But there was no answer—only the ragged dancing in the wind.

She shut her eyes, reached out her hand, and touched a sleeve. She found a coat and inside that an emptiness, cold as ice.

"You scarecrow," she said. Her face lighted. "I ought to be shut up for good," she said with laughter. "My senses is gone. I too old. I the oldest people I ever know. Dance, old scarecrow," she said, "while I dancing with you."

She kicked her foot over the furrow, and with mouth drawn down, shook her head once or twice in a little strutting way. Some husks blew down and whirled in streamers about her skirts.

Then she went on, parting her way from side to side with the cane, through the whispering field. At last she came to the end, to a wagon track where the silver grass blew between the red ruts. The quail were walking around like pullets, seeming all dainty and unseen.

"Walk pretty," she said. "This the easy place. This the easy going."

She followed the track, swaying through the quiet bare fields, through the little strings of trees silver in their dead leaves, past cabins silver from weather, with the doors and windows boarded shut, all like old women under a spell sitting there. "I walking in their sleep," she said, nodding her head vigorously.

In a ravine she went where a spring was silently flowing through a hollow log. Old Phoenix bent and drank. "Sweet-gum makes the water sweet," she said, and drank more. "Nobody know who made this well, for it was here when I was born."

The track crossed a swampy part where the moss hung as white as lace from every limb. "Sleep on, alligators, and blow your bubbles." Then the track went into the road.

Deep, deep the road went down between the high green-colored banks. Overhead the live-oaks met, and it was as dark as a cave.

A black dog with a lolling tongue came up out of the weeds by the ditch. She was meditating, and not ready, and when he came at her she only hit him a little with her cane. Over she went in the ditch, like a little puff of milk-weed.

Down there, her senses drifted away. A dream visited her, and she reached her hand up, but nothing reached down and gave her a pull. So she lay there and presently went to talking. "Old woman," she said to herself, "that black dog come up out of the weeds to stall you off, and now there he sitting on his fine tail, smiling at you."

A white man finally came along and found her—a hunter, a young man, with his dog on a chain.

"Well, Granny!" he laughed. "What are you doing there?"

"Lying on my back like a June-bug waiting to be turned over, mister," she said, reaching up her hand.

He lifted her up, gave her a swing in the air, and set her down, "Anything broken, Granny?"

"No sir, them old dead weeds is springy enough," said Phoenix, when she had got her breath. "I thank you for your trouble."

"Where do you live, Granny?" he asked, while the two dogs were growling at each other.

"Away back yonder, sir, behind the ridge. You can't even see it from here."

"On your way home?"

"No, sir, I going to town."

"Why, that's too far! That's as far as I walk when I come out myself, and I get something for my trouble." He patted the stuffed bag he carried, and there hung down a little closed claw. It was one of the bob-whites, with its beak hooked bitterly to show it was dead. "Now you go on home, Granny!"

"I bound to go to town, mister," said Phoenix. "The time come around."

He gave another laugh, filling the whole landscape. "I know you old colored people! Wouldn't miss going to town to see Santa Claus!"

But something held Old Phoenix very still. The deep lines in her face went into a fierce and different radiation. Without warning, she had seen with her own eyes a flashing nickel fall out of the man's pocket onto the ground.

"How old are you, Granny?" he was saying.

"There is no telling, mister," she said, "no telling."

Then she gave a little cry and clapped her hands and said, "Git on away from here, dog! Look! Look at that dog!" She laughed as if in admiration. "He ain't scared of nobody. He a big black dog." She whispered, "Sic him!"

"Watch me get rid of that cur," said the man. "Sic him, Pete! Sic him!"

Phoenix heard the dogs fighting, and heard the man running and throwing sticks. She even heard a gunshot. But she was slowly bending forward by that time, further and further forward, the lids stretched down over her eyes, as if she were doing this in her sleep. Her chin was lowered almost to her knees. The yellow palm of her hand came out from the fold of her apron. Her fingers slid down and along the ground under the piece of money with the grace and care they would have in lifting an egg from under a sitting hen. Then she slowly straightened up, she stood erect, and the nickel was in her apron pocket. A bird flew by. Her lips moved. "God watching me the whole time. I come to stealing."

The man came back, and his own dog panted about them. "Well, I scared him off that time," he said, and then he laughed and lifted his gun and pointed it at Phoenix.

She stood straight and faced him.

"Doesn't the gun scare you?" he said, still pointing it.

"No, sir, I seen plenty go off closer by, in my day, and for less than what I done," she said, holding utterly still.

He smiled, and shouldered the gun. "Well, Granny," he said, "you must be a hundred years old, and scared of nothing. I'd give you a dime if I had any money with me. But you take my advice and stay home, and nothing will happen to you."

"I bound to go on my way, mister," said Phoenix. She inclined her head in the red rag. Then they went in different directions, but she could hear the gun shooting again and again over the hill.

She walked on. The shadows hung from the oak trees to the road like curtains. Then she smelled wood-smoke, and smelled the river, and she saw a steeple and the cabins on their steep steps. Dozens of little black children whirled around her. There ahead was Natchez shining. Bells were ringing. She walked on.

In the paved city it was Christmas time. There were red and green electric lights strung and crisscrossed everywhere, and all turned on in the daytime. Old Phoenix would have been lost if she had not distrusted her eyesight and depended on her feet to know where to take her.

She paused quietly on the sidewalk where people were passing by. A lady came along in the crowd, carrying an armful of red-, green-, and silver-wrapped presents; she gave off perfume like the red roses in hot summer, and Phoenix stopped her.

"Please, missy, will you lace up my shoe?" She held up her foot.

"What do you want, Grandma?"

"See my shoe," said Phoenix. "Do all right for out in the country, but wouldn't look right to go in a big building."

"Stand still then, Grandma," said the lady. She put her packages down on the sidewalk beside her and laced and tied both shoes tightly.

"Can't lace 'em with a cane," said Phoenix. "Thank you, missy. I doesn't mind asking a nice lady to tie up my shoe, when I gets out on the street."

Moving slowly and from side to side, she went into the big building and into a tower of steps, where she walked up and around and around until her feet knew to stop.

She entered a door, and there she saw nailed up on the wall the document that had been stamped with the gold seal and framed in the gold frame, which matched the dream that was hung up in her head.

"Here I be," she said. There was a fixed and ceremonial stiffness over her body.

"A charity case, I suppose," said an attendant who sat at the desk before her.

But Phoenix only looked above her head. There was sweat on her face, the wrinkles in her skin shone like a bright net.

"Speak up, Grandma," the woman said. "What's your name? We must have your history, you know. Have you been here before? What seems to be the trouble with you?"

Old Phoenix only gave a twitch to her face as if a fly were bothering her.

"Are you deaf?" cried the attendant.

But then the nurse came in.

"Oh, that's just old Aunt Phoenix," she said. "She doesn't come for herself—she has a little grandson. She makes these trips just as regular as clockwork. She lives away back off the Old Natchez Trace." She bent down. "Well, Aunt Phoenix, why don't you just take a seat? We won't keep you standing after your long trip." She pointed.

The old woman sat down, bolt upright in the chair.

"Now, how is the boy?" asked the nurse.

Old Phoenix did not speak.

"I said, how is the boy?"

But Phoenix only waited and stared straight ahead, her face very solemn and withdrawn into rigidity.

"Is his throat any better?" asked the nurse. "Aunt Phoenix, don't you hear me? Is your grandson's throat any better since the last time you came for the medicine?"

With her hands on her knees, the old woman waited, silent, erect and motionless, just as if she were in armour.

"You mustn't take up our time this way, Aunt Phoenix," the nurse said. "Tell us quickly about your grandson, and get it over. He isn't dead, is he?"

At last there came a flicker and then a flame of comprehension across her face, and she spoke.

"My grandson. It was my memory had left me. There I sat and forgot why I made my long trip."

"Forgot?" The nurse frowned. "After you came so far?"

Then Phoenix was like an old woman begging a dignified forgiveness for waking up frightened in the night. "I never did go to school, I was too old at the Surrender," she said in a soft voice. "I'm an old woman without an education. It was my memory fail me. My little grandson, he is just the same, and I forgot it in the coming."

"Throat never heals, does it?" said the nurse, speaking in a loud, sure voice to Old Phoenix. By now she had a card with something written on it, a little list. "Yes. Swallowed lye. When was it—January—two-three years ago—"

Phoenix spoke unasked now. "No, missy, he not dead, he just the same. Every little while his throat begin to close up again, and he not able to swallow. He not get his breath. He not able to help himself. So the time come around, and I go on another trip for the soothingmedicine."

"All right. The doctor said as long as you came to get it, you could have it," said the nurse. "But it's an obstinate case."

"My little grandson, he sit up there in the house all wrapped up, waiting by himself," Phoenix went on. "We is the only two left in the world. He suffer and it don't seem to put him back at all. He got a sweet look. He going to last. He wear a little patch quilt and peep out holding his mouth open like a little bird. I remembers so plain now. I not going to forget him again, no, the whole enduring time. I could tell him from all the others in creation."

"All right." The nurse was trying to hush her now. She brought her a bottle of medicine. "Charity," she said, making a check mark in a book.

Old Phoenix held the bottle close to her eyes and then carefully put it into her pocket.

"I thank you," she said.

"It's Christmas time, Grandma," said the attendant. "Could I give you a few pennies out of my purse?"

"Five pennies is a nickel," said Phoenix stiffly.

"Here's a nickel," said the attendant.

Phoenix rose carefully and held out her hand. She received the nickel and then fished the other nickel out of her pocket and laid it beside the new one. She stared at her palm closely, with her head on one side.

Then she gave a tap with her cane on the floor.

"This is what come to me to do," she said. "I going to the store and buy my child a little windmill they sells, made out of paper. He going to find it hard to believe there such a thing in the world. I'll march myself back where he waiting, holding it straight up in this hand."

She lifted her free hand, gave a little nod, turned round, and walked out of the doctor's office. Then her slow step began on the stairs, going down.

Tillie Olsen (1913–   )

Born in 1913 in Nebraska, Tillie Olsen wrote copiously during her teen years but then spent the next twenty-odd years as a wife, a mother of four daughters, and an office worker. Only when she was over forty did she embark upon the career that has brought her a first-rank reputation among critics and teachers of writing. This reputation is based on half a dozen stories, four of which were collected as *Tell Me a Riddle* (1960), and a novel, *Yonnondio,* which was written when she was nineteen but not published until 1974. She remains relatively obscure to the general reading public.

Olsen's great strength as a writer is the compelling nature of her tone. (See Introduction, p. 15.) Unlike James Joyce, who believed the author should stand aside, "paring his fingernails," Olsen is right in the thick of the story. She is not merely directing traffic, as did eighteenth-century novelists and to some extent present writers like Katherine Anne Porter; nor is "Tell Me a Riddle" written in the voice of a character, like Updike's "Wife-wooing" or Mansfield's third-person narration "Marriage à la Mode." Nor is she to be grouped with anti-fiction writers who call attention to themselves as authors in order to destroy the illusion of fiction as reality. Rather, Olsen believes so completely in the truth of her fiction that she as author cannot stand back from it. It is the author's feelings that create the emotional universe of the story. The reader must relate to the author who exercises an immediate and forceful authorial presence.

Most writers would find Olsen's themes too immense for the confines of the short story. Indeed, they have little in common with the epiphanies or ironies or absurdities that mark many modern stories. The cancer death of an old woman might seem to run the risk of romantic sentimentality. But Olsen's presence—passionately committed, profoundly caring—cuts through the armor of the sophisticated reader and overcomes his protective distance. The reader enters the center of the story with the author and dares to release feelings deeper than those of everyday reality. One can put down an Olsen story profoundly shaken.

The writer's emotional concern dictates her technique. Without thought of the "rules" of fiction, or the theories of Henry James, Olsen "tells" her story, "shows" only to reinforce. She shifts point of view whenever the emotional center of the story shifts, will plunge right into the minds of a whole family in an instant, articulating their feelings with a grandeur of which they are incapable.

The narrative line is far from smooth; she moves always to the big scenes, does not even bother to summarize the little ones. In an Olsen story, people don't light cigarettes, say good morning, walk down hallways—gestures other writers use for verisimilitude, for showing, for creating breathing space. There is no breathing space in "Tell Me a Riddle," no relaxation of emotion, no easy opportunity to "observe the fine writing." The language is in the service of the emotion: "While he struggled with the motor, it seethed in him." "Blows, screams, a call. . . . Hide, hunch beind the dresser. . . ." Whatever power of sound or connotation the words or images have is transferred immediately into the story. Every word carries a burden of feeling.

Tell Me a Riddle

1

For forty-seven years they had been married. How deep back the stubborn, gnarled roots of the quarrel reached, no one could say—but only now, when tending to the needs of others no longer shackled them together, the roots swelled up visible, split the earth between them, and the tearing shook even to the children, long since grown.

Why now, why now? wailed Hannah.

As if when we grew up weren't enough, said Paul.

Poor Ma. Poor Dad. It hurts so for both of them, said Vivi. They never had very much; at least in old age they should be happy.

Knock their heads together, insisted Sammy; tell 'em: you're too old for this kind of thing; no reason not to get along now.

Lennie wrote to Clara: They've lived over so much together; what could possibly tear them apart?

Something tangible enough.

Arthritic hands, and such work as he got, occasional. Poverty all his life, and there was little breath left for running. He could not, could not turn away from this desire: to have the troubling of responsibility, the fretting with money, over and done with; to be free, to be *care*free where success was not measured by accumulation, and there was use for the vitality still in him.

There was a way. They could sell the house, and with the money join his lodge's Haven, cooperative for the aged. Happy communal life, and was he not already an official; had he not helped organize it, raise funds, served as a trustee?

But she—would not consider it.

"What do we need all this for?" he would ask loudly, for her hearing aid was turned down and the vacuum was shrilling. "Five rooms" (pushing the sofa so she could get into the corner) "furniture" (smoothing down the rug) "floors and surfaces to make work. Tell me, why do we need it?" And he was glad he could ask in a scream.

"Because I'm use't."

"Because you're use't. This is a reason, Mrs. Word Miser? Used to can get unused!"

"Tell Me A Riddle" is from the book, *Tell Me A Riddle* by Tillie Olsen. Copyright © 1960, 1961 by Tillie Olsen. Reprinted by permission of the publisher, Delacorte Press/Seymour Lawrence.

"Enough unused I have to get used to already. . . . Not enough words?" turning off the vacuum a moment to hear herself answer. "Because soon enough we'll need only a little closet, no windows, no furniture, nothing to make work, but for worms. Because now I want room. . . . Screech and blow like you're doing, you'll need that closet even sooner. . . . Ha, again!" for the vacuum bag wailed, puffed half up, hung stubbornly limp. "This time fix it so it stays; quick before the phone rings and you get too important-busy."

But while he struggled with the motor, it seethed in him. Why fix it? Why have to bother? And if it can't be fixed, have to wring the mind with how to pay the repair? At the Haven they come in with their own machines to clean your room or your cottage; you fish, or play cards, or make jokes in the sun, not with knotty fingers fight to mend vacuums.

Over the dishes, coaxingly: "For once in your life, to be free, to have everything done for you, like a queen."

"I never liked queens."

"No dishes, no garbage, no towel to sop, no worry what to buy, what to eat."

"And what else would I do with my empty hands? Better to eat at my own table when I want, and to cook and eat how I want."

"In the cottages they buy what you ask, and cook it how you like. *You* are the one who always used to say: better mankind born without mouths and stomachs than always to worry for money to buy, to shop, to fix, to cook, to wash, to clean."

"How cleverly you hid that you heard. I said it then because eighteen hours a day I ran. And you never scraped a carrot or knew a dish towel sops. Now—for you and me—who cares? A herring out of a jar is enough. But when *I* want, and nobody to bother." And she turned off her ear button, so she would not have to hear.

But as *he* had no peace, juggling and rejuggling the money to figure: how will I pay for this now?; prying out the storm windows (there they take care of this); jolting in the streetcar on errands (there I would not have to ride to take care of this or that); fending the patronizing relatives just back from Florida (at the Haven it matters what one is, not what one can afford), he gave *her* no peace.

"Look! In their bulletin. A reading circle. Twice a week it meets."

"Haumm," her answer of not listening.

"A reading circle. Chekhov they read that you like, and Peretz. Cultured people at the Haven that you would enjoy."

"Enjoy!" She tasted the word. "Now, when it pleases you, you find a reading circle for me. And forty years ago when the children were morsels and there was a Circle, did you stay home with them once so I could go? Even once? You trained me well. I do not need others to enjoy. Others!" Her voice trembled. "Because *you* want to be there with others. Already it makes me sick to think of you always around others. Clown, grimacer, floormat, yesman, entertainer, whatever they want of you."

And now it was he who turned on the television loud so he need not hear.

Old scar tissue ruptured and the wounds festered anew. Chekhov indeed. She thought without softness of that young wife, who in the deep night hours while she nursed the current baby, and perhaps held another in her lap, would try to stay awake for the only time there was to read. She would feel again the weather of the outside on his cheek when, coming late from a meeting, he would find her so, and stimulated and ardent, sniffing her skin, coax: "I'll put the baby to bed, and you—put the book away, don't read, don't read."

That had been the most beguiling of all the "don't read, put your book away" her life had been. Chekhov indeed!

"Money?" She shrugged him off. "Could we get poorer than once we were? And in America, who starves to death?"

But as still he pressed:

"Let me alone about money. Was there ever enough? Seven little ones—for every penny I had to ask—and sometimes, remember, there was nothing. But always *I* had to manage. Now *you* manage. Rub your nose in it good."

But from those years she had had to manage, old humiliations and terrors rose up, lived again, and forced her to relive them. The children's needings; that grocer's face or this merchant's wife she had had to beg credit from when credit was a disgrace; the scenery of the long blocks walked around when she could not pay; school coming, and the desperate going over the old to see what could yet be remade; the soups of meat bones begged "for-the-dog" one winter. . . .

Enough. Now they had no children. Let *him* wrack his head for how they would live. She would not exchange her solitude for anything. *Never again to be forced to move to the rhythms of others.*

For in this solitude she had won to a reconciled peace.

Tranquillity from having the empty house no longer an enemy, for it stayed clean—not as in the days when it was her family, the life in it, that had seemed the enemy: tracking, smudging, littering, dirtying, engaging her in endless defeating battle—and on whom her endless defeat had been spewed.

The few old books, memorized from rereading; the pictures to ponder (the magnifying glass superimposed on her heavy eyeglasses). Or if she wishes, when he is gone, the phonograph, that if she turns up very loud and strains, she can hear: the ordered sounds and the struggling.

Out in the garden, growing things to nurture. Birds to be kept out of the pear tree, and when the pears are heavy and ripe, the old fury of work, for all must be canned, nothing wasted.

And her one social duty (for she will not go to luncheons or meetings) the boxes of old clothes left with her, as with a life-practised eye for finding what is still wearable within the worn (again the magnifying glass superimposed on the heavy glasses) she scans and sorts—this for rag or rummage, that for mending and cleaning, and this for sending away.

Being able at last to live within, and not move to the rhythms of others, as life had helped her to: denying; removing; isolating; taking the children one by one; then deafening, half-blinding—and at last, presenting her solitude.

And in it she had won to a reconciled peace.

Now he was violating it with his constant campaigning: *Sell the house and move to the Haven.* (You sit, you sit—there too you could sit like a stone.) He was making of her a battleground where old grievances tore. (Turn on your ear button—I am talking.) And stubbornly she resisted—so that from wheedling, reasoning manipulation, it was bitterness he now started with.

And it came to where every happening lashed up a quarrel.

"I will sell the house anyway," he flung at her one night. "I am putting it up for sale. There will be a way to make you sign."

The television blared, as always it did on the evenings he stayed home, and as always it reached her only as noise. She did not know if the tumult was in her or outside. Snap! she turned the sound off. "Shadows," she whispered to him, pointing to the screen, "look, it is only shadows." And in a scream: "Did you say that you will sell the house? Look at me, not at that. I am no shadow. You cannot sell without me."

"Leave on the television. I am watching."

"Like Paulie, like Jenny, a four-year-old. Staring at shadows. *You cannot sell the house.*"

"I will. We are going to the Haven. There you would not hear the television when you do not want it. I could sit in the social room and watch. You could lock yourself up to smell your unpleasantness in a room by yourself—for who would want to come near you?"

"No, no selling." A whisper now.

"The television is shadows. Mrs. Enlightened! Mrs. Cultured! A world comes into your house—and it is shadows. People you would never meet in a thousand lifetimes. Wonders. When you were four years old, yes, like Paulie, like Jenny, did you know of Indian dances, alligators, how they use bamboo in Malaya? No, you scratched in your dirt with the chickens and thought Olshana was the world. Yes, Mrs. Unpleasant, I will sell the house, for there better can we be rid of each other than here."

She did not know if the tumult was outside, or in her. Always a ravening inside, a pull to the bed, to lie down, to succumb.

"Have you thought maybe Ma should let a doctor have a look at her?" asked their son Paul after Sunday dinner, regarding his mother crumpled on the couch, instead of, as was her custom, busying herself in Nancy's kitchen.

"Why not the President too?"

"Seriously, Dad. This is the third Sunday she's lain down like that after dinner. Is she that way at home?"

"A regular love affair with the bed. Every time I start to talk to her."

Good protective reaction, observed Nancy to herself. The workings of hos-til-ity.

"Nancy could take her. I just don't like how she looks. Let's have Nancy arrange an appointment."

"You think she'll go?" regarding his wife gloomily. "All right, we have to have doctor bills, we have to have doctor bills." Loudly: "Something hurts you?"

She startled, looked to his lips. He repeated: "Mrs. Take It Easy, something hurts?"

"Nothing. . . . Only you."

"A woman of honey. That's why you're lying down?"

"Soon I'll get up to do the dishes, Nancy."

"Leave them, Mother, I like it better this way."

"Mrs. Take It Easy, Paul says you should start ballet. You should go to see a doctor and ask: how soon can you start ballet?"

"A doctor?" she begged. "Ballet?"

"We were talking, Ma," explained Paul, "you don't seem any too well. It would be a good idea for you to see a doctor for a checkup."

"I get up now to do the kitchen. Doctors are bills and foolishness, my son. I need no doctors."

"At the Haven," he could not resist pointing out, "a doctor is *not* bills. He lives beside you. You start to sneeze, he is there before you open up a Kleenex. You can be sick there for free, all you want."

"Diarrhea of the mouth, is there a doctor to make you dumb?"

"Ma. Promise me you'll go. Nancy will arrange it."

"It's all of a piece when you think of it," said Nancy, "the way she attacks my kitchen, scrubbing under every cup hook, doing the inside of the oven so I can't enjoy Sunday dinner, knowing that half-blind or not, she's going to find every speck of dirt. . . ."

"Don't, Nancy, I've told you—it's the only way she knows to be useful. What did the *doctor* say?"

"A real fatherly lecture. Sixty-nine is young these days. Go out, enjoy life, find interests. Get a new hearing aid, this one is antiquated. Old age is sickness only if one makes it so. Geriatrics, Inc."

"So there was nothing physical."

"Of course there was. How can you live to yourself like she does without there being? Evidence of a kidney disorder, and her blood count is low. He gave her a diet, and she's to come back for follow-up and lab work. . . . But he was clear enough: Number One prescription—start living like a human being. . . . When I think of your dad, who could really play the invalid with that arthritis of his, as active as a teenager, and twice as much fun. . . ."

"You didn't tell me the doctor says your sickness is in you, how you live." He pushed his advantage. "Life and enjoyments you need better than medicine. And this diet, how can you keep it? To weigh each morsel and scrape away each bit of fat, to make this soup, that pudding. There, at the Haven, they have a dietician, they would do it for you."

She is silent.

"You would feel better there, I know it," he says gently. "There there is life and enjoyments all around."

"What is the matter, Mr. Importantbusy, you have no card game or meeting you can go to?"—turning her face to the pillow.

For a while he cut his meetings and going out, fussed over her diet, tried to wheedle her into leaving the house, brought in visitors:

"I should come to a fashion tea. I should sit and look at pretty babies in clothes I cannot buy. This is pleasure?"

"Always you are better than everyone else. The doctor said you should go out. Mrs. Brem comes to you with goodness and you turn her away."

"Because *you* asked her to, she asked me."

"They won't come back. People you need, the doctor said. Your own cousins I asked; they were willing to come and make peace as if nothing had happened. . . ."

"No more crushers of people, pushers, hypocrites, around me. No more in *my* house. You go to them if you like."

"Kind he is to visit. And you, like ice."

"A babbler. All my life around babblers. Enough!"

"She's even worse, Dad? Then let her stew a while," advised Nancy. "You can't let it destroy you; it's a psychological thing, maybe too far gone for any of us to help."

So he let her stew. More and more she lay silent in bed, and sometimes did not even get up to make the meals. No longer was the tongue-lashing inevitable if he left the coffee cup where it did not belong, or forgot to take out the garbage or mislaid the broom. The birds grew bold that summer and for once pocked the pears, undisturbed.

A bellyful of bitterness and every day the same quarrel in a new way and a different old grievance the quarrel forced her to enter and relive. And the new torment: I am not really sick, the doctor said it, then why do I feel so sick?

One night she asked him: "You have a meeting tonight? Do not go. Stay . . . with me."

He had planned to watch "This Is Your Life," but half sick himself from the heavy heat, and sickening therefore the more after the brooks and woods of the Haven, with satisfaction he grated:

"Hah, Mrs. Live Alone And Like It wants company all of a sudden. It doesn't seem so good the time of solitary when she was a girl exile in Siberia. 'Do not go. Stay with me.' A new song for Mrs. Free As A Bird. Yes, I am going out, and while I am gone chew this aloneness good, and think how you keep us both from where if you want people, you do not need to be alone."

"Go, go. All your life you have gone without me."

After him she sobbed curses he had not heard in years, old-country curses from their childhood: Grow, oh shall you grow like an onion, with your head in the ground. Like the hide of a drum shall you be, beaten in life, beaten in death. Oh shall you be like a chandelier, to hang, and to burn. . . .

She was not in their bed when he came back. She lay on the cot on the sun porch. All week she did not speak or come near him; nor did he try to make peace or care for her.

He slept badly, so used to her next to him. After all the years, old harmonies and dependencies deep in their bodies; she curled to him, or he coiled to her, each warmed, warming, turning as the other turned, the nights a long embrace.

It was not the empty bed or the storm that woke him, but a faint singing. *She* was singing. Shaking off the drops of rain, the lightning riving her lifted face, he saw her so; the cot covers on the floor.

"This is a private concert?" he asked. "Come in, you are wet."

"I can breathe now," she answered; "my lungs are rich." Though indeed the sound was hardly a breath.

"Come in, come in." Loosing the bamboo shades. "Look how wet you are." Half helping, half carrying her, still faint-breathing her song.

A Russian love song of fifty years ago.

He had found a buyer, but before he told her, he called together those children who were close enough to come. Paul, of course, Sammy from New Jersey, Hannah from Connecticut, Vivi from Ohio.

With a kindling of energy for her beloved visitors, she arrayed the house, cooked and baked. She was not prepared for the solemn after-dinner conclave, they too probing in and tearing. Her frightened eyes watched from mouth to mouth as each spoke.

His stories were eloquent and funny of her refusal to go back to the doctor; of the scorned invitations; of her stubborn silence or the bile "like a Niagara"; of her contrariness: "If I clean it's no good how I cleaned; if I don't clean, I'm still a master who thinks he has a slave."

(Vinegar he poured on me all his life; I am well marinated; how can I be honey now?)

Deftly he marched in the rightness for moving to the Haven; their money from social security free for visiting the children, not sucked into daily needs and into the house; the activities in the Haven for him; but mostly the Haven for *her:* her health, her need of care, distraction, amusement, friends who shared her interests.

"This does offer an outlet for Dad," said Paul; "he's always been an active person. And economic peace of mind isn't to be sneezed at, either. I could use a little of that myself."

But when they asked: "And you, Ma, how do you feel about it?" could only whisper:

"For him it is good. It is not for me. I can no longer live between people."

"You lived all your life *for* people," Vivi cried.

"Not with." Suffering doubly for the unhappiness on her children's faces.

"You have to find some compromise," Sammy insisted. "Maybe sell the house and buy a trailer. After forty-seven years there's surely some way you can find to live in peace."

"There is no help, my children. Different things we need."

"Then live alone!" He could control himself no longer. "I have a buyer for the house. Half the money for you, half for me. Either alone or with me to the Haven. You think I can live any longer as we are doing now?"

"Ma doesn't have to make a decision this minute, however you feel, Dad," Paul said quickly, "and you wouldn't want her to. Let's let it lay a few months, and then talk some more."

"I think I can work it out to take Mother home with me for a while," Hannah said. "You both look terrible, but especially you, Mother. I'm going to ask Phil to have a look at you."

"Sure," cracked Sammy. "What's the use of a doctor husband if you can't get free service out of him once in a while for the family? And absence might make the heart . . . you know."

"There was something after all," Paul told Nancy in a colorless voice. "That was Hannah's Phil calling. Her gall bladder. . . . Surgery."

"Her *gall* bladder. If that isn't classic. 'Bitter as gall'—talk of psychosom————"

He stepped closer, put his hand over her mouth, and said in the same colorless, plodding voice, "We have to get Dad. They operated at once. The cancer was everywhere, surrounding the liver, everywhere. They did what they could . . . at best she has a year. Dad . . . we have to tell him."

2

Honest in his weakness when they told him, and that she was not to know. "I'm not an actor. She'll know right away by how I am. Oh that poor woman. I am old too, it will break me into pieces. Oh that poor woman. She will spit on me: 'So my sickness was how I live.' Oh Paulie, how she will be, that poor woman. Only she should not suffer. . . . I can't stand sickness, Paulie, I can't go with you."

But went. And play-acted.

"A grand opening and you did not even wait for me. . . . A good thing Hannah took you with her."

"Fashion teas I needed. They cut out what tore in me; just in my throat something hurts yet. . . . Look! so many flowers, like a funeral. Vivi called, did Hannah tell you? And Lennie from San Francisco, and Clara; and Sammy is coming." Her gnome's face pressed happily into the flowers.

It is impossible to predict in these cases, but once over the immediate effects of the operation, she should have several months of comparative well-being.

The money, where will come the money?

Travel with her, Dad. Don't take her home to the old associations. The other children will want to see her.

The money, where will I wring the money?

Whatever happens, she is not to know. No, you can't ask her to sign papers to sell the house; nothing to upset her. Borrow instead, then after. . . .

I had wanted to leave you each a few dollars to make life easier, as other fathers do. There will be nothing left now. (Failure! you and your "business is exploitation." Why didn't you make it when it could be made?—Is that what you're thinking, Sammy?)

Sure she's unreasonable, Dad—but you have to stay with her; if there's to be any happiness in what's left of her life, it depends on you.

Prop me up, children, think of me, too. Shuffled, chained with her, bitter woman. No Haven, and the little money going. . . . How happy she looks, poor creature.

The look of excitement. The straining to hear everything (the new hearing aid turned full). Why are you so happy, dying woman?

How the petals are, fold on fold, and the gladioli color. The autumn air.

Stranger grandsons, tall above the little gnome grandmother, the little spry grandfather. Paul in a frenzy of picture-taking before going.

She, wandering the great house. Feeling the books; laughing at the maple shoemaker's bench of a hundred years ago used as a table. The ear turned to music.

"Let us go home. See how good I walk now." "One step from the hospital," he answers, "and she wants to fly. Wait till Doctor Phil says."

"Look—the birds too are flying home. Very good Phil is and will not show it, but he is sick of sickness by the time he comes home."

"Mrs. Telepathy, to read minds," he answers; "read mine what it says: when the trunks of medicines become a suitcase, then we will go."

The grandboys, they do not know what to say to us. . . . Hannah, she runs around here, there, when is there time for herself?

Let us go home. Let us go home.

Musing; gentleness—*but for the incidents of the rabbi in the hospital, and of the candles of benediction.*

Of the rabbi in the hospital:

Now tell me what happened, Mother.

From the sleep I awoke, Hannah's Phil, and he stands there like a devil in a dream and calls me by name. I cannot hear. I think he prays. Go away, please, I tell him, I am not a believer. Still he stands, while my heart knocks with fright.

You scared *him* Mother. He thought you were delirious.

Who sent him? Why did he come to me?

It is a custom. The men of God come to visit those of their religion they might help. The hospital makes up the list for them—race, religion—and you are on the Jewish list.

Not for rabbis. At once go and make them change. Tell them to write: Race, human; Religion, none.

And of the candles of benediction:

Look how you have upset yourself, Mrs. Excited Over Nothing. Pleasant memories you should leave.

Go in, go back to Hannah and the lights. Two weeks I saw candles and said nothing. But she asked me.

So what was so terrible? She forgets you never did, she asks you to light the Friday candles and say the benediction like Phil's mother when she visits. If the candles give her pleasure, why shouldn't she have the pleasure?

Not for pleasure she does it. For emptiness. Because his family does. Because all around her do.

That is not a good reason too? But you did not hear her. For heritage, she told you. For the boys, from the past they should have tradition.

Superstition! From the savages, afraid of the dark, of themselves: mumbo words and magic lights to scare away ghosts.

She told you: How it started does not take away the goodness. For centuries, peace in the house it means.

Swindler! does she look back on the dark centuries? Candles bought instead of bread and stuck into a potato for a candlestick? Religion that stifled and said: In Paradise, woman, you will be the footstool of your husband, and in life—poor chosen Jew—ground under, despised, trembling in cellars. And cremated. And cremated.

This is religion's fault? You think you are still an orator of the 1905 revolution? Where are the pills for quieting? Which are they?

Heritage. How have we come from the savages, how no longer to be savages—this to teach. To look back and learn what humanizes—this to teach. To smash all ghettos that divide us—not to go back, not to go back—this to teach. Learned books in the house, will humankind live or die, and she gives to her boys—superstition.

Hannah that is so good to you. Take your pill, Mrs. Excited For Nothing, swallow.

Heritage! But when did I have time to teach? Of Hannah I asked only hands to help.

Swallow.

Otherwise—musing; gentleness.

Not to travel. To go home.

The children want to see you. We have to show them you are as thorny a flower as ever.

Not to travel.

Vivi wants you should see her new baby. She sent the tickets—airplane tickets—a Mrs. Roosevelt she wants to make of you. To Vivi's we have to go.

A new baby. How many warm, seductive babies. She holds him stiffly, *away* from her, so that he wails. And a long shudder begins, and the sweat beads on her forehead.

"Hush, shush," croons the grandfather, lifting him back. "You should forgive your grandmamma, little prince, she has never held a baby before, only seen them in glass cases. Hush, shush."

"You're tired, Ma," says Vivi. "The travel and the noisy dinner. I'll take you to lie down."

(A long travel from, to, what the feel of a baby evokes.)

In the airplane, cunningly designed to encase from motion (no wind, no feel of flight), she had sat severely and still, her face turned to the sky through which they cleaved and left no scar.

So this was how it looked, the determining, the crucial sky, and this was how man moved through it, remote above the dwindled earth, the concealed human life. Vulnerable life, that could scar.

There was a steerage ship of memory that shook across a great, circular sea: clustered, ill human beings; and through the thick-stained air, tiny fretting waters in a window round like the airplane's—sun round, moon round. (The round thatched roofs of Olshana.) Eye round—like the smaller window that framed distance the solitary year of exile when only her eyes could travel, and no voice spoke. And the polar winds hurled themselves across snows trackless and endless and white—like the clouds which had closed together below and hidden the earth.

Now they put a baby in her lap. Do not ask me, she would have liked to beg. Enough the worn face of Vivi, the remembered grandchildren. I cannot, cannot. . . .

Cannot what? Unnatural grandmother, not able to make herself embrace a baby.

She lay there in the bed of the two little girls, her new hearing aid turned full, listening to the sound of the children going to sleep, the baby's fretful crying and hushing, the clatter of dishes being washed and put away. They thought she slept. Still she rode on.

It was not that she had not loved her babies, her children. The love—the passion of tending—had risen with the need like a torrent; and like a torrent drowned and immolated all else. But when the need was done—oh the power that was lost in the painful damming back and drying up of what still surged, but had nowhere to go. Only the thin pulsing left that could not quiet, suffering over lives one felt, but could no longer hold nor help.

On that torrent she had borne them to their own lives, and the riverbed was desert long years now. Not there would she dwell, a memoried wraith. Surely that was not all, surely there was more. Still the springs, the springs were in her seeking. Somewhere an older power that beat for life. Somewhere coherence, transport, meaning. If they would but leave her in the air now stilled of clamor, in the reconciled solitude, to journey to her self.

And they put a baby in her lap. Immediacy to embrace, and the breath of *that* past: warm flesh like this that had claims and nuzzled away all else and with lovely mouths devoured; hot-living like an animal—intensely and now; the turning maze; the long drunkenness; the drowning into needing and being needed. Severely she looked back—and the shudder seized her again, and the sweat. Not that way. Not there, not now could she, not yet. . . .

And all that visit, she could not touch the baby.

"Daddy, is it the . . . sickness she's like that?" asked Vivi. "I was so glad to be having the baby—for her. I told Tim, it'll give her more happiness than anything, being around a baby again. And she hasn't played with him once."

He was not listening, "Aahh little seed of life, little charmer," he crooned, "Hollywood should see you. A heart of ice you would melt. Kick, kick. The future you'll have for a ball. In 2050 still kick. Kick for your grandaddy then."

Attentive with the older children; sat through their performances (command performance; we command you to be the audience); helped Ann sort autumn leaves to find the best for a school program; listened gravely to Richard tell about his rock collection, while her lips mutely formed the words to remember: *igneous, sedimentary, metamorphic;* looked for missing socks, books, and bus tickets; watched the children whoop after their grandfather who knew how to tickle, chuck, lift, toss, do tricks, tell secrets, make jokes, match riddle for riddle. (Tell me a riddle, Grammy. I know no riddles, child.) Scrubbed sills and woodwork and furniture in every room; folded the laundry; straightened drawers; emptied the heaped baskets waiting for ironing (while he or Vivi or Tim nagged: You're supposed to rest here, you've been sick) but to none tended or gave food—and could not touch the baby.

After a week she said: "Let us go home. Today call about the tickets."

"You have important business, Mrs. Inahurry? The President waits to consult with you?" He shouted, for the fear of the future raced in him. "The clothes are still warm from the suitcase, your children cannot show enough how glad they are to see you, and you want home. There is plenty of time for home. We cannot be with the children at home."

"Blind to around you as always: the little ones sleep four in a room because we take their bed. We are two more people in a house with a new baby, and no help."

"Vivi is happy so. The children should have their grandparents a while, she told to me. I should have my mommy and daddy. . . ."

"Babbler and blind. Do you look at her so tired? How she starts to talk and she cries? I am not strong enough yet to help. Let us go home."

(To reconciled solitude.)

For it seemed to her the crowded noisy house was listening to her, listening for *her. She could feel it like a great ear pressed under her heart. And everything knocked: quick constant raps: let me in, let me in.*

How was it that soft reaching tendrils also became blows that knocked?

C'mon, Grandma, I want to show you. . . .

Tell me a riddle, Grandma. *(I know no riddles.)*

Look, Grammy, he's so dumb he can't even find his hands. (Dody and the baby on a blanket over the fermenting autumn mould.)

I made them—for you. (Ann) (Flat paper dolls with aprons that lifted on scalloped skirts that lifted on flowered pants; hair of yarn and great ringed questioning eyes.)

Watch me, Grandma. (Richard snaking up the tree, hanging exultant, free, with one hand at the top. Below Dody hunching over in pretend-cooking.) *(Climb too, Dody, Climb and look.)*

Be my nap bed, Grammy. (The "No!" too late.) Morty's abandoned heaviness, while his fingers ladder up and down her hearing-aid cord to his drowsy chant: eentsiebeentsiespider. *(Children trust.)*

It's to start off your own rock collection, Grandma. That's a trilobite fossil, 200 million years old (millions of years on a child's mouth) and that one's obsidian, black glass.

Knocked and knocked.

Mother, I *told* you the teacher said we had to bring it back all filled out this morning. Didn't you even ask Daddy? Then tell *me* which plan and I'll check it: evacuate or stay in the city or wait for you to come and take me away. (Seeing the look of straining to hear.) It's for Disaster, Grandma. *(Children trust.)*

Vivi in the maze of the long, the lovely drunkenness. The old old noises: baby sounds; screaming of a mother flayed to exasperation; children quarreling; children playing; singing; laughter.

And Vivi's tears and memories, spilling so fast, half the words not understood.

She had started remembering out loud deliberately, so her mother would know the past was cherished, still lived in her.

Nursing the baby: My friends marvel, and I tell them, oh it's easy to be such a cow. I remember how beautiful my mother seemed nursing my brother, and the milk just flows. . . . Was that Davy? It must have been Davy. . . .

Lowering a hem: How did you ever . . . when I think how you made everything we wore . . . Tim, just think, seven kids and Mommy sewed everything . . . do I remember you sang while you sewed? That white dress with the red apples on the skirt you fixed over for me, was it Hannah's or Clara's before it was mine?

Washing sweaters: Ma, I'll never forget, one of those days so nice you washed clothes outside; one of the first spring days it must have been. The bubbles just danced while you scrubbed, and we chased after, and you stopped to show us how to blow our own bubbles with green onion stalks . . . you always. . . .

"Strong onion, to still make you cry after so many years," her father said, to turn the tears into laughter.

While Richard bent over his homework: Where is it now, do we still have it, the Book of the Martyrs? It always seemed so, well—exalted, when you'd put it on the round table and we'd all look at it together; there was even a halo from the lamp. The lamp with the beaded fringe you could move up and down; they're in style again, pulley lamps like that, but without the fringe. You know the book I'm talking about, Daddy, the Book of the Martyrs, the first picture was a bust of Socrates? I wish there was something like that for the children, Mommy, to give them what you. . . . (And the tears splashed again.)

(What I intended and did not? Stop it, daughter, stop it, leave that time. And he, the hypocrite, sitting there with tears in his eyes—it was nothing to you then, nothing.)

. . . The time you came to school and I almost died of shame because of your accent and because I knew you knew I was ashamed; how could I? . . . Sammy's harmonica and you danced to it once, yes you did, you and Davy squealing in your arms. . . . That time you bundled us up and walked us down to the railway station to stay the night 'cause it was heated and we didn't have any coal, that winter of the strike, you didn't think I remembered that, did you, Mommy? . . . How you'd call us out to see the sunsets. . . .

Day after day, the spilling memories. Worse now, questions, too. Even the grandchildren: Grandma, in the olden days, when you were little. . . .

It was the afternoons that saved.

While they thought she napped, she would leave the mosaic on the wall (of children's drawings, maps, calendars, pictures, Ann's cardboard dolls with their great ringed questioning eyes) and hunch in the girls' cupboard, on the low shelf where the shoes stood, and the girls' dresses covered.

For that while she would painfully sheathe against the listening house, the tendrils and noises that knocked, and Vivi's spilling memories. Sometimes it helped to braid and unbraid the sashes that dangled, or to trace the pattern on the hoop slips.

Today she had jacks and children under jet trails to forget. Last night, Ann and Dody silhouetted in the window against a sunset of flaming man-made clouds of jet trail, their jacks ball accenting the peaceful noise of dinner being made. Had she told them, yes she had told them of how they played jacks in her village though there was no ball, no jacks. Six stones, round and flat, toss them out, the seventh on the back of the hand, toss, catch and swoop up as many as possible, toss again. . . .

Of stones (repeating Richard) there are three kinds: earth's fire jetting; rock of layered centuries; crucibled new out of the old *(igneous, sedimentary, metamorphic).* But there was that other—frozen to black glass, never to transform or hold the fossil memory . . . (let not my seed fall on stone). There was an ancient man who fought to heights a great rock that crashed back down eternally—eternal labor, freedom, labor . . . (stone will perish, but the word remain). And you, David, who with a stone slew, screaming: Lord, take my heart of stone and give me flesh.

Who was screaming? Why was she back in the common room of the prison, the sun motes dancing in the shafts of light, and the informer being brought in, a prisoner now, like themselves. And Lisa leaping, yes, Lisa, the gentle and tender, biting at the betrayer's jugular. Screaming and screaming.

No, it is the children screaming. Another of Paul and Sammy's terrible fights? In Vivi's house. Severely: you are in Vivi's house.

Blows, screams, a call: "Grandma!" For her? Oh please not for her. Hide, hunch behind the dresses deeper. But a trembling little body hurls itself beside her—surprised, smothered laughter, arms surround her neck, tears rub dry on her cheek, and words too soft to understand whisper into her ear (Is this where you hide too, Grammy? It's my secret place, we have a secret now).

And the sweat beads, and the long shudder seizes.

It seemed the great ear pressed inside now, and the knocking. "We have to go home," she told him, "I grow ill here."

"It's your own fault, Mrs. Bodybusy, you do not rest, you do too much." He raged, but the fear was in his eyes. "It was a serious operation, they told you to take care. . . . All right, we will go to where you can rest."

But where? Not home to death, not yet. He had thought to Lennie's, to Clara's; beautiful visits with each of the children. She would have to rest first, be stronger. If they could but go to Florida—it glittered before him, the never-realized promise of Florida. California: of course. (The money, the money, dwindling!) Los Angeles first for sun and rest, then to Lennie's in San Francisco.

He told her the next day. "You saw what Nancy wrote: snow and wind back home, a terrible winter. And look at you—all bones and a swollen belly. I called Phil: he said: 'A prescription, Los Angeles sun and rest.'"

She watched the words on his lips. "You have sold the house," she cried, "that is why we do not go home. That is why you talk no more of the Haven, why there is money for travel. After the children you will drag me to the Haven."

"The Haven! Who thinks of the Haven any more? Tell her, Vivi, tell Mrs. Suspicious: a prescription, sun and rest, to make you healthy. . . . And how could I sell the house without *you?*"

At the place of farewells and greetings, of winds of coming and winds of going, they say their good-byes.

They look back at her with the eyes of others before them: Richard with her own blue blaze; Ann with the nordic eyes of Tim; Morty's dreaming brown of a great-grandmother he will never know; Dody with the laughing eyes of him who had been her springtide love (who stands beside her now); Vivi's, all tears.

The baby's eyes are closed in sleep.

Good-bye, my children.

3

It is to the back of the great city he brought her, to the dwelling places of the cast-off old. Bounded by two lines of amusement piers to the north and to the south, and between a long straight paving rimmed with black benches facing the sand—sands so wide the ocean is only a far fluting.

In the brief vacation season, some of the boarded stores fronting the sands open, and families, young people and children, may be seen. A little tasselled tram shuttles between the piers, and the lights of roller coasters prink and tweak over those who come to have sensation made in them.

The rest of the year it is abandoned to the old, all else boarded up and still; seemingly empty, except the occasional days and hours when the sun, like a tide, sucks them out of the low rooming houses, casts them onto the benches and sandy rim of the walk—and sweeps them into decaying enclosures once again.

A few newer apartments glint among the low bleached squares. It is in one of these Lennie's Jeannie has arranged their rooms. "Only a few miles north and south people pay hundreds of dollars a month for just this gorgeous air, Grandaddy, just this ocean closeness."

She had been ill on the plane, lay ill for days in the unfamiliar room. Several times the doctor came by—left medicine she would not take. Several times Jeannie drove in the twenty miles from work, still in her Visiting Nurse uniform, the lightness and brightness of her like a healing.

"Who can believe it is winter?" he asked one morning. "Beautiful it is outside like an ad. Come, Mrs. Invalid, come to taste it. You are well enough to sit in here, you are well enough to sit outside. The doctor said it too."

But the benches were encrusted with people, and the sands at the sidewalk's edge. Besides, she had seen the far ruffle of the sea: "there take me," and though she leaned against him, it was she who led.

Plodding and plodding, sitting often to rest, he grumbling. Patting the sand so warm. Once she scooped up a handful, cradling it close to her better eye; peered, and flung it back. And as they came almost to the brink and she could see the glistening wet, she sat down, pulled off her shoes and stockings, left him and began to run. "You'll catch cold," he screamed, but the sand in his shoes weighed him down—he who had always been the agile one—and already the white spray creamed her feet.

He pulled her back, took a handkerchief to wipe off the wet and the sand. "Oh no," she said, "the sun will dry," seized the square and smoothed it flat, dropped on it a mound of sand, knotted the kerchief corners and tied it to a bag—"to look at with the strong glass" (for the first time in years explaining an action of hers)—and lay down with the little bag against her cheek, looking toward the shore that nurtured life as it first crawled toward consciousness the millions of years ago.

He took her one Sunday in the evil-smelling bus, past flat miles of blister houses, to the home of relatives. Oh what is this? she cried as the light began to smoke and the houses to dim and recede. Smog, he said, everyone knows but you. . . . Outside he kept his arms about her, but she walked with hands pushing the heavy air as if to open it, whispered: who has done this? sat down suddenly to vomit at the curb and for a long while refused to rise.

One's age as seen on the altered face of those known in youth. Is this they he has come to visit? This Max and Rose, smooth and pleasant, introducing them to polite children, disinterested grandchildren, "the whole family, once a month on Sundays. And why not? We have the room, the help, the food."

Talk of cars, of houses, of success: this son that, that daughter this. And *your* children? Hastily skimped over, the intermarriages, the obscure work—"my doctor son-in-law, Phil"—all he has to offer. She silent in a corner. (Car-sick like a baby, he explains.) Years since he has taken her to visit anyone but the children, and old apprehensions prickle: "no incidents," he silently begs, "no incidents." He itched to tell them. "A very sick woman," significantly, indicating her with his eyes, "a very sick woman." Their restricted faces did not react. "Have you thought maybe she'd do better at Palm Springs?" Rose asked. "Or at least a nicer section of the beach, nicer people, a pool." Not to have to say "money" he said instead: "would she have sand to look at through a magnifying glass?" and went on, detail after detail, the old habit betraying of parading the queerness of her for laughter.

After dinner—the others into the living room in men- or women-clusters, or into the den to watch TV—the four of them alone. She sat close to him, and did not speak. Jokes, stories, people they had known, beginning of reminiscence, Russia fifty-sixty years ago. Strange words across the Duncan Phyfe table: *hunger; secret meetings; human rights; spies; betrayals; prison; escape*—interrupted by one of the grandchildren: "Commercial's on; any Coke left? Gee, you're missing a real hair-raiser." And then a granddaughter (Max proudly: "look at her, an American queen") drove them home on her way back to U.C.L.A. No incident—except that there had been no incidents.

The first few mornings she had taken with her the magnifying glass, but he would sit only on the benches, so she rested at the foot, where slatted bench shadows fell, and unless she turned her hearing aid down, other voices invaded.

Now on the days when the sun shone and she felt well enough, he took her on the tram to where the benches ranged in oblongs, some with tables for checkers or cards. Again the blanket on the sand in the striped shadows, but she no longer brought the magnifying glass. He played cards, and she lay in the sun and looked towards the waters; or they walked—two blocks down to the scaling hotel, two blocks back—past chili-hamburger stands, open-doored bars, Next to New and Perpetual Rummage Sale stores.

Once, out of the aimless walkers, slow and shuffling like themselves, someone ran unevenly towards them, embraced, kissed, wept: "dear friends, old friends." A friend of *hers,* not his: Mrs. Mays who had lived next door to them in Denver when the children were small.

Thirty years are compressed into a dozen sentences; and the present, not even in three. All is told: the children scattered; the husband dead; she lives in a room two blocks up from the sing hall—and points to the domed auditorium jutting before the pier. The leg? plebitis; the heavy breathing? that, one does not ask. She, too, comes to the benches each day to sit. And tomorrow, tomorrow, are they going to the community sing? Of course he would have heard of it, everybody goes—the big doings they wait for all week. They have never been? She will come to them for dinner tomorrow and they will all go together.

So it is that she sits in the wind of the singing, among the thousand various faces of age.

She had turned off her hearing aid at once they came into the auditorium—as she would have wished to turn off sight.

One by one they streamed by and imprinted on her—and though the savage zest of their singing came voicelessly soft and distant, the faces still roared—the faces densened the air—chorded into

children-chants, mother-croons, singing of the chained
love serenades, Beethoven storms, mad Lucia's scream
drunken joy-songs, keens for the dead, work-singing

while from floor to balcony to dome a bare-footed sore-covered little girl threaded the sound-thronged tumult, danced her ecstasy of grimace to flutes that scratched at a crossroads village wedding

Yes, faces became sound, and the sound became faces; and faces and sound became weight—pushed, pressed

"Air"—her hands claw his.

"Whenever I enjoy myself. . . ." Then he saw the gray sweat on her face. "Here. Up. Help me, Mrs. Mays," and they support her out to where she can gulp the air in sob after sob.

"A doctor, we should get for her a doctor."

"Tch, it's nothing," says Ellen Mays, "I get it all the time. You've missed the tram; come to my place. Fix your hearing aid, honey . . . close . . . tea. My view. See, she *wants* to come. Steady now, that's how." Adding mysteriously: "Remember your advice, easy to keep your head above water, empty things float. Float."

The singing a fading march for them, tall woman with a swollen leg, weaving little man, and the swollen thinness they help between.

The stench in the hall: mildew? decay? "We sit and rest then climb. My gorgeous view. We help each other and here we are."

The stench along into the slab of room. A washstand for a sink, a box with oilcloth tacked around for a cupboard, a three-burner gas plate. Artificial flowers, colorless with dust. Everywhere pictures foaming: wedding, baby, party, vacation, graduation, family pictures. From the narrow couch under a slit of window, sure enough the view: lurching rooftops and a scallop of ocean heaving, preening, twitching under the moon.

"While the water heats. Excuse me . . . down the hall." Ellen Mays has gone.

"You'll live?" he asks mechanically, sat down to feel his fright; tried to pull her alongside.

She pushed him away. "For air," she said; stood clinging to the dresser. Then, in a terrible voice:

After a lifetime of room. Of many rooms.

Shhh.

You remember how she lived. Eight children. And now one room   like a coffin. She pays rent!

Shrinking the life of her   into one room   like a coffin.   Rooms and rooms like this   I lie on the quilt and hear them talk

Please, Mrs. Orator-without-Breath.

Once you went for coffee   I walked   I saw.   A Balzac   a Chekhov to write it Rummage   Alone   On scraps

Better old here than in the old country!

On scraps   Yet they sang like   like . . .   Wondrous! *Humankind   one has to believe*   So strong   for what? To rot   not grow?

Your poor lungs beg you. They sob between each word.

Singing.   Unused   the life in them.   She   in this poor room   with her   pic-tures.   Max.   You.   The children.   Everywhere   unused   the life   And who has meaning?   Century after century   still all in us   not   to grow?

Coffins, rummage, plants: sick woman. Oh lay down. We will get for you the doctor.

"And when will it end. Oh, *the end.*" *That* nightmare thought, and this time she writhed, crumpled against him, seized his hand (for a moment again the weight, the soft distant roaring of humanity) and on the strangled-for breath, begged: "Man . . . we'll destroy ourselves?"

And looking for answer—in the helpless pity and fear for her (for *her*) that distorted his face—she understood the last months, and knew that she was dying.

4

"Let us go home," she said after several days.

"You are in training for a cross-country race? That is why you do not even walk across the room? Here, like a prescription Phil said, till you are stronger from the operation. You want to break doctor's orders?"

She saw the fiction was necessary to him, was silent; then: "At home I will get better. If the doctor here says?"

"And winter? And the visits to Lennie and to Clara? All right," for he saw the tears in her eyes, "I will write Phil, and talk to the doctor."

Days passed. He reported nothing. Jeannie came and took her out for air, past the boarded concessions, the hooded and tented amusement rides, to the end of the pier. They watched the spent waves feeding the new, the gulls in the clouded sky; even up where they sat, the wind-blown sand stung.

She did not ask to go down the crooked steps to the sea.

Back in her bed, while he was gone to the store, she said: "Jeannie, this doctor, he is not one I can ask questions. Ask him for me, can I go home?"

Jeannie looked at her, said quickly: "Of course, poor Granny. You want your own things around you, don't you? I'll call him tonight. . . . Look, I've something to show you," and from her purse unwrapped a large cookie, intricately shaped like a little girl. "Look at the curls—can you hear me well, Granny?—and the darling eye-lashes. I just came from a house where they were baking them."

"The dimples, there in the knees," she marveled, holding it to the better light, turning, studying, "like art. Each singly they cut, or a mold?"

"Singly," said Jeannie, "and if it is a child only the mother can make them. Oh Granny, it's the likeness of a real little girl who died yesterday—Rosita. She was three years old. *Pan del Muerto,* the Bread of the Dead. It was the custom in the part of Mexico they came from."

Still she turned and inspected. "Look, the hollow in the throat, the little cross necklace. . . . I think for the mother it is a good thing to be busy with such bread. You know the family?"

Jeannie nodded. "On my rounds. I nursed. . . . Oh Granny, it is like a party; they play songs she liked to dance to. The coffin is lined with pink velvet and she wears a white dress. There are candles. . . ."

"In the house?" Surprised, "They keep her in the house?"

"Yes," said Jeannie, "and it *is* against the health law. I think she is . . . prepared there. The father said it will be sad to bury her in this country; in Oaxaca they have a feast night with candles each year; everyone picnics on the graves of those they loved until dawn."

"Yes, Jeannie, the living must comfort themselves." And closed her eyes.

"You want to sleep, Granny?"

"Yes, tired from the pleasure of you. I may keep the Rosita? There stand it, on the dresser, where I can see; something of my own around me."

In the kitchenette, helping her grandfather unpack the groceries, Jeannie said in her light voice:

"I'm resigning my job, Grandaddy."

"Ah, the lucky young man. Which one is he?"

"Too late. You're spoken for." She made a pyramid of cans, unstacked, and built again.

"Something is wrong with the job?"

"With me. I can't be"—she searched for the word—"What they call professional enough. I let myself feel things. And tomorrow I have to report a family. . . ." The cans clicked again. "It's not that, either. I just don't know what I want to do, maybe go back to school, maybe go to art school, maybe . . . I thought if you went to San Francisco I'd come along and talk it over with Momma and Daddy. But I don't see how you can go. She wants to go home. She asked me to ask the doctor."

The doctor told her himself. "Next week you may travel, when you are a little stronger." But next week there was the fever of an infection, and by the time that was over, she could not leave the bed—a rented hospital bed that stood beside the double bed he slept in alone now.

Outwardly the days repeated themselves. Every other afternoon and evening he went out to his newfound cronies, to talk and play cards. Twice a week, Mrs. Mays came. And the rest of the time, Jeannie was there.

By the sickbed stood Jeannie's FM radio. Often into the room the shapes of music came. She would lie curled on her side, her knees drawn up, intense in listening (Jeannie sketched her so, coiled, convoluted like an ear), then thresh her hand out and abruptly snap the radio mute—still to lie in her attitude of listening, concealing tears.

Once Jeannie brought in a young Marine to visit, a friend from high-school days she had found wandering near the empty pier. Because Jeannie asked him to, gravely, without self-consciousness, he sat himself cross-legged on the floor and performed for them a dance of his native Samoa.

Long after they left, a tiny thrumming sound could be heard where, in her bed, she strove to repeat the beckon, flight, surrender of his hands, the fluttering footbeats, and his low plaintive calls.

Hannah and Phil sent flowers. To deepen her pleasure, he placed one in her hair. "Like a girl," he said, and brought the hand mirror so she could see. She looked at the pulsing red flower, the yellow skull face; a desolate, excited laugh shuddered from her, and she pushed the mirror away—but let the flower burn.

The week Lennie and Helen came, the fever returned. With it the excited laugh, and incessant words. She, who in her life had spoken but seldom and then only when necessary (never having learned the easy, social uses of words), now in dying, spoke incessantly.

In a half-whisper: "Like Lisa she is, your Jeannie. Have I told you of Lisa who taught me to read? Of the highborn she was, but noble in herself. I was sixteen; they beat me; my father beat me so I would not go to her. It was forbidden, she was a Tolstoyan. At night, past dogs that howled, terrible dogs, my son, in the snows of winter to the road, I to ride in her carriage like a lady, to books. To her, life was holy, knowledge was holy, and she taught me to read. They hung her. Everything that happens one must try to understand why. She killed one who betrayed many. Because of betrayal, betrayed all she lived and believed. In one minute she killed, before my eyes (there is so much blood in a human being, my son), in prison with me. All that happens, one must try to understand.

"The name?" Her lips would work. "The name that was their pole star; the doors of the death houses fixed to open on it; I read of it my year of penal servitude. Thuban!" very excited, "Thuban, in ancient Egypt the pole star. Can you see, look out to see it, Jeannie, if it swings around *our* pole star that seems to *us* not to move.

"Yes, Jeannie, at your age my mother and grandmother had already buried children . . . yes, Jeannie, it is more than oceans between Olshana and you . . . yes, Jeannie, they danced, and for all the bodies they had they might as well be chickens, and indeed, they scratched and flapped their arms and hopped.

"And Andrei Yefimitch, who for twenty years had never known of it and never wanted to know, said as if he wanted to cry: but why my dear friend this malicious laughter?" Telling to herself half-memorized phrases from her few books. "Pain I answer with tears and cries, baseness with indignation, meanness with repulsion . . . for life may be hated or wearied of, but never despised."

Delirious: "Tell me, my neighbor, Mrs. Mays, the pictures never lived, but what of the flowers? Tell them who ask: no rabbis, no ministers, no priests, no speeches, no ceremonies: ah, false—let the living comfort themselves. Tell Sammy's boy, he who flies, tell him to go to Stuttgart and see where Davy has no grave. And what?" A conspirator's laugh. "And what? where millions have no graves—save air."

In delirium or not, wanting the radio on; not seeming to listen, the words still jetting, wanting the music on. Once, silencing it abruptly as of old, she began to cry, unconcealed tears this time. "You have pain, Granny?" Jeannie asked.

"The music," she said, "still it is there and we do not hear; knocks, and our poor human ears too weak. What else, what else we do not hear?"

Once she knocked his hand aside as he gave her a pill, swept the bottles from her bedside table: "no pills, let me feel what I feel," and laughed as on his hands and knees he groped to pick them up.

Nighttimes her hand reached across the bed to hold his.

A constant retching began. Her breath was too faint for sustained speech now, but still the lips moved:

When no longer necessary   to injure others
Pick   pick pick   Blind chicken
As a human being   responsibility

"David!" imperious, "Basin!" and she would vomit, rinse her mouth, the wasted throat working to swallow, and begin the chant again.

She will be better off in the hospital now, the doctor said.

He sent the telegrams to the children, was packing her suitcase, when her hoarse voice startled. She had roused, was pulling herself to sitting.

"Where now?" she asked. "Where now do you drag me?"

"You do not even have to have a baby to go this time," he soothed, looking for the brush to pack. "Remember, after Davy you told me—worthy to have a baby for the pleasure of the ten days rest in the hospital?"

"Where now? Not home yet?" Her voice mourned. "Where *is* my home?"

He rose to ease her back. "The doctor, the hospital," he started to explain, but deftly, like a snake, she had slithered out of bed and stood swaying, propped behind the night table.

"Coward," she hissed, "runner."

"You stand," he said senselessly.

"To take me there and run. Afraid of a little vomit."

He reached her as she fell. She struggled against him, half slipped from his arms, pulled herself up again.

"Weakling," she taunted, "to leave me there and run. Betrayer. All your life you have run."

He sobbed, telling Jeannie. "A Marilyn Monroe to run for her virtue. Fifty-nine pounds she weighs, the doctor said, and she beats at me like a Dempsey. Betrayer, she cries, and I running like a dog when she calls; day and night, running to her, her vomit, the bedpan. . . ."

"She needs you, Grandaddy," said Jeannie. "Isn't that what they call love? I'll see if she sleeps, and if she does, poor worn-out darling, we'll have a party, you and I: I brought us rum babas."

They did not move her. By her bed now stood the tall hooked pillar that held the solutions—blood and dextrose—to feed her veins. Jeannie moved down the hall to take over the sickroom, her face so radiant, her grandfather asked her once: "you are in love?" (Shameful the joy, the pure overwhelming joy from being with her grandmother; the peace, the serenity that breathed.) "My darling escape," she answered incoherently, "my darling Granny"—as if that explained.

Now one by one the children came, those that were able. Hannah, Paul, Sammy. Too late to ask: and what did you learn with your living, Mother, and what do we need to know?

Clara, the eldest, clenched:

Pay me back, Mother, pay me back for all you took from me. Those others you crowded into your heart. The hands I needed to be for you, the heaviness, the responsibility.

Is this she? Noises the dying make, the crablike hands crawling over the covers. The ethereal singing.

She hears that music, that singing from childhood; forgotten sound—not heard since, since. . . . And the hardness breaks like a cry: Where did we lose each other, first mother, singing mother?

Annulled: the quarrels, the gibing, the harshness between; the fall into silence and the withdrawal.

I do not know you, Mother. Mother, I never knew you.

Lennie, suffering not alone for her who was dying, but for that in her which never lived (for that which in him might never live). From him too, unspoken words: *goodbye Mother who taught me to mother myself.*

Not Vivi, who must stay with her children; not Davy, but he is already here, having to die again with *her* this time, for the living take their dead with them when they die.

Light she grew, like a bird, and, like a bird, sound bubbled in her throat while the body fluttered in agony. Night and day, asleep or awake (though indeed there was no difference now) the songs and the phrases leaping.

And he, who had once dreaded a long dying (from fear of himself, from horror of the dwindling money) now desired her quick death profoundly, for *her* sake. He no longer went out, except when Jeannie forced him; no longer laughed, except when, in the bright kitchenette, Jeannie coaxed his laughter (and she, who seemed to hear nothing else, would laugh too, conspiratorial wisps of laughter).

Light, like a bird, the fluttering body, the little claw hands, the beaked shadow on her face; and the throat, bubbling, straining.

He tried not to listen, as he tried not to look on the face in which only the forehead remained familiar, but trapped with her the long nights in that little room, the sounds worked themselves into his consciousness, with their punctuation of death swallows, whimpers, gurglings.

Even in reality (swallow) *life's lack of it*
Slaveships   death trains   clubs   eeenough
The bell   summon what enobles
78,000 in one minute (whisper of a scream) *78,000 human beings   we'll destroy ourselves?*

"Aah, Mrs. Miserable," he said, as if she could hear, "all your life working, and now in bed you lie, servants to tend, you do not even need to call to be tended, and still you work. Such hard work it is to die? Such hard work?"

The body threshed, her hand clung in his. A melody, ghost-thin, hovered on her lips, and like a guilty ghost, the vision of her bent in listening to it, silencing the record instantly he was near. Now, heedless of his presence, she floated the melody on and on.

"Hid it from me," he complained, "how many times you listened to remember it so?" And tried to think when she had first played it, or first begun to silence her few records when he came near—but could reconstruct nothing. There was only this room with its tall hooked pillar and its swarm of sounds.

No man one   except through others
Strong   with the not yet   in the now
Dogma dead   war dead   one country

"It helps, Mrs. Philosopher, words from books? It helps?" And it seemed to him that for seventy years she had hidden a tape recorder, infinitely miscroscopic, within her, that it had coiled infinite mile on mile, trapping every song, every melody, every word read, heard, and spoken—and that maliciously she was playing back only what said nothing of him, of the children, of their intimate life together.

"Left us indeed, Mrs. Babbler," he reproached, "you who called others babbler and cunningly saved your words. A lifetime you tended and loved, and now not a word of us, for us. Left us indeed? Left me."

And he took out his solitaire deck, shuffled the cards loudly, slapped them down.

Lift high   banner of reason (tatter of an orator's voice) *justice   freedom   light*
Humankind   life worthy   capacities
Seeks (blur of shudder) *belong   human being*

"Words, words," he accused, "and what human beings did *you* seek around you, Mrs. Live Alone, and what humankind think worthy?"

Though even as he spoke, he remembered she had not always been isolated, had not always wanted to be alone (as he knew there had been a voice before this gossamer one; before the hoarse voice that broke from silence to lash, make incidents, shame him—a girl's voice of eloquence that spoke their holiest dreams). But again he could reconstruct, image, nothing of what had been before, or when, or how, it had changed.

Ace, queen, jack. The pillar shadow fell, so, in two tracks; in the mirror depths glistened a moonlike blob, the empty solution bottle. And it worked in him: *of reason and justice and freedom . . . Dogma dead:* he remembered the full quotation, laughed bitterly. "Hah, good you do not know what you say; good Victor Hugo died and did not see it, his twentieth century."

Deuce, ten, five. Dauntlessly she began a song of their youth of belief:

These things shall be, a loftier race
than e'er the world hath known shall rise
with flame of freedom in their souls
and light of knowledge in their eyes

King, four jack. "In the twentieth century, hah!"

They shall be gentle, brave and strong
to spill no drop of blood, but dare
all . . .

. . . on earth and fire and sea and air

"To spill no drop of blood, hah! So, cadaver, and you too, cadaver Hugo, 'in the twentieth century ignorance will be dead, dogma will be dead, war will be dead, and for all mankind one country—of fulfilment?' Hah!"

And every life (long strangling cough) *shall be a song*

The cards fell from his fingers. Without warning, the bereavement and betrayal he had sheltered—compounded through the years—hidden even from himself—revealed itself,
     uncoiled,
     released,
     sprung

and with it the monstrous shapes of what had actually happened in the century.

A ravening hunger or thirst seized him. He groped into the kitchenette, switched on all three lights, piled a tray—"you have finished your night snack, Mrs. Cadaver, now I will have mine." And he was shocked at the tears that splashed on the tray.

"Salt tears. For free. I forgot to shake on salt?"

Whispered: "Lost, how much I lost."

Escaped to the grandchildren whose childhoods were childish, who had never hungered, who lived unravaged by disease in warm houses of many rooms, had all the school for which they cared, could walk on any street, stood a head taller than their grandparents, towered above—beautiful skins, straight backs, clear straightforward eyes. "Yes, you in Olshana," he said to the town of sixty years ago, "they would be nobility to you."

And was this not the dream then, come true in ways undreamed? he asked.

And are there no other children in the world? he answered, as if in her harsh voice.

And the flame of freedom, the light of knowledge?

And the drop, to spill no drop of blood?

And he thought that at six Jeannie would get up and it would be his turn to go to her room and sleep, that he could press the buzzer and she would come now; that in the afternoon Ellen Mays was coming, and this time they would play cards and he could marvel at how rouge can stand half an inch on the cheek; that in the evening the doctor would come, and he could beg him to be merciful, to stop the feeding solutions, to let her die.

To let her die, and with her their youth of belief out of which her bright, betrayed words foamed; stained words, that on her working lips came stainless.

Hours yet before Jeannie's turn. He could press the buzzer and wake her to come now; he could take a pill, and with it sleep; he could pour more brandy into his milk glass, though what he had poured was not yet touched.

Instead he went back, checked her pulse, gently tended with his knotty fingers as Jeannie had taught.

She was whimpering; her hand crawled across the covers for his. Compassionately he enfolded it, and with his free hand gathered up the cards again. Still was there thirst or hunger ravening in him.

That world of their youth—ignorant, terrible with hate, hunger, disease—how was it that living in it, in the midst of corruption, filth, treachery, degradation, they had not mistrusted man nor themselves; had believed so beautifully, so . . . falsely?

"Aaah, children," he said out loud, "how we believed, how we belonged." And he yearned to package for each of the children, the grandchildren, for everyone, *that joyous certainty, that sense of mattering, of moving and being moved, of being one and indivisible with the great of the past, with all that freed, ennobled.* Package it, stand on corners, in front of stadiums and on crowded beaches, knock on doors, give it as a fabled gift.

"And why not in cereal boxes, in soap packages?" he mocked himself. "Aah. You have taken my senses, cadaver."

Words foamed, died unsounded. Her body writhed; she made kissing motions with her mouth. (Her lips moving as she read, poring over the Book of the Martyrs, the magnifying glass superimposed over the heavy eyeglasses.) *Still she believed?* "Eva!" he whispered. "Still you believed? You lived by it? These Things *Shall* Be?"

"One pound soup meat," she answered distinctly, "one soup bone."

"My ears heard you! Ellen Mays was witness: 'Humankind . . . one has to believe.'" Imploringly: "Eva!"

"Bread, day-old." She was mumbling. "Please, in a wooden box . . . for kindling. The thread, hah, the thread breaks. Cheap thread"—and a gurgling, enormously loud, began in her throat.

"I ask for stone; she gives me bread—day-old." He pulled his hand away, shouted: "Who wanted questions? Everything you have to wake?" Then dully, "Ah, let me help you turn, poor creature."

Words jumbled, cleared. In a voice of crowded terror:

"Paul, Sammy, don't fight.

"Hannah, have I ten hands?

"How can I give it, Clara, how can I give it if I don't have?"

"You lie," he said sturdily, "there was joy too." Bitterly: "Ah how cheap you speak of us at the last."

As if to rebuke him, as if her voice had no relationship with her flailing body, she sang clearly, beautifully, a school song the children had taught her when they were little; begged:

"Not look   my hair   where they cut. . . ."

(The crown of braids shorn.) And instantly he left the mute old woman poring over the Book of the Martyrs; went past the mother treading at the sewing machine, singing with the children; past the girl in her wrinkled prison dress, hiding her hair with scarred hands, lifting to him her awkward, shamed, imploring eyes of love; and took her in his arms, dear, personal, fleshed, in all the heavy passion he had loved to rouse from her.

"Eva!"

Her little claw hand beat the covers. How much, how much can a man stand? He took up the cards, put them down, circled the beds, walked to the dresser, opened, shut drawers, brushed his hair, moved his hand bit by bit over the mirror to see what of the reflection he could blot out with each move, and felt that at any moment he would die of what was unendurable. Went to press the buzzer to wake Jeannie, looked down, saw on Jeannie's sketch pad the hospital bed, with *her;* the double bed alongside, with him; the tall pillar feeding into her veins, and their hands, his and hers, clasped, feeding each other. And as if he had been instructed he went to his bed, lay down, holding the sketch (as if it could shield against the monstrous shapes of loss, of betrayal, of death) and with his free hand took hers back into his.

So Jeannie found them in the morning.

That last day the agony was perpetual. Time after time it lifted her almost off the bed, so they had to fight to hold her down. He could not endure and left the room; wept as if there never would be tears enough.

Jeannie came to comfort him. In her light voice she said: Grandaddy, Grandaddy don't cry. She is not there, she promised me. On the last day, she said she would go back to when she first heard music, a little girl on the road of the village where she was born. She promised me. It is a wedding and they dance, while the flutes so joyous and vibrant tremble in the air. Leave her there, Grandaddy, it is all right. She promised me. Come back, come back and help her poor body to die.

For two of that generation
Seevya and Genya
Dauntless, Infinite, Incorruptible
Death deepens the wonder

Bernard Malamud (1914–   )

Bernard Malamud's first novel *The Natural* (1952) was a mythic treatment of a base-ball player; it signaled the advent of a writer who combines fantasy and realism to create works of imagination that are fresh, humorous, and profound. His imagery, cadences, metaphors, his themes, plots, and characters express a unique modern tragicomic vision. He is easily one of the most distinctive voices in American fiction, and he seems equally at home in the short story and the novel. In 1957 his novel *The Assistant* appeared and instantly won a high place among American novels of our era, and in 1959 his volume of short stories *The Magic Barrel,* whose title story follows this note, received the National Book Award. He has since published several volumes of stories and several novels.

Although his work transcends its subject matter and has universal implications for our age, it deals almost always with the Jewish experience, an experience which provided him an approach to reality and a tone for presenting it. The mixture of the tragic and comic is common in the literature of the people whose will to survive was fueled in part by comic irony.

Malamud's characters, like Leo Finkle in "The Magic Barrel," are often caught in a "ghetto" of the spirit, unable to experience human love or understanding. Suffering and defeat are their lot, but out of suffering comes a hint of redemption and out of defeat perhaps an approximate victory of the spirit. But Malamud's end-ings hardly provide the kind of uplift the reader may hope for: for at the heart of his vision lies ironic ambiguity.

Thus, after Finkle has persuaded the reader that he will "convert [the prosti-tute] to goodness, himself to God," and "Violins and lit candles revolved in the sky," then Malamud points out that "Around the corner, Salzman leaning against the wall, chanted prayers for the dead." Prayers for the dead! Just as the reader relaxes into satisfaction, the writer undercuts him.

Hopes dashed can be hard on a reader. What makes this ending endurable is the comic quality which has prepared us to expect almost anything. All of Malamud has this comic quality (even *The Fixer,* which takes place largely in a prison). Theo-dore Solotaroff says that Malamud's is an "implacably comic world of absurd rever-sals and last straws and of uncertain stairs that lead seemingly nowhere."

Often, as in "The Magic Barrel," the beginning of a Malamud story is flat, matter-of-fact, comically prosaic, accepting the bizarre (the rabbinical student who seeks a wife in order to get a better congregation) as if it were perfectly usual. That same flat tone tells the reader that the matchmaker "appeared one night out of the dark fourth-floor hallway" and was of "slight but dignified build" and "smelled frankly of fish." These hints prepare the reader to accept the later fantasy.

Soon the incongruities deepen: between piety and rascality, the satiric and the portentous, the ironic and the spiritual. The most significant disparity is between naturalism (lonely widows, elderly spinsters, lame girls, all craving love, all losers) and the marvelous (the sudden appearances of the matchmaker, the picture of his daughter falling from the packet). And over the whole story hovers the quality of Yiddish speech: inversions, questions, analogies, exaggerations, the persistent rhythms, the cadence.

But comedy is certainly not the whole story. Important notions find expression. Leo comes to understand that his life has been empty. He suffers, and out of his suffering, a little miracle occurs, and he is redeemed. Or is he?

The Magic Barrel

Not long ago there lived in uptown New York, in a small almost meager room, though crowded with books, Leo Finkle, a rabbinical student in the Yeshivah University. Finkle, after six years of study, was to be ordained in June and had been advised by an acquaintance that he might find it easier to win himself a congregation if he were married. Since he had no present prospects of marriage, after two tormented days of turning it over in his mind, he called in Pinye Salzman, a marriage broker whose two-line advertisement he had read in the *Forward*.

The matchmaker appeared one night out of the dark fourth-floor hallway of the graystone rooming house where Finkle lived, grasping a black, strapped portfolio that had been worn thin with use. Salzman, who had been long in the business, was of slight but dignified build, wearing an old hat, and an overcoat too short and tight for him. He smelled frankly of fish, which he loved to eat, and although he was missing a few teeth, his presence was not displeasing, because of an amiable manner curiously contrasted with mournful eyes. His voice, his lips, his wisp of beard, his bony fingers were animated, but give him a moment of repose and his mild blue eyes revealed a depth of sadness, a characteristic that put Leo a little at ease although the situation, for him, was inherently tense.

He at once informed Salzman why he had asked him to come, explaining that his home was in Cleveland, and that but for his parents, who had married comparatively late in life, he was alone in the world. He had for six years devoted himself almost entirely to his studies, as a result of which, understandably, he had found himself without time for a social life and the company of young women. Therefore he thought it the better part of trial and error—of embarrassing fumbling—to call in an experi-

Bernard Malamud, "The Magic Barrel," from *The Magic Barrel*, Copyright 1950, 1951, 1952, 1953, 1954, 1955, 1956, 1958 Bernard Malamud. Copyright 1953 by the *American Mercury* magazine. Reprinted by permission of Farrar, Strauss & Giroux, Inc.

enced person to advise him on these matters. He remarked in passing that the function
of the marriage broker was ancient and honorable, highly approved in the Jewish
community, because it made practical the necessary without hindering joy. Moreover,
his own parents had been brought together by a matchmaker. They had made, if not
a financially profitable marriage—since neither had possessed any worldly goods to
speak of—at least a successful one in the sense of their everlasting devotion to each
other. Salzman listened in embarrassed surprise, sensing a sort of apology. Later,
however, he experienced a glow of pride in his work, an emotion that had left him
years ago, and he heartily approved of Finkle.

The two went to their business. Leo had led Salzman to the only clear place in the
room, a table near a window that overlooked the lamp-lit city. He seated himself at the
matchmaker's side but facing him, attempting by an act of will to suppress the unpleasant tickle in his throat. Salzman eagerly unstrapped his portfolio and removed a
loose rubber band from a thin packet of much-handled cards. As he flipped through
them, a gesture and sound that physically hurt Leo, the student pretended not to see
and gazed steadfastly out the window. Although it was still February, winter was on
its last legs, signs of which he had for the first time in years begun to notice. He now
observed the round white moon, moving high in the sky through a cloud menagerie,
and watched with half-open mouth as it penetrated a huge hen, and dropped out of
her like an egg laying itself. Salzman, though pretending through eyeglasses he had
just slipped on, to be engaged in scanning the writing on the cards, stole occasional
glances at the young man's distinguished face, noting with pleasure the long, severe
scholar's nose, brown eyes heavy with learning, sensitive yet ascetic lips, and a certain,
almost hollow quality of the dark cheeks. He gazed around at shelves upon shelves of
books and let out a soft, contented sigh.

When Leo's eyes fell upon the cards, he counted six spread out in Salzman's
hand.

"So few?" he asked in disappointment.

"You wouldn't believe me how much cards I got in my office," Salzman replied.
"The drawers are already filled to the top, so I keep them now in a barrel, but is every
girl good for a new rabbi?"

Leo blushed at this, regretting all he had revealed of himself in a curriculum vitae
he had sent to Salzman. He had thought it best to acquaint him with his strict stan-
dards and specifications, but in having done so, felt he had told the marriage broker
more than was absolutely necessary.

He hesitantly inquired, "Do you keep photographs of your clients on file?"

"First comes family, amount of dowry, also what kind promises," Salzman replied, unbuttoning his tight coat and settling himself in the chair. "After comes pictures, rabbi."

"Call me Mr. Finkle. I'm not yet a rabbi."

Salzman said he would, but instead called him doctor, which he changed to rabbi
when Leo was not listening too attentively.

Salzman adjusted his horn-rimmed spectacles, gently cleared his throat and read
in an eager voice the contents of the top card:

"Sophie P. Twenty four years. Widow one year. No children. Educated high
school and two years college. Father promises eight thousand dollars. Has wonderful
wholesale business. Also real estate. On the mother's side comes teachers, also one
actor. Well known on Second Avenue."

Leo gazed up in surprise. "Did you say a widow?"

"A widow don't mean spoiled, rabbi. She lived with her husband maybe four months. He was a sick boy she made a mistake to marry him."

"Marrying a widow has never entered my mind."

"This is because you have no experience. A widow, especially if she is young and healthy like this girl, is a wonderful person to marry. She will be thankful to you the rest of her life. Believe me, if I was looking now for a bride, I would marry a widow."

Leo reflected, then shook his head.

Salzman hunched his shoulders in an almost imperceptible gesture of disappointment. He placed the card down on the wooden table and began to read another:

"Lily H. High school teacher. Regular. Not a substitute. Has savings and new Dodge car. Lived in Paris one year. Father is successful dentist thirty-five years. Interested in professional man. Well Americanized family. Wonderful opportunity."

"I knew her personally," said Salzman. "I wish you could see this girl. She is a doll. Also very intelligent. All day you could talk to her about books and theyater and what not. She also knows current events."

"I don't believe you mentioned her age?"

"Her age?" Salzman said, raising his brows. "Her age is thirty-two years."

Leo said after a while, "I'm afraid that seems a little too old."

Salzman let out a laugh. "So how old are you, rabbi?"

"Twenty-seven."

"So what is the difference, tell me, between twenty-seven and thirty-two? My own wife is seven years older than me. So what did I suffer?—Nothing. If Rothschild's a daughter wants to marry you, would you say on account her age, no?"

"Yes," Leo said dryly.

Salzman shook off the no in the yes. "Five years don't mean a thing. I give you my word that when you will live with her for one week you will forget her age. What does it mean five years—that she lived more and knows more than somebody who is younger? On this girl, God bless her, years are not wasted. Each one that it comes makes better the bargain."

"What subject does she teach in high school?"

"Languages. If you heard the way she speaks French, you will think it is music. I am in the business twenty-five years, and I recommend her with my whole heart. Believe me, I know what I'm talking, rabbi."

"What's on the next card?" Leo said abruptly.

Salzman reluctantly turned up the third card:

"Ruth K. Nineteen years. Honor student. Father offers thirteen thousand cash to the right bridegroom. He is a medical doctor. Stomach specialist with marvelous practice. Brother in law owns own garment business. Particular people."

Salzman looked as if he had read his trump card.

"Did you say nineteen?" Leo asked with interest.

"On the dot."

"Is she attractive?" He blushed. "Pretty?"

Salzman kissed his finger tips. "A little doll. On this I give you my word. Let me call the father tonight and you will see what means pretty."

But Leo was troubled. "You're sure she's that young?"

"This I am positive. The father will show you the birth certificate."

"Are you positive there isn't something wrong with her?" Leo insisted.

"Who says there is wrong?"

"I don't understand why an American girl her age should go to a marriage broker."

A smile spread over Salzman's face.

"So for the same reason you went, she comes."

Leo flushed. "I am pressed for time."

Salzman, realizing he had been tactless, quickly explained. "The father came, not her. He wants she should have the best, so he looks around himself. When we will locate the right boy he will introduce him and encourage. This makes a better marriage than if a young girl without experience takes for herself. I don't have to tell you this."

"But don't you think this young girl believes in love?" Leo spoke uneasily.

Salzman was about to guffaw but caught himself and said soberly, "Love comes with the right person, not before."

Leo parted dry lips but did not speak. Noticing that Salzman had snatched a glance at the next card, he cleverly asked, "How is her health?"

"Perfect," Salzman said, breathing with difficulty. "Of course, she is a little lame on her right foot from an auto accident that it happened to her when she was twelve years, but nobody notices on account she is so brilliant and also beautiful."

Leo got up heavily and went to the window. He felt curiously bitter and upbraided himself for having called in the marriage broker. Finally, he shook his head.

"Why not?" Salzman persisted, the pitch of his voice rising.

"Because I detest stomach specialists."

"So what do you care what is his business? After you marry her do you need him? Who says he must come every Friday night in your house?"

Ashamed of the way the talk was going, Leo dismissed Salzman, who went home with heavy, melancholy eyes.

Though he had felt only relief at the marriage broker's departure, Leo was in low spirits the next day. He explained it as arising from Salzman's failure to produce a suitable bride for him. He did not care for his type of clientele. But when Leo found himself hesitating whether to seek out another matchmaker, one more polished than Pinye, he wondered if it could be—his protestations to the contrary, and although he honored his father and mother—that he did not, in essence, care for the matchmaking institution? This thought he quickly put out of mind yet found himself still upset. All day he ran around in the woods—missed an important appointment, forgot to give out his laundry, walked out of a Broadway cafeteria without paying and had to run back with the ticket in his hand; had even not recognized his landlady in the street when she passed with a friend and courteously called out, "A good evening to you, Doctor Finkle." By nightfall, however, he had regained sufficient calm to sink his nose into a book and there found peace from his thoughts.

Almost at once there came a knock on the door. Before Leo could say enter, Salzman, commercial cupid, was standing in the room. His face was gray and meager, his expression hungry, and he looked as if he would expire on his feet. Yet the marriage broker managed, by some trick of the muscles, to display a broad smile.

"So good evening. I am invited?"

Leo nodded, disturbed to see him again, yet unwilling to ask the man to leave.

Beaming still, Salzman laid his portfolio on the table, "Rabbi, I got for you tonight good news."

"I've asked you not to call me rabbi. I'm still a student."

"Your worries are finished. I have for you a first-class bride."

"Leave me in peace concerning this subject." Leo pretended lack of interest.

"The world will dance at your wedding."

"Please, Mr. Salzman, no more."

"But first must come back my strength," Salzman said weakly. He fumbled with the portfolio straps and took out of the leather case an oily paper bag, from which he extracted a hard, seeded roll and a small, smoked white fish. With a quick motion of his hand he stripped the fish out of its skin and began ravenously to chew. "All day in a rush," he muttered.

Leo watched him eat.

"A sliced tomato you have maybe?" Salzman hesitantly inquired.

"No."

The marriage broker shut his eyes and ate. When he had finished he carefully cleaned up the crumbs and rolled up the remains of the fish, in the paper bag. His spectacled eyes roamed the room until he discovered, amid some piles of books, a one-burner gas stove. Lifting his hat he humbly asked, "A glass tea you got, rabbi?"

Conscience-stricken, Leo rose and brewed the tea. He served it with a chunk of lemon and two cubes of lump sugar, delighting Salzman.

After he had drunk his tea, Salzman's strength and good spirits were restored.

"So tell me, rabbi," he said amiably, "you considered some more the three clients I mentioned yesterday?"

"There was no need to consider."

"Why not?"

"None of them suits me."

"What then suits you?"

Leo let it pass because he could give only a confused answer.

Without waiting for a reply, Salzman asked, "You remember this girl I talked to you—the high school teacher?"

"Age thirty-two?"

But, surprisingly, Salzman's face lit in a smile. "Age twenty-nine."

Leo shot him a look. "Reduced from thirty-two?"

"A mistake," Salzman avowed. "I talked today with the dentist. He took me to his safety deposit box and showed me the birth certificate. She was twenty-nine years last August. They made her a party in the mountains where she went for her vacation. When her father spoke to me the first time I forgot to write the age and I told you thirty-two, but now I remember this was a different client, a widow."

"The same one you told me about? I thought she was twenty-four?"

"A different. Am I responsible that the world is filled with widows?"

"No, but I'm not interested in them, nor for that matter, in school teachers."

Salzman pulled his clasped hands to his breast. Looking at the ceiling he devoutly exclaimed, "Yiddishe kinder, what can I say to somebody that he is not interested in high school teachers? So what then you are interested?"

Leo flushed but controlled himself.

"In what else will you be interested," Salzman went on, "if you not interested in this fine girl that speaks four languages and has personally in the bank ten thousand dollars? Also her father guarantees further twelve thousand. Also she has a new car, wonderful clothes, talks on all subjects, and she will give you a first-class home and children. How near do we come in our life to paradise?"

"If she's so wonderful, why hasn't she married ten years ago?"

"Why?" said Salzman with a heavy laugh. "—Why? Because she is *partikiler*. This is why. She wants the *best*."

Leo was silent, amused at how he had entangled himself. But Salzman had aroused his interest in Lily H., and he began seriously to consider calling on her. When the marriage broker observed how intently Leo's mind was at work on the facts he had supplied, he felt certain they would soon come to an agreement.

Late Saturday afternoon, conscious of Salzman, Leo Finkle walked with Lily Hirschorn along Riverside Drive. He walked briskly and erectly, wearing with distinction the black fedora he had that morning taken with trepidation out of the dusty hat box on his closet shelf, and the heavy black Saturday coat he had thoroughly whisked clean. Leo also owned a walking stick, a present from a distant relative, but quickly put temptation aside and did not use it. Lily, petite and not unpretty, had on something signifying the approach of spring. She was au courant, animatedly, with all sorts of subjects, and he weighed her words and found her surprisingly sound—score another for Salzman, whom he uneasily sensed to be somewhere around, hiding perhaps high in a tree along the street, flashing the lady signals with a pocket mirror; or perhaps a cloven-hoofed Pan, piping nuptial ditties as he danced his invisible way before them, strewing wild buds on the walk and purple grapes in their path, symbolizing fruit of a union, though there was of course still none.

Lily startled Leo by remarking, "I was thinking of Mr. Salzman, a curious figure, wouldn't you say?"

Not certain what to answer, he nodded.

She bravely went on, blushing, "I for one am grateful for his introducing us. Aren't you?"

He courteously replied, "I am."

"I mean," she said with a little laugh—and it was all in good taste, or at least gave the effect of being not in bad—"do you mind that we came together so?"

He was not displeased with her honesty, recognizing that she meant to set the relationship aright, and understanding that it took a certain amount of experience in life, and courage, to want to do it quite that way. One had to have some sort of past to make that kind of beginning.

He said that he did not mind. Salzman's function was traditional and honorable—valuable for what it might achieve, which, he pointed out, was frequently nothing.

Lily agreed with a sigh. They walked on for a while and she said after a long silence, again with a nervous laugh, "Would you mind if I asked you something a little bit personal? Frankly, I find the subject fascinating." Although Leo shrugged, she went on half embarrassedly, "How was it that you came to your calling? I mean was it a sudden passionate inspiration?"

Leo, after a time, slowly replied, "I was always interested in the Law."

"You saw revealed in it the presence of the Highest?"

He nodded and changed the subject. "I understand that you spent a little time in Paris, Miss Hirschorn?"

"Oh, did Mr. Salzman tell you, Rabbi Finkle?" Leo winced but she went on, "It was ages ago and almost forgotten. I remember I had to return for my sister's wedding."

And Lily would not be put off. "When," she asked in a trembly voice, "did you become enamored of God?"

He stared at her. Then it came to him that she was talking not about Leo Finkle, but of a total stranger, some mystical figure, perhaps even passionate prophet that Salzman had dreamed up for her—no relation to the living or dead. Leo trembled with rage and weakness. The trickster had obviously sold her a bill of goods, just as he had him, who'd expected to become acquainted with a young lady of twenty-nine, only to behold, the moment he laid eyes upon her strained and anxious face, a woman past thirty-five and aging rapidly. Only his self control had kept him this long in her presence.

"I am not," he said gravely, "a talented religious person," and in seeking words to go on, found himself possessed by shame and fear. "I think," he said in a strained manner, "that I came to God not because I loved Him, but because I did not."

This confession he spoke harshly because its unexpectedness shook him.

Lily wilted. Leo saw a profusion of loaves of bread go flying like ducks high over his head, not unlike the winged loaves by which he had counted himself to sleep last night. Mercifully, then, it snowed, which he would not put past Salzman's machinations.

He was infuriated with the marriage broker and swore he would throw him out of the room the minute he reappeared. But Salzman did not come that night, and when Leo's anger had subsided, an unaccountable despair grew in its place. At first he thought this was caused by his disappointment in Lily, but before long it became evident that he had involved himself with Salzman without a true knowledge of his own intent. He gradually realized—with an emptiness that seized him with six hands—that he had called in the broker to find him a bride because he was incapable of doing it himself. This terrifying insight he had derived as a result of his meeting and conversation with Lily Hirschorn. Her probing questions had somehow irritated him into revealing—to himself more than her—the true nature of his relationship to God, and from that it had come upon him, with shocking force, that apart from his parents, he had never loved anyone. Or perhaps it went the other way, that he did not love God so well as he might, because he had not loved man. It seemed to Leo that his whole life stood starkly revealed and he saw himself for the first time as he truly was—unloved and loveless. This bitter but somehow not fully unexpected revelation brought him to a point of panic, controlled only by extraordinary effort. He covered his face with his hands and cried.

The week that followed was the worst of his life. He did not eat and lost weight. His beard darkened and grew ragged. He stopped attending seminars and almost never opened a book. He seriously considered leaving the Yeshivah, although he was deeply troubled at the thought of the loss of all his years of study—saw them like pages torn from a book, strewn over the city—and at the devastating effect of this decision upon his parents. But he had lived without knowledge of himself, and never in the Five Books and all the Commentaries—mea culpa—had the truth been revealed to him. He did not know where to turn, and in all this desolating loneliness there was no *to whom,* although he often thought of Lily but not once could bring himself to go downstairs and make the call. He became touchy and irritable, especially with his landlady, who asked him all manner of personal questions; on the other hand, sensing his own disagreeableness, he waylaid her on the stairs and apologized abjectly, until mortified, she ran from him. Out of this, however, he drew the consolation that he was a Jew and that a Jew suffered. But gradually, as the long and terrible week drew to a close, he regained his composure and some idea of purpose in life: to go on as planned.

Although he was imperfect, the ideal was not. As for his quest of a bride, the thought of continuing afflicted him with anxiety and heartburn, yet perhaps with this new knowledge of himself he would be more successful than in the past. Perhaps love would now come to him and a bride to that love. And for this sanctified seeking who needed a Salzman?

The marriage broker, a skeleton with haunted eyes, returned that very night. He looked, withal, the picture of frustrated expectancy—as if he had steadfastly waited the week at Miss Lily Hirschorn's side for a telephone call that never came.

Casually coughing, Salzman came immediately to the point: "So how did you like her?"

Leo's anger rose and he could not refrain from chiding the matchmaker: "Why did you lie to me, Salzman?"

Salzman's pale face went dead white, the world had snowed on him.

"Did you not state that she was twenty-nine?" Leo insisted.

"I give you my word—"

"She was thirty-five, if a day. *At least* thirty-five."

"Of this don't be too sure. Her father told me—"

"Never mind. The worst of it was that you lied to her."

"How did I lie to her, tell me?"

"You told her things about me that weren't true. You made me out to be more, consequently less than I am. She had in mind a totally different person, a sort of semimystical Wonder Rabbi."

"All I said, you was a religious man."

"I can imagine."

Salzman sighed. "This is my weakness that I have," he confessed. "My wife says to me I shouldn't be a salesman, but when I have two fine people that they would be wonderful to be married, I am so happy that I talk too much." He smiled wanly. "This is why Salzman is a poor man."

Leo's anger left him. "Well, Salzman, I'm afraid that's all."

The marriage broker fastened hungry eyes on him.

"You don't want any more a bride?"

"I do," said Leo, "but I have decided to seek her in a different way. I am no longer interested in an arranged marriage. To be frank, I now admit the necessity of premarital love. That is, I want to be in love with the one I marry."

"Love?" said Salzman, astounded. After a moment he remarked, "For us, our love is our life, not for the ladies. In the ghetto they—"

"I know, I know," said Leo. "I've thought of it often. Love, I have said to myself, should be a by-product of living and worship rather than its own end. Yet for myself I find it necessary to establish the level of my need and fulfill it."

Salzman shrugged but answered, "Listen, rabbi, if you want love, this I can find for you also. I have such beautiful clients that you will love them the minute your eyes will see them."

Leo smiled unhappily. "I'm afraid you don't understand."

But Salzman hastily unstrapped his portfolio and withdrew a manila packet from it.

"Pictures," he said, quickly laying the envelope on the table.

Leo called after him to take the pictures away, but as if on the wings of the wind, Salzman had disappeared.

March came. Leo had returned to his regular routine. Although he felt not quite himself yet—lacked energy—he was making plans for a more active social life. Of course it would cost something, but he was an expert in cutting corners; and when there were no corners left he would make circles rounder. All the while Salzman's pictures had lain on the table, gathering dust. Occasionally as Leo sat studying, or enjoying a cup of tea, his eyes fell on the manila envelope, but he never opened it.

The days went by and no social life to speak of developed with a member of the opposite sex—it was difficult, given the circumstances of his situation. One morning Leo toiled up the stairs to his room and stared out the window at the city. Although the day was bright his view of it was dark. For some time he watched the people in the street below hurrying along and then turned with a heavy heart to his little room. On the table was the packet. With a sudden relentless gesture he tore it open. For a half-hour he stood by the table in a state of excitement, examining the photographs of the ladies Salzman had included. Finally, with a deep sigh he put them down. There were six, of varying degrees of attractiveness, but look at them long enough and they all became Lily Hirschorn: all past their prime, all starved behind bright smiles, not a true personality in the lot. Life, despite their frantic yoohooings, had passed them by; they were pictures in a brief case that stank of fish. After a while, however, as Leo attempted to return the photographs into the envelope, he found in it another, a snapshot of the type taken by a machine for a quarter. He gazed at it a moment and let out a cry.

Her face deeply moved him. Why, he could at first not say. It gave him the impression of youth—spring flowers, yet age—a sense of having been used to the bone, wasted; this came from the eyes which were hauntingly familiar, yet absolutely strange. He had a vivid impression that he had met her before, but try as he might he could not place her although he could almost recall her name, as if he had read it in her own handwriting. No, this couldn't be; he would have remembered her. It was not, he affirmed, that she had an extraordinary beauty—no, though her face was attractive enough; it was that *something* about her moved him. Feature for feature, even some of the ladies of the photographs could do better; but she leaped forth to his heart—had *lived,* or wanted to—more than just wanted, perhaps regretted how she had lived—had somehow deeply suffered: it could be seen in the depths of those reluctant eyes, and from the way the light enclosed and shone from her, and within her, opening realms of possibility: this was her own. Her he desired. His head ached and eyes narrowed with the intensity of his gazing, then as if an obscure fog had blown up in the mind, he experienced fear of her and was aware that he had received an impression, somehow, of evil. He shuddered, saying softly, it is thus with us all. Leo brewed some tea in a small pot and sat sipping it without sugar, to calm himself. But before he had finished drinking, again with excitement he examined the face and found it good: good for Leo Finkle. Only such a one could understand him and help him seek whatever he was seeking. She might, perhaps, love him. How she had happened to be among the discards in Salzman's barrel he could never guess, but he knew he must urgently go find her.

Leo rushed downstairs, grabbed up the Bronx telephone book, and searched for Salzman's home address. He was not listed, nor was his office. Neither was he in the Manhattan book. But Leo remembered having written down the address on a slip of paper after he had read Salzman's advertisement in the "personals" column of the *Forward.* He ran up to his room and tore through his papers, without luck. It was exasperating. Just when he needed the matchmaker he was nowhere to be found. Fortunately Leo remembered to look in his wallet. There on a card he found his name written and a Bronx address. No phone number was listed, the reason—Leo now recalled—he had originally communicated with Salzman by letter. He got on his coat, put a hat on over his skull cap and hurried to the subway station. All the way to the far end of the Bronx he sat on the edge of his seat. He was more than once tempted to take out the picture and see if the girl's face was as he remembered it, but he refrained, allowing the snapshot to remain in his inside coat pocket, content to have her so close. When the train pulled into the station he was waiting at the door and bolted out. He quickly located the street Salzman had advertised.

The building he sought was less than a block from the subway, but it was not an office building, nor even a loft, nor a store in which one could rent office space. It was a very old tenement house. Leo found Salzman's name in pencil on a soiled tag under the bell and climbed three dark flights to his apartment. When he knocked, the door was opened by a thin, asthmatic, gray-haired woman, in felt slippers.

"Yes?" she said, expecting nothing. She listened without listening. He could have sworn he had seen her, too, before but knew it was an illusion.

"Salzman—does he live here? Pinye Salzman," he said, "the matchmaker?"

She stared at him a long minute. "Of course."

He felt embarrassed. "Is he in?"

"No." Her mouth, though left open, offered nothing more.

"The matter is urgent. Can you tell me where his office is?"

"In the air." She pointed upward.

"You mean he has no office?" Leo asked.

"In his socks."

He peered into the apartment. It was sunless and dingy, one large room divided by a half-open curtain, beyond which he could see a sagging metal bed. The near side of a room was crowded with rickety chairs, old bureaus, a three-legged table, racks of cooking utensils, and all the apparatus of a kitchen. But there was no sign of Salzman or his magic barrel, probably also a figment of the imagination. An odor of frying fish made Leo weak to the knees.

"Where is he?" he insisted. "I've got to see your husband."

At length she answered, "So who knows where he is? Every time he thinks a new thought he runs to a different place. Go home, he will find you."

"Tell him Leo Finkle."

She gave no sign she had heard.

He walked downstairs, depressed.

But Salzman, breathless, stood waiting at his door.

Leo was astounded and overjoyed. "How did you get here before me?"

"I rushed."

"Come inside."

They entered. Leo fixed tea, and a sardine sandwich for Salzman. As they were drinking he reached behind him for the packet of pictures and handed them to the marriage broker.

Salzman put down his glass and said expectantly, "You found somebody you like?"

"Not among these."

The marriage broker turned away.

"Here is the one I want." Leo held forth the snapshot.

Salzman slipped on his glasses and took the picture into his trembling hand. He turned ghastly and let out a groan.

"What's the matter?" cried Leo.

"Excuse me. Was an accident this picture. She isn't for you."

Salzman frantically shoved the manila packet into his portfolio. He thrust the snapshot into his pocket and fled down the stairs.

Leo, after momentary paralysis, gave chase and cornered the marriage broker in the vestibule. The landlady made hysterical outcries but neither of them listened.

"Give me back the picture, Salzman."

"No." The pain in his eyes was terrible.

"Tell me who she is then."

"This I can't tell you. Excuse me."

He made to depart, but Leo, forgetting himself, seized the matchmaker by his tight coat and shook him frenziedly.

"Please," sighed Salzman. *"Please."*

Leo ashamedly let him go. "Tell me who she is," he begged. "It's very important for me to know."

"She is not for you. She is a wild one—wild, without shame. This is not a bride for a rabbi."

"What do you mean wild?"

"Like an animal. Like a dog. For her to be poor was a sin. This is why to me she is dead now."

"In God's name, what do you mean?"

"Her I can't introduce to you," Salzman cried.

"Why are you so excited?"

"Why, he asks," Salzman said, bursting into tears. "This is my baby, my Stella, she should burn in hell."

Leo hurried up to bed and hid under the covers. Under the covers he thought his life through. Although he soon fell asleep he could not sleep her out of his mind. He woke, beating his breast. Though he prayed to be rid of her, his prayers went unanswered. Through days of torment he endlessly struggled not to love her; fearing success, he escaped it. He then concluded to convert her to goodness, himself to God. The idea alternately nauseated and exalted him.

He perhaps did not know that he had come to a final decision until he encountered Salzman in a Broadway cafeteria. He was sitting alone at a rear table, sucking the bony remains of a fish. The marriage broker appeared haggard, and transparent to the point of vanishing.

Salzman looked up at first without recognizing him. Leo had grown a pointed beard and his eyes were weighted with wisdom.

"Salzman," he said, "love has at last come to my heart."

"Who can love from a picture?" mocked the marriage broker.

"It is not impossible."

"If you can love her, then you can love anybody. Let me show you some new clients that they just sent me their photographs. One is a little doll."

"Just her I want," Leo murmured.

"Don't be a fool, doctor. Don't bother with her."

"Put me in touch with her, Salzman," Leo said humbly. "Perhaps I can be of service."

Salzman had stopped eating and Leo understood with emotion that it was now arranged.

Leaving the cafeteria, he was, however, afflicted by a tormenting suspicion that Salzman had planned it all to happen this way.

Leo was informed by letter that she would meet him on a certain corner, and she was there one spring night, waiting under a street lamp. He appeared, carrying a small bouquet of violets and rosebuds. Stella stood by the lamp post, smoking. She wore white with red shoes, which fitted his expectations, although in a troubled moment he had imagined the dress red, and only the shoes white. She waited uneasily and shyly. From afar he saw that her eyes—clearly her father's—were filled with desperate innocence. He pictured, in her, his own redemption. Violins and lit candles revolved in the sky. Leo ran forward with flowers outthrust.

Around the corner, Salzman, leaning against a wall, chanted prayers for the dead.

Saul Bellow (1915–   )

"Bellow's novels," writes R. R. Dutton, "never really probe the depth and breadth of anyone. What they do is explore thoroughly a particular human condition through character." That "human condition" is Bellow's essential subject, and all his novels have a single individual at their center. Though Bellow continually pictures man as alienated, victimized, adrift in a hostile or indifferent society, he never—like some "modernist" writers—backs the premise that man is fundamentally absurd or meaningless. He has a "strong sense of self," and the human individual is to him "subangelic." No facile optimist, he nevertheless rejects the knee-jerk pessimism of those who would picture man as "wretched by nature." In his important essay "Distractions of a Fiction Writer," Bellow writes:

> If man wretched by nature is represented, what we have . . . is only accurate reporting. But if it is man in the image of God, man a little lower than the angels who is impotent, the case is not the same. . . . Why should wretched man need power or wish to inflate himself with imaginary glory? If this is what power signifies it can only be vanity to suffer from impotence. On the nobler assumption he should have at least sufficient power to overcome ignominy and to complete his own life.

Bellow's novels can be read as progressive case studies in individuals trying to "overcome ignominy" and to "complete" their own lives. In *Dangling Man* (1944) and *The Victim* (1947) we are given studies in, mainly, defeat and impotence; but in the novels that followed—*The Adventures of Augie March* (1953), *Seize the Day* (1956), *Henderson the Rain King* (1959), *Herzog* (1964), *Mosby's Memoirs* (1968), and *Mr. Sammler's Planet* (1971)—we meet protagonists who move in spite of their own weaknesses and society's road blocks, toward self-realization. Serious as they are, these books are also often outrageously funny. In his last novel the conflict becomes one between science (which he elsewhere calls the "fictive superself") and the intuitive, "subangelic" individual—an issue which he has spelled out as well in his recent essay "Machines and Storybooks":

> Yes, technology is the product of science and capital, and of socialization and the division of labor. It is a triumph of the accurate power of innumerable brains and wills acting in unison to produce a machine or a commodity. These many wills constitute a fictive superself, astonishingly effective in converting dreams into machines. Literature, by contrast, is produced by the single individual, concerns itself with individuals, and is read by separate persons. And the single individual—this unit of vital being, of nerve and brain, which judges or knows, is happy or mourns, actually lives and actually dies—is unfavorably compared with that fictive superself, which, acting in unison and according to plan, produces jet planes, atom smashers, computers, rockets, and other modern technological wonders.

Needless to say, Bellow's writings are attempts to right the balance.

The story "Looking for Mr. Green" can be read, like much of Bellow's fiction, on both a realistic and allegorical level. George Grebe is looking for Mr. Green in order to give him his relief check. But the inhabitants of the slum tenement are suspicious and hostile toward this "outsider," this alien. Yet Grebe persists in his search ("it was important that there was a real Mr. Green whom they could not keep him from reaching"), just as in his fiction Bellow persists in his search for the "real" individual in spite of society's hostility and indifference. Yet the story is also as realistic as anything in Richard Wright or Ernest Hemingway. It is a real world that Bellow inhabits, though he brings to it a romantic vision.

Bellow's home is Chicago, though he was born in Quebec of Russian immigrant parents. Thrice married, he has taught at many American universities, and among his many honors are the National Book Award, the French *Croix de Chevalier des Arts et Lettres,* and an honorary Doctor of Letters from Northwestern University.

Looking for Mr. Green

Whatsoever thy hand findeth to do, do it with thy might. . . .

Hard work? No, it wasn't really so hard. He wasn't used to walking and stair-climbing, but the physical difficulty of his new job was not what George Grebe felt most. He was delivering relief checks in the Negro district, and although he was a native Chicagoan this was not a part of the city he knew much about—it needed a depression to introduce him to it. No, it wasn't literally hard work, not as reckoned in foot-pounds, but yet he was beginning to feel the strain of it, to grow aware of its peculiar difficulty. He could find the streets and numbers, but the clients were not where they were supposed to be, and he felt like a hunter inexperienced in the camouflage of his game. It was an

From *Mosby's Memoirs* by Saul Bellow. Copyright 1951 by Saul Bellow. Reprinted by permission of The Viking Press, Inc.

unfavorable day, too—fall, and cold, dark weather, windy. But, anyway, instead of shells in his deep trenchcoat pocket he had the cardboard of checks, punctured for the spindles of the file, the holes reminding him of the holes in player-piano paper. And he didn't look much like a hunter, either; his was a city figure entirely, belted up in this Irish conspirator's coat. He was slender without being tall, stiff in the back, his legs looking shabby in a pair of old tweed pants gone through and fringy at the cuffs. With this stiffness, he kept his head forward, so that his face was red from the sharpness of the weather; and it was an indoors sort of face with gray eyes that persisted in some kind of thought and yet seemed to avoid definiteness of conclusion. He wore sideburns that surprised you somewhat by the tough curl of the blond hair and the effect of assertion in their length. He was not so mild as he looked, nor so youthful; and nevertheless there was no effort on his part to seem what he was not. He was an educated man; he was a bachelor; he was in some ways simple; without lushing, he liked a drink; his luck had not been good. Nothing was deliberately hidden.

He felt that his luck was better than usual today. When he had reported for work that morning he had expected to be shut up in the relief office at a clerk's job, for he had been hired downtown as a clerk, and he was glad to have, instead, the freedom of the streets and welcomed, at least at first, the vigor of the cold and even the blowing of the hard wind. But on the other hand he was not getting on with the distribution of the checks. It was true that it was a city job; nobody expected you to push too hard at a city job. His supervisor, that young Mr. Raynor, had practically told him that. Still, he wanted to do well at it. For one thing, when he knew how quickly he could deliver a batch of checks, he would know also how much time he could expect to clip for himself. And then, too, the clients would be waiting for their money. That was not the most important consideration, though it certainly mattered to him. No, but he wanted to do well, simply for doing-well's sake, to acquit himself decently of a job because he so rarely had a job to do that required just this sort of energy. Of the peculiar energy he now had a superabundance; once it had started to flow, it flowed all too heavily. And, for the time being anyway, he was balked. He could not find Mr. Green.

So he stood in his big-skirted trenchcoat with a large envelope in his hand and papers showing from his pocket, wondering why people should be so hard to locate who were too feeble or sick to come to the station to collect their own checks. But Raynor had told him that tracking them down was not easy at first and had offered him some advice on how to proceed. "If you can see the postman, he's your first man to ask, and your best bet. If you can't connect with him, try the stores and tradespeople around. Then the janitor and the neighbors. But you'll find the closer you come to your man the less people will tell you. They don't want to tell you anything."

"Because I'm a stranger."

"Because you're white. We ought to have a Negro doing this, but we don't at the moment, and of course you've got to eat, too, and this is public employment. Jobs have to be made. Oh, that holds for me too. Mind you, I'm not letting myself out. I've got three years of seniority on you, that's all. And a law degree. Otherwise, you might be back of the desk and I might be going out into the field this cold day. The same dough pays us both and for the same, exact, identical reason. What's my law degree got to do with it? But you have to pass out these checks, Mr. Grebe, and it'll help if you're stubborn, so I hope you are."

"Yes, I'm fairly stubborn."

Raynor sketched hard with an eraser in the old dirt of his desk, left-handed, and said, "Sure, what else can you answer to such a question. Anyhow, the trouble you're going to have is that they don't like to give information about anybody. They think you're a plain-clothes dick or an installment collector, or summons-server or something like that. Till you've been seen around the neighborhood for a few months and people know you're only from the relief."

It was dark, ground-freezing, pre-Thanksgiving weather; the wind played hob with the smoke, rushing it down, and Grebe missed his gloves, which he had left in Raynor's office. And no one would admit knowing Green. It was past three o'clock and the postman had made his last delivery. The nearest grocer, himself a Negro, had never heard the name Tulliver Green, or said he hadn't. Grebe was inclined to think that it was true, that he had in the end convinced the man that he wanted only to deliver a check. But he wasn't sure. He needed experience in interpreting looks and signs and, even more, the will not to be put off or denied and even the force to bully if need be. If the grocer did know, he had got rid of him easily. But since most of his trade was with reliefers, why should he prevent the delivery of a check? Maybe Green, or Mrs. Green, if there was a Mrs. Green, patronized another grocer. And was there a Mrs. Green? It was one of Grebe's great handicaps that he hadn't looked at any of the case records. Raynor should have let him read files for a few hours. But he apparently saw no need for that, probably considering the job unimportant. Why prepare systematically to deliver a few checks?

But now it was time to look for the janitor. Grebe took in the building in the wind and gloom of the late November day—trampled, frost-hardened lots on one side; on the other, an automobile junk yard and then the infinite work of Elevated frames, weak-looking, gaping with rubbish fires; two sets of leaning brick porches three stories high and a flight of cement stairs to the celler. Descending, he entered the underground passage, where he tried the doors until one opened and he found himself in the furnace room. There someone rose toward him and approached, scraping on the coal grit and bending under the canvas-jacketed pipes.

"Are you the janitor?"

"What do you want?"

"I'm looking for a man who's supposed to be living here. Green."

"What Green?"

"Oh, you maybe have more than one Green?" said Grebe with new, pleasant hope. "This is Tulliver Green."

"I don't think I c'n help you, mister. I don't know any."

"A crippled man."

The janitor stood bent before him. Could it be that he was crippled? Oh, God! what if he was. Grebe's gray eyes sought with excited difficulty to see. But no, he was only very short and stooped. A head awakened from meditation, a strong-haired beard, low, wide shoulders. A staleness of sweat and coal rose from his black shirt and the burlap sack he wore as an apron.

"Crippled how?"

Grebe thought and then answered with the light voice of unmixed candor, "I don't know. I've never seen him." This was damaging, but his only other choice was to make a lying guess, and he was not up to it. "I'm delivering checks for the relief to shut-in cases. If he weren't crippled he'd come to collect himself. That's why I said crippled. Bedridden, chair-ridden—is there anybody like that?"

This sort of frankness was one of Grebe's oldest talents, going back to childhood. But it gained him nothing here.

"No suh. I've got four buildin's same as this that I take care of. I don' know all the tenants, leave alone the tenants' tenants. The rooms turn over so fast, people movin' in and out every day. I can't tell you."

The janitor opened his grimy lips but Grebe did not hear him in the piping of the valves and the consuming pull of air to flame in the body of the furnace. He knew, however, what he had said.

"Well, all the same, thanks. Sorry I bothered you. I'll prowl around upstairs again and see if I can turn up someone who knows him."

Once more in the cold air and early darkness he made the short circle from the cellarway to the entrance crowded between the brickwood pillars and began to climb to the third floor. Pieces of plaster ground under his feet; strips of brass tape from which the carpeting had been torn away marked old boundaries at the sides. In the passage, the cold reached him worse than in the street; it touched him to the bone. The hall toilets ran like springs. He thought grimly as he heard the wind burning around the building with a sound like that of the furnace, that this was a great piece of constructed shelter. Then he struck a match in the gloom and searched for names and numbers among the writings and scribbles on the walls. He saw WHOODY-DOODY GO TO JESUS and zigzags, caricatures, sexual scrawls, and curses. So the sealed rooms of pyramids were also decorated, and the caves of human dawn.

The information on his card was, TULLIVER GREEN-APT 3D. There were no names, however, and no numbers. His shoulders drawn up, tears of cold in his eyes, breathing vapor, he went the length of the corridor and told himself that if he had been lucky enough to have the temperament for it he would bang on one of the doors and bawl out "Tulliver Green!" until he got results. But it wasn't in him to make an uproar and he continued to burn matches, passing the light over the walls. At the rear, in a corner off the hall, he discovered a door he had not seen before and he thought it best to investigate. It sounded empty when he knocked, but a young Negress answered, hardly more than a girl. She opened only a bit, to guard the warmth of the room.

"Yes suh?"

"I'm from the district station on Prairie Avenue. I'm looking for a man named Tulliver Green to give him his check. Do you know him?"

No, she didn't; but he thought she had not understood anything of what he had said. She had a dream-bound, dream-blind face, very soft and black, shut off. She wore a man's jacket and pulled the ends together at her throat. Her hair was parted in three directions, at the sides and transversely, standing up at the front in a dull puff.

"Is there somebody around here who might know?"

"I jus' taken this room las' week."

He observed that she shivered, but even her shiver was somnambulistic and there was no sharp consciousness of cold in the big smooth eyes of her handsome face.

"All right, miss, thank you. Thanks," he said, and went to try another place.

Here he was admitted. He was grateful, for the room was warm. It was full of people, and they were silent as he entered—ten people, or a dozen, perhaps more, sitting on benches like a parliament. There was no light, properly speaking, but a tempered darkness that the window gave, and everyone seemed to him enormous, the men padded out in heavy work clothes, and winter coats, and the women huge, too, in their sweaters, hats, and old furs. And, besides, bed and bedding, a black cooking range, a piano piled towering to the ceiling with papers, a dining-room table of the old style of prosperous Chicago. Among these people Grebe, with his cold-heightened fresh color and his smaller stature, entered like a schoolboy. Even though he was met with smiles and good will, he knew, before a single word was spoken, that all the currents ran against him and that he would make no headway. Nevertheless he began. "Does anybody here know how I can deliver a check to Mr. Tulliver Green?"

"Green?" It was the man that had let him in who answered. He was in short sleeves, in a checkered shirt, and had a queer, high head, profusely overgrown and long as a shako; the veins entered it strongly from his forehead. "I never heard mention of him. Is this where he live?"

"This is the address they gave me at the station. He's a sick man, and he'll need his check. Can't anybody tell me where to find him?"

He stood his ground and waited for a reply, his crimson wool scarf wound around his neck and drooping outside his trenchcoat, pockets weighted with the block af checks and official forms. They must have realized that he was not a college boy employed afternoons by a bill collector, trying foxily to pass for a relief clerk, recognized that he was an older man who knew himself what need was, who had had more than an average seasoning in hardship. It was evident enough if you looked at the marks under his eyes and at the sides of his mouth.

"Anybody know this sick man?"

"No suh." On all sides he saw heads shaken and smiles of denial. No one knew. And maybe it was true, he considered, standing silent in the earthen, musky human gloom of the place as the rumble continued. But he could never really be sure.

"What's the matter with this man?" said shako-head.

"I've never seen him. All I can tell you is that he can't come in person for his money. It's my first day in this district."

"Maybe they given you the wrong number?"

"I don't believe so. But where else can I ask about him?" He felt that this persistence amused them deeply, and in a way he shared their amusement that he should stand up so tenaciously to them. Though smaller, though slight, he was his own man, he retracted nothing about himself, and he looked back at them, gray-eyed, with amusement and also with a sort of courage. On the bench some man spoke in his throat, the words impossible to catch, and a woman answered with a wild, shrieking laugh, which was quickly cut off.

"Well, so nobody will tell me?"

"Ain't nobody who knows."

"At least, if he lives here, he pays rent to someone. Who manages the building?"

"Greatham Company. That's on Thirty-ninth Street."

Grebe wrote it in his pad. But, in the street again, a sheet of wind-driven paper clinging to his leg while he deliberated what direction to take next, it seemed a feeble lead to follow. Probably this Green didn't rent a flat, but a room. Sometimes there were as many as twenty people in an apartment; the real-estate agent would know only the lessee. And not even the agent could tell who the renters were. In some places the beds were even used in shifts, watchmen or jitney drivers or short-order cooks in night joints turning out after a day's sleep and surrendering their beds to a sister, a nephew, or perhaps a stranger, just off the bus. There were large numbers of newcomers in this terrific, blight-bitten portion of the city between Cottage Grove and Ashland, wandering from house to house and room to room. When you saw them, how could you know them? They didn't carry bundles on their backs or look picturesque. You only saw a man, a Negro, walking in the street or riding in the car, like everyone else, with his thumb closed on a transfer. And therefore how were you supposed to tell? Grebe thought the Greatham agent would only laugh at his question.

But how much it would have simplified the job to be able to say that Green was old, or blind, or consumptive. An hour in the files, taking a few notes, and he needn't have been at such a disadvantage. When Raynor gave him the block of checks he asked, "How much should I know about these people?" Then Raynor had looked as though he were preparing to accuse him of trying to make the job more important than it was. He smiled, because by then they were on fine terms, but nevertheless he had been getting ready to say something like that when the confusion began in the station over Staika and her children.

Grebe had waited a long time for this job. It came to him through the pull of an old schoolmate in the Corporation Counsel's office, never a close friend, but suddenly sympathetic and interested—pleased to show, moreover, how well he had done, how strongly he was coming on even in these miserable times. Well, he was coming through strongly, along with the Democratic administration itself. Grebe had gone to see him in City Hall, and they had had a counter lunch or beers at least once a month for a year, and finally it had been possible to swing the job. He didn't mind being assigned the lowest clerical grade, nor even being a messenger, though Raynor thought he did.

This Raynor was an original sort of guy and Grebe had taken to him immediately. As was proper on the first day, Grebe had come early, but he waited long, for Raynor was late. At last he darted into his cubicle of an office as though he had just jumped from one of those hurtling huge red Indian Avenue cars. His thin, rough face was wind-stung and he was grinning and saying something breathlessly to himself. In his hat, a small fedora, and his coat, the velvet collar a neat fit about his neck, and his silk muffler that set off the nervous twist of his chin, he swayed and turned himself in his swivel chair, feet leaving the ground; so that he pranced a little as he sat. Meanwhile he took Grebe's measure out of his eyes, eyes of an unusual vertical length and slightly sardonic. So the two men sat for a while, saying nothing, while the supervisor raised his hat from his miscombed hair and put it in his lap. His cold-darkened hands were not clean. A steel beam passed through the little makeshift room, from which machine belts once had hung. The building was an old factory.

"I'm younger than you; I hope you won't find it hard taking orders from me," said Raynor. "But I don't make them up, either. You're how old, about?"

"Thirty-five."

"And you thought you'd be inside doing paper work. But it so happens I have to send you out."

"I don't mind."

"And it's mostly a Negro load we have in this district."

"So I thought it would be."

"Fine. You'll get along. *C'est un bon boulot*[1] Do you know French?"

"Some."

"I thought you'd be a university man."

"Have you been in France?" said Grebe.

"No, that's the French of the Berlitz School. I've been at it for more than a year, just as I'm sure people have been, all over the world, office boys in China and braves in Tanganyika. In fact, I damn well know it. Such is the attractive power of civilization. It's overrated, but what do you want? *Que voulez-vous?* I get *Le Rire* and all the spicy papers, just like in Tanganyika. It must be mystifying, out there. But my reason is that I'm aiming at the diplomatic service. I have a cousin who's a courier, and the

[1] It's a good meal.

way he describes it is awfully attractive. He rides in the *wagon-lits* and reads books. While we—What did you do before?"

"I sold."

"Where?"

"Canned meat at Stop and Shop. In the basement."

"And before that?"

"Window shades at Goldblatt's."

"Steady work?"

"No, Thursdays and Saturdays. I also sold shoes."

"You've been a shoe-dog too. Well. And prior to that? Here it is in your folder." He opened the record. "Saint Olaf's College, instructor in classical languages. Fellow, University of Chicago, 1926-27. I've had Latin, too. Let's trade quotations—'*Dum spiro spero.*' "[1]

"'*Da dextram misero.*'"[2]

"'*Alea jacta est.*'"[3]

"'*Excelsior.*'"

Raynor shouted with laughter, and other workers came to look at him over the partition. Grebe also laughed, feeling pleased and easy. The luxury of fun on a nervous morning.

When they were done and no one was watching or listening, Raynor said rather seriously, "What made you study Latin in the first place? Was it for the priesthood?"

"No."

"Just for the hell of it? For the culture? Oh, the things people think they can pull!" He made his cry hilarious and tragic. "I ran my pants off so I could study for the bar, and I've passed the bar, so I get twelve dollars a week more than you as a bonus for having seen life straight and whole. I'll tell you, as a man of culture, that even though nothing looks to be real, and everything stands for something else, and that thing for another thing, and that thing for a still another one—there ain't any comparison between twenty-five and thirty-seven dollars a week, regardless of the last reality. Don't you think that was clear to your Greeks? They were a thoughtful people, but they didn't part with their slaves."

This was a great deal more than Grebe had looked for in his first interview with his supervisor. He was too shy to show all the astonishment he felt. He laughed a little, aroused, and brushed at the sunbeam that covered his head with its dust. "Do you think my mistake was so terrible?"

"Damn right it was terrible, and you know it now that you've had the whip of hard times laid on your back. You should have been preparing yourself for trouble. Your people must have been well off to send you to the university. Stop me, if I'm stepping on your toes. Did your mother pamper you? Did your father give in to you? Were you brought up tenderly, with permission to go and find out what were the last things that everybody else stands for while everybody else labored in the fallen world of appearances?"

"Well, no, it wasn't exactly like that." Grebe smiled. *The fallen world of appearances!* no less. But now it was his turn to deliver a surprise. "We weren't rich. My father was the last genuine English butler in Chicago—"

"Are you kidding?"

---

[1] While I breathe, I hope.

[2] Misery strikes from strange quarters.

[3] The die is cast.

"Why should I be?"

"In a livery?"

"In livery. Up on the Gold Coast."

"And he wanted you to be educated like a gentleman?"

"He did not. He sent me to the Armour Institute to study chemical engineering. But when he died I changed schools."

He stopped himself and considered how quickly Raynor had reached him. In no time he had your valise on the table and all your stuff unpacked. And afterward, in the streets, he was still reviewing how far he might have gone, and how much he might have been led to tell if they had not been interrupted by Mrs. Staika's great noise.

But just then a young woman, one of Raynor's workers, ran into the cubicle exclaiming, "Haven't you heard all the fuss?"

"We haven't heard anything."

"It's Staika, giving out with all her might. The reporters are coming. She said she phoned the papers, and you know she did."

"But what is she up to?" said Raynor.

"She brought her wash and she's ironing it here, with our current, because the relief won't pay her electric bill. She has her ironing board set up by the admitting desk, and her kids are with her, all six. They never are in school more than once a week. She's always dragging them around with her because of her reputation."

"I don't want to miss any of this," said Raynor, jumping up. Grebe, as she followed with the secretary, said, "Who is this Staika?"

"They call her the 'Blood Mother of Federal Street.' She's a professional donor at the hospitals. I think they pay ten dollars a pint. Of course it's no joke, but she makes a very big thing out of it and she and the kids are in the papers all the time."

A small crowd, staff and clients divided by a plywood barrier, stood in the narrow space of the entrance, and Staika was shouting in a gruff, mannish voice, plunging the iron on the board and slamming it on the metal rest.

"My father and mother came in a steerage, and I was born in our house, Robey by Huron. I'm no dirty immigrant. I'm a U.S. citizen. My husband is a gassed veteran from France with lungs weaker'n paper, that hardly can he go to the toilet by himself. These six children of mine, I have to buy the shoes for their feet with my own blood. Even a lousy little white Communion necktie, that's a couple of drops of blood; a little piece of mosquito veil for my Vadja so she won't be ashamed in church for the other girls, they take my blood for it by Goldblatt. That's how I keep goin'. A fine thing if I had to depend on the relief. And there's plenty of people on the rolls—fakes! There's nothin' *they* can't get, that can go and wrap bacon at Swift and Armour any time. They're lookin' for them by the Yards. They never have to be out of work. Only they rather lay in their lousy beds and eat the public's money." She was not afraid, in a predominantly Negro station, to shout this way about Negroes.

Grebe and Raynor worked themselves forward to get a closer view of the woman. She was flaming with anger and with pleasure at herself, broad and huge, a golden-headed woman, who wore a cotton cap laced with pink ribbon. She was barelegged and had on black gym shoes, her Hoover apron was open and her great breasts, not much restrained by a man's undershirt, hampered her arms as she worked at the kid's dress on the ironing board. And the children, silent and white, with a kind of locked obstinacy, in sheepskins and lumberjackets, stood behind her. She had captured the station, and the pleasure this gave her was enormous. Yet her grievances were true grievances. She was telling the truth. But she behaved like a liar. The look of her small eyes was hidden, and while she raged she also seemed to be spinning and planning.

"They send me out college case workers in silk pants to talk me out of what I got comin.' Are they better'n me? Who told them? Fire them. Let 'em go and get married, and then you won't have to cut electric from people's budget."

The chief supervisor, Mr. Ewing, couldn't silence her and he stood with folded arms at the head of his staff, bald, bald-headed, saying to his subordinates like the ex-school principal he was, "Pretty soon she'll be tired and go."

"No she won't," said Raynor to Grebe. "She'll get what she wants. She knows more about the relief than Ewing. She's been on the rolls for years, and she always gets what she wants because she puts on a noisy show. Ewing knows it. He'll give in soon. He's only saving face. If he gets bad publicity, the Commissioner'll have him on the carpet, downtown. She's got him submerged; she'll submerge everybody in time, and that includes nations and governments."

Grebe replied with his characteristic smile, disagreeing completely. Who would take Staika's orders, and what changes could her yelling ever bring about?

No, what Grebe saw in her, the power that made people listen, was that her cry expressed the war of flesh and blood, perhaps turned a little crazy and certainly ugly, on this place and this condition. And at first, when he went out, the spirit of Staika somehow presided over the whole district for him, and it took color from her; he saw her color, in the spotty curb fires, and the fires under the El, the straight alley of flamy gloom. Later, too, when he went into a tavern for a shot of rye, the sweat of beer, association with West Side Polish streets, made him think of her again.

He wiped the corners of his mouth with his muffler, his hankerchief being inconvenient to reach for, and went out again to get on with the delivery of his checks. The air bit cold and hard and a few flakes of snow formed near him. A train struck by and left a quiver in the frames and a bristling icy hiss over the rails.

Crossing the street, he descended a flight of board steps into a basement grocery, setting off a little bell. It was a dark, long store and it caught you with its stinks of smoked meat, soap, dried peaches, and fish. There was a fire wrinkling and flapping in the little stove, and the proprietor was waiting, an Italian with a long, hollow face and stubborn bristles. He kept his hands warm under his apron.

No, he didn't know Green. You knew people but not names. The same man might not have the same name twice. The police didn't know, either, and mostly didn't care. When somebody was shot or knifed they took the body away and didn't look for the murderer. In the first place, nobody would tell them anything. So they made up a name for the coroner and called it quits. And in the second place, they didn't give a goddamn anyhow. But they couldn't get to the bottom of a thing even if they wanted to. Nobody would get to know even a tenth of what went on among these people. They stabbed and stole, they did every crime and abomination you ever heard of, men and men, women and women, parents and children, worse than the animals. They carried on their own way, and the horrors passed off like a smoke. There was never anything like it in the history of the whole world.

It was a long speech, deepening with every word in its fantasy and passion and becoming increasingly senseless and terrible: a swarm amassed by suggestion and invention, a huge, hugging, despairing knot, a human wheel of heads, legs, bellies, arms, rolling through his shop.

Grebe felt that he must interrupt him. He said sharply, "What are you talking about! All I asked was whether you knew this man."

"That isn't even the half of it. I been here six years. You probably don't want to believe this. But suppose it's true?"

"All the same," said Grebe, "there must be a way to find a person."

The Italian's close-spaced eyes had been queerly concentrated, as were his muscles, while he leaned across the counter trying to convince Grebe. Now he gave up the effort and sat down on his stool. "Oh—I suppose. Once in a while. But I been telling you, even the cops don't get anywhere."

"They're always after somebody. It's not the same thing."

"Well, keep trying if you want. I can't help you."

But he didn't keep trying. He had no more time to spend on Green. He slipped Green's check to the back of the block. The next name on the list was FIELD, WINSTON.

He found the back-yard bungalow without the least trouble; it shared a lot with another house, a few feet of yard between. Grebe knew these two-shack arrangements. They had been built in vast numbers in the days before the swamps were filled and the streets raised, and they were all the same—a boardwalk along the fence, well under street level, three or four ball-headed posts for clotheslines, greening wood, dead shingles, and a long, long flight of stairs to the rear door.

A twelve-year-old boy let him into the kitchen, and there the old man was, sitting by the table in a wheel chair.

"Oh, it's d' Government man," he said to the boy when Grebe drew out his checks. "Go bring me my box of papers." He cleared a space on the table.

"Oh, you don't have to go to all that trouble," said Grebe. But Field laid out his papers: Social Security card, relief certification, letters from the state hospital in Manteno, and a naval discharge dated San Diego, 1920.

"That's plenty," Grebe said. "Just sign."

"You got to know who I am," the old man said. "You're from the Government. It's not your check, it's a Government check and you got no business to hand it over till everything is proved."

He loved the ceremony of it, and Grebe made no more objections. Field emptied his box and finished out the circle of cards and letters.

"There's everything I done and been. Just the death certificate and they can close book on me." He said this with a certain happy pride and magnificence. Still he did not sign; he merely held the little pen upright on the golden-green corduroy of his thigh. Grebe did not hurry him. He felt the old man's hunger for conversation.

"I got to get better coal," he said. "I send my little gran'son to the yard with my order and they fill his wagon with screening. The stove ain't made for it. It fall through the grate. The order says Franklin County egg-size coal."

"I'll report it and see what can be done."

"Nothing can be done, I expect. You know and I know. There ain't no little ways to make things better, and the only big thing is money. That's the only sunbeams, money. Nothing is black where it shines, and the only place you see black is where it ain't shining. What we colored have to have is our own rich. There ain't no other way."

Grebe sat, his reddened forehead bridged levelly by his close-cut hair and his cheeks lowered in the wings of his collar—the caked fire shone hard within the isinglass-and-iron frames but the room was not comfortable—sat and listened while the old man unfolded his scheme. This was to create one Negro millionaire a month by subscription. One clever, good-hearted young fellow elected every month would sign a contract to use the money to start a business employing Negroes. This would be advertised by chain letters and word of mouth, and every Negro wage earner would contribute a dollar a month. Within five years there would be sixty millionaires.

"That'll fetch respect," he said with a throat-stopped sound that came out like a foreign syllable. "You got to take and organize all the money that gets thrown away on the policy wheel and horse race. As long as they can take it away from you, they got no respect for you. Money, that's d' sun of human kind!" Field was a Negro of mixed blood, perhaps Cherokee, or Natchez; his skin was reddish. And he sounded, speaking about a golden sun in this dark room, and looked, shaggy, and slab-headed, with the mingled blood of his face and broad lips, the little pen still upright in his hand, like one of the underground kings of mythology, old judge Minos himself.

And now he accepted the check and signed. Not to soil the slip, he held it down with his knuckles. The table budged and creaked, the center of the gloomy, heathen midden of the kitchen covered with bread, meat, and cans, and the scramble of papers.

"Don't you think my scheme'd work?"

"It's worth thinking about. Something ought to be done, I agree."

"It'll work if people will do it. That's all. That's the only thing, any time. When they understand it in the same way, all of them."

"That's true," said Grebe, rising. His glance met the old man's.

"I know you got to go," he said. "Well, God bless you, boy you ain't been sly with me. I can tell it in a minute."

He went back through the buried yard. Someone nursed a candle in a shed, where a man unloaded kindling wood from a sprawl-wheeled baby buggy and two voices carried on a high conversation. As he came up the sheltered passage he heard the hard boost of the wind in the branches and against the house fronts, and then, reaching the sidewalk, he saw the needle-eye red of cable towers in the open icy height hundreds of feet above the river and the factories—those keen points. From here, his view was obstructed all the way to the South Branch and its timber banks, and the cranes beside the water. Rebuilt after the Great Fire, this part of the city was, not fifty years later, in ruins again, factories boarded up, buildings deserted or fallen, gaps of prairie between. But it wasn't desolation that this made you feel, but rather a faltering of organization that set free a huge energy, an escaped, unattached, unregulated power from the giant raw place. Not only must people feel it but, it seemed to Grebe, they were compelled to match it. In their very bodies. He no less than others, he realized. Say that his parents had been servants in their time, whereas he was not supposed to be one. He thought that they had never done any service like this, which no one visible asked for, and probably flesh and blood could not even perform. Nor could anyone show why it should be performed; or see where the performance would lead. That did not mean that he wanted to be released from it, he realized with a grimly pensive face. On the contrary. He had something to do. To be compelled to feel this energy and yet have no task to do—that was horrible; that was suffering; he knew what that was. It was now quitting time. Six o'clock. He could go home if he liked, to his room, that is, to wash in hot water, to pour a drink, lie down on his quilt, read the paper, eat some liver paste on crackers before going out to dinner. But to think of this actually made him feel a little sick, as though he had swallowed hard air. He had six checks left, and he was determined to deliver at least one of these: Mr. Green's check.

So he started again. He had four or five dark blocks to go, past open lots, condemned houses, old foundations, closed schools, black churches, mounds, and he reflected that there must be many people alive who had once seen the neighborhood rebuilt and new. Now there was a second layer of ruins; centuries of history accomplished through human massing. Numbers had given the place forced growth; enormous numbers had also broken it down. Objects once so new, so concrete that it could have occurred to anyone they stood for other things, had crumbled. Therefore, reflected Grebe, the secret of them was out. It was that they stood for themselves by agreement, and were natural and not unnatural by agreement, and when the things themselves collapsed the agreement became visible. What was it, otherwise, that kept cities from looking peculiar? Rome, that was almost permanent, did not give rise to thoughts like these. And was it abidingly real? But in Chicago, where the cycles were so fast and the familiar died out, and again rose, changed, and died again in thirty years, you saw the common agreement or covenant, and you were forced to think about appearances and realities. (He remembered Raynor and he smiled. Raynor was a clever boy.) Once you had grasped this, a great many things became intelligible. For instance, why Mr. Field should conceive such a scheme. Of course, if people were to agree to create a millionaire, a real millionaire would come into existence. And if you wanted to know how Mr. Field was inspired to think of this, why, he had within sight of his kitchen window the chart, the very bones of a successful scheme—the El with its blue and green confetti of signals. People consented to pay dimes and ride the crash-box cars, and so it was a success. Yet how absurd it looked; how little reality there was to start with. And yet Yerkes, the great financier who built it, had known that he could get people to agree to do it. Viewed as itself, what a scheme of a scheme it seemed, how close to an appearance. Then why wonder at Mr. Field's idea? He had grasped a principle. And then Grebe remembered, too, that Mr. Yerkes had established the Yerkes Observatory and endowed it with millions. Now how did the notion come to him in his New York museum of a palace or his Aegean-bound yacht to give money to astronomers? Was he awed by the success of his bizarre enterprise and therefore ready to spend money to find out where in the universe being and seeming were identical? Yes, he wanted to know what abides; and whether flesh is Bible grass; and he offered money to be burned in the fire of suns. Okay, then, Grebe thought further, these things exist because people consent to exist with them—we have got so far—and also there is a reality which doesn't depend on consent but within which consent is a game. But what need, the need that keeps so many vast thousands in position? You tell me that, you *private* little gentleman and *decent* soul—he used these words against himself scornfully. Why is the consent given to misery? And why so painfully ugly? Because there is *something* that is dismal and permanently ugly? Here he sighed and gave it up, and thought it was enough for the present moment that he had a real check in his pocket for a Mr. Green who must be real beyond question. If only his neighbors didn't think they had to conceal him.

This time he stopped at the second floor. He struck a match and found a door. Presently a man answered his knock and Grebe had the check ready and showed it even before he began. "Does Tulliver Green live here? I'm from the relief."

The man narrowed the opening and spoke to someone at his back.

"Does he live here?"

"Uh-uh. No."

"Or anywhere in this building? He's a sick man and can't come for his dough." He exhibited the check in the light, which was smoky—the air smelled of charred lard—and the man held off the brim of his cap to study it.

"Uh-uh. Never seen the name."

"There's no body around here that uses crutches?"

He seemed to think, but it was Grebe's impression that he was simply waiting for a decent interval to pass.

"No, suh. Nobody I ever see."

"I've been looking for this man all afternoon"—Grebe spoke out with sudden force—"and I'm going to have to carry this check back to the station. It seems strange not to be able to find a person to *give* him something when you're looking for him for a good reason. I suppose if I had bad news for him I'd find him quick enough."

There was a responsive motion in the other man's face. "That's right, I reckon."

"It almost doesn't do any good to have a name if you can't be found by it. It doesn't stand for anything. He might as well not have any," he went on, smiling. It was as much of a concession as he could make to his desire to laugh.

"Well, now, there's a little old knot-back man I see once in a while. He might be the one you lookin' for. Downstairs."

"Where? Right side or left? Which door?"

"I don't know which. Thin-face little knot-back with a stick."

But no one answered to any of the doors on the first floor. He went to the end of the corridor, searching by matchlight, and found only a stairless exit to the yard, a drop of about six feet. But there was a bungalow near the alley, an old house like Mr. Field's. To jump was unsafe. He ran from the front door, through the underground passage and into the yard. The place was occupied. There was a light through the curtains, upstairs. The name on the ticket under the broken, scoop-shaped mailbox was Green! He exultantly rang the bell and pressed against the locked door. Then the lock clicked faintly and a long staircase opened before him. Someone was slowly coming down—a woman. He had the impression in the weak light that she was shaping her hair as she came, making herself presentable, for he saw her arms raised. But it was for support that they were raised, she was feeling her way downward, down the wall, stumbling. Next he wondered about the pressure of her feet on the treads; she did not seem to be wearing shoes. And it was a freezing stairway. His ring had got her out of bed, perhaps, and she had forgotten to put them on. And then he saw that she was not only shoeless but naked; she was entirely naked, climbing down while she talked to herself, a heavy woman, naked and drunk. She blundered into him. The contact of her breasts, though they touched only his coat, made him go back against the door with a blind shock. See what he had tracked down, in his hunting game!

The woman was saying to herself, furious with insult, "So I cain't———k, huh? I'll show that son-of-a-bitch kin I, cain't I."

What should he do now? Grebe asked himself. Why, he should go. He should turn away and go. He couldn't talk to this woman. He couldn't keep her standing naked in the cold. But when he tried he found himself unable to turn away.

He said, "Is this where Mr. Green lives?"

But she was still talking to herself and did not hear him.

"Is this Mr. Green's house?"

At last she turned her furious drunken glance on him. "What do you want?"

Again her eyes wandered from him; there was a dot of blood in their enraged brilliance. He wondered why she didn't feel the cold.

"I'm from the relief."

"Awright, what?"

"I've got a check for Tulliver Green."

This time she heard him and put out her hand.

"No, no, for *Mr.* Green. He's got to sign," he said. How was he going to get Green's signature tonight!

"I'll take it. He can't."

He desperately shook his head, thinking of Mr. Field's precautions about identification. "I can't let you have it. It's for him. Are you Mrs. Green?"

"Maybe I is, and maybe I ain't. Who want to know?"

"Is he upstairs?"

"Awright. Take it up yourself, you gaddamn fool."

Sure, he was a goddamn fool. Of course he could not go up because Green would probably be drunk and naked, too. And perhaps he would appear on the landing soon. He looked eagerly upward. Under the light was a high narrow brown wall. Empty! It remained empty!

"Hell with you, then!" he heard her cry. To deliver a check for coal and clothes, he was keeping her in the cold. She did not feel it, but his face was burning with frost and self-ridicule. He backed away from her.

"I'll come tomorrow, tell him."

"Ah, hell with you. Don' never come. What you doin' here in the nighttime? Don' come back." She yelled so that he saw the breadth of her tongue. She stood astride in the long cold box of the hall and held on to the banister and the wall. The bungalow itself was shaped something like a box, a clumsy, high box pointing into the freezing air with its sharp, wintry lights.

"If you are Mrs. Green, I'll give you the check," he said, changing his mind.

"Give here, then." She took it, took the pen offered with it in her left hand, and tried to sign the receipt on the wall. He looked around, almost as though to see whether his madness was being observed, and came near believing that someone was standing on a mountain of used tires in the auto-junking shop next door.

"But are you Mrs. Green?" he now thought to ask. But she was already climbing the stairs with the check, and it was too late, if he had made an error, if he was now in trouble, to undo the thing. But he wasn't going to worry about it. Though she might not be Mrs. Green, he was convinced that Mr. Green was upstairs. Whoever she was, the woman stood for Green, whom he was not to see this time. Well, you silly bastard, he said to himself, so you think you found him. So what? Maybe you really did find him—what of it? But it was important that there was a real Mr. Green whom they could not keep him from reaching because he seemed to come as an emissary from hostile appearances. And though the self-ridicule was slow to diminish, and his face still blazed with it, he had, nevertheless, a feeling of elation, too. "For after all," he said, "he *could* be found!"

Carson McCullers (1917–1967)

Carson McCullers was born in Columbus, Georgia, and, as with so many Southern writers, the South is a powerful presence in nearly all of her fiction. Her original ambition was to become a concert pianist, and at the age of seventeen she came to New York to attend the Juilliard School of Music. Unfortunately, she lost her tuition money in the subway on her second day in the city. Her musical career thus quickly ended, she found work to support herself while taking writing courses at Columbia University. Between 4 A.M. and 8 A.M. she worked at her writing and then set off to a full-time clerical job. One of her reviewers reported that she lost one job when her boss caught her reading Proust. In 1936 she suffered a severe attack of rheumatic fever, the first in an almost unbelievable series of illnesses and accidents. In 1940 her first novel, *The Heart is a Lonely Hunter,* was published. It caused an immediate sensation, and to many critics it seemed incredible that it had been written by someone only twenty-two years old. Her next novel, *Reflections in a Golden Eye* (1941), was a critical disaster, but in 1946 she published *The Member of the Wedding,* and in 1951 the dramatic version of that third novel opened on Broadway to overwhelming critical and popular success. In that same year she had the pleasure, at age thirty-four, of seeing a single volume of her collected works appear, the three novels, six stories, and a moving new novella that served as a title piece, *The Ballad of the Sad Café.* From this point on, however, her health and her personal life began to fall apart, and the work she published during the last sixteen years of her life fell far short of the promise and achievement she had already realized. She died of a stroke in 1967.

Many readers have felt the influence of Sherwood Anderson on Carson McCullers's work. Her characters, who are often physically, mentally, or sexually deformed, are "grotesques" in the Anderson tradition. Her constant theme is the search of these alienated misfits for love and understanding. As Louise Gossett says,

> The motif of Carson Smith McCullers' fiction is love, its modes, demands, successes, defeats, grace, and shame. Whatever force, instinct, or need holds the human community together, this is love. The falling apart of the community is signaled by the breakdown of communications between persons, by physical and spiritual isolation, by hatred and fear, by sexual perversion, or by economic and racial injustice, and violence accompanies all negations. Within each negation, however, there is a drive toward a positive alliance. No matter how distorted the relationship may be, Mrs. McCullers has compassion for every attempt of the human being to become a *we* instead of an *I*. . . . Thus the author is charitable toward the violence and grotesqueness which develop when the impulse to love goes astray, and she treats deviations more with mercy than with horror.

We have discussed "A Tree • A Rock • A Cloud" with some fullness in our main introduction. The ending of the story—the old man leaving the boy, going "cautious" into the "gray damp light of the early morning"—receives a most sensitive reaction from Mark Schorer: "They move off, each into his own separateness. The very periods in her title suggest the character of the human situation as she saw it."

A Tree • A Rock • A Cloud

It was raining that morning, and still very dark. When the boy reached the streetcar café he had almost finished his route and he went in for a cup of coffee. The place was an all-night café owned by a bitter and stingy man called Leo. After the raw, empty street, the café seemed friendly and bright: along the counter there were a couple of

From Carson McCullers, *Collected Short Stories and the Novel, The Ballad of the Sad Cafe.* Copyright by Carson McCullers, 1955. Reprinted by permission of Houghton Mifflin Company.

soldiers, three spinners from the cotton mill, and in a corner a man who sat hunched over with his nose and half his face down in a beer mug. The boy wore a helmet such as aviators wear. When he went into the café he unbuckled the chin strap and raised the right flap up over his pink little ear; often as he drank his coffee someone would speak to him in a friendly way. But this morning Leo did not look into his face and none of the men were talking. He paid and was leaving the café when a voice called out to him:

"Son! Hey Son!"

He turned back and the man in the corner was crooking his finger and nodding to him. He had brought his face out of the beer mug and he seemed suddenly very happy. The man was long and pale, with a big nose and faded orange hair.

"Hey Son!"

The boy went toward him. He was an undersized boy of about twelve, with one shoulder drawn higher than the other because of the weight of the paper sack. His face was shallow, freckled, and his eyes were round child eyes.

"Yeah Mister?"

The man laid one hand on the paper boy's shoulders, then grasped the boy's chin and turned his face slowly from one side to the other. The boy shrank back uneasily.

"Say! What's the big idea?"

The boy's voice was shrill; inside the café it was suddenly very quiet.

The man said slowly: "I love you."

All along the counter the men laughed. The boy, who had scowled and sidled away, did not know what to do. He looked over the counter at Leo, and Leo watched him with a weary, brittle jeer. The boy tried to laugh also. But the man was serious and sad.

"I did not mean to tease you, Son," he said. "Sit down and have a beer with me. There is something I have to explain."

Cautiously, out of the corner of his eye, the paper boy questioned the men along the counter to see what he should do. But they had gone back to their beer or their breakfast and did not notice him. Leo put a cup of coffee on the counter and a little jug of cream.

"He is a minor," Leo said.

The paper boy slid himself up onto the stool. His ear beneath the upturned flap of the helmet was very small and red. The man was nodding at him soberly. "It is important," he said. Then he reached in his hip pocket and brought out something which he held up in the palm of his hand for the boy to see.

"Look very carefully," he said.

The boy stared, but there was nothing to look at very carefully. The man held in his big, grimy palm a photograph. It was the face of a woman, but blurred, so that only the hat and the dress she was wearing stood out clearly.

"See?" the man asked.

The boy nodded and the man placed another picture in his palm. The woman was standing on a beach in a bathing suit. The suit made her stomach very big, and that was the main thing you noticed.

"Got a good look?" He leaned over closer and finally asked: "You ever seen her before?"

The boy sat motionless, staring slantwise at the man. "Not so I know of."

"Very well." The man blew on the photographs and put them back into his pocket. "That was my wife."

"Dead?" the boy asked.

Slowly the man shook his head. He pursed his lips as though about to whistle and answered in a long-drawn way; "Nuuu—" he said. "I will explain."

The beer on the counter before the man was in a large brown mug. He did not pick it up to drink. Instead he bent down and, putting his face over the rim, he rested there for a moment. Then with both hands he tilted the mug and sipped.

"Some night you'll go to sleep with your nose in a mug and drown," said Leo. "Prominent transient drowns in beer. That would be a cute death."

The paper boy tried to signal to Leo. While the man was not looking he screwed up his face and worked his mouth to question soundlessly: "Drunk?" But Leo only raised his eyebrows and turned away to put some pink strips of bacon on the grill. The man pushed the mug away from him, straightened himself, and folded his loose crooked hands on the counter. His face was sad as he looked at the paper boy. He did not blink, but from time to time the lids closed down with delicate gravity over his pale green eyes. It was nearing dawn and the boy shifted the weight of the paper sack.

"I am talking about love," the man said. "With me it is a science."

The boy half slid down from the stool. But the man raised his forefinger, and there was something about him that held the boy and would not let him go away.

"Twelve years ago I married the woman in the photograph. She was my wife for one year, nine months, three days, and two nights. I loved her. Yes. . ." He tightened his blurred, rambling voice and said again: "I loved her. I thought also that she loved me. I was a railroad engineer. She had all home comforts and luxuries. It never crept into my brain that she was not satisfied. But do you know what happened?"

"Mgneeow!" said Leo.

The man did not take his eyes from the boy's face. "She left me. I came in one night and the house was empty and she was gone. She left me."

"With a fellow?" the boy asked.

Gently the man placed his palm down on the counter. "Why naturally, Son. A woman does not run off like that alone."

The café was quiet, the soft rain black and endless in the street outside. Leo pressed down the frying bacon with the prongs of his long fork. "So you have been chasing the floozie for eleven years. You frazzled old rascal!"

For the first time the man glanced at Leo. "Please don't be vulgar. Besides, I was not speaking to you." He turned back to the boy and said in a trusting and secretive undertone: "Let's not pay any attention to him. O.K.?"

The paper boy nodded doubtfully.

"It was like this," the man continued. "I am a person who feels many things. All my life one thing after another has impressed me. Moonlight. The leg of a pretty girl. One thing after another. But the point is that when I had enjoyed anything there was a peculiar sensation as though it was laying around loose in me. Nothing seemed to finish itself up or fit in with the other things. Women? I had my portion of them. The same. Afterwards laying around loose in me. I was a man who had never loved."

Very slowly he closed his eyelids, and the gesture was like a curtain drawn at the end of a scene in a play. When he spoke again his voice was excited and the words came fast—the lobes of his large, loose ears seemed to tremble.

"Then I met this woman. I was fifty-one years old and she always said she was thirty. I met her at a filling station and we were married within three days. And do you know what it was like? I just can't tell you. All I had ever felt was gathered together around this woman. Nothing lay around loose in me any more but was finished up by her."

The man stopped suddenly and stroked his long nose. His voice sank down to a steady and reproachful undertone: "I'm not explaining this right. What happened was this. There were these beautiful feelings and loose little pleasures inside me. And this woman was something like an assembly line for my soul. I run these little pieces of myself through her and I come out complete. Now do you follow me?"

"What was her name?" the boy asked.

"Oh," he said. "I called her Dodo. But that is immaterial."

"Did you try to make her come back?"

The man did not seem to hear. "Under the circumstances you can imagine how I felt when she left me."

Leo took the bacon from the grill and folded two strips of it between a bun. He had a gray face, with slitted eyes, and a pinched nose saddled by faint blue shadows. One of the mill workers signaled for more coffee and Leo poured it. He did not give refills on coffee free. The spinner ate breakfast there every morning, but the better Leo knew his customers the stingier he treated them. He nibbled his own bun as though he grudged it to himself.

"And you never got hold of her again?"

The boy did not know what to think of the man, and his child's face was uncertain with mingled curiosity and doubt. He was new on the paper route; it was still strange to him to be out in the town in the black, queer early morning.

"Yes," the man said. "I took a number of steps to get her back. I went around trying to locate her. I went to Tulsa where she had folks. And to Mobile. I went to every town she had ever mentioned to me, and I hunted down every man she had formerly been connected with. Tulsa, Atlanta, Chicago, Cheehaw, Memphis. . . . For the better part of two years I chased around the country trying to lay hold of her."

"But the pair of them had vanished from the face of the earth!" said Leo.

"Don't listen to him," the man said confidentially. "And also just forget those two years. They are not important. What matters is that around the third year a curious thing begun to happen to me."

"What?" the boy asked.

The man leaned down and tilted his mug to take a sip of beer. But as he hovered over the mug his nostrils fluttered slightly; he sniffed the staleness of the beer and did not drink. "Love is a curious thing to begin with. At first I thought only of getting her back. It was a kind of mania. But then as time went on I tried to remember her. But do you know what happened?"

"No," the boy said.

"When I laid myself down on a bed and tried to think about her my mind became a blank. I couldn't see her. I would take out her pictures and look. No good. Nothing doing. A blank. Can you imagine it?"

"Say Mac!" Leo called down the counter. "Can you imagine this bozo's mind a blank!"

Slowly, as though fanning away flies, the man waved his hand. His green eyes were concentrated and fixed on the shallow little face of the paper boy.

"But a sudden piece of glass on a sidewalk. Or a nickel tune in a music box. A shadow on a wall at night. And I would remember. It might happen in a street and I would cry or bang my head against a lamppost. You follow me?"

"A piece of glass . . ." the boy said.

"Anything. I would walk around and I had no power of how and when to remember her. You think you can put up a kind of shield. But remembering don't come to a man face forward—it corners around sideways. I was at the mercy of everything I saw and heard. Suddenly instead of me combing the countryside to find her she begun to chase me around in my very soul. *She* chasing *me,* mind you! And in my soul."

The boy asked finally: "What part of the country were you in then?"

"Ooh," the man groaned. "I was a sick mortal. It was like smallpox. I confess, Son, that I boozed. I fornicated. I committed any sin that suddenly appealed to me. I am loath to confess it but I will do so. When I recall that period it is all curdled in my mind, it was so terrible."

The man leaned his head down and tapped his forehead on the counter. For a few seconds he stayed bowed over in this position, the back of his stringy neck covered with orange furze, his hands with their long warped fingers held palm to palm in an attitude of prayer. Then the man straightened himself; he was smiling and suddenly his face was bright and tremulous and old.

"It was in the fifth year that it happened," he said. "And with it I started my science."

Leo's mouth jerked with a pale, quick grin. "Well none of we boys are getting any younger," he said. Then with sudden anger he balled up a dishcloth he was holding and threw it down hard on the floor. "You draggle-tailed old Romeo!"

"What happened?" the boy asked.

The old man's voice was high and clear: "Peace," he answered.

"Huh?"

"It is hard to explain scientifically, Son," he said. "I guess the logical explanation is that she and I had fleed around from each other for so long that finally we just got tangled up together and lay down and quit. Peace. A queer and beautiful blankness. It was spring in Portland and the rain came every afternoon. All evening I just stayed there on my bed in the dark. And that is how the science come to me."

The windows in the streetcar were pale blue with light. The two soldiers paid for their beers and opened the door—one of the soldiers combed his hair and wiped off his muddy puttees before they went outside. The three mill workers bent silently over their breakfasts. Leo's clock was ticking on the wall.

"It is this. And listen carefully. I meditated on love and reasoned it out. I realized what is wrong with us. Men fall in love for the first time. And what do they fall in love with?"

The boy's soft mouth was partly open and he did not answer.

"A woman," the old man said. "Without science, with nothing to go by, they undertake the most dangerous and sacred experience in God's earth. They fall in love with a woman. Is that correct, Son?"

"Yeah," the boy said faintly.

"They start at the wrong end of love. They begin at the climax. Can you wonder it is so miserable? Do you know how men should love?"

The old man reached over and grasped the boy by the collar of his leather jacket. He gave him a gentle little shake and his green eyes gazed down unblinking and grave.

"Son, do you know how love should be begun?"

The boy sat small and listening and still. Slowly he shook his head. The old man leaned closer and whispered:

"A tree. A rock. A cloud."

It was still raining outside in the street: a mild, gray, endless rain. The mill whistle blew for the six o'clock shift and the three spinners paid and went away. There was no one in the café but Leo, the old man, and the little paper boy.

"The weather was like this in Portland," he said. "At the time my science was begun. I meditated and I started very cautious. I would pick up something from the street and take it home with me. I bought a goldfish and I concentrated on the goldfish and I loved it. I graduated from one thing to another. Day by day I was getting this technique. On the road from Portland to San Diego—"

"Aw shut up!" screamed Leo suddenly. "Shut up! Shut up!"

The old man still held the collar of the boy's jacket; he was trembling and his face was earnest and bright and wild. "For six years now I have gone around by myself and built up my science. And now I am a master. Son. I can love anything. No longer do I have to think about it even. I see a street full of people and a beautiful light comes in me. I watch a bird in the sky. Or I meet a traveler on the road. Everything, Son. And anybody. All stranger and all loved! Do you realize what a science like mine can mean?"

The boy held himself stiffly, his hands curled tight around the counter edge. Finally he asked: "Did you ever really find that lady?"

"What? What say, Son?"

"I mean," the boy asked timidly. "Have you fallen in love with a woman again?"

The old man loosened his grasp on the boy's collar. He turned away and for the first time his green eyes had a vague and scattered look. He lifted the mug from the counter, drank down the yellow beer. His head was shaking slowly from side to side. Then finally he answered: "No, Son. You see that is the last step in my science. I go cautious. And I am not quite ready yet."

"Well!" said Leo. "Well well well!"

The old man stood in the open doorway. "Remember," he said. Framed there in the gray damp light of the early morning he looked shrunken and seedy and frail. But his smile was bright. "Remember I love you." he said with a last nod. And the door closed quietly behind him.

The boy did not speak for a long time. He pulled down the bangs on his forehead and slid his grimy little forefinger around the rim of his empty cup. Then without looking at Leo he finally asked:

"Was he drunk?"

"No," said Leo shortly.

The boy raised his clear voice higher. "Then was he a dope fiend?"

"No."

The boy looked up at Leo, and his flat little face was desperate, his voice urgent and shrill. "Was he crazy? Do you think he was a lunatic?" The paper boy's voice dropped suddenly with doubt. "Leo? Or not?"

But Leo would not answer him. Leo had run a night café for fourteen years, and he held himself to be a critic of craziness. There were the town characters and also the transients who roamed in from the night. He knew the manias of all of them. But he did not want to satisfy the questions of the waiting child. He tightened his pale face and was silent.

So the boy pulled down the right flap of his helmet and as he turned to leave he made the only comment that seemed safe to him, the only remark that could not be laughed down and despised:

"He sure has done a lot of traveling."

Juan Rulfo (1918–   )

Although the recent (1972) *Who's Notable in Mexico* makes no mention of Juan Rulfo, reviewers of the English translation of his novel *Pedro Páramo,* which appeared in 1959, claimed that his Mexican confreres regarded Rulfo as "the most eminent new writer among them" and that "only the poet Octavio Paz is similarly expected to rank among the immortals." That high estimation still stands, perhaps partly because Rulfo has done so little to alter it. He has published only two books, the novel *Pedro Páramo* (1955) and a volume of short stories, *El llano en llamas* (1953) which was translated by George D. Schade as *The Burning Plain and Other Stories* (1967). A second novel, *La Cordillera,* has been in preparation for many years. Yet in spite of this slender production, Rulfo promises to stand along with Carlos Fuentes and Agustin Ýañez as one of the most powerful and influential fiction writers of postrevolutionary Mexico. His work is at once traditional and innovative: it embodies on the one hand qualities of myth and folktale that evoke comparisons with Greek tragedy, and on the other with those radical experiments with time, narrative sequence, and causality that we associate with the work of Faulkner, Woolf, and more "modernist" writers. As Joseph Somers writes in his fine book *After the Storm: Landmarks of the Modern Mexican Novel* (1968): "The dominant process in *Pedro Páramo* is neither development nor progression, but the relevation of finality—the static, permanent qualities inherent in human existence. Events flow backward and forward, with the future and present merged in the past."

"Macario," the first story in *The Burning Plain,* renders most powerfully those "static, permanent qualities" Somers mentions. Told from the point of view of a feebleminded boy, like Part I of Faulkner's *The Sound and the Fury,* the story is one long interior monologue, the simple, stark account of bitter poverty and hunger, and the blunt tenderness of the one person who cares for him, the girl Felipa. Daily she confesses for him, since he can't confess for himself, asking God to drive out the devils that cause him continually to bang his head on the floors and pillars: "That's why I love her so much—Still, having a head so hard is a great thing." A character in *Pedro Páramo* asks, "And what do you think life is, if not sin?" It is the underlying question of this story as well. Rulfo's is a tragic vision, remorseless as the arid, half-deserted region of southern Jalisco, which is the setting for all his fiction. "Life seems to have come to a stop in this paralyzed region, producing a static quality in many of the stories," writes George D. Schade: "Macario . . . starts out on his rambling monologue, 'I am sitting by the sewer waiting for the frogs to come out.' And he is still waiting there at the end of the story." There is no action and no conversation, though the illusion of dialogue is strong; and though we never actually hear or see Felipa, we end by knowing her, as people are always known, as a presence in the life of others.

Rulfo was, like Macario, orphaned as a boy, his family having been destroyed in the wars of the church against the government in the late 1920s. After a minimal education in a Guadalajara orphanage (which he left at age fifteen) he attended a few classes at the National University in Mexico City. But essentially he educated himself through reading. He has been an editor for the National Indian Institute and an adviser to young writers at the Mexican Writers' Center, as well as a worker in publicity, films, and television. He continues, so his admirers hope, to work on that long-awaited second novel.

Macario

I am sitting by the sewer waiting for the frogs to come out. While we were having supper last night they started making a great racket and they didn't stop singing till dawn. Godmother says so too—the cries of the frogs scared her sleep away. And now she would really like to sleep. That's why she ordered me to sit here, by the sewer, with a board in my hand to whack to smithereens every frog that may come hopping out— Frogs are green all over except on the belly. Toads are black. Godmother's eyes are also black. Frogs make good eating. Toads don't. People just don't eat toads. People don't, but I do, and they taste just like frogs. Felipa is the one who says it's bad to eat toads. Felipa has green eyes like a cat's eyes. She feeds me in the kitchen whenever I get to eat. She doesn't want me to hurt frogs. But then Godmother is the one who orders me to do things—I love Felipa more than Godmother. But Godmother is the one who takes money out of her purse so Felipa can buy all the food. Felipa stays alone in the kitchen cooking food for the three of us. Since I've known her, that's all she does. Washing the dishes is up to me. Carrying in wood for the stove is my job too. Then Godmother is the one who dishes out food to us. After she has eaten, she makes two little piles with her hands, one for Felipa, the other for me. But sometimes Felipa doesn't feel like eating and then the two little piles are for me. That's why I love Felipa, because I'm always hungry and I never get filled up—never, not even when I eat up her food. They say a person does get filled up eating, but I know very well that I don't even though I eat all they give me. And Felipa knows it too—They say in the street that I'm crazy because I never stop being hungry. Godmother has heard them say that. I haven't. Godmother won't let me go out alone on the street. When she takes me out, it's to go to church to hear Mass. There she sets me down next to her and ties my hands with the fringe of her shawl. I don't know why she ties my hands, but she says it's because they say I do crazy things. One day they found me hanging somebody; I was hanging a lady just to be doing it. I don't remember. But then Godmother is the one who says what I do and she never goes about telling lies. When she calls me to eat, it's to give me my part of the food. She's not like other people who invite me to eat with them and then when I get close throw rocks at me until I run away without eating anything. No, Godmother is good to me. That's why I'm content in her house. Besides, Felipa lives here. Felipa is very good to me. That's why I love her—Felipa's milk is as sweet as hibiscus flowers. I've drunk goat's milk and also the milk of a sow that had recently had pigs. But no, it isn't as good as Felipa's milk—Now it's been a

From Juan Rulfo, *The Burning Plain and Other Stories,* translated by George D. Schade. Reprinted by permission of University of Texas Press.

long time since she has let me nurse the breasts that she has where we just have ribs, and where there comes out, if you know how to get it, a better milk than the one Godmother gives us for lunch on Sundays—Felipa used to come every night to the room where I sleep, and snuggle up to me, leaning over me or a little to one side. Then she would fix her breasts so that I could suck the sweet, hot milk that came out in streams on my tongue— Many times I've eaten hibiscus flowers to try to forget my hunger. And Felipa's milk had the same flavor, except that I liked it better because, at the same time that she let me nurse, Felipa would tickle me all over. Then almost always she would stay there sleeping by me until dawn. And that was very good for me, because I didn't worry about the cold and I wasn't afraid of being damned to hell if I died there alone some night—Sometimes I'm not so afraid of hell. But sometimes I am. And then I like to scare myself about going to hell any day now, because my head is so hard and I like to bang it against the first thing I come across. But Felipa comes and scares away my fears. She tickles me with her hands like she knows how to do and she stops that fear of mine that I have of dying. And for a little while I even forget it—Felipa says, when she feels like being with me, that she will tell the Lord all my sins. She will go to heaven very soon and will talk with Him, asking Him to pardon me for all the great wickedness that fills my body from head to toe. She will tell Him to pardon me so I won't worry about it any more. That's why she goes to confession every day. Not because she's bad, but because I'm full of devils inside, and she has to drive them out of my body by confessing for me. Every single day. Every single afternoon of every single day. She will do that favor for me her whole life. That's what Felipa says. That's why I love her so much—Still, having a head so hard is the great thing. I bang it against the pillars of the corridor hours on end and nothing happens to it. It stands banging and doesn't crack. I bang it against the floor—first slowly, then harder—and that sounds like a drum. Just like the drum that goes with the wood flute when I hear them through the window of the church, tied to Godmother, and hearing outside the boom boom of the drum— And Godmother says that if there are chinches and cockroaches and scorpions in my room it's because I'm going to burn in hell if I keep on with this business of banging my head on the floor. But what I like is to hear the drum. She should know that. Even when I'm in church, waiting to go out soon into the street to see why the drum is heard from so far away, deep inside the church and above the damning of the priest— "The road of good things is filled with light. The road of bad things is dark." That's what the priest says— I get up and go out of my room while it's still dark. I sweep the street and I go back in my room before daylight grabs me. On the street things happen. There are lots of people who will hit me on the head with rocks as soon as they see me. Big sharp rocks rain from every side. And then my shirt has to be mended and I have to wait many days for the scabs on my face or knees to heal. And go through having my hands tied again, because if I don't they'll hurry to scratch off the scabs and a stream of blood will come out again. Blood has a good flavor too, although it isn't really like the flavor of Felipa's milk— That's why I always live shut up in my house—so they won't throw rocks at me. As soon as they feed me I lock myself in my room and bar the door so my sins won't find me out, because it's dark. And I don't even light the torch to see where the cockroaches are climbing on me. Now I keep quiet. I go to bed on my sacks, and as soon as I feel a cockroach walking along my neck with its scratchy feet I give it a slap with my hand and squash it. But I don't light the torch. I'm not going to let my sins catch me off guard with my torch lit looking for cockroaches under my blanket—Cockroaches pop like firecrackers when you mash them. I don't know whether crickets pop. I never kill crickets. Felipa says that crickets always make noise so you can't hear the cries of souls suffering in purgatory. The day there are no more crickets the world will be filled with the screams of holy souls and we'll all start running scared out of our wits. Besides, I like very much to prick my ears up and listen to the noise of the crickets. There are lots of them in my room. Maybe there are more crickets than cockroaches among the folds of the sacks where I sleep. There are scorpions too. Every once in a while they fall from the ceiling and I have to hold my breath until they've made their way across me to reach the floor. Because if an arm moves or one of my bones begins to tremble, I feel the burn of the sting right away. That hurts. Once Felipa got stung on the behind by one of them. She started moaning and making soft little cries to the Holy Virgin that her behind wouldn't be ruined. I rubbed spit on her. All night I spent rubbing spit on her and praying with her, and after a while, when I saw that my spit wasn't making her any better, I also helped her to cry with my eyes all that I could— Anyway, I like it better in my room than out on the street, attracting the attention of those who love to throw rocks at people. Here nobody does anything to me. Godmother doesn't even scold me when she sees me eating up her hibiscus flowers, or her myrtles, or her pomegranates. She knows how awfully hungry I am all the time. She knows that I'm always hungry. She knows that no meal is enough to fill up my insides, even though I go about snitching things to eat here and there all the time. She knows that I gobble up the chick-pea slop I give to the fat pigs and the dry-corn slop I give to the skinny pigs. So she knows how hungry I go around from the time I get up until the time I go to bed. And as long as I find something to eat here in this house I'll stay here. Because I think that the day I quit eating I'm going to die, and then I'll surely go straight to hell. And nobody will get me out of there, not even Felipa, who is so good to me, or the scapular that Godmother gave to me and that I wear hung around my neck— Now I'm by the sewer waiting for the frogs to come out. And not one has come out all this while I've been talking. If they take much longer to come out I may go to sleep and then there won't be any way to kill them and Godmother won't be able to sleep at all if she hears them singing and she'll get very angry. And then she'll ask one of that string of saints she has in her room to send the devils after me, to take me off to eternal damnation, right now, without even passing through purgatory, and then I won't be able to see my papa or mamma, because that's where they are—So I just better keep on talking— What I would really like to do is take a few swallows of Felipa's milk, that good milk as sweet as honey that comes from under the hibiscus flowers—

Flannery O'Connor (1925–1964)

Flannery O'Connor was a woman, a Southerner, a cripple, and a Catholic and, though all her complex background and experience find their way into her fiction, the theme that runs most strongly is religion. She wrote,

> I see from the standpoint of Christian orthodoxy. This means that for me the meaning of life is centered in our Redemption by Christ and what I see in the world I see in its relation to that.

Hers is no simple or easily grasped vision. She said that she discovered from reading her work that "my subject in fiction is the action of grace in territory held largely by the devil."

Sometimes the violence of the action and the grotesqueness of the characters seem to preclude the manifestation of grace. But she believed that when the audience viewed the repugnant as normal, the writer must shock: "To the hard of hearing you shout and for the almost-blind you draw large and startling pictures." She also found that "violence is strangely capable of returning my characters to reality and preparing them to accept their moment of grace."

But she is not propagandistic, and the reader who does not share her theology or values can still enjoy and benefit from her work. She does not oversimplify human experience in order to fit it neatly in a mold or to "prove" a point. Though often her characters seem larger than life, perhaps caricatured, they lead their own lives, find their own destinies, make their own hells. Also, O'Connor tells good, exciting yarns in which important things happen to people, usually her fellow Georgians.

"Greenleaf" is sometimes thought to be sociologically specific, that is, a story about declining gentry and rising poor whites. And so it is, but it is more than that. The first sentences introduce the major themes: the intertwined mystery of sex and religion, the possibility of the sudden manifestation of the deity, here in the form of a bull. Soon, other themes emerge: Mrs. May's pride, snobbery, arrogance, and rage; the idea of death, foreshadowed by Mrs. May's dreams of approaching doom; her struggle with Mr. Greenleaf for dominance. And most important is Mrs. May's complacent nonbelief. She had a "large respect for religion, though she did not, of course, believe any of it was true." Church is where her sons can meet nice girls. When she is confronted with Mrs. Greenleaf's fundamentalist faith, she says, "Jesus would be ashamed of you."

The ending ties the themes together. The bull charges toward her "as if he were overjoyed to see her again." She remains in "freezing disbelief" until he buries his head in her lap "like a tormented lover." Dying, she has the look of a person "whose sight had been restored but who finds the light unbearable." And then Mr. Greenleaf, who has been closely identified with the bull throughout, comes to shoot the animal in the eye. Is it too late for Mrs. May, or is *this* the action of grace? O'Connor does not presume to say.

But despite the seriousness of her themes and the power of her commitment, Flannery O'Connor is a comic writer. She can make a reader laugh out loud, at the outrageous imagery, at the twists of countrified speech, at characters who are exaggerated and grotesque but somehow not horrible, and even at the comic absurdity she sees in the spiritual condition of modern man.

Greenleaf

Mrs. May's bedroom window was low and faced on the east and the bull, silvered in the moonlight, stood under it, his head raised as if he listened—like some patient god

Flannery O'Connor, "Greenleaf," from *Contemporary American Short Stories,* selected and intro. Douglas & Sylvia Angus, Fawcett Publications, Greenwich, Conn., 1967. Originally from *Everything That Rises Must Converge.* Copyright 1956 Estate of Mary Flannery O'Connor.

come down to woo her—for a stir inside the room. The window was dark and the sound of her breathing too light to be carried outside. Clouds crossing the moon blackened him and in the dark he began to tear at the hedge. Presently they passed and he appeared again in the same spot, chewing steadily, with a hedge-wreath that he had ripped loose for himself caught in the tips of his horns. When the moon drifted into retirement again, there was nothing to mark his place but the sound of steady chewing. Then abruptly a pink glow filled the window. Bars of light slid across him as the venetian blind was slit. He took a step backward and lowered his head as if to show the wreath across his horns.

For almost a minute there was no sound from inside, then as he raised his crowned head again, a woman's voice, guttural as if addressed to a dog, said, "Get away from here, Sir!" and in a second muttered, "Some nigger's scrub bull."

The animal pawed the ground and Mrs. May, standing bent forward behind the blind, closed it quickly lest the light make him charge into the shrubbery. For a second she waited, still bent forward, her nightgown hanging loosely from her narrow shoulders. Green rubber curlers sprouted neatly over her forehead and her face beneath them was smooth as concrete with an egg-white paste that drew the wrinkles out while she slept.

She had been conscious in her sleep of a steady rhythmic chewing as if something were eating one wall of the house. She had been aware that whatever it was had been eating as long as she had had the place and had eaten everything from the beginning of her fence line up to the house and now was eating the house and calmly with the same steady rhythm would continue through the house, eating her and the boys, and then on, eating everything but the Greenleafs, on and on, eating everything until nothing was left but the Greenleafs on a little island all their own in the middle of what had been her place. When the munching reached her elbow, she jumped up and found herself, fully awake, standing in the middle of her room. She identified the sound at once: a cow was tearing at the shrubbery under her window. Mr. Greenleaf had left the lane gate open and she didn't doubt that the entire herd was on her lawn. She turned on the dim pink table lamp and then went to the window and slit the blind. The bull, gaunt and long-legged, was standing about four feet from her, chewing calmly like an uncouth country suitor.

For fifteen years, she thought as she squinted at him fiercely, she had been having shiftless people's hogs root up her oats, their mules wallow on her lawn, their scrub bulls breed her cows. If this one was not put up now, he would be over the fence, ruining her herd before morning—and Mr. Greenleaf was soundly sleeping a half mile down the road in the tenant house. There was no way to get him unless she dressed and got in her car and rode down there and woke him up. He would come but his expression, his whole figure, his every pause, would say: "Hit looks to me like one or both of them boys would not make their maw ride out in the middle of the night thisaway. If hit was my boys, they would have got thet bull up theirself."

The bull lowered his head and shook it and the wreath slipped down to the base of his horns where it looked like a menacing prickly crown. She had closed the blind then; in a few seconds she heard him move off heavily.

Mr. Greenleaf would say, "If hit was my boys they would never have allowed their maw to go after hired help in the middle of the night. They would have did it theirself."

Weighing it, she decided not to bother Mr. Greenleaf. She returned to bed thinking that if the Greenleaf boys had risen in the world it was because she had given their father employment when no one else would have him. She had had Mr. Greenleaf fifteen years but no one else would have had him five minutes. Just the way he approached an object was enough to tell anybody with eyes what kind of a worker he was. He walked with a high-shouldered creep and he never appeared to come directly forward. He walked on the perimeter of some invisible circle and if you wanted to look him in the face, you had to move and get in front of him. She had not fired him because she had always doubted she could do better. He was too shiftless to go out and look for another job; he didn't have the initiative to steal, and after she had told him three or four times to do a thing, he did it; but he never told her about a sick cow until it was too late to call the veterinarian and if her barn had caught on fire, he would have called his wife to see the flames before he began to put them out. And of the wife, she didn't even like to think. Beside the wife, Mr. Greenleaf was an aristocrat.

"If it had been my boys," he would have said, "they would have cut off their right arm before they would have allowed their maw to . . . ."

"If your boys had any pride, Mr. Greenleaf," she would like to say to him some day, "there are many things that they would not *allow* their mother to do."

The next morning as soon as Mr. Greenleaf came to the back door, she told him there was a stray bull on the place and that she wanted him penned up at once.

"Done already been here three days," he said, addressing his right foot which he held forward, turned slightly as if he were trying to look at the sole. He was standing at the bottom of the three back steps while she leaned out the kitchen door, a small woman with pale near-sighted eyes and grey hair that rose on top like the crest of some disturbed bird.

"Three days!" she said in the restrained screech that had become habitual with her.

Mr. Greenleaf, looking into the distance over the near pasture, removed a package of cigarets from his shirt pocket and let one fall into his hand. He put the package back and stood for a while looking at the cigaret. "I put him in the bull pen but he torn out of there," he said presently. "I didn't see him none after that." He bent over the cigaret and lit it and then turned his head briefly in her direction. The upper part of his face sloped gradually into the lower which was long and narrow, shaped like a rough chalice. He had deepset fox-colored eyes shadowed under a grey felt hat that he wore slanted forward following the line of his nose. His build was insignificant.

"Mr. Greenleaf," she said, "get that bull up this morning before you do anything else. You know he'll ruin the breeding schedule. Get him up and keep him up and the next time there's a stray bull on this place, tell me at once. Do you understand?"

"Where you want him put at?" Mr. Greenleaf asked.

"I don't care where you put him," she said. "You are supposed to have some sense. Put him where he can't get out. Whose bull is he?"

For a moment Mr. Greenleaf seemed to hesitate between silence and speech. He studied the air to the left of him. "He must be somebody's bull," he said after a while.

"Yes, he must!" she said and shut the door with a precise little slam.

She went into the dining room where the two boys were eating breakfast and sat down on the edge of her chair at the head of the table. She never ate breakfast but she sat with them to see that they had what they wanted. "Honestly!" she said, and began to tell about the bull, aping Mr. Greenleaf saying, "It must be *somebody's* bull."

Wesley continued to read the newspaper folded beside his plate but Scofield interrupted his eating from time to time to look at her and laugh. The two boys never had the same reaction to anything. They were as different, she said, as night and day. The only thing they did have in common was that neither of them cared what happened on the place. Scofield was a business type and Wesley was an intellectual.

Wesley, the younger child, had had rheumatic fever when he was seven and Mrs. May thought that this was what had caused him to be an intellectual. Scofield, who had never had a day's sickness in his life, was an insurance salesman. She would not have minded his selling insurance if he had sold a nicer kind but he sold the kind that only Negroes buy. He was what Negroes call a "policy man." He said there was more money in nigger-insurance than any other kind, and before company, he was very loud about it. He would shout, "Mamma don't like to hear me say it but I'm the best nigger-insurance salesman in this county!"

Scofield was thirty-six and he had a broad pleasant smiling face but he was not married. "Yes," Mrs. May would say, "and if you sold decent insurance, some *nice* girl would be willing to marry you. What nice girl wants to marry a nigger-insurance man? You'll wake up some day and it'll be too late."

And at this Scofield would yodel and say, "Why Mamma, I'm not going to marry until you're dead and gone and then I'm going to marry me some nice fat farm girl that can take over this place!" And once he had added, "—some nice lady like Mrs. Greenleaf." When he had said this, Mrs. May had risen from her chair, her back stiff as a rake handle, and had gone to her room. There she had sat down on the edge of her bed for some time with her small face drawn. Finally she had whispered, "I work and slave, I struggle and sweat to keep this place for them and soon as I'm dead, they'll marry trash and bring it in here and ruin everything. They'll marry trash and ruin everything I've done," and she had made up her mind at that moment to change her will. The next day she had gone to her lawyer and had had the property entailed so that if they married, they could not leave it to their wives.

The idea that one of them might marry a woman even remotely like Mrs. Greenleaf was enough to make her ill. She had put up with Mr. Greenleaf for fifteen years, but the only way she had endured his wife had been by keeping entirely out of her sight. Mrs. Greenleaf was large and loose. The yard around her house looked like a dump and her five girls were always filthy; even the youngest one dipped snuff. Instead of making a garden or washing their clothes, her preoccupation was what she called "prayer healing."

Every day she cut all the morbid stories out of the newspaper—the accounts of women who had been raped and criminals who had escaped and children who had been burned and of train wrecks and plane crashes and the divorces of movie stars. She took these to the woods and dug a hole and buried them and then she fell on the ground over them and mumbled and groaned for an hour or so, moving her huge arms back and forth under her and out again and finally just lying down flat and, Mrs. May suspected, going to sleep in the dirt.

She had not found out about this until the Greenleafs had been with her a few months. One morning she had been out to inspect a field that she had wanted planted in rye but that had come up in clover because Mr. Greenfield had used the wrong seeds in the grain drill. She was returning through a wooded path that separated two pastures, muttering to herself and hitting the ground methodically with a long stick she carried in case she saw a snake. "Mr. Greenleaf," she was saying in a low voice, "I cannot afford to pay for your mistakes. I am a poor woman and this place is all I have. I have two boys to educate. I cannot . . . ."

Out of nowhere a guttural agonized voice groaned, "Jesus! Jesus!" In a second it came again with a terrible urgency. "Jesus! Jesus!"

Mrs. May stopped still, one hand lifted to her throat. The sound was so piercing that she felt as if some violent unleashed force had broken out of the ground and was charging toward her. Her second thought was more reasonable: somebody had been hurt on the place and would sue her for everything she had. She had no insurance. She rushed forward and turning a bend in the path, she saw Mrs. Greenleaf sprawled on her hands and knees off the side of the road, her head down.

"Mrs. Greenleaf!" she shrilled, "what's happened?"

Mrs. Greenleaf raised her head. Her face was a patchwork of dirt and tears and her small eyes, the color of two field peas, were red-rimmed and swollen, but her expression was as composed as a bulldog's. She swayed back and forth on her hands and knees and groaned, "Jesus! Jesus!"

Mrs. May winced. She thought the word, Jesus, should be kept inside the church building like other words inside the bedroom. She was a good Christian woman with a large respect for religion, though she did not, of course, believe any of it was true. "What is the matter with you?" she asked sharply.

"You broken my healing," Mrs. Greenleaf said, waving her aside. "I can't talk to you until I finish."

Mrs. May stood, bent forward, her mouth open and her stick raised off the ground as if she were not sure what she wanted to strike with it.

"Oh Jesus, stab me in the heart!" Mrs. Greenleaf shrieked. "Jesus, stab me in the heart!" and she fell back flat in the dirt, a huge human mound, her legs and arms spread out as if she were trying to wrap them around the earth.

Mrs. May felt as furious and helpless as if she had been insulted by a child. "Jesus," she said, drawing herself back, "would be *ashamed* of you. He would tell you to get up from there this instant and go wash your children's clothes!" and she had turned and walked off as fast as she could.

Whenever she thought of how the Greenleaf boys had advanced in the world, she had only to think of Mrs. Greenleaf sprawled obscenely on the ground, and say to herself, "Well, no matter how far they *go,* they *came* from that."

She would like to have been able to put in her will that when she died, Wesley and Scofield were not to continue to employ Mr. Greenleaf. She was capable of handling Mr. Greenleaf; they were not. Mr. Greenleaf had pointed out to her once that her boys didn't know hay from silage. She had pointed out to him that they had other talents, that Scofield was a successful business man and Wesley a successful intellectual. Mr. Greenleaf did not comment, but he never lost an opportunity of letting her see, by his expression or some simple gesture, that he held the two of them in infinite contempt. As scrub-human as the Greenleafs were, he never hesitated to let her know that in any like circumstance in which his own boys might have been involved, they—O. T. and E. T. Greenleaf—would have acted to better advantage.

The Greenleaf boys were two or three years younger than the May boys. They were twins and you never knew when you spoke to one of them whether you were speaking to O. T. or E. T, and they never had the politeness to enlighten you. They were long-legged and raw-boned and red-skinned, with bright grasping fox-colored eyes like their father's. Mr. Greenleaf's pride in them began with the fact that they were twins. He acted, Mrs. May said, as if this were something smart they had thought of themselves. They were energetic and hardworking and she would admit to anyone that they had come a long way—and that the Second World War was responsible for it.

They had both joined the service and, disguised in their uniforms, they could not be told from other people's children. You could tell, of course, when they opened their mouths but they did that seldom. The smartest thing they had done was to get sent overseas and there to marry French wives. They hadn't married French trash either. They had married nice girls who naturally couldn't tell that they murdered the king's English or that the Greenleafs were who they were.

Wesley's heart condition had not permitted him to serve his country but Scofield had been in the army for two years. He had not cared for it and at the end of his military service, he was only a Private First Class. The Greenleaf boys were both some kind of sergeants, and Mr. Greenleaf, in those days, had never lost an opportunity of referring to them by their rank. They had both managed to get wounded and now they both had pensions. Further, as soon as they were released from the army, they took advantage of all the benefits and went to the school of agriculture at the university— the taxpayers meanwhile supporting their French wives. The two of them were living now about two miles down the highway on a piece of land that the government had helped them to buy and in a brick duplex bungalow that the government had helped to build and pay for. If the war had made anyone, Mrs. May said, it had made the Greenleaf boys. They each had three little children apiece, who spoke Greenleaf English and French, and who, on account of their mothers' background, would be sent to the convent school and brought up with manners. "And in twenty years," Mrs. May asked Scofield and Wesley, "do you know what those people will be?"

"*Society,*" she said blackly.

She had spent fifteen years coping with Mr. Greenleaf and, by now, handling him had become second nature with her. His disposition on any particular day was as much a factor in what she could and couldn't do as the weather was, and she had learned to read his face the way real country people read the sunrise and sunset.

She was a country woman only by persuasion. The late Mr. May, a business man, had bought the place when land was down, and when he died it was all he had to leave her. The boys had not been happy to move to the country to a broken-down farm, but there was nothing else for her to do. She had the timber on the place cut and with the proceeds had set herself up in the dairy business after Mr. Greenleaf had answered her ad. "I seen yor ad and i will come have 2 boys," was all his letter said, but he arrived the next day in a pieced-together truck, his wife and five daughters sitting on the floor in back, himself and the two boys in the cab.

Over the years they had been on her place, Mr. and Mrs. Greenleaf had aged hardly at all. They had no worries, no responsibilities. They lived like the lilies of the field, off the fat that she struggled to put into the land. When she was dead and gone from overwork and worry, the Greenleafs, healthy and thriving, would be just ready to begin draining Scofield and Wesley.

Wesley said the reason Mrs. Greenleaf had not aged was because she released all her emotions in prayer healing. "You ought to start praying, Sweetheart," he had said in the voice that, poor boy, he could not help making deliberately nasty.

Scofield only exasperated her beyond endurance but Wesley caused her real anxiety. He was thin and nervous and bald and being an intellectual was a terrible strain on his disposition. She doubted if he would marry until she died but she was certain that then the wrong woman would get him. Nice girls didn't like Scofield but Wesley didn't like nice girls. He didn't like anything. He drove twenty miles every day to the university where he taught and twenty miles back every night, but he said he hated the twenty-mile drive and he hated the second-rate university and he hated the morons who attended it. He hated the country and he hated the life he lived; he hated living with his mother and his idiot brother and he hated hearing about the damn dairy and the damn help and the damn broken machinery. But in spite of all he said, he never made any move to leave. He talked about Paris and Rome but he never went even to Atlanta.

"You'd go to those places and you'd get sick," Mrs. May would say. "Who in Paris is going to see that you get a salt-free diet? And do you think if you married one of those odd numbers you take out that *she* would cook a salt-free diet for you? No indeed, she would not!" When she took this line, Wesley would turn himself roughly around in his chair and ignore her. Once when she had kept it up too long, he had snarled, "Well, why don't you do something practical, Woman? Why don't you pray for me like Mrs. Greenleaf would?"

"I don't like to hear you boys make jokes about religion," she had said. "If you would go to church, you would meet some nice girls."

But it was impossible to tell them anything. When she looked at the two of them now, sitting on either side of the table, neither one caring the least if a stray bull ruined her herd—which was their herd, their future—when she looked at the two of them, one hunched over a paper and the other teetering back in his chair, grinning at her like an idiot, she wanted to jump up and beat her fist on the table and shout, "You'll find out one of these days, you'll find out what *Reality* is when it's too late!"

"Mamma," Scofield said, "don't you get excited now but I'll tell you whose bull that is." He was looking at her wickedly. He let his chair drop forward and he got up. Then with his shoulders bent and his hands held up to cover his head, he tiptoed to the door. He backed into the hall and pulled the door almost to so that it hid all of him but his face. "You want to know, Sugarpie?" he asked.

Mrs. May sat looking at him coldly.

"That's O. T. and E. T.'s bull," he said. "I collected from their nigger yesterday and he told me they were missing it," and he showed her an exaggerated expanse of teeth and disappeared silently.

Wesley looked up and laughed.

Mrs. May turned her head forward again, her expression unaltered. "I am the only *adult* on this place," she said. She leaned across the table and pulled the paper from the side of his plate. "Do you see how it's going to be when I die and you boys have to handle him?" she began. "Do you see why he didn't know whose bull that was? Because it was theirs. Do you see what I have to put up with? Do you see that if I hadn't kept my foot on his neck all these years, you boys might be milking cows every morning at four o'clock?"

Wesley pulled the paper back toward his plate and staring at her full in the face, he murmured, "I wouldn't milk a cow to save your soul from hell."

"I know you wouldn't," she said in a brittle voice. She sat back and began rapidly turning her knife over at the side of her plate. "O. T. and E. T. are fine boys," she said. "They ought to have been my sons." The thought of this was so horrible that her vision of Wesley was blurred at once by a wall of tears. All she saw was his dark shape, rising quickly from the table. "And you two," she cried, "you two should have belonged to that woman!"

He was heading for the door.

"When I die," she said in a thin voice, "I don't know what's going to become of you."

"You're always yapping about when-you-die," he growled as he rushed out, "but you look pretty healthy to me."

For some time she sat where she was, looking straight ahead through the window across the room into a scene of indistinct greys and greens. She stretched her face and her neck muscles and drew in a long breath but the scene in front of her flowed together anyway into a watery grey mass. "They needn't think I'm going to die any time soon," she muttered, and some more defiant voice in her added: I'll die when I get good and ready.

She wiped her eyes with the table napkin and got up and went to the window and gazed at the scene in front of her. The cows were grazing on two pale green pastures across the road and behind them, fencing them in, was a black wall of trees with a sharp sawtooth edge that held off the indifferent sky. The pastures were enough to calm her. When she looked out any window in her house, she saw the reflection of her own character. Her city friends said she was the most remarkable woman they knew, to go, practically penniless and with no experience, out to a rundown farm and make a success of it. "Everything is against you," she would say, "the weather is against you and the dirt is against you and the help is against you. They're all in league against you. There's nothing for it but an iron hand!"

"Look at Mamma's iron hand!" Scofield would yell and grab her arm and hold it up so that her delicate blue-veined little hand would dangle from her wrist like the head of a broken lily. The company always laughed.

The sun, moving over the black and white grazing cows, was just a little brighter than the rest of the sky. Looking down, she saw a darker shape that might have been its shadow cast at an angle, moving among them. She uttered a sharp cry and turned and marched out of the house.

Mr. Greenleaf was in the trench silo, filling a wheelbarrow. She stood on the edge and looked down at him. "I told you to get up that bull. Now he's in with the milk herd."

"You can't do two things at oncet," Mr. Greenleaf remarked.

"I told you to do that first."

He wheeled the barrow out of the open end of the trench toward the barn and she followed close behind him. "And you needn't think, Mr. Greenleaf," she said, "that I don't know exactly whose bull that is or why you haven't been in any hurry to notify me he was here. I might as well feed O. T. and E. T.'s bull as long as I'm going to have him here ruining my herd."

Mr. Greenleaf paused with the wheelbarrow and looked behind him. "Is that them boy's bull?" he asked in an incredulous tone.

She did not say a word. She merely looked away with her mouth taut.

"They told me their bull was out but I never known that was him," he said.

"I want that bull put up now," she said, "and I'm going to drive over to O. T. and E. T.'s and tell them they'll have to come get him today. I ought to charge for the time he's been here—then it wouldn't happen again."

"They didn't pay but seventy-five dollars for him," Mr. Greenleaf offered.

"I wouldn't have had him as a gift," she said.

"They was just going to beef him," Mr. Greenleaf went on, "but he got loose and run his head into their pickup truck. He don't like cars and trucks. They had a time getting his horn out the fender and when they finally got him loose, he took off and they was too tired to run after him—but I never known that was him there."

"It wouldn't have paid you to know, Mr. Greenleaf," she said. "But you know now. Get a horse and get him."

In a half hour, from her front window she saw the bull, squirrel-colored, with jutting hips and long light horns, ambling down the dirt road that ran in front of the house. Mr. Greenleaf was behind him on the horse. "That's a Greenleaf bull if I ever saw one," she muttered. She went out on the porch and called, "Put him where he can't get out."

"He likes to bust loose," Mr. Greenleaf said, looking with approval at the bull's rump. "This gentleman is a sport."

"If those boys don't come for him, he's going to be a dead sport," she said. "I'm just warning you."

He heard her but he didn't answer.

"That the awfullest looking bull I ever saw," she called but he was too far down the road to hear.

It was mid-morning when she turned into O. T. and E. T.'s driveway. The house, a new red-brick, low-to-the-ground building that looked like a warehouse with windows, was on top of a treeless hill. The sun was beating down directly on the white roof of it. It was the kind of house that everybody built now and nothing marked it as belonging to Greenleafs except three dogs, part hound and part spitz, that rushed out from behind it as soon as she stopped her car. She reminded herself that you could always tell the class of people by the class of dog, and honked her horn. While she sat waiting for someone to come, she continued to study the house. All the windows were down and she wondered if the government could have air-conditioned the thing. No one came and she honked again. Presently a door opened and several children appeared in it and stood looking at her, making no move to come forward. She recognized this as a true Greenleaf trait—they could hang in a door, looking at you for hours.

"Can't one of you children come here?" she called.

After a minute they all began to move forward, slowly. They had on overalls and were barefooted but they were not as dirty as she might have expected. There were two or three that looked distinctly like Greenleafs; the others not so much so. The smallest child was a girl with untidy black hair. They stopped about six feet from the automobile and stood looking at her.

"You're mighty pretty," Mrs. May said, addressing herself to the smallest girl.

There was no answer. They appeared to share one dispassionate expression between them.

"Where's your Mamma?" she asked.

There was no answer to this for some time. Then one of them said something in French. Mrs. May did not speak French.

"Where's your daddy?" she asked.

After a while, one of the boys said, "He ain't hyar neither."

"Ahhhh," Mrs. May said as if something had been proven. "Where's the colored man?"

She waited and decided no one was going to answer. "The cat has six little tongues," she said. "How would you like to come home with me and let me teach you how to talk?" She laughed and her laugh died on the silent air. She felt as if she were on trial for her life, facing a jury of Greenleafs. "I'll go down and see if I can find the colored man," she said.

"You can go if you want to," one of the boys said.

"Well, thank you," she murmured and drove off.

The barn was down the lane from the house. She had not seen it before but Mr. Greenleaf had described it in detail for it had been built according to the latest specifications. It was a milking parlor arrangement where the cows are milked from below. The milk ran in pipes from the machines to the milk house and was never carried in no bucket, Mr. Greenleaf said, by no human hand. "When you gonter get you one?" he had asked.

"Mr. Greenleaf," she said, "I have to do for myself. I am not assisted hand and foot by the government. It would cost me $20,000 to install a milking parlor. I barely make ends meet as it is."

"My boys done it," Mr. Greenleaf had murmured, and then—"but all boys ain't alike."

"No indeed!" she had said. "I thank God for that!"

"I thank Gawd for ever-thang," Mr. Greenleaf had drawled.

You might as well, she had thought in the fierce silence that followed; you've never done anything for yourself.

She stopped by the side of the barn and honked but no one appeared. For several minutes she sat in the car, observing the various machines parked around, wondering how many of them were paid for. They had a forage harvester and a rotary hay baler. She had those too. She decided that since no one was here, she would get out and have a look at the milking parlor and see if they kept it clean.

She opened the milking room door and stuck her head in and for the first second she felt as if she were going to lose her breath. The spotless white concrete room was filled with sunlight that came from a row of windows head-high along both walls. The metal stanchions gleamed ferociously and she had to squint to be able to look at all. She drew her head out of the room quickly and closed the door and leaned against it, frowning. The light outside was not so bright but she was conscious that the sun was directly on top of her head, like a silver bullet ready to drop into her brain.

A Negro carrying a yellow calf-feed bucket appeared from around the corner of the machine shed and came toward her. He was a light yellow boy dressed in the cast-off army clothes of the Greenleaf twins. He stopped at a respectable distance and set the bucket on the ground.

"Where's Mr. O. T. and Mr. E. T.?" she asked.

"Mist O. T. he in town, Mist E. T. he off yonder in the field," the Negro said, pointing first to the left and then to the right as if he were naming the position of two planets.

"Can you remember a message?" she asked, looking as if she thought this doubtful.

"I'll remember it if I don't forget it," he said with a touch of sullenness.

"Well, I'll write it down then," she said. She got in her car and took a stub of pencil from her pocket book and began to write on the back of an empty envelope. The Negro came and stood at the window. "I'm Mrs. May," she said as she wrote. "Their bull is on my place and I want him off *today*. You can tell them I'm furious about it."

"That bull lef here Sareday," the Negro said, "and none of us ain't seen him since. We ain't knowed where he was."

"Well, you know now," she said, "and you can tell Mr. O. T. and Mr. E. T. that if they don't come and get him today, I'm going to have their daddy shoot him the first thing in the morning. I can't have that bull ruining my herd." She handed him the note.

"If I knows Mist O. T. and Mist E. T.," he said, taking it, "they goin to say you go ahead on and shoot him. He done busted up one of our trucks already and we be glad to see the last of him."

She pulled her head back and gave him a look from slightly bleared eyes. "Do they expect me to take my time and my worker to shoot their bull?" she asked. "They don't want him so they just let him loose and expect somebody else to kill him? He's eating my oats and ruining my herd and I'm expected to shoot him too?"

"I speck you is," he said softly. "He done busted up . . ."

She gave him a very sharp look and said, "Well, I'm not surprised. That's just the way some people are," and after a second she asked, "Which is boss, Mr. O. T. or Mr. E. T.?" She had always suspected that they fought between themselves secretly.

"They never quarls," the boy said. "They like one man in two skins."

"Hmp. I expect you just never heard them quarrel."

"Nor nobody else heard them neither," he said, looking away as if this insolence were addressed to some one else.

"Well," she said, "I haven't put up with their father for fifteen years not to know a few things about Greenleafs."

The Negro looked at her suddenly with a gleam of recognition. "Is you my policy man's mother?" he asked.

"I don't know who your policy man is," she said sharply. "You give them that note and tell them if they don't come for that bull today, they'll be making their father shoot it tomorrow," and she drove off.

She stayed at home all afternoon waiting for the Greenleaf twins to come for the bull. They did not come. I might as well be working for them, she thought furiously. They are simply going to use me to the limit. At the supper table, she went over it again for the boys' benefit because she wanted them to see exactly what O. T. and E. T. would do. "They don't want that bull," she said, "—pass the butter—so they simply turn him loose and let somebody else worry about getting rid of him for them. How do you like that? I'm the victim. I've always been the victim."

"Pass the butter to the victim," Wesley said. He was in a worse humor than usual because he had had a flat tire on the way home from the university.

Scofield handed her the butter and said, "Why Mamma, ain't you ashamed to shoot an old bull that ain't done nothing but give you a little scrub strain in your herd? I declare," he said, "with the Mamma I got it's a wonder I turned out to be such a nice boy!"

"You ain't her boy, Son," Wesley said.

She eased back in her chair, her fingertips on the edge of the table.

"All I know is," Scofield said, "I done mighty well to be as nice as I am seeing what I come from."

When they teased her they spoke Greenleaf English but Wesley made his own particular tone come through it like a knife edge. 'Well lemme tell you one thang, Brother," he said, leaning over the table, "that if you had half a mind you would already know."

"What's that, Brother?" Scofield asked, his broad face grinning into the thin constricted one across from him.

"That is," Wesley said, "that neither you nor me is her boy . . .," but he stopped abruptly as she gave a kind of hoarse wheeze like an old horse lashed unexpectedly. She reared up and ran from the room.

"Oh, for God's sake," Wesley growled, "What did you start her off for?"

"I never started her off," Scofield said. "You started her off."

"Hah."

"She's not as young as she used to be and she can't take it."

"She can only give it out," Wesley said. "I'm the one that takes it."

His brother's pleasant face had changed so that an ugly family resemblance showed between them. "Nobody feels sorry for a lousy bastard like you," he said and grabbed across the table for the other's shirtfront.

From her room she heard a crash of dishes and she rushed back through the kitchen into the dining room. The hall door was open and Scofield was going out of it. Wesley was lying like a large bug on his back with the edge of the over-turned table cutting him across the middle and broken dishes scattered on top of him. She pulled the table off him and caught his arm to help him rise but he scrambled up and pushed her off with a furious charge of energy and flung himself out of the door after his brother.

She would have collapsed but a knock on the back door stiffened her and she swung around. Across the kitchen and back porch, she could see Mr. Greenleaf peering eagerly through the screenwire. All her resources returned in full strength as if she had only needed to be challenged by the devil himself to regain them. "I heard a thump," he called, "and I thought the plastering might have fell on you."

If he had been wanted someone would have had to go on a horse to find him. She crossed the kitchen and the porch and stood inside the screen and said, "No, nothing happened but the table turned over. One of the legs was weak," and without pausing, "the boys didn't come for the bull so tomorrow you'll have to shoot him."

The sky was crossed with thin red and purple bars and behind them the sun was moving down slowly as if it were descending a ladder. Mr. Greenleaf squatted down on the step, his back to her, the top of his hat on a level with her feet. "Tomorrow I'll drive him home for you," he said.

"Oh no, Mr. Greenleaf," she said in a mocking voice, "you drive him home tomorrow and next week he'll be back here. I know better than that." Then in a mournful tone, she said, "I'm surprised at O. T. and E. T. to treat me this way. I thought they'd have more gratitude. Those boys spent some mighty happy days on this place, didn't they, Mr. Greenleaf?"

Mr. Greenleaf didn't say anything.

"I think they did," she said. "I think they did. But they've forgotten all the nice little things I did for them now. If I recall, they wore my boys' old clothes and played with my boys' old toys and hunted with my boys' old guns. They swam in my pond and shot my birds and fished in my stream and I never forgot their birthday and Christmas seemed to roll around very often if I remember it right. And do they think of any of those things now?" she asked. "NOOOOO," she said.

For a few seconds she looked at the disappearing sun and Mr. Greenleaf examined the palms of his hands. Presently as if it had just occurred to her, she asked, "Do you know the real reason they didn't come for that bull?"

"Naw I don't," Mr. Greenleaf said in a surly voice.

"They didn't come because I'm a woman," she said. "You can get away with anything when you're dealing with a woman. If there were a man running this place . . ."

Quick as a snake striking Mr. Greenleaf said, "You got two boys. They know you got two men on the place."

The sun had disappeared behind the tree line. She looked down at the dark crafty face, upturned now, and at the wary eyes, bright under the shadow of the hatbrim. She waited long enough for him to see that she was hurt and then she said, "Some people learn gratitude too late, Mr. Greenleaf, and some never learn it at all," and she turned and left him sitting on the steps.

Half the night in her sleep she heard a sound as if some large stone were grinding a hole on the outside wall of her brain. She was walking on the inside, over a succession of beautiful rolling hills, planting her stick in front of each step. She became aware after a time that the noise was the sun trying to burn through the tree line and she stopped to watch, safe in the knowledge that it couldn't, that it had to sink the way it always did outside of her property. When she first stopped it was a swollen red ball, but as she stood watching it began to narrow and pale until it looked like a bullet. Then suddenly it burst through the tree line and raced down the hill toward her. She woke up with her hand over her mouth and the same noise, diminished but distinct, in her ear. It was the bull munching under her window. Mr. Greenleaf had let him out.

She got up and made her way to the window in the dark and looked out through the slit blind, but the bull had moved away from the hedge and at first she didn't see him. Then she saw a heavy form some distance away, paused as if observing her. This is the last night I am going to put up with this, she said, and watched until the iron shadow moved away in the darkness.

The next morning she waited until exactly eleven o'clock. Then she got in her car and drove to the barn. Mr. Greenleaf was cleaning milk cans. He had seven of them standing up outside the milk room to get the sun. She had been telling him to do this for two weeks. "All right, Mr. Greenleaf," she said, "go get your gun. We're going to shoot that bull."

"I thought you wanted theseyer cans . . ."

"Go get your gun, Mr. Greenleaf," she said. Her voice and face were expressionless.

"That gentleman torn out of there last night," he murmured in a tone of regret and bent again to the can he had his arm in.

"Go get your gun, Mr. Greenleaf," she said in the same triumphant toneless voice. "The bull is in the pasture with the dry cows. I saw him from my upstairs window. I'm going to drive you up to the field and you can run him into the empty pasture and shoot him there."

He detached himself from the can slowly. "Ain't nobody ever ast me to shoot my boys' own bull!" he said in a high rasping voice. He removed the rag from his back pocket and began to wipe his hands violently, then his nose.

She turned as if she had not heard this and said, "I'll wait for you in the car. Go get your gun."

She sat in the car and watched him stalk off toward the harness room where he kept a gun. After he had entered the room, there was a crash as if he had kicked something out of his way. Presently he emerged again with the gun, circled behind the car, opened the door violently and threw himself onto the seat beside her. He held the gun between his knees and looked straight ahead. He'd like to shoot me instead of the bull, she thought, and turned her face away so that he could not see her smile.

The morning was dry and clear. She drove through the woods for a quarter of a mile and then out into the open where there were fields on either side of the narrow road. The exhilaration of carrying her point had sharpened her senses. Birds were screaming everywhere, the grass was almost too bright to look at, the sky was an even piercing blue. "Spring is here!" she said gaily. Mr. Greenleaf lifted one muscle some-where near his mouth as if he found this the most asinine remark ever made. When she stopped at the second pasture gate, he flung himself out of the car door and slammed it behind him. Then he opened the gate and she drove through. He closed it and flung himself back in, silently, and she drove around the rim of the pasture until she spotted the bull, almost in the center of it, grazing peacefully among the cows.

"The gentleman is waiting on you," she said and gave Mr. Greenleaf's furious profile a sly look. "Run him into that next pasture and when you get him in, I'll drive in behind you and shut the gate myself."

He flung himself out again, this time deliberately leaving the car door open so that she had to lean across the seat and close it. She sat smiling as she watched him make his way across the pasture toward the opposite gate. He seemed to throw himself forward at each step and then pull back as if he were calling on some power to witness that he was being forced. "Well," she said aloud as if he were still in the car, "it's your own boys who are making you do this, Mr. Greenleaf." O. T. and E. T. were probably splitting their sides laughing at him now. She could hear their identical nasal voices saying, "Made Daddy shoot our bull for us. Daddy don't know no better than to think that's a fine bull he's shooting. Gonna kill Daddy to shoot that bull!"

"If those boys cared a thing about you, Mr. Greenleaf," she said, "they would have come for that bull. I'm surprised at them."

He was circling around to open the gate first. The bull, dark among the spotted cows, had not moved. He kept his head down, eating constantly. Mr. Greenleaf opened the gate and then began circling back to approach him from the rear. When he was about ten feet behind him, he flapped his arms at his sides. The bull lifted his head indolently and then lowered it again and continued to eat. Mr. Greenleaf stooped again and picked up something and threw it at him with a vicious swing. She decided it was a sharp rock for the bull leapt and then began to gallop until he disappeared over the rim of the hill. Mr. Greenleaf followed at his leisure.

"You needn't think you're going to lose him!" she cried and started the car straight across the pasture. She had to drive slowly over the terraces and when she reached the gate, Mr. Greenleaf and the bull were nowhere in sight. This pasture was smaller than the last, a green arena, encircled almost entirely by woods. She got out and closed the gate and stood looking for some sign of Mr. Greenleaf but he had disappeared completely. She knew at once that his plan was to lose the bull in the woods. Eventually, she would see him emerge somewhere from the circle of trees and come limping toward her and when he finally reached her, he would say, "If you can find that gentleman in them woods, you're better than me."

She was going to say, "Mr. Greenleaf, if I have to walk into those woods with you and stay all afternoon, we are going to find that bull and shoot him. You are going to shoot him if I have to pull the trigger for you." When he saw she meant business he would return and shoot the bull quickly himself.

She got back into the car and drove to the center of the pasture where he would not have so far to walk to reach her when he came out of the woods. At this moment she could picture him sitting on a stump, marking lines in the ground with a stick. She decided she would wait exactly ten minutes by her watch. Then she would begin to honk. She got out of the car and walked around a little and then sat down on the front bumper to wait and rest. She was very tired and she lay her head back against the hood and closed her eyes. She did not understand why she should be so tired when it was only mid-morning. Through her closed eyes, she could feel the sun, red-hot overhead. She opened her eyes slightly but the white light forced her to close them again.

For some time she lay back against the hood, wondering drowsily why she was so tired. With her eyes closed, she didn't think of time as divided into days and nights but into past and future. She decided she was tired because she had been working continuously for fifteen years. She decided she had every right to be tired, and to rest for a few minutes before she began working again. Before any kind of judgement seat, she would be able to say: I've worked, I have not wallowed. At this very instant while she was recalling a lifetime of work, Mr. Greenleaf was loitering in the woods and Mrs. Greenleaf was probably flat on the ground, asleep over her holeful of clippings. The woman had got worse over the years and Mrs. May believed that now she was actually demented. "I'm afraid your wife has let religion warp her," she said once tactfully to Mr. Greenleaf. "Everything in moderation, you know."

"She cured a man oncet that half his gut was eat out with worms," Mr. Greenleaf said, and she had turned away, half-sickened. Poor souls, she thought now, so simple. For a few seconds she dozed.

When she sat up and looked at her watch, more than ten minutes had passed. She had not heard any shot. A new thought occurred to her: suppose Mr. Greenleaf had aroused the bull chunking stones at him and the animal had turned on him and run him up against a tree and gored him? The irony of it deepened: O. T. and E. T. would then get a shyster lawyer and sue her. It would be the fitting end to her fifteen years with the Greenleafs. She thought of it almost with pleasure as if she had hit on the perfect ending for a story she was telling her friends. Then she dropped it, for Mr. Greenleaf had a gun with him and she had insurance.

She decided to honk. She got up and reached inside the car window and gave three sustained honks and two or three shorter ones to let him know she was getting impatient. Then she went back and sat down on the bumper again.

In a few minutes something emerged from the tree line, a black heavy shadow that tossed its head several times and then bounded forward. After a second she saw it was the bull. He was crossing the pasture toward her at a slow gallop, a gay almost rocking gait as if he were overjoyed to find her again. She looked beyond him to see if Mr. Greenleaf was coming out of the woods too but he was not. "Here he is, Mr. Greenleaf!" she called and looked on the other side of the pasture to see if he could be coming out there but he was not in sight. She looked back and saw that the bull, his head lowered, was racing toward her. She remained perfectly still, not in fright, but in a freezing unbelief. She stared at the violent black streak bounding toward her as if she had no sense of distance, as if she could not decide at once what his intention was, and the bull had buried his head in her lap, like a wild tormented lover, before her expression changed. One of his horns sank until it pierced her heart and the other curved around her side and held her in an unbreakable grip. She continued to stare straight ahead but the entire scene in front of her had changed—the tree line was a dark wound in a world that was nothing but sky—and she had the look of a person whose sight had been suddenly restored but who finds the light unbearable.

Mr. Greenleaf was running toward her from the side with his gun raised and she saw him coming though she was not looking in his direction. She saw him approaching on the outside of some invisible circle, the tree line gaping behind him and nothing under his feet. He shot the bull four times through the eye. She did not hear the shots but she felt the quake in the huge body as it sank, pulling her forward on its head, so that she seemed, when Mr. Greenleaf reached her, to be bent over whispering some last discovery into the animal's ear.

Yukio Mishima (1925–1970)

In November 1970 Yukio Mishima, together with some of his fanatical followers from the ultranationalistic Shield Society (which he had founded in 1968), broke into the headquarters of Japan's Eastern Defense Forces armed with swords and daggers, overpowered some aides, tied up the commanding general, and demanded that the troops be assembled to hear a speech. Mishima, wearing a kamikaze headband, addressed the troops for ten minutes, inciting them to rebel against the constitutional government (imposed by the United States) that had, in his words, "turned Japan spineless." Receiving only ridicule in response, he returned to the general's office and there, before the general's unbelieving eyes, proceeded to kill himself in strict accordance with the traditional samurai ritual of *seppuku,* or hara-kiri. After Mishima had driven a dagger deep into his left abdomen, one of his aides severed his head with a sword. The aide likewise killed himself and was beheaded; the others surrendered.

In 1936 there had been a similar revolt and, though equally unsuccessful, it had foreshadowed the repressive regime of General Tojo that was to stage the attack on Pearl Harbor in 1941. That earlier revolt is the one referred to in "Patriotism," one of Mishima's most powerful stories. Here life and fiction become joined. The act of *seppuku* was for Mishima (born Kimitake Hiraoka) a fulfillment, 'the ultimate dream of my life.' Born of an ancient samurai family, he longed to die a hero's death in accordance with the ancient samurai code; but his weak body kept him from service in the war, and he had to compensate through body-building (he became expert at *karate* and *kendo*) and, most important, through the discipline of writing. In his short lifetime he turned out twenty novels, thirty-three plays, many essays, and more than eighty stories; he also produced, directed, and acted in movies, and even sang on stage. His first book of stories, *A Forest in Flower,* appeared in 1943, but it was *Confessions of a Mask* (1948), dealing with the meditations of a young man of homosexual leanings in a repressive society, that brought him fame. A later book, *Forbidden Colors* (1968) also dealt with homosexuality, revealing that strain of aestheticism and even decadence which, throughout Mishima's work, seems strangely out of place in one so given to the samurai spirit. But his love of death was itself erotic, a kind of *liebestod,* and his self-discipline inseparable from a desire to create a body beautiful enough to be sacrificed. His last book, *Spring Snow* (1971), was the first of a four-volume posthumous cycle entitled *The Sea of Fertility,* of which the others are *Runaway Horses* (1973), *The Temple of Dawn* (1973), and *The Decay of the Angel* (1974). This last novel, translated by Edward G. Seidensticker, has been called "a death rattle in prose," but "a surpassingly chilling, subtle, and original novel" as well.

Mishima has been called "Japan's Hemingway," while others have compared him to "aesthetic" writers like Walter Pater and Oscar Wilde. He is not easy to define. His writing sometimes approaches the slick and the sentimental, but at its best—as in "Patriotism"—it is elegant, polished, austere. From an outsider's point of view there can be something simply silly or melodramatic about the enactment of archaic rituals that, for most, have lost their meaning; but Mishima by his heroic seriousness has, at least in his art, redeemed the ceremonial. He was a man out of his time. He hated, in Lawrence Olson's words, "the gritty selfishness and hypocrisy of much of postwar Japanese society," and this—together with his disposition toward theatricalism and sexual fantasy—"set him to writing books about young men in search of perfect beauty." In "Patriotism" we see the disciplined ardor of a fanatical romantic.

Patriotism

On the twenty-eighth of February, 1936 (on the third day, that is, of the February 26 Incident), Lieutenant Shinji Takeyama of the Konoe Transport Battalion—profoundly disturbed by the knowledge that his closest colleagues had been with the mutineers from the beginning, and indignant at the imminent prospect of Imperial troops attacking Imperial troops—took his officer's sword and ceremonially disemboweled himself in the eight-mat room of his private residence in the sixth block of Aoba-chō, in Yotsuya Ward. His wife, Reiko, followed him, stabbing herself to death. The lieutenant's farewell note consisted of one sentence: "Long live the Imperial Forces." His wife's, after apologies for her unfilial conduct in thus preceding her parents to the grave, concluded: "The day which, for a soldier's wife, had to come, has come. . . ." The last moments of this heroic and dedicated couple were such as to make the gods themselves weep. The lieutenant's age, it should be noted, was thirty-one, his wife's twenty-three; and it was not half a year since the celebration of their marriage.

2

Those who saw the bride and bridegroom in the commemorative photograph—perhaps no less than those actually present at the lieutenant's wedding—had exclaimed in wonder at the bearing of this handsome couple. The lieutenant, majestic in military uniform, stood protectively beside his bride, his right hand resting upon his sword, his officer's cap held at his left side. His expression was severe, and his dark brows and wide-gazing eyes well conveyed the clear integrity of youth. For the beauty of the bride in her white over-robe no comparisons were adequate. In the eyes, round beneath soft brows, in the slender, finely shaped nose, and in the full lips, there was both sensuousness and refinement. One hand, emerging shyly from a sleeve of the over-robe, held a fan, and the tips of the fingers, clustering delicately, were like the bud of a moonflower.

Yukio Mishima, *Death in Midsummer and Other Stories.* Translated by Geoffrey W. Sargeant. Copyright © 1966 by New Directions Publishing Corporation. Reprinted by permission of New Directions Publishing Corporation.

After the suicide, people would take out this photograph and examine it, and sadly reflect that too often there was a curse on these seemingly flawless unions. Perhaps it was no more than imagination, but looking at the picture after the tragedy it almost seemed as if the two young people before the gold-lacquered screen were gazing, each with equal clarity, at the deaths which lay before them.

Thanks to the good offices of their go-between, Lieutenant General Ozeki, they had been able to set themselves up in a new home at Aoba-chō in Yotsuya. "New home" is perhaps misleading. It was an old three-room rented house backing onto a small garden. As neither the six- nor the four-and-a-half mat room downstairs was favored by the sun, they used the upstairs eight-mat room as both bedroom and guest room. There was no maid, so Reiko was left alone to guard the house in her husband's absence.

The honeymoon trip was dispensed with on the grounds that these were times of national emergency. The two of them had spent the first night of their marriage at this house. Before going to bed, Shinji, sitting erect on the floor with his sword laid before him, had bestowed upon his wife a soldierly lecture. A woman who had become the wife of a soldier should know and resolutely accept that her husband's death might come at any moment. It could be tomorrow. It could be the day after. But, no matter when it came—he asked—was she steadfast in her resolve to accept it? Reiko rose to her feet, pulled open a drawer of the cabinet, and took out what was the most prized of her new possessions, the dagger her mother had given her. Returning to her place, she laid the dagger without a word on the mat before her, just as her husband had laid his sword. A silent understanding was achieved at once, and the lieutenant never again sought to test his wife's resolve.

In the first few months of her marriage Reiko's beauty grew daily more radiant, shining serene like the moon after rain.

As both were possessed of young, vigorous bodies, their relationship was passionate. Nor was this merely a matter of the night. On more than one occasion, returning home straight from maneuvers, and begrudging even the time it took to remove his mud-splashed uniform, the lieutenant had pushed his wife to the floor almost as soon as he had entered the house. Reiko was equally ardent in her response. For a little more or a little less than a month, from the first night of their marriage Reiko knew happiness, and the lieutenant, seeing this, was happy too.

Reiko's body was white and pure, and her swelling breasts conveyed a firm and chaste refusal; but, upon consent, those breasts were lavish with their intimate, welcoming warmth. Even in bed these two were frighteningly and awesomely serious. In the very midst of wild, intoxicating passions, their hearts were sober and serious.

By day the lieutenant would think of his wife in the brief rest periods between training; and all day long, at home, Reiko would recall the image of her husband. Even when apart, however, they had only to look at the wedding photograph for their happiness to be once more confirmed. Reiko felt not the slightest surprise that a man who had been a complete stranger until a few months ago should now have become the sun about which her whole world revolved.

All these things had a moral basis, and were in accordance with the Education Rescript's injunction that "husband and wife should be harmonious." Not once did Reiko contradict her husband, nor did the lieutenant ever find reason to scold his wife. On the god shelf below the stairway, alongside the tablet from the Great Ise Shrine, were set photographs of their Imperial Majesties, and regularly every morning, before leaving for duty, the lieutenant would stand with his wife at this hallowed place and together they would bow their heads low. The offering water was renewed each morning, and the sacred sprig of *sasaki* was always green and fresh. Their lives were lived beneath the solemn protection of the gods and were filled with an intense happiness which set every fiber in their bodies trembling.

3

Although Lord Privy Seal Saitō's house was in their neighborhood, neither of them heard any noise of gunfire on the morning of February 26. It was a bugle, sounding muster in the dim, snowy dawn, when the ten-minute tragedy had already ended, which first disrupted the lieutenant's slumbers. Leaping at once from his bed, and without speaking a word, the lieutenant donned his uniform, buckled on the sword held ready for him by his wife, and hurried swiftly out into the snow-covered streets of the still darkened morning. He did not return until the evening of the twenty-eighth.

Later, from the radio news, Reiko learned the full extent of this sudden eruption of violence. Her life throughout the subsequent two days was lived alone, in complete tranquillity, and behind locked doors.

In the lieutenant's face, as he hurried silently out into the snowy morning, Reiko had read the determination to die. If her husband did not return, her own decision was made: she too would die. Quietly she attended to the disposition of her personal possessions. She chose her sets of visiting kimonos as keepsakes for friends of her schooldays, and she wrote a name and address on the stiff paper wrapping in which each was folded. Constantly admonished by her husband never to think of the morrow, Reiko had not even kept a diary and was now denied the pleasure of assiduously rereading her record of the happiness of the past few months and consigning each page to the fire as she did so. Ranged across the top of the radio were a small china dog, a rabbit, a squirrel, a bear, and a fox. There were also a small vase and a water pitcher. These comprised Reiko's one and only collection. But it would hardly do, she imagined, to give such things as keepsakes. Nor again would it be quite proper to ask specifically for them to be included in the coffin. It seemed to Reiko, as these thoughts passed through her mind, that the expressions on the small animals' faces grew even more lost and forlorn.

Reiko took the squirrel in her hand and looked at it. And then, her thoughts turning to a realm far beyond these childlike affections, she gazed up into the distance at the great sunlike principle which her husband embodied. She was ready, and happy, to be hurtled along to her destruction in that gleaming sun chariot—but now, for these few moments of solitude, she allowed herself to luxuriate in this innocent attachment to trifles. The time when she had genuinely loved these things, however, was long past. Now she merely loved the memory of having once loved them, and their place in her heart had been filled by more intense passions, by a more frenzied happiness. . . . For Reiko had never, even to herself, thought of those soaring joys of the flesh as a mere pleasure. The February cold, and the icy touch of the china squirrel, had numbed Reiko's slender fingers; yet, even so, in her lower limbs, beneath the ordered repetition of the pattern which crossed the skirt of her trim *meisen* kimono, she could feel now, as she thought of the lieutenant's powerful arms reaching out toward her, a hot moistness of the flesh which defied the snows.

She was not in the least afraid of the death hovering in her mind. Waiting alone at home, Reiko firmly believed that everything her husband was feeling or thinking now, his anguish and distress, was leading her—just as surely as the power in his flesh—to a welcome death. She felt as if her body could melt away with ease and be transformed to the merest fraction of her husband's thought.

Listening to the frequent announcements on the radio, she heard the names of several of her husband's colleagues mentioned among those of the insurgents. This was news of death. She followed the developments closely, wondering anxiously, as the situation became daily more irrevocable, why no Imperial ordinance was sent down, and watching what had at first been taken as a movement to restore the nation's honor come gradually to be branded with the infamous name of mutiny. There was no communication from the regiment. At any moment, it seemed, fighting might commence in the city streets where the remains of the snow still lay.

Toward sundown on the twenty-eighth Reiko was startled by a furious pounding on the front door. She hurried downstairs. As she pulled with fumbling fingers at the bolt, the shape dimly outlined beyond the frosted-glass panel made no sound, but she knew it was her husband. Reiko had never known the bolt on the sliding door to be so stiff. Still it resisted. The door just would not open.

In a moment, almost before she knew she had succeeded, the lieutenant was standing before her on the cement floor inside the porch, muffled in a khaki greatcoat, his top boots heavy with slush from the street. Closing the door behind him, he returned the bolt once more to its socket. With what significance, Reiko did not understand.

"Welcome home."

Reiko bowed deeply, but her husband made no response. As he had already unfastened his sword and was about to remove his greatcoat, Reiko moved around behind to assist. The coat, which was cold and damp and had lost the odor of horse dung it normally exuded when exposed to the sun, weighed heavily upon her arm. Draping it across a hanger, and cradling the sword and leather belt in her sleeves, she waited while her husband removed his top boots and then followed behind him into the "living room." This was the six-mat room downstairs.

Seen in the clear light from the lamp, her husband's face, covered with a heavy growth of bristle, was almost unrecognizably wasted and thin. The cheeks were hollow, their luster and resilience gone. In his normal good spirits he would have changed into old clothes as soon as he was home and have pressed her to get supper at once, but now he sat before the table still in his uniform, his head drooping dejectedly. Reiko refrained from asking whether she should prepare the supper.

After an interval the lieutenant spoke.

"I knew nothing. They hadn't asked me to join. Perhaps out of consideration, because I was newly married. Kanō, and Homma too, and Yamaguchi."

Reiko recalled momentarily the faces of high-spirited young officers, friends of her husband, who had come to the house occasionally as guests.

"There may be an Imperial ordinance sent down tomorrow. They'll be posted as rebels, I imagine. I shall be in command of a unit with orders to attack them. . . . I can't do it. It's impossible to do a thing like that."

He spoke again.

"They've taken me off guard duty, and I have permission to return home for one night. Tomorrow morning, without question, I must leave to join the attack. I can't do it, Reiko."

Reiko sat erect with lowered eyes. She understood clearly that her husband had spoken of his death. The lieutenant was resolved. Each word, being rooted in death, emerged sharply and with powerful significance against this dark, unmovable background. Although the lieutenant was speaking of his dilemma, already there was no room in his mind for vacillation.

However, there was a clarity, like the clarity of a stream fed from melting snows, in the silence which rested between them. Sitting in his own home after the long two-day ordeal, and looking across at the face of his beautiful wife, the lieutenant was for the first time experiencing true peace of mind. For he had at once known, though she said nothing, that his wife divined the resolve which lay beneath his words.

"Well, then . . ." The lieutenant's eyes opened wide. Despite his exhaustion they were strong and clear, and now for the first time they looked straight into the eyes of his wife. "Tonight I shall cut my stomach."

Reiko did not flinch.

Her round eyes showed tension, as taut as the clang of a bell.

"I am ready," she said. "I ask permission to accompany you."

The lieutenant felt almost mesmerized by the strength in those eyes. His words flowed swiftly and easily, like the utterances of a man in delirium, and it was beyond his understanding how permission in a matter of such weight could be expressed so casually.

"Good. We'll go together. But I want you as a witness, first, for my own suicide. Agreed?"

When this was said a sudden release of abundant happiness welled up in both their hearts. Reiko was deeply affected by the greatness of her husband's trust in her. It was vital for the lieutenant, whatever else might happen, that there should be no irregularity in his death. For that reason there had to be a witness. The fact that he had chosen his wife for this was the first mark of his trust. The second, and even greater mark, was that though he had pledged that they should die together he did not intend to kill his wife first—he had deferred her death to a time when he would no longer be there to verify it. If the lieutenant had been a suspicious husband, he would doubtless, as in the usual suicide pact, have chosen to kill his wife first.

When Reiko said, "I ask permission to accompany you," the lieutenant felt these words to be the final fruit of the education which he had himself given his wife, starting on the first night of their marriage, and which had schooled her, when the moment came, to say what had to be said without a shadow of hesitation. This flattered the lieutenant's opinion of himself as a self-reliant man. He was not so romantic or conceited as to imagine that the words were spoken spontaneously, out of love for her husband.

With happiness welling almost too abundantly in their hearts, they could not help smiling at each other. Reiko felt as if she had returned to her wedding night.

Before her eyes was neither pain nor death. She seemed to see only a free and limitless expanse opening out into vast distances.

"The water is hot. Will you take your bath now?"

"Ah yes, of course."

"And supper . . .?"

The words were delivered in such level, domestic tones that the lieutenant came near to thinking, for the fraction of a second, that everything had been a hallucination.

"I don't think we'll need supper. But perhaps you could warm some sake?"

"As you wish."

As Reiko rose and took a *tanzen* gown from the cabinet for after the bath, she purposely directed her husband's attention to the opened drawer. The lieutenant rose, crossed to the cabinet, and looked inside. From the ordered array of paper wrappings he read, one by one, the addresses of the keepsakes. There was no grief in the lieutenant's response to this demonstration of heroic resolve. His heart was filled with tenderness. Like a husband who is proudly shown the childish purchases of a young wife, the lieutenant, overwhelmed by affection, lovingly embraced his wife from behind and implanted a kiss upon her neck.

Reiko felt the roughness of the lieutenant's unshaven skin against her neck. This sensation, more than being just a thing of this world, was for Reiko almost the world itself, but now—with the feeling that it was soon to be lost forever—it had freshness beyond all her experience. Each moment had its own vital strength, and the senses in every corner of her body were reawakened. Accepting her husband's caresses from behind, Reiko raised herself on the tips of her toes, letting the vitality seep through her entire body.

"First the bath, and then, after some sake . . . lay out the bedding upstairs, will you?"

The lieutenant whispered the words into his wife's ear. Reiko silently nodded.

Flinging off his uniform, the lieutenant went to the bath. To faint background noises of slopping water Reiko tended the charcoal brazier in the living room and began the preparations for warming the sake.

Taking the *tanzen*, a sash, and some underclothes, she went to the bathroom to ask how the water was. In the midst of a coiling cloud of steam the lieutenant was sitting cross-legged on the floor, shaving, and she could dimly discern the rippling movements of the muscles on his damp, powerful back as they responded to the movement of his arms.

There was nothing to suggest a time of any special significance. Reiko, going busily about her tasks, was preparing side dishes from odds and ends in stock. Her hands did not tremble. If anything, she managed even more efficiently and smoothly than usual. From time to time, it is true, there was a strange throbbing deep within her breast. Like distant lightning, it had a moment of sharp intensity and then vanished without trace. Apart from that, nothing was in any way out of the ordinary.

The lieutenant, shaving in the bathroom, felt his warmed body miraculously healed at last of the desperate tiredness of the days of indecision and filled—in spite of the death which lay ahead—with pleasurable anticipation. The sound of his wife going about her work came to him faintly. A healthy physical craving, submerged for two days, reasserted itself.

The lieutenant was confident there had been no impurity in that joy they had experienced when resolving upon death. They had both sensed at that moment— though not, of course, in any clear and conscious way—that those permissible pleasures which they shared in private were once more beneath the protection of Righteousness and Divine Power, and of a complete and unassailable morality. On looking into each other's eyes and discovering there an honorable death, they had felt themselves safe once more behind steel walls which none could destroy, encased in an impenetrable armor of Beauty and Truth. Thus, so far from seeing any inconsistency or conflict between the urges of his flesh and the sincerity of his patriotism, the lieutenant was even able to regard the two as parts of the same thing.

Thrusting his face close to the dark, cracked, misted wall mirror, the lieutenant shaved himself with great care. This would be his death face. There must be no unsightly blemishes. The clean-shaven face gleamed once more with a youthful luster, seeming to brighten the darkness of the mirror. There was a certain elegance, he even felt, in the association of death with this radiantly healthy face.

Just as it looked now, this would become his death face! Already, in fact, it had half departed from the lieutenant's personal possession and had become the bust above a dead soldier's memorial. As an experiment he closed his eyes tight. Everything was wrapped in blackness, and he was no longer a living, seeing creature.

Returning from the bath, the traces of the shave glowing faintly blue beneath his smooth cheeks, he seated himself beside the now well-kindled charcoal brazier. Busy though Reiko was, he noticed, she had found time lightly to touch up her face. Her cheeks were gay and her lips moist. There was no shadow of sadness to be seen. Truly, the lieutenant felt, as he saw this mark of his young wife's passionate nature, he had chosen the wife he ought to have chosen.

As soon as the lieutenant had drained his sake cup he offered it to Reiko. Reiko had never before tasted sake, but she accepted without hesitation and sipped timidly.

"Come here," the lieutenant said.

Reiko moved to her husband's side and was embraced as she leaned backward across his lap. Her breast was in violent commotion, as if sadness, joy, and the potent sake were mingling and reacting within her. The lieutenant looked down into his wife's face. It was the last face he would see in this world, the last face he would see of his wife. The lieutenant scrutinized the face minutely, with the eyes of a traveler bidding farewell to splendid vistas which he will never revisit. It was a face he could not tire of looking at—the features regular yet not cold, the lips lightly closed with a soft strength. The lieutenant kissed those lips, unthinkingly. And suddenly, though there was not the slightest distortion of the face into the unsightliness of sobbing, he noticed that tears were welling slowly from beneath the long lashes of the closed eyes and brimming over into a glistening stream.

When, a little later, the lieutenant urged that they should move to the upstairs bedroom, his wife replied that she would follow after taking a bath. Climbing the stairs alone to the bedroom, where the air was already warmed by the gas heater, the lieutenant lay down on the bedding with arms outstretched and legs apart. Even the time at which he lay waiting for his wife to join him was no later and no earlier than usual.

He folded his hands beneath his head and gazed at the dark boards of the ceiling in the dimness beyond the range of the standard lamp. Was it death he was now waiting for? Or a wild ecstasy of the senses? The two seemed to overlap, almost as if the object of this bodily desire was death itself. But, however that might be, it was certain that never before had the lieutenant tasted such total freedom.

There was the sound of a car outside the window. He could hear the screech of its tires skidding in the snow piled at the side of the street. The sound of its horn re-echoed from near-by walls. . . . Listening to these noises he had the feeling that this house rose like a solitary island in the ocean of a society going as restlessly about its business as ever. All around, vastly and untidily, stretched the country for which he grieved. He was to give his life for it. But would that great country, with which he was prepared to remonstrate to the extent of destroying himself, take the slightest heed of his death? He did not know; and it did not matter. His was a battlefield without glory, a battlefield where none could display deeds of valor: it was the front line of the spirit.

Reiko's footsteps sounded on the stairway. The steep stairs in this old house creaked badly. There were fond memories in that creaking, and many a time, while waiting in bed, the lieutenant had listened to its welcome sound. At the thought that he would hear it no more he listened with intense concentration, striving for every corner of every moment of this precious time to be filled with the sound of those soft footfalls on the creaking stairway. The moments seemed transformed to jewels, sparkling with inner light.

Reiko wore a Nagoya sash about the waist of her *yukata,* but as the lieutenant reached toward it, its redness sobered by the dimness of the light, Reiko's hand moved to his assistance and the sash fell away, slithering swiftly to the floor. As she stood before him, still in her *yukata,* the lieutenant inserted his hands through the side slits beneath each sleeve, intending to embrace her as she was; but at the touch of his finger tips upon the warm naked flesh, and as the armpits closed gently about his hands, his whole body was suddenly aflame.

In a few moments the two lay naked before the glowing gas heater.

Neither spoke the thought, but their hearts, their bodies, and their pounding breasts blazed with the knowledge that this was the very last time. It was as if the words "The Last Time" were spelled out, in invisible brushstrokes, across every inch of their bodies.

The lieutenant drew his wife close and kissed her vehemently. As their tongues explored each other's mouths, reaching out into the smooth, moist interior, they felt as if the still unknown agonies of death had tempered their senses to the keenness of red-hot steel. The agonies they could not yet feel, the distant pains of death, had refined their awareness of pleasure.

"This is the last time I shall see your body," said the lieutenant. "Let me look at it closely." And, tilting the shade on the lampstand to one side, he directed the rays along the full length of Reiko's outstretched form.

Reiko lay still with her eyes closed. The light from the low lamp clearly revealed the majestic sweep of her white flesh. The lieutenant, not without a touch of egocentricity, rejoiced that he would never see this beauty crumble in death.

At his leisure, the lieutenant allowed the unforgettable spectacle to engrave itself upon his mind. With one hand he fondled the hair, with the other he softly stroked the magnificent face, implanting kisses here and there where his eyes lingered. The quiet coldness of the high, tapering forehead, the closed eyes with their long lashes beneath faintly etched brows, the set of the finely shaped nose, the gleam of teeth glimpsed between full, regular lips, the soft cheeks and the small, wise chin . . . these things conjured up in the lieutenant's mind the vision of a truly radiant death face, and again and again he pressed his lips tight against the white throat—where Reiko's own hand was soon to strike—and the throat reddened faintly beneath his kisses. Returning to the mouth he laid his lips against it with the gentlest of pressures, and moved them rhythmically over Reiko's with the light rolling motion of a small boat. If he closed his eyes, the world became a rocking cradle.

Wherever the lieutenant's eyes moved his lips faithfully followed. The high, swelling breasts, surmounted by nipples like the buds of a wild cherry, hardened as the lieutenant's lips closed about them. The arms flowed smoothly downward from each side of the breast, tapering toward the wrists, yet losing nothing of their roundness or symmetry, and at their tips were those delicate fingers which had held the fan at the wedding ceremony. One by one, as the lieutenant kissed them, the fingers withdrew behind their neighbor as if in shame. . . . The natural hollow curving between the bosom and the stomach carried in its lines a suggestion not only of softness but of resilient strength, and while it gave forewarning of the rich curves spreading outward from here to the hips it had, in itself, an appearance only of restraint and proper discipline. The whiteness and richness of the stomach and hips was like milk brimming in a great bowl, and the sharply shadowed dip of the navel could have been the fresh impress of a raindrop, fallen there that very moment. Where the shadows gathered more thickly, hair clustered, gentle and sensitive, and as the agitation mounted in the now no longer passive body there hung over this region a scent like the smoldering of fragrant blossoms, growing steadily more pervasive.

At length, in a tremulous voice, Reiko spoke.

"Show me. . . . Let me look too, for the last time."

Never before had he heard from his wife's lips so strong and unequivocal a request. It was as if something which her modesty had wished to keep hidden to the end had suddenly burst its bonds of constraint. The lieutenant obediently lay back and surrendered himself to his wife. Lithely she raised her white, trembling body, and— burning with an innocent desire to return to her husband what he had done for her— placed two white fingers on the lieutenant's eyes, which gazed fixedly up at her, and gently stroked them shut.

Suddenly overwhelmed by tenderness, her cheeks flushed by a dizzying uprush of emotion, Reiko threw her arms about the lieutenant's close-cropped head. The bristly hairs rubbed painfully against her breast, the prominent nose was cold as it dug into her flesh, and his breath was hot. Relaxing her embrace, she gazed down at her husband's masculine face. The severe brows, the closed eyes, the splendid bridge of the nose, the shapely lips drawn firmly together . . . the blue, cleanshaven cheeks reflecting the light and gleaming smoothly. Reiko kissed each of these. She kissed the broad nape of the neck, the strong, erect shoulders, the powerful chest with its twin circles like shields and its russet nipples. In the armpits, deeply shadowed by the ample flesh of the shoulders and chest, a sweet and melancholy odor emanated from the growth of hair, and in the sweetness of this odor was contained, somehow, the essence of young death. The lieutenant's naked skin glowed like a field of barley, and everywhere the muscles showed in sharp relief, converging on the lower abdomen about the small, unassuming navel. Gazing at the youthful, firm stomach, modestly covered by a vigorous growth of hair, Reiko thought of it as it was soon to be, cruelly cut by the sword, and she laid her head upon it, sobbing in pity, and bathed it with kisses.

At the touch of his wife's tears upon his stomach the lieutenant felt ready to endure with courage the cruelest agonies of his suicide.

What ecstasies they experienced after these tender exchanges may well be imagined. The lieutenant raised himself and enfolded his wife in a powerful embrace, her body now limp with exhaustion after her grief and tears. Passionately they held their faces close, rubbing cheek against cheek. Reiko's body was trembling. Their breasts, moist with sweat, were tightly joined, and every inch of the young and beautiful bodies had become so much one with the other that it seemed impossible there should ever again be a separation. Reiko cried out. From the heights they plunged into the abyss, and from the abyss they took wing and soared once more to dizzying heights. The lieutenant panted like the regimental standard-bearer on a route march. . . . As one cycle ended, almost immediately a new wave of passion would be generated, and together—with no trace of fatigue—they would climb again in a single breathless movement to the very summit.

4

When the lieutenant at last turned away, it was not from weariness. For one thing, he was anxious not to undermine the considerable strength he would need in carrying out his suicide. For another, he would have been sorry to mar the sweetness of these last memories by overindulgence.

Since the lieutenant had clearly desisted, Reiko too, with her usual compliance, followed his example. The two lay naked on their backs, with fingers interlaced, staring fixedly at the dark ceiling. The room was warm from the heater, and even when the sweat had ceased to pour from their bodies they felt no cold. Outside, in the hushed night, the sounds of passing traffic had ceased. Even the noises of the trains and streetcars around Yotsuya station did not penetrate this far. After echoing through the region bounded by the moat, they were lost in the heavily wooded park fronting the broad driveway before Akasaka Palace. It was hard to believe in the tension gripping this whole quarter, where the two factions of the bitterly divided Imperial Army now confronted each other, poised for battle.

Savoring the warmth glowing within themselves, they lay still and recalled the ecstasies they had just known. Each moment of the experience was relived. They remembered the taste of kisses which had never wearied, the touch of naked flesh, episode after episode of dizzying bliss. But already, from the dark boards of the ceiling, the face of death was peering down. These joys had been final, and their bodies would never know them again. Not that joy of this intensity—and the same thought had occurred to them both—was ever likely to be reexperienced, even if they should live on to old age.

The feel of their fingers intertwined—this too would soon be lost. Even the woodgrain patterns they now gazed at on the dark ceiling boards would be taken from them. They could feel death edging in, nearer and nearer. There could be no hesitation now. They must have the courage to reach out to death themselves, and to seize it.

"Well, let's make our preparations," said the lieutenant. The note of determination in the words was unmistakable, but at the same time Reiko had never heard her husband's voice so warm and tender.

After they had risen, a variety of tasks awaited them.

The lieutenant, who had never once before helped with the bedding, now cheerfully slid back the door of the closet, lifted the mattress across the room by himself, and stowed it away inside.

Reiko turned off the gas heater and put away the lamp standard. During the lieutenant's absence she had arranged this room carefully, sweeping and dusting it to a fresh cleanness, and now—if one overlooked the rosewood table drawn into one corner—the eight-mat room gave all the appearance of a reception room ready to welcome an important guest.

"We've seen some drinking here, haven't we? With Kanō and Homma and Noguchi . . ."

"Yes, they were great drinkers, all of them."

"We'll be meeting them before long, in the other world. They'll tease us, I imagine, when they find I've brought you with me."

Descending the stairs, the lieutenant turned to look back into this calm clean room, now brightly illuminated by the ceiling lamp. There floated across his mind the faces of the young officers who had drunk there, and laughed, and innocently bragged. He had never dreamed then that he would one day cut open his stomach in this room.

In the two rooms downstairs husband and wife busied themselves smoothly and serenely with their respective preparations. The lieutenant went to the toilet, and then to the bathroom to wash. Meanwhile Reiko folded away her husband's padded robe, placed his uniform tunic, his trousers, and a newly cut bleached loincloth in the bathroom, and set out sheets of paper on the livingroom table for the farewell notes.

Then she removed the lid from the writing box and began rubbing ink from the ink tablet. She had already decided upon the wording of her own note.

Reiko's fingers pressed hard upon the cold gilt letters of the ink tablet, and the water in the shallow well at once darkened, as if a black cloud had spread across it. She stopped thinking that this repeated action, this pressure from her fingers, this rise and fall of faint sound, was all and solely for death. It was a routine domestic task, a simple paring away of time until death should finally stand before her. But somehow, in the increasingly smooth motion of the tablet rubbing on the stone, and in the scent from the thickening ink, there was unspeakable darkness.

Neat in his uniform, which he now wore next to his skin, the lieutenant emerged from the bathroom. Without a word he seated himself at the table, bolt upright, took a brush in his hand, and stared undecidedly at the paper before him.

Reiko took a white silk kimono with her and entered the bathroom. When she reappeared in the living room, clad in the white kimono and with her face lightly made up, the farewell note lay completed on the table beneath the lamp. The thick black brushstrokes said simply:

"Long Live the Imperial Forces—Army Lieutenant Takeyama Shinji."

While Reiko sat opposite him writing her own note, the lieutenant gazed in silence, intensely serious, at the controlled movement of his wife's pale fingers as they manipulated the brush.

With their respective notes in their hands—the lieutenant's sword strapped to his side, Reiko's small dagger thrust into the sash of her white Kimono—the two of them stood before the god shelf and silently prayed. Then they put out all the downstairs lights. As he mounted the stairs the lieutenant turned his head and gazed back at the striking, white-clad figure of his wife, climbing behind him, with lowered eyes, from the darkness beneath.

The farewell notes were laid side by side in the alcove of the upstairs room. They wondered whether they ought not to remove the hanging scroll, but since it had been written by their go-between, Lieutenant General Ozeki, and consisted, moreover, of two Chinese characters signifying "Sincerity," they left it where it was. Even if it were to become stained with splashes of blood, they felt that the lieutenant general would understand.

The lieutenant sitting erect with his back to the alcove, laid his sword on the floor before him.

Reiko set facing him, a mat's width away. With the rest of her so severely white the touch of rouge on her lips seemed remarkably seductive.

Across the dividing mat they gazed intently into each other's eyes. The lieutenant's sword lay before his knees. Seeing it, Reiko recalled their first night and was overwhelmed with sadness. The lieutenant spoke, in a hoarse voice:

"As I have no second to help me I shall cut deep. It may look unpleasant, but please do not panic. Death of any sort is a fearful thing to watch. You must not be discouraged by what you see. Is that all right?"

"Yes."

Reiko nodded deeply.

Looking at the slender white figure of his wife the lieutenant experienced a bizarre excitement. What he was about to perform was an act in his public capacity as a soldier, something he had never previously shown his wife. It called for a resolution equal to the courage to enter battle; it was a death of no less degree and quality than death in the front line. It was his conduct on the battlefield that he was now to display.

Momentarily the thought led the lieutenant to a strange fantasy. A lonely death on the battlefield, a death beneath the eyes of his beautiful wife . . . in the sensation that he was now to die in these two dimensions, realizing an impossible union of them both, there was sweetness beyond words. This must be the very pinnacle of good fortune, he thought. To have every moment of his death observed by those beautiful eyes—it was like being borne to death on a gentle, fragrant breeze. There was some special favor here. He did not understand precisely what it was, but it was a domain unknown to others: a dispensation granted to no one else had been permitted to himself. In the radiant, bridelike figure of his white-robed wife the lieutenant seemed to see a vision of all those things he had loved and for which he was to lay down his life—the Imperial Household, the Nation, the Army Flag. All these, no less than the wife who sat before him, were presences observing him closely with clear and never-faltering eyes.

Reiko too was gazing intently at her husband, so soon to die, and she thought that never in this world had she seen anything so beautiful. The lieutenant always looked well in uniform, but now, as he contemplated death with severe brows and firmly closed lips, he revealed what was perhaps masculine beauty at its most superb.

"It's time to go," the lieutenant said at last.

Reiko bent her body low to the mat in a deep bow. She could not raise her face. She did not wish to spoil her make-up with tears, but the tears could not be held back.

When at length she looked up she saw hazily through the tears that her husband had wound a white bandage around the blade of his now unsheathed sword, leaving five or six inches of naked steel showing at the point.

Resting the sword in its cloth wrapping on the mat before him, the lieutenant rose from his knees, resettled himself cross-legged, and unfastened the hooks of his uniform collar. His eyes no longer saw his wife. Slowly, one by one, he undid the flat brass buttons. The dusky brown chest was revealed, and then the stomach. He unclasped his belt and undid the buttons of his trousers. The pure whiteness of the thickly coiled loincloth showed itself. The lieutenant pushed the cloth down with both hands, further to ease his stomach, and then reached for the white-bandaged blade of his sword. With his left hand he massaged his abdomen, glancing downward as he did so.

To reassure himself on the sharpness of his sword's cutting edge the lieutenant folded back the left trouser flap, exposing a little of his thigh, and lightly drew the blade across the skin. Blood welled up in the wound at once, and several streaks of red trickled downward, glistening in the strong light.

It was the first time Reiko had ever seen her husband's blood, and she felt a violent throbbing in her chest. She looked at her husband's face. The lieutenant was looking at the blood with calm appraisal. For a moment—though thinking at the same time that it was hollow comfort—Reiko experienced a sense of relief.

The lieutenant's eyes fixed his wife with an intense, hawk-like stare. Moving the sword around to his front, he raised himself slightly on his hips and let the upper half of his body lean over the sword point. That he was mustering his whole strength was apparent from the angry tension of the uniform at his shoulders. The lieutenant aimed to strike deep into the left of his stomach. His sharp cry pierced the silence of the room.

Despite the effort he had himself put into the blow, the lieutenant had the impression that someone else had struck the side of his stomach agonizingly with a thick rod of iron. For a second or so his head reeled and he had no idea what had happened.

The five or six inches of naked point had vanished completely into his flesh, and the white bandage, gripped in his clenched fist, pressed directly against his stomach.

He returned to consciousness. The blade had certainly pierced the wall of the stomach, he thought. His breathing was difficult, his chest thumped violently, and in some far deep region, which he could hardly believe was a part of himself, a fearful and excruciating pain came welling up as if the ground had split open to disgorge a boiling stream of molten rock. The pain came suddenly nearer, with terrifying speed. The lieutenant bit his lower lip and stiffled an instinctive moan.

Was this *seppuku?*—he was thinking. It was a sensation of utter chaos, as if the sky had fallen on his head and the world was reeling drunkenly. His will power and courage, which had seemed so robust before he made the incision, had now dwindled to something like a single hairlike thread of steel, and he was assailed by the uneasy feeling that he must advance along this thread, clinging to it with desperation. His clenched fist had grown moist. Looking down, he saw that both his hand and the cloth were drenched in blood. His loincloth too was dyed a deep red. It struck him as incredible that, amidst this terrible agony, things which could be seen could still be seen, and existing things existed still.

The moment the lieutenant thrust the sword into his left side and she saw the deathly pallor fall across his face, like an abruptly lowered curtain, Reiko had to struggle to prevent herself from rushing to his side. Whatever happened, she must watch. She must be a witness. That was the duty her husband had lain upon her. Opposite her, a mat's space away, she could clearly see her husband biting his lip to stifle the pain. The pain was there, with absolute certainty, before her eyes. And Reiko had no means of rescuing him from it.

The sweat glistened on her husband's forehead. The lieutenant closed his eyes, and then opened them again, as if experimenting. The eyes had lost their luster, and seemed innocent and empty like the eyes of a small animal.

The agony before Reiko's eyes burned as strong as the summer sun, utterly remote from the grief which seemed to be tearing herself apart within. The pain grew steadily in stature, stretching upward. Reiko felt that her husband had already become a man in a separate world, a man whose whole being had been resolved into pain, a prisoner in a cage of pain where no hand could reach out to him. But Reiko felt no pain at all. Her grief was not pain. As she thought about this, Reiko began to feel as if someone had raised a cruel wall of glass high between herself and her husband.

Ever since her marriage her husband's existence had been her own existence, and every breath of his had been a breath drawn by herself. But now, while her husband's existence in pain was a vivid reality, Reiko could find in this grief of hers no certain proof at all of her own existence.

With only his right hand on the sword the lieutenant began to cut sideways across his stomach. But as the blade became entangled with the entrails it was pushed constantly outward by their soft resilience; and the lieutenant realized that it would be necessary, as he cut, to use both hands to keep the point pressed deep into his stomach. He pulled the blade across. It did not cut as easily as he had expected. He directed the strength of his whole body into his right hand and pulled again. There was a cut of three or four inches.

The pain spread slowly outward from the inner depths until the whole stomach reverberated. It was like the wild clanging of a bell. Or like a thousand bells which jangled simultaneously at every breath he breathed and every throb of his pulse, rocking his whole being. The lieutenant could no longer stop himself from moaning.

But by now the blade had cut its way through to below the navel, and when he noticed this he felt a sense of satisfaction, and a renewal of courage.

The volume of blood had steadily increased, and now it spurted from the wound as if propelled by the beat of the pulse. The mat before the lieutenant was drenched red with splattered blood, and more blood overflowed onto it from pools which gathered in folds of the lieutenant's khaki trousers. A spot, like a bird, came flying across to Reiko and settled on the lap of her white silk kimono.

By the time the lieutenant had at last drawn the sword across to the right side of his stomach, the blade was already cutting shallow and had revealed its naked tip, slippery with blood and grease. But, suddenly stricken by a fit of vomiting, the lieutenant cried out hoarsely. The vomiting made the fierce pain fiercer still, and the stomach, which had thus far remained firm and compact, now abruptly heaved, opening wide its wound, and the entrails burst through, as if the wound too were vomiting. Seemingly ignorant of their master's suffering, the entrails gave an impression of robust health and almost disagreeable vitality as they slipped smoothly out and spilled over into the crotch. The lieutenant's head drooped, his shoulders heaved, his eyes opened to narrow slits, and a thin trickle of saliva dribbled from his mouth. The gold markings on his epaulettes caught the light and glinted.

Blood was scattered everywhere. The lieutenant was soaked in it to his knees, and he sat now in a crumpled and listless posture, one hand on the floor. A raw smell filled the room. The lieutenant his head drooping, retched repeatedly, and the movement showed vividly in his shoulders. The blade of the sword, now pushed back by the entrails and exposed to its tip, was still in the lieutenant's right hand.

It would be difficult to imagine a more heroic sight than that of the lieutenant at this moment, as he mustered his strength and flung back his head. The movement was performed with sudden violence, and the back of his head struck with a sharp crack against the alcove pillar. Reiko had been sitting until now with her face lowered, gazing in fascination at the tide of blood advancing toward her knees, but the sound took her by surprise and she looked up.

The lieutenant's face was not the face of a living man. The eyes were hollow, the skin parched, the once so lustrous cheeks and lips the color of dried mud. The right hand alone was moving. Laboriously gripping the sword, it hovered shakily in the air like the hand of a marionette and strove to direct the point at the base of the lieutenant's throat. Reiko watched her husband make this last, most heart-rending, futile exertion. Glistening with blood and grease, the point was thrust at the throat again and again. And each time it missed its aim. The strength to guide it was no longer there. The straying point struck the collar and the collar badges. Although its hooks had been unfastened, the stiff military collar had closed together again and was protecting the throat.

Reiko could bear the sight no longer. She tried to go to her husband's help, but she could not stand. She moved through the blood on her knees, and her white skirts grew deep red. Moving to the rear of her husband, she helped no more than by loosening the collar. The quivering blade at last contacted the naked flesh of the throat. At that moment Reiko's impression was that she herself had propelled her husband forward; but that was not the case. It was a movement planned by the lieutenant himself, his last exertion of strength. Abruptly he threw his body at the blade, and the blade pierced his neck, emerging at the nape. There was a tremendous spurt of blood and the lieutenant lay still, cold blue-tinged steel protruding from his neck at the back.

5

Slowly, her socks slippery with blood, Reiko descended the stairway. The upstairs room was now completely still.

Switching on the ground-floor lights, she checked the gas jet and the main gas plug and poured water over the smoldering, half-buried charcoal in the brazier. She stood before the upright mirror in the four-and-a-half-mat room and held up her skirts. The blood stains made it seem as if a bold, vivid pattern was printed across the lower half of her white kimono. When she sat down before the mirror, she was conscious of the dampness and coldness of her husband's blood in the region of her thighs, and she shivered. Then, for a long while, she lingered over her toilet preparations. She applied the rouge generously to her cheeks, and her lips too she painted heavily. This was no longer make-up to please her husband. It was make-up for the world which she would leave behind, and there was a touch of the magnificent and the spectacular in her brushwork. When she rose, the mat before the mirror was wet with blood. Reiko was not concerned about this. Returning from the toilet, Reiko stood finally on the cement floor of the porchway. When her husband had bolted the door here last night it had been in preparation for death. For a while she stood immersed in the consideration of a simple problem. Should she now leave the bolt drawn? If she were to lock the door, it could be that the neighbors might not notice their suicide for several days. Reiko did not relish the thought of their two corpses putrifying before discovery. After all, it seemed, it would be best to leave it open. . . . She released the bolt, and also drew open the frosted-glass door a fraction. . . . At once a chill wind blew in. There was no sign of anyone in the midnight streets and stars glittered ice-cold through the trees in the large house opposite.

Leaving the door as it was, Reiko mounted the stairs. She had walked here and there for some time and her socks were no longer slippery. About halfway up, her nostrils were already assailed by a peculiar smell.

The lieutenant was lying on his face in a sea of blood. The point protruding from his neck seemed to have grown even more prominent than before. Reiko walked heedlessly across the blood. Sitting beside the lieutenant's corpse, she stared intently at the face, which lay on one cheek on the mat. The eyes were opened wide, as if the lieutenant's attention had been attracted by something. She raised the head, folding it in her sleeve, wiped the blood from the lips, and bestowed a last kiss.

Then she rose and took from the closet a new white blanket and a waist cord. To prevent any derangement of her skirts, she wrapped the blanket about her waist and bound it there firmly with the cord.

Reiko sat herself on a spot about one foot distant from the lieutenant's body. Drawing the dagger from her sash, she examined its dully gleaming blade intently, and held it to her tongue. The taste of the polished steel was slightly sweet.

Reiko did not linger. When she thought how the pain which had previously opened such a gulf between herself and her dying husband was now to become a part of her own experience, she saw before her only the joy of herself entering a realm her husband had already made his own. In her husband's agonized face there had been something inexplicable which she was seeing for the first time. Now she would solve that riddle. Reiko sensed that at last she too would be able to taste the true bitterness and sweetness of that great moral principle in which her husband believed. What had until now been tasted only faintly through her husband's example she was about to savor directly with her own tongue.

Reiko rested the point of the blade against the base of her throat. She thrust hard. The wound was only shallow. Her head blazed, and her hands shook uncontrollably. She gave the blade a strong pull sideways. A warm substance flooded into her mouth, and everything before her eyes reddened, in a vision of spouting blood. She gathered her strength and plunged the point of the blade deep into her throat.

John Updike (1932–   )

Perhaps no important writer of his generation can lay claim to a more prodigious and varied output than John Updike. Born in 1932, he has published eight novels, four collections of short stories, three volumes of verse, a play, and a book of prose pieces. Since his twenties he has been considered one of the outstanding writers of America.

For the most part, his fiction is traditional and his concern is the middle range of experience. His characters are not of heroic measure, nor are they evil, cruel, bizarre, or mad, as are many of the characters of his contemporaries. The hero of his most acclaimed work, *Rabbit, Run,* is a former basketball star, now a salesman of kitchen gadgets, who makes one failed effort to shake off the mediocrity and "quiet desperation" of his middle-American life. *The Centaur* (1963) is about the family of a high school science teacher. Even the protagonist of *Bech: a Book* (1970), albeit a writer of celebrated novels, is only a man who works at his craft, and leads a relatively normal life. Basically, he is no more unusual and eccentric than any man next door.

Updike's characters, like the narrator of "Wife-wooing," are concerned with common experiences: the loss of youth, sexuality, the generation gap, marriage and its discontents, religious faith, the saving grace of love, even in-law conflicts. His fiction is a transformation of material familiar to most of us. Though his subject matter is plain, his style is far from it. It seems to be an expression of his early training as a painter, his continuing experience as a poet, and his concern for the homely facts of real life. His rhythms are pronounced, his perceptions are precisely delineated, his language is exact and yet surprising, his imagery is often luscious.

"Wife-wooing" is a prosaic story magically transformed by Updike's rich style. It begins with a homely scene, a family eating hamburgers in front of the fire, a baby in an Easybaby sucking a bottle. Updike drops into this scene carefully conceived and emotionally laden images (the baby's "selfish, contemplative eyes stealing glitter from the center of the flames;" he sees his wife's skirt slide "off your raised knees down your thighs, slide *up* your thighs. . . ."). Some of Updike's images are difficult to grasp. One cannot skim over the "absolute geography" of the wife's body, or over the comparison of the baby with a jewel that makes simple reflections within itself. The perceptions often require pondering before they will yield up their meaning and their pleasure.

His stories are written as if to be sounded silently or read aloud. There are many alliterations, rhymes and near-rhymes, repetitions of sounds, balanced phrasings, tensions between words and ideas. In the third sentence of the second paragraph, Updike juxtaposes "back" and "black," "air" and "fire," "intimate" and "winter," "halloo" and "hurrah," "agape" and "gushing," "deer" and "dead."

The reader is soon aware, upon reading an Updike story, that he is in the presence of a craftsman who uses his style to make alive and significant the experiences that for many have grown stale with custom.

Wife-wooing

Oh my love. Yes. Here we sit, on warm broad floorboards, before a fire, the children between us, in a crescent, eating. The girl and I share one halfpint of French-fried potatoes; you and the boy share another; and in the center, sharing nothing, making simple reflections within himself like a jewel, the baby, mounted in an Easybaby, sucks at his bottle with frowning mastery, his selfish, contemplative eyes stealing glitter from the center of the flames. And you. You. You allow your skirt, the same black skirt in which this morning you with woman's soft bravery mounted a bicycle and sallied forth to play hymns in difficult keys on the Sunday school's old piano—you allow this black skirt to slide off your raised knees down your thighs, slide *up* your thighs in your body's absolute geography, so the parallel whiteness of their undersides is exposed to the fire's warmth and to my sight. Oh. There is a line of Joyce. I try to recover it from the legendary, imperfectly explored grottoes of *Ulysses:* a garter snapped, to please Blazes Boylan, in a deep Dublin den. What? Smackwarm. That was the crucial word. Smacked smackwarm on her smackable warm woman's thigh. Something like that. A splendid man, to feel that. Smackwarm woman's. Splendid also to feel the curious and potent, inexplicable and irrefutably magical life language leads within itself. What soul took thought and knew that adding "wo" to man would make a woman? The difference exactly. The wide w, the receptive o. Womb. In our crescent the children for all their size seem to come out of you toward me, wet fingers and eyes, tinted bronze. Three children, five persons, seven years. Seven years since I wed wide warm woman, white-thighed. Wooed and wed. Wife. A knife of a word that for all its final bite did not end the wooing. To my wonderment.

We eat meat, meat I wrested warm from the raw hands of the hamburger girl in the diner a mile away, a ferocious place, slick with savagery, wild with chrome; young predators snarling dirty jokes menaced me, old men reached for me with coffee-warmed paws; I wielded my wallet, and won my way back. The fat brown bag of buns was warm beside me in the cold car; the smaller bag holding the two tiny cartons of French-fries emitted an even more urgent heat. Back through the black winter air to the fire, the intimate cave, where halloos and hurrahs greeted me, the deer, mouth agape and its cotton throat gushing, stretched dead across my shoulders. And now you, beside the white O of the plate upon which the children discarded with squeals of disgust the rings of translucent onion that came squeezed in the hamburgers—you push your toes an inch closer to the blaze, and the ashy white of the inside of your deep thigh is lazily laid bare, and the eternally elastic garter snaps smackwarm against my hidden heart.

Who would have thought, wide wife, back there in the white tremble of the ceremony (in the corner of my eye I held, despite the distracting hail of ominous vows, the vibration of the cluster of stephanotis clutched against your waist), that seven

Copyright © 1960 by John Updike. Reprinted from *Pigeon Feathers and Other Stories,* by John Updike, by permission of Alfred A. Knopf, Inc. Originally appeared in *The New Yorker.*

years would bring us no distance, through all those warm beds, to the same trembling point, of beginning? The cells change every seven years, and down in the atom, apparently, there is a strange discontinuity; as if God wills the universe anew every instant. (Ah God, dear God, tall friend of my childhood, I will never forget you, though they say dreadful things. They say rose windows in cathedrals are vaginal symbols.) Your legs, exposed as fully as by a bathing suit, yearn deeper into the amber wash of heat. Well: begin. A green jet of flame spits out sideways from a pocket of resin in a log, crying, and the orange shadows on the ceiling sway with fresh life. Begin.

"Remember, on our honeymoon, how the top of the kerosene heater made a great big rose window on the ceiling?"

"Vnn." Your chin goes to your knees, your shins draw in, all is retracted. Not much to remember, perhaps, for you; blood badly spilled, clumsiness of all sorts. "It was cold for June."

"Mommy, what was cold? What did you say?" the girl asks, enunciating angrily, determined not to let language slip on her tongue and tumble her so that we laugh.

"A house where Daddy and I stayed one time."

"I don't like dat," the boy says, and throws a half bun painted with chartreuse mustard onto the floor.

You pick it up and with beautiful sombre musing ask, "Isn't that funny? Did any of the others have mustard on them?"

"I *hate* dat," the boy insists; he is two. Language is to him thick vague handles swirling by; he grabs what he can.

"Here. He can have mine. Give me his." I pass my hamburger over, you take it, he takes it from you, there is nowhere a ripple of gratitude. There is no more praise of my heroism in fetching Sunday supper, saving you labor. Cunning, you sense, and sense that I sense your knowledge, that I had hoped to hoard your energy toward a more ecstatic spending. We sense everything between us, every ripple, existent and nonexistent; it is tiring. Courting a wife takes tenfold the strength of winning an ignorant girl. The fire shifts, shattering fragments of newspaper that carry in lighter gray the ghost of the ink of their message. You huddle your legs and bring the skirt back over them. With a sizzling noise like the sighs of the exhausted logs, the baby sucks the last from his bottle, drops it to the floor with its distasteful hoax of vacant suds, and begins to cry. His egotist's mouth opens; the delicate membrane of his satisfaction tears. You pick him up and stand. You love the baby more than me.

Who would have thought, blood once spilled, that no barrier would be broken, that you would be each time healed into a virgin again? Tall, fair, obscure, remote, and courteous.

We put the children to bed, one by one, in reverse order of birth. I am limitlessly patient, paternal, good. Yet you know. We watch the paper bags and cartons ignite on the breathing pillow of embers, read, watch television, eat crackers, it does not matter. Eleven comes. For a tingling moment you stand on the bedroom rug in your underpants, untangling your nightie; oh, fat white sweet fat fatness. In bed you read. About Richard Nixon. He fascinates you; you hate him. You know how he defeated Jerry Voorhis, martyred Mrs. Douglas, how he played poker in the Navy despite being a Quaker, every fiendish trick, every low adaptation. Oh my Lord. Let's let the poor man go to bed. We're none of us perfect. "Hey let's turn out the light."

"Wait. He's just about to get Hiss convicted. It's very strange. It says he acted honorably."

"I'm sure he did." I reach for the switch.

"No. Wait. Just till I finish this chapter. I'm sure there'll be something at the end."

"Honey, Hiss was guilty. We're all guilty. Conceived in concupiscence, we die unrepentant." Once my ornate words wooed you.

I lie against your filmy convex back. You read side ways, a sleepy trick. I see the page through the fringe of your hair, sharp and white as a wedge of crystal. Suddenly it slips. The book has slipped from your hand. You are asleep. Oh cunning trick, cunning. In the darkness I consider. Cunning. The headlights of cars accidentally slide fanning slits of light around our walls and ceiling. The great rose window was projected upward through the petal-shaped perforations in the top of the black kerosene stove, which we stood in the center of the floor. As the flame on the circular wick flickered, the wide soft star of interlocked penumbrae moved and waved as if it were printed on a silk cloth being gently tugged or slowly blown. Its color soft blurred blood. We pay dear in blood for our peaceful homes.

In the morning, to my relief, you are ugly. Monday's wan breakfast light bleaches you blotchily, drains the goodness from your thickness, makes the bathrobe a limp stained tube flapping disconsolately, exposing sallow décolletage. The skin between your breasts a sad yellow. I feast with the coffee on your drabness. Every wrinkle and sickly tint a relief and a revenge. The children yammer. The toaster sticks. Seven years have worn this woman.

The man, he arrows off to work, jousting for right-of-way, veering on the thin hard edge of the legal speed limit. Out of domestic muddle, softness, pallor, flaccidity: into the city. Stone is his province. The winning of coin. The maneuvering of abstractions. Making heartless things run. Oh the inanimate, adamant joys of job!

I return with my head enmeshed in a machine. A technicality it would take weeks to explain to you snags my brain; I fiddle with phrases and numbers all the blind evening. You serve me supper as a waitress—as less than a waitress, for I have known you. The children touch me timidly, as they would a steep girder bolted into a framework whose height they don't understand. They drift into sleep securely. We survive their passing in calm parallelity. My thoughts rework in chronic right angles the same snagging circuits on the same professional grid. You rustle the book about Nixon; vanish upstairs into the plumbing; the bathtub pipes cry. In my head I seem to have found the stuck switch at last: I push at it; it jams; I push; it is jammed. I grow dizzy, churning with cigarettes. I circle the room aimlessly.

So I am taken by surprise at a turning when at the meaningful hour of ten you come with a kiss of toothpaste to me moist and girlish and quick; the momentous moral of this story being, An expected gift is not worth giving.

Le Roi Jones (Imamu Amiri Baraka) (1934–   )

As playwright, poet, storyteller, and essayist—and one of the busiest—LeRoi Jones has made himself one of the leading spokesmen of Black Liberation in the United States. Born in Newark of middle-class parents, Jones started writing stories in high school and, upon graduation, was offered several scholarships, accepting the one from Rutgers. For social reasons, however, he transferred from Rutgers to Howard University where, after dabbling in religion and pre-med, he settled on English and philosophy, and outside of class acquired a passion for jazz. But Howard, to him a citadel of bourgeois values, was a mixed influence ("The Howard thing let me understand the Negro sickness. They teach you how to pretend to be white"), and there is a (possibly apocryphal) story of how he outraged the dean by eating watermelon in front of Douglass Hall. But, apocryphal or not, it is typical of how Jones, from then on, became more and more uneasy in his middle-classness. After graduation he entered the air force ("the error farce"), where he learned something about the "white sickness" ("how the oppressors suffered by virtue of their oppressions"). He served in Germany and Puerto Rico (where he did mountains of writing) and following his discharge settled in Greenwich Village, where in 1958 he met and married Hettie Cohen, who worked on a Village magazine called *The Record Changer.* Their apartment became a salon for such avant-garde poets, painters, intellectuals, and jazz musicians as Allen Ginsberg, Gregory Corso, Robert Creeley, and Thelonious Monk. The years that followed were immensely busy: Jones won Whitney and Guggenheim awards, taught poetry writing at The New School and drama at Columbia, studied German philology, founded the American Theatre for Poets (1961), sponsored jazz concerts, and wrote criticism, poetry, and plays. His play *Dutchman* opened in 1964 and won the Obie prize for the best off-Broadway play of the year; as Toni Cade writes, the LeRoi Jones plays between 1962 and 1964 were more than a beginning of black theater, they *were* black theater. By the mid-sixties, says another critic, he was "the most discussed—and admired—Negro writer since James Baldwin," and not for his plays only. Some of his work (of this period and later) includes: *Preface to a Twenty Volume Suicide Note* (1961), *The System of Dante's Hell* (1963), *The Dead Lecturer* (1964), *The Slave* (a play) (1964), *Home: Social Essays* (1966), *Tales* (1967), Jello (1970), and *In Our Terribleness* (1970).

But in the mid-sixties came the break with the Village, with Hettie, with white America—and with "the American Bitch Goddess of Success." He moved to Harlem, in 1969 assumed the Muslim name of Imamu Amiri Baraka, and devoted his prodigious energy and talent to the betterment of his own race. To carry his "consciousness" to black people became his mission, a mission that has resulted in his work being fundamentally autobiographical—and, ironically, of greater influence with white intellectuals than with blacks.

"The Death of Horatio Alger" (from *Tales*) records one of those testing points before his break with the white world. The prose spills out almost like words in a dream, the free associations of one talking to an opposing self. Baraka's prose is often a hard-to-understand, fractured syntax, demonstrating "the mind's inability to articulate what the senses perceive," but it has, as one critic says, "a strong cumulative effect." The fight in this story is more internal than external, a testament—as Theodore R. Hudson puts it—"of the internal inferno the narrator lives simply because he is black." And while it marks a stage in his abandonment of the American Dream (in which the Horatio Alger myth was central), it also records the recognition that that Dream is shattered for whites as well. Out of such words Baraka makes the magic of what redemption he can find: "In the alien language of another tribe, I make these documents for some heart who will recognize me truthfully."

The Death of Horatio Alger

The cold red building burned my eyes. The bricks hung together, like the city, the nation, under the dubious cement of rationalism and need. A need so controlled, it only erupted out of the used-car lots, or sat parked, Saturdays, in front of our orange house, for Orlando, or Algernon, or Danny, or J.D. to polish. There was silence, or summers, noise. But this was a few days after Christmas, and the ice melted from the roofs and the almost frozen water knocked lethargically against windows, tar roofs and slow dogs moping through the yards. The building was Central Avenue School. And its tired red sat on the corner of Central Avenue and Dey (pronounced *die* by the natives, *day* by the teachers, or any non-resident whites) Street. Then, on Dey, halfway up the block, the playground took over. A tarred-over yard, though once there had been gravel, surrounded by cement and a wire metal fence.

The snow was dirty as it sat dull and melting near the Greek restaurants, and the dimly lit "grocey" stores of the Negroes. The rich boys had metal wagons, the poor rode in. The poor made up games, the rich played them. The poor won the games, or as an emergency measure, the fights. No one thought of the snow except Mr. Feld, the playground director, who was in charge of it, or Miss Martin, the husky gym teacher Matthew Stodges had pushed into the cloakroom, who had no chains on her car. Grey slush ran over the curbs, and our dogs drank it out of boredom, shaking their heads and snorting.

I had said something about J.D.'s father, as to who he was, or had he ever been. And J., usually a confederate, and private strong arm, broke bad because Augie, Norman, and white Johnny were there, and laughed, misunderstanding simple "dozens" with ugly insult, in that curious scholarship the white man affects when he suspects a stronger link than sociology, or the tired cultural lies of Harcourt, Brace sixth-grade histories. And under their naïveté he grabbed my shirt and pushed me in the snow. I got up, brushing dead ice from my ears, and he pushed me down again, this time dumping a couple pounds of cold dirty slush down my neck, calmly hysterical at his act.

J. moved away and stood on an icy garbage hamper, sullenly throwing wet snow at the trucks on Central Avenue. I pushed myself into a sitting position, shaking my head. Tears full in my eyes, and the cold slicing minutes from my life. I wasn't making a sound. I wasn't thinking any thought I could make someone else understand. Just the rush of young fear and anger and disgust. I could have murdered God, in that simple practical way we kick dogs off the bottom step.

Augie (my best white friend), fat Norman, whose hook shots usually hit the rim, and were good for easy tip-ins by our big men, and useless white Johnny who had some weird disease that made him stare, even in the middle of a game, he'd freeze, and sometimes line drives almost knocked his head off while he shuddered slightly, cracking and recracking his huge knuckles. They were howling and hopping, they thought it was so funny that J. and I had come to blows. And especially, I guess, that I had got my lumps. "Hey, wiseass, somebody's gonna break your nose!" fat Norman would say over and over whenever I did something to him. Hold his pants when he tried his jump

From *Tales* by Le Roi Jones. Copyright © 1967 by LeRoi Jones. Reprinted by permission of Grove Press, Inc.

shot; spike him sliding into home (he was a lousy catcher); talk about his brother who hung out under the El and got naked in alleyways.

(The clucks of Autumn could have, right at that moment, easily seduced me. Away, and into school. To masquerade as a half-rich nigra with shiny feet. Back through the clean station, and up the street. Stopping to talk on the way. One beer gets you drunk and you stand in an empty corridor, lined with Italian paintings, talking about the glamours of sodomy.)

Rise and Slay.

I hurt so bad, and inside without bleeding I realized the filthy grey scratches my blood would carry to my heart. John walked off staring, and Augie and Norman disappeared, so easily there in the snow. And J.D. too, my first love, drifted against the easy sky. Weeping at what he'd done. No one there but me. THE SHORT SKINNY BOY WITH THE BUBBLE EYES.

Could leap up and slay them. Could hammer my fist and misery through their faces. Could strangle and bake them in the crude jungle of my feeling. Could stuff them in the sewie hole with the collected garbage of children's guilt. Could elevate them into heroic images of my own despair. A righteous messenger from the wrong side of the tracks. Gym teachers, cut-throats, aging pickets, ease by in the cold. The same lyric chart, exchange of particulars, that held me in my minutes, the time "Brownie" rammed the glass door down and ate up my suit. Even my mother, in a desperate fit of rhythm, was not equal to the task. Which was simple economics. I.e., a white man's dog cannot bite your son if he has been taught that something very ugly will happen to him if he does. He might pace stupidly in his ugly fur, but he will never never bite.

But what really stays to be found completely out, except stupid enterprises like art? The word on the page, the paint on the canvas (Marzette dragging in used-up canvases to revive their hopeless correspondence with the times), stone clinging to air, as if it were real. Or something a Deacon would admit was beautiful. The conscience rules against ideas. The point was to be where you wanted to, and do what you wanted to. After all is "said and done," what is left but those sheepish constructions. "I've got to go to the toilet" is no less pressing than the Puritans taking off for Massachusetts, and dragging their devils with them. (There is in those parts, even now, the peculiar smell of roasted sex organs. And when a good New Englander leaves his house in the earnestly moral sub-towns to go into the smoking hells of soon to be destroyed Yankee Gomorrahs, you watch him pull very firmly at his tie, or strapping on very tightly his evil watch.) The penitence there. The masochism. So complete and conscious a phenomenon. Like a standard of beauty; for instance, the bespectacled, soft-breasted, gently pigeon-toed maidens of America. Neither rich nor poor, with intelligent smiles and straight lovely noses. No one would think of them as beautiful but these mysterious scions of the puritans. They value health and devotion, and their good women, the lefty power of all our nation, are unpresuming subtle beauties, who could even live with poets (if they are from the right stock), if pushed to that. But mostly they are where they should be, reading good books and opening windows to air out their bedrooms. And it is a useful memory here, because such things as these were the vague images that had even so early, helped shape me. Light freckles, sandy hair, narrow clean bodies. Though none lived where I lived then. And I don't remember a direct look at them even, with clear knowledge of my desire, until one afternoon I gave a speech at East Orange High, as sports editor of our high school paper, which should have been printed in Italian, and I saw there, in the auditorium, young American girls, for the first time. And have loved them as flesh things emanating from real life, that is, in contrast to my own, a scraping and floating through the last three red and blue stripes of the flag, that settles the hash of the lower middle class. So that even sprawled there in the snow, with my blood and pompous isolation, I vaguely knew of a glamorous world and was mistaken into thinking it could be gotten from books. Negroes and Italians beat and shaped me, and my allegiance is there. But the triumph of romanticism was parquet floors, yellow dresses, gardens and sandy hair. I must have felt the loss and could not rise against a cardboard world of dark hair and linoleum. Reality was something I was convinced I could not have.

And thus to be flogged or put to the rack. For all our secret energies. The first leap over the barrier: when the victim finds he can no longer stomach his own "group." Politics whinnies, but is still correct, and asleep in a windy barn. The beautiful statue of victory, whose arms were called duty. And they curdle in her snatch thrust there by angry minorities, along with their own consciences. Poets climb, briefly, off their motorcycles, to find out who owns their words. We are named by all the things we will never understand. Whether we can fight or not, or even at the moment of our hugest triumph we stare off into space remembering the snow melting in our cuts, and all the pimps of reason who've ever conquered us. It is the harshest form of love.

I could not see when I "chased" Norman and Augie. Chased in quotes because, they really did not have to run. They could have turned, and myth aside, calmly whipped my ass. But they ran, laughing and keeping warm. And J.D. kicked snow from around a fire hydrant flatly into the gutter. Smiling and broken, with his head hung just slanted towards the yellow dog ice running down a hole. I took six or seven long running steps and tripped. I couldn't have been less interested, but the whole project had gotten out of hand. I was crying, and my hands were freezing, and the two white boys leaned against the pointed metal fence and laughed and slapped their knees. I threw snow stupidly in their direction. It fell short and was not even noticed as it dropped.

(All of it rings in your ears for a long time. But the payback . . . in simple terms against such actual sin as supposing quite confidently that the big sweating purple whore staring from her peed up hall very casually at your whipping has *never* been loved . . . is hard. We used to say.)

Then I pushed to my knees and could only see J. leaning there against the hydrant looking just over my head. I called to him, for help really. But the words rang full of dead venom. I screamed his mother a purple nigger with alligator titties. His father a bilious white man with sores on his jowls. I was screaming for help in my hatred and loss, and only the hatred would show. And he came over shouting for me to shut up. Shut Up skinny bastard. I'll break your ass if you don't. Norman had both hands on his stomach, his laugh was getting so violent, and he danced awkwardly toward us howling to agitate J. to beat me some more. But J. whirled on him perfectly and rapped him hard under his second chin. Norman was going to say, "Hey me-an," in that hated twist of our speech, and J. hit him again, between his shoulder and chest, and almost dropped him to his knees. Augie cooled his howl to a giggle of concern and backed up until Norman turned and they both went shouting up the street.

I got to my feet, wiping my freezing hands on my jacket. J. was looking at me hard, like country boys do, when their language, or the new tone they need to take on once they come to this cold climate (1940's New Jersey) fails, and they are left with only the old Southern tongue, which cruel farts like me used to deride their lack of interest in America. I turned to walk away. Both my eyes were nothing but water, though it held at their rims, stoically refusing to blink and thus begin to sob uncontrollably. And to keep from breaking down I wheeled and hid the weeping by screaming at that boy. You nigger without a father. You eat your mother's pussy. And he wheeled me around and started to hit me again.

Someone called my house and my mother and father and grandmother and sister were strung along Dey street, in some odd order. (They couldn't have come out of the house "together.") And I was conscious first of my father saying, "Go on Mickey, hit him. Fight back." And for a few seconds, under the weight of that plea for my dignity, I tried. I feinted and danced, but I couldn't even roll up my fists. The whole street was blurred and hot as my eyes. I swung and swung, but J.D. bashed me when he wanted to.

My mother stopped the fight finally, shuddering at the thing she'd made. "His hands are frozen, Michael. His hands are frozen." And my father looks at me even now, wondering if they'll ever thaw.

Joyce Carol Oates (1938–   )

"I would be unable to write about anything that did not seem to me both unique and universal," says Joyce Carol Oates,

> —an event I have lived through myself, or experienced intensely through my imagination, and an event that has some meaning, some larger appeal, which may go far beyond the temporal limitations of the subject. If art has any general evolutionary function, it must be to enhance the race, to work somehow toward an essential unity and harmony—survival and growth—and perhaps an integration of the human world with the natural world.

This is the credo of a young writer who burst, as it were, full-armed upon the world of fiction. Acclaimed from the beginning for its quality, the very quantity of her work is prodigious. Born in 1938, by the time she was thirty-one she had published her fourth novel, *them,* for which she received the prestigious National Book Award. Her short stories have nine times received the O. Henry Prize Award, and in 1970 she was awarded an O. Henry Special Award for Continuing Achievement. By 1973, she had published half a dozen novels, four volumes of short stories, and a book of critical pieces. In addition, she teaches at the University of Windsor, Ontario.

In discussing the sources of her work, she says, "my own fantasies, however intriguing, simply don't seem substantial enough for me to formalize into art." Her stories start in her imagination usually with an objective event, a personal experience, or perhaps a newspaper item, which then works "its way through my imagination" into consciousness. But "Without the conscious and intelligent *formalization* of one's deepest, instinctive fantasies, no communication at all is possible." Artistry there most certainly is; her scenes are brilliantly realized, her characters palpable. But the reader is more likely to be struck by the energy and emotional intensity of the writing itself.

The protagonist of "Stalking" is apparently schizophrenic, delusionary, and profoundly and pointlessly antisocial. But even the presumably normal Oates's characters are obsessive. Their lives seem controlled not by reason or morality, or custom or convention, but rather by urgencies that burst from the unconscious.

As well as describing them, the language reflects the characters. When dealing with the girl, the imagery and sounds are sluggish, dull, relentless: "walking slowly, deliberately . . .," "big, square, strong feet jammed into white leather boots. . . ." For the Invisible Adversary, the words are staccato, sharply visible, quick: He is "fleeing across a field . . . on long spiky legs brisk as colts' legs." The sentences are, in T. S. Eliot's phrase, "the objective correlatives" of the characters and happenings. The writing itself seems to participate in the dark forces of the protagonist's unconscious.

"Stalking" is the story about a sick girl who, through a series of destructive and dangerous episodes, conquers her alter ego. It is also a story about a society that is, Oates seems to think, equally sick. It is no accident that the girl pursues her alter ego amidst half-built freeways, bulldozers, shopping malls, ludicrously marked parking stalls. She is a fitting symbol of the society, as well as its inevitable consequence. As anomie and materialism rule it, so alienation and affectlessness rule her. As it destroys the landscape to build a gas station that is in turn destroyed, so she assaults all that lies in her path.

She finally, back home, achieves a moment of tranquillity. The final paragraph, when the Adversary is conquered, is bland, almost restful in content and in tone. Oates does not attempt to tell us what she sees for the society.

Stalking

The Invisible Adversary is fleeing across a field.

Gretchen, walking slowly, deliberately, watches with her keen unblinking eyes the figure of the Invisible Adversary some distance ahead. The Adversary has run boldly in front of all that traffic—on long spiky legs brisk as colts' legs—and jumped up onto a curb of new concrete, and now is running across a vacant field. The Adversary glances over his shoulder at Gretchen.

Bastard, Gretchen thinks.

Saturday afternoon. November. A cold gritty day. Gretchen is out stalking. She has hours for her game. Hours. She is dressed for the hunt, her solid legs crammed into old blue jeans, her big, square, strong feet jammed into white leather boots that cost her mother forty dollars not long ago, but are now scuffed and filthy with mud. Hopeless to get them clean again, Gretchen doesn't give a damn. She is wearing a dark green corduroy jacket that is worn out at the elbows and the rear, with a zipper that can be zipped swiftly up or down, attached to a fringed leather strip. On her head nothing, though it is windy today.

She has hours ahead.

Cars and trucks and buses from the city and enormous interstate trucks hauling automobiles pass by on the highway; Gretchen waits until the way is nearly clear, then starts out. A single car is approaching. *Slow down, you bastard,* Gretchen thinks; and like magic he does.

Following the footprints of the Invisible Adversary. There is no sidewalk here yet, so she might as well cut right across the field. A gigantic sign announces the site of the

Reprinted from *Marriages and Infidelities and Other Stories* by Joyce Carol Oates by permission of the publisher, Vanguard Press, Inc. Copyright © 1968, 1969, 1970, 1971, 1972 by Joyce Carol Oates.

new Pace & Fischbach Building, an office building of fifteen floors to be completed the following year. The land around here is all dug up and muddy; she can see the Adversary's footsteps leading right past the gouged-up area . . . and there he is, smirking back at her, pretending panic.

I'll get you. Don't worry, Gretchen thinks carefully.

Because the Adversary is so light-footed and invisible, Gretchen doesn't make any effort to be that way. She plods along as she does at school, passing from classroom to classroom, unhurried and not even sullen, just unhurried. She knows she is very visible. She is thirteen years old and weighs one hundred and thirty-five pounds. She's only five feet three—stocky, muscular, squat in the torso and shoulders, with good strong legs and thighs. She could be good at gym, if she bothered; instead, she just stands around, her face empty, her arms crossed and her shoulders a little slumped. If forced, she takes part in the games of volleyball and basketball, but she runs heavily, without spirit, and sometimes bumps into other girls, hurting them. *Out of my way,* she thinks; at such times her face shows no expression.

And now? . . . The Adversary is peeking out at her from around the corner of a gas station. Something flickers in her brain. *I see you,* she thinks, with quiet excitement. The Adversary ducks back out of sight. Gretchen heads in his direction, plodding through a jumbled, bulldozed field of mud and thistles and debris that is mainly rocks and chunks of glass. The gas station is brand new and not yet opened for business. It is all white tile, white concrete, perfect plate-glass windows with whitewashed X's on them, a large driveway and eight gasoline pumps, all proudly erect and ready for business. But the gas station has not opened since Gretchen and her family moved here—about six months ago. Something must have gone wrong. Gretchen fixes her eyes on the corner where the Adversary was last seen. He can't escape.

One wall of the gas station's white tile has been smeared with something like tar. Dreamy, snakelike, thick twistings of black. Black tar. Several windows have been broken. Gretchen stands in the empty driveway, her hands jammed into her pockets. Traffic is moving slowly over here. A barricade has been set up that directs traffic out onto the shoulder of the highway, on a narrow, bumpy, muddy lane that loops out and back again onto the pavement. Cars move slowly, carefully. Their bottoms scrape against the road. The detour signs are great rectangular things, bright yellow with black zigzag lines. SLOW. DETOUR. In the two center lanes of the highway are bulldozers not being used today, and gigantic concrete pipes to be used for storm sewers. Eight pipes. They are really enormous; Gretchen's eyes crinkle with awe, just to see them.

She remembers the Adversary.

There he is—headed for the shopping plaza. *He won't get away in the crowds,* Gretchen promises herself. She follows. Now she is approaching an area that is more completed, though there are still no sidewalks and some of the buildings are brand-new and yet unoccupied, vacant. She jumps over a concrete ditch that is stained with rust-colored water and heads up a slight incline to the service drive of the Federal Savings Bank. The drive-in tellers' windows are all dark today, behind their green-tinted glass. The whole bank is dark, closed. Is this the bank her parents go to now? It takes Gretchen a minute to recognize it.

Now a steady line of traffic, a single lane, turns onto the service drive that leads to the shopping plaza. BUCKINGHAM MALL. 101 STORES. Gretchen notices a few kids her own age, boys or girls, trudging in jeans and jackets ahead of her, through the mud. They might be classmates of hers. Her attention is captured again by the Invisible Adversary, who has run all the way up to the Mall and is hanging around the entrance of the Cunningham Drug Store, teasing her.

You'll be sorry for that, you bastard, Gretchen thinks with a smile.

Automobiles pass her slowly. The parking lot for the Mall is enormous, many acres. A city of cars on a Saturday afternoon. Gretchen sees a car that might be her mother's, but she isn't sure. Cars are parked slanted here, in lanes marked LOT K, LANE 15; LOT K, LANE 16. The signs are spheres, bubbles, perched up on long slender poles. At night they are illuminated.

Ten or twelve older kids are hanging around the drugstore entrance. One of them is sitting on top of a mailbox, rocking it back and forth. Gretchen pushes past them— they are kidding around, trying to block people—and inside the store her eye darts rapidly up and down the aisles, looking for the Invisible Adversary.

Hiding here? Hiding?

She strolls along, cunning and patient. At the cosmetics counter a girl is showing an older woman some liquid make-up. She smears a small oval onto the back of the woman's hand, rubs it in gently. "That's Peach Pride," the girl says. She has shimmering blond hair and eyes that are penciled to show a permanent exclamatory interest. She does not notice Gretchen, who lets one hand drift idly over a display of marked-down lipsticks, each for only $1.59.

Gretchen slips the tube of lipstick into her pocket. Neatly. Nimbly. Ignoring the Invisible Adversary, who is shaking a finger at her, she drifts over to the newsstand, looks at the magazine covers without reading them, and edges over to another display. Packages in a cardboard barrel, out in the aisle. Big bargains. Gretchen doesn't even glance in the barrel to see what is being offered . . . she just slips one of the packages in her pocket. No trouble.

She leaves by the other door, the side exit. A small smile tugs at her mouth.

The Adversary is trotting ahead of her. The Mall is divided into geometric areas, each colored differently; the Adversary leaves the blue pavement and is now on the green. Gretchen follows. She notices the Adversary going into a Franklin Joseph store.

Gretchen enters the store, sniffs in the perfumy, overheated smell, sees nothing that interests her on the counters or at the dress racks, and so walks right to the back of the store, to the Ladies Room. No one inside. She takes the tube of lipstick out of her pocket, opens it, examines the lipstick. It has a tart, sweet smell. A very light pink: *Spring Blossom.* Gretchen goes to the mirror and smears the lipstick onto it, at first lightly, then coarsely; part of the lipstick breaks and falls into a hair-littered sink. Gretchen goes into one of the toilet stalls and tosses the tube into the toilet bowl. She takes handfuls of toilet paper and crumbles them into a ball and throws them into the toilet. Remembering the package from the drugstore, she takes it out of her pocket— just toothpaste. She throws it, cardboard package and all, into the toilet bowl, then, her mind glimmering with an idea, she goes to the apparatus that holds the towel—a single cloth towel on a roll—and tugs at it until it comes loose, then pulls it out hand over hand, patiently, until the entire towel is out. She scoops it up and carries it to the toilet. She pushes it in and flushes the toilet.

The stuff doesn't go down, so she tries again. This time it goes part-way down before it gets stuck.

Gretchen leaves the rest room and strolls unhurried through the store. The Adversary is waiting for her outside—peeking through the window—wagging a finger at her. *Don't you wag no finger at me,* she thinks, with a small tight smile. Outside, she follows him at a distance. Loud music is blaring around her head. It is rock music, piped out onto the colored squares and rectangles of the Mall, blown everywhere by the November wind, but Gretchen hardly hears it.

Some boys are fooling around in front of the record store. One of them bumps into Gretchen and they all laugh as she is pushed against a trash can. "Watch it, babe!" the boy sings out. Her leg hurts. Gretchen doesn't look at them but, with a cold, swift anger, her face averted, she knocks the trash can over onto the sidewalk. Junk falls out. The can rolls. Some women shoppers scurry to get out of the way and the boys laugh.

Gretchen walks away without looking back.

She wanders through Sampson Furniture, which has two entrances. In one door and out the other, as always; it is a ritual with her. Again she notices the sofa that is like the sofa in their family room at home—covered with black and white fur, real goatskin. All over the store there are sofas, chairs, tables, beds. A jumble of furnishings. People stroll around them, in and out of little displays, displays meant to be living rooms, dining rooms, bedrooms, family rooms. . . . It makes Gretchen's eyes squint to see so many displays: like seeing the inside of a hundred houses. She slows down, almost comes to a stop. Gazing at a living-room display on a raised platform. Only after a moment does she remember why she is here—whom she is following—and she turns to see the Adversary beckoning to her.

She follows him outside again. He goes into Dodi's Boutique and, with her head lowered so that her eyes seem to move to the bottom of her eyebrows, pressing up against her forehead, Gretchen follows him. *You'll regret this,* she thinks. Dodi's Boutique is decorated in silver and black. Metallic strips hang down from a dark ceiling, quivering. Salesgirls dressed in pants suits stand around with nothing to do except giggle with one another and nod their heads in time to the music amplified throughout the store. It is music from a local radio station. Gretchen wanders over to the dress rack, for the hell of it. Size 14. "The time is now 2:35," a radio announcer says cheerfully. "The weather is 32 degrees with a chance of showers and possible sleet tonight. You're listening to WCKK, Radio Wonderful. . . ." Gretchen selects several dresses and a salesgirl shows her to a dressing room.

"Need any help?" the girl asks. She has long swinging hair and a high-shouldered, indifferent, bright manner.

"No," Gretchen mutters.

Alone, Gretchen takes off her jacket. She is wearing a navy blue sweater. She zips one of the dresses open and it falls off the flimsy plastic hanger before she can catch it. She steps on it, smearing mud onto the white wool. *The hell with it.* She lets it lie there and holds up another dress, gazing at herself in the mirror.

She has untidy, curly hair that looks like a wig set loosely on her head. Light brown curls spill out everywhere, bouncy, a little frizzy, a cascade, a tumbling of curls. Her eyes are deep set, her eyebrows heavy and dark. She has a stern, staring look, like an adult man. Her nose is perfectly formed, neat and noble. Her upper lip is long, as if it were stretched to close with difficulty over the front teeth. She wears no make-up, her lips are perfectly colorless, pale, a little chapped, and they are usually held tight, pursed tightly shut. She has a firm, rounded chin. Her facial structure is strong, pensive, its features stern and symmetrical as a statue's, blank, neutral, withdrawn. Her face is attractive. But there is a blunt, neutral, sexless stillness to it, as if she were detached from it and somewhere else, uninterested.

She holds the dress up to her body, smooths it down over her breasts, staring.

After a moment she hangs the dress up again, and runs down the zipper so roughly that it breaks. The other dress she doesn't bother with. She leaves the dressing room, putting on her jacket.

At the front of the store the salesgirl glances at her . . . "—Didn't fit?—"

"No," says Gretchen.

She wanders around for a while, in and out of Carmichael's, the Mall's big famous store, where she catches sight of her mother on an escalator going up. Her mother doesn't notice her. She pauses by a display of "winter homes." Her family owns a home like this, in the Upper Peninsula, except theirs is larger. This one comes complete for only $5330: PACKAGE ERECTED ON YOUR LOT—YEAR-ROUND HOME FIBER GLASS INSULATION—BEAUTIFUL ROUGH-SAWN VERTICAL B. C. CEDAR SIDING WITH DEEP SIMULATED SHADOW LINES FOR A RUGGED EXTERIOR.

Only 3:15. For the hell of it, Gretchen goes into the Big Boy restaurant and orders a ground-round hamburger with French fries. Also a Coke. She sits at the crowded counter and eats slowly, her jaws grinding slowly, as she glances at her reflection in the mirror directly in front of her—her mop of hair moving almost imperceptibly with the grinding of her jaws—and occasionally she sees the Adversary waiting outside, coyly. *You'll get yours,* she thinks.

She leaves the Big Boy and wanders out into the parking lot, eating from a bag of potato chips. She wipes her greasy hands on her thighs. The afternoon has turned dark and cold. Shivering a little, she scans the maze of cars for the Adversary—yes, there he is—and starts after him. He runs ahead of her. He runs through the parking lot, waits teasingly at the edge of a field, and as she approaches he runs across the field, trotting along with a noisy crowd of four or five loose dogs that don't seem to notice him.

Gretchen follows him through that field, trudging in the mud, and through another muddy field, her eyes fixed on him. Now he is at the highway—hesitating there—now he is about to run across in front of traffic—now, now—now he darts out—

Now! He is struck by a car! His body knocked backward, spinning backward. Ah, now, *now how does it feel?* Gretchen asks.

He picks himself up. Gets to his feet. Is he bleeding? Yes, bleeding! He stumbles across the highway to the other side, where there is a sidewalk. Gretchen follows him as soon as the traffic lets up. He is staggering now, like a drunken man. *How does it feel? Do you like it now?*

The Adversary staggers along the sidewalk. He turns onto a side street, beneath an archway. *Piney Woods.* He is leading Gretchen into the Piney Woods subdivision. Here the homes are quite large, on artificial hills that show them to good advantage. Most of the homes are white colonials with attached garages. There are no sidewalks here, so the Adversary has to walk in the street, limping like an old man, and Gretchen follows him in the street, with her eyes fixed on him.

Are you happy now? Does it hurt? Does it?

She giggles at the way he walks. He looks like a drunken man. He glances back at her, white-faced, and turns up a flagstone walk . . . goes right up to a big white colonial house. . . .

Gretchen follows him inside. She inspects the simulated brick of the foyer: yes, there are blood spots. He is dripping blood. Entranced, she follows the splashes of blood into the hall, to the stairs . . . forgets her own boots, which are muddy . . . but she doesn't feel like going back to wipe her feet. The hell with it.

Nobody seems to be home. Her mother is probably still shopping, her father is out of town for the weekend. The house empty. Gretchen goes into the kitchen, opens the refrigerator, takes out a Coke, and wanders to the rear of the house, to the family room. It is two steps down from the rest of the house. She takes off her jacket and tosses it somewhere. Turns on the television set. Sits on the goatskin sofa and stares at the screen: a return of a Shotgun Steve show, which she has already seen.

If the Adversary comes crawling behind her, groaning in pain, weeping, she won't even bother to glance at him.

Towards 1984

Franz Kafka (1883–1924)

At least one reader has suggested that the best description of Kafka's fictional world—more exactly, of our response to its symbolic labyrinths—is to be found in a portion of a sentence from "A Country Doctor": "The air was almost unbreathable; . . . I wanted to push open a window." In his stories and novels we often feel as though we were experiencing a waking nightmare, the more terrifying because at the end of the tale we have not waked up. Yet, as Philip Rahv reminds us, it is important to perceive that Kafka is considerably more than a neurotic artist; "he is also an artist of neurosis." His greatness is by now fully established, but the character and meaning of his work are still much in dispute. Claimed as one of their own by Freudians, existentialists, expressionists, antitotalitarians, and by Jews and Christians, Kafka continues to baffle even as he magnetizes his readers.

He was born into an upper-middle-class Jewish family in Prague in 1883. From youth onward the central force in his life was his father, an authoritarian figure who generated in his son ambivalent feelings of admiration and fear. So profound was his father's effect on him that, while he spoke easily and well in the company of others, in the presence of the disquieting parent he stuttered. The need for his father's approval was obsessive, and it stayed with Kafka to the end of his life. Many critics find the father- or authority-figure, in its multiple symbolic manifestations, indispensable to any accounting of what happens in Kafka's fiction. For example, in "A Country Doctor" the physician, so long as he remains in a superior relationship to the boy, is powerless to help him. The boy in turn, clinging to his sacrificial role, says, "A fine wound is all I brought into the world; that was my sole endowment." And it is only after the doctor, stripped of clothes and status, lies beside the boy and his rose-red wound that he can be of aid.

The events of Kafka's adult life are quickly told. He received a doctorate in jurisprudence in 1906 and entered the civil service two years later, already a writer in private. Although his duties were not in themselves taxing, he experienced only annoyance in his position, and his fear of bureaucracy became terror in his fiction. In 1917 he discovered that he had tuberculosis and resigned. Treatment was unsuccessful; he died in 1924, known only to a small literary circle.

During his life Kafka published very little. He owes his fame to his friend and literary executor, Max Brod, who, against Kafka's expressed wish, refused to burn his unpublished manuscripts, much the greater part of his work. Following their initial publication in the decade after Kafka's death, the stories and novels began to appear in English translation in 1930. All of the novels—*The Trial, The Castle,* and *Amerika*—focus on the impotence, felt sinfulness, and frustration of man brought before a tribunal that seems to exist outside of time, a perpetual court of perpetual conviction. No innocent verdicts are rendered. There is no hope, because for man hope may not even be conceptualized.

In the story that follows, we would seem to be in the realm of dream literature, for it is only the shifting images and metamorphoses of dreams that enable us to ascribe any literal meaning to the action. The figures, gestures, and motions are so firmly rooted in symbolism "that any certain dichotomy between the literal and the symbolic vanishes." From another point of view, according to Stanley Cooperman:

> the story becomes a symbolic restatement of the classic existentialist situation. On the one hand, we have a respectable and adjusted life; on the other, the swift insight, the crisis erupting within the placidly flowing sequence of "duties" and prosaic tasks. "I could see no way out," the doctor cries, and his words are an echo of the philosophers of crisis from Kierkegaard to Sartre.

A Country Doctor

I was in great perplexity; I had to start on an urgent journey; a seriously ill patient was waiting for me in a village ten miles off; a thick blizzard of snow filled all the wide spaces between him and me; I had a gig, a light gig with big wheels, exactly right for our country roads; muffled in furs, my bag of instruments in my hand, I was in the courtyard all ready for the journey; but there was no horse to be had, no horse. My own horse had died in the night, worn out by the fatigues of this icy winter; my servant girl was now running round the village trying to borrow a horse; but it was hopeless, I knew it, and I stood there forlornly, with the snow gathering more and more thickly upon me, more and more unable to move. In the gateway the girl appeared, alone, and waved the lantern; of course, who would lend a horse at this time for such a journey? I strode through the courtyard once more; I could see no way out; in my confused distress I kicked at the dilapidated door of the year-long uninhabited pigsty. It flew open and flapped to and fro on its hinges. A steam and smell as of horses came out from it. A dim stable lantern was swinging inside from a rope. A man, crouching on his hams in that low space, showed an open blue-eyed face. "Shall I yoke up?" he asked, crawling out on all fours. I did not know what to say and merely stooped down to see what else was in the sty. The servant girl was standing beside me.

Reprinted by permission of Schocken Books, Inc. from *The Penal Colony* by Franz Kafka, translated by Willa and Edwin Muir. Copyright © 1948 by Schocken Books, Inc.

"You never know what you're going to find in your own house," she said, and we both laughed. "Hey there, Brother, hey there, Sister!" called the groom, and two horses, enormous creatures with powerful flanks, one after the other, their legs tucked close to their bodies, each well-shaped head lowered like a camel's, by sheer strength of buttocking squeezed out through the door hole which they filled entirely. But at once they were standing up, their legs long and their bodies steaming thickly. "Give him a hand," I said, and the willing girl hurried to help the groom with the harnessing. Yet hardly was she beside him when the groom clipped hold of her and pushed his face against hers. She screamed and fled back to me; on her cheek stood out in red the marks of two rows of teeth. "You brute," I yelled in fury, "do you want a whipping?" but in the same moment reflected that the man was a stranger; that I did not know where he came from, and that of his own free will he was helping me out when everyone else had failed me. As if he knew my thoughts he took no offense at my threat but, still busied with the horses, only turned round once towards me. "Get in," he said then, and indeed: everything was ready. A magnificent pair of horses, I observed, such as I had never sat behind, and I climbed in happily. "But I'll drive, you don't know the way," I said. "Of course," said he, "I'm not coming with you anyway, I'm staying with Rose." "No," shrieked Rose, fleeing into the house with a justified presentiment that her fate was inescapable; I heard the door chain rattle as she put it up; I heard the key turn in the lock; I could see, moreover, how she put out the lights in the entrance hall and in further flight all through the rooms to keep herself from being discovered. "You're coming with me," I said to the groom, "or I won't go, urgent as my journey is. I'm not thinking of paying for it by handing the girl over to you." "Gee up!" he said; clapped his hands; the gig whirled off like a log in a freshet; I could just hear the door of my house splitting and bursting as the groom charged at it and then I was deafened and blinded by a storming rush that steadily buffeted all my senses. But this only for a moment, since, as if my patient's farmyard had opened out just before my courtyard gate, I was already there; the horses had come quietly to a standstill; the blizzard had stopped; moonlight all around; my patient's parents hurried out of the house, his sister behind them; I was almost lifted out of the gig; from their confused ejaculations I gathered not a word; in the sickroom the air was almost unbreathable; the neglected stove was smoking; I wanted to push open a window; but first I had to look at my patient. Gaunt, without any fever, not cold, not warm, with vacant eyes, without a shirt, the youngster heaved himself up from under the feather bedding, threw his arms round my neck, and whispered in my ear: "Doctor, let me die." I glanced round the room; no one had heard it; the parents were leaning forward in silence waiting for my verdict; the sister had set a chair for my handbag; I opened the bag and hunted among my instruments; the boy kept clutching at me from his bed to remind me of his entreaty; I picked up a pair of tweezers, examined them in the candlelight and laid them down again. "Yes," I thought blasphemously, "in cases like this the gods are helpful, send the missing horse, add to it a second because of the urgency, and to crown everything bestow even a groom—" And only now did I remember Rose again; what was I to do, how could I rescue her, how could I pull her away from under that groom at ten miles' distance, with a team of horses I couldn't control. These horses, now, they had somehow slipped the reins loose, pushed the windows open from outside, I did not know how; each of them had stuck a head in at a window and, quite unmoved by the startled cries of the family, stood eyeing the patient. "Better go back at once," I thought, as if the horses were summoning me to the return journey, yet I permitted the patient's sister, who fancied that I was dazed by the heat, to take my fur coat from me. A glass of rum was poured out for me, the old man clapped me on the shoulder, a familiarity justified by this offer of his treasure. I shook my head; in the narrow confines of the old man's thoughts I felt ill; that was my only reason for refusing the drink. The mother stood by the bedside and cajoled me towards it; I yielded, and, while one of the horses whinnied loudly to the ceiling, laid my head to the boy's breast, which shivered under my wet beard. I confirmed what I already knew; the boy was quite sound, something a little wrong with his circulation, saturated with coffee by his solicitous mother, but sound and best turned out of bed with one shove. I am no world reformer and so I let him lie. I was the district doctor and did my duty to the uttermost, to the point where it became almost too much. I was badly paid and yet generous and helpful to the poor. I had still to see that Rose was all right, and then the boy might have his way and I wanted to die too. What was I doing there in that endless winter! My horse was dead, and not a single person in the village would lend me another. I had to get my team out of the pigsty; if they hadn't chanced to be horses I should have had to travel with swine. That was how it was. And I nodded to the family. They knew nothing about it, and, had they known, would not have believed it. To write prescriptions is easy, but to come to an understanding with people is hard. Well, this should be the end of my visit, I had once more been called out needlessly, I was used to that, the whole district made my life a torment with my night bell, but that I should have to sacrifice Rose this time as well, the pretty girl who had lived in my house for years almost without my noticing her—that sacrifice was too much to ask, and I had somehow to get it reasoned out in my head with the help of what craft I could muster, in order not to let fly at this family, which with the best will in the world could not restore Rose to me. But as I shut my bag and put an arm out for my fur coat, the family meanwhile standing together, the father sniffing at the glass of rum in his hand, the mother, apparently disappointed in me—why, what do people expect?—biting her lips with tears in her eyes, the sister fluttering a blood-soaked towel, I was somehow ready to admit conditionally that the boy might be ill after all. I went towards him, he welcomed me smiling as if I were bringing him the most nourishing invalid broth—ah, now both horses were whinnying together; the noise, I suppose, was ordained by heaven to assist my examination of the patient—and this time I discovered that the boy was indeed ill. In his right side, near the hip, was an open wound as big as the palm of my hand. Rose-red, in many variations of shade, dark in the hollows, lighter at the edges, softly granulated, with irregular clots of blood, open as a surface mine to the daylight. That was how it looked from a distance. But on a closer inspection there was another complication. I could not help a low whistle of surprise. Worms, as thick and as long as my little finger, themselves rose-red and blood-spotted as well, were wriggling from their fastness in the interior of the wound towards the light, with small white heads and many little legs. Poor boy, you were past helping. I had discovered your great wound; this blossom in your side was destroying you. The family was pleased; they saw me busying myself; the sister told the mother, the mother the father, the father told several guests who were coming in, through the moonlight at the open door, walking on tiptoe, keeping their balance with outstretched arms. "Will you save me?" whispered the boy with a sob, quite blinded by the life within his wound. That is what people are like in my district. Always expecting the impossible from the doctor. They have lost their ancient beliefs; the parson sits at home and unravels his vestments, one after another; but the doctor is supposed to be omnipotent with his merciful surgeon's hand. Well, as it pleases them; I have not thrust my services on them; if they misuse me for sacred ends, I let that happen to me too; what better do I want, old country doctor that I am, bereft of my servant girl! And so they came, the family and the village elders, and stripped my clothes off me; a school choir with the teacher at the head of it stood before the house and sang these words to an utterly simple tune:

> Strip his clothes off, then he'll heal us,
> If he doesn't, kill him dead!
> Only a doctor, only a doctor.

Then my clothes were off and I looked at the people quietly, my fingers in my beard and my head cocked to one side. I was altogether composed and equal to the situation and remained so, although it was no help to me, since they now took me by the head and feet and carried me to the bed. They laid me down in it next to the wall, on the side of the wound. Then they all left the room; the door was shut; the singing stopped; clouds covered the moon; the bedding was warm around me; the horses' heads in the open windows wavered like shadows. "Do you know," said a voice in my ear, "I have very little confidence in you. Why, you were only blown in here, you didn't come on your own feet. Instead of helping me, you're cramping me on my deathbed. What I'd like best is to scratch your eyes out." "Right," I said, "it is a shame. And yet I am a doctor. What am I to do? Believe me, it is not too easy for me either." "Am I supposed to be content with this apology? Oh, I must be, I can't help it. I always have to put up with things. A fine wound is all I brought into the world; that was my sole endowment." "My young friend," said I, "your mistake is: you have not a wide enough view. I have been in all the sickrooms, far and wide, and I tell you: your wound is not so bad. Done in a tight corner with two strokes of the ax. Many a one proffers his side and can hardly hear the ax in the forest, far less that it is coming nearer to him." "Is that really so, or are you deluding me in my fever?" "It is really so, take the word of honor of an official doctor." And he took it and lay still. But now it was time for me to think of escaping. The horses were still standing faithfully in their places. My clothes, my fur coat, my bag were quickly collected; I didn't want to waste time dressing; if the horses raced home as they had come, I should only be springing, as it were, out of this bed into my own. Obediently a horse backed away from the window; I threw my bundle into the gig; the fur coat missed its mark and was caught on a hook only by the sleeve. Good enough. I swung myself onto the horse. With the reins loosely trailing, one horse barely fastened to the other, the gig swaying behind, my fur coat last of all in the snow. "Gee up!" I said, but there was no galloping; slowly, like old men, we crawled through the snowy wastes; a long time echoed behind us the new but faulty song of the children:

> O be joyful, all you patients,
> The doctor's laid in bed beside you!

Never shall I reach home at this rate; my flourishing practice is done for; my successor is robbing me, but in vain, for he cannot take my place; in my house the disgusting groom is raging; Rose is his victim; I do not want to think about it any more. Naked, exposed to the frost of this most unhappy of ages, with an earthly vehicle, unearthly horses, old man that I am, I wander astray. My fur coat is hanging from the back of the gig, but I cannot reach it and none of my limber pack of patients lifts a finger. Betrayed! Betrayed! A false alarm on the night bell once answered—it cannot be made good, not ever.

Karel Čapek (1890–1938)

In 1929 Čapek published in Czech two volumes of stories, which were later translated as *Tales from One Pocket* (including "The Last Judgment") and *Tales from the Other Pocket*. They are frequently described as detective stories, though only a few of them follow traditional forms and conventions of detective fiction. "Police tales" might better describe many of them, for the principal investigator is not the familiar amateur sleuth, but one or more professional policemen. And a considerable number of the tales are concerned with other aspects of crime altogether. Here is Čapek's own comment on the *Tales* and their themes:

> The kernel of *Tales from One Pocket* was the intention to write *noetic* [i.e., cognitive] stories about the various roads that lead to the knowledge of the truth; and so . . . the detective *genre* forced itself upon me. Here you have discoveries which are pseudo-occult, poetical, matter of routine, purely empirical, and so forth. But involuntarily, in the course of the work another *motif* came up, an ethical one, the problem of *justice*. You will find it in most of the tales of the second half of *One Pocket* [where "The Last Judgment" is located].

In earlier stories Čapek had used the detective genre as a parable of man's quest for truth, but in them the search was for the mystery of the Absolute, and the search regularly ended in failure. In the *Pocket* tales, however, belief in absolute truth or in its possible accessibility has been totally rejected: "Relative truth is all that is accessible to man. But man frequently mistakes this relative truth for absolute truth, or at least for relative truth of a wider application than in fact it possesses." The limitations, confusions, and contradictions of human knowledge thus constitute the organizing theme for *Tales from One Pocket*.

The setting of "The Last Judgment" is a tribunal in Heaven. On trial is a criminal who had been a multiple killer in this life and who has himself just been killed by a policeman. God is present, but only as a witness. He will not judge the accused, for he knows everything about him: the history of his entire life, including all of the experiences and conditioning forces that have made him what he is. To know everything is to understand everything; to understand everything is to know the necessary causes of everything. In the eyes of omniscience, therefore, there can be no guilt, only comprehension. *Tout comprendre, c'est tout pardonner.*

The dialogue of the story is at once merciful and severe. God speaks to Kugler with a kind of "mateyness," almost like an old friend bringing him up to date on events and consequences of events that Kugler may have missed simply because he was out of town. It is as though they had grown up together in the same neighborhood. Indeed, the domestic handling of cosmic issues is one source of Čapek's wry humor. But severity is the final order of the story: man, and only man, whose knowledge is relative and limited, can judge. As God puts it in the story: "Man belongs to man. . . . Man isn't worthy of divine judgment. He deserves to be judged only by other men." It is at once an epistemological solution and dramatic resolution.

During the 1930s Čapek did his best to alert his native Czechoslovakia and the rest of Europe to the menace of Hitler, but his voice was not heard, and he died in 1939 as Nazi troops marched into Prague. An enormously productive author, Čapek wrote travel sketches, criticism, fiction, and plays. He was a close friend of the founder and first president of the 1918 Czechoslovak Republic, Tomáš Masaryk, who established the National Theater with Čapek and his brother Josef as its leaders.

The Last Judgment

The notorious multiple-killer Kugler, pursued by several warrants and a whole army of policemen and detectives, swore that he'd never be taken. He wasn't either—at least not alive. The last of his nine murderous deeds was shooting a policeman who tried to arrest him. The policeman indeed died, but not before putting a total of seven bullets into Kugler. Of these seven, three were fatal. Kugler's death came so quickly that he felt no pain. And so it seemed Kugler had escaped earthly justice.

When his soul left his body, it should have been surprised at the sight of the next world—a world beyond space, grey, and infinitely desolate—but it wasn't. A man who has been jailed on two continents looks upon the next life merely as new surroundings. Kugler expected to struggle through, equipped only with a bit of courage, as he had in the last world.

At length the inevitable Last Judgment got around to Kugler.

Heaven being eternally in a state of emergency, Kugler was brought before a special court of three judges and not, as his previous conduct would ordinarily merit, before a jury. The courtroom was furnished simply, almost like courtrooms on earth, with this one exception: there was no provision for swearing in witnesses. In time, however, the reason for this will become apparent.

The judges were old and worthy councillors with austere, bored faces. Kugler complied with the usual tedious formalities: Ferdinand Kugler, unemployed, born on such and such a date, died . . . at this point it was shown Kugler didn't know the date of his own death. Immediately he realized this was a damaging omission in the eyes of the judges; his spirit of helpfulness faded.

"Do you plead guilty or not guilty?" asked the presiding judge.

"Not guilty," said Kugler obdurately.

"Bring in the first witness," the judge sighed.

Opposite Kugler appeared an extraordinary gentleman, stately, bearded, and clothed in a blue robe strewn with golden stars.

At his entrance the judges arose. Even Kugler stood up, reluctant but fascinated. Only when the old gentleman took a seat did the judges again sit down.

From *The Realm of Fiction: 61 Short Stories,* edited by James B. Hall. Copyright © 1965 by McGraw-Hill, Inc. Used with permission of McGraw-Hill Book Company.

"Witness," began the presiding judge, "Omniscient God, this court has summoned You in order to hear Your testimony in the case against Kugler, Ferdinand. As You are the Supreme Truth, You need not take the oath. In the interest of the proceedings, however, we ask You to keep to the subject at hand rather than branch out into particulars—unless they have a bearing on this case.

"And you, Kugler, don't interrupt the Witness. He knows everything, so there's no use denying anything.

"And now, Witness, if You would please begin."

That said, the presiding judge took off his spectacles and leaned comfortably on the bench before him, evidently in preparation for a long speech by the Witness. The oldest of the three judges nestled down in sleep. The recording angel opened the Book of Life.

God, the Witness, coughed lightly and began:

"Yes, Kugler, Ferdinand. Ferdinand Kugler, son of a factory worker, was a bad, unmanageable child from his earliest days. He loved his mother dearly, but was unable to show it; this made him unruly and defiant. Young man, you irked everyone! Do you remember how you bit your father on the thumb when he tried to spank you? You had stolen a rose from the notary's garden."

"The rose was for Irma, the tax collector's daughter," Kugler said.

"I know," said God. "Irma was seven years old at that time. Did you ever hear what happened to her?"

"No, I didn't"

"She married Oscar, the son of the factory owner. But she contracted a venereal disease from him and died of a miscarriage. You remember Rudy Zaruba?"

"What happened to him?"

"Why, he joined the navy and died accidentally in Bombay. You two were the worst boys in the whole town. Kugler, Ferdinand, was a thief before his tenth year and an inveterate liar. He kept bad company, too: old Gribble, for instance, a drunkard and an idler, living on handouts. Nevertheless, Kugler shared many of his own meals with Gribble."

The presiding judge motioned with his hand, as if much of this was perhaps unnecessary, but Kugler himself asked hesitantly, "And . . . what happened to his daughter?"

"Mary?" asked God, "She lowered herself considerably. In her fourteenth year she married. In her twentieth year she died, remembering you in the agony of her death. By your fourteenth year you were nearly a drunkard yourself, and you often ran away from home. Your father's death came about from grief and worry; your mother's eyes faded from crying. You brought dishonor to your home, and your sister, your pretty sister Martha, never married. No young man would come calling at the home of a thief. She's still living alone and in poverty, sewing until late each night. Scrimping has exhausted her, and patronizing customers hurt her pride."

"What's she doing right now?"

"This very minute she's buying thread at Wolfe's. Do you remember that shop? Once, when you were six years old, you bought a colored glass marble there. On that very same day you lost it and never, never found it. Do you remember how you cried with rage?"

"Whatever happened to it?" Kugler asked eagerly.

"Well, it rolled into the drain and under the gutterspout. As a matter of fact, it's still there, after thirty years. Right now it's raining on earth and your marble is shivering in the gush of cold water."

Kugler bent his head, overcome by this revelation.

But the presiding judge fitted his spectacles back on his nose and said mildly, "Witness, we are obliged to get on with the case. Has the accused committed murder?"

Here the Witness nodded his head.

"He murdered nine people. The first one he killed in a brawl, and it was during his prison term for this crime that he became completely corrupted. The second victim was his unfaithful sweetheart. For that he was sentenced to death, but he escaped. The third was an old man whom he robbed. The fourth was a night watchman."

"Then he died?" Kugler asked.

"He died after three days in terrible pain," God said. "And he left six children behind him. The fifth and sixth victims were an old married couple. He killed them with an axe and found only sixteen dollars, although they had twenty thousand hidden away."

Kugler jumped up.

"Where?"

"In the straw mattress," God said. "In a linen sack inside the mattress. That's where they hid all the money they acquired from greed and penny-pinching. The seventh man he killed in America; a countryman of his, a bewildered, friendless immigrant."

"So it was in the mattress," whispered Kugler in amazement.

"Yes," continued God. "The eighth man was merely a passerby who happened to be in Kugler's way when Kugler was trying to outrun the police. At that time Kugler had periostitis and was delirious from the pain. Young man, you were suffering terribly. The ninth and last was the policeman who killed Kugler exactly when Kugler shot him."

"And why did the accused commit murder?" asked the presiding judge.

"For the same reasons others have," answered God. "Out of anger or desire for money; both deliberately and accidentally—some with pleasure, others from necessity. However, he was generous and often helpful. He was kind to women, gentle with animals, and he kept his word. Am I to mention his good deeds?"

"Thank You," said the presiding judge, "but it isn't necessary. Does the accused have anything to say in his own defense?"

"No," Kugler replied with honest indifference.

"The judges of this court will now take this matter under advisement," declared the presiding judge, and the three of them withdrew.

Only God and Kugler remained in the courtroom.

"Who are they?" asked Kugler, indicating with his head the men who had just left.

"People like you," answered God. "They were judges on earth, so they're judges here as well."

Kugler nibbled his fingertips. "I expected . . . I mean, I never really thought about it. But I figured You would judge, since—"

"Since I'm God," finished the Stately Gentleman. "But that's just it, don't you see? Because I know everything, I can't possibly judge. That wouldn't do at all. By the way, do you know who turned you in this time?"

"No, I don't," said Kugler, surprised.

"Lucky, the waitress. She did it out of jealousy."

"Excuse me," Kugler ventured, "but You forgot about that good-for-nothing Teddy I shot in Chicago."

"Not at all," God said. "He recovered and is alive this very minute. I know he's an informer, but otherwise he's a very good man and terribly fond of children. You shouldn't think of any person as being completely worthless."

"But I still don't understand why You aren't the judge," Kugler said thoughtfully.

"Because my knowledge is infinite. If judges knew everything, absolutely everything, then they would also understand everything. Their hearts would ache. They couldn't sit in judgment—and neither can I. As it is, they know only about your crimes. I know all about you. The entire Kugler. And that's why I cannot judge."

"But why are they judging . . . the same people who were judges on earth?"

"Because man belongs to man. As you see, I'm only the witness. But the verdict is determined by man, even in heaven. Believe me, Kugler, this is the way it should be. Man isn't worthy of divine judgment. He deserves to be judged only by other men."

At that moment the three returned from their deliberation.

In heavy tones the presiding judge announced, "For repeated crimes of first degree murder, manslaughter, robbery, disrespect for the law, illegally carrying weapons, and for the theft of a rose: Kugler, Ferdinand, is sentenced to lifelong punishment in hell. The sentence is to begin immediately.

"Next case, please: Torrance, Frank.

"Is the accused present in court?"

Jorge Luis Borges (1899–   )

Jorge Luis Borges is considered by many to be the greatest living master of Spanish prose. Born in Buenos Aires in 1899, he was educated in Switzerland; in 1919 he went to Spain, where he met a number of writers interested in European avant-garde literary movements. When he returned to Argentina in 1921, he helped found *Ultraísmo,* a movement of Argentinian and Spanish poets trying to develop Spanish into an instrument of the new poetry. One of their magazines, *Prisma, revista mural,* was devised to be stuck on walls in order to bring poetry to the people. Here is an excerpt from one of the manifestos appearing in that magazine:

> We have synthesized poetry into its primordial element: the metaphor, to which we grant the greatest independence, beyond the little games of those who compare things like each other *to* each other, equating a circus with the moon. Each line of our poems has its individual life and represents an original vision. Ultraísmo thus propounds the formation of an emotional, changeable, varied mythology.

By the early thirties Borges had turned from poetry to the short story, but some of the same principles were evident in his new efforts. Granting "the greatest independence" to his metaphors, he turned out a dazzling series of stories in a modernist and experimental mode. His first important collection of stories was *Fic-*

ciones (1945) (translated into English in 1962). These "fictions" were a unique blending of the essay and the stort story, and a demonstration of his fundamental artistic contention: that truth eludes matter-of-fact. Works that followed were *El Aleph* (in which "Emma Zunz" appeared) in 1949; *El hacedor* (containing "Borges and I") in 1960, and translated as *Dreamtigers* in 1964; and *Antología personal* in 1961, a volume containing Borges' favorite short stories, sketches, essays, and poems, including all three of the selections reproduced here. This is but a fraction of Borges's work; he is probably the most widely known and translated author in Latin America today.

"The fantastic structure of Borges' stories," writes Victor Lange, "conjured as though by magic or sleight of hand, are the product of acts of calculated deception. What is in one breath stated as corroborated fact is at the same time obscured and blurred by doubts, denials, and open questions." The dream, the labyrinth, the mirror, and the double are characteristic devices by which the "coolly cerebral" Borges achieves and manipulates this deception, confusing the line between subject and object, history and fantasy, appearance and reality. His fictions are flights of imagination; they are also models of scholarly erudition. As Victor Lange says, his marshaling of recondite learning with such "ceremonious care" is itself an irony, "and points to his fundamental conviction of the fictitious character of reality." In "Emma Zunz" the act of revenge to be performed has already been performed, since the intention, becoming fate, makes irrelevant the time-space for its execution. In "Everything and Nothing," that brilliant parable (see pp. 34–35), we engage in a search for identity in a dream within a dream: the Shakespeare who has imagined so many selves desires to be "one and myself," but God denies him, saying, "Neither am I anyone; I have dreamt the world as you dreamt your work, my Shakespeare. . . ." And in "Borges and I"—more a sketch than a story—the author confronts himself as "other" in a similar, but more personal and exacting, search for identity. "I live, let myself go on living, so that Borges may contrive his literature"— and in this exchange between person and persona we are never given the easy comfort of knowing which is which.

Borges has been called a "calculating hallucinator," but his fictional sleights of hand exist not only to baffle, tease, and amuse, but to probe the unknown for "the one word that contains the universe." Some "engaged" critics feel that these practices make Borges an irrelevant aesthete, but most honor him as the artistic genuis who did more than anyone to turn Spanish into a vehicle for the new literature.

Emma Zunz

Returning home from the Tarbuch and Loewenthal textile mills on the 14th of January, 1922, Emma Zunz discovered in the rear of the entrance hall a letter, posted in Brazil, which informed her that her father had died. The stamp and the envelope deceived her at first; then the unfamiliar handwriting made her uneasy. Nine or ten

Jorge Luis Borges, *Labyrinths: Selected Stories and Other Writings.* Translated by Donald A. Yates. Copyright © 1962 by New Directions Publishing Corporation. Reprinted by permission of New Directions Publishing Corporation.

lines tried to fill up the page; Emma read that Mr. Maier had taken by mistake a large dose of veronal and had died on the third of the month in the hospital of Bagé. A boarding-house friend of her father had signed the letter, some Fein or Fain from Río Grande, with no way of knowing that he was addressing the deceased's daughter.

Emma dropped the paper. Her first impression was of a weak feeling in her stomach and in her knees; then of blind guilt, of unreality, of coldness, of fear; then she wished that it were already the next day. Immediately afterward she realized that that wish was futile because the death of her father was the only thing that had happened in the world, and it would go on happening endlessly. She picked up the piece of paper and went to her room. Furtively, she hid it in a drawer, as if somehow she already knew the ulterior facts. She had already begun to suspect them, perhaps; she had already become the person she would be.

In the growing darkness, Emma wept until the end of that day for the suicide of Manuel Maier, who in the old happy days was Emmanuel Zunz. She remembered summer vacations at a little farm near Gualeguay, she remembered (tried to remember) her mother, she remembered the little house at Lanús which had been auctioned off, she remembered the yellow lozenges of a window, she remembered the warrant for arrest, the ignominy, she remembered the poison-pen letters with the newspaper's account of "the cashier's embezzlement," she remembered (but this she never forgot) that her father, on the last night, had sworn to her that the thief was Loewenthal. Loewenthal, Aaron Loewenthal, formerly the manager of the factory and now one of the owners. Since 1916 Emma had guarded the secret. She had revealed it to no one, not even to her best friend, Elsa Urstein. Perhaps she was shunning profane incredulity; perhaps she believed that the secret was a link between herself and the absent parent. Loewenthal did not know that she knew; Emma Zunz derived from this slight fact a feeling of power.

She did not sleep that night and when the first light of dawn defined the rectangle of the window, her plan was already perfected. She tried to make the day, which seemed interminable to her, like any other. At the factory there were rumors of a strike. Emma declared herself, as usual, against all violence. At six o'clock, with work over, she went with Elsa to a women's club that had a gymnasium and a swimming pool. They signed their names; she had to repeat and spell out her first and her last name, she had to respond to the vulgar jokes that accompanied the medical examination. With Elsa and with the youngest of the Kronfuss girls she discussed what movie they would go to Sunday afternoon. Then they talked about boyfriends and no one expected Emma to speak. In April she would be nineteen years old, but men inspired in her, still, an almost pathological fear . . . Having returned home, she prepared a tapioca soup and a few vegetables, ate early, went to bed and forced herself to sleep. In this way, laborious and trivial, Friday the fifteenth, the day before, elapsed.

Impatience awoke her on Saturday. Impatience it was, not uneasiness, and the special relief of it being that day at last. No longer did she have to plan and imagine; within a few hours the simplicity of the facts would suffice. She read in *La Prensa* that the *Nordstjärnan,* out of Malmö, would sail that evening from Pier 3. She phoned Loewenthal, insinuated that she wanted to confide in him, without the other girls knowing, something pertaining to the strike; and she promised to stop by at his office at nightfall. Her voice trembled; the tremor was suitable to an informer. Nothing else of note happened that morning. Emma worked until twelve o'clock and then settled with Elas and Perla Kronfuss the details of their Sunday stroll. She lay down after lunch and reviewed, with her eyes closed, the plan she had devised. She thought that the final step would be less horrible than the first and that it would doubtlessly afford her the taste of victory and justice. Suddenly, alarmed, she got up and ran to the dresser drawer. She opened it; beneath the picture of Milton Sills, where she had left it the night before, was Fain's letter. No one could have seen it; she began to read it and tore it up.

To relate with some reality the events of that afternoon would be difficult and perhaps unrighteous. One attribute of a hellish experience is unreality, an attribute that seems to allay its terrors and which aggravates them perhaps. How could one make credible an action which was scarcely believed in by the person who executed it, how to recover that brief chaos which today the memory of Emma Zunz repudiates and confuses? Emma lived in Almagro, on Liniers Street: we are certain that in the afternoon she went down to the waterfront. Perhaps on the infamous Paseo de Julio she saw herself multiplied in mirrors, revealed by lights and denuded by hungry eyes, but it is more reasonable to suppose that at first she wandered, unnoticed, through the indifferent portico . . . She entered two or three bars, noted the routine or technique of the other women. Finally she came across men from the *Nordstjärnan*. One of them, very young, she feared might inspire some tenderness in her and she chose instead another, perhaps shorter than she and coarse, in order that the purity of the horror might not be mitigated. The man led her to a door, then to a murky entrance hall and afterwards to a narrow stairway and then a vestibule (in which there was a window with lozenges identical to those in the house at Lanús) and then to a passageway and then to a door which was closed behind her. The arduous events are outside of time, either because the immediate past is as if disconnected from the future, or because the parts which form these events do not seem to be consecutive.

During that time outside of time, in that perplexing disorder of disconnected and atrocious sensations, did Emma Zunz think *once* about the dead man who motivated the sacrifice? It is my belief that she did think once, and in that moment she endangered her desperate undertaking. She thought (she was unable not to think) that her father had done to her mother the hideous thing that was being done to her now. She thought of it with weak amazement and took refuge, quickly, in vertigo. The man, a Swede or Finn, did not speak Spanish. He was a tool for Emma, as she was for him, but she served him for pleasure whereas he served her for justice.

When she was alone, Emma did not open her eyes immediately. On the little night table was the money that the man had left: Emma sat up and tore it to pieces as before she had torn the letter. Tearing money is an impiety, like throwing away bread; Emma repented the moment after she did it. An act of pride and on that day . . . Her fear was lost in the grief of her body, in her disgust. The grief and the nausea were chaining her, but Emma got up slowly and proceeded to dress herself. In the room there were no longer any bright colors; the last light of dusk was weakening. Emma was able to leave without anyone seeing her; at the corner she got on a Lacroze streetcar heading west. She selected, in keeping with her plan, the seat farthest toward the front, so that her face would not be seen. Perhaps it comforted her to verify in the insipid movement along the streets that what had happened had not contaminated things. She rode through the diminishing opaque suburbs, seeing them and forgetting them at the same instant, and got off on one of the side streets of Warnes. Paradoxically her fatigue was turning out to be a strength, since it obligated her to concentrate on the details of the adventure and concealed from her the background and the objective.

Aaron Loewenthal was to all persons a serious man, to his intimate friends a miser. He lived above the factory, alone. Situated in the barren outskirts of the town, he feared thieves; in the patio of the factory there was a large dog and in the drawer of his desk, everyone knew, a revolver. He had mourned with gravity, the year before, the unexpected death of his wife—a Gauss who had brought him a fine dowry—but money was his real passion. With intimate embarrassment, he knew himself to be less apt at earning it than at saving it. He was very religious; he believed he had a secret pact with God which exempted him from doing good in exchange for prayers and piety. Bald, fat, wearing the band of mourning, with smoked glasses and blond beard, he was standing next to the window awaiting the confidential report of worker Zunz.

He saw her push the iron gate (which he had left open for her) and cross the gloomy patio. He saw her make a little detour when the chained dog barked. Emma's lips were moving rapidly, like those of someone praying in a low voice; weary, they were repeating the sentence which Mr. Loewenthal would hear before dying.

Things did not happen as Emma Zunz had anticipated. Ever since the morning before she had imagined herself wielding the firm revolver, forcing the wretched creature to confess his wretched guilt and exposing the daring stratagem which would permit the Justice of God to triumph over human justice. (Not out of fear but because of being an instrument of Justice she did not want to be punished.) Then, one single shot in the center of his chest would seal Loewenthal's fate. But things did not happen that way.

In Aaron Loewenthal's presence, more than the urgency of avenging her father, Emma felt the need of inflicting punishment for the outrage she had suffered. She was unable not to kill him after that thorough dishonor. Nor did she have time for theatrics. Seated, timid, she made excuses to Loewenthal, she invoked (as a privilege of the informer) the obligation of loyalty, uttered a few names, inferred others and broke off as if fear had conquered her. She managed to have Loewenthal leave to get a glass of water for her. When the former, unconvinced by such a fuss but indulgent, returned from the dining room, Emma had already taken the heavy revolver out of the drawer. She squeezed the trigger twice. The large body collapsed as if the reports and the smoke had shattered it, the glass of water smashed, the face looked at her with amazement and anger, the mouth of the face swore at her in Spanish and Yiddish. The evil words did not slacken; Emma had to fire again. In the patio the chained dog broke out barking, and a gush of rude blood flowed from the obscene lips and soiled the beard and the clothing. Emma began the accusation she had prepared ("I have avenged my father and they will not be able to punish me . . ."), but she did not finish it, because Mr. Loewenthal had already died. She never knew if he managed to understand.

The straining barks reminded her that she could not, yet, rest. She disarranged the divan, unbuttoned the dead man's jacket, took off the bespattered glasses and left them on the filing cabinet. Then she picked up the telephone and repeated what she would repeat so many times again, with these and with other words: *Something incredible has happened . . . Mr. Loewenthal had me come over on the pretext of the strike . . . He abused me, I killed him . . .*

Actually, the story *was* incredible, but it impressed everyone because substantially it was true. True was Emma Zunz' tone, true was her shame, true was her hate. True also was the outrage she had suffered: only the circumstances were false, the time, and one or two proper names.

Borges and I

The other one, the one called Borges, is the one things happen to. I walk through the streets of Buenos Aires and stop for a moment, perhaps mechanically now, to look at the arch of an entrance hall and the grillwork on the gate; I know of Borges from the mail and see his name on a list of professors or in a biographical dictionary. I like hourglasses, maps, eighteenth-century typography, the taste of coffee and the prose of Stevenson;[1] he shares these preferences, but in a vain way that turns them into the attributes of an actor. It would be an exaggeration to say that ours is a hostile relationship; I live, let myself go on living, so that Borges may contrive his literature, and this literature justifies me. It is no effort for me to confess that he has achieved some valid pages, but those pages cannot save me, perhaps because what is good belongs to no one, not even to him, but rather to the language and to tradition. Besides, I am destined to perish, definitively, and only some instant of myself can survive in him. Little by little, I am giving over everything to him, though I am quite aware of his perverse custom of falsifying and magnifying things. Spinoza knew that all things long to persist in their being; the stone eternally wants to be a stone and the tiger a tiger. I shall remain in Borges, not in myself (if it is true that I am someone), but I recognize myself less in his books than in many others or in the laborious strumming of a guitar. Years ago I tried to free myself from him and went from the mythologies of the suburbs to the games with time and infinity, but those games belong to Borges now and I shall have to imagine other things. Thus my life is a flight and I lose everything and everything belongs to oblivion, or to him.

I do not know which of us has written this page.

Everything and Nothing

There was no one in him; behind his face (which even through the bad paintings of those times resembles no other) and his words, which were copious, fantastic and stormy, there was only a bit of coldness, a dream dreamt by no one. At first he thought that all people were like him, but the astonishment of a friend to whom he had begun to speak of this emptiness showed him his error and made him feel always that an individual should not differ in outward appearance. Once he thought that in books he would find a cure for his ill and thus he learned the small Latin and less Greek a contemporary would speak of; later he considered that what he sought might well be found in an elemental rite of humanity, and let himself be initiated by Anne Hathaway one long June afternoon. At the age of twenty-odd years he went to London. Instinc-

[1] Robert Louis Stevenson. Borges in 1955 was appointed Professor of English and American Literature at the University of Buenos Aires.

Jorge Luis Borges, *Labyrinths: Selected Stories & Other Writings*. Translated by James E. Irby. Copyright © 1962 by New Directions Publishing Corporation. Reprinted by permission of New Directions Publishing Corporation.

tively he had already become proficient in the habit of simulating that he was some-one, so that others would not discover his condition as no one; in London he found the profession to which he was predestined, that of the actor, who on a stage plays at being another before a gathering of people who play at taking him for that other person. His histrionic tasks brought him a singular satisfaction, perhaps the first he had ever known; but once the last verse had been acclaimed and the last dead man withdrawn from the stage, the hated flavor of unreality returned to him. He ceased to be Ferrex or Tamerlane[1] and became no one again. Thus hounded, he took to imagin-ing other heroes and other tragic fables. And so, while his flesh fulfilled its destiny as flesh in the taverns and brothels of London, the soul that inhabited him was Caesar, who disregards the augur's admonition, and Juliet, who abhors the lark, and Macbeth, who converses on the plain with the witches who are also Fates. No one has ever been so many men as this man, who like the Egyptian Proteus could exhaust all the guises of reality. At times he would leave a confession hidden away in some corner of his work, certain that it would not be deciphered; Richard affirms that in his person he plays the part of many and Iago claims with curious words "I am not what I am." The fundamental identity of existing, dreaming and acting inspired famous passages of his.

For twenty years he persisted in that controlled hallucination, but one morning he was suddenly gripped by the tedium and the terror of being so many kings who die by the sword and so many suffering lovers who converge, diverge and melodiously expire. That very day he arranged to sell his theater. Within a week he had returned to his native village, where he recovered the trees and rivers of his childhood and did not relate them to the others his muse had celebrated, illustrious with mythological allu-sions and Latin terms. He had to be someone; he was a retired impresario who had made his fortune and concerned himself with loans, lawsuits and petty usury. It was in this character that he dictated the arid will and testament known to us, from which he deliberately excluded all traces of pathos or literature. His friends from London would visit his retreat and for them he would take up again his role as poet.

History adds that before or after dying he found himself in the presence of God and told Him: "I who have been so many men in vain want to be one and myself." The voice of the Lord answered from a whirlwind: "Neither am I anyone; I have dreamt the world as you dreamt your work, my Shakespeare, and among the forms in my dream are you, who like myself are many and no one."

Tomasso Landolfi (1908-   )

Gogol was a Russian writer, the author of the first modern short story in this collec-tion. Landolfi is an Italian writer who has been profoundly influenced by his reading of nineteenth-century Russian literature—Tolstoy and, especially, Dostoevsky. Go-gol may have been a case of adolescent arrest: he never married and apparently never felt an erotic interest in women, though there is no evidence of homosexual-

---

[1] See *Ferrex and Porrex* (c.1570), one of the earliest English tragedies, and *Tamerlane* (1590), a play by Christopher Marlowe.

ity. He died, mad, in 1852. It is also reported authoritatively that his descent into madness was accompanied by an accelerating sensation of coldness, plus an intensifying vision of steadily accumulating snow (enough to arouse and rivet the recollection of anyone who has read Conrad Aiken's "Silent Snow, Secret Snow," p. 318).

We may begin by wondering how much Landolfi might have known of Gogol's life and career. Something, surely; how else to account for the title of the story and for references to such Russian critics of Gogol as Belinsky and Vershiny? But the story's point is no more the historical Gogol than the point of "Wakefield" (p. 97) is what Hawthorne claimed to have read in a newspaper. At the same time we may remember Gogol's extraordinary importance to contemporary Russian authors (pp. 67–68), a reputation and influence the scholarly monologist of this story assumes we are perfectly familiar with: "so lofty a genius," "these privileged natures," "the Master." The setting, then, formally considered, is perfectly clear: we are in the presence of an official biographer, probably young, diffident, hesitant, but one who has run into something disturbing in the course of his research on "the Master," and who, given his own uncertainties about "the present stage of development of Gogol studies," seems to have to talk himself into disclosing what he has discovered.

Given everything that follows in the story, that whole pose becomes hilarious, if hilariously unnerving. It is, however, a fine example of Landolfi's characteristic technique as described by the Italian critic Giacomo Debenedetti:

> Imagine that you have come as a guest to a castle and the host, accompanying you to the room set aside for you, opens the shutters, shows you the beautiful view and acquaints you with the room's comforts and conveniences. But when night falls you begin to hear all around you an insidious concert of squeaks and groans. The next morning, after a sleepless night, you learn that this is the room haunted by ghosts. And the host's politeness and exaggerated concern now appear to you in another light.

When we come to the climactic last evening of the story, our modest biographer alludes to "the famous 'pyre of vanities'—the burning of his manuscripts"—as though we had all heard of how Gogol, near the end of his life and in precipitously deteriorating health, had in fact burned the manuscript of the sequel he was trying to write to his novel *Dead Souls*. And when Caracas hits the coals, the only commentary we are offered is that Gogol, "like all Russians, had a passion for throwing important things in the fire."

A more strictly symbolic reading of the story (see Introduction, p. 21)—without reference to the historical Gogol—might suggest that as the doll-like "wife" begins to take on a life and character of her own, the husband cannot stand it, in fact wants her and her offspring dead. She has, after all, never *really* existed in her own right. And the minute she begins to emerge into vascular and circulatory existence (symbolized by her one spoken utterance?), steps have to be taken. Is not a death wish implicit in all such ego-centered, alienated "love"? And—more unnerving still—may not Caracas symbolize what can happen when we turn life into art?

Landolfi has been Italy's pre-eminent avant-garde short-story writer for a good many years now, and he is also well known as a critic and translator of Russian literature. Two volumes of his stories have recently become available in English: *Cancerqueen and Other Stories* (1971) and *Gogol's Wife and Other Stories* (1961).

Gogol's Wife

At this point, confronted with the whole complicated affair of Nikolai Vassilevitch's wife, I am overcome by hesitation. Have I any right to disclose something which is unknown to the whole world, which my unforgettable friend himself kept hidden from the world (and he had his reasons), and which I am sure will give rise to all sorts of malicious and stupid misunderstandings? Something, moreover, which will very probably offend the sensibilities of all sorts of base, hypocritical people, and possibly of some honest people too, if there are any left? And finally, have I any right to disclose something before which my own spirit recoils, and even tends toward a more or less open disapproval?

But the fact remains that, as a biographer, I have certain firm obligations. Believing as I do that every bit of information about so lofty a genius will turn out to be of value to us and to future generations, I cannot conceal something which in any case has no hope of being judged fairly and wisely until the end of time. Moreover, what right have we to condemn? Is it given to us to know, not only what intimate needs, but even what higher and wider ends may have been served by those very deeds of a lofty genius which perchance may appear to us vile? No indeed, for we understand so little of these privileged natures. "Is it true," a great man once said, "that I also have to pee, but for quite different reasons."

But without more ado I will come to what I know beyond doubt, and can prove beyond question, about this controversial matter, which will now—I dare to hope—no longer be so. I will not trouble to recapitulate what is already known of it, since I do not think this should be necessary at the present stage of development of Gogol studies.

Let me say it at once: Nikolai Vassilevitch's wife was not a woman. Nor was she any sort of human being, nor any sort of living creature at all, whether animal or vegetable (although something of the sort has sometimes been hinted). She was quite simply a balloon. Yes, a balloon; and this will explain the perplexity, or even indignation, of certain biographers who were also the personal friends of the Master, and who complained that, although they often went to his house, they never saw her and "never even heard her voice." From this they deduced all sorts of dark and disgraceful complications—yes, and criminal ones too. No, gentlemen, everything is always simpler than it appears. You did not hear her voice simply because she could not speak, or to be more exact, she could only speak in certain conditions, as we shall see. And it was always, except once, in tête-à-tête with Nikolai Vassilevitch. So let us not waste time with any cheap or empty refutations but come at once to as exact and complete a description as possible of the being or object in question.

Gogol's so-called wife was an ordinary dummy made of thick rubber, naked at all seasons, buff in tint, or as is more commonly said, flesh-colored. But since women's skins are not all of the same color, I should specify that hers was a light-colored, polished skin, like that of certain brunettes. It, or she, was, it is hardly necessary to add, of feminine sex. Perhaps I should say at once that she was capable of very wide alterations of her attributes without, of course, being able to alter her sex itself. She could sometimes appear to be thin, with hardly any breasts and with narrow hips more like a young lad than a woman, and at other times to be excessively well-endowed or—

Tommaso Landolfi, *Gogol's Wife and Other Stories.* Translated by Wayland Young. Copyright © 1963 by New Directions Publishing Corporation. Reprinted by permission of New Directions Publishing Corporation.

let us not mince matters—fat. And she often changed the color of her hair, both on her head and elsewhere on her body, though not necessarily at the same time. She could also seem to change in all sorts of other tiny particulars, such as the position of moles, the vitality of the mucous membranes and so forth. She could even to a certain extent change the very color of her skin. One is faced with the necessity of asking oneself who she really was, or whether it would be proper to speak of a single "person"—and in fact we shall see that it would be imprudent to press this point.

The cause of these changes, as my readers will already have understood, was nothing else but the will of Nikolai Vassilevitch himself. He would inflate her to a greater or lesser degree, would change her wig and her other tufts of hair, would grease her with ointments and touch her up in various ways so as to obtain more or less the type of woman which suited him at that moment. Following the natural inclinations of his fancy, he even amused himself sometimes by producing grotesque or monstrous forms; as will be readily understood, she became deformed when inflated beyond a certain point or if she remained below a certain pressure.

But Gogol soon tired of these experiments, which he held to be "after all, not very respectful" to his wife, whom he loved in his own way—however inscrutable it may remain to us. He loved her, but which of these incarnations, we may ask ourselves, did he love? Alas, I have already indicated that the end of the present account will furnish some sort of an answer. And how can I have stated above that it was Nikolai Vassilev-itch's will which ruled that woman? In a certain sense, yes, it is true; but it is equally certain that she soon became no longer his slave but his tyrant. And here yawns the abyss, or if you prefer it, the Jaws of Tartarus. But let us not anticipate.

I have said that Gogol obtained with his manipulations *more or less* the type of woman which he needed from time to time. I should add that when, in rare cases, the form he obtained perfectly incarnated his desire, Nikolai Vassilevitch fell in love with it "exclusively," as he said in his own words, and that this was enough to render "her" stable for a certain time—until he fell out of love with "her." I counted no more than three or four of these violent passions—or, as I suppose they would be called today, infatuations—in the life (dare I say in the conjugal life?) of the great writer. It will be convenient to add here that a few years after what one may call his marriage, Gogol had even given a name to his wife. It was Caracas, which is, unless I am mistaken, the capital of Venezuela. I have never been able to discover the reason for this choice: great minds are so capricious!

Speaking only of her normal appearance, Caracas was what is called a fine woman—well built and proportioned in every part. She had every smallest attribute of her sex properly disposed in the proper location. Particularly worthy of attention were her genital organs (if the adjective is permissible in such a context). They were formed by means of ingenious folds in the rubber. Nothing was forgotten, and their operation was rendered easy by various devices, as well as by the internal pressure of the air.

Caracas also had a skeleton, even though a rudimentary one. Perhaps it was made of whalebone. Special care had been devoted to the construction of the thoracic cage, of the pelvic basin and of the cranium. The first two systems were more or less visible in accordance with the thickness of the fatty layer, if I may so describe it, which covered them. It is a great pity that Gogol never let me know the name of the creator of such a fine piece of work. There was an obstinacy in his refusal which was never quite clear to me.

Nikolai Vassilevitch blew his wife up through the anal sphincter with a pump of his own invention, rather like those which you hold down with your two feet and which are used today in all sorts of mechanical workshops. Situated in the anus was a little one-way valve, or whatever the correct technical description would be, like the mitral valve of the heart, which, once the body was inflated, allowed more air to come in but none to go out. To deflate, one unscrewed a stopper in the mouth, at the back of the throat.

And that, I think, exhausts the description of the most noteworthy peculiarities of this being. Unless perhaps I should mention the splendid rows of white teeth which adorned her mouth and the dark eyes which, in spite of their immobility, perfectly simulated life. Did I say simulate? Good heavens, simulate is not the word! Nothing seems to be the word, when one is speaking of Caracas! Even these eyes could undergo a change of color, by means of a special process to which, since it was long and tiresome, Gogol seldom had recourse. Finally, I should speak of her voice, which it was only once given to me to hear. But I cannot do that without going more fully into the relationship between husband and wife, and in this I shall no longer be able to answer to the truth of everything with absolute certitude. On my conscience I could not—so confused, both in itself and in my memory, is that which I now have to tell.

Here, then, as they occur to me, are some of my memories.

The first and, as I said, the last time I ever heard Caracus speak to Nikolai Vassilevitch was one evening when we were absolutely alone. We were in the room where the woman, if I may be allowed the expression, lived. Entrance to this room was strictly forbidden to everybody. It was furnished more or less in the Oriental manner, had no windows and was situated in the most inaccessible part of the house. I did know that she could talk, but Gogol had never explained to me the circumstances under which this happened. There were only the two of us, or three, in there. Nikolai Vassilevitch and I were drinking vodka and discussing Butkov's[1] novel. I remember that we left this topic, and he was maintaining the necessity for radical reforms in the laws of inheritance. We had almost forgotten her. It was then that, with a husky and submissive voice, like Venus on the nuptial couch, she said point-blank: "I want to go poo poo."

I jumped, thinking I had misheard, and looked across at her. She was sitting on a pile of cushions against the wall; that evening she was a soft, blonde beauty, rather well-covered. Her expression seemed commingled of shrewdness and slyness, childishness and irresponsibility. As for Gogol, he blushed violently and, leaping on her, stuck two fingers down her throat. She immediately began to shrink and to turn pale; she took on once again that lost and astonished air which was especially hers, and was in the end reduced to no more than a flabby skin on a perfunctory bony armature. Since, for practical reasons which will readily be divined, she had an extraordinarily flexible back-bone, she folded up almost in two, and for the rest of the evening she looked up at us from where she had slithered to the floor, in utter abjection.

All Gogol said was: "She only does it for a joke, or to annoy me, because as a matter of fact she does not have such needs." In the presence of other people, that is to say of me, he generally made a point of treating her with a certain disdain.

We went on drinking and talking, but Nikolai Vassilevitch seemed very much disturbed and absent in spirit. Once he suddenly interrupted what he was saying, seized my hand in his and burst into tears. "What can I do now?" he exclaimed. "You understand, Foma Paskalovitch, that I loved her?"

---

[1] This is probably *Peter Burgskie Vershiny,* 2 vols., 1844-45. The novels of Yakov Petrovich Butkov (1815-1856) showed Gogol's influence.

It is necessary to point out that it was impossible, except by a miracle, ever to repeat any of Caracas' forms. She was a fresh creation every time, and it would have been wasted effort to seek to find again the exact proportions, the exact pressure, and so forth, of a former Caracas. Therefore the plumpish blonde of that evening was lost to Gogol from that time forth forever; this was in fact the tragic end of one of those few loves of Nikolai Vassilevitch, which I described above. He gave me no explanation; he sadly rejected my proffered comfort, and that evening we parted early. But his heart had been laid bare to me in that outburst. He was no longer so reticent with me, and soon had hardly any secrets left. And this, I may say in parenthesis, caused me very great pride.

It seems that things had gone well for the "couple" at the beginning of their life together. Nikolai Vassilevitch had been content with Caracas and slept regularly with her in the same bed. He continued to observe this custom till the end, saying with a timid smile that no companion could be quieter or less importunate than she. But I soon began to doubt this, especially judging by the state he was sometimes in when he woke up. Then, after several years, their relationship began strangely to deteriorate.

All this, let it be said once and for all, is no more than a schematic attempt at an explanation. About that time the woman actually began to show signs of independence or, as one might say, of autonomy. Nikolai Vassilevitch had the extraordinary impression that she was acquiring a personality of her own, indecipherable perhaps, but still distinct from his, and one which slipped through his fingers. It is certain that some sort of continuity was established between each of her appearances— between all those brunettes, those blondes, those redheads and auburn-headed girls, between those plump, those slim, those dusky or snowy or golden beauties, there was a certain something in common. At the beginning of this chapter I cast some doubt on the propriety of considering Caracas as a unitary personality; nevertheless I myself could not quite, whenever I saw her, free myself of the impression that, however unheard of it may seem, this was fundamentally the same woman. And it may be that this was why Gogol felt he had to give her a name.

An attempt to establish in what precisely subsisted the common attributes of the different forms would be quite another thing. Perhaps it was no more and no less than the creative afflatus of Nikolai Vassilevitch himself. But no, it would have been too singular and strange if he had been so much divided off from himself, so much averse to himself. Because whoever she was, Caracas was a disturbing presence and even—it is better to be quite clear—a hostile one. Yet neither Gogol nor I ever succeeded in formulating a remotely tenable hypothesis as to her true nature; when I say formulate, I mean in terms which would be at once rational and accessible to all. But I cannot pass over an extraordinary event which took place at this time.

Caracas fell ill of a shameful disease—or rather Gogol did—though he was not then having, nor had he ever had, any contact with other women. I will not even try to describe how this happened, or where the filthy complaint came from; all I know is that it happened. And that my great, unhappy friend would say to me: "So, Foma Paskalovitch, you see what lay at the heart of Caracas; it was the spirit of syphilis."

Sometimes he would even blame himself in a quite absurd manner; he was always prone to self-accusation. This incident was a real catastrophe as far as the already obscure relationship between husband and wife, and the hostile feelings of Nikolai Vassilevitch himself, were concerned. He was compelled to undergo long-drawn-out and painful treatment—the treatment of those days—and the situation was aggravated by the fact that the disease in the woman did not seem to be easily curable.

Gogol deluded himself for some time that, by blowing his wife up and down and furnishing her with the most widely divergent aspects, he could obtain a woman immune from the contagion, but he was forced to desist when no results were forthcoming.

I shall be brief, seeking not to tire my readers, and also because what I remember seems to become more and more confused. I shall therefore hasten to the tragic conclusion. As to this last, however, let there be no mistake. I must once again make it clear that I am very sure of my ground. I was an eyewitness. Would that I had not been!

The years went by. Nikolai Vassilevitch's distaste for his wife became stronger, though his love for her did not show any signs of diminishing. Toward the end, aversion and attachment struggled so fiercely with each other in his heart that he became quite stricken, almost broken up. His restless eyes, which habitually assumed so many different expressions and sometimes spoke so sweetly to the heart of his interlocutor, now almost always shone with a fevered light, as if he were under the effect of a drug. The strangest impulses arose in him, accompanied by the most senseless fears. He spoke to me of Caracas more and more often, accusing her of unthinkable and amazing things. In these regions I could not follow him, since I had but a sketchy acquaintance with his wife, and hardly any intimacy—and above all since my sensibility was so limited compared with his. I shall accordingly restrict myself to reporting some of his accusations, without reference to my personal impressions.

"Believe it or not, Foma Paskalovitch," he would, for example, often say to me: "Believe it or not, *she's aging!*" Then, unspeakably moved, he would, as was his way, take my hands in his. He also accused Caracas of giving herself up to solitary pleasures, which he had expressly forbidden. He even went so far as to charge her with betraying him, but the things he said became so extremely obscure that I must excuse myself from any further account of them.

One thing that appears certain is that toward the end Caracas, whether aged or not, had turned into a bitter creature, querulous, hypocritical and subject to religious excess. I do not exclude the possibility that she may have had an influence on Gogol's moral position during the last period of his life, a position which is sufficiently well known. The tragic climax came one night quite unexpectedly when Nikolai Vassilevitch and I were celebrating his silver wedding—one of the last evenings we were to spend together. I neither can nor should attempt to set down what it was that led to his decision, at a time when to all appearances he was resigned to tolerating his consort. I know not what new events had taken place that day. I shall confine myself to the facts; my readers must make what they can of them.

That evening Nikolai Vassilevitch was unusually agitated. His distaste for Caracas seemed to have reached an unprecedented intensity. The famous "pyre of vanities"—the burning of his manuscripts—had already taken place; I should not like to say whether or not at the instigation of his wife. His state of mind had been further inflamed by other causes. As to his physical condition, this was ever more pitiful, and strengthened my impression that he took drugs. All the same, he began to talk in a more or less normal way about Belinsky,[2] who was giving him some trouble with his attacks on the *Selected Correspondence.* Then suddenly, tears rising to his eyes, he

---

[2] Vissarion Grigoryevitch Belinsky (1811-1848), the founder of literary criticism in Russia, who wrote a famous *Letter to Gogol* in 1847 in which he attacked the czarist autocracy and Gogol's "conversion" to reaction.

interrupted himself and cried out: "No. No. It's too much, too much. I can't go on any longer," as well as other obscure and disconnected phrases which he would not clarify. He seemed to be talking to himself. He wrung his hands, shook his head, got up and sat down again after having taken four or five anxious steps round the room. When Caracas appeared, or rather when we went in to her later in the evening in her Oriental chamber, he controlled himself no longer and began to behave like an old man, if I may so express myself, in his second childhood, quite giving way to his absurd impulses. For instance, he kept nudging me and winking and senselessly repeating: "There she is, Foma Paskalovitch; there she is!" Meanwhile she seemed to look up at us with a disdainful attention. But behind these "mannerisms" one could feel in him a real repugnance, a repugnance which had, I suppose, now reached the limits of the endurable. Indeed . . .

After a certain time Nikolai Vassilevitch seemed to pluck up courage. He burst into tears, but somehow they were more manly tears. He wrung his hands again, seized mine in his, and walked up and down, muttering: "That's enough! We can't have any more of this. This is an unheard of thing. How can such a thing be happening to me? How can a man be expected to put up with *this*?"

He then leapt furiously upon the pump, the existence of which he seemed just to have remembered, and, with it in his hand, dashed like a whirlwind to Caracas. He inserted the tube in her anus and began to inflate her. . . . Weeping the while, he shouted like one possessed: "Oh, how I love her, how I love her, my poor, poor darling! . . . But she's going to burst! Unhappy Caracas, most pitiable of God's creatures! But die she must!"

Caracas was swelling up. Nikolai Vassilevitch sweated, wept and pumped. I wished to stop him but, I know not why, I had not the courage. She began to become deformed and shortly assumed the most monstrous aspect; and yet she had not given any signs of alarm—she was used to these jokes. But when she began to feel unbearably full, or perhaps when Nikolai Vassilevitch's intentions became plain to her, she took on an expression of bestial amazement, even a little beseeching, but still without losing that disdainful look. She was afraid, she was even committing herself to his mercy, but still she could not believe in the immediate approach of her fate; she could not believe in the frightful audacity of her husband. He could not see her face because he was behind her. But I looked at her with fascination, and did not move a finger.

At last the internal pressure came through the fragile bones at the base of her skull, and printed on her face an indescribable rictus. Her belly, her thighs, her lips, her breasts and what I could see of her buttocks had swollen to incredible proportions. All of a sudden she belched, and gave a long hissing groan; both these phenomena one could explain by the increase in pressure, which had suddenly forced a way out through the valve in her throat. Then her eyes bulged frantically, threatening to jump out of their sockets. Her ribs flared wide apart and were no longer attached to the sternum, and she resembled a python digesting a donkey. A donkey, did I say? An ox! An elephant! At this point I believed her already dead, but Nikolai Vassilevitch, sweating, weeping and repeating: "My dearest! My beloved! My best!" continued to pump.

She went off unexpectedly and, as it were, all of a piece. It was not one part of her skin which gave way and the rest which followed, but her whole surface at the same instant. She scattered in the air. The pieces fell more or less slowly, according to their size, which was in no case above a very restricted one. I distinctly remember a piece of her cheek, with some lip attached, hanging on the corner of the mantlepiece. Nikolai

Vassilevitch stared at me like a madman. Then he pulled himself together and, once more with furious determination, he began carefully to collect those poor rags which once had been the shining skin of Caracas, and all of her.

"Good-by, Caracas," I thought I heard him murmur, "Good-by! You were too pitiable!" And then suddenly and quite audibly: "The fire! The fire! She too must end up in the fire." He crossed himself—with his left hand, of course. Then, when he had picked up all those shriveled rags, even climbing on the furniture so as not to miss any, he threw them straight on the fire in the hearth, where they began to burn slowly and with an excessively unpleasant smell. Nikolai Vassilevitch, like all Russians, had a passion for throwing important things in the fire.

Red in the face, with an inexpressible look of despair, and yet of sinister triumph too, he gazed on the pyre of those miserable remains. He had seized my arm and was squeezing it convulsively. But those traces of what had once been a being were hardly well alight when he seemed yet again to pull himself together, as if he were suddenly remembering something or taking a painful decision. In one bound he was out of the room.

A few seconds later I heard him speaking to me through the door in a broken, plaintive voice: "Foma Paskalovitch, I want you to promise not to look. *Golubchik,* promise not to look at me when I come in."

I don't know what I answered, or whether I tried to reassure him in any way. But he insisted, and I had to promise him, as if he were a child, to hide my face against the wall and only turn round when he said I might. The door then opened violently and Nikolai Vassilevitch burst into the room and ran to the fireplace.

And here I must confess my weakness, though I consider it justified by the extraordinary circumstances. I looked round before Nikolai Vassilevitch told me I could; it was stronger than me. I was just in time to see him carrying something in his arms, something which he threw on the fire with all the rest, so that it suddenly flared up. At that, since the desire to *see* had entirely mastered every other thought in me, I dashed to the fireplace. But Nikolai Vassilevitch placed himself between me and it and pushed me back with a strength of which I had not believed him capable. Meanwhile the object was burning and giving off clouds of smoke. And before he showed any sign of calming down there was nothing left but a heap of silent ashes.

The true reason why I wished to see was because I had already glimpsed. But it was only a glimpse, and perhaps I should not allow myself to introduce even the slightest element of uncertainty into this true story. And yet, an eyewitness account is not complete without a mention of that which the witness knows with less than complete certainty. To cut a long story short, that something was a baby. Not a flesh and blood baby, of course, but more something in the line of a rubber doll or a model. Something, which, to judge by its appearance, could have been called *Caracas' son.*

Was I mad too? That I do not know, but I do know that this was what I saw, not clearly, but with my own eyes. And I wonder why it was that when I was writing this just now I didn't mention that when Nikolai Vassilevitch came back into the room he was muttering between his clenched teeth: "Him too! Him too!"

And that is the sum of my knowledge of Nikolai Vassilevitch's wife. In the next chapter I shall tell what happened to him afterwards, and that will be the last chapter of his life. But to give an interpretation of his feelings for his wife, or indeed for anything, is quite another and more difficult matter, though I have attempted it elsewhere in this volume, and refer the reader to that modest effort. I hope I have thrown sufficient light on a most controversial question and that I have unveiled the mystery, if not of Gogol, then at least of his wife. In the course of this I have implicitly given the lie to the insensate accusation that he ill-treated or even beat his wife, as well as other like absurdities. And what else can be the goal of a humble biographer such as the present writer but to serve the memory of that lofty genius who is the object of his study?

Delmore Schwartz (1913–1966)

Delmore Schwartz, short-story writer, critic, teacher, poet, and famed talker, was born in Brooklyn in 1913. A brilliant student, Schwartz took a degree in philosophy at New York University in 1935, and continued at Harvard in literature. He taught on and off at universities most of his life (Harvard, New York University, Kenyon, Princeton, Chicago, State University of New York at Buffalo, and elsewhere): he was an editor of the *Partisan Review* (1943 to 1955) and poetry editor of *The New Republic* (1955 to 1957). *Summer Knowledge* (1959), a volume of his selected poems, won the Bollingen Prize and the Shelley Memorial Award for 1960.

Schwartz's first book, *In Dreams Begin Responsibilities* (1938), was published when the author was twenty-five and still at Harvard. It included the story that follows as well as poems, a lyric drama, and a play. His recognition as a poet and story writer was immediate, and Robert Lowell, John Berryman, and Randall Jarrell, to name but a few, admired his work and became lifelong friends. Five volumes of poetry, translations from the French, a book of essays, and other collections of short stories—including *The World Is a Wedding* (1948) and *Successful Love, and Other Stories* (1961)—appeared over the next twenty years. But the precocious, perpetually "young" man lived as close to despair as the characters in his created work. "Even paranoids have real enemies," he once said. He spent years in and out of mental hospitals, and when he died in July, l966 he was alone in a New York hotel room. His friends had not seen him for a year and were to find a large body of unpublished writings among his papers.

"In Dreams Begin Responsibilities" (the title is a line from John Butler Yeats) reveals the complexity of his thought and the kind of unresolved contradictions that beset him throughout his life. Dreams, we might believe, are a part of life for which we are not responsible, but dreams to Schwartz, a Freudian, were anything but free knowledge. They were fruit stolen from the tree of knowledge by night. The scene of the theft starts hesitantly, with images flickering jumpily across a movie screen: "I think it is the year 1909," the narrator tells us, as the silent movie begins; "The light is bad." By the end we realize that the movie is going on within a dream and that its content (the day the narrator's future father proposed to his future mother in a Coney Island restaurant) had condemned him to live with its knowledge forever. He awakens to the day of his twenty-first birthday; the dream was a ritual coming-of-age. The "omniscient" narrator has subsumed his parents, and suffers not only for himself but for their unhappy marriage as well. At first a passive spectator, he cannot hold back from becoming an actor in their courtship: at the end of the "film" he rises from his seat to yell at his still unmarried parents, "Don't do it! It's not too late to change your minds, both of you. Nothing good will come of it, only remorse, hatred, scandal, and two children whose characters are monstrous." His parents vanish before the light of day, replaced by the *audience*—which plays a decisive role in the story. At first it is sympathetic (an old lady even comforts the narrator), but finally the audience turns on him, his grief having interrupted the story once too often; an usher throws him out, saying, "You can't act like this even if other people aren't about!" The monologist, the compulsive talker, offends others even in his dreams: the narrator's self-pity has interfered with the audience's pleasure, and the audience *must* be entertained.

Irving Howe has called Schwartz a "comedian of alienation." He must turn his own nightmare into a half-comic movie in order to please the audience, an audience he hates but needs, since he must have listeners for his confession. A later generation of American writers often insults that audience, since they feel more hopeless about their alienation.

"In Dreams Begin Responsibilities"

1

I think it is the year 1909. I feel as if I were in a moving-picture theatre, the long arm of light crossing the darkness and spinning, my eyes fixed upon the screen. It is a silent picture, as if an old Biograph one, in which the actors are dressed in ridiculously old-fashioned clothes, and one flash succeeds another with sudden jumps, and the actors, too, seem to jump about, walking too fast. The shots are full of rays and dots, as if it had been raining when the picture was photographed. The light is bad.

It is Sunday afternoon, June 12th, 1909, and my father is walking down the quiet streets of Brooklyn on his way to visit my mother. His clothes are newly pressed, and his tie is too tight in his high collar. He jingles the coins in his pocket, thinking of the witty things he will say. I feel as if I had by now relaxed entirely in the soft darkness of the theatre; the organist peals out the obvious approximate emotions on which the audience rocks unknowingly. I am anonymous. I have forgotten myself: it is always so when one goes to a movie, it is, as they say, a drug.

My father walks from street to street of trees, lawns and houses, once in a while coming to an avenue on which a street-car skates and gnaws, progressing slowly. The motorman, who has a handle-bar mustache, helps a young lady wearing a hat like a feathered bowl onto the car. He leisurely makes change and rings his bell as the passengers mount the car. It is obviously Sunday, for everyone is wearing Sunday clothes and the street-car's noises emphasize the quiet of the holiday (Brooklyn is said to be the city of churches). The shops are closed and their shades drawn but for an occasional stationery store or drugstore with great green balls in the window.

My father has chosen to take this long walk because he likes to walk and think. He thinks about himself in the future and so arrives at the place he is to visit in a mild state of exaltation. He pays no attention to the houses he is passing, in which the Sunday dinner is being eaten, nor to the many trees which line each street, now coming to their full green and the time when they will enclose the whole street in leafy

Delmore Schwartz, *In Dreams Begin Responsibilities.* Copyright 1938 by New Directions © 1966 by Delmore Schwartz. A revised version of this story is published in Schwartz's *The World Is a Wedding.* Copyright 1948 by Delmore Schwartz. Reprinted by permission of New Directions Publishing Corporation.

shadow. An occasional carriage passes, the horses' hooves falling like stones in the quiet afternoon, and once in a while an automobile, looking like an enormous upholstered sofa, puffs and passes.

My father thinks of my mother, of how lady-like she is, and of the pride which will be his when he introduces her to his family. They are not yet engaged and he is not yet sure that he loves my mother, so that, once in a while, he becomes panicky about the bond already established. But then he reassures himself by thinking of the big men he admires who are married: William Randolph Hearst and William Howard Taft, who has just become the President of the United States.

My father arrives at my mother's house. He has come too early and so is suddenly embarrassed. My aunt, my mother's younger sister, answers the loud bell with her napkin in her hand, for the family is still at dinner. As my father enters, my grandfather rises from the table and shakes hands with him. My mother has run upstairs to tidy herself. My grandmother asks my father if he has had dinner and tells him that my mother will be down soon. My grandfather opens the conversation by remarking about the mild June weather. My father sits uncomfortably near the table, holding his hat in his hand. My grandmother tells my aunt to take my father's hat. My uncle, twelve years old, runs into the house, his hair tousled. He shouts a greeting to my father, who has often given him nickels, and then runs upstairs, as my grandmother shouts after him. It is evident that the respect in which my father is held in this house is tempered by a good deal of mirth. He is impressive, but also very awkward.

2

Finally my mother comes downstairs and my father, being at the moment engaged in conversation with my grandfather, is made uneasy by her entrance, for he does not know whether to greet my mother or to continue the conversation. He gets up from his chair clumsily and says "Hello" gruffly. My grandfather watches this, examining their congruence, such as it is, with a critical eye, and meanwhile rubbing his bearded cheek roughly, as he always does when he reasons. He is worried; he is afraid that my father will not make a good husband for his oldest daughter. At this point something happens to the film, just as my father says something funny to my mother: I am awakened to myself and my unhappiness just as my interest has become most intense.The audience begins to clap impatiently. Then the trouble is attended to, but the film has been returned to a portion just shown, and once more I see my grandfather rubbing his bearded cheek, pondering my father's character. It is difficult to get back into the picture once more and forget myself, but as my mother giggles at my father's words, the darkness drowns me.

My father and mother depart from the house, my father shaking hands with my grandfather once more, out of some unknown uneasiness. I stir uneasily also, slouched in the hard chair of the theatre. Where is the older uncle, my mother's older brother? He is studying in his bedroom upstairs, studying for his final examinations at the College of the City of New York, having been dead of double pneumonia for the last twenty-one years. My mother and father walk down the same quiet streets once more. My mother is holding my father's arm and telling him of the novel she has been reading and my father utters judgments of the characters as the plot is made clear to him. This is a habit which he very much enjoys, for he feels the utmost superiority and confidence when he is approving or condemning the behavior of other people. At times he feels moved to utter a brief "Ugh," whenever the story becomes what he would call sugary. This tribute is the assertion of his manliness. My mother feels satisfied by the interest she has awakened; and she is showing my father how intelligent she is and how interesting.

They reach the avenue, and the street-car leisurely arrives. They are going to Coney Island this afternoon, although my mother really considers such pleasures inferior. She has made up her mind to indulge only in a walk on the boardwalk and a pleasant dinner, avoiding the riotous amusements as being beneath the dignity of so dignified a couple. My father tells my mother how much money he has made in the week just past, exaggerating an amount which need not have been exaggerated. But my father has always felt that actualities somehow fall short, no matter how fine they are. Suddenly I begin to weep. The determined old lady who sits next to me in the theatre is annoyed and looks at me with an angry face, and being intimidated, I stop. I drag out my handerchief and dry my face, licking the drop which has fallen near my lips. Meanwhile I have missed something, for here are my father and mother alighting from the street-car at the last stop, Coney Island.

3

They walk toward the boardwalk and my mother commands my father to inhale the pungent air from the sea. They both breathe in deeply, both of them laughing as they do so. They have in common a great interest in health, although my father is strong and husky, and my mother is frail. They are both full of theories about what is good to eat and not good to eat, and sometimes have heated discussions about it, the whole matter ending in my father's announcement, made with a scornful bluster, that you have to die sooner or later anyway. On the boardwalk's flagpole, the American flag is pulsing in an intermittent wind from the sea.

My father and mother go to the rail of the boardwalk and look down on the beach where a good many bathers are casually walking about. A few are in the surf. A peanut whistle pierces the air with its pleasant and active whine, and my father goes to buy peanuts. My mother remains at the rail and stares at the ocean. The ocean seems merry to her; it pointedly sparkles and again and again the pony waves are released. She notices the children digging in the wet sand, and the bathing costumes of the girls who are her own age. My father returns with the peanuts. Overhead the sun's lightning strikes and strikes, but neither of them are at all aware of it. The boardwalk is full of people dressed in their Sunday clothes and casually strolling. The tide does not reach as far as the boardwalk, and the strollers would feel no danger if it did. My father and mother lean on the rail of the boardwalk and absently stare at the ocean. The ocean is becoming rough: the waves come in slowly, tugging strength from far back. The moment before they somersault, the moment when they arch their backs so beautifully, showing white veins in the green and black, that moment is intolerable. They finally crack, dashing fiercely upon the sand, actually driving, full force downward, against it, bouncing upward and forward, and at last petering out into a small stream of bubbles which slides up the beach and then is recalled. The sun overhead does not disturb my father and my mother. They gaze idly at the ocean, scarcely interested in its harshness. But I stare at the terrible sun which breaks up sight, and the fatal merciless passionate ocean. I forget my parents. I stare fascinated, and finally, shocked by their indifference, I burst out weeping once more. The old lady next to me pats my shoulder and says "There, there, young man, all of this is only a movie, only a movie," but I look up once more at the terrifying sun and the terrifying ocean, and being unable to control my tears I get up and go to the men's room, stumbling over the feet of the other people seated in my row.

4

When I return, feeling as if I had just awakened in the morning sick for lack of sleep, several hours have apparently passed and my parents are riding on the merry-go-round. My father is on a black horse, my mother on a white one, and they seem to be making an eternal circuit for the single purpose of snatching the nickel rings which are attached to an arm of one of the posts. A hand organ is playing; it is inseparable from the ceaseless circling of the merry-go-round.

For a moment it seems that they will never get off the carousel, for it will never stop, and I feel as if I were looking down from the fiftieth story of a building. But at length they do get off; even the hand-organ has ceased for a moment. There is a sudden and sweet stillness, as if the achievement of so much motion. My mother has acquired only two rings, my father, however, ten of them, although it was my mother who really wanted them.

They walk on along the boardwalk as the afternoon descends by imperceptible degrees into the incredible violet of dusk. Everything fades into a relaxed glow, even the ceaseless murmuring from the beach. They look for a place to have dinner. My father suggests the best restaurant on the boardwalk and my mother demurs, according to her principles of economy and housewifeliness.

However they do go to the best place, asking for a table near the window so that they can look out upon the boardwalk and the mobile ocean. My father feels omnipotent as he places a quarter in the waiter's hand in asking for a table. The place is crowded and here too there is music, this time from a kind of string trio. My father orders with a fine confidence.

As their dinner goes on, my father tells of his plans for the future and my mother shows with expressive face how interested she is, and how impressed. My father becomes exultant, lifted up by the waltz that is being played and his own future begins to intoxicate him. My father tells my mother that he is going to expand his business, for there is a great deal of money to be made. He wants to settle down. After all, he is twenty-nine, he has lived by himself since his thirteenth year, he is making more and more money, and he is envious of his friends when he visits them in the security of their homes, surrounded, it seems, by the calm domestic pleasures, and by delightful children, and then as the waltz reaches the moment when the dancers all swing madly, then, then with awful daring, then he asks my mother to marry him, although awkwardly enough and puzzled as to how he had arrived at the question, and she, to make the whole business worse, begins to cry, and my father looks nervously about, not knowing at all what to do now, and my mother says: "It's all I've wanted from the first moment I saw you," sobbing, and he finds all of this very difficult, scarcely to his taste, scarcely as he thought it would be, on his long walks over Brooklyn Bridge in the revery of a fine cigar, and it was then, at that point, that I stood up in the theatre and shouted:"Don't do it! It's not too late to change your minds, both of you. Nothing good will come of it, only remorse, hatred, scandal, and two children whose characters are monstrous." The whole audience turned to look at me, annoyed, the usher came hurrying down the aisle flashing his searchlight, and the old lady next to me tugged me down into my seat, saying: "Be quiet. You'll be put out, and you paid thirty-five cents to come in." And so I shut my eyes because I could not bear to see what was happening. I sat there quietly.

5

But after a while I begin to take brief glimpses and at length I watch again with thirsty interest, like a child who tries to maintain his sulk when he is offered the bribe of candy. My parents are now having their picture taken in a photographer's booth along the boardwalk. The place is shadowed in the mauve light which is apparently necessary. The camera is set to the side on its tripod and looks like a Martian man. The photographer is instructing my parents in how to pose. My father has his arm over my mother's shoulder, and both of them smile emphatically. The photographer brings my mother a bouquet of flowers to hold in her hand, but she holds it at the wrong angle. Then the photographer covers himself with the black cloth which drapes the camera and all that one sees of him is one protruding arm and his hand with which he holds tightly to the rubber ball which he squeezes when the picture is taken. But he is not satisfied with their appearance. He feels that somehow there is something wrong in their pose. Again and again he comes out from his hiding place with new directions. Each suggestion merely makes matters worse. My father is becoming impatient. They try a seated pose. The photographer explains that he has his pride, he wants to make beautiful pictures, he is not merely interested in all of this for the money. My father says: "Hurry up, will you? We haven't got all night." But the photographer only scurries about apologetically, issuing new directions. The photographer charms me, and I approve of him with all my heart, for I know exactly how he feels, and as he criticizes each revised pose according to some obscure idea of rightness, I become quite hopeful. But then my father says angrily: "Come on, you've had enough time, we're not going to wait any longer." And the photographer, sighing unhappily, goes back into the black covering, and holds out his hand, saying: "One, two, three, Now!", and the picture is taken, with my father's smile turned to a grimace and my mother's bright and false. It takes a few minutes for the picture to be developed and as my parents sit in the curious light they become depressed.

6

They have passed a fortune-teller's booth and my mother wishes to go in, but my father does not. They begin to argue about it. My mother becomes stubborn, my father once more impatient. What my father would like to do now is walk off and leave my mother there, but he knows that that would never do. My mother refuses to budge. She is near tears, but she feels an uncontrollable desire to hear what the palm-reader will say. My father consents angrily and they both go into the booth which is, in a way, like the photographer's, since it is draped in black cloth and its light is colored and shadowed. The place is too warm, and my father keeps saying that this is all nonsense, pointing to the crystal ball on the table. The fortune-teller, a short, fat woman garbed in robes supposedly exotic, comes into the room and greets them, speaking with an accent. But suddenly my father feels that the whole thing is intolerable; he tugs at my mother's arm but my mother refuses to budge. And then, in terrible anger, my father lets go of my mother's arm and strides out, leaving my mother stunned. She makes a movement as if to go after him, but the fortune-teller holds her and begs her not to do so, and I in my seat in the darkness am shocked and horrified. I feel as if I were walking a tight-rope one hundred feet over a circus audience and suddenly the rope is showing signs of breaking, and I get up from my seat and begin to shout once more the first words I can think of to communicate my terrible fear, and once more the usher comes hurrying down the aisle flashing his searchlight, and the old lady pleads with me, and the shocked audience has turned to stare at me, and I keep shouting: "What are they doing? Don't they know what they are doing? Why doesn't my mother go after my father and beg him not to be angry? If she does not do that, what will she do? Doesn't my father know what he is doing?" But the usher has seized my arm, and is dragging me away, and as he does so, he says: "What are *you* doing? Don't you know you can't do things like this, you can't do whatever you want to do, even if other people aren't about? You will be sorry if you do not do what you should do. You can't carry on like this, it is not right, you will find that out soon enough, everything you do matters too much," and as he said that, dragging me through the lobby of the theatre, into the cold light, I woke up into the bleak winter morning of my twenty-first birthday, the window-sill shining with its lip of snow, and the morning already begun.

Julio Cortàzar (1914–   )

Literature in Latin America is experiencing a new burst of energy which has lifted it from obscurity into international importance. As Jean Franco says, "At the moment when many European countries are going through a dead period in the novel, the genre has attained totally new dimensions in Spanish America."

A major element of this quickening is "magic realism." This term was first used in the late forties to describe a new kind of writing in Spanish America that went beyond regionalism, social realism, and imitation of European literary modes. Magic realism combines reality and fantasy, sometimes by way of folktales and supernaturalism or myth, and sometimes by way of purely intellectual constructs that express the disorientation of modern culture. Although the language can be beautifully lyrical, the imagery is often grotesque or surreal. Time and space are distorted, the vision is frequently apocalyptic. Among the magic realists are Jorge Luis Borges, Gabriel Garcia Marquez, Alejo Carpentier, Carlos Fuentes, and Julio Cortàzar. Cortàzar has taken one strand of magic realism and in novels and short stories like "Axolōtl" has carried it to an unusual extreme, where it transects some aspects of anti-realist fiction in the United States.

Cortàzar was born in 1914 in Brussels of Argentine parentage. He grew up in Buenos Aires. At the age of twenty he took a post as a provincial teacher and there began his long and deliberate apprenticeship as a writer. He was especially influenced by Poe, whose work he spent two years translating; William Faulkner, whose influence has been great throughout Latin America; and Borges, who befriended Cortàzar and helped to promote his career. In 1941, Cortàzar published a book of sonnets but nothing after that until 1949, when *Los Reyes,* a dramatic prose poem based on the legend of the minotaur, came out. In 1951 he moved permanently to Paris. Three volumes of short stories appeared in the fifties, one of which was the basis of the movie *Blow Up.* His first novel, *Los Premios,* came out in 1960. His most acclaimed work, *Rayuela* (1963), which was translated as *Hopscotch,* is in the anti-novel tradition. Of it Jean Franco says that "the entire form of the book is a questioning of literature and . . . art in its relation to reality" and that "it represents the disintegration of all that constitutes culture and morality, and the demonstration of the conventional nature of thought, action, and literary activity." He has since published more stories and several novels in the same vein.

In an interview Cortàzar said of his stories, "They're charms, they're a way out, but above all, they're exorcisms. Many of these stories . . . are purgative, a sort of self-analysis." Although in view of his later work, his stories "may seem like games," Cortàzar said,

> when I wrote them I didn't think of them that way at all. They were glimpses, dimensions, or hints of possibilities that terrified or fascinated me and that I had to exhaust by working them off in the story.

"Sometimes," he says, "it takes six months of tension to produce a long story that comes out in a single night. . . . The best are packed full of a sort of explosive charge."

Whether "Axolōtl" is a glimpse or a possibility, fascinating or terrifying, may depend on the reader. As the narrator himself, through an act of perception, becomes the axolōtl, so may the reader. The act of apprehending (to grasp mentally) is one and the same as the act of being apprehended (taken into custody). For some readers, this may seem a bewitching game; for others, it may create a moment of existential terror. This story carries the literary trend toward subjectivity to its furthest reaches.

Axolōtl

There was a time when I thought a great deal about the axolotls. I went to see them in the aquarium at the Jardin des Plantes[1] and stayed for hours watching them, observing their immobility, their faint movements. Now I am an axolotl.

I got to them by chance one spring morning when Paris was spreading its peacock tail after a wintry Lent. I was heading down the boulevard Port-Royal, then I took Saint-Marcel and L'Hôpital and saw green among all that grey and remembered the lions. I was friend of the lions and panthers, but had never gone into the dark, humid building that was the aquarium. I left my bike against the gratings and went to look at the tulips. The lions were sad and ugly and my panther was asleep. I decided on the aquarium, looked obliquely at banal fish until, unexpectedly, I hit it off with the axolotls. I stayed watching them for an hour and left, unable to think of anything else.

In the library at Sainte-Geneviève, I consulted a dictionary and learned that axolotls are the larval stage (provided with gills) of a species of salamander of the genus Ambystoma. That they were Mexican I knew already by looking at them and

[1] In Paris

From *End of the Game and Other Stories,* by Julio Cortàzar, translated by Paul Blackburn. Copyright © 1967 by Random House, Inc. Reprinted by permission of Pantheon Books, a Division of Random House, Inc.

their little pink Aztec faces and the placard at the top of the tank. I read that specimens of them had been found in Africa capable of living on dry land during the
periods of drought, and continuing their life under water when the rainy season came.
I found their Spanish name, *ajolote,* and the mention that they were edible, and that
their oil was used (no longer used, it said) like cod-liver oil.

I didn't care to look up any of the specialized works, but the next day I went back
to the Jardin des Plantes. I began to go every morning, morning and afternoon some
days. The aquarium guard smiled perplexedly taking my ticket. I would lean up
against the iron bar in front of the tanks and set to watching them. There's nothing
strange in this, because after the first minute I knew that we were linked, that something infinitely lost and distant kept pulling us together. It had been enough to detain
me that first morning in front of the sheet of glass where some bubbles rose through
the water. The axolotls huddled on the wretched narrow (only I can know how narrow
and wretched) floor of moss and stone in the tank. There were nine specimens, and the
majority pressed their heads against the glass, looking with their eyes of gold at whoever came near them. Disconcerted, almost ashamed, I felt it a lewdness to be peering
at these silent and immobile figures heaped at the bottom of the tank. Mentally I
isolated one, situated on the right and somewhat apart from the others, to study it
better. I saw a rosy little body, translucent (I thought of those Chinese figurines of
milky glass), looking like a small lizard about six inches long, ending in a fish's tail of
extraordinary delicacy, the most sensitive part of our body. Along the back ran a
transparent fin which joined with the tail, but what obsessed me was the feet, of the
slenderest nicety, ending in tiny fingers with minutely human nails. And then I discovered its eyes, its face. Inexpressive features, with no other trait save the eyes, two
orifices, like brooches, wholly of transparent gold, lacking any life but looking, letting
themselves be penetrated by my look, which seemed to travel past the golden level and
lose itself in a diaphanous interior mystery. A very slender black halo ringed the eye
and etched it onto the pink flesh, onto the rosy stone of the head, vaguely triangular,
but with curved and irregular sides which gave it a total likeness to a statuette cor-
roded by time. The mouth was masked by the triangular plane of the face, its considerable size would be guessed only in profile; in front a delicate crevice barely slit the
lifeless stone. On both sides of the head where the ears should have been, there grew
three tiny sprigs red as coral, a vegetal outgrowth, the gills, I suppose. And they were
the only thing quick about it; every ten or fifteen seconds the sprig pricked up stiffly
and again subsided. Once in a while a foot would barely move, I saw the diminutive
toes poise mildly on the moss. It's that we don't enjoy moving a lot, and the tank is so
cramped—we barely move in any direction and we're hitting one of the others with
our tail or our head—difficulties arise, fights, tiredness. The time feels like it's less if we
stay quietly.

It was their quietness that made me lean toward them fascinated the first time I
saw the axolotls. Obscurely I seemed to understand their secret will, to abolish space
and time with an indifferent immobility. I knew better later; the gill contraction, the
tentative reckoning of the delicate feet on the stones, the abrupt swimming (some of
them swim with a simple undulation of the body) proved to me that they were capable
of escaping that mineral lethargy in which they spent whole hours. Above all else,
their eyes obsessed me. In the standing tanks on either side of them, different fishes
showed me the simple stupidity of their handsome eyes so similar to our own. The eyes
of the axolotls spoke to me of the presence of a different life, of another way of seeing.
Glueing my face to the glass (the guard would cough fussily once in a while), I tried to

see better those diminutive golden points, that entrance to the infinitely slow and remote world of these rosy creatures. It was useless to tap with one finger on the glass directly in front of their faces; they never gave the least reaction. The golden eyes continued burning with their soft, terrible light; they continued looking at me from an unfathomable depth which made me dizzy.

And nevertheless they were close. I knew it before this, before being an axolotl. I learned it the day I came near them for the first time. The anthropomorphic features of a monkey reveal the reverse of what most people believe, the distance that is traveled from them to us. The absolute lack of similarity between axolotls and human beings proved to me that my recognition was valid, that I was not propping myself up with easy analogies. Only the little hands . . . But an eft, the common newt, has such hands also, and we are not at all alike. I think it was the axolotls' heads, that triangular pink shape with the tiny eyes of gold. That looked and knew. That laid the claim. They were not *animals*.

It would seem easy, almost obvious, to fall into mythology. I began seeing in the axolotls a metamorphosis which did not succeed in revoking a mysterious humanity. I imagined them aware, slaves of their bodies, condemned infinitely to the silence of the abyss, to a hopeless meditation. Their blind gaze, the diminutive gold disc without expression and nonetheless terribly shining, went through me like a message: "Save us, save us." I caught myself mumbling words of advice, conveying childish hopes. They continued to look at me, immobile; from time to time the rosy branches of the gills stiffened. In that instant I felt a muted pain; perhaps they were seeing me, attracting my strength to penetrate into the impenetrable thing of their lives. They were not human beings, but I had found in no animal such a profound relation with myself. The axolotls were like witnesses of something, and at times like horrible judges. I felt ignoble in front of them; there was such a terrifying purity in those transparent eyes. They were larvas, but larva means disguise and also phantom. Behind those Aztec faces, without expression but of an implacable cruelty, what semblance was awaiting its hour?

I was afraid of them. I think that had it not been for feeling the proximity of other visitors and the guard, I would not have been bold enough to remain alone with them. "You eat them alive with your eyes, hey," the guard said, laughing; he likely thought I was a little cracked. What he didn't notice was that it was they devouring me slowly with their eyes, in a cannabalism of gold. At any distance from the aquarium, I had only to think of them, it was as though I were being affected from a distance. It got to the point that I was going every day, and at night I thought of them immobile in the darkness, slowly putting a hand out which immediately encountered another. Perhaps their eyes could see in the dead of night, and for them the day continued indefinitely. The eyes of axolotls have no lids.

I know now that there was nothing strange, that that had to occur. Leaning over in front of the tank each morning, the recognition was greater. They were suffering, every fiber of my body reached toward that stifled pain, that stiff torment at the bottom of the tank. They were lying in wait for something, a remote dominion destroyed, an age of liberty when the world had been that of the axolotls. Not possible that such a terrible expression which was attaining the overthrow of that forced blankness on their stone faces should carry any message other than one of pain, proof of that eternal sentence, of that liquid hell they were undergoing. Hopelessly, I wanted to prove to myself that my own sensibility was projecting a nonexistent consciousness upon the axolotls. They and I knew. So there was nothing strange in what happened. My face was pressed against the glass of the aquarium, my eyes were attempting once more to penetrate the mystery of those eyes of gold without iris, without pupil. I saw from very close up the face of an axolotl immobile next to the glass. No transition and no surprise, I saw my face against the glass, I saw it on the outside of the tank, I saw it on the other side of the glass. Then my face drew back and I understood.

Only one thing was strange: to go on thinking as usual, to know. To realize that was, for the first moment, like the horror of a man buried alive awaking to his fate. Outside, my face came close to the glass again, I saw my mouth, the lips compressed with the effort of understanding the axolotls. I was an axolotl and now I knew instantly that no understanding was possible. He was outside the aquarium, his thinking was a thinking outside the tank. Recognizing him, being him himself, I was an axolotl and in my world. The horror began—I learned in the same moment—of believing myself prisoner in the body of an axolotl, metamorphosed into him with my human mind intact, buried alive in an axolotl, condemned to move lucidly among unconscious creatures. But that stopped when a foot just grazed my face, when I moved just a little to one side and saw an axolotl next to me who was looking at me, and understood that he knew also, no communication possible, but very clearly. Or I was also in him, or all of us were thinking humanlike, incapable of expression, limited to the golden splendor of our eyes looking at the face of the man pressed against the aquarium.

He returned many times, but he comes less often now. Weeks pass without his showing up. I saw him yesterday, he looked at me for a long time and left briskly. It seemed to me that he was not so much interested in us any more, that he was coming out of habit. Since the only thing I do is think, I could think about him a lot. It occurs to me that at the beginning we continued to communicate, that he felt more than ever one with the mystery which was claiming him. But the bridges were broken between him and me, because what was his obsession is now an axolotl, alien to his human life. I think that at the beginning I was capable of returning to him in a certain way—ah, only in a certain way—and of keeping awake his desire to know us better. I am an axolotl for good now, and if I think like a man it's only because every axolotl thinks like a man inside his rosy stone resemblance. I believe that all this succeeded in communicating something to him in those first days, when I was still he. And in this final solitude to which he no longer comes, I console myself by thinking that perhaps he is going to write a story about us, that, believing he's making up a story, he's going to write all this about axolotls.

Shirley Jackson (1919–1965)

Shirley Jackson was born in San Francisco, went east to attend college, and received a bachelor's degree from Syracuse University in 1941. By the end of the 1940s she had become a frequent contributor to *The New Yorker,* where "The Lottery," her best-known story, first appeared in 1948. She spent most of the rest of her life in Vermont, where her husband, a literary critic and folklorist, taught at Bennington College.

In addition to a collection of short stories *(The Lottery or, The Adventures of James Harris, 1949)*, Jackson wrote six novels, including *Hangsaman* (1951), *The Bird's Nest* (1954), and *The Haunting of Hill House* (1959). They conduct us variously through worlds of cruelty and fear, and through episodes of alienation, derangement, and delirium. Yet this versatile author also turned out two witty autobiographical works about the life led by an intellectual family in a small New England village—with a special emphasis on the rearing of her own children, as their waggish titles signal: *Life among the Demons* (1953) and *Raising Demons* (1957). One of her very funniest stories, also autobiographical, is called "My Life with R. H. Macy."

In all of her serious fiction, Jackson was considerably influenced by her study of anthropology. Strange psychological states, ritualistic mumbo jumbo, magical spells—all are widely treated in her writing. In one of the earliest notices to appear following publication of the 1949 short-story gathering, the reviewer Robert Halsband, having divided the contents of the book into three kinds of stories, offered the following characterization:

> Her final group deals with fantasy, ranging from humorous whimsy to horrifying shock. Her method is to establish with meticulous detail a concretely realistic setting, and then to allow the story to crumble (or, as in "The Lottery," to explode) into unreality.

That representation seems just. The story is clearly the work of a brilliant craftsman who knows exactly how to jolt a reader by setting in sudden and violent juxtaposition the familiar and the bizarre. It is a favorite Jackson device.

But the review goes on to assert that "as a horror story it is a failure." Arguing first that the story's setting and characters are "unmistakably twentieth-century New England," the reviewer makes the following case:

> In *The Golden Bough* Frazer records the ritual of making human sacrifices for crops as occurring in savage cultures, and the stoning of human scapegoats in ancient Athens. What Miss Jackson has done, then, is to superimpose a barbaric ritual ceremony onto a contemporary scene . . . , translating exactly the same ritual into events that coalesce with their time and place. . . . If "The Lottery" is intended to be a symbolic action which the reader must translate, it may be provocative, intellectually, but it is hardly horrifying, emotionally.

We may or may not agree that the setting is necessarily New England, and some might even quibble over "twentieth century." What is important, however, is that the reviewer seems to be arguing that the story cannot move us to horror because we cannot believe such things can happen in contemporary America. But can they not? One thinks of the *new forms of extremity* implicit in Philip Stevick's "Against the Middle Range of Experience" (see Introduction, p. 4); one thinks also of the some forty-odd thousand soldiers picked by lottery for slaughter in Vietnam, in what history surely will record as America's most unnecessary war. Ritual slaughter, it can be argued, is still quite in style. Is Shirley Jackson's story only about what happened in that village on that day? Or is it about the persistence of certain forms of human behavior (in particular the need for blood sacrifice) even though the reasons for such rituals are no longer understood or even thought about? Her story can be read on many levels, but one of them surely concerns the secularization of death in our time, and our separation from a daily sense of holiness in life—and death.

The Lottery

The morning of June 27th was clear and sunny, with the fresh warmth of a full-summer day; the flowers were blossoming profusely and the grass was richly green. The people of the village began to gather in the square, between the post office and the bank, around ten o'clock; in some towns there were so many people that the lottery took two days and had to be started on June 26th, but in this village, where there were only about three hundred people, the whole lottery took less than two hours, so it could begin at ten o'clock in the morning and still be through in time to allow the villagers to get home for noon dinner.

The children assembled first, of course. School was recently over for the summer, and the feeling of liberty sat uneasily on most of them; they tended to gather together quietly for a while before they broke into boisterous play, and their talk was still of the classroom and the teacher, of books and reprimands. Bobby Martin had already stuffed his pockets full of stones, and the other boys soon followed his example, selecting the smoothest and roundest stones; Bobby and Harry Jones and Dickie Delacroix—the villagers pronounced this name "Dellacroy"—eventually made a great pile of stones in one corner of the square and guarded it against the raids of the other boys. The girls stood aside, talking among themselves, looking over their shoulders at the boys, and the very small children rolled in the dust or clung to the hands of their older brothers or sisters.

Soon the men began to gather, surveying their own children, speaking of planting and rain, tractors and taxes. They stood together, away from the pile of stones in the corner, and their jokes were quiet and they smiled rather than laughed. The women, wearing faded house dresses and sweaters, came shortly after their menfolk. They greeted one another and exchanged bits of gossip as they went to join their husbands. Soon the women, standing by their husbands, began to call to their children, and the children came reluctantly, having to be called four or five times. Bobby Martin ducked under his mother's grasping hand and ran, laughing, back to the pile of stones. His father spoke up sharply, and Bobby came quickly and took his place between his father and his oldest brother.

The lottery was conducted—as were the square dances, the teen-age club, the Halloween program—by Mr. Summers, who had time and energy to devote to civic activities. He was a round-faced, jovial man and he ran the coal business, and people were sorry for him, because he had no children and his wife was a scold. When he arrived in the square, carrying the black wooden box, there was a murmur of conversation among the villagers, and he waved and called, "Little late today, folks." The postmaster, Mr. Graves, followed him, carrying a three-legged stool, and the stool was put in the center of the square and Mr. Summers set the black box down on it. The

Shirley Jackson, "The Lottery," from *The Lottery or, The Adventure of James Harris*. Copyright 1948 *The New Yorker Magazine,* Inc. 1949 Shirley Jackson.

villagers kept their distance, leaving a space between themselves and the stool, and when Mr. Summers said, "Some of you fellows want to give me a hand?" there was a hesitation before two men, Mr. Martin and his oldest son, Baxter, came forward to hold the box steady on the stool while Mr. Summers stirred up the papers inside it.

The original paraphernalia for the lottery had been lost long ago, and the black box now resting on the stool had been put into use even before Old Man Warner, the oldest man in town, was born. Mr. Summers spoke frequently to the villagers about making a new box, but no one liked to upset even as much tradition as was represented by the black box. There was a story that the present box had been made with some pieces of the box that had preceded it, the one that had been constructed when the first people settled down to make a village here. Every year, after the lottery, Mr. Summers began talking again about a new box, but every year the subject was allowed to fade off without anything's being done. The black box grew shabbier each year; by now it was no longer completely black but splintered badly along one side to show the original wood color, and in some places faded or stained.

Mr. Martin and his oldest son, Baxter, held the black box securely on the stool until Mr. Summers had stirred the papers thoroughly with his hand. Because so much of the ritual had been forgotten or discarded, Mr. Summers had been successful in having slips of paper substituted for the chips of wood that had been used for generations. Chips of wood, Mr. Summers had argued, had been all very well when the village was tiny, but now that the population was more than three hundred and likely to keep on growing, it was necessary to use something that would fit more easily into the black box. The night before the lottery, Mr. Summers and Mr. Graves made up the slips of paper and put them in the box, and it was then taken to the safe of Mr. Summers' coal company and locked up until Mr. Summers was ready to take it to the square next morning. The rest of the year, the box was put away, sometimes one place, sometimes another; it had spent one year in Mr. Grave's barn and another year underfoot in the post office, and sometimes it was set on a shelf in the Martin grocery and left there.

There was a great deal of fussing to be done before Mr. Summers declared the lottery open. There were lists to make up—of heads of families, heads of households in each family, members of each household in each family. There was the proper swearing-in of Mr. Summers by the postmaster, as the official of the lottery; at one time, some people remembered, there had been a recital of some sort, performed by the official of the lottery, a perfunctory, tuneless chant that had been rattled off duly each year; some people believed that the official of the lottery used to stand just so when he said or sang it, others believed that he was supposed to walk among the people, but years and years ago this part of the ritual had been allowed to lapse. There had been, also, a ritual salute, which the official of the lottery had had to use in addressing each person who came up to draw from the box, but this also had changed with time, until now it was felt necessary only for the official to speak to each person approaching. Mr. Summers was very good at all this; in his clean white shirt and blue jeans, with one hand resting carelessly on the black box, he seemed very proper and important as he talked interminably to Mr. Graves and the Martins.

Just as Mr. Summers finally left off talking and turned to the assembled villagers, Mrs. Hutchinson came hurriedly along the path to the square, her sweater thrown over her shoulders, and slid into place in the back of the crowd. "Clean forgot what day it was," she said to Mrs. Delacroix, who stood next to her, and they both laughed softly. "Thought my old man was out back stacking wood," Mrs. Hutchinson went on, "and then I looked out the window and the kids were gone, and then I remembered it was the twenty-seventh and came a-running." She dried her hands on her apron, and Mrs. Delacroix said, "You're in time, though. They're still talking away up there."

Mrs. Hutchinson craned her neck to see through the crowd and found her husband and children standing near the front. She tapped Mrs. Delacroix on the arm as a farewell and began to make her way through the crowd. The people separated good-humoredly to let her through; two or three people said, in voices just loud enough to be heard across the crowd, "Here comes your Missus, Hutchinson," and "Bill, she made it after all." Mrs. Hutchinson reached her husband, and Mr. Summers, who had been waiting, said cheerfully, "Thought we were going to have to get on without you, Tessie." Mrs. Hutchinson said, grinning. "Wouldn't have me leave m'dishes in the sink, now would you, Joe?," and soft laughter ran through the crowd as the people stirred back into position after Mrs. Hutchinson's arrival.

"Well, now," Mr. Summers said soberly, "guess we better get started, get this over with, so's we can go back to work. Anybody ain't here?"

"Dunbar," several people said. "Dunbar, Dunbar."

Mr Summers consulted his list. "Clyde Dunbar," he said. "That's right. He's broke his leg, hasn't he? Who's drawing for him?"

"Me, I guess," a woman said, and Mr. Summers turned to look at her. "Wife draws for her husband," Mr. Summers said. "Don't you have a grown boy to do it for you, Janey?" Although Mr. Summers and everyone else in the village knew the answer perfectly well, it was the business of the official of the lottery to ask such questions formally. Mr. Summers waited with an expression of polite interest while Mrs. Dunbar answered.

"Horace's not but sixteen yet," Mrs. Dunbar said regretfully. "Guess I gotta fill in for the old man this year."

"Right," Mr. Summers said. He made a note on the list he was holding. Then he asked, "Watson boy drawing this year?"

A tall boy in the crowd raised his hand. "Here," he said. "I'm drawing for m'mother and me." He blinked his eyes nervously and ducked his head as several voices in the crowd said things like "Good fellow, Jack," and "Glad to see your mother's got a man to do it."

"Well," Mr. Summers said, "guess that's everyone. Old Man Warner make it?"

"Here," a voice said, and Mr. Summers nodded.

A sudden hush fell on the crowd as Mr. Summers cleared his throat and looked at the list. "All ready?" he called. "Now, I'll read the names—heads of families first—and the men come up and take a paper out of the box. Keep the paper folded in your hand without looking at it until everyone has had a turn. Everything clear?"

The people had done it so many times that they only half listened to the directions, most of them were quiet, wetting their lips, not looking around. Then Mr. Summers raised one hand high and said, "Adams." A man disengaged himself from the crowd and came forward. "Hi, Steve," Mr. Summers said, and Mr. Adams said, "Hi Joe." They grinned at one another humorlessly and nervously. Then Mr. Adams reached into the black box and took out a folded paper. He held it firmly by one corner as he turned and went hastily back to his place in the crowd, where he stood a little apart from his family, not looking down at his hand.

"Allen," Mr. Summers said. "Anderson. . . . Bentham."

"Seems like there's no time at all between lotteries any more," Mrs. Delacroix said to Mrs. Graves in the back row. "Seems like we got through with the last one only last week."

"Time sure goes fast," Mrs. Graves said.

"Clark. . . . Delacroix."

"There goes my old man," Mrs. Delacroix said. She held her breath while her husband went forward.

"Dunbar," Mr. Summers said, and Mrs. Dunbar went steadily to the box while one of the women said, "Go on, Janey," and another said, "There she goes."

"We're next," Mrs. Graves said. She watched while Mr. Graves came around from the side of the box, greeted Mr. Summers gravely, and selected a slip of paper from the box. By now, all through the crowd there were men holding the small folded papers in their large hands, turning them over and over nervously. Mrs. Dunbar and her two sons stood together, Mrs. Dunbar holding the slip of paper.

"Harburt. . . . Hutchinson."

"Get up there, Bill," Mrs. Hutchinson said, and the people near her laughed.

"Jones."

"They do say," Mr. Adams said to Old Man Warner, who stood next to him, "that over in the north village they're talking of giving up the lottery."

Old Man Warner snorted, "Pack of crazy fools," he said. "Listening to the young folks, nothing's good enough for *them*. Next thing you know, they'll be wanting to go back to living in caves, nobody work any more, live *that* way for a while. Used to be a saying about 'Lottery in June, corn be heavy soon.' First thing you know, we'd all be eating stewed chickweed and acorns. There's *always* been a lottery," he added petulantly. "Bad enough to see young Joe Summers up there joking with everybody."

"Some places have already quit lotteries," Mrs. Adams said.

"Nothing but trouble in *that*," Old Man Warner said stoutly. "Pack of young fools."

"Martin." And Bobby Martin watched his father go forward. "Overdyke. . . . Percy."

"I wish they'd hurry," Mrs. Dunbar said to her older son. "I wish they'd hurry."

"They're almost through," her son said.

"You get ready to run tell Dad," Mrs. Dunbar said.

Mr. Summers called his own name and then stepped forward precisely and selected a slip from the box. Then he called, "Warner."

"Seventy-seventh year I been in the lottery," Old Man Warner said as he went through the crowd. "Seventy-seventh time."

"Watson." The tall boy came awkwardly through the crowd. Someone said, "Don't be nervous, Jack," and Mr. Summers said, "Take your time, son."

"Zanini."

After that, there was a long pause, a breathless pause, until Mr. Summers, holding his slip of paper in the air, said, "All right, fellows." For a minute, no one moved, and then all the slips of paper were opened. Suddenly, all women began to speak at once, saying, "Who is it?," "Who's got it?," "Is it the Dunbars?," "Is it the Watsons?" Then the voices began to say, "It's Hutchinson. It's Bill." "Bill Hutchinson's got it."

"Go tell your father," Mrs. Dunbar said to her older son.

People began to look around to see the Hutchinsons. Bill Hutchinson was standing quiet, staring down at the paper in his hand. Suddenly, Tessie Hutchinson shouted to Mr. Summers, "You didn't give him time enough to take any paper he wanted. I saw you. It wasn't fair!"

"Be a good sport, Tessie," Mrs. Delacroix called, and Mrs. Graves said, "All of us took the same chance."

"Shut up, Tessie," Bill Hutchinson said.

"Well, everyone," Mr. Summers said, "that was done pretty fast, and now we've got to be hurrying a little more to get done in time." He consulted his next list. "Bill," he said, "you draw for the Hutchinson family. You got any other households in the Hutchinsons?"

"There's Don and Eva," Mrs. Hutchinson yelled. "Make *them* take their chance!"

"Daughters draw with their husbands' families, Tessie," Mr. Summers said gently. "You know that as well as anyone else."

"It wasn't *fair*," Tessie said.

"I guess not, Joe," Bill Hutchinson said regretfully. "My daughter draws with her husband's family, that's only fair. And I've got no other family except the kids."

"Then, as far as drawing for families is concerned, it's you," Mr. Summers said in explanation, "and as far as drawing for households is concerned, that's you, too. Right?"

"Right," Bill Hutchinson said.

"How many kids, Bill?" Mr. Summers asked formally.

"Three," Bill Hutchinson said. "There's Bill, Jr., and Nancy, and little Dave. And Tessie and me."

"All right, then," Mr. Summers said. "Harry, you got their tickets back?"

Mr. Graves nodded and held up the slips of paper. "Put them in the box, then," Mr. Summers directed. "Take Bill's and put it in."

"I think we ought to start over," Mrs. Hutchinson said, as quietly as she could. "I tell you it wasn't *fair*. You didn't give him time enough to choose. *Every*body saw that."

Mr. Graves had selected the five slips and put them in the box, and he dropped all the papers but those onto the ground, where the breeze caught them and lifted them off.

"Listen, everybody," Mrs. Hutchinson was saying to the people around her.

"Ready, Bill?" Mr. Summers asked, and Bill Hutchinson, with one quick glance around at his wife and children, nodded.

"Remember," Mr. Summers said, "take the slips and keep them folded until each person has taken one. Harry, you help little Dave." Mr. Graves took the hand of the little boy, who came willingly with him up to the box. "Take a paper out of the box, Davy," Mr. Summers said. Davy put his hand into the box and laughed. "Take just *one* paper," Mr. Summers said. "Harry, you hold it for him." Mr. Graves took the child's hand and removed the folded paper from the tight fist and held it while little Dave stood next to him and looked up at him wonderingly.

"Nancy next," Mr. Summers said. Nancy was twelve, and her school friends breathed heavily as she went forward, switching her skirt, and took a slip daintily from the box. "Bill, Jr.," Mr. Summers said, and Billy, his face red and his feet over-large, nearly knocked the box over as he got a paper out. "Tessie," Mr. Summers said. She hesitated for a minute, looking around defiantly, and then set her lips and went up to the box. She snatched a paper out and held it behind her.

"Bill," Mr. Summers said, and Bill Hutchinson reached into the box and felt around, bringing his hand out at last with the slip of paper in it.

The crowd was quiet. A girl whispered, "I hope it's not Nancy," and the sound of the whisper reached the edges of the crowd.

"It's not the way it used to be," Old Man Warner said clearly. "People ain't the way they used to be."

"All right," Mr. Summers said. "Open the papers. Harry, you open little Dave's."

Mr. Graves opened the slip of paper and there was a general sigh through the crowd as he held it up and everyone could see that it was blank. Nancy and Bill, Jr., opened theirs at the same time, and both beamed and laughed, turning around to the crowd and holding their slips of papers above their heads.

"Tessie," Mr. Summers said. There was a pause, and then Mr. Summers looked at Bill Hutchinson, and Bill unfolded his paper and showed it. It was blank.

"It's Tessie," Mr. Summers said, and his voice was hushed. "Show us her paper, Bill."

Bill Hutchinson went over to his wife and forced the slip of paper out of her hand. It had a black spot on it, the black spot Mr. Summers had made the night before with the heavy pencil in the coal-company office. Bill Hutchinson held it up, and there was a stir in the crowd.

"All right, folks," Mr. Summers said, "Let's finish quickly."

Although the villagers had forgotten the ritual and lost the original black box, they still remembered to use stones. The pile of stones the boys had made earlier was ready; there were stones on the ground with the blowing scraps of paper that had come out of the box. Mrs. Delacroix selected a stone so large she had to pick it up with both hands and turned to Mrs. Dunbar. "Come on," she said. "Hurry up."

Mrs. Dunbar had small stones in both hands, and she said, gasping for breath, "I can't run at all. You'll have to go ahead and I'll catch up with you."

The children had stones already, and someone gave little Davy Hutchinson a few pebbles.

Tessie Hutchinson was in the center of a cleared space by now, and she held her hands out desperately as the villagers moved in on her. "It isn't fair," she said. A stone hit her on the side of the head.

Old Man Warner was saying, "Come on, come on, everyone." Steve Adams was in the front of the crowd of villagers, with Mrs. Graves beside him.

"It isn't fair, it isn't right," Mrs. Hutchinson screamed, and then they were upon her.

Heinrich Böll (1917–   )

Heinrich Böll was born in Cologne of Catholic parents. His youth was overshadowed by the emergence of Hitler's regime, and he was forced to serve in the Nazi infantry from 1939 to 1945. It was the experience of World War II and of postwar Germany that provided him with his subjects when he began to write, and his was the strongest literary voice to arise from Germany of the 1950s. According to W. B. Fleishmann, the books and plays of that period record "the brutalities of racial persecution, the lethal vacuity of *Wehrmacht* life, and the grim aspects of daily existence under the Nazis, which allows the full horror of recent German existence to emerge. . . ." In his attacks on the corruptions and spiritual sterility of postwar bourgeois society he was no more sparing.

Böll's experiments with language, his use of symbolism, his mordant satire—though often tempered by a playful and wistful strain—all constitute a continuous and major contribution to experimental literature of the continent over the past quarter century. Among his more important works that have been translated into English are *Acquainted with the Night* (1954), *Traveller, If You Come to Spa* (1956), *The Train Was on Time* (1956), *Billiards at Half-Past Nine* (1962), *The Clown* (1965), *18 Stories* —in which "Action Will Be Taken" appeared—(1966), and *End of a Mission* (1968). His works brought him the Nobel Prize for Literature in 1972, the citation acknowledging his part in aiding the "renewal of German literature." In recent years he has been somewhat eclipsed in vogue by newer German writers like Günter Grass and Peter Handke, but he still ranks pre-eminent among those experimental writers who have tried with high seriousness to make the short story an expressive vehicle for the mixed horror and absurdity of our time.

Earlier in the twentieth century, before television, when popular American "slick" magazines still enjoyed mammoth circulations, a story like "Action Will Be Taken" would have been recognized by all readers as belonging to a category known as the "short, short story." Both *Liberty* (now defunct) and *The Reader's Digest* regularly included the type in every issue, with *Liberty* offering a stopwatch guide: "Reading Time: 2 minutes, 40 seconds." In a story of such brevity, much depends upon the author's skill in exploiting the opportunities and versatilities of economy. If that is so, the story's opening is crucial. Consider what we discover in Böll's first two paragraphs. How does the speaker characterize himself? Is that characterization important to the rest of the tale? What kind of person works only when he is out of money? Why "a *so-called* job"? Note the parallelism between his aversion to well-lit buildings and well-lit rooms, and to work. Does "pensiveness" properly require the quiet, inactive, but honest dark, while busyness invariably courts a hypocritical daylight? Why "pensive" instead of "thoughtful"?

Broschek, Wunsiedel's "right-hand man," supports seven children and a paralyzed wife; Wunsiedel's secretary supports four children and a paralyzed husband. Does the grotesque parallelism have any symbolic overtones? To inquire more largely, is the story a genuine (if seriocomic) attack upon the Great Gospel of Getting On, or does its doubleness of tone and point of view—whereby the speaker mocks himself as much as he satirizes the conditions and relationships he is describing—leave us with the memory of an inside joke, a supersophisticated and only partially penetrable cartoon? Why, do you suppose, *soap?*

Action Will Be Taken

AN ACTION-PACKED STORY

Probably one of the strangest interludes in my life was the time I spent as an employee in Alfred Wunsiedel's factory. By nature I am inclined more to pensiveness and inactivity than to work, but now and again prolonged financial difficulties compel me—for pensiveness is no more profitable than inactivity—to take on a so-called job. Finding myself once again at a low ebb of this kind, I put myself in the hands of the employment office and was sent with seven other fellow-sufferers to Wunsiedel's factory, where we were to undergo an aptitude test.

From *18 Stories* by Heinrich Böll. Translated by Leila Vennewitz. Copyright © 1966 by Heinrich Böll. Used with permission of McGraw-Hill Book Company.

The exterior of the factory was enough to arouse my suspicions: the factory was built entirely of glass brick, and my aversion to well-lit buildings and well-lit rooms is as strong as my aversion to work. I became even more suspicious when we were immediately served breakfast in the well-lit, cheerful coffee shop: pretty waitresses brought us eggs, coffee and toast, orange juice was served in tastefully designed jugs, goldfish pressed their bored faces against the sides of pale-green aquariums. The waitresses were so cheerful that they appeared to be bursting with good cheer. Only a strong effort of will—so it seemed to me—restrained them from singing away all day long. They were as crammed with unsung songs as chickens with unlaid eggs.

Right away I realized something that my fellow-sufferers evidently failed to realize: that this breakfast was already part of the test; so I chewed away reverently, with the full appreciation of a person who knows he is supplying his body with valuable elements. I did something which normally no power on earth can make me do: I drank orange juice on an empty stomach, left the coffee and egg untouched, as well as most of the toast, got up, and paced up and down in the coffee shop, pregnant with action.

As a result I was the first to be ushered into the room where the questionnaires were spread out on attractive tables. The walls were done in a shade of green that would have summoned the word "delightful" to the lips of interior decoration enthusiasts. The room appeared to be empty, and yet I was so sure of being observed that I behaved as someone pregnant with action behaves when he believes himself unobserved: I ripped my pen impatiently from my pocket, unscrewed the top, sat down at the nearest table and pulled the questionnaire toward me, the way irritable customers snatch at the bill in a restaurant.

Question No. 1: Do you consider it right for a human being to possess only two arms, two legs, eyes, and ears?

Here for the first time I reaped the harvest of my pensive nature and wrote without hesitation: "Even four arms, legs and ears would not be adequate for my driving energy. Human beings are very poorly equipped."

Question No. 2: How many telephones can you handle at one time?

Here again the answer was as easy as simple arithmetic: "When there are only seven telephones," I wrote, "I get impatient; there have to be nine before I feel I am working to capacity."

Question No. 3: How do you spend your free time?

My answer: "I no longer acknowledge the term free time—on my fifteenth birthday I eliminated it from my vocabulary, for in the beginning was the act."

I got the job. Even with nine telephones I really didn't feel I was working to capacity. I shouted into the mouthpieces: "Take immediate action!" or: "Do something!—We must have some action—Action will be taken—Action has been taken—Action should be taken." But as a rule—for I felt this was in keeping with the tone of the place—I used the imperative.

Of considerable interest were the noon-hour breaks, when we consumed nutritious foods in an atmosphere of silent good cheer. Wunsiedel's factory was swarming with people who were obsessed with telling you the story of their lives, as indeed vigorous personalities are fond of doing. The story of their lives is more important to them than their lives, you have only to press a button, and immediately it is covered with spewed-out exploits.

Wunsiedel had a right-hand man called Broschek, who had in turn made a name for himself by supporting seven children and a paralyzed wife by working night-shifts in his student days, and successfully carrying on four business agencies, besides which he had passed two examinations with honors in two years. When asked by reporters: "When do you sleep, Mr. Broschek?" he had replied: "It's a crime to sleep!"

Wunsiedel's secretary had supported a paralyzed husband and four children by knitting, at the same time graduating in psychology and German history as well as breeding shepherd dogs, and she had become famous as a night-club singer where she was known as *Vamp Number Seven.*

Wunsiedel himself was one of those people who every morning, as they open their eyes, make up their minds to act. "I must act," they think as they briskly tie their bathrobe belts around them. "I must act," they think as they shave, triumphantly watching their beard hairs being washed away with the lather: these hirsute vestiges are the first daily sacrifices to their driving energy. The more intimate functions also give these people a sense of satisfaction: water swishes, paper is used. Action has been taken. Bread gets eaten, eggs are decapitated.

With Wunsiedel, the most trivial activity looked like action: the way he put on his hat, the way—quivering with energy—he buttoned up his overcoat, the kiss he gave his wife, everything was action.

When he arrived at his office he greeted his secretary with a cry of "Let's have some action!" And in ringing tones she would call back: "Action will be taken!" Wunsiedel then went from department to department, calling out his cheerful: "Let's have some action!" Everyone would answer: "Action will be taken!" And I would call back to him too, with a radiant smile, when he looked into my office: "Action will be taken!"

Within a week I had increased the number of telephones on my desk to eleven, within two weeks to thirteen, and every morning on the streetcar I enjoyed thinking up new imperatives, or chasing the words *take action* through various tenses and modulations: for two whole days I kept saying the same sentence over and over again because I thought it sounded so marvelous: "Action ought to have been taken;" for another two days it was: "Such action ought not to have been taken."

So I was really beginning to feel I was working to capacity when there actually was some action. One Tuesday morning—I had hardly settled down at my desk— Wunsiedel rushed into my office crying his "Let's have some action!" But an inexplicable something in his face made me hesitate to reply, in a cheerful gay voice as the rules dictated: "Action will be taken!" I must have paused too long, for Wunsiedel, who seldom raised his voice, shouted at me: "Answer! Answer, you know the rules!" And I answered, under my breath, reluctantly, like a child who is forced to say: I am a naughty child. It was only by a great effort that I managed to bring out the sentence: "Action will be taken," and hardly had I uttered it when there really was some action: Wunsiedel dropped to the floor. As he fell he rolled over onto his side and lay right across the open doorway. I knew at once, and I confirmed it when I went slowly around my desk and approached the body on the floor: he was dead.

Shaking my head I stepped over Wunsiedel, walked slowly along the corridor to Broschek's office, and entered without knocking. Broschek was sitting at his desk, a telephone receiver in each hand, between his teeth a ballpoint pen with which he was making notes on a writing pad, while with his bare feet he was operating a knitting machine under the desk. In this way he helps to clothe his family. "We've had some action," I said in a low voice.

Broschek spat out the ballpoint pen, put down the two receivers, reluctantly detached his toes from the knitting machine.

"What action?" he asked.

"Wunsiedel is dead," I said.

"No," said Broschek.

"Yes," I said, "come and have a look!"

"No," said Broschek, "that's impossible," but he put on his slippers and followed me along the corridor.

"No," he said, when we stood beside Wunsiedel's corpse, "no no!" I did not contradict him. I carefully turned Wunsiedel over onto his back, closed his eyes, and looked at him pensively.

I felt something like tenderness for him, and realized for the first time that I had never hated him. On his face was that expression which one sees on children who obstinately refuse to give up their faith in Santa Claus, even though the arguments of their playmates sound so convincing.

"No," said Broschek, "no."

"We must take action," I said quietly to Broschek.

"Yes," said Broschek, "we must take action."

Action was taken: Wunsiedel was buried, and I was delegated to carry a wreath of artificial roses behind his coffin, for I am equipped with not only a penchant for pensiveness and inactivity but also a face and figure that go extremely well with dark suits. Apparently as I walked along behind Wunsiedel's coffin carrying the wreath of artificial roses I looked superb. I received an offer from a fashionable firm of funeral directors to join their staff as a professional mourner. "You are a born mourner," said the manager, "your outfit would be provided by the firm. Your face—simply superb!"

I handed in my notice to Broschek, explaining that I had never really felt I was working to capacity there; that, in spite of the thirteen telephones, some of my talents were going to waste. As soon as my first professional appearance as a mourner was over I knew: This is where I belong, this is what I am cut out for.

Pensively I stand behind the coffin in the funeral chapel, holding a simple bouquet, while the organ plays Handel's *Largo,* a piece that does not receive nearly the respect it deserves. The cemetery café is my regular haunt; there I spend the intervals between my professional engagements, although sometimes I walk behind coffins which I have not been engaged to follow, I pay for flowers out of my own pocket and join the welfare worker who walks behind the coffin of some homeless person. From time to time I also visit Wunsiedel's grave, for after all I owe it to him that I discovered my true vocation, a vocation in which pensiveness is essential and inactivity my duty.

It was not till much later that I realized I had never bothered to find out what was being produced in Wunsiedel's factory. I expect it was soap.

Isaac Rosenfeld (1918–1956)

In 1956, at the age of thirty-eight, Isaac Rosenfeld died of a heart attack, just as he was beginning a brilliant career as creative writer and critic. Graduating from the University of Chicago in 1941, in the following years he taught literature at New York

University, the University of Minnesota, and the University of Chicago. As his friend and editor Theodore Solotaroff says, "in these places and elsewhere he has become a legend: the wise and tender, the charming and fated 'Isaac' of the various stories that are remembered far more vividly than those he wrote." But he was always a marginal, if not an underground, man, moving from job to job and living in lonely rooms. In 1941 he left off work for a Ph.D. in philosophy at New York University to become a regular contributor to *The New Republic*, and later a staff editor; he was also for a time literary editor of *The New Yorker*. As a literary journalist he mastered, as Solotaroff says, "the firm, tense, intellectually ambitious prose" that was characteristic of Jewish New York writers of his generation—men like Saul Bellow, Delmore Schwartz, Alfred Kazin, Irving Howe, and Leslie Fiedler. His reviews and articles have been collected in a volume entitled *An Age of Enormity: Life and Writing in the Forties and Fifties* (1962), and the title is indicative of Rosenfeld's relationship to his age. In reviewing the work of the Marxist Walter Morris, he wrote a passage out of his own experience:

> The frustrations he encountered were the same that have turned almost his entire generation into underground men—men who are not so much beyond belief as below it, incapable of the desperate exertion of rising which an affirmation of our time demands. This is the generation which remembers the last war dimly, and the Depression clearly; which was sustained by the WPA only to see the rise and flourishing of fascism, the death of Spain and the disgrace of the democracies; which lost, in Stalin, the last hope of imminent socialism and in the present war the hope of its own survival.

Yet Rosenfeld never despaired of transcending his own alienation; the words "joy" and "love" are large in his vocabulary, and he did not use them sentimentally. In "The Meaning of Terror" (*Partisan Review*, 1949) he called Hitler's slaughtering of the Jews "the evil greater than evil" which can be transcended only by "the good greater than good," a state of joy which does not yet exist on earth.

Rosenfeld's first book was *Passage from Home* (1946), an autobiographical novel, and at the time of his death he was working on a book about the Chicago fire of 1871. His stories have been collected in *Alpha and Omega* (1966). "The Brigadier" was one part of a novel called *The Enemy* which was finished in 1951, but, for some puzzling reason, rejected by the publishers; but three parts were separately published: "The Brigadier" (*Partisan Review*, 1947), "In the Monastery" (*Kenyon Review*, 1951), and "In the Holy City" (*New World Writing*, 1962). The Brigadier sets out to determine the nature of the "enemy." He begins with interrogation, and when that doesn't work, takes to torture and murder; when they don't work, he disguises himself as Pathfinder and penetrates the "enemy" country. He has tried hating the prisoners and loving them, and even submitting to torture himself, "as if there might . . . be lurking in me an essential particle of their enemy's nature. . . ." But the war goes on, and he ends no closer to the truth. Even when he investigates the fact that "in certain respects we come to resemble the enemy," he got no hint of a solution. Paranoia has seldom had a more telling literary expression. As Norman Mailer has said, "the seed of paranoia is the arrival of the conviction that the truth about oneself is never told."

The Brigadier

We have been fighting the enemy a very long time. So long that I, who entered the war as a foot soldier, have had time to receive more than the usual number of decorations and promotions and to become a brigadier, attached to staff headquarters. I forget how many times I have been wounded and the names of all the battles and campaigns in which I have participated. The greater number of them, however, are not to be forgotten: Striplitz, Bougaumères, Trèle, Bzelokhorets, Kovinitsa, Laud Ingaume, El Khabhar, Woozi-Fassam, and so on. I am the oldest man in our field office, though not in the brigade itself. Lately, the newcomers have not been rising from the ranks, but from the Academy. They are young men who have not proved themselves in any way; some have not even fought.

I am settled into my work, which for many years, I am pleased to say, has been of an absorbing nature. It is difficult to recall the time when I fretted with impatience to return to what I considered my natural life as a citizen. I am happy that I am no longer impatient. I have developed, instead, a great eagerness—an eagerness, however, which is thoroughly disciplined and in every way related to our military enterprise. I do not hesitate to call our enterprise the most glorious and far-reaching that has ever been undertaken.

Far-reaching is not quite the word—though it is only in an unofficial capacity that I admit as much. Let me say that it is not the word for me to use. As a matter, simply, of objective fact, what we are engaged in is, of course, that—I mean far-reaching—and much else besides. But for myself it is not enough, and the work I do must be otherwise defined. I have been studying the ends of our warfare while pursuing them; I have tried to make them a part of myself. I should not want it to be said that the Objective is one thing, and the brigadier's effort in its behalf is quite another, not related to it as the word one and the number one are related. My work is the war itself.

The office in which I do my work was once a schoolhouse; it stands in what used to be enemy country. A section of blackboard, cracked down the middle, is still affixed to the wall near my desk and on it you can read a lesson in the enemy's language, written by one of his children; when the chalk began to fade, I had it carefully restored and covered with a coat of shellac. I can read the enemy's hand—which is sometimes difficult even for scholars, as the script is spidery and irregular and varies not only with the dialect but with the very temperament of the writer. The broken lines read: ". . . of the cat and the dog? What will she . . .;" here the first line ends, broken off at the jagged edge of the board. "We," runs the second line, "know that the . . . [several words are obliterated] while the bird was singing. . . ." The third and last line: ". . . is what we all love. It makes us very happy." I like to imagine, although I know this is nothing but a child's exercise, that these broken lines, could I only complete them, would tell me more about the enemy than all the work of our specialists combined. As for my subordinates, I have led them to believe that these scraps of writing have something to do with logistics—which is all they care about.

The benches, the charts, the books and other blackboards of the schoolhouse have long since been removed. The rooms are now occupied by sturdy desks of our

From *Alpha and Omega* by Isaac Rosenfeld. Copyright © 1966 by the Estate of Isaac Rosenfeld. All rights reserved. Reprinted by permission of The Viking Press, Inc.

own design, developed during the war, and the walls are lined with filing cabinets and hung with maps of the region. The sides of the house have been reinforced against blast with sandbags, and the windows have been covered with interesting strips of wire and tape which, when the sun is right, cast patterns of shadow upon our papers. If there were nothing else to do, it would be a pleasure to trace some of these patterns. The glass—these are the enemy's original panes—is very bright and clear. The enemy is known for the quality of his glass works. A strange people.

Our office is a relay station among the various fronts. The position of the fronts has grown so complicated through the years, that I never attempt to give our location with reference to the lines of battle. We are well in the center of one circle of fighting, on the periphery of a second, and connected by a long tangent with a third. From time to time our position appears enveloped, and we pack our papers, dismantle our immobile equipment, and prepare to retreat. Subsequent intelligence, however, informs us that the first reports, owing to the complexity of the warfare, were erroneous in many respects and that, far from being encircled, our position may be described as part of an arc thrown round the enemy's flank. The lines of battle, the longer I study them, seem to me more and more like the arms of many embracing bodies.

It is our general purpose, but not my specific task, to supply logistical information to headquarters in the front and in the rear. We are one of a number of stations that co-ordinate the numerous reports both of the enemy's movements and of our own, and relay these back and forth. These reports never fail to conflict with one another, and no matter how well trained our spies, pilots, observers, and scouts may be, we must keep a large staff working round the clock to prevent mistakes, repetitions, and inconsistencies from appearing in our dispatches. Even so we have blundered many times, and our only consolation, and at the same time the reason that reprimands from headquarters have not been more severe, is the fact that the enemy must work under the same disadvantages. Very often a report so complicated and contradictory that it seems impossible to submit, is nevertheless a true picture of the fighting. You can see what we are up against. And then there are the many spontaneous breakdowns of routine for which no one is to blame, the impatience of my superiors which is always interfering with the work, the orders handed down from above, countermanding orders that have already been carried out, and so many other difficulties that are part of the day's normal detail. To make matters worse a training class for scouts is held in the basement of our schoolhouse and we often hear them laughing or crying out in pain as they tumble about on the mats. I have been trying to get this class removed, thus far without success.

My own work developed as a subsidiary of the main logistical operation. My superiors are not yet convinced of the importance of my task (I have been at it for eleven years!), but some of them are interested, and all my equals and subordinates support me in it, so I am not required to give up my investigations. I work in a semiofficial capacity, filling in and sending out my own reports and as much corroborative material as I can lay my hands on—all this in addition to my regular duties. I am kept very busy indeed, seldom working less than sixteen hours at a stretch. I sometimes think, sitting as I do in an old schoolhouse, that I am both schoolmaster and pupil: a teacher to those who are beneath me in rank and an idiot child to my superiors.

I work on the enemy proper. I am trying to discover what he is, what motivates him, what his nature is. And if you say, as so many of my superiors do, that this is known, I reply that I am attacking his very essence. This is not known. In spite of the many long years that we have been at war with him, and the periods of time, in the past, when we lived at his side in restless peace, we know nothing of him that is really worth knowing and that must be known. I myself am convinced that victory will be impossible until we gain this knowledge—and it is precisely to this knowledge that I am devoting my life.

What do we know? The enemy is darker than we, and shorter in stature. His language, as I have indicated, has nothing in common with our own; his religion is an obscenity to all of us who have not made a specialty of studying it. Well then, as I say, he is shorter and darker, two positive facts. His language, though it would be too much trouble to go into it here, is of such and such a kind—a third fact—and his religion is this, that and the other thing, which gives us still another fact. So much we know. Still, what is he?

I have gone many times to the camps and hospitals in the rear to interview the prisoners we have taken. It teaches me nothing, but I nevertheless make my regular visits, and just the other week I returned from one of our hospitals. There was the usual sight in the wards; I am hardened to it. (And yet, almost as if to test myself, I try to recall what I have seen. Am I absolutely hardened?) There were the lightly wounded, their personalities not distorted by pain, and the natural qualities of these men could be observed: their churlishness, stupidity, sullenness, or good nature. They are much like our own soldiers, especially in their boredom. I spoke with them, I took my usual sampling—so many boys (as with our own troops, eleven-year-olds are not uncommon), so many youths, so many of the middle-aged, so many old men, old campaigners. The usual questions, the usual answers—home, parents, occupation, the government, women, disease, God, the purpose of the war, of life, of history, etc. There is nothing to be learned here that we don't already know. Then the wards of the severely wounded—the amputations, the blinded, the infected. The stench is the same as our own stench (the hospital orderlies deny this, maintaining that the enemy's is worse!). The ones with fever have fever, though their skins and eyes show it differently from ours. The delirious rave, the chilled shiver, the poisoned vomit and groan. There are outcries, the usual hysteria, weeping, coughing, and hemorrhage. One lies in a coma, the stump of his leg is gangrenous, it is too late, he cannot be saved. Another soldier has nearly every bone in his body broken: he has both his thighs in traction, a broken back, a broken arm, his skull wound in bandages. Can he be said to suffer either more or less than one of our own men in similar circumstances, or in any way differently from him? I attend an operation—it is the same thing over and over again. The mental casualties in their guarded ward are no different from ours. Some in straightjackets, strapped to their beds, some screaming, some colorless, lifeless, forever immobile. Here and there a dead body, not yet removed. I lift the sheet; the face is already puffed up. The shock of it is gone, and I can no longer remember what it actually used to be like. I poke a finger into a puffy cheek, leaving a depression which takes a long time to fill up again. It is the same death as our own.

I go to the hospitals, though I learn nothing there, and I go to the prison camps, also in vain. Once I had myself incarcerated, disguised as an enemy soldier. I slept with the men in their barracks, ate with them, studied them, was soon infested with the same lice. I was involved in a plan to escape, of which I informed our guards. No one saw through my disguise, and I, in turn, failed to see through the undisguised men and learned nothing. In fact, the few weeks I spent in prison camp were extremely discouraging, for if the gap between the enemy and ourselves is so small that I can pose, undetected, as one of his men, why is it that I can't cross over to him?

I have even suspected my project of a subtle treason. By "cross over to him," I mean of course, "cross the gulf that separates us from knowledge of his true nature." Now I know where I stand in this regard and it no longer troubles me; but at one time I feared that the second expression really meant nothing more than the first and I thought surely that my whole ambition was only to desert to the enemy. Perhaps he fascinated me in the precise sense of attraction, drawing me, through my desire to know, closer and closer to his side. My conscience drove me to my superior, Major General Box. He believes in my project and follows my reports with interest. The General reassured me; it is his opinion that we are all drawn to the enemy, particularly in such a long war, and that the enemy is drawn to us. In certain respects we even begin to resemble each other. But this is only natural, and has nothing to do with my project, which, far from being treason, remains the most important of the war.

I was reassured, but was soon taken with a fresh disquietude. A suggestion that the General had made, without meaning to do so, set me on a new course of activity. The General had said that in certain respects we come to resemble the enemy. What are these respects? Perhaps the knowledge that I was seeking really lay in myself? The resemblance to the enemy might have grown so strong in my case, that it was my own nature I would have to know in order to know his. I took a leave from the service, the only one I have had in the entire campaign, and spent a month in one of the enemy's mountain villages that had been captured by our troops. I lived away from the men, attended only by goats which forage high up among the rocks in this region. I had a hut to myself, and all the mountains necessary to a great introspection. But I learned nothing, nothing that I did not already know.

It was when I returned to active service that I began the most desperate work that I have as yet undertaken. I selected a group of twenty prisoners, all young, sturdy, healthy men. I lived with them until I grew to know them well; some were like my own sons, and one in particular, a peasant boy named Reri, I will say that I loved. I spent long hours out of doors with my companions, joined them in races and various sports, their own as well as ours. We went on long camping and fishing trips about the country, and I developed so great a trust in them that I even provided them with firearms and let them hunt with me. Evenings, when we were not camping under the open sky, we entertained ourselves in my lodge, drinking, playing cards or chess, listening to music, or holding the most intimate conversations—conversations and confidences that verged on love. We became very intimate; there has never been a group of men whom I have known or loved so well, never a youth as my Reri for whom I have had such a close and tender feeling. It was above all with Reri that I carried on my desperate yet gentle work; I strove to know him as completely as one man can ever hope to know another, and something in his response to me, perhaps an intuitive comprehension of my motive, promised that my effort would be rewarded. He was a handsome boy, taller than the average among the enemy, and fairer in color and complexion. Certainly one such as his could be known, a face as open as his could not long conceal the secrets of the inner nature. Often when I was not with him I would picture his face to myself, trusting that a chance moment of insight might reveal him, and therefore his whole people, to me. And I studied his image, sketching him and taking many photographs while he sat patiently before me. (I have kept these sketches and photographs, and look at them from time to time as I once looked at the living Reri. His image still saddens and perplexes me.) So, with all my companions, I engaged in an unceasing search after friendship and understanding, hoping that love would teach me what I was determined to know.

But my ultimate means were not to be gentle, and when I failed again I had to resort, with great reluctance, in shame and disgust, to the final means I had selected to attain my objective. As I had been their friend and lover and father, their teacher in the ways of our people and their pupil in the ways of theirs, so, at last, I became their torturer, hoping now to break them down and force them to yield what they had not been able to give freely. One day I ordered them whipped, the next, beaten; all of them, including Reri. I stood by, directing their tortures and noting their surprise, their hatred of me, their screams and their pleas for mercy. I could not help feeling that I had betrayed them; but my guilt only excited me the more and made me inflict always greater agony and humiliation upon them. It must have been guilt that was responsible for my extreme excitement, in the grip of which, while supervising the tortures, I would feel an overwhelming hatred of the enemy, and become convinced that my hatred had brought me so much farther than love, to the very brink of knowledge. When my companions died, I trained, in much the same manner, a new group, in which I included some of the enemy's women. The experiment was repeated. This time I did not spare myself, but submitted in their company to some of the same tortures, as if there might still be lurking in me an essential particle of their enemy's nature which was itself either capable of yielding the truth, or of preventing me from finding it. The experiment failed again. Again I learned nothing, nothing at all.

I still go to the wards and the camps, and from time to time I still conduct tortures. I have devised many other means of coping with my problem, some of them not yet tested. Over the years, I have grown hardened to failure: I more or less expect it now as an essential element of my work. But though I am hardened and toughened and experienced, I find that my work grows more and more difficult. Because of my interest in prisoners, new duties have been assigned to me. Recently negotiations for the exchange of prisoners broke down between the enemy and ourselves, and their number keeps piling up, as ours does in their camps; it is now my duty to arrange for their transportation to the interior. And then there are still the many administrative details of my department, to which I must somehow find time to attend; there are still the hazards and ever greater complications of our old war, which we have not yet won, and which, I have become absolutely certain, we will never win unless I succeed in my task. To know the enemy! It is the whole purpose and nature of our war, its ultimate meaning, its glory and its greatness. Already I have succeeded in my own character, for I have become my task in my whole being. Nothing comes between me and the work I do. I have triumphed in my character and in my person, but I must still triumph over the enemy. Sometimes I see his armies standing before me, clearly revealed in their dark, powerful mass, and I rush out of the schoolhouse, out of our office, and I feel that in a moment, but one moment more, I will know the truth. And when I hear our gunfire from the front that winds around us in all directions, I know that if my faith is only great enough, the knowledge will come to me and I will win.

Alain Robbe-Grillet (1922–   )

The fictional techniques and concerns of Alain Robbe-Grillet are an extension of his existential philosophy. According to Bruce Morrissette, the existential author "must, to express the content of consciousness, attach himself to objects, rejecting the verbiage of psychological analysis, ideological commentary, and omniscient rumination." This is what Robbe-Grillet does. His purpose is to render not concepts, or abstract thoughts, but percepts, or the sensory building blocks of experience. For some critics, he is the most original, innovative and influential exponent of "anti-realist" fiction.

His approach to point of view and narrative voice is at the heart of his fiction. He attempts to eliminate the narrative voice that analyzes, summarizes, and evaluates and that controls the reader's moral and psychological relation to the story. (See Introduction, p. 3.) By confining the reader to the character's sense impressions rendered as objectively as possible, he seeks to collapse the distance between the reader and the material of the story. The reader perceives not the character but what the character perceives. Personality (often sadomasochistic in Robbe-Grillet) must be inferred from the sense impressions. No motives, ideas, generalities, or values are allowed into the work. Even the action must be inferred from the recorded sensations of the actor. The reader is locked into the reality of the character. In discussing Robbe-Grillet's novel *Jealousy* (1959), Wayne Booth writes that

> The effect of such a novel is of an extended dramatic monologue, an intense expression of one quality of mind and soul, deliberately not judged, deliberately left unplaced, isolated from the rest of human experience. It is, thus, less closely related to the traditional forms of fiction than to lyric poetry.

Robbe-Grillet was born in Brest, France, in 1922. His first occupation was as an agronomist, and from this perhaps he learned the skills of minute observation we see in his work. He abandoned agronomy for literature, and his first novel, *The Erasers,* appeared in 1953. In 1961, his film script "Last Year at Marienbad" was produced by Resnais and became an instant controversy. It was as startling and inaccessible to many viewers as his novels and stories have been to many readers. But it, like the fiction, forged new possibilities of aesthetic excitement and meaning. Some themes reappear throughout his work: psychosadism, uncertainty, accident.

The story we have included in this volume is a rendering of three children walking along the beach, a common setting for Robbe-Grillet who grew up on the Breton seacoast. The reader is placed at the center of a sensuous awareness that is focused on the children. Everything is rendered sharply and objectively: the tracks the children leave in the sand, the recurrent waves, the birds circling, the bell. Robbe-Grillet has eliminated all except the external objects. Yet there remains a sinister element, an unspoken threat as the awareness relentlessly tracks the children.

The Shore

Three children are walking along a beach. They walk side by side, holding each other by the hand. They are about the same height, and probably the same age: about twelve. The one in the center, nevertheless, is slightly shorter than the other two.

From Alain Robbe-Grillet, *Snapshots,* translated by Bruce Morrissette, Copyright © 1968 by Grove Press. Reprinted by permission of Grove Press, Inc.

Except for these three children, the long shore is empty. The band of sand is fairly wide, unbroken, free of scattered rocks and water holes, sloping gently from the steep cliff, which seems unending, to the sea.

The weather is fine. The sun illuminates the yellow sand with a violent, vertical light. There is not a single cloud in the sky. Nor is there any wind. The water is blue, calm, without a trace of a swell coming in from the distance, although the beach faces the open sea and the horizon.

But at regular intervals, a quick wave, always the same, originating a few yards from the shore, suddenly rises and immediately breaks, always along the same line. The water does not seem to move forward, and then rush back; it is rather as if the whole movement occurred in a stationary position. The swelling of the water produces first a shallow trough, along the side next to the shore, and the wave draws back slightiy, with a rustling noise of gravel rolling; then it bursts and spreads milkily over the slope of the beach's edge, but only to recover the space which it had lost. At most, a stronger surge rises, here and there, to moisten, for a moment, a few extra inches of sand.

And all is again motionless, the sea, flat and blue, stationary at precisely the same height on the yellow sand of the beach, on which the three children walk side by side.

They are blond, and almost the same color as the sand: their skin a little darker, their hair a little lighter. All three are dressed in the same way, short trousers and sleeveless shirts, both of a faded thick blue cloth. They are walking side by side, holding each other by the hand, in a straight line, parallel to the sea and parallel to the cliff, almost equidistant between the two, yet a little closer to the water. The sun, now at the zenith, throws no shadow at their feet.

In front of them the sand is absolutely unmarked, yellow and smooth from the rock cliff to the water. The children walk forward in a straight line, at a constant pace, without the slightest movement to either side, calmly and holding each other by the hand. Behind them the sand, barely damp, is marked by three lines of footprints left by their bare feet, three regular series of similar and equally spaced prints, clearly hollowed out, and without a seam.

The children look straight ahead. They never glance at the high cliff, on their left, or at the sea, with its little waves breaking periodically, in the other direction. Nor, even more certainly, do they turn around to look behind them at the space which they have covered. They continue on their way with a rapid and uniform step.

In front of them, a flock of sea birds walk briskly along the shore, just at the edge of the waves. They move parallel with the children, in the same direction, about a hundred yards farther on. But, as the birds do not move as fast as they, the children gain upon them. And while the sea constantly wipes out the starry tracks of the birds, the children's footsteps remain clearly inscribed in the barely damp sand, in which the three lines of footsteps grow longer and longer.

The depth of these footprints is unchanging: a little less than an inch. They are not deformed either by a crumbling of the edges or by an excessively deep impression of the heel, or of the toe. They appear as if punched out by machine in an upper, and more malleable, crust of the beach.

Thus their triple line extends, always farther, and seems at the same time to grow narrower, to slow down, to blend into a single line, which separates the beach into two bands, throughout its length, and which comes to an end in a tiny mechanical movement, far off, occurring as if in a stationary position: the alternate lifting and setting down of six bare feet.

But as the bare feet move farther along, they gain upon the birds. Not only do they cover the ground rapidly, but the relative distance which separates the two groups diminishes even faster, compared with the space already covered. Soon there is only the gap of a few steps between them. . . .

But, when the children finally seem about to catch up with the birds, there is a flapping of wings as the birds take flight, first one, then two, then ten. . . . And the whole flock, white and gray, describes a curve above the sea as it returns to light upon the sand and begins to walk quickly again, always in the same direction, just at the edge of the waves, about a hundred yards farther on.

At this distance, the movements of the water are almost imperceptible, except for a sudden change in color, every ten seconds, at the moment when the dazzling foam shines in the sunlight.

Heedless of the footprints that they continue to press so precisely into the bare sand, indifferent to the little waves on their right, to the birds—now flying, now walking—that advance before them, the three blond children walk along side by side, with a rapid and uniform step, holding each other by the hand.

Their three sunburned faces, darker than their hair, look alike. They have the same expression: serious, thoughtful, perhaps concerned. Their features are also identical, although, obviously, two of the children are boys and the third a girl. The girl's hair is just a little longer, a little bit more curly, and her limbs appear a shade more slender. But her clothes are exactly the same: short trousers and sleeveless shirt, both of a faded thick blue cloth.

The girl is at the far right, next to the sea. At her left walks the boy who is slightly less tall. The other boy, nearest the cliff, is as tall as the girl.

Before them extends the smooth, unbroken sand, as far as the eye can see. On their left rises the wall of brown rock, almost vertical, and seemingly unending. On their right, motionless and blue out to the horizon, is the flat surface of the water, bordered by a sudden hem, which immediately bursts and spreads out in white foam.

Then, ten seconds later, the wave which wells up hollows out again the same shallow trough, on the side next to the beach, with a rustling noise of gravel rolling.

The tiny wave unfurls; the milky foam again climbs up the slope of sand, recovering the few inches of lost space. During the silence that follows, the tolling of a bell, from very far away, reverberates dimly in the quiet air.

"There's the bell," says the smallest of the children, the boy who is walking in the middle.

But the noise of the gravel sucked in by the sea muffles the weak echoes of the bell. Only at the end of the wave cycle can a few sounds, distorted by the distance, be heard again.

"It's the first bell," says the tall boy.

The tiny wave unfurls, on their right.

When silence returns, they hear nothing further. The three blond children still walk at the same regular pace, holding each other by the hand. In front of them the flock of birds, only a few steps away, is suddenly overcome by a contagious excitement. The birds flap their wings and fly upward.

They describe the same curve above the sea, and return to light upon the sand and begin to walk quickly again, always in the same direction, just at the edge of the waves, about a hundred yards farther on.

"Maybe it isn't the first," says the small boy, "maybe we didn't hear the other one, before. . . ."
"We would have heard it the same as this one," the tall boy answers.
The children have not in any way changed their pace; and the same footprints, behind them, continue to appear, as they walk forward, under the six bare feet.
"We weren't as near before," says the girl.
After a moment, the taller of the two boys, the one next to the cliff, says:
"We still aren't near."
And all three walk on in silence.
They remain silent thus until the bell, still just as faint, sounds again in the quiet air. The taller of the boys says then, "There's the bell." The others make no answer.
The birds, as the children are about to overtake them, flap their wings and fly upward, first one, then two, then ten. . . .
Then the whole flock is again back upon the sand, moving along the shore, about a hundred yards ahead of the children.
The sea continually wipes out the starry tracks left by their feet. The children, on the other hand, who are walking closer to the cliff, side by side, holding each other by the hand, leave behind them deep prints, in a triple line which stretches out parallel to the seashore, down the long beach.
On the right, near the edge of the motionless, flat water, and always at the same spot, the same small wave wells up and breaks.

Italo Calvino (1923–   )

Italo Calvino, one of the most innovative writers alive today, was born in Cuba of Italian parents—both scientists—who returned to their native Italy in 1925. Their scientific interests (agronomy and natural science) together with their political activism both found reflection in their son. During World War II Calvino interrupted his university studies at Turin to fight against the Nazis in a Partisan brigade, and first emerged as a writer in 1947 with *Il sentiero dei nidi di ragno* (*The Path of the Nest of Spiders*), a realistic account of some of his experiences. (In the same year he received his degree in Letters with a thesis on Joseph Conrad.) Besides his fiction writing he was active in politics, contributing regularly to the Communist journal *L'Unità* until he broke with the party in 1957. He was an editor for the Einaudi Press and a frequent contributor to *Botteghe Oscure, Officina, Nouvi Argomenti,* and other journals. But fiction was his forte, and after his first success Calvino turned from realism to fantasy, or rather to a unique blend of realism and fantasy that was to become Calvino's special signature. In 1952 he published the long story *La formica argentina* (translated by William Weaver in 1957 as *The Argentine Ant*), which Gore Vidal called "a masterpiece of twentieth century prose writing" and added: "It is also hideously funny." A comparable masterpiece is the story translated as "Smog"

(1958) which reveals, besides Calvino's great writing talent, his social awareness: at a time when most Italians were celebrating the Italian economic "miracle," Calvino was counting the cost in pollution of that industrial prosperity. His major work in the fifties was a mock-epic trilogy, *Il visconte dimezzato* (1952), *Il barone rampante* (1957), and *Il cavaliere inesistente* (1959), translated by Archibald Colquhon as *The Cloven Viscount* (1962), *The Baron in the Trees* (1959), and *The Nonexistent Knight* (1962). These are bizarre and brilliant fantasies. In *The Cloven Viscount,* for example, the Viscount is split in two, one half being utterly evil and the other utterly good, and both in love with Pamela. In one exchange the good half says, "Doing good together is the only way to love." Pamela replies: "A pity. I thought there were other ways." A volume of *Italian Fables* (*Fiabe italiane*) appeared in 1956, *t zero* in 1967, and his last volume, *Le città invisibili* (1972), appeared as *The Invisible City* in a translation by William Weaver in 1974.

But perhaps Calvino's greatest book is *Cosmicomiche* (1965), translated by Weaver as *Cosmicomics* (1968), from which "The Spiral" is taken. These twelve stories all deal with the creation of the universe and man and human society and are narrated by Qfwfq, a being who was miraculously *there* as the moon separated from the earth, as the dinosaurs died out, as the solar system was made, as the mollusks make their shells ("The Spiral"). Calvino's imagination enters these unknowns with brilliant inductiveness: but we sense that the force making it a thing of surpassing beauty (where there are no eyes to see) was, in some remote and nonverbal way, a force of love. Afterward came sight—"corneas and irises and pupils"—to see what evolution had made. Is this science fiction? It is far more than that. It is a great writer entering his imagination into the processes of life itself. Though Calvino has been compared with Borges and Robbe-Grillet, there is no one quite like him. He is, quite literally, fabulous and incomparable.

The Spiral

For the majority of mollusks, the visible organic form has little importance in the life of the members of a species, since they cannot see one another and have, at most, only a vague perception of other individuals and of their surroundings. This does not prevent brightly colored stripings and forms which seem very beautiful to our eyes (as in many gastropod shells) from existing independently of any relationship to visibility.

1

Like me, when I was clinging to that rock, you mean?—*Qfwfq asked,*—With the waves rising and falling, and me there, still, flat, sucking what there was to suck and thinking about it all the time? If that's the time you want to know about, there isn't much I can tell you. Form? I didn't have any; that is, I didn't know I had one, or rather I didn't know you *could* have one. I grew more or less on all sides, at random; if this is what you call radial symmetry, I suppose I had radial symmetry, but to tell you the truth I

"The Spiral" from *Cosmicomics*, by Italo Calvino, translated by William Weaver. Copyright © 1965 by Giulio Einaudi editore s.p.a. Torino; English translation copyright © 1968 by Harcourt Brace Jovanovich, Inc. and Jonathan Cape Ltd. Reprinted by permission of the publishers.

never paid any attention to it. Why should I have grown more on one side than on the other? I had no eyes, no head, no part of the body that was different from my other part; now I try to persuade myself that the two holes I had were a mouth and an anus, and that I therefore already had my bilateral symmetry, just like the trilobites and the rest of you, but in my memory I really can't tell those holes apart, I passed stuff from whatever side I felt like, inside or outside was the same, differences and repugnances came along much later. Every now and then I was seized by fantasies, that's true; for example, the notion of scratching my armpit, or crossing my legs, or once even of growing a mustache. I use these words here with you, to make myself clear; then there were many details I couldn't foresee: I had some cells, one more or less the same as another, and they all did more or less the same job. But since I had no form I could feel all possible forms in myself, and all actions and expressions and possibilities of making noises, even rude ones. In short, there were no limitations to my thoughts, which weren't thoughts, after all, because I had no brain to think them; every cell on its own thought every thinkable thing all at once, not through images, since we had no images of any kind at our disposal, but simply in that indeterminate way of feeling oneself there, which did not prevent us from feeling ourselves equally there in some other way.

It was a rich and free and contented condition, my condition at that time, quite the contrary of what you might think. I was a bachelor (our system of reproduction in those days didn't require even temporary couplings), healthy, without too many ambitions. When you're young, all evolution lies before you, every road is open to you, and at the same time you can enjoy the fact of being there on the rock, flat mollusk-pulp, damp and happy. If you compare yourself with the limitations that came afterwards, if you think of how having one form excludes other forms, of the monotonous routine where you finally feel trapped, well, I don't mind saying life was beautiful in those days.

To be sure, I lived a bit withdrawn into myself, that's true, no comparison with our interrelated life nowadays; and I'll also admit that—partly because of my age and partly under the influence of my surroundings—I was what they call a narcissist to a slight extent; I mean I stayed there observing myself all the time, I saw all my good points and all my defects, and I liked myself for the former and for the latter; I had no terms of comparison, you must remember that, too.

But I wasn't so backward that I didn't know something else existed beyond me: the rock where I clung, obviously, and also the water that reached me with every wave, but other stuff, too, farther on: that is, the world. The water was a source of information, reliable and precise: it brought me edible substances which I absorbed through all my surface, and other inedible ones which still helped me form an idea of what there was around. The system worked like this: a wave would come, and I, still sticking to the rock, would raise myself up a little bit, imperceptibly—all I had to do was loosen the pressure slightly—and, splat the water passed beneath me, full of substances and sensations and stimuli. You never knew how those stimuli were going to turn out, sometimes a tickling that made you die laughing, other times a shudder, a burning, an itch; so it was a constant seesaw of amusement and emotion. But you mustn't think I just lay there passively, dumbly accepting everything that came: after a while I had acquired some experience and I was quick to analyze what sort of stuff was arriving and to decide how I should behave, to make the best use of it or to avoid the more unpleasant consequences. It was all a kind of game of contractions, with each of the cells I had, or of relaxing at the right moment: and I could make my choices, reject, attract, even spit.

And so I learned that there were *the others,* the element surrounding me was filled with traces of them, *others* hostile and different from me or else disgustingly similar. No, now I'm giving you a disagreeable idea of my character, which is all wrong. Naturally, each of us went about on his own business, but the presence of the *others* reassured me, created an inhabited zone around me, freed me from the fear of being an alarming exception, which I would have been if the fact of existing had been my fate alone, a kind of exile.

So I knew that some of the *others* were female. The water transmitted a special vibration, a kind of brrrum brrrum brrrum, I remember when I became aware of it the first time, or rather, not the first, I remember when I became aware of being aware of it as a thing I had always known. At the discovery of these vibrations' existence, I was seized with a great curiosity, not so much to see them, or to be seen by them either— since, first, we hadn't any sight, and secondly, the sexes weren't yet differentiated, each individual was identical with every other individual and at looking at one or another I would have felt no more pleasure than in looking at myself—but a curiosity to know whether something would happen between me and them. A desperation filled me, a desire not to do anything special, which would have been out of place, knowing that there was nothing special to do, or nonspecial either, but to respond in some way to that vibration with a corresponding vibration, or rather, with a personal vibration of my own, because, sure enough, there was something there that wasn't exactly the same as the other, I mean now you might say it came from hormones, but for me it was very beautiful.

So then, one of them, shlup shlup shlup, emitted her eggs, and I, shlup shlup shlup, fertilized them: all down inside the sea, mingling in the water tepid from the sun; oh, I forgot to tell you, I could feel the sun, which warmed the sea and heated the rock.

One of them, I said. Because, among all those female messages that the sea slammed against me like an indistinct soup at first where everything was all right with me and I grubbed about paying no attention to what one was like or another, suddenly I understood what corresponded best to my tastes, tastes which I hadn't known before that moment, of course. In other words, I had fallen in love. What I mean is: I had begun to recognize, to isolate the signs of one of those from the others, in fact I waited for these signs I had begun to recognize, I sought them, responded to those signs I awaited with other signs I made myself, or rather it was I who aroused them, these signs from her, which I answered with other signs of my own, I mean I was in love with her and she with me, so what more could I want from life?

Now habits have changed, and it already seems inconceivable to you that one could love a female like that, without having spent any time with her. And yet, through that unmistakable part of her still in solution in the sea water, which the waves placed at my disposal, I received a quantity of information about her, more than you can imagine: not the superficial, generic information you get now, seeing and smelling and touching and hearing a voice, but essential information, which I could then develop at length in my imagination. I could think of her with minute precision, thinking not so much of how she was made, which would have been a banal and vulgar way of thinking of her, but of how from her present formlessness she would be transformed into one of the infinite possible forms, still remaining herself, however. I didn't imagine the forms that she might assume, but I imagined the special quality that, in taking them, she would give to those forms.

I knew her well, in other words. And I wasn't sure of her. Every now and then I was overcome with suspicion, anxiety, rage. I didn't let anything show, you know my character, but beneath that impassive mask passed suppositions I can't bring myself to confess even now. More than once I suspected she was unfaithful to me, that she sent messages not only to me but also to others; more than once I thought I had intercepted one, or that I had discovered a tone of insincerity in a message addressed to me. I was jealous, I can admit it now, not so much out of distrust of her as out of unsureness of myself: who could assure me that she had really understood who I was? Or that she had understood the fact that I was? This relationship achieved between us thanks to the sea water—a full, complete relationship, what more could I ask for?— was for me something absolutely personal, between two unique and distinct individualities; but for her? Who could assure me that what she might find in me she hadn't also found in another, or in another two or three or ten or a hundred like me? Who could assure me that her abandon in our shared relations wasn't an indiscriminate abandon, slapdash, a kind of—who's next?—collective ecstasy?

The fact that these suspicions did not correspond to the truth was confirmed, for me, by the subtle, soft, private vibration, at times still trembling with modesty, in our correspondences; but what if, precisely out of shyness and inexperience, she didn't pay enough attention to my characteristics and others took advantage of this innocence to worm their way in? And what if she, a novice, believed it was still I and couldn't distinguish one from the other, and so our most intimate play was extended to a circle of strangers . . .?

It was then that I began to secrete calcareous matter. I wanted to make something to mark my presence in an unmistakable fashion, something that would defend this individual presence of mine from the indiscriminate instability of all the rest. Now it's no use my piling up words, trying to explain the novelty of this intention I had; the first word I said is more than enough: *make,* I wanted to *make,* and considering the fact that I had never made anything or thought you could make anything, this in itself was a big event. So I began to make the first thing that occurred to me, and it was a shell. From the margin of that fleshy cloak on my body, using certain glands, I began to give off secretions which took on a curving shape all around, until I was covered with a hard and variegated shield, rough on the outside and smooth and shiny inside. Naturally, I had no way of controlling the form of what I was making: I just stayed there all huddled up, silent and sluggish, and I secreted. I went on even after the shell covered my whole body; I began another turn; in short, I was getting one of those shells all twisted into a spiral, which you, when you see them, think are so hard to make, but all you have to do is keep working and giving off the same matter without stopping, and they grow like that, one turn after the other.

Once it existed, this shell was also a necessary and indispensable place to stay inside of, a defense for my survival; it was a lucky thing I had made it, but while I was making it I had no idea of making it because I needed it; on the contrary, it was like when somebody lets out an exclamation he could perfectly well not make, and yet he makes it, like "Ha" or "hmph!," that's how I made the shell: simply to express myself. And in this self-expression I put all the thoughts I had about her, I released the anger she made me feel, my amorous way of thinking about her, my determination to exist for her, the desire for me to be me, and for her to be her, and the love for myself that

I put in my love for her—all the things that could be said only in that conch shell wound into a spiral.

At regular intervals the calcareous matter I was secreting came out colored, so a number of lovely stripes were formed running straight through the spirals, and this shell was a thing different from me but also the truest part of me, the explanation of who I was, my portrait translated into a rhythmic system of volumes and stripes and colors and hard matter, and it was the portrait of her as she was, because at the same time she was making herself a shell identical to mine and without knowing it I was copying what she was doing and she without knowing it was copying what I was doing, and all the others were copying all the others, so we would be back where we had been before except for the fact that in saying these shells were the same I was a bit hasty, because when you looked closer you discovered all sorts of little differences that later on might become enormous.

So I can say that my shell made itself, without my taking any special pains to have it come out one way rather than another, but this doesn't mean that I was absent-minded during that time; I applied myself, instead, to that act of secreting, without allowing myself a moment's distraction, never thinking of anything else, or rather: thinking always of something else, since I didn't know how to think of the shell, just as, for that matter, I didn't know how to think of anything else either, but I accompanied the effort of making the shell with the effort of thinking I was making something, that is anything: that is, I thought of all the things it would be possible to make. So it wasn't even a monotonous task, because the effort of thinking which accompanied it spread toward countless types of thoughts which spread, each one, toward countless types of actions that might each serve to make countless things, and making each of these things was implicit in making the shell grow, turn after turn . . .

2

(And so now, after five hundred million years have gone by, I look around and, above the rock, I see the railway embankment and the train passing along it with a party of Dutch girls looking out of the window and, in the last compartment, a solitary traveler reading Herodotus in a bilingual edition, and the train vanishes into the tunnel under the highway, where there is a sign with the pyramids and the words "VISIT EGYPT," and a little ice-cream wagon tries to pass a big truck laden with installments of Rh-Stijl, a periodical encyclopedia that comes out in paperback, but then it puts its brakes on because its visibility is blocked by a cloud of bees which crosses the road coming from a row of hives in a field from which surely a queen bee is flying away, drawing behind her a swarm in the direction opposite to the smoke of the train, which has reappeared at the other end of the tunnel, so you can see hardly anything thanks to the cloudy stream of bees and coal smoke, except a few yards farther up there is a peasant breaking the ground with his mattock and, unaware, he brings to light and reburies a fragment of a Neolithic mattock similar to his own, in a garden that surrounds an astronomical observatory with its telescopes aimed at the sky and on whose threshold the keeper's daughter sits reading the horoscopes in a weekly whose cover displays the face of the star of Cleopatra: I see all this and I feel no amazement because making the shell implied also making the honey in the wax comb and the coal and the telescopes and the reign of Cleopatra and the films about Cleopatra and the pyramids and the design of the zodiac of the Chaldean astrologers and the wars and empires Herodotus speaks of and the words written by Herodotus and the works written in all languages including those of Spinoza in Dutch and the fourteen-line summary of Spino-

za's life and works in the installment of the encyclopedia in the truck passed by the ice-cream wagon, and so I feel as if, in making the shell, I had also made the rest.

I look around, and whom am I looking for? She is still the one I seek; I've been in love for five hundred million years, and if I see a Dutch girl on the sand with a beachboy wearing a gold chain around his neck and showing her the swarm of bees to frighten her, there she is: I recognize her from her inimitable way of raising one shoulder until it almost touches her cheek, I'm almost sure, or rather I'd say absolutely sure if it weren't for a certain resemblance that I find also in the daughter of the keeper of the observatory, and in the photograph of the actress made up as Cleopatra, or perhaps in Cleopatra as she really was in person, for what part of the true Cleopatra they say every representation of Cleopatra contains, or in the queen bee flying at the head of the swarm with that forward impetuousness, or in the paper woman cut out and pasted on the plastic windshield of the little ice-cream wagon, wearing a bathing suit like the Dutch girl on the beach now listening over a little transistor radio to the voice of a woman singing, the same voice that the encyclopedia truck driver hears over his radio, and the same one I'm now sure I've heard for five million years, it is surely she I hear singing and whose image I look for all around, seeing only gulls volplaning on the surface of the sea where a school of anchovies glistens and for a moment I am certain I recognize her in a female gull and a moment later I suspect that instead she's an anchovy, though she might just as well be any queen or slave-girl named by Herodotus or only hinted at in the pages of the volume left to mark the seat of the reader who has stepped into the corridor of the train to strike up a conversation with the party of Dutch tourists; I might say I am in love with each of those girls and at the same time I am sure of being in love always with her alone.

And the more I torment myself with love for each of them, the less I can bring myself to say to them: "Here I am!," afraid of being mistaken and even more afraid that she is mistaken, taking me for somebody else, for somebody who, for all she knows of me, might easily take my place, for example the beachboy with the gold chain, or the director of the observatory, or a gull, or a male anchovy, or the reader of Herodotus, or Herodotus himself, or the vendor of ice cream, who has come down to the beach along a dusty road among the prickly pears and is now surrounded by the Dutch girls in their bathing suits, or Spinoza, or the truck driver who is transporting the life and works of Spinoza summarized and repeated two thousand times, or one of the drones dying at the bottom of the hive after having fulfilled his role in the continuation of the species.)

3

. . . Which doesn't mean that the shell wasn't, first and foremost, a shell, with its particular form, which couldn't be any different because it was the very form I had given it, the only one I could or would give it. Since the shell had a form, the form of the world was also changed, in the sense that now it included the form of the world as it had been without a shell plus the form of the shell.

And that had great consequences: because the waving vibrations of light, striking bodies, produce particular effects from them, color first of all, namely, that matter I used to make stripes with which vibrated in a different way from the rest; but there was also the fact that a volume enters into a special relationship of volumes with other volumes, all phenomena I couldn't be aware of, though they existed.

The shell in this way was able to create visual images of shells, which are things very similar—as far as we know—to the shell itself, except that the shell is here, whereas the images of it are formed elsewhere, possibly on a retina. An image therefore presupposes a retina, which in turn presupposes a complex system stemming from an encephalon. So, in producing the shell, I also produced its image—not one, of course, but many, because with one shell you can make as many shell-images as you want—but only potential images because to form an image you need all the requisites I mentioned before: an encephalon with its optic ganglia, and an optic nerve to carry the vibrations from outside to inside, and this optic nerve, at the other extremity, ends in something made purposely to see what there is outside, namely the eye. Now it's ridiculous to think that, having an encephalon, one would simply drop a nerve like a fishing line cast into the darkness; until the eyes crop up, one can't know whether there is something to be seen outside or not. For myself, I had none of this equipment, so I was the least authorized to speak of it; however, I had conceived an idea of my own, namely that the important thing was to form some visual images, and the eyes would come later in consequence. So I concentrated on making the part of me that was outside (and even the interior part of me that conditioned the exterior) give rise to an image, or rather to what would later be called a lovely image (when compared to other images considered less lovely, or rather ugly, or simply revoltingly hideous).

When a body succeeds in emitting or in reflecting luminous vibrations in a distinct and recognizable order—I thought—what does it do with these vibrations? Put them in its pocket? No, it releases them on the first passer-by. And how will the latter behave in the face of vibrations he can't utilize and which, taken in this way, might even be annoying? Hide his head in a hole? No, he'll thrust it out in that direction until the point most exposed to the optic vibrations becomes sensitized and develops the mechanism for exploiting them in the form of images. In short, I conceived of the eye-encephalon link as a kind of tunnel dug from the outside by the force of what was ready to become image, rather than from within by the intention of picking up any old image.

And I wasn't mistaken: even today I'm sure that the project—in its over-all aspect—was right. But my error lay in thinking that sight would also come to us, that is to me and to her. I elaborated a harmonious, colored image of myself to enter her visual receptivity, to occupy its center, to settle there, so that she could utilize me constantly, in dreaming and in memory, with thought as well as with sight. And I felt at the same time she was radiating an image of herself so perfect that it would impose itself on my foggy, backward senses, developing in me an interior visual field where it would blaze forth definitely.

So our efforts led us to become those perfect objects of a sense whose nature nobody quite knew yet, and which later became perfect precisely through the perfection of its object, which was, in fact, us. I'm talking about sight, the eyes; only I had failed to foresee one thing: the eyes that finally opened to see us didn't belong to us but to others.

Shapeless, colorless beings, sacks of guts stuck together carelessly, peopled the world all around us, without giving the slightest thought to what they should make of themselves, to how to express themselves and identify themselves in a stable, complete form, such as to enrich the visual possibilities of whoever saw them. They came and went, sank a while, then emerged, in that space between air and water and rock, wandering about absently; and we in the meanwhile, she and I and all those intent on squeezing out a form of ourselves, were there slaving away at our dark task. Thanks to us, that badly defined space became a visual field; and who reaped the benefit? These intruders, who had never before given a thought to the possibility of eyesight (ugly as they were, they wouldn't have gained a thing by seeing one another), these creatures who had always turned a deaf ear to the vocation of form. While we were bent over, doing the hardest part of the job, that is, creating something to be seen, they were quietly taking on the easiest part: adapting their lazy, embryonic receptive organs to what there was to receive; our images. And they needn't try telling me now that their job was toilsome too: from that gluey mess that filled their heads anything could have come out, and a photosensitive mechanism doesn't take all that much trouble to put together. But when it comes to perfecting it, that's another story! How can you, if you don't have visible objects to see, gaudy ones even, the kind that impose themselves on the eyesight? To sum it up in a few words: they developed eyes at our expense.

So sight, *our* sight, which we were obscurely waiting for, was the sight that the others had of us. In one way or another, the great revolution had taken place: all of a sudden, around us, eyes were opening, and corneas and irises and pupils: the swollen, colorless eye of polyps and cuttlefish, the dazed and gelatinous eyes of bream and mullet, the protruding and peduncled eyes of crayfish and lobsters, the bulging and faceted eyes of flies and ants. A seal now comes forward, black and shiny, winking little eyes like pinheads. A snail extends ball-like eyes at the end of long antennae. The inexpressive eyes of the gull examine the surface of the water. Beyond a glass mask the frowning eyes of an underwater fisherman explore the depths. Through the lens of a spyglass a sea captain's eyes and the eyes of a woman bathing converge on my shell, then look at each other, forgetting me. Framed by far-sighted lenses I feel on me the far-sighted eyes of a zoologist, trying to frame me in the eye of a Rolleiflex. At that moment a school of tiny anchovies, barely born, passes before me, so tiny that in each little white fish it seems there is room only for the eye's black dot, and it is a kind of eye-dust that crosses the sea.

All these eyes were mine. I had made them possible; I had had the active part; I furnished them the raw material, the image. With eyes had come all the rest, so everything that the others, having eyes, had become, their every form and function, and the quantity of things that, thanks to eyes, they had managed to do, in their every form and function, came from what I had done. Of course, they were not just casually implicit in my being there, in my having relations with others, male and female, et cetera, in my setting out to make a shell, et cetera. In other words, I had foreseen absolutely everything.

And at the bottom of each of those eyes I lived, or rather another me lived, one of the images of me, and it encountered the image of her, the most faithful image of her, in that beyond which opens, past the semiliquid sphere of the irises, in the darkness of the pupils, the mirrored hall of the retinas, in our true element which extends without shores, without boundaries.

William Gass (1924–   )

William Gass was born in Fargo, North Dakota. He attended Kenyon College, Ohio Wesleyan, and finally Cornell University, where he received his Ph.D. His stories have appeared in numerous publications, including *The Best American Short Stories* of 1959, 1961, and 1962. A recipient of both a Rockefeller Grant in 1967 and a Guggenheim Fellowship in 1969, he is at present Professor of Philosophy at Washington University in St. Louis, Missouri. His other publications include *Omensetter's Luck* (1966), a widely praised first novel; *Willie Masters' Lonesome Wife* (1968); and a collection of critical essays called *Fiction and the Figures of Life* (1970), which Gass himself describes "as the work of a novelist insufficiently off duty."

The book for which the following story serves as title piece (though it is placed at the end) appeared in 1968 and consists of a collection of two novellas and three short stories. We are in the presence of a poet-narrator who is "in retirement from love," and our experience of the story is one of *overhearing* him as he comments variously on the limitations, constrictions, and frustrations of life in the "vacant and barren and loveless . . . heart of the country." Like the speaker in Yeats's "Sailing to Byzantium," he too has "sailed the seas and come . . . to B. . . ." But what kind of a Byzantium has he come to? Is it like the timeless, ideal realm that Yeats envisions, a world of singing-masters, of "sages standing in God's holy fire," "of hammered gold and gold enamelling," a world of art, unsubject to decay, so perfected and spiritualized that it releases us from the flux and decay of natural life? No, it is a gray world:

> The sides of the buildings, the roofs, the limbs of the trees are gray. Streets, sidewalks, faces, feelings—they are gray. Speech is gray, and the grass where it shows. Every flank and front, each top is gray. Everything is gray: hair, eyes, window glass, the hawkers' bills and touters' posters, lips, teeth, poles and metal signs—they're gray, quite gray.

The author wants us to feel the sad discrepancy between his drab and cheerless B, and the world of life and vitality to which art—and men who are alive to art—aspire. (If we just happen to know that Gass was a professor at the University of Indiana at Bloomington when he wrote the piece, the irony is doubled.)

But surely the Midwestern meadows can't be all that bad. They have to be better than "the slums, the cities, and the crowds." Oh, the speaker seems to say, is that what you think? "Come into the country, then. The air nimbly and sweetly recommends itself unto our gentle senses." The words are those of King Duncan as he arrives at Macbeth's castle at Inverness:

> This castle hath a pleasant seat; the air
> Nimbly and sweetly recommends itself
> Unto our gentle senses.

For Duncan, Inverness will be a place where his "gentle senses" will be violently extinguished, and those who come as guests to Gass's place will discover another kind of death—in life.

But what of the people who live in B? Aren't they "close to the land, . . . good companions to the soil"? Do they not "live in harmony with the alternating seasons," like the innocent but noble rustics of the pastoral tradition? Aren't those farmer-citizens, descendants of remote Arcadian hillsides, in intimate touch with the spirit and mystery of the life process itself? Not so: all that is "a lie of old poetry":

> The modern husbandman uses chemicals from cylinders and sacks, spike-ball-and-claw machines, metal sheds, and cost accounting.

> Nature in the old sense does not matter. It does not exist. Our farmer's
> only mystical attachment is to parity.

For "mystical," read imaginative, spiritual.

Gass's writing is brilliantly precise. He knows, as Jack Richardson wrote
in a review, "as well as any writer I've read the secret of freezing a character
in an attitude of mortality that is forever memorable; he knows, too, how to
make objects and nature cluster about his people until they are all active on
the page." He does not set out to prove something. He simply builds his town,
its citizens, their attitudes, and in so doing *creates* the experience he is talking
about.

Finally, the heart is not only the Midwestern heartland. There is another
heart present in the story. It is, to quote Richardson once more,

> that of the narrator, a poet, alone in a house with memories of a de-
> parted lover. His passions work in counterpoint to the town's, their very
> human, sensual base opposed to the mass angers and suspicions of the
> Midwest. This juxtaposition, helping to etch his subject more clearly,
> also creates the sort of tension that one finds, oddly enough, in a spy
> novel; for, after a while, one begins to feel that the narrator is indeed a
> secret agent in alien territory, and should the inhabitants discover what
> lay in his heart, they might rip it out between halves of the high-school
> basketball game.

In the Heart of the Heart of the Country

A PLACE

SO I HAVE sailed the seas and come . . .

to B . . .

a small town fastened to a field in Indiana. Twice there have been twelve hundred
people here to answer to the census. The town is outstandingly neat and shady, and
always puts its best side to the highway. On one lawn there's even a wood or plastic
iron deer.

You can reach us by crossing a creek. In the spring the lawns are green, the
forsythia is singing, and even the railroad that guts the town has straight bright rails
which hum when the train is coming, and the train itself has a welcome horning sound.

Down the back streets the asphalt crumbles into gravel. There's Westbrook's,
with the geraniums, Horsefall's, Mott's. The sidewalk shatters. Gravel dust rises like
breath behind the wagons. And I am in retirement from love.

WEATHER

In the Midwest, around the lower Lakes, the sky in the winter is heavy and close, and
it is a rare day, a day to remark on, when the sky lifts and allows the heart up. I am
keeping count, and as I write this page, it is eleven days since I have seen the sun.

"In the Heart of the Heart of the Country" from *In The Heart of the Heart of the Country* by William H.
Gass. Copyright © 1967 by William H. Gass. By permission of Harper & Row, Publishers, Inc.

MY HOUSE

There's a row of headless maples behind my house, cut to free the passage of electric wires. High stumps, ten feet tall, remain, and I climb these like a boy to watch the country sail away from me. They are ordinary fields, a little more uneven than they should be, since in the spring they puddle. The top-soil's thin, but only moderately stony. Corn is grown one year, soybeans another. At dusk starlings darken the single tree—a larch—which stands in the middle. When the sky moves, fields move under it. I feel, on my perch, that I've lost my years. It's as though I were living at last in my eyes, as I have always dreamed of doing, and I think then I know why I've come here: to see, and so to go out against new things—oh god how easily—like air in a breeze. It's true there are moments—foolish moments, ecstasy on a tree stump—when I'm all but gone, scattered I like to think like seed, for I'm the sort now in the fool's position of having love left over which I'd like to lose; what good is it now to me, candy ungiven after Halloween?

A PERSON

There are vacant lots on either side of Billy Holsclaw's house. As the weather improves, they fill with hollyhocks. From spring through fall, Billy collects coal and wood and puts the lumps and pieces in piles near his door, for keeping warm is his one work. I see him most often on mild days sitting on his doorsill in the sun. I notice he's squinting a little, which is perhaps the reason he doesn't cackle as I pass. His house is the size of a single garage, and very old. It shed its paint with its youth, and its boards are a warped and weathered gray. So is Billy. He wears a short lumpy faded black coat when it's cold, otherwise he always goes about in the same loose, grease-spotted shirt and trousers. I suspect his galluses were yellow once, when they were new.

WIRES

These wires offend me. Three trees were maimed on their account, and now these wires deface the sky. They cross like a fence in front of me, enclosing the crows with the clouds. I can't reach in, but like a stick, I throw my feelings over. What is it that offends me? I am on my stump, I've built a platform there and the wires prevent my going out. The cut trees, the black wires, all the beyond birds therefore anger me. When I've wormed through a fence to reach a meadow, do I ever feel the same about the field?

THE CHURCH

The church has a steeple like the hat of a witch, and five birds, all doves, perch in its gutters.

MY HOUSE

Leaves move in the windows. I cannot tell you yet how beautiful it is, what it means. But they do move. They move in the glass.

POLITICS

. . . for all those not in love.

I've heard Batista described as a Mason. A farmer who'd seen him in Miami made this claim. He's as nice a fellow as you'd ever want to meet. Of Castro, of course, no one speaks.

For all those not in love there's law: to rule . . . to regulate . . . to rectify. I cannot write the poetry of such proposals, the poetry of politics, though sometimes—often— always now—I am in that uneasy peace of equal powers which makes a State; then I communicate by passing papers, proclamations, orders, through my bowels. Yet I was not a State with you, nor were we both together any Indiana. A squad of Pershing Rifles at the moment, I make myself Right Face! Legislation packs the screw of my intestines. Well, king of the classroom's king of the hill. You used to waddle when you walked because my sperm between your legs was draining to a towel. Teacher, poet, folded lover—like the politician, like those drunkards, ill, or those who faucet-off while pissing heartily to preach upon the force and fullness of that stream, or pause from vomiting to praise the purity and passion of their puke—I chant, I beg, I orate, I command, I sing—

> Come back to Indiana—not too late!
> (Or will you be a ranger to the end?)
> Good-bye . . . Good-bye . . . oh, I shall always wait
> You, Larry, traveler—stranger, son,—my friend—

my little girl, my poem by heart, my self, my childhood.

But I've heard Batista described as a Mason. That dries up my pity, melts my hate. Back from the garage where I have overheard it, I slap the mended fender of my car to laugh, and listen to the metal stinging tartly in my hand.

PEOPLE

Their hair in curlers and their heads wrapped in loud scarves, young mothers, fattish in trousers, lounge about in the speedwash, smoking cigarettes, eating candy, drinking pop, thumbing magazines, and screaming at their children above the whir and rumble of the machines.

At the bank a young man freshly pressed is letting himself in with a key. Along the street, delicately teetering, many grandfathers move in a dream. During the murderous heat of summer, they perch on window ledges, their feet dangling just inside the narrow shelf of shade the store has made, staring steadily into the street. Where their consciousness has gone I can't say. It's not in the eyes. Perhaps it's diffuse, all temperature and skin, like an infant's, though more mild. Near the corner there are several large overalled men employed in standing. A truck turns to be weighed on the scales at the Feed and Grain. Images drift on the drugstore window. The wind has blown the smell of cattle into town. Our eyes have been driven in like the eyes of the old men. And there's no one to have mercy on us.

VITAL DATA

There are two restaurants here and a tearoom. two bars. one bank. three barbers, one with a green shade with which he blinds his window. two groceries. a dealer in Fords. one drug, one hardware, and one appliance store. several that sell feed, grain, and farm equipment. an antique shop. a poolroom. a laundromat. three doctors. a dentist. a plumber. a vet. a funeral home in elegant repair the color of a buttercup. numerous beauty parlors which open and shut like night-blooming plants. a tiny dime and department store of no width but several floors. a hutch, homemade, where you can order, after lying down or squirming in, furniture that's been fashioned from bent lengths of stainless tubing, glowing plastic, metallic thread, and clear shellac. an American Legion Post and a root beer stand. little agencies for this and that: cosmetics, brushes, insurance, greeting cards and garden produce—anything—sample shoes—which do their business out of hats and satchels, over coffee cups and dissolving sugar. a factory for making paper sacks and pasteboard boxes that's lodged in an old brick building bearing the legend OPERA HOUSE, still faintly golden, on its roof. a library given by Carnegie. a post office. a school. a railroad station. fire station. lumberyard. telephone company. welding shop. garage . . . and spotted through the town from one end to the other in a line along the highway, gas stations to the number five.

EDUCATION

In 1833, Colin Goodykoontz, an itinerant preacher with a name from a fairytale, summed up the situation in one Indiana town this way:
Ignorance and her squalid brood. A universal dearth of intellect. Total abstinence from literature is very generally practiced. . . . There is not a scholar in grammar or geography, or a *teacher capable of instructing* in them, to my knowledge. . . . Others are supplied a few months of the year with the most antiquated & unreasonable forms of teaching reading, writing & cyphering. . . . Need I stop to remind you of the host of loathsome reptiles such a stagnant pool is fitted to breed! Croaking jealousy; bloated bigotry; coiling suspicion; wormish blindness; crocodile malice!
Things have changed since then, but in none of the respects mentioned.

BUSINESS

One side section of street is blocked off with sawhorses. Hard, thin, bitter men in blue jeans, cowboy boots and hats, untruck a dinky carnival. The merchants are promoting themselves. There will be free rides, raucous music, parades and coneys, pop, popcorn, candy, cones, awards and drawings, with all you can endure of pinch, push, bawl, shove, shout, scream, shriek, and bellow. Children pedal past on decorated bicycles, their wheels a blur of color, streaming crinkled paper and excited dogs. A little later there's a pet show for a prize—dogs, cats, birds, sheep, ponies, goats—none of which wins. The whirlabouts whirl about. The Ferris wheel climbs dizzily into the sky as far as a tall man on tiptoe might be persuaded to reach, and the irritated operators measure the height and weight of every child with sour eyes to see if they are safe for the machines. An electrical megaphone repeatedly trumpets the names of the generous sponsors. The following day they do not allow the refuse to remain long in the street.

MY HOUSE, THIS PLACE AND BODY

I have met with some mischance, wings withering, as Plato says obscurely, and across the breadth of Ohio, like heaven on a table, I've fallen as far as the poet, to the sixth sort of body, this house in B, in Indiana, with its blue and gray bewitching windows, holy magical insides. Great thick evergreens protect its entry. And I live *in.*
    Lost in the corn rows, I remember feeling just another stalk, and thus this country takes me over in the way I occupy myself when I am well . . . completely—to the edge of both my house and body. No one notices, when they walk by, that I am brimming

in the doorways. My house, this place and body, I've come in mourning to be born in. To anybody else it's pretty silly: love. Why should I feel a loss? How am I bereft? She was never mine; she was a fiction, always a golden tomgirl, barefoot, with an adolescent's slouch and a boy's taste for sports and fishing, a figure out of Twain, or worse, in Riley.[1] Age cannot be kind.

There's little hand-in-hand here . . . not in B. No one touches except in rage. Occasionally girls will twine their arms about each other and lurch along, school out, toward home and play. I dreamed my lips would drift down your back like a skiff on a river. I'd follow a vein with the point of my finger, hold your bare feet in my naked hands.

THE SAME PERSON

Billy Holsclaw lives alone—how alone it is impossible to fathom. In the post office he talks greedily to me about the weather. His head bobs on a wild flood of words, and I take this violence to be a measure of his eagerness for speech. He badly needs a shave, coal dust has layered his face, he spits when he speaks, and his fingers pick at his tatters. He wobbles out in the wind when I leave him, a paper sack mashed in the fold of his arm, the leaves blowing past him, and our encounter drives me sadly home to poetry—where there's no answer. Billy closes his door and carries coal or wood to his fire and closes his eyes, and there's simply no way of knowing how lonely and empty he is or whether he's as vacant and barren and loveless as the rest of us are—here in the heart of the country.

WEATHER

For we're always out of luck here. That's just how it is—for instance in the winter. The sides of the buildings, the roofs, the limbs of the trees are gray. Streets, sidewalks, faces, feelings—they are gray. Speech is gray, and the grass where it shows. Every flank and front, each top is gray. Everything is gray: hair, eyes, window glass, the hawkers' bills and touters' posters, lips, teeth, poles and metal signs—they're gray, quite gray. Cars are gray. Boots, shoes, suits, hats, gloves are gray. Horses, sheep, and cows, cats killed in the road, squirrels in the same way, sparrows, doves, and pigeons, all are gray, everything is gray, and everyone is out of luck who lives here.

A similar haze turns the summer sky milky, and the air muffles your head and shoulders like a sweater you've got caught in. In the summer light, too, the sky darkens a moment when you open your eyes. The heat is pure distraction. Steeped in our fluids, miserable in the folds of our bodies, we can scarcely think of anything but our sticky parts. Hot cyclonic winds and storms of dust crisscross the country. In many places, given an indifferent push, the wind will still coast for miles, gathering resource and edge as it goes, cunning and force. According to the season, paper, leaves, field litter, seeds, snow, fill up the fences. Sometimes I think the land is flat because the winds have leveled it, they blow so constantly. In any case, a gale can grow in a field of corn that's as hot as a draft from hell, and to receive it is one of the most dismaying experiences of this life, though the smart of the same wind in winter is more humiliating, and in that sense even worse. But in the spring it rains as well, and the trees fill with ice.

[1] James Whitcomb Riley (1849-1916), often called "the Hoosier poet."

PLACE

Many small Midwestern towns are nothing more than rural slums, and this community could easily become one. Principally during the first decade of the century, though there were many earlier instances, well-to-do farmers moved to town and built fine homes to contain them in their retirement. Others desired a more social life, and so lived in, driving to their fields like storekeepers to their businesses. These houses are now dying like the bereaved who inhabit them; they are slowly losing their senses—deafness, blindness, forgetfulness, mumbling, an insecure gait, an uncontrollable trembling has overcome them. Some kind of Northern Snopes[2] will occupy them next: large-familied, Catholic, Democratic, scrambling, vigorous, poor; and since the parents will work in larger, nearby towns, the children will be loosed upon themselves and upon the hapless neighbors much as the fabulous Khan loosed his legendary horde. These Snopes will undertake makeshift repairs with materials that other people have thrown away; paint halfway round their house, then quit; almost certainly maintain an ugly loud cantankerous dog and underfeed a pair of cats to keep the rodents down. They will collect piles of possibly useful junk in the back yard, park their cars in the front, live largely leaning over engines, give not a hoot for the land, the old community, the hallowed ways, the established clans. Weakening widow ladies have already begun to hire large rude youths from families such as these to rake and mow and tidy the grounds they will inherit.

PEOPLE

In the cinders at the station boys sit smoking steadily in darkened cars, their arms bent out the windows, white shirts glowing behind the glass. Nine o'clock is the best time. They sit in a line facing the highway—two or three or four of them—idling their engines. As you walk by a machine may growl at you or a pair of headlights flare up briefly. In a moment one will pull out, spinning cinders behind it, to stalk impatiently up and down the dark streets or roar half a mile into the country before returning to its place in line and pulling up.

MY HOUSE, MY CAT, MY COMPANY

I must organize myself. I must, as they say, pull myself together, dump this cat from my lap, stir—yes, resolve, move, do. But do what? My will is like the rosy dustlike light in this room: soft, diffuse, and gently comforting. It lets me do . . . anything . . . nothing. My ears hear what they happen to; I eat what's put before me; my eyes see what blunders into them; my thoughts are not thoughts, they are dreams. I'm empty or I'm full . . . depending; and I cannot choose. I sink my claws in Tick's fur and scratch the bones of his back until his rear rises amorously. Mr. Tick, I murmur, I must organize myself. I must pull myself together. And Mr. Tick rolls over on his belly, all ooze.

I spill Mr. Tick when I've rubbed his stomach. Shoo. He steps away slowly, his long tail rhyming with his paws. How beautifully he moves, I think; how beautifully, like you, he commands his loving, how beautifully he accepts. So I rise and wander

---

[2] Reference to Abner Snopes, a character in Faulkner's fiction. A man of low tastes and origins, he was a ruthless "climber."

from room to room, up and down, gazing through most of my forty-one windows. How well this house receives its loving too. Let out like Mr. Tick, my eyes sink in the shrubbery. I am not here; I've passed the glass, passed second-story spaces, flown by branches, brilliant berries, to the ground, grass high in seed and leafage every season; and it is the same as when I passed above you in my aged, ardent body; it's, in short, a kind of love; and I am learning to restore myself, my house, my body, by paying court to gardens, cats, and running water, and with neighbors keeping company.

Mrs. Desmond is my right-hand friend; she's eighty-five. A thin white mist of hair, fine and tangled, manifests the climate of her mind. She is habitually suspicious, fretful, nervous. Burglars break in at noon. Children trespass. Even now they are shaking the pear tree, stealing rhubarb, denting lawn. Flies caught in the screens and numbed by frost awake in the heat to buzz and scrape the metal cloth and frighten her, though she is deaf to me, and consequently cannot hear them. Boards creak, the wind whistles across the chimney mouth, drafts cruise like fish through the hollow rooms. It is herself she hears, her own flesh failing, for only death will preserve her from those daily chores she climbs like stairs, and all that anxious waiting. It is now, she wonders. No? Then: is it now?

We do not converse. She visits me to talk. My task to murmur. She talks about her grandsons, her daughter who lives in Delphi, her sister or her husband—both gone—obscure friends—dead—obscurer aunts and uncles—lost—ancient neighbors, members of her church or of her clubs—passed or passing on; and in this way she brings the ends of her life together with a terrifying rush: she is a girl, a wife, a mother, widow, all at once. All at once—appalling—but I believe it; I wince in expectation of the clap. Her talk's a fence—a shade drawn, window fastened, door that's locked—for no one dies taking tea in a kitchen; and as her years compress and begin to jumble, I really believe in the brevity of life; I sweat in my wonder; death is the dog down the street, the angry gander, bedroom spider, goblin who's come to get her; and it occurs to me that in my listening posture I'm the boy who suffered the winds of my grandfather with an exactly similar politeness, that I am, right now, all my ages, out in elbows, as angular as badly stacked cards. Thus was I, when I loved you, every man I could be, youth and child—far from enough—and you, so strangely ambiguous a being, met me, heart for spade, play after play, the whole run of our suits.

Mr. Tick, you do me honor. You not only lie in my lap, but you remain alive there, coiled like a fetus. Through your deep nap, I feel you hum. You are, and are not, a machine. You are alive, alive exactly, and it means nothing to you—much to me. You are a cat—you cannot understand—you are a cat so easily. Your nature is not something you must rise to. You, not I, live in: in house, in skin, in shrubbery. Yes. I think I shall hat my head with a steeple: turn church; devour people. Mr. Tick, though, has a tail he can twitch, he need not fly his Fancy. Claws, not metrical schema, poetry his paws; while smoothing . . . smoothing . . . smoothing roughly, his tongue laps its neatness. O Mr. Tick, I know you; you are an electrical penis. Go on now, shoo. Mrs. Desmond doesn't like you. She thinks you will tangle yourself in her legs and she will fall. You murder her birds, she knows, and walk upon her roof with death in your jaws. I must gather myself together for a bound. What age is it I'm at right now, I wonder. The heart, don't they always say, keeps the true time. Mrs. Desmond is knocking. Faintly, you'd think, but she pounds. She's brought me a cucumber. I believe she believes I'm a woman. Come in, Mrs. Desmond, thank you, be my company, it looks lovely, and have tea. I'll slice it, crisp, with cream, for luncheon, each slice as thin as me.

POLITICS

O all ye isolate and separate powers, Sing! Sing, and sing in such a way that from a distance it will seem a harmony, a Strindberg play, a friendship ring . . . so happy—happy, happy, happy—as here we go hand in handling, up and down. Our union was a singing, though we were silent in the songs we sang like single notes are silent in a symphony. In no sense sober, we barbershopped together and never heard the discords in our music or saw ourselves as dirty, cheap, or silly. Yet cats have worn out better shoes than those thrown through our love songs at us. Hush. Be patient—prudent—politic. Still, Cleveland killed you, Mr. Crane. Were you not politic enough and fond of being beaten? Like a piece of sewage, the city shat you from its stern three hundred miles from history—beyond the loving reach of sailors. Well, I'm not a poet who puts Paris to his temple in his youth to blow himself from Idaho, or—fancy that—Missouri. My god, I said, this my country, but must my country go so far as Terre Haute or Whiting, go so far as Gary?

When the Russians first announced the launching of their satellite, many people naturally refused to believe them. Later others were outraged that they had sent a dog around the earth. I wouldn't want to take that mutt from out that metal flying thing if he's still living when he lands, our own dog catcher said; anybody knows you shut a dog up by himself to toss around the first thing he'll be setting on to do you let him out is bite somebody.

This Midwest. A dissonance of parts and people, we are a consonance of Towns. Like a man grown fat in everything but heart, we overlabor; our outlook never really urban, never rural either, we enlarge and linger at the same time, as Alice both changed and remained in her story. You are blond. I put my hand upon your belly; feel it tremble from my trembling. We always drive large cars in my section of the country. How could you be a comfort to me now?

MORE VITAL DATA

The town is exactly fifty houses, trailers, stores, and miscellaneous buildings long, but in places no streets deep. It takes on width as you drive south, always adding to the east. Most of the dwellings are fairly spacious farm houses in the customary white, with wide wraparound porches and tall narrow windows, though there are many of the grander kind—fretted, scalloped, turreted, and decorated with clapboards set at angles or on end, with stained-glass windows at the stair landings and lots of wrought iron full of fancy curls—and a few of these look like castles in their rarer brick. Old stables serve as garages now, and the lots are large to contain them and the vegetable and flower gardens which, ultimately widows plant and weed and then entirely disappear in. The shade is ample, the grass is good, the sky a glorious fall violet; the apple trees are heavy and red, the roads are calm and empty; corn has sifted from the chains of tractored wagons to speckle the streets with gold and with the russet fragments of the cob, and a man would be a fool who wanted, blessed with this, to live anywhere else in the world.

EDUCATION

Buses like great orange animals move through the early light to school. There the children will be taught to read and warned against Communism. By Miss Janet Jakes. That's not her name. Her name is Helen something—Scott or James. A teacher twenty years. She's now worn fine and smooth, and has a face, Wilfred says, like a mail-order ax. Her voice is hoarse, and she has a cough. For she screams abuse. The children stare, their faces blank. This is the thirteenth week. They are used to it. You will all, she shouts, you will all draw pictures of me. No. She is a Mrs.—someone's missus. And in silence they set to work while Miss Jakes jabs hairpins in her hair. Wilfred says an ax, but she has those rimless tinted glasses, graying hair, an almost dimpled chin. I must concentrate. I must stop making up things. I must give myself to life; let it mold me: that's what they say in *Wisdom's Monthly Digest* every day. Enough, enough— you've been at it long enough; and the children rise formally a row at a time to present their work to her desk. No, she wears rims; it's her chin that's dimpleless. Well, it will take more than a tablespoon of features to sweeten that face. So she grimly shuffles their sheets, examines her reflection crayoned on them. I would not dare . . . allow a child . . . to put a line around me. Though now and then she smiles like a nick in the blade, in the end these drawings depress her. I could not bear it—how can she ask?— that anyone . . . draw me. Her anger's lit. That's why she does it: flame. There go her eyes; the pink in her glasses brightens, dims. She is a pumpkin, and her rage is breathing like the candle in. No, she shouts, no—the cartoon trembling—no, John Mauck, John Stewart Mauck, this will not do. The picture flutters from her fingers. You've made me too muscular.

I work on my poetry. I remember my friends, associates, my students, by their names. Their names are Maypop, Dormouse, Upsydaisy. Their names are Gladiolus, Callow Bladder, Prince and Princess Oleo, Hieronymus, Cardinal Mummum, Mr. Fitchew, The Silken Howdah, Spot. Sometimes you're Tom Sawyer, Huckleberry Finn; it is perpetually summer; your buttocks are my pillow; we are adrift on a raft; your back is our river. Sometimes you are Major Barbara, sometimes a goddess who kills men in battle, sometimes you are soft like a shower of water; you are bread in my mouth.

I do not work on my poetry. I forget my friends, associates, my students, and their names: Gramophone, Blowgun, Pickle, Serenade . . . Marge the Barge, Arena, Uberhaupt . . . Doctor Dildoe, The Fog Machine. For I am now in B, in Indiana: out of job and out of patience, out of love and time and money, out of bread and out of body, in a temper, Mrs. Desmond, out of tea. So shut your fist up, bitch, you bag of death; go bang another door; go die, my dearie. Die, life-deaf old lady. Spill your breath. Fall over like a frozen board. Gray hair grows from the nose of your mind. You are a skull already—*memento mori*—the foreskin retracts from your teeth. Will your plastic gums last longer than your bones, and color their grinning? And is your twot still hazel-hairy, or are you bald as a ditch? . . . bitch . . . . . . bitch . . . . bitch. I wanted to be famous, but you bring me age—my emptiness. Was it *that* which I thought would balloon me above the rest? Love? where are you? . . . love me. I want to rise so high, I said, that when I shit I won't miss anybody.

BUSINESS

For most people, business is poor. Nearby cities have siphoned off all but a neighborhood trade. Except for feed and grain and farm supplies, you stand a chance to sell only what one runs out to buy. Chevrolet has quit, and Frigidaire. A locker plant has left its afterimage. The lumberyard has been, so far, six months about its going. Gas stations change hands clumsily, a restaurant becomes available, a grocery closes. One day they came and knocked the cornices from the watch repair and pasted campaign posters on the windows. Torn across, by now, by boys, they urge you still to vote for half an orange beblazoned man who as a whole one failed two years ago to win at his election. Everywhere, in this manner, the past speaks, and it mostly speaks of failure. The empty stores, the old signs and dusty fixtures, the debris in alleys, the flaking paint and rusty gutters, the heavy locks and sagging boards: they say the same disagreeable things. What do the sightless windows see, I wonder, when the sun throws a passerby against them? Here a stair unfolds toward the street—dark, rickety, and treacherous— and I always feel, as I pass it, that if I just went carefully up and turned the corner at the landing, I would find myself out of the world. But I've never had the courage.

THAT SAME PERSON

The weeds catch up with Billy. In pursuit of the hollyhocks, they rise in coarse clumps all around the front of his house. Billy has to stamp down a circle by his door like a dog or cat does turning round to nest up, they're so thick. What particularly troubles me is that winter will find the weeds still standing stiff and tindery to take the sparks which Billy's little mortarless chimney spouts. It's true that fires are fun here. The town whistle, which otherwise only blows for noon (and there's no noon on Sunday), signals the direction of the fire by the length and number of its blasts, the volunteer firemen rush past in their cars and trucks, houses empty their owners along the street every time like an illustration in a children's book. There are many bikes, too, and barking dogs, and sometimes—halleluiah—the fire's right here in town—a vacant lot of weeds and stubble flaming up. But I'd rather it weren't Billy or Billy's lot or house. Quite selfishly I want him to remain the way he is—counting his sticks and logs, sitting on his sill in the soft early sun—though I'm not sure what his presence means to me . . . or to anyone. Nevertheless, I keep wondering whether, given time, I might not someday find a figure in our language which would serve him faithfully, and furnish his poverty and loneliness richly out.

WIRES

Where sparrows sit like fists. Doves fly the steeple. In mist the wires change perspective, rise and twist. If they led to you, I would know what they were. Thoughts passing often, like the starlings who flock these fields at evening to sleep in the trees beyond, would form a family of paths like this; they'd foot down the natural height of air to just about a bird's perch. But they do not lead to you.

> Of whose beauty it was sung
> She shall make the old man young.

They fasten me.

If I walked straight on, in my present mood, I would reach the Wabash. It's not a mood in which I'd choose to conjure you. Similes dangle like baubles from me. This time of year the river is slow and shallow, the clay banks crack in the sun, weeds surprise the sandbars. The air is moist and I am sweating. It's impossible to rhyme in this dust. Everything—sky, the cornfield, stump, wild daisies, my old clothes and pressless feelings—seem fabricated for installment purchase. Yes. Christ. I am suffering a summer Christmas; and I cannot walk under the wires. The sparrows scatter like handfuls of gravel. Really, wires are voices in thin strips. They are words wound in cables. Bars of connection.

WEATHER

I would rather it were the weather that was to blame for what I am and what my friends and neighbors are—we who live here in the heart of the country. Better the weather, the wind, the pale dying snow . . . the snow—why not the snow? There's never much really, not around the lower Lakes anyway, not enough to boast about, not enough to be useful. My father tells how the snow in the Dakotas would sweep to the roofs of the barns in the old days, and he and his friends could sled on the crust that would form because the snow was so fiercely driven. In Bemidji trees have been known to explode. That would be something—if the trees in Davenport or Francisville or Carbondale or Niles were to go blam some winter—blam! blam! blam! all the way down the gray, cindery, snow-sick streets.

A cold fall rain is blackening the trees or the air is like lilac and full of parachuting seeds. Who cares to live in any season but his own? Still I suspect the secret's in this snow, the secret of our sickness, if we could only diagnose it, for we are all dying like the elms in Urbana. This snow—like our skin it covers the country. Later dust will do it. Right now—snow. Mud presently. But it is snow without any laughter in it, a pale gray pudding thinly spread on stiff toast, and if that seems a strange description, it's accurate all the same. Of course soot blackens everything, but apart from that, we are never sufficiently cold here. The flakes as they come, alive and burning, we cannot retain, for if our temperatures fall, they rise promptly again, just as, in the summer, they bob about in the same feckless way. Suppose though . . . suppose they were to rise some August, climb and rise, and then hang in the hundreds like a hawk through December, what a desert we could make of ourselves—from Chicago to Cairo, from Hammond to Columbus—what beautiful Death Valleys.

PLACE

I would rather it were the weather. It drives us in upon ourselves—an unlucky fate. Of course there is enough to stir our wonder anywhere; there's enough to love, anywhere, if one is strong enough, if one is diligent enough, if one is perceptive, patient, kind enough—whatever it takes; and surely it's better to live in the country, to live on a prairie by a drawing of rivers, in Iowa or Illinois or Indiana, say, than in any city, in any stinking fog of human beings, in any blooming orchard of machines. It ought to be. The cities are swollen and poisonous with people. It ought to be better. Man has never been a fit environment for man—for rats, maybe, rats do nicely, or for dogs or cats and the household beetle.

And how long the street is, nowadays. These endless walls are fallen to keep back the tides of earth. Brick could be beautiful but we have covered it gradually with gray industrial vomits. Age does not make concrete genial, and asphalt is always—like America—twenty-one, until it breaks up in crumbs like stale cake. The brick, the asphalt, the concrete, the dancing signs and garish posters, the feed and excrement of the automobile, the litter of its inhabitants: they compose, they decorate, they line our streets, and there is nowhere, nowadays, our streets can't reach.

A man in the city has no natural thing by which to measure himself. His parks are potted plants. Nothing can live and remain free where he resides but the pigeon, starling, sparrow, spider, cockroach, mouse, moth, fly and weed, and he laments the existence of even these and makes his plans to poison them. The zoo? There *is* the zoo. Through its bars the city man stares at the great cats and dully sucks his ice. Living, alas, among men and their marvels, the city man supposes that his happiness depends on establishing, somehow, a special kind of harmonious accord with others. The novelists of the city, of slums and crowds, they call it love—and break their pens.

Wordsworth feared the accumulation of men in cities. He foresaw their "degrading thirst after outrageous stimulation," and some of their hunger for love. Living in a city, among so many, dwelling in the heat and tumult of incessant movement, a man's affairs are touch and go—that's all. It's not surprising that the novelists of the slums, the cities, and the crowds, should find that sex is but a scratch to ease a tickle, that we're most human when we're sitting on the john, and that the justest image of our life is in full passage through the plumbing.

> That man, immur'd in cities, still retains
> His inborn inextinguishable thirst
> Of rural scenes, compensating his loss
> By supplemental shifts, the best he may.

Come into the country, then. The air nimbly and sweetly recommends itself unto our gentle senses. Here, growling tractors tear the earth. Dust roils up behind them. Drivers sit jouncing under bright umbrellas. They wear refrigerated hats and steer by looking at the tracks they've cut behind them, their transistors blaring. Close to the land, are they? good companions to the soil? Tell me: do they live in harmony with the alternating seasons?

It's a lie of old poetry. The modern husbandman uses chemicals from cylinders and sacks, spike-ball-and-claw machines, metal sheds, and cost accounting. Nature in the old sense does not matter. It does not exist. Our farmer's only mystical attachment is to parity. And if he does not realize that cows and corn are simply different kinds of chemical engine, he cannot expect to make a go of it.

It isn't necessary to suppose our cows have feelings; our neighbor hasn't as many as he used to have either; but think of it this way a moment, you can correct for the human imputations later: how would it feel to nurse those strange tentacled calves with their rubber, glass, and metal lips, their stainless eyes?

PEOPLE

Aunt Pet's still able to drive her car—a high square Ford—even though she walks with difficulty and a stout stick. She has a watery gaze, a smooth plump face despite her age, and jet black hair in a bun. She has the slowest smile of anyone I ever saw, but she hates dogs, and not very long ago cracked the back of one she cornered in her garden. To prove her vigor she will tell you this, her smile breaking gently while she raises the knob of her stick to the level of your eyes.

HOUSE, MY BREATH AND WINDOW

My window is a grave, and all that lies within it's dead. No snow is falling. There's no haze. It is not still, not silent. Its images are not an animal that waits, for movement is no demonstration. I have seen the sea slack, life bubble through a body without a trace, its spheres impervious as soda's. Downwound, the whore at wagtag clicks and clacks. Leaves wiggle. Grass sways. A bird chirps, pecks the ground. An auto wheel in penning circles keeps its rigid spokes. These images are stones; they are memorials. Beneath this sea lies sea: god rest it . . . rest the world beyond my window, me in front of my reflection, above this page, my shade. Death is not so still, so silent, since silence implies a falling quiet, stillness a stopping, containing, holding in; for death is time in a clock, like Mr. Tick, electric . . . like wind through a windup poet. And my blear floats out to visible against the glass, befog its country and bespill myself. The mist lifts slowly from the fields in the morning. No one now would say: the Earth throws back its covers; it is rising from sleep. Why is the feeling foolish? The image is too Greek. I used to gaze at you so wantonly your body blushed. Imagine: wonder: that my eyes could cause such flowering. Ah, my friend, your face is pale, the weather cloudy; a street has been felled through your chin, bare trees do nothing, houses take root in their rectangles, a steeple stands up in your head. You speak of loving; then give me a kiss. The pane is cold. On icy mornings the fog rises to greet me (as you always did); the barns and other buildings, rather than ghostly, seem all the more substantial for looming, as if they grew in themselves while I watched (as you always did). Oh my approach, I suppose, was like breath in a rubber monkey. Nevertheless, on the road along the Wabash in the morning, though the trees are sometimes obscured by fog, their reflection floats serenely on the river, reasoning the banks, the sycamores in French rows. Magically, the world tips. I'm led to think that only those who grow down live (which will scarcely win me twenty-five from *Wisdom's Monthly Digest*), but I find I write that only those who live down grow; and what I write, I hold, whatever I really know. My every word's inverted, or reversed—or I am. I held you, too, that way. You were so utterly provisional, subject to my change. I could inflate your bosom with a kiss, disperse your skin with gentleness, enter your vagina from within, and make my love emerge like a fresh sex. The pane is cold. Honesty is cold, my inside lover. The sun looks, through the mist, like a plum on the tree of heaven, or a bruise on the slope of your belly. Which? The grass crawls with frost. We meet on this window, the world and I, inelegantly, swimmers of the glass; and swung wrong way round to one another, the world seems in. The world—how grand, how monumental, grave and deadly, that word is: the world, my house and poetry. All poets have their inside lovers. Wee penis does not belong to me, or any of this foggery. It is *his* property which he's thrust through what's womanly of me to set down this. These wooden houses in their squares, gray streets and fallen sidewalks, standing trees, your name I've written sentimentally across my breath into the whitening air, pale birds: they exist in me now because of him. I gazed with what intensity . . . A bush in the excitement of its roses could not have bloomed so beautifully as you did then. It was a look I'd like to give this page. For that is poetry: to bring within about, to change.

POLITICS

Sports, politics, and religion are the three passions of the badly educated. They are the Midwest's open sores. Ugly to see, a source of constant discontent, they sap the body's strength. Appalling quantities of money, time, and energy are wasted on them. The rural mind is narrow, passionate, and reckless on these matters. Greed, however short-sighted and direct, will not alone account for it. I have known men, for instance, who for years have voted squarely against their interests. Nor have I ever noticed that their surly Christian views prevented them from urging forward the smithereening, say, of Russia, China, Cuba, or Korea. And they tend to back their country like they back their local team: they have a fanatical desire to win; yelling is their forte; and if things go badly, they are inclined to sack the coach. All in all, then, Birch is a good name. It stands for the bigot's stick, the wild-child-tamer's cane.

Forgetfulness—is that their object?

Oh, I was new, I thought. A fresh start: new cunt, new climate, and new country—there you were, and I was pioneer, and had no history. That language hurts me, too, my dear. You'll never hear it.

FINAL VITAL DATA

The Modern Homemakers' Demonstration Club. The Prairie Home Demonstration Club. The Night-outers' Home Demonstration Club. the IOOF, FFF, VFW, WCTU, WSCS, 4-H, 40 and 8, Psi Iota Chi, and PTA. The Boy and Girl Scouts, Rainbows, Masons, Indians and Rebekah Lodge. Also the Past Noble Grand Club of the Rebekah Lodge. As well as the Moose and the Ladies of the Moose. The Elks, the Eagles, the Jaynettes and the Eastern Star. The Women's Literary Club, the Hobby Club, the Art Club, the Sunshine Society, the Dorcas Society, the Pythian Sisters, the Pilgrim Youth Fellowship, the American Legion, the American Legion Auxiliary, the American Legion Junior Auxiliary, the Gardez Club, the Bridge for Fun Club, the What-can-you-do? Club, the Get Together Club, the Coterie Club, the Worthwhile Club, the Let's Help Our Town Club, the No Name Club, the Forget-me-not Club, the Merry-go-round Club . . .

EDUCATION

Has a quarter disappeared from Paula Frosty's pocket book? Imagine the landscape of that face: no crayon could engender it; soft wax is wrong; thin wire in trifling snips might do the trick. Paul Frosty and Christopher Roger accuse the pale and splotchy Cheryl Pipes. But Miss Jakes, I *saw* her. Miss Jakes is so extremely vexed she snaps her pencil. What else is missing? I appoint you a detective, John: search her desk. Gum, candy, paper, pencils, marble, round eraser—whose? A thief. I can't watch her all the time, I'm here to teach. Poor pale fosseted[3] Cheryl, it's determined, can't return the money because she took it home and spent it. Cindy, Janice, John, and Pete—you four who sit around her—you will be detectives this whole term to watch her. A thief. In all my time. Miss Jakes turns, unfists, and turns again. I'll handle you, she cries. To think. A thief. In all my years. Then she writes on the blackboard the name of Cheryl Pipes and beneath that the figure twenty-five with a large sign for cents. Now Cheryl, she says, this won't be taken off until you bring that money out of home, out of home straight up to here, Miss Jakes says, tapping her desk.

Which is three days.

ANOTHER PERSON

I was raking leaves when Uncle Halley introduced himself to me. He said his name came from the comet, and that his mother had borne him prematurely in her fright of it. I thought of Hobbes, whom fear of the Spanish Armada had hurried into birth,[4]

---

[3] Submerged, in a hole.

[4] Thomas Hobbes (1588–1679), English philosopher who was born in the year and on the day that the Spanish Armada was repulsed by the British fleet.

and so I believed Uncle Halley to honor the philosopher, though Uncle Halley is a liar, and neither the one hundred twenty-nine nor the fifty-three he ought to be. That fall the leaves had burned themselves out on the trees, the leaf lobes had curled, and now they flocked noisily down the street and were broken in the wires of my rake. Uncle Halley was himself (like Mrs. Desmond and history generally) both deaf and implacable, and he shooed me down his basement stairs to a room set aside there for stacks of newspapers reaching to the ceiling, boxes of leaflets and letters and programs, racks of photo albums, scrapbooks, bundles of rolled-up posters and maps, flags and pennants and slanting piles of dusty magazines devoted mostly to motoring and the Christian ethic. I saw a bird cage, a tray of butterflies, a bugle, a stiff straw boater, and all kinds of tassels tied to a coat tree. He still possessed and had on display the steering lever from his first car, a linen duster, driving gloves and goggles, photographs along the wall of himself, his friends, and his various machines, a shell from the first war, a record of "Ramona" nailed through its hole to a post, walking sticks and fanciful umbrellas, shoes of all sorts (his baby shoes, their counters broken, were held in sorrow beneath my nose—they had not been bronzed, but he might have them done someday before he died, he said), countless boxes of medals, pins, beads, trinkets, toys, and keys (I scarcely saw—they flowed like jewels from his palms), pictures of downtown when it was only a path by the railroad station, a brightly colored globe of the world with a dent in Poland, antique guns, belt buckles, buttons, souvenir plates and cups and saucers (I can't remember all of it—I won't), but I recall how shamefully, how rudely, how abruptly, I fled, a good story in my mouth but death in my nostrils; and how afterward I busily, righteously, burned my leaves as if I were purging the world of its years. I still wonder if this town—its life, and mine now—isn't really a record like the one of "Ramona" that I used to crank around on my grandmother's mahogany Victrola through lonely rainy days as a kid.

THE FIRST PERSON

Billy's like the coal he's found: spilled, mislaid, discarded. The sky's no comfort. His house and his body are dying together. His windows are boarded. And now he's reduced to his hands. I suspect he has glaucoma. At any rate he can scarcely see, and weeds his yard of rubble on his hands and knees. Perhaps he's a surgeon cleansing a wound or an ardent and tactile lover. I watch, I must say, apprehensively. Like mine-war detectors, his hands graze in circles ahead of him. Your nipples were the color of your eyes. Pebble. Snarl of paper. Length of twine. He leans down closely, picks up something silvery, holds it near his nose. Foil? cap? coin? He has within him—what, I wonder? Does he know more now because he fingers everything and has to sniff to see? It would be romantic cruelty to think so. He bends the down on your arms like a breeze. You wrote me: something is strange when we don't understand. I write in return: I think when I loved you I fell to my death.

Billy, I could read to you from Beddoes[5] he's your man perhaps; he held with dying, freed his blood of its arteries; and he said that there were many wretched love-ill fools like me lying alongside the last bone of their former selves, as full of spirit and speech, nonetheless, as Mrs. Desmond, Uncle Halley and the Ferris wheel, Aunt Pet, Miss Jakes, Ramona or the megaphone; yet I reverse him finally, Billy, on no evidence but braggadocio, and I declare that though my inner organs were devoured long ago, the worm which swallowed down my parts still throbs and glows like a crystal palace.

[5] Thomas Lovell Beddoes (1803-1849), English poet and dramatist.

Yes, you were younger. I was Uncle Halley, the museum man and infrequent meteor. Here is my first piece of ass. They weren't so flat in those days, had more round, more juice. And over here's the sperm I've spilled, nicely jarred and clearly labeled. Look at this tape like lengths of intestine where I've stored my spew, the endless worm of words I've written, a hundred million emissions or more: oh I was quite a man right from the start; even when unconscious in my cradle, from crotch to cranium, I was erectile tissue; though mostly, after the manner approved by Plato, I had intercourse by eye. Never mind, old Holsclaw, you are blind. We pull down darkness when we go to bed; put out like Oedipus the actually offending organ, and train our touch to lies. All cats are gray, says Mr. Tick; so under cover of glaucoma you are sack gray too, and cannot be distinguished from a stallion.

I must pull myself together, get a grip, just as they say, but I feel spilled, bewildered, quite mislaid. I did not restore my house to its youth, but to its age. Hunting, you hitch through the hollyhocks. I'm inclined to say you aren't half the cripple I am, for there is nothing left of me but mouth. However, I resist the impulse. It is another lie of poetry. My organs are all there, though it's there where I fail—at the roots of my experience. Poet of the spiritual, Rilke,[6] weren't you? yet that's what you said. Poetry, like love, is—in and out—a physical caress. I can't tolerate any more of my sophistries about spirit, mind, and breath. Body equals being, and if your weight goes down, you are the less.

HOUSEHOLD APPLES

I knew nothing about apples. Why should I? My country came in my childhood, and I dreamed of sitting among the blooms like the bees. I failed to spray the pear tree too. I doubled up under them at first, admiring the sturdy low branches I should have pruned, and later I acclaimed the blossoms. Shortly after the fruit formed there were falls—not many—apples the size of goodish stones which made me wobble on my ankles when I walked about the yard. Sometimes a piece crushed by a heel would cling on the shoe to track the house. I gathered a few and heaved them over the wires. A slingshot would have been splendid. Hard, an unattractive green, the worms had them. Before long I realized the worms had them all. Even as the apples reddened, lit their tree, they were being swallowed. The birds preferred the pears, which were small— sugar pears I think they're called—with thick skins of graying green that ripen on toward violet. So the fruit fell, and once I made some applesause by quartering and paring hundreds; but mostly I did nothing, left them, until suddenly, overnight it seemed, in that ugly late September heat we often have in Indiana, my problem was upon me.

My childhood came in the country. I remember, now, the flies on our snowy luncheon table. As we cleared away they would settle, fastidiously scrub themselves and stroll to the crumbs to feed where I would kill them in crowds with a swatter. It was quite a game to catch them taking off. I struck heavily since I didn't mind a few stains; they'd wash. The swatter was a square of screen bound down in red cloth. It drove no air ahead of it to give them warning. They might have thought they'd flown head-long into a summered window. The faint pink dot where they had died did not rub out as I'd supposed, and after years of use our luncheon linen would faintly, pinkly, speckle.

[6] Rainer Maria Rilke (1875-1926), Austrian lyric poet and writer.

The country became my childhood. Flies braided themselves on the flypaper in my grandmother's house. I can smell the bakery and the grocery and the stables and the dairy in that small Dakota town I knew as a kid; knew as I dreamed I'd know your body, as I've known nothing, before or since; knew as the flies knew, in the honest, unchaste sense: the burned house, hose-wet, which drew a mist of insects like the blue smoke of its smolder, and gangs of boys, moist-lipped, destructive as its burning. Flies have always impressed me; they are so persistently alive. Now they were coating the ground beneath my trees. Some were ordinary flies; there were the large blue-green ones; there were swarms of fruit flies too, and the red-spotted scavenger beetle; there were a few wasps, several sorts of bees and butterflies—checkers, sulphurs, monarchs, commas, question marks—and delicate dragonflies . . . but principally houseflies and horseflies and bottleflies, flies and more flies in clusters around the rotting fruit. They loved the pears. Inside, they fed. If you picked up a pear, they flew, and the pear became skin and stem. They were everywhere the fruit was: in the tree still—apples like a hive for them—or where the fruit littered the ground, squashing itself as you stepped . . . there was no help for it. The flies droned, feasting on the sweet juice. No one could go near the trees; I could not climb; so I determined at last to labor like Hercules. There were fruit baskets in the barn. Collecting them and kneeling under the branches, I began to gather remains. Deep in the strong rich smell of the fruit, I began to hum myself. The fruit caved in at the touch. Glistening red apples, my lifting disclosed, had families of beetles, flies, and bugs, devouring their rotten undersides. There were streams of flies; there were lakes and cataracts and rivers of flies, seas and oceans. The hum was heavier, higher, than the hum of the bees when they came to the blooms in the spring, though the bees were there, among the flies, ignoring me— ignoring everyone. As my work went on and juice covered my hands and arms, they would form a sleeve, black and moving, like knotty wool. No caress could have been more indifferently complete. Still I rose fearfully, ramming my head in the branches, apples bumping against me before falling, bursting with bugs. I'd snap my hand sharply but the flies would cling to the sweet. I could toss a whole cluster into a basket from several feet. As the pear or apple lit, they would explosively rise, like monads for a moment, windowless, certainly, with respect to one another, sugar their harmony. I had to admit, though, despite my distaste, that my arm had never been more alive, oftener or more gently kissed. Those hundreds of feet were light. In washing them off, I pretended the hose was a pump. What have I missed? Childhood is a lie of poetry.

THE CHURCH

Friday night. Girls in dark skirts and white blouses sit in ranks and scream in concert. They carry funnels loosely stuffed with orange and black paper which they shake wildly, and small megaphones through which, as drilled, they direct and magnify their shouting. Their leaders, barely pubescent girls, prance and shake and whirl their skirts above their bloomers. The young men, leaping, extend their arms and race through puddles of amber light, their bodies glistening. In a lull, though it rarely occurs, you can hear the squeak of tennis shoes against the floor. Then the yelling begins again, and then continues; fathers, mothers, neighbors joining in to form a single pulsing ululation—a cry of the whole community—for in this gymnasium each body becomes the bodies beside it, pressed as they are together, thigh to thigh, and the same shudder runs through all of them, and runs toward the same release. Only the ball moves serenely through this dazzling din. Obedient to law it scarcely speaks but caroms quietly and lives at peace.

BUSINESS

It is the week of Christmas and the stores, to accommodate the rush they hope for, are remaining open in the evening. You can see snow falling in the cones of the street lamps. The roads are filling—undisturbed. Strings of red and green lights droop over the principal highway, and the water tower wears a star. The windows of the stores have been bedizened. Shamelessly they beckon. But I am alone, leaning against a pole—no . . . there is no one in sight. They're all at home, perhaps by their instruments, tuning in on their evenings, and like Ramona, tirelessly playing and replaying themselves. There's a speaker perched in the tower, and through the boughs of falling snow and over the vacant streets, it drapes the twisted and metallic strains of a tune that can barely be distinguished—yes, I believe it's one of the jolly ones, it's "Joy to the World." There's no one to hear the music but myself, and though I'm listening, I'm no longer certain. Perhaps the record's playing something else.

Donald Barthelme (1933–   )

"Fragments are the only forms I trust," Barthelme has said, and it is a social as well as aesthetic statement. For his fiction tells us, in funny as well as horrifying detail, of the awfulness of our order, which is to him a disorder, of the endlessness of the "damned accumulations" of a mass-production society in which the gross national product becomes continually more gross. *Dreck* is one of his favorite terms, by which he means—as Tony Tanner in his book *City of Words* reminds us—the flow of things, trash, junk, stuff, and sludge that fills and is filling our environment. In his novel *Snow White* a voice says: "The percapita production of trash in this country is up from 2.75 pounds per day in 1920 to 4.5 pounds per day in 1965 . . . that rate will probably go up, because it's *been* going up, and I hazard that we may very well soon reach a point where it's 100 percent. Now at such a point you will agree, the question turns from a question of disposing of this 'trash' to a question of appreciating its qualities, because, after all, it's 100 percent, right?" And part of that dreck is words, the words and syntax pouring out from the mass media, and corrupted to the purposes of commercialism, militarism, and government persiflage. For this reason, Barthelme in his stories and novels deliberately treats us to the "circus of the mind in motion" and to "the odd linguistic trip, stutter and fall." "For," as Tony Tanner says, "it is a language circus, and Barthelme has such sport with the words and things which make up 'the trash phenomenon' that one registers a spirit of resilience and carnival countering the deadening accumulations which make up the materials he handles."

Besides the novel *Snow White* (1967), Barthelme has published two volumes of stories, *Come Back, Dr. Caligari* (1974) and *Unspeakable Practices, Unnatural Acts* (1967). Of Donald Barthelme's personal life we know very little. He was born in Philadelphia and raised and educated in Houston, Texas, where his father, an architect, imparted to him something of his love for modernism in all its forms, literary as well as architectural. Barthelme has worked as a newspaperman, magazine editor, curator of an art gallery, and a university public relations director; and he has served in the army in Korea and Japan. His first fiction was published under the auspices of a Houston friend; these pieces attracted the editors of *The New Yorker,* and Barthelme has been a frequent contributor to that and other periodicals ever since. He makes his home in Greenwich Village.

"Report" is one of Barthelme's less lighthearted pieces, in that it does not seem to recommend that one "go with the flow" but that one oppose, or at least distrust it. The language is that "doublespeak" of the military by which instruments of torture and holocaustic destruction are talked about in the level language of applied science, a language that makes the human element conspicuous by its absence. "The banality of evil"—in the phrase of Hannah Arendt—is here manifest, the business-as-usual guise in which terror has come dressed in our time. Or, as Karl Kraus has said, in our epoch the Horsemen of the Apocalypse are "Tom, Dick, and Harry." Ah, but we need not worry, the technicians have thought of the dangers; they have built a "moral sense" into the computer that governs our destiny. Aristotle said "Character is fate," but here is a world in which "the computer is fate." More polemical than usual, Barthelme tells us frankly at the end of his story that no one back home believed in that "moral sense"!

Report

Our group is against the war. But the war goes on. I was sent to Cleveland to talk to the engineers. The engineers were meeting in Cleveland. I was supposed to persuade them not to do what they are going to do. I took United's 4:45 from LaGuardia arriving in Cleveland at 6:13. Cleveland is dark blue at that hour. I went directly to the motel, where the engineers were meeting. Hundreds of engineers attended the Cleveland meeting. I noticed many fractures among the engineers, bandages, traction. I noticed what appeared to be fracture of the carpal scaphoid in six examples. I noticed numerous fractures of the humeral shaft, of the os calcis, of the pelvic girdle. I noticed a high incidence of clay-shoveller's fracture. I could not account for these fractures. The engineers were making calculations, taking measurements, sketching on the blackboard, drinking beer, throwing bread, buttonholing employers, hurling glasses into the fireplace. They were friendly.

They were friendly. They were full of love and information. The chief engineer wore shades. Patella in Monk's traction, clamshell fracture by the look of it. He was standing in a slum of beer bottles and microphone cable. "Have some of this chicken à la Isambard Kingdom Brunel the Great Ingineer," he said. "And declare who you are and what we can do for you. What is your line, distinguished guest?"

"Software," I said. "In every sense. I am here representing a small group of interested parties. We are interested in your thing, which seems to be functioning. In the midst of so much dysfunction, function is interesting. Other people's things don't seem to be working. The State Department's thing doesn't seem to be working. The

From Donald Barthelme, *Unspeakable Practices, Unnatural Acts.* Copyright © 1967 by Barthelme. Reprinted by permission of Farrar, Straus & Giroux, Inc.

U.N.'s thing doesn't seem to be working. The democratic left's thing doesn't seem to be working. Buddha's thing—"

"Ask us anything about our thing, which seems to be working," the chief engineer said. "We will open our hearts and heads to you, Software Man, because we want to be understood and loved by the great lay public, and have our marvels appreciated by that public, for which we daily unsung produce tons of new marvels each more life-enhancing than the last. Ask us anything. Do you want to know about evaporated thin-film metallurgy? Monolithic and hybrid integrated-circuit processes? The algebra of inequalities? Optimization theory? Complex high-speed micro-miniature closed and open loop systems? Fixed variable mathematical cost searches? Epitaxial deposition of semi-conductor materials? Gross interfaced space gropes? We also have specialists in the cuckooflower, the doctorfish, and the dumdum bullet as these relate to aspects of today's expanding technology, and they do in the damnedest ways."

I spoke to him then about the war. I said the same things people always say when they speak against the war. I said that the war was wrong. I said that large countries should not burn down small countries. I said that the government had made a series of errors. I said that these errors once small and forgivable were now immense and unforgivable. I said that the government was attempting to conceal its original errors under layers of new errors. I said that the government was sick with error, giddy with it. I said that ten thousand of our soldiers had already been killed in pursuit of the government's errors. I said that tens of thousands of the enemy's soldiers and civilians had been killed because of various errors, ours and theirs. I said that we are responsible for errors made in our name. I said that the government should not be allowed to make additional errors.

"Yes, yes," the chief engineer said, "there is doubtless much truth in what you say, but we can't possibly *lose* the war, can we? And stopping is losing, isn't it? The war regarded as a process, stopping regarded as an abort? We don't know *how* to lose a war. That skill is not among our skills. Our array smashes their array, that is what we know. That is the process. That is what is.

"But let's not have any more of this dispiriting downbeat counterproductive talk. I have a few new marvels here I'd like to discuss with you just briefly. A few new marvels that are just about ready to be gaped at by the admiring layman. Consider for instance the area of realtime online computer-controlled wish evaporation. Wish evaporation is going to be crucial in meeting the rising expectations of the world's peoples, which are as you know rising entirely too fast."

I noticed then distributed about the room a great many transverse fractures of the ulna. "The development of the pseudo-ruminant stomach for underdeveloped peoples," he went on, "is one of our interesting things you should be interested in. With the pseudo-ruminant stomach they can chew cuds, that is to say, eat grass. Blue is the most popular color worldwide and for that reason we are working with certain strains of your native Kentucky *Poa pratensis,* or bluegrass, as the staple input for the p/r stomach cycle, which would also give a shot in the arm to our balance-of-payments thing don't you know. . . ." I noticed about me then a great number of metatarsal fractures in banjo splints. "The kangaroo initiative . . . eight hundred thousand harvested last year . . . highest percentage of edible protein of any herbivore yet studied . . ."

"Have new kangaroos been planted?"

The engineer looked at me.

"I intuit your hatred and jealousy of our thing," he said. "The ineffectual always hate our thing and speak of it as anti-human, which is not at all a meaningful way to speak of our thing. Nothing mechanical is alien to me," he said (amber spots making bursts of light in his shades), "because I am human, in a sense, and if I think it up, then 'it' is human too, whatever 'it' may be. Let me tell you, Software Man, we have been damned forbearing in the matter of this little war you declare yourself to be interested in. Function is the cry, and our thing is functioning like crazy. There are things we could do that we have not done. Steps we could take that we have not taken. These steps are, regarded in a certain light, the light of our enlightened self-interest, quite justifiable steps. We could, of course, get irritated. We could, of course, *lose patience.*

"We could, of course, release thousands upon thousands of self-powered crawl-ing-along-the-ground lengths of titanium wire eighteen inches long with a diameter of .0005 centimeters (that is to say, invisible) which, scenting an enemy, climb up his trouser leg and wrap themselves around his neck. We have developed those. They are within our capabilities. We could, of course, release in the arena of the upper air our new improved pufferfish toxin which precipitates an identity crisis. No special techni-cal problems there. That is almost laughably easy. We could, of course, place up to two million maggots in their rice within twenty-four hours. The maggots are ready, massed in secret staging areas in Alabama. We have hypodermic darts capable of piebalding the enemy's pigmentation. We have rots, blights, and rusts capable of attacking his alphabet. Those are dandies. We have a hut-shrinking chemical which penetrates the fibres of the bamboo, causing it, the hut, to strangle its occupants. This operates only after 10 P.M., when people are sleeping. Their mathematics are at the mercy of a suppurating surd we have invented. We have a family of fishes trained to attack their fishes. We have the deadly testicle-destroying telegram. The cable compa-nies are coöperating. We have a green substance that, well, I'd rather not talk about. We have a secret word that, if pronounced, produces multiple fractures in all living things in an area the size of four football fields."

"That's why—"

"Yes. Some damned fool couldn't keep his mouth shut. The point is that the whole structure of enemy life is within our power to *rend, vitiate, devour,* and *crush.* But that's not the interesting thing."

"You recount these possibilities with uncommon relish."

"Yes I realize that there is too much relish here. But *you* must realize that these capabilities represent in and of themselves highly technical and complex and interest-ing problems and hurdles on which our boys have expended many thousands of hours of hard work and brilliance. And that the effects are often grossly exaggerated by irresponsible victims. And that the whole thing represents a fantastic series of tri-umphs for the multi-disciplined problem-solving team concept."

"I appreciate that."

"We *could* unleash all this technology at once. You can imagine what would happen then. But that's not the interesting thing."

"What is the interesting thing?"

"The interesting thing is that we have a *moral sense.* It is on punched cards, perhaps the most advanced and sensitive moral sense the world has ever known."

"Because it is on punched cards?"

"It considers all considerations in endless and subtle detail," he said. "It even quibbles. With this great new moral tool, how can we go wrong? I confidently predict that, although we *could* employ all this splendid new weaponry I've been telling you about, *we're not going to do it.*"

"We're not going to do it?"

I took United's 5:44 from Cleveland arriving at Newark at 7:19. New Jersey is bright pink at that hour. Living things move about the surface of New Jersey at that hour molesting each other only in traditional ways. I made my report to the group. I stressed the friendliness of the engineers. I said, It's all right. I said, We have a moral sense. I said, *We're not going to do it.* They didn't believe me.

Richard Brautigan (1935–   )

Richard Brautigan was born in Tacoma, Washington in 1935. He first published his poetry and fiction in small San Francisco presses, but by the late sixties a New York publisher picked up on his local popularity and republished half a dozen of his novels and collections of verse. Today Brautigan, whose Wild Bill Hickock mustachios and lovely, or eccentric, girl friends adorn the covers of his books with their curious expressions, enjoys the enviable position of keeping his former audience while he gains a growing popularity in the universities. Mark Schorer recently said that the current generation of undergraduates are reading "Lawrence, Hermann Hesse, Kurt Vonnegut, Jr., J. R. R. Tolkien, in that order . . . with Anaïs Nin, Richard Brautigan, and perhaps Thomas Pynchon tailing along." Brautigan has ten books of prose and fiction to his credit, the most important being: *In Watermelon Sugar* (1968), *A Confederate General from Big Sur* (1964), *The Pill Versus the Springhill Mine Disaster* (1968), *Rommel Drives on Deep into Egypt* (1970), *The Abortion: An Historical Romance 1966* (1971), and *Trout Fishing in America* (1967), from which "The Cleveland Wrecking Yard" is taken.

As Tony Tanner says, "Trout Fishing in America becomes a person, a place, an hotel, a cripple, a pen nib, and of course a book. Protean and amorphous, it is a dream to be pursued, a sense of something lost, a quality of life, a spirit that is present or absent in many forms." The book is on one level a lighthearted fantasy, gay, gentle, and often hilariously funny. Brautigan's humor has a quality of innocence that wears his unique signature. Thus he describes a mansion built for a movie actor at Big Sur: "The mansion had been brought over the mountains on the backs of mules, strung out like ants, bringing visions of the good life to the poison oak, the ticks, and the salmon." Brautigan seems to have no axe to grind; his gentle fantasies have a surface manner of happy acceptance.

But on another level *Trout Fishing* can be read more seriously, not as a polemic to be sure, but as a kind of satire, a sort of picaresque fantasy where the narrator is eternally disappointed in his quest. He never finds Trout Fishing in America, though he finds evidence of its past existence that makes him nostalgic. He encounters, as Tanner says, "a pastoral America which has vanished or been despoiled by mechanization, crime, accumulating garbage, and various kinds of poison and violence." The narrator never raises his voice, but when in his quest he comes to the Cleveland Wrecking Yard, it is innocence not recognizing experience. In that garden of ambiguous riches, full of the waste products of the American dream, he looks to put together a second Eden out of the *things*. "The junk of the psyche [has] the deepest things to tell us," says Saul Bellow (citing Freud), for "the unconscious [does] not distinguish between major and minor matters as conscious judgment [does]," and Brautigan is a happy tourist in that unconscious realm. In the Wrecking Yard, the "unpolluted" streams are stacked like so many automobile fenders, though "they were practically out of animals," except for the mice. The narrator is an innocent, more a voice than a character, and he demands nothing of us except our suspension of disbelief. Yet his happy delight ("O, I had never in my life seen anything like that trout stream") creates an irony we cannot miss. Part of Brautigan's technique is a simple naming of things, like that of the primitive myth maker: "Whatever has been fixed by a name," said Ernst Cassirer, "is not only real, but is Reality," and Brautigan's story has many similarities with the Kiowa myths early in this volume. They both have a kind of simple magic.

The Cleveland Wrecking Yard

Until recently my knowledge about the Cleveland Wrecking Yard had come from a couple of friends who'd bought things there. One of them bought a huge window: the frame, glass and everything for just a few dollars. It was a fine-looking window.

Then he chopped a hole in the side of his house up on Potrero Hill and put the window in. Now he has a panoramic view of the San Francisco County Hospital.

He can practically look right down into the wards and see old magazines eroded like the Grand Canyon from endless readings. He can practically hear the patients thinking about breakfast: *I hate milk,* and thinking about dinner: *I hate peas,* and then he can watch the hospital slowly drown at night, hopelessly entangled in huge bunches of brick seaweed.

He bought that window at the Cleveland Wrecking Yard.

My other friend bought an iron roof at the Cleveland Wrecking Yard and took the roof down to Big Sur in an old station wagon and then he carried the iron roof on his back up the side of a mountain. He carried up half the roof on his back. It was no picnic. Then he bought a mule, George, from Pleasanton. George carried up the other half of the roof.

The mule didn't like what was happening at all. He lost a lot of weight because of the ticks, and the smell of the wildcats up on the plateau made him too nervous to graze there. My friend said jokingly that George had lost around two hundred pounds. The good wine country around Pleasanton in the Livermore Valley probably had looked a lot better to George than the wild side of the Santa Lucia Mountains.

My friend's place was a shack right beside a huge fireplace where there had once been a great mansion during the 1920s, built by a famous movie actor. The mansion was built before there was even a road down at Big Sur. The mansion had been brought over the mountains on the backs of mules, strung out like ants, bringing visions of the good life to the poison oak, the ticks, and the salmon.

The mansion was on a promontory, high over the Pacific. Money could see far-

"The Cleveland Wrecking Yard" is from the book, *Trout Fishing in America* by Richard Brautigan. Copyright © 1967 by Richard Brautigan. Reprinted with permission of Delacorte Press/ Seymour Lawrence.

ther in the 1920s, and one could look out and see whales and the Hawaiian Islands and the Kuomintang in China.

The mansion burned down years ago.

The actor died.

His mules were made into soap.

His mistresses became bird nests of wrinkles.

Now only the fireplace remains as a sort of Carthaginian homage to Hollywood.

I was down there a few weeks ago to see my friend's roof. I wouldn't have passed up the chance for a million dollars, as they say. The roof looked like a colander to me. If that roof and the rain were running against each other at Bay Meadows, I'd bet on the rain and plan to spend my winnings at the World's Fair in Seattle.

My own experience with the Cleveland Wrecking Yard began two days ago when I heard about a used trout stream they had on sale out at the Yard. So I caught the Number 15 bus on Columbus Avenue and went out there for the first time.

There were two Negro boys sitting behind me on the bus. They were talking about Chubby Checker and the Twist. They thought that Chubby Checker was only fifteen years old because he didn't have a mustache. Then they talked about some other guy who did the twist forty-four hours in a row until he saw George Washington crossing the Delaware.

"Man, that's what I call twisting," one of the kids said.

"I don't think I could twist no forty-four hours in a row," the other kid said. "That's a lot of twisting."

I got off the bus right next to an abandoned Time Gasoline filling station and an abandoned fifty-cent self-service car wash. There was a long field on one side of the filling station. The field had once been covered with a housing project during the war, put there for the shipyard workers.

On the other side of the Time filling station was the Cleveland Wrecking Yard. I walked down there to have a look at the used trout stream. The Cleveland Wrecking Yard has a very long front window filled with signs and merchandise.

There was a sign in the window advertising a laundry marking machine for $65.00. The original cost of the machine was $175.00. Quite a saving.

There was another sign advertising new and used two and three ton hoists. I wondered how many hoists it would take to move a trout stream.

There was another sign that said:

THE FAMILY GIFT CENTER,
GIFT SUGGESTIONS FOR THE ENTIRE FAMILY

The window was filled with hundreds of items for the entire family. *Daddy, do you know what I want for Christmas? What, son? A bathroom. Mommy, do you know what I want for Christmas? What, Patricia? Some roofing material.*

There were jungle hammocks in the window for distant relatives and dollar-ten-cent gallons of earth-brown enamel paint for other loved ones.

There was also a big sign that said:

USED TROUT STREAM FOR SALE.
MUST BE SEEN TO BE APPRECIATED.

I went inside and looked at some ship's lanterns that were for sale next to the door. Then a salesman came up to me and said in a pleasant voice, "Can I help you?"

"Yes," I said. "I'm curious about the trout stream you have for sale. Can you tell me something about it? How are you selling it?"

"We're selling it by the foot length. You can buy as little as you want or you can buy all we've got left. A man came in here this morning and bought 563 feet. He's going to give it to his niece for a birthday present," the salesman said.

"We're selling the waterfalls separately of course, and the trees and birds, flowers, grass and ferns we're also selling extra. The insects we're giving away free with a minimum purchase of ten feet of stream."

"How much are you selling the stream for?" I asked.

"Six dollars and fifty cents a foot," he said. "That's for the first hundred feet. After that it's five dollars a foot."

"How much are the birds?" I asked.

"Thirty-five cents apiece," he said. "But of course they're used. We can't guarantee anything."

"How wide is the stream?" I asked. "You said you were selling it by the length, didn't you?"

"Yes," he said. "We're selling it by the length. Its width runs between five and eleven feet. You don't have to pay anything extra for width. It's not a big stream, but it very pleasant."

"What kinds of animals do you have?" I asked.

"We only have three deer left," he said.

"Oh . . . What about flowers?"

"By the dozen," he said.

"Is the stream clear?" I asked.

"Sir," the salesman said. "I wouldn't want you to think that we would ever sell a murky trout stream here. We always make sure they're running crystal clear before we even think about moving them."

"Where did the stream come from?" I asked.

"Colorado," he said. "We moved it with loving care. We've never damaged a trout stream yet. We treat them all as if they were china."

"You're probably asked this all the time, but how's fishing in the stream?" I asked.

"Very good," he said. "Mostly German browns, but there are a few rainbows."

"What do the trout cost?" I asked.

"They come with the stream," he said. "Of course it's all luck. You never know how many you're going to get or how big they are. But the fishing's very good, you might say it's excellent. Both bait and dry fly," he said smiling.

"Where's the stream at?" I asked. "I'd like to take a look at it."

"It's around in back," he said. "You go straight through that door and then turn right until you're outside. It's stacked in lengths. You can't miss it. The waterfalls are upstairs in the used plumbing department."

"What about the animals?"

"Well, what's left of the animals are straight back from the stream. You'll see a bunch of our trucks parked on a road by the railroad tracks. Turn right on the road and follow it down past the piles of lumber. The animal shed's right at the end of the lot."

"Thanks," I said. "I think I'll look at the waterfalls first. You don't have to come with me. Just tell me how to get there and I'll find my own way."

"All right," he said. "Go up those stairs. You'll see a bunch of doors and windows, turn left and you'll find the used plumbing department. Here's my card if you need any help."

"Okay," I said. "You've been a great help already. Thanks a lot. I'll take a look around."

"Good luck," he said.

I went upstairs and there were thousands of doors there. I'd never seen so many doors before in my life. You could have built an entire city out of those doors. Doors-town. And there were enough windows up there to build a little suburb entirely out of windows. Windowville.

I turned left and went back and saw the faint glow of pearl-colored light. The light got stronger and stronger as I went farther back, and then I was in the used plumbing department, surrounded by hundreds of toilets.

The toilets were stacked on shelves. They were stacked five toilets high. There was a skylight above the toilets that made them glow like the Great Taboo Pearl of the South Sea movies.

Stacked over against the wall were the waterfalls. There were about a dozen of them, ranging from a drop of a few feet to a drop of ten or fifteen feet.

There was one waterfall that was over sixty feet long. There were tags on the pieces of the big falls describing the correct order for putting the falls back together again.

The waterfalls all had price tags on them. They were more expensive than the stream. The waterfalls were selling for $19.00 a foot.

I went into another room where there were piles of sweet-smelling lumber, glowing a soft yellow from a different color skylight above the lumber. In the shadows at the edge of the room under the sloping roof of the building were many sinks and urinals covered with dust, and there was also another waterfall about seventeen feet long, lying there in two lengths and already beginning to gather dust.

I had seen all I wanted of the waterfalls, and now I was very curious about the trout stream, so I followed the salesman's directions and ended up outside the building.

O I had never in my life seen anything like that trout stream. It was stacked in piles of various lengths: ten, fifteen, twenty feet, etc. There was one pile of hundred-foot lengths. There was also a box of scraps. The scraps were in odd sizes ranging from six inches to a couple of feet.

There was a loudspeaker on the side of the building and soft music was coming out. It was a cloudy day and seagulls were circling high overhead.

Behind the stream were big bundles of trees and bushes. They were covered with sheets of patched canvas. You could see the tops and roots sticking out the ends of the bundles.

I went up close and looked at the lengths of stream. I could see some trout in them. I saw one good fish. I saw some crawdads crawling around the rocks at the bottom.

It looked like a fine stream. I put my hand in the water. It was cold and felt good.

I decided to go around to the side and look at the animals. I saw where the trucks were parked beside the railroad tracks. I followed the road down past the piles of lumber, back to the shed where the animals were.

The salesman had been right. They were practically out of animals. About the only thing they had left in any abundance were mice. There were hundreds of mice.

Beside the shed was a huge wire birdcage, maybe fifty feet high, filled with many kinds of birds. The top of the cage had a piece of canvas over it, so the birds wouldn't get wet when it rained. There were woodpeckers and wild canaries and sparrows.

On my way back to where the trout stream was piled, I found the insects. They were inside a prefabricated steel building that was selling for eighty cents a square foot. There was a sign over the door. It said:

INSECTS

Alternative Tables of Contents: Theme and Subject

For readers who want alternative entries into these stories, we have listed below some themes and subjects represented in this volume. A theme must be distinguished from a subject. A story may have *war* as its subject, but *self-discovery* as its theme. The subject is the raw material of the story, its subject *matter,* but the theme is its meaning, its point.

Themes are obviously, from a critical point of view, more important than subjects, but the two are often closely allied (and sometimes indistinguishable). We have, therefore, included both, themes under Part I and subjects under Part II.

No such lists as these can be more than crude indicators, since the categories overlap, and since we cannot possibly be exhaustive. It would be the rare story whose theme, by another reader, could not be called by another name: one reader might call the theme of Joyce's "Araby" "self-realization," while another might call it "escape from romantic illusion." Likewise, a story might have "war" as its subject, but it surely has "human nature" or "courage" or "suffering" as subjects as well. Therefore, we have listed stories under more than one heading. We believe that a careful look at these lists will help readers to compare and distinguish the stories and thus to increase their understanding and response.

PART I: THEMES

In naming the following themes, we have followed the image of a widening circle, beginning in childhood and expanding outward to the experiences of adulthood and of responsibility.

I. Childhood and Youth

Sherwood Anderson	The Egg
Conrad Aiken	Silent Snow, Secret Snow
William Faulkner	Barn Burning
Delmore Schwartz	In Dreams Begin Responsibilities
Joyce Carol Oates	Stalking

II. Rites of Passage

James Joyce	Araby
Katherine Anne Porter	The Grave
Isaac Babel	My First Goose
William Faulkner	Barn Burning
Richard Wright	The Man Who Was Almost a Man
Delmore Schwartz	In Dreams Begin Responsibilities

III. Identity and Self-discovery

Nikolai Gogol	The Overcoat
Henry James	The Beast in the Jungle
James Joyce	Araby
Virginia Woolf	The Mark on the Wall
Jorge Luis Borges	Borges and I
	Everything and Nothing

IV. Fantasy and Absurdity

Nikolai Gogol	The Overcoat
Edgar Allan Poe	The Black Cat
James Joyce	Araby
Conrad Aiken	Silent Snow, Secret Snow
James Thurber	The Secret Life of Walter Mitty
Virginia Woolf	The Mark on the Wall
Franz Kafka	A Country Doctor
Karel Čapek	The Last Judgment
Jorge Luis Borges	Everything and Nothing
Bernard Malamud	The Magic Barrel
Heinrich Böll	Action Will Be Taken
Julio Cortázar	Axolotl
Isaac Rosenfeld	The Brigadier
Italo Calvino	The Spiral
Donald Barthelme	Report
Richard Brautigan	The Cleveland Wrecking Yard

V. Adventure and Mystery

Edgar Allan Poe	The Black Cat
Thomas Hardy	The Three Strangers
Stephen Crane	The Open Boat
Jorge Luis Borges	Emma Zunz
Julio Cortázar	Axolotl
Alain Robbe-Grillet	The Shore

VI. Loneliness and Alienation

| Nathaniel Hawthorne | Wakefield |
| Herman Melville | Bartleby, The Scrivener |

Gustave Flaubert	A Simple Heart
Anton Chekhov	Vierochka
Thomas Mann	Little Herr Friedemann
D. H. Lawrence	The Blind Man
Katherine Mansfield	Marriage à la Mode
Isaac Babel	My First Goose
Ernest Hemingway	Hills Like White Elephants
Eudora Welty	A Worn Path
Tillie Olsen	Tell Me a Riddle
Juan Rulfo	Macario
Heinrich Böll	Action Will Be Taken
Isaac Rosenfeld	The Brigadier
William Gass	In the Heart of the Heart of The Country
John Updike	Wife-wooing
Joyce Carol Oates	Stalking

VII. Love and Sex

Ivan Turgenev	Ermolai and the Miller's Wife
Giovanni Verga	The She-Wolf
Guy de Maupassant	A Country Outing
Anton Chekhov	Ninochka: A Love Story
Rudyard Kipling	The Wish House
D. H. Lawrence	The Blind Man
Katherine Mansfield	Marriage à la Mode
Isaac Babel	The Sin of Jesus
Ernest Hemingway	Hills Like White Elephants
Tillie Olsen	Tell Me a Riddle
Bernard Malamud	The Magic Barrel
Yukio Mishima	Patriotism
Italo Calvino	The Spiral
John Updike	Wife-wooing

VIII. Justice and Injustice

Nikolai Gogol	The Overcoat
Ivan Turgenev	Ermolai and the Miller's Wife
Thomas Hardy	The Three Strangers
E. M. Forster	The Rock
William Faulkner	Barn Burning
Karel Čapek	The Last Judgment
Jorge Luis Borges	Emma Zunz
Shirley Jackson	The Lottery
Flannery O'Connor	Greenleaf
LeRoi Jones	The Death of Horatio Alger

IX. Cruelty and Suffering

Edgar Allan Poe	The Black Cat
Anton Chekhov	Heartache
Isaac Babel	The Sin of Jesus
Eudora Welty	A Worn Path
Richard Wright	The Man Who Was Almost a Man
Franz Kafka	A Country Doctor

Virginia Woolf	The Mark on the Wall
Conrad Aiken	Silent Snow, Secret Snow
Katherine Anne Porter	The Grave
Eudora Welty	A Worn Path
Tillie Olsen	Tell Me a Riddle
Joyce Carol Oates	Stalking
Franz Kafka	A Country Doctor
Jorge Luis Borges	Everything and Nothing

III. Sex, Marriage, Family, Children

Nathaniel Hawthorne	Wakefield
Guy de Maupassant	A Country Outing
Anton Chekhov	Ninochka: A Love Story
Sherwood Anderson	The Egg
D. H. Lawrence	The Blind Man
Katherine Mansfield	Marriage à la Mode
James Thurber	The Secret Life of Walter Mitty
Ernest Hemingway	Hills Like White Elephants
Carson McCullers	A Tree • A Rock • A Cloud
Tillie Olsen	Tell Me a Riddle
Bernard Malamud	The Magic Barrel
Yukio Mishima	Patriotism
John Updike	Wife-wooing
Tomasso Landolfi	Gogol's Wife
Delmore Schwartz	In Dreams Begin Responsibilities
Alain Robbe-Grillet	The Shore

IV. Animals and People

Aesop	Fables
Kiowa Indians	Kiowa Legends
Edgar Allan Poe	The Black Cat
Giovanni Verga	The She-Wolf
Sherwood Anderson	The Egg
Isaac Babel	My First Goose
Flannery O'Connor	Greenleaf
Julio Cortázar	Axolōtl
Italo Calvino	The Spiral
Gustave Flaubert	A Simple Heart

V. Country and City

Guy de Maupassant	A Country Outing
Thomas Hardy	The Three Strangers
Anton Chekhov	Vierochka
E. M. Forster	The Rock
D. H. Lawrence	The Blind Man
Eudora Welty	A Worn Path
Saul Bellow	Looking for Mr. Green
Flannery O'Connor	Greenleaf
Franz Kafka	A Country Doctor
William Gass	In the Heart of the Heart of the Country

Brief Glossary of Terms

The following are some brief and necessarily simple definitions of the *genres* represented in this volume.

ALLEGORY   (See discussion, p. 35.)

ANTI-REALISM   Anti-realists reject traditional techniques of fiction—plots, character, point of view, "showing" versus "telling"—which they believe are inadequate for modern experience. They are drawn to the farther reaches of imagination—fairy tales, fantasy, grotesquerie, utter subjectivity, absurdity, outrageous satire, wild inventive humor. (See discussions, pp. 3-5.)

AVANT-GARDE   (See Modernism).

COMEDY   It is impossible to define comedy in a short space, but it may be of value to suggest some of its parameters. In his essay "Laughter," Henri Bergson says that we laugh whenever we encounter "the mechanical encrusted on the living." When a human being acts like a robot instead of the living creature he is supposed to be, then we laugh—unconsciously trying to laugh him out of his mechanicalness and back into his humanity. But *comedy* is a bigger word than *laughter*: it exists on a spectrum stretching from lighthearted farce and horseplay (at which we laugh) to such deadly serious forms as "black humor" or "gallows humor" which are, quite literally, no laughing matter—though we sometimes laugh anyway. Irony (see p. 16) can be comic or not, depending on the context. Comedy, in short, is a profound and complex subject, as is shown by the fact that it can apply to stories as various as Thurber's "The Secret Life of Walter Mitty" and Barthelme's "Report" or Kafka's "A Country Doctor" and Brautigan's "The Cleveland Wrecking Yard."

EXPRESSIONISM   Expressionism began in the late nineteenth century as a reaction against realism, which was thought to be inadequate for expressing the anguish of modern experience. Expressionists project onto external objects and events internal states of mind. This inner experience is apt to be troubled, anxious, or otherwise abnormal. Chief exponents have been the playwrights August Strindberg (1849-1912) and Bertolt Brecht (1898-1956) and the painters Edvard Münch (1863-1944) and Emile Nolde (1867-1956). Though not frequently used in relation to fiction, the term can be useful in understanding certain anti-realists and absurdists in whose work chronology is disrupted, time dislocated, place distorted in order to express the inner condition.

FABLE   (See discussion, pp. 34-35.)

FABLIAU   (See discussion, p. 40.)

FANTASY   Fantasy is as old as fairy tales, as old as dreams, and as new as Anti-Realism, or Modernism. In fiction, it is the tapping of the world of imagination or dream as opposed to the world of actuality. The elements of play, sport, whimsy, and light-hearted absurdity are often strong in fantasy, but Freud said: "A happy person never fantasies, only an unsatisfied one. . . . every single fantasy is the fulfillment of a wish, a correction of unsatisfied reality." (See discussion, pp. 3-5.)

FOLKTALE   (See discussion, pp. 25-26.)

GOTHIC TALE (GOTHICISM)   The word *Gothic* (from *Goths,* a German tribe) came to refer to a style of medieval architecture, to stone-vaulted churches and castles with pointed arches and grotesque decorations. Popular in the late eighteenth and early nineteenth centuries were novels set against backgrounds of Gothic architecture, tales fraught with horror, supernaturalism, perversity. The term has come to signify any fiction that is violent and melodramatic, with abnormal characters and a chilling atmosphere, as in the works of Poe and the "Southern Gothic" writers. (See discussion, p. 90.)

IMPRESSIONISM   In literature, as in art and music, impressionism is the effort to portray the effects of experience on consciousness rather than to render reality objectively. Impressionist painters—Monet, Renoir, Pissarro, among others—eschewed formal "Academy" approaches and explored ways of representing the effects of light and air in broken color. To them the "feel" of the scene was more important than attention to detail. Likewise in music, impressionists—like Debussy and Ravel—broke with traditional methods of composition in their desire to evoke a "mood" in the listener.

IRONY   (See discussions, p. 16.)

LEGEND   (See discussion, pp. 25-26.)

MODERNISM   Modernism refers loosely to a group ("school" would be too definite) of writers who have been engaging in radical experiments with fictional structure and subject matter. These writers have become most evident and increasingly influential since about 1950, and the group includes Borges, Robbe-Grillet, Barthelme, Brautigan, Landolfi.

MYTH   (See discussions, pp. 25-26.)

NATURALISM   Naturalism is a literary movement based on the belief that man is the product of heredity and environment, and that his behavior is completely—or mainly—controlled by social, economic, and biologic forces. Naturalist writers, therefore, tend to render reality in cross section, as a "slice of life," much as a scientist might dissect a specimen for study. As James T. Farrell put it, "Just as science helps man to understand nature, literature helps man to understand himself." Characteristically, naturalist writers tend to be concerned with people in the lower economic strata of society who are victimized by a destructive social environment. Their mode of narration tends to be detached, remote, yet sometimes brutally frank about sexual behavior, bodily functions, and the bestial aspects of human beings. The movement took root in nineteenth century France in the work of Flaubert, Daudet, Maupassant, and especially Émile Zola. In the United States a vigorous school of naturalist writers grew up, led by Stephen Crane, Theodore Dreiser, Frank Norris, and James T. Farrell. Thomas Hardy, among other British writers, also shows the influence of the movement.

NOVELLA (See discussions, p. 40.)

ORIENTAL TALE (See discussion, pp. 40-41.)

PARABLE (See discussion, pp. 34-35.)

REALISM Realism in fiction took its rise from writers like Flaubert in France and George Eliot in England. It is an attempt to render "actual" life in recognizable veri-similitude, to present scenes so that the reader has the sense of witnessing everyday experiences. Realism is opposed to Romance, since the characters in realistic fiction are life-size and the events subject to credible cause-effect sequence. No one has put the case for realism better than George Eliot in her novel *Adam Bede:* "I turn, without shrinking, from cloud-borne angels, from prophets, sibyls, and heroic warriors, to an old woman bending over her flower-pot, or eating her solitary dinner, while the noonday light, softened perhaps by a screen of leaves, falls on her mob-cap, and just touches the rim of her spinning wheel, and her stone jug, and all those cheap common things which are the precious necessaries of life to her. . . ."

ROMANCE Romance is best defined in contrast to Realism. Northrop Frye says, "The romancer does not attempt to create 'real people' so much as stylized figures which expand into psychological archetypes. . . . The romance, which deals with heroes, is intermediate between the novel, which deals with men, and the myth, which deals with gods." The traditional subject matter of romance is courtly love and chivalric deeds often made mysterious with magic and marvels. But in reference to the short story Romance is a generic term embracing a wide range of nonrealistic writing, from allegories and fables to fantasies and Gothic tales.

SATIRE Satire in fiction is an exposure of the follies and foibles, the vices and shortcomings, of men or societies, or almost anything. It is a conservative genre since the satirist does not wish to destroy but to reinvoke normalcy, to rebuild. Satire can be gentle or harsh, laughter-provoking or denunciatory. Irony is often employed in satire; invective is just as likely.

SCIENCE FICTION This genre goes far back in literature and includes such works as the Faust legend and Mary Wollstonecraft Shelley's *Frankenstein.* It is an attempt to explore and present in fictional terms the wonders of science, past and future. Although it has tended to portray utopias, science fiction recently has rendered dystopias as well—visions of science become master rather than servant of man. Although no story in this volume is strictly or exclusively science fiction, many stories contain elements of it, and many of the writers here represented have worked in or near it, most notably Poe and Wells, but also Hawthorne, Forster, Cortázar, Calvino, Pynchon.

SURREALISM   The intention of surrealists is to release the energy and knowledge of the unconscious mind. Dreams, nightmares, free associations, hallucinations (occasionally drug-induced) were its subject matter. The movement became important in the twenties, and though more influential in painting (Chirico, Dali, Magritte), it had an important impact on prose, sometimes directly (as with its founder André Breton) and sometimes indirectly (as with Henry Miller and William Burroughs). It is a direct descendant of Dadaism, an art movement that exploited the absurd, the meaningless, and the irreverent in order to tell a vicious modern society that it too was irrational and without values. In surrealism (though it is less radical) some of the same impulses survive, and stories like Brautigan's "The Cleveland Wrecking Yard" and Böll's "Action Will Be Taken" embody some of these qualities. (See discussion, pp. 3-5.)

SYMBOLISM   (See discussions, pp. 21-23.)

List of Useful Books

Aldridge, John W., ed. *Critiques and Essays on Modern Fiction,* 1920-1951. New York: Ronald Press Co., 1952.

Auerbach, Erich. *Mimesis.* Princeton: Princeton University Press, 1953.

Bates, H. E. *The Modern Short Story, A Critical Survey.* Boston: The Writer, Inc., 1941.

Booth, Wayne C. *The Rhetoric of Fiction.* Chicago: University of Chicago Press, 1961.

Brooks, Cleanth, Jr., and Robert Penn Warren, eds. *Understanding Fiction.* New York: Appleton-Century-Crofts, Inc., 1943.

Canby, Henry Seidel and Alfred Dashiel. *A Study of the Short Story,* Revised. New York: Henry Holt, 1935.

Chekhov, Anton. *Letters of Anton Chekhov,* Avram Yarmolinsky, ed. New York: The Viking Press, 1973.

Cowley, Malcolm, ed. *Writers At Work: The Paris Review Interviews.* New York: The Viking Press, 1958.

Current-García, Eugene, and Walton R. Patrick, eds. *Realism and Romanticism in Fiction.* Chicago: Scott, Foresman and Co., 1962.

Ellmann, Richard, and Charles Feidelson, Jr. *The Modern Tradition: Backgrounds of Modern Literature.* New York: Oxford University Press, 1965.

Ferguson, Suzanne. *Formal Developments in the English Short Story, 1880-1910.* Ph.D. Thesis. Stanford University, 1966.

Fletcher, Angus. *Allegory. The Theory of a Symbolic Mode.* Ithaca: Cornell University Press, 1964.

Forster, E. M. *Aspects of the Novel.* New York: Harcourt, Brace, & World, Inc., 1927.

Franco, Jean. *Spanish American Literature Since Independence.* New York: Barnes and Noble Publications, 1973.

Frye, Northrop. *Anatomy of Criticism.* Princeton: Princeton University Press, 1957.

Gass, William. *Fiction and the Figures of Life.* New York: Alfred A. Knopf, Inc., 1970.

Gordon, Caroline, and Allen Tate. *The House of Fiction.* New York: Charles Scribner's Sons, 1960.

James, Henry. *The Art of Fiction and Other Essays,* Morris Roberts, ed. New York: Oxford University Press, 1948.

Joyce, James. *Stephen Hero.* New York: New Directions, 1944.

Kazin, Alfred. *Bright Book of Life: American Novelists and Storytellers from Hemingway to Mailer.* Boston: Little, Brown & Co., 1973.

Kermode, Frank. *The Sense of an Ending: Studies in the Theory of Fiction.* London and New York: Oxford University Press, 1966.

Klinkowitz, Jerome, and John Somer, eds. *Innovative Fiction Stories for the Seventies.* New York: Dell Publishing Co., Inc., 1972.

Levin, Harry. *The Gates of Horn: A Study of Five French Realists.* London and New York: Oxford University Press, 1963.

Lubbock, Percy. *The Craft of Fiction.* New York: The Viking Press, 1957.

Matthews, Brander. *The Philosophy of the Short Story.* New York: Folcroft, 1912.

Mirrielees, Edith R. *Story Writing.* Boston: The Writer, Inc., 1947.

O'Connor, Flannery. *Mystery and Manners.* Sally and Robert Fitzgerald, eds. New York: Farrar, Straus & Giroux, 1969.

O'Connor, Frank [Michael O'Donovan, pseud.]. *The Lonely Voice.* New York: The World Publishing Co., 1962.

O'Connor, William Van, ed. *Form of Modern Fiction.* Bloomington: Indiana University Press, 1948.

O'Faolain, Sean. *The Short Story.* Old Greenwich, Conn.: The Devin-Adair Co., 1964.

Ross, Danforth. *The American Short Story.* Minneapolis: The University of Minnesota Press, 1961.

Sarraute, Nathalie. *The Age of Suspicion: Essays on the Novel.* New York: George Braziller, Inc., 1963.

Stegner, Wallace. *Teaching the Short Story.* Berkeley: University of California Press, 1965.

Steiner, George. *Language and Silence: Essays on Language, Literature and the Inhuman* New York: Atheneum, 1967.

Stevick, Philip, ed. *Anti-Story: An Anthology of Experimental Fiction.* New York and London: The Free Press and Collier-Macmillan Ltd., 1971.

Sukenick, Ronald. *The Death of the Novel and Other Stories.* New York: The Dial Press, 1969.

Tanner, Tony. *City of Words: American Fiction 1950-1970.* New York: Harper & Row, 1971.

Trilling, Lionel. *The Liberal Imagination: Essays on Literature and Society.* New York: The Viking Press, Inc., 1950.

Wellek, René, and Austin Warren. *Theory of Literature.* New York: Harcourt Brace & Co., 1942. See Chapter XVI, "The Nature and Modes of Narrative Fiction."

Woolf, Virginia. *A Writer's Diary.* New York: Harcourt, Brace & World, Inc., 1953.

Woolf, Virginia. "Mr. Bennett and Mrs. Brown" in *The Captain's Death Bed and Other Essays.* London: Hogarth Press, 1950.

Wright, Austin McGiffert. *The American Short Story in the Twenties.* Chicago: University of Chicago Press, 1965.

ADDITIONAL ACKNOWLEDGMENTS

Donald Barthelme, from *Snow White.* Copyright © 1967. With permission of Atheneum Publishers.

Saul Bellow, from "Distractions of a Fiction Writer," in *The Living Novel,* edited by Granville Hicks. Copyright © 1957 by Macmillan Publishing Company, Inc. With permission of Macmillan Publishing Company, Inc.

E. Caracciolo-Trejo, from *The Penguin Book of Latin American Verse.* Copyright © 1971. With permission of Penguin Books, Ltd.

Giacomo Debendetti, from "A Note on Landolfi," in *Cancerqueen and Other Stories,* translated by Raymond Rosenthal. With permission of The Dial Press.

William Faulkner in *Writers at Work, The 'Paris Review' Interviews, First Series,* edited by Malcolm Cowley. With permission of Martin Secker & Warburg Ltd.

Suzanne Carol Ferguson, from *Formal Development in the English Short Story,* 1966. With permission of the author.

David Galloway, from Edgar Allan Poe's *Selected Writings.* Copyright © 1967. With permission of Penguin Books Ltd.

Louise Y. Gossett, from *Violence In Recent Southern Fiction.* Copyright © 1973. With permission of Duke University Press.

Robert Halsband, from "Sketch Potpourri," in *The Saturday Review,* May 7, 1949. With permission of the publisher.

William E. Harkins, from *Karel Capek.* Copyright © 1962. With permission of Columbia University Press.

Nathaniel Hawthorne, from "Letter to Longfellow," in *A Scarlet Letter Handbook,* by Seymour L. Gross. Copyright © 1960. Published by Wadsworth Publishing Co., Inc.

Frederick J. Hoffman, from *Conrad Aiken.* Copyright 1962 by Twayne Publishers, Inc.; reprinted by permission of Twayne Publishers, A Division of G. K. Hall & Co.

Victor Lange, from *Dreamtigers.* Copyright © 1964. With permission of The University of Texas Press.

Joyce Carol Oates, from "The Unique/Universal in Fiction," in *The Writer.* Copyright © 1972 by The Writer, Inc. With permission of the publisher.

Flannery O'Connor, from *Mystery and Manners.* Copyright © 1969. With permission of Farrar, Straus and Giroux, Inc.

Sean O'Faolain, from *Short Stories: A Study in Pleasure.* Copyright © 1961. With permission of Little, Brown and Company.

Katherine Anne Porter, excerpts from *The Collected Essays and Occasional Writings of Katherine Anne Porter.* Copyright © 1970 by Katherine Anne Porter. Reprinted with the permission of Delacorte Press/Seymour Lawrence.

V. S. Pritchett, from *The Sailor, Sense of Humor and Other Stories.* With permission of Harold Matson Company, Inc.

Geza Róhéim, from "Myth and Folktale," in *Myth and Literature,* by John B. Vickery. Copyright © 1966. With permission of The University of Nebraska Press.

Francis Steegmuller, from *Flaubert and Madame Bovary.* Copyright © 1939, 1966 by Francis Steegmuller. With permission of the author.

Philip Stevick, from *Anti-Story.* Copyright © 1971. With permission of Macmillan Publishing Co., Inc.

Ronald Sukenick, from *The Death of the Novel and Other Stories.* Copyright © 1969. With permission of The Dial Press.

Tony Tanner, from *City of Words: American Fiction 1950-1970.* Copyright © 1971. With permission of Harper and Row.

Richard C. Tobias, from *The Art of James Thurber.* Copyright © 1970. With permission of The Ohio University Press.

INDEX